The **Rough Guide** to

Tokyo

written and researched by

Jan Dodd and Simon Richmond

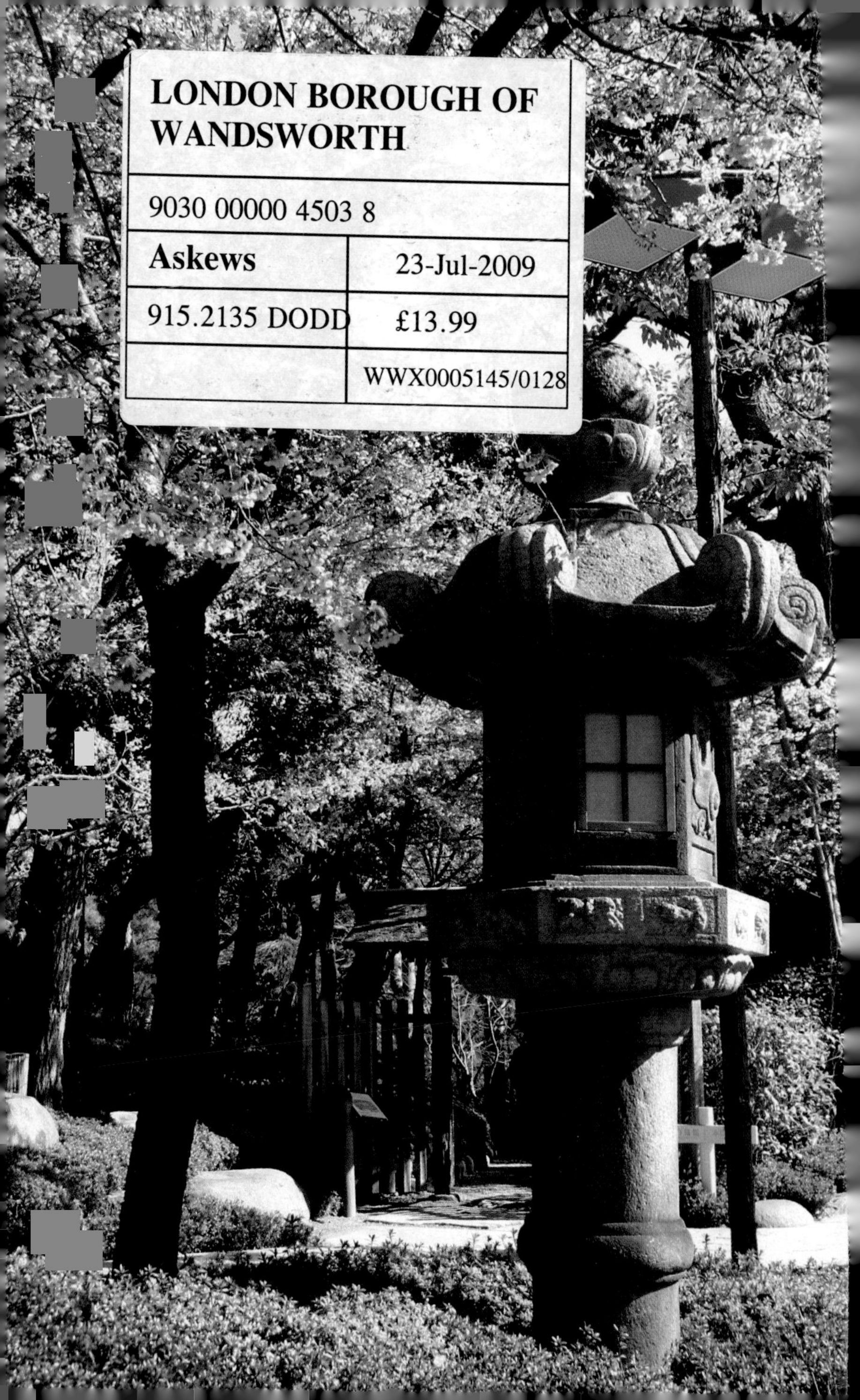

Contents

Shrines and temples colour section following p.80

Tokyo architecture colour section following p.112

Colour maps following p.352

◀◀ A busy intersection in Shibuya ◀ Stone lantern, Happōen

Introduction to
Tokyo

One of the world's most exciting cities, Tokyo is a fuel-injected adrenaline rush into a neon-bright future. But for all its cutting-edge modernity, Tokyo remains a city which is fiercely proud of its heritage. Lively neighbourhood festivals are held virtually every day of the year, and people regularly visit their local shrine or temple and scrupulously observe the passing seasons in manicured gardens. And at the centre of it all lies the mysterious Imperial Palace – the inviolate home of the emperor and a tangible link to the past.

But at first glance, the city's beauty and traditions are not readily apparent. Untidily hung about overhead cables, plagued by seemingly incessant noise, its freeways often clogged with bumper-to-bumper traffic, this concrete-and-steel sardine can – the heart of which is home to at least eight million people – can come across as the stereotypical urban nightmare. Yet step back from the frenetic main roads and chances are you'll find yourself in a world of tranquil backstreets, where dinky wooden houses are fronted by neatly clipped bonsai trees; wander beyond the hi-tech emporia, and you'll discover temples and shrines where the trappings of contemporary Japan dissolve in wisps of smoking incense.

Centuries-long experience of organizing itself to cope with the daily demands of millions of inhabitants has made Tokyo something of a model urban environment. Trains run on time and to practically every corner of the city, crime is hardly worth worrying about, and shops and vending machines provide everything you could need (and many things you never thought you

did) 24 hours a day. This is impressive enough, but as if to keep challenging itself, Tokyo keeps on changing, like some cartoon creature from a manga. Buildings go up one day, only to be torn down the next, and whole neighbourhoods are now being re-imagined.

With so much going on, first-time visitors should be prepared for a massive assault on the senses – just walking the streets of this hyperactive city can be an energizing experience. It need not be an expensive one, either. Tokyo's reputation as a costly city is ill-deserved these days, and you'll be pleasantly surprised by how affordable many things are. Cheap-and-cheerful *izakaya* – bars that serve food – and casual cafés serving noodles and rice dishes are plentiful, the metro is a bargain, and tickets for a sumo tournament or a Kabuki play can be bought for the price of a few drinks. Browsing the shops and marvelling at the passing parade can be great fun – the next best thing to having a ringside seat at the hippest of fashion shows. Likewise, in Tokyo's *über*-chic bars, restaurants and clubs you'll see today what the rest of the world will get tomorrow.

Underscoring – and adding a certain frisson to – Tokyo's cutting-edge modernity and effervescent trends is its incredibly volatile geographical position. Legend says that a giant catfish sleeps beneath Tokyo Bay, and its wriggling can be felt in the hundreds of small tremors that rumble the capital each year. Around every seventy years, the catfish awakes, resulting in the kind of major earthquake seen in 1995 in the Japanese city of Kōbe. Yet, despite the fact that the city is well overdue for the Big One, talk of relocating the capital remains just talk. Now, more than ever before, Tokyo is the centre of Japanese life, and nobody wants to leave and miss any of the action.

> In Tokyo's *über*-chic bars, restaurants and clubs you'll see today what the rest of the world will get tomorrow.

The Manga City

Across Tokyo cartoon mascots are used to promote everything from baseball teams and banks to the image of the local police – proof of the huge popularity of **manga** (cartoon images), books and magazines devoted to which account for a third of all published material in Japan.

It doesn't take much exposure to Japanese manga and **anime** (animation) to discern that both have a distinctive visual feel, the characters often having unusually large eyes and cutesy Westernized features. Both art forms appeal to young and old alike, with plots that are frequently complex and which embrace genres such as romance, the psychological thriller and the historical epic, as well as the more typical ones of science fiction and fantasy.

The increasing popularity overseas of anime and manga has not escaped the Japanese government, who are officially promoting them as pop cultural highlights. Whether you're an *otaku* (obsessive fan) or not, it's worth heading to Akihabara to experience the brilliant invention of the manga/anime scene at the new Anime Centre (see p.69), while out in the city's west are the excellent Suginami Animation Museum (see p.112) and the charming Ghibli Museum (p.112), where you can enter the wonderful world of the Oscar-winning Studio Ghibli, a brand that's arguably more loved in Japan than Sony or Toyota. For more on manga, see the box on p.222.

What to see

One way to ease yourself into the city is by taking a relatively crowd-free turn around the **Imperial Palace** – although most of the grounds remain tantalizingly off-limits. From here it's a quick hop to Tokyo's most famous high-class shopping *and* entertainment district, **Ginza**, where you'll also find the **Kabuki-za**, the best theatre in which to watch this quintessential Japanese performing art form. Ginza's elite shops have faced stiff competition recently from the new boutiques of Roppongi Hills and Omotesandō, but the area is fighting back with new urban developments in **Marunouchi** and **Shiodome**, both dominated by shiny commercial towers, as well as the **Tokyo International Forum**, a great example of contemporary architecture.

More obviously oriental scenes can be found in the evocative **Shitamachi** area, covering Asakusa, Ueno, Nezu and Yanaka, where the spirit of old Tokyo remains. **Asakusa**'s primary focus is the major Buddhist temple of **Sensō-ji**, surrounded by a plethora of traditional craft shops. The leafy precincts of **Ueno Park** contain several major museums, including the **Tokyo National Museum**. From here it's an easy stroll to the charming and tranquil districts of **Nezu** and **Yanaka**, packed with small temples, shrines and shops. The spirit of old Tokyo also lives on in **Kanda**, where you'll find the **Kanda Myōjin**, one of Tokyo's oldest shrines and home to one the city's top three festivals, and across the Sumida-gawa to **Ryōguku**, home to the colossal **Edo-Tokyo Museum** and the **National Sumo Stadium**. Cross the river back again to drop into the weird, wired and wonderful world of **Akihabara**, the one-time "electric town" rebooted as the epicentre of Tokyo's dynamic manga and anime scene.

> **More obviously oriental scenes can be found in the evocative Shitamachi area.**

If Akihabara has a rival as the city's most happening district, it has to be **Roppongi**. The nightlife here can exhaust the most committed hedonist, but save some energy to return by day to explore the art triangle formed by the dazzling new **National Arts Centre**, the various art and design institutes of the mammoth **Tokyo Midtown** development, and the excellent Mori Arts Centre atop the **Roppongi Hills** complex.

Fashionistas should head towards the teenage shopping meccas of **Shibuya** and **Harajuku** and the super-chic, boutique-lined boulevards of **Aoyama**. When you've reached consumer saturation point, retreat to the wooded grounds of nearby **Meiji-jingū**, the city's most venerable Shinto shrine, or peruse the delicate woodblock prints and crafts and artworks in the **Ōta Memorial Museum of Art**, or the **Japan Folk Crafts Museum**.

West of the Imperial Palace lies **Shinjuku**, an archetypal Tokyo district bursting with towering skyscrapers, endless amounts of neon, TV screens several storeys tall, and arguably the world's most complicated railway station. The attractions include the monumental **Tokyo Metropolitan Government Building**, the beautiful gardens of **Shinjuku Gyoen**, and lively and raffish **Kabukichō** entertainment area.

▼ Akihabara

Pampered pooches

In the country that gave us Tamagotchi virtual pets, it's surprising to find that the real thing – in the form of walking, woofing, tail-wagging canines – are currently all the rage. There are an estimated 120 million dogs nationwide, almost one for every person. While many of these are farm dogs, thousands live out their lives as the mollycoddled fashion accessories of an urban elite. The favoured status symbol is a small, pedigree lap dog that scores high in the *kawaii* (cute) stakes.

No expense is spared on these pampered pets. Specialist outfitters such as Adachiya in Asakusa (see p.87) sell diamond-studded collars and little leopard-skin numbers for that special occasion. Around Valentine's Day, department stores peddle bone-shaped chocolates in a heart-shaped dish. There are bakeries specializing in gourmet biscuits, birthday cakes and other doggie delights, while more health-conscious dog owners can treat their hound to a yoga workout or a "Happy Dog Cruise" around Tokyo Bay. You'll find examples of doggie devotion all over the city, but to see where the most privileged of pooches hang out, head for the Dogdays store (daily 11am–10pm; ⓦwww.dogdays.co.jp) in the Tokyo Midtown complex (see p.80). In addition to holistic pet products, it offers a doggy spa and even a "hotel" where you can leave your little darling while you browse the shopping malls.

Similar to Shinjuku, though not so full-on in scale, is **Ikebukuro**, dominated by the giant Seibu and Tōbu department stores. Offbeat pleasures of this part of northern Tokyo include the rickety **Toden-Arakawa Line**, Tokyo's last tramway, and a couple of pretty Japanese gardens: **Rikugi-en** and the **Kyū Furukawa Gardens**.

It costs nothing (other than a few hours' sleep) to experience the frenetic early-morning fish market at **Tsukiji**, on the edge of **Tokyo Bay**, while **Hama Rikyū Teien**, one of the city's loveliest traditional gardens, lies close by. Across the bay from here, and linked to the main city by the impressive Rainbow Bridge, is **Odaiba**, a futuristic man-made island, where you'll find **MeSci**, Tokyo's most fascinating science museum, and a passable beach, also man-made.

High-speed trains put several important sights within **day-trip** range of Tokyo, including the ancient temple and shrine towns of **Kamakura** to the south and **Nikkō** to the north. **Mount Fuji**, 100km southwest of the capital, can be climbed between June and September, while the adjoining national park area of **Hakone** offers relaxed hiking amid beautiful lakeland scenery and the chance to take a dip in an onsen – a Japanese mineral bath.

If you're looking for a quick and convenient trip to the countryside, sacred **Mount Takao**, just an hour west of the capital, provides a verdant escape. Just 40km north of Tokyo is **Kawagoe**, a great place to wander through nineteenth-century streetscapes and indulge in some serious souvenir shopping. Pop pilgrims will also want to make time for the **John Lennon Museum** at Saitama Shintoshin.

Last, but not least, there's **Yokohama**, a whole other city – Japan's second largest in fact – right on Tokyo's doorstep and well worth a look for its vibrant Chinatown and breezy waterfront districts.

▲ Conveyor-belt sushi

When to visit

One of the best times to visit Tokyo is in the **spring**, from April to early May. At the start of this period flurries of falling cherry blossom give the city a soft pink hue and by the end the temperatures are pleasant. October and November are also good months to come; this is when you'll catch the fireburst of **autumn** leaves in Tokyo's parks and gardens.

▲ Mural in a Tokyo underpass

Avoid the steamy height of **summer** in August and early September, when the city's humidity sees its citizens scurrying from one air-conditioned haven to another. From January through to March temperatures can dip to freezing, but the crisp blue **winter** skies are rarely disturbed by rain or snow showers. Carrying an umbrella in any season is a good idea but particularly so during *tsuyu*, the rainy season in June and July, and in September, when typhoons occasionally strike the coast.

Before deciding when to visit, check the city's calendar of **festivals** and special events (see pp.31–33), which range from grand sumo tournaments to the spectacular Sannō and Kanda *matsuri* (festivals) held in alternate years. Note also that many attractions shut for several days around New Year when Tokyo becomes a ghost town, as many people return to their family homes elsewhere in the country.

▼ Lanterns at Sensō-ji, Asakusa

Average temperatures and rainfall

	Average daily temperature (°F)		Average daily temperature (°C)		Average monthly rainfall	
	Max	Min	Max	Min	Inches	mm
January	49	33	10	1	4.3	110
February	50	34	10	1	6.1	155
March	55	40	13	4	9	228
April	65	50	18	10	10	254
May	73	58	23	15	9.6	244
June	78	65	25	18	12	305
July	84	72	29	22	10	254
August	87	75	31	24	8	203
September	80	68	27	20	11	279
October	70	57	21	14	9	228
November	62	47	17	8	6.4	162
December	58	38	12	3	3.8	96

22

things not to miss

It's impossible to see everything that Tokyo has to offer in one trip – and we don't suggest you try. What follows, in no particular order, is a selective and subjective taste of the city's highlights, from the most impressive museums to tranquil tea gardens, and the best day-trip destinations around the city – all arranged in colour-coded categories to help you find the best things to see, do and experience. All entries have a page reference to take you straight into the Guide, where you can find out more.

| ACTIVITIES | CONSUME | EVENTS | NATURE | SIGHTS |

01 **Rikugi-en** Page **102** • A quintessential Japanese-style garden designed to reflect scenes from ancient Japanese poetry.

02 Drinking in Shinjuku

Page **95** • From the rarified heights of the *Park Hyatt's New York Bar* to the tiny drinking dens of Golden Gai and the gay district of Ni-chōme, Shinjuku has a bar for you.

04 Happōen
Page **130** • Sip *matcha* – thick green tea – in one of Tokyo's loveliest traditional gardens.

03 Kamakura
Page **276** • Japan's ancient seaside capital offers great walks between temples and shrines, plus a giant bronze Buddha.

05 Shinjuku Gyoen
Page **111** • Japanese, English and French styles of landscape gardening combine in delightful Shinjuku Gyoen.

06 **National Art Centre** Page **81** • Set aside a chunk of time to explore this enormous new gallery, the highlight of the so-called Roppongi art triangle.

07 **Onsen bath** Page **238** • Soak your stresses away in an old neighbourhood bathhouse such as the Azabu-Jūban Onsen or the resort-like spa complex of Ōedo Onsen Monogatari in Odaiba.

08 **Harajuku** Page **113** • Pick through the Sunday flea market at Tōgō-jinja and trawl the funky backstreet boutiques and galleries.

09 **Rainbow Bridge** Page **140** • Walk across this elegant, 918-metre-long suspension bridge for fabulous views across Tokyo Harbour towards the futuristic mini-city of Odaiba.

10 **Tsukiji** Page **134** • Get up early to see the nation's top fish market in full flight and to enjoy a fresh sushi breakfast.

12 **Kabuki** Page **205** • Enjoy the liveliest of Japan's traditional performing arts at the grand Kabuki-za theatre in Ginza.

11 **Naka-Meguro** Page **127** • Discover some of the city's coolest boutiques, cafés, restaurants and bars along the tranquil banks of the Meguro River.

13 **Yūrakuchō** Page **167** • Join off-duty salarymen over a beer and a plate of *yakitori* – small meat kebabs – at the many raucous joints beneath the railway tracks in this part of town.

14 **Nikkō** Page **245** • This dazzling Tōshō-gū shrine is the star turn of this mountain town, which also boasts some of the most beautiful countryside in Japan.

16 **Meiji-jingū** Page **113** • Enjoy one of the many annual festivals or regular wedding ceremonies held at Tokyo's most venerable Shinto shrine.

15 **Hanami parties** Page **32** • Unpack your bentō and sake in Ueno Park or around the Imperial Palace moat for a picnic under the falling blossoms.

17 **River buses** Page **28** • Cruise down the Sumida-gawa or across Tokyo Bay on one of the city's river buses, including the manga-inspired *Himiko* sightseeing boat.

19 **Tokyo's fireworks** Page **33** • Spectacular displays are held every July and August over the Sumida-gawa in Asakusa and in Tokyo Bay.

20 **Ghibli Museum** Page **112** • This imaginative museum, a short journey west of Tokyo, is dedicated to the animated movies of Studio Ghibli.

18 **Asakusa** Page **84** • The city's most colourful and evocative district, home to old craft shops, traditional inns, restaurants and the bustling Sensō-ji temple.

21 **Sumo** Page **215** • Witness the titanic clashes of sumo giants at the Ryōgoku National Stadium in Ryōgoku.

22 **Yanaka** Page **96** • Charming old-fashioned district crammed with small temples and wooden houses on twisting byways.

Basics

Basics

Getting there

Airfares to Tokyo largely depend on how far in advance you book: in general, the earlier the better. Prices also reflect the season when you want to travel, with fares at their highest around the Japanese holiday periods of Golden Week (early May) and the Obon festival in mid-August, as well as at Christmas and New Year, when seats are at a premium. You'll get the best deals in the low season (Jan–March, plus Nov & Dec, excluding Christmas and New Year). Note also that flying at weekends is generally more expensive; prices quoted below assume mid-week travel.

If Tokyo is only one stop on a longer journey, you might want to consider buying a **Round the World (RTW)** ticket. The big three airline alliances – oneworld (Ⓦwww.oneworld.com), Sky Team (Ⓦwww.skyteam.com) and Star Alliance (Ⓦwww.staralliance.com) – all offer RTW tickets routed through Tokyo. Prices depend on your itinerary, but count on at least £1200 from the UK, US$4000 from the US and Aus$3200 from Australia, excluding taxes and surcharges. It may also be worth checking out the **regional air passes** and **Circle Pacific** tickets offered by some airlines.

Tokyo isn't a difficult city for the independent traveller to negotiate, nor need it be horrendously expensive. However, if you're worried about the cost or potential language problems, a **package tour** is worth considering. Flight-and-accommodation packages are often cheaper than booking the two separately, particularly if you want to stay in the more upmarket hotels. Prices for a return flight, five nights' accommodation at a three- or four-star hotel and airport transfers begin at around £800 from the UK, US$1000 from the US and Aus$1800 from Australia, based on double occupancy.

Flights from the US and Canada

A number of airlines fly nonstop from the US and Canada to Tokyo, including Air Canada, ANA, American Airlines, Continental, Japan Airlines, United and Northwest, with connections from virtually every regional airport. Flying time is around fifteen hours from New York, thirteen hours from Chicago and ten hours from Los Angeles.

Many flights are offered at substantial discounts, so keep an eye out for special offers. In general, return fares to Tokyo start at around US$1000 from Chicago or New York; from Los Angeles, US$800; and from Vancouver, Can$1200.

Flights from the UK and Ireland

All Nippon Airways, British Airways, Japan Airlines and Virgin fly nonstop **from London** to Tokyo, taking about twelve hours. Flying from elsewhere in the UK or **from Ireland**, you'll need to stop over en route; the cheapest options usually involve changing planes in London or Paris.

Return fares to Tokyo from London start from around £500. However, you can find occasional special deals from as low as £400, so it pays to shop around. From Dublin, expect to pay in the region of €800.

Flights from Australia, New Zealand and South Africa

Qantas, Japan Airlines and Air New Zealand operate **nonstop** flights to Tokyo from Australia and New Zealand. Flying time is around ten hours from Australia and twelve hours from New Zealand. Alternatively, you can also reach Japan from either country with one of the southeast Asian carriers, flying via their home base. **Return fares** from Australia to Tokyo kick off at around Aus$1300 with one stopover, or Aus$1500

Fly less – stay longer! Travel and climate change

Climate change is a serious threat to the ecosystems that humans rely upon, and air travel is among the fastest-growing contributors to the problem. Rough Guides regard travel, overall, as a global benefit, and feel strongly that the advantages to developing economies are important, as is the opportunity of greater contact and awareness among peoples. But we all have a responsibility to limit our personal impact on global warming, and that means giving thought to how often we fly, and what we can do to redress the harm that our trips create.

Flying and climate change

Pretty much every form of motorized travel generates CO_2 – the main cause of human-induced climate change – but planes also generate climate-warming contrails and cirrus clouds and emit oxides of nitrogen, which create ozone (another greenhouse gas) at flight levels. Furthermore, flying simply allows us to travel much further than we otherwise would do. The figures are frightening: one person taking a return flight between Europe and California produces the equivalent impact of 2.5 tonnes of CO_2 – similar to the yearly output of the average UK car.

Fuel-cell and other less harmful types of plane may emerge eventually. But until then, there are really just two options for concerned travellers: to reduce the amount we travel by air (take fewer trips – stay for longer!), and to make the trips we do take "climate neutral" via a carbon offset scheme.

Carbon offset schemes

Offset schemes run by ⓦwww.climatecare.org, ⓦwww.carbonneutral.com and others allow you to make up for some or all of the greenhouse gases that you are responsible for releasing. To do this, they provide "carbon calculators" for working out the global-warming contribution of a specific flight (or even your entire existence), and then let you contribute an appropriate amount of money to fund offsetting measures. These include rainforest reforestation and initiatives to reduce future energy demand – often run in conjunction with sustainable development schemes.

Rough Guides, together with Lonely Planet and other concerned partners in the travel industry, are supporting a carbon offset scheme run by climatecare.org. Please take the time to view our website and see how you can help to make your trip climate neutral.

ⓦ**www.roughguides.com/climatechange**

for a nonstop flight. From New Zealand prices start at roughly NZ$1700, though the most direct routings will cost at least NZ$2000.

Flying **from South Africa**, you'll be routed through southeast Asia or the Middle East, since there are no direct services to Japan. Promotional fares can be as cheap as R8000, though you're more likely to be paying in the region of R10,000 and above.

Airlines, agents and operators

Contact details for airlines in the listings below are given selectively, reflecting the territories from which they offer flights to Tokyo.

Online booking

ⓦ**www.ebookers.com** (in UK), ⓦ**www.ebookers.ie** (in Ireland)
ⓦ**www.expedia.co.uk** (in UK), ⓦ**www.expedia.com** (in US) ⓦ**www.expedia.ca** (in Canada)
ⓦ**www.lastminute.com**
ⓦ**www.opodo.co.uk** (in UK)
ⓦ**www.orbitz.com** (in US)
ⓦ**www.travelocity.co.uk** (in UK), ⓦ**www.travelocity.com** (in US), ⓦ**www.travelocity.ca** (in Canada)
ⓦ**www.zuji.com** (in Australia and New Zealand)

Airlines

Air Canada US & Canada ☏1-888/247-2262, ⓦwww.aircanada.ca.

Air France UK ☎ 0870/142 4343,
🖳 www.airfrance.com, Republic of Ireland
☎ 01/605 0383, 🖳 www.airfrance.ie.
Air New Zealand Australia ☎ 13 24 76, New
Zealand ☎ 0800/737 000, 🖳 www.airnz.com.
Alitalia UK ☎ 0870/544 8259, 🖳 www.alitalia.com.
All Nippon Airways (ANA) US & Canada
☎ 1-800/235-9262, UK ☎ 0870/837 8866,
🖳 www.anaskyweb.com.
American Airlines US & Canada ☎ 1-800/433-
7300, 🖳 www.aa.com.
Asiana Airlines US ☎ 1-800/227-4262,
UK ☎ 020/7304 9900, Australia ☎ 02/9767 4334,
🖳 www.flyasiana.com.
Austrian Airlines UK ☎ 0870/460 0191, Republic
of Ireland ☎ 1800/509 142, 🖳 www.aua.com.
British Airways US & Canada ☎ 1-800/247-9297,
UK ☎ 0870/850 9850, Republic of Ireland
☎ 1890/626 747, 🖳 www.britishairways.com.
Cathay Pacific US ☎ 1-800/233-2742, Canada
☎ 1-800/268-6868, UK ☎ 020/8834 8888,
Australia ☎ 13 17 47, New Zealand ☎ 09/379
0861, South Africa ☎ 011/700 8900,
🖳 www.cathaypacific.com.
China Airlines Australia ☎ 02/9231 5588,
🖳 www.china-airlines.com.
China Eastern UK ☎ 0870/760 6232, Australia
☎ 02/9290 1148, 🖳 www.flychinaeastern.com.
Continental Airlines US & Canada ☎ 1-800/231-
0856, 🖳 www.continental.com.
Delta US & Canada ☎ 1-800/221-1212,
🖳 www.delta.com.
Emirates South Africa ☎ 0861/364 728,
🖳 www.emirates.com/za.
Garuda Indonesia Australia ☎ 02/9334 9944,
New Zealand ☎ 09/366 1862,
🖳 www.garuda-indonesia.com.
Japan Airlines (JAL) US & Canada ☎ 1-800/525-
3663, UK ☎ 0845/774 7700, Republic of Ireland
☎ 01/408 3757, Australia ☎ 02/9272 1111,
New Zealand ☎ 09/379 9906, South Africa
☎ 011/214 2560 🖳 www.jal.com.
KLM Royal Dutch Airlines UK ☎ 0870/507 4074,
Republic of Ireland ☎ 1850/747 400,
🖳 www.klm.com.
Korean Airlines US & Canada ☎ 1-800/438-5000,
UK ☎ 0800/413 000, Republic of Ireland ☎ 01/799
7990, Australia ☎ 02/9262 6000, New Zealand
☎ 09/914 2000, 🖳 www.koreanair.com.
Lufthansa UK ☎ 0870/837 7747, Republic of
Ireland ☎ 01/844 5544, 🖳 www.lufthansa.co.uk.
Malaysia Airlines Australia ☎ 13 26 27,
New Zealand ☎ 09/373 2741, South Africa
☎ 011/880 9614, 🖳 www.mas.com.my.
Northwest Airlines US & Canada ☎ 1-800/225-
2525, 🖳 www.nwa.com.

Qantas Australia ☎ 13 13 13, New Zealand
☎ 09/357 8900, 🖳 www.qantas.com.au.
Qatar Airways South Africa ☎ 011/523 2928,
🖳 www.qatarairways.com.
Scandinavian Airlines UK ☎ 0870/6072 7727,
Republic of Ireland ☎ 01/844 5440,
🖳 www.flysas.com.
Singapore Airlines US ☎ 1-800/742-3333,
Canada ☎ 1-800/663-3046, Australia ☎ 13 10 11,
New Zealand ☎ 0800/808 909, South Africa
☎ 011/880 8560, 🖳 www.singaporeair.com.
South African Airways South Africa ☎ 011/978
5313, 🖳 www.flysaa.com.
Swiss International Airlines UK ☎ 0845/601
0956, 🖳 www.swiss.com.
Thai Airways International Australia
☎ 1300/651 960, New Zealand ☎ 09/377 3886,
🖳 www.thaiair.com.
United Airlines US & Canada ☎ 1-800/864-8331,
🖳 www.united.com.
Virgin Atlantic UK ☎ 0870/380 2007,
🖳 www.virgin-atlantic.com.

Travel agents and tour operators

Adventure Center US ☎ 1-800/228-8747,
🖳 www.adventurecenter.com. Among their offerings
is a two-week tour based around Tokyo, including the
chance to climb Mount Fuji.

Artisans of Leisure US ☎1-800/214-8144, ⓦwww.artisansofleisure.com. Luxury private tours staying in ryokan and top hotels. Options include a culinary tour of Tokyo, Kyoto and Hakone, and a classic Japan family tour.

AsiaFare UK ☎020/7038 3945, ⓦwww.asia-fare.co.uk. Accommodation packages and customized itineraries.

AWL Pitt Australia ☎02/9264 7384, ⓦwww.japanpackage.com.au. Sydney-based agent offering Japan packages with time in Tokyo, plus accommodation packages, customized tours, Japan Rail passes and so forth.

AWL Travel UK ☎020/7222 1144, ⓦwww.awlt.com. Specialists in travel to Japan, offering discount airfares, tours and Japan Rail passes.

Baumann Travel US ☎914/419-8470, ⓦwww.baumanntravel.com. Arts and cultural tours, covering themes such as Japanese gardens, cuisine and cherry blossom.

Elite Orient Tours US & Canada ☎1-800/668-8100 or 416/977-3026, ⓦwww.elitetours.com. Tokyo mini-tours for independent travellers, fully escorted tours and accommodation packages.

eTours Online UK ☎020/7312 1708, ⓦwww.etours-online.com. Flights plus well-priced semi-escorted, independent and special-interest tours.

Exodus UK ☎020/8675 5550, ⓦwww.exodus.co.uk. Options include a fourteen-day tour of "Ancient and Modern Japan" ending in Tokyo.

Explore Worldwide UK ☎0870/333 4001, Republic of Ireland c/o Maxwells Travel ☎01/677 9479, ⓦwww.exploreworldwide.com. Offers a "Shogun Trail" two-week guided tour of Japan, flying into Tokyo and out of Fukuoka.

Explorient Travel Services US ☎1-800/785-1233, ⓦwww.explorient.com. Broad range of options, from family-oriented holidays to climbing Mount Fuji. Also offers unescorted programmes and tailor-made tours.

Far East Gateways UK ☎0161/437 4371, ⓦwww.gateways.co.uk. Escorted sightseeing tours and accommodation packages. The "Golden Route" comprises an eleven-day trip including Tokyo, Nikkō, Kamakura and Hakone.

Frank Lloyd Wright Preservation Trust US ☎708/848-1976, ⓦwww.wrightplus.org. The trust runs an annual tour to Tokyo and Japan, focusing around the work and legacy of architect Frank Lloyd Wright.

GET Educational Tours Australia ☎02/9221 5911, ⓦwww.getours.com.au. Study tours, holidays and homestays from this education specialist.

H.I.S. Travel Japan Australia ☎02/9267 0555, New Zealand ☎09/336 1336, ⓦwww.traveljapan.com.au. Long-established specialist Japan agent

providing everything from flights to Tokyo packages and customized itineraries.

IACE Travel US ☎1-866/735-4223, ⓦwww.iace-asia.com. The International Association for Cultural Exchange offers youth exchange programmes, sumo- and kabuki-themed tours and the like.

Imaginative Traveller UK ☎0800/316 2717, Republic of Ireland ☎0147/366 7337, ⓦwww.imaginative-traveller.com. Small-group adventure tour operator. Their fifteen-day "Empire of the Sun" tour includes climbing Mount Fuji and time in Tokyo.

Inside Japan UK ☎0870/120 5600, ⓦwww.insidejapan.com. Interesting range of well-designed small-group, self-guided and fully tailored trips, ranging from Tokyo stopovers to climbing Mount Fuji.

Into Japan UK ☎01865/841 443, ⓦwww.intojapan.co.uk. Upmarket tailor-made and special-interest tours. Options at the time of writing included a fifteen-day Kabuki tour.

Intrepid Travel UK ☎020/7354 6169, Australia ☎1300/364 512 or 03/9473 2626, ⓦwww.intrepidtravel.com. This adventure specialist offers some interesting Tokyo tours, including a Flavours of Tokyo culinary tour and an Old Edo, New Tokyo cultural programme – plus a guided climb of Mount Fuji, of course.

Jalpak/Jaltour US ☎1-800/221-1081, ⓦwww.jalpak.com; UK ☎0870/111 8830, ⓦwww.jaltour.co.uk; Australia ☎02/9285 6603, ⓦwww.jalpak.com.au. Japan Airlines' tour arm sells a range of holiday packages and can put together personalized itineraries.

Japan Journeys UK ☎020/7766 5267, ⓦwww.japanjourneys.co.uk. Tokyo options include a six-night "Manga Tour" and a shopping tour.

Japan Package Tours Australia ☎03/9909 7212, ⓦwww.japanpackagetours.com.au. Fully escorted and self-guided tours, tailor-made itineraries, accommodation packages and rail passes.

Japan Travel Bureau (JTB) US ☎1-800/235-3523, ⓦwww.jtbusa.com; Canada ☎416/367 5824, ⓦwww.jtbi.ca; Australia ☎1800/800 956 or 03/8623 0000, ⓦwww.japantravel.com.au. In addition to flights, Tokyo stopovers and hotel options, they handle Sunrise Tours (see p.29) taking in the capital and surrounding region, and can put together individual escorted programmes.

Japan Travel Centre UK ☎0870/890 0360, ⓦwww.japantravel.co.uk. Offers flights, accommodation packages, Japan Rail passes and guided tours, including five nights in Tokyo or Tokyo plus Kyoto.

Journeys East US ☎1-800/527-2612, ⓦwww.journeyseast.com. Small-group cultural tours focusing on art and architecture.

Kintetsu International Express US ☏ 212/422-3481, ⓦ www.japanforyou.com; Australia ☏ 02/8251 3300, ⓦ www.kintetsu.com.au. Package-and day-tour operator with a good variety of trips on offer, covering everything from architecture to onsen.

Magical Japan UK ☏ 0161/962 9054, ⓦ www.magicaljapan.co.uk. Their guided tours all offer at least three days in and around Tokyo; customized packages possible.

Mitsui Travel Australia ☏ 02/9262 5100, ⓦ www.mitsuitravel.com.au. Options include a three-night onsen tour to Tokyo and Hakone and an eight-night traditional Tokyo and Kyoto tour.

Nippon Travel Agency Australia ☏ 02/9338 2300, New Zealand ☏ 09/309 5750, ⓦ www.nta.com.au. This giant Japanese travel agency offers standard and bespoke tours.

North South Travel UK ☏ 01245/608291, ⓦ www.northsouthtravel.co.uk. Friendly travel agency offering discount fares; profits support projects in the developing world, especially the promotion of sustainable tourism.

Oxalis Holidays UK ☏ 020/7099 6147, ⓦ www.oxalis-adventures.com. Broad range of escorted small-group tours, many including Tokyo, such as the classic two-week "Shogun and Samurai" tour or the ten-day "Bushido" cultural tour.

Price Travel Services Australia ☏ 1800/221 707 or 02/9247 3086, ⓦ www.pricetravelservices.com.au. Over twenty years' experience in running tours to Japan, with a number of Tokyo options.

STA Travel US ☏ 1-800/781-4040, ⓦ www.statravel.com; UK ☏ 0871/230 0040, ⓦ www.statravel.co.uk; Australia ☏ 13 47 82, ⓦ www.statravel.com.au; New Zealand ☏ 0800/474 400 or 09/356 1550, ⓦ www.statravel.co.nz; South Africa ☏ 0861/781 781, ⓦ www.statravel.co.za. Worldwide specialists in low-cost flights, overland and holiday deals. Good discounts for students and under-26s. Also arranges student IDs.

Trailfinders UK ☏ 0845/054 6060, Republic of Ireland ☏ 01/677 7888, ⓦ www.trailfinders.com. Well-established agent for independent travellers offering a four-day Tokyo Discovery tour, among other Japan options. Also does tailor-made holidays, flights and accommodation packages.

Travel Cuts US ☏ 1-800/592-2887, Canada ☏ 1-866/246-9762, ⓦ www.travelcuts.com. Student fares, IDs, insurance and other travel services run by the Canadian Federation of Students.

USIT Northern Ireland ☏ 028/9032 7111, Republic of Ireland ☏ 01/602 1904, ⓦ www.usit.ie. Specialists in student, youth and independent travel – flights, trains, accommodation, study tours, visas and more.

Arrival

If you're arriving in Tokyo from abroad, you'll almost certainly touch down at Narita International Airport; flying in from elsewhere in Japan, you'll land at Haneda Airport on Tokyo Bay. Otherwise, you'll be arriving at one of the main train stations or long-distance bus terminals, or at the ferry port at Ariake on Tokyo Bay.

By air

Narita International Airport (成田国際空港; ☏ 0476/34-8000, ⓦ www.narita-airport.jp) is some 66km east of the city centre. There are two terminals, both with **cash machines** which accept foreign credit and debit cards, and **bureaux de change** (daily 6.30am–11pm), which offer the same rates as city banks. Both terminals also have **tourist information** and **Welcome Inn Reservation** Centres for accommodation bookings (daily 8am–8pm; ⓦ www.itcj.jp). If you have a Japan Rail Pass (see p.27) exchange order, you can arrange to use your pass either immediately or at a later date at the JR travel agencies (not the ticket offices) in the basement; English signs indicate where these are.

Located on a spit of land jutting into Tokyo Bay 20km south of the Imperial

Palace, **Haneda Airport** (羽田空港; flight information ☏03/5757-8111, ⓦwww.tokyo -airport-bldg.co.jp) is where most domestic flights touch down. There are plans to expand international routes from here, specifically in the immediate Asian region. The airport has a small branch of the **Tokyo Tourist Information Centre** (daily 9am–10pm; ☏03/5757-9345), and the airport's information desk can provide you with an English-language map of Tokyo.

There are frequent bus (1hr 20min; ¥3000) and rail (1hr 10min; ¥1580) connections between Narita and Haneda.

Transport between the airports and Tokyo

The fastest way into Tokyo **from Narita** is on one of the frequent Japan Rail (JR) or Keisei **trains** that depart from the basements of both terminals. **Keisei** (ⓦwww.keisei.co.jp), located on the left side of the basements, offers the cheapest connection into town in the form of the no-frills *tokkyū* (limited express) service, which costs ¥1000 to Ueno (every 30min; 1hr 11min). This service also stops at Nippori, a few minutes north of Ueno, where it's easy to transfer to the Yamanote or the Keihin Tōhoku lines. If you're staying around Ueno, or you're not carrying much luggage, this – or Keisei's slightly faster and fancier Skyliner (¥1920; 56min) – is a good option.

JR, who operate from the right-hand side of the basements, run the more luxurious red and silver **Narita Express** (**N'EX**; ⓦwww .jreast.co.jp/e/nex) to several city stations. The cheapest fare is ¥2940 to Tokyo Station (every 30min; 1hr), and there are frequent direct N'EX services to Shinjuku (hourly; 1hr 20min) for ¥3110. The N'EX services to Ikebukuro (¥3110) and Yokohama (¥4180) via Shinagawa are much less frequent; heading for Ikebukoro, you're better off going to Shinjuku and changing onto the Yamanote line, while there are plenty of trains to Yokohama from Tokyo Station.

If you have a non-Japanese passport, JR offers a great **discount package**: for ¥3500 you can get a ticket on the N'EX to any Tokyo stations it serves, or Yokohama, plus a Suica card (see p.27) to the value of ¥2000 (comprising a ¥500 deposit plus ¥1500 of train and subway travel). This actually makes travelling on the N'EX a way better deal than the JR *kaisoku* (rapid) trains which, despite the name, chug slowly into Tokyo Station (hourly; 1hr 20min) for ¥1280.

The travel agency HIS has started offering a new **free bus service** into Tokyo, specifically eight buses daily to Akihabara and Shinjuku; to use this, you need first to register and book online at ⓦen.wa-shoi.com. The paid alternative, **Airport Limousine buses** (☏03/3665-7220, ⓦwww.limousinebus.co.jp), is prone to delays in traffic, but can be useful if you're weighed down by luggage. You buy tickets from the limousine bus counters in each of the arrival lobbies; the buses depart directly outside (check which platform you need) and stop at a wide range of places around the city, including all the major hotels and train stations. Journeys to hotels in central Tokyo cost around ¥3000 and take at least ninety minutes. Although tickets are pricier than the train, once you factor in the cost of a taxi from one of the train stations to your hotel, these buses can be a good deal. Their ¥3100 **Limousine & Metro Pass** combines a one-way bus trip from Narita to central Tokyo and a one-day pass for the Tokyo Metro, valid on nine of Tokyo's thirteen subway lines.

Taxis to the city centre can be caught from stand 15 outside Terminal One and stands 29 and 30 outside Terminal Two; the journey will set you back around ¥20,000, and is no faster than going by bus.

From Haneda Airport, it's a twenty-minute monorail journey to Hamamatsuchō Station on the Yamanote line (daily 5.20am–11.15pm; every 5–10min; ¥460). Alternatively you can board a Keihin Kūkō-line train to Shinagawa

Departing Tokyo from Narita

If you're **leaving Tokyo** from Narita airport, it's important to set off around four hours before your flight. Nevertheless, during peak holiday periods, queues at the baggage check-in and immigration desks at Narita are lengthy. **International departure tax** from Narita is included in the price of your ticket.

or Sengakuji and connect directly with other rail and subway lines. A taxi from Haneda to central Tokyo costs ¥6000, while a limousine bus to Tokyo Station is ¥900.

By train and bus

If you're coming into Tokyo by Shinkansen **JR train** from Ōsaka, Kyoto and other points west, you'll pull in to **Tokyo Station** (東京駅), close to the Imperial Palace, or **Shinagawa Station** (品川駅), around 6km southwest. Most Shinkansen services from the north (the Hokuriku line from Nagano, the Jōetsu line from Niigata and the Tōhoku lines from Akita, Hachinohe and Yamagata) arrive at Tokyo Station, though a few services go only as far as **Ueno Station** (上野駅), some 4km north-east of the Imperial Palace. Tokyo, Shinagawa and Ueno stations are all on the Yamanote line and are connected to several subway lines, putting them within reach of most of the capital. Other long-distance JR services stop at Tokyo and Ueno stations, Shinjuku Station on Tokyo's west side and Ikebukuro Station in the city's northwest corner.

Non-JR trains terminate at different stations: the Tōkyū Tōyoko line from Yokohama ends at **Shibuya Station** (渋谷駅), southwest of the Imperial Palace; the Tōbu Nikkō line runs from Nikkō to **Asakusa Station** (浅草駅), east of Ueno; and the Odakyū line from Hakone finishes at **Shinjuku Station** (新宿駅), which is also the terminus for the Seibu Shinjuku line from Kawagoe. All these stations have subway connections and (apart from Asakusa) are on the Yamanote rail line.

Long-distance buses pull in at several major stations around the city, making transport connections straightforward. The main overnight services from Kyoto and Ōsaka arrive at the bus station beside the eastern Yaesu exit of Tokyo Station; other buses arrive at Ikebukuro, Shibuya, Shinagawa and Shinjuku.

By boat

The most memorable way to arrive in the capital is by long-distance **ferry**, sailing past the suspended roads and monorail on the Rainbow Bridge and the harbour wharves to dock at Tokyo Ferry Terminal (東京フェリーターミナル) at Ariake, on the man-made island of Odaiba (see p.138) in Tokyo Bay. There are ferry connections to Tokyo from Kōchi and Tokushima on Shikoku and Tomakomai on Hokkaidō. For more details see the website of the **Tokyo Port Terminal Corporation** (@www.tptc.or.jp). Buses run from the port to Shin-Kiba Station, which is both on the subway and ten minutes' ride from Tokyo Station on the JR Keiyō line. A taxi from the port to central Tokyo shouldn't cost more than ¥2000.

Getting around

All of Tokyo's public transport system is efficient, clean and safe. As a visitor you'll probably find the trains and subways the best way of getting around; a lack of signs in English makes the bus system a lot more challenging. For short, cross-town journeys, taxis are handy and, if shared by a group of people, not that expensive. Cycling (see p.240 for bike-rental outlets) can also be a good way of zipping around if you stick to the quiet backstreets.

If you'd prefer someone else to take care of the transport logistics, Tokyo has a wide range of sightseeing **tours** that are worth considering if you are pushed for time or want a guided commentary.

By subway

Its colourful map may look like a messy plate of noodles, but Tokyo's **subway** is relatively easy to negotiate: the simple colour-coding

Tokyo transport passes

If you're on a short visit and making minimal use of the subway or trains, you could buy **kaisūken**, carnet-type tickets. Regular *kaisūken* give you eleven tickets of a specific value for the price of ten; there are also offpeak *kaisūken*, twelve tickets for the price of ten, but valid only between 10am and 4pm on weekdays; and Saturday/Sunday and public holiday *kaisūken*, fourteen weekend/holiday tickets for the price of ten. *Kaisūken* can be bought using the special buttons, labelled in Japanese, on ticket machines at stations, or from ticket offices.

If you need to ride the metro and trains a lot in the space of a day, you'll find both Tokyo Metro and Toei have day tickets for use exclusively on their own subway systems (¥710 and ¥700 respectively), the Toei pass also covering the city's buses. However, it's far more convenient to get a one-day **economy pass** covering both systems for ¥1000. For day-use of the city's subways, JR trains and buses there's the **Tokyo Free Ticket** (¥1580), but you'd really have to be tearing all over town to get your money's worth.

The most convenient pass, however, is **PASMO** (ⓦ www.pasmo.co.jp), a stored-value card that can be used on all subways and both JR and private trains in the wider Tokyo area, and which will eventually be usable on city buses when they're fitted with the required sensors. Tap the pass on the electronic sensor as you go through the ticket barriers and the appropriate fare will be deducted. The card can be recharged at ticket machines and ticket offices as the value runs down.

PASMO is basically an extension of JR's **Suica** card, which covers not just JR but also private trains, as well as buses. To get either card, you have to spend a minimum of ¥2000, of which ¥500 is a deposit, ¥1500 stored value.

Otherwise, there's the **SF Metro Card** (or **Passnet Card**) which can be used on Tokyo Metro and Toei subways and all the private railways (but not JR) in the Tokyo area. As you go through a ticket barrier, the appropriate fare is deducted from the card's stored value (¥1000, ¥3000 or ¥5000, no deposit needed); cards can be bought from ticket offices and machines, and also used in machines to pay for a supplementary ticket if there isn't enough value left to allow you through the barrier.

Finally, if you're here for a month or more and will be travelling the same route most days, look into getting a **teiki** season ticket, which runs for one, three or six months, and covers your specified route and stations in between.

on trains and maps, as well as clear signposts (many in English), directional arrows, and alpha-numeric codes for all central subway stations, make this by far the most *gaijin*-friendly form of transport. And while during rush hour (7.30–9am & 5.30–7.30pm) you may find yourself crushed between someone's armpit and another person's back, only rarely do the infamous white-gloved platform attendants shove commuters into carriages.

There are two systems, the privately owned nine-line **Tokyo Metro** (ⓦ www .tokyometro.jp) and the four-line **Toei** (ⓦ www.kotsu.metro.tokyo.jp), run by the city authority. The systems share some stations, but unless you buy a special ticket from the vending machines that specifies your route from one system to the other, or you have a pass (see box above), you cannot switch mid-journey between the two sets of lines without paying extra at the ticket barrier. Subways have connecting passageways to overland train lines, such as the Yamanote. A colour **map** of the subway system appears at the back of the book.

You'll generally pay for your **ticket** at the vending machines beside the electronic ticket gates. There are no ticket sales windows other than at major stations. Most trips across central Tokyo cost no more than ¥190, but if you're fazed by the wide range of price buttons, buy the cheapest ticket (¥160) and sort out the difference with the gatekeeper at the other end. A useful alternative to buying individual tickets is to get one of the many types of passes (see box opposite).

Trains run daily from around 5am to just after midnight, and during peak daytime hours as frequently as every five minutes (and at least every fifteen minutes at other times). Leaving a station can be complicated by the number of exits (sixty in Shinjuku, for example), but there are maps close to the ticket barriers and on the platforms indicating where the exits emerge, and strips of yellow tiles on the floor mark the routes to the ticket barriers.

By rail

Japan Railways East (Ⓦwww.jreast.co.jp), part of the national rail network, runs the main overland services in and around Tokyo, and there also several private railways, including lines run by Odakyū, Tobu, Seibu and Tokyu. Spend any length of time in the city and you'll become very familiar with the JR **Yamanote train line** (shown in green on network maps) that loops around the city centre. Another useful JR route is the **Chūō line** (orange on network maps; the trains are also painted orange), which starts at Tokyo Station and runs west to Shinjuku and the suburbs beyond, to terminate beside the mountains at Takao; the rapid services (look for the red *kanji* characters on the side of the train) miss out on some stations. JR's **Sōbu line** (dark yellow on maps; trains are pale yellow or deep orange) goes from Chiba in the east to Mitaka in the west, and runs parallel to the Chūō line in the centre of Tokyo, doubling as a local service stopping at all stations. Finally, you might have reason to use the blue JR **Keihin Tōhoku line**, which runs from Ōmiya in the north through Tokyo Station and on to Yokohama and beyond. It's fine to transfer between JR lines on the same ticket, but you'll have to buy a new ticket if you transfer to a subway line.

As on the subway, **tickets** are bought from vending machines. The lowest fare on JR lines is ¥130. Like the subways, JR offers prepaid cards and *kaisūken* (carnet) deals on tickets. One of the handiest is the **Suica**, a stored-value card, which is available from ticket machines in all JR stations. Also a good deal is the one-day **Tokunai Pass** (¥730), which gives unlimited travel on JR trains within the Tokyo Metropolitan District Area.

If you're planning a lot of travel around Japan in a short period of time by train, then the **Japan Rail Pass** (Ⓦwww.japanrailpass.net) can be a good deal. JR East offers its own versions of the pass, covering just its network in the Tokyo region and northern Japan. Possibly worth considering if you intend to travel to destinations around Tokyo such as Nikkō, or further afield, is the flexible three-day pass (¥10,000; valid between July 1 and Oct 31 only), which can be used either on three consecutive days or on three separate days within a month. For more details, see Ⓦwww.jreast .co.jp/e/eastpass_sp.

By monorail

Tokyo has a couple of monorail systems – the **Tokyo monorail**, which runs from Hamamatsuchō to Haneda Airport, and the **Yurikamome monorail**, which connects Shinbashi with Toyosu via Odaiba. These services operate like the city's private rail lines – you buy separate tickets for journeys on them or you can travel using the various stored-value cards, such as Passnet and Pasmo.

By bus

Once you've got a feel for the city, **buses** can be a good way of cutting across the few areas of Tokyo not served by a subway or train line. Only a small number of the buses or routes are labelled in English, so you'll have to get used to recognizing *kanji* place names or memorize the numbers of useful bus routes. The final destination is on the front of the bus, along with the route number. You pay on entry, by dropping the flat rate of ¥200 into the fare box by the driver (there's a machine in the box for changing notes). A recorded voice announces the next stop in advance, as well as issuing constant warnings about not forgetting your belongings when you get off the bus. If you're not sure when your stop is, ask your fellow passengers. The Transport Bureau of Tokyo Metropolitan Government issues a useful English pamphlet and map of all the bus routes; pick one up from one of the tourist information centres (see p.47).

By ferry

The Tokyo Cruise Ship Company (☎0120-977311, ⓦwww.suijobus.co.jp) runs several **ferry** services, known as *suijō basu* (water buses), in and around Tokyo Bay. The most popular is the double-decker Sumida-gawa river service (daily 10am–6.30pm; every 30–50min), plying the 40-minute route between **Hinode Pier** (aka Hinode Sanbashi), on Tokyo Bay, and **Asakusa**, northeast of the city centre, where they dock under Azuma-bashi opposite Philippe Starck's eye-catching Super Dry Building. Heading downriver, boats call at the gardens of **Hama Rikyū Teien** near Ginza, though note that 3.40pm is usually the last departure calling here. The ferries' large picture windows, which give a completely different view of the city from the one you'll get on the streets, are reason enough for hopping aboard. The **fare**

from one end of the route to the other is ¥760; you can buy a combination ticket for the ferry and gardens for around ¥1020.

For a few hundred extra yen you can travel on the *Himiko*, a space-age ferry (4 daily between Asakusa and Odaiba via Hinode). Designed by Matsumoto Reiji, a famous manga artist, this silver-painted ship changes its name to *Jicoo* at night, when it becomes a floating bar (see p.177).

Hinode Pier (close by Hinode Station on the Yurikamome monorail or a 10min walk from Hamamatsuchō Station on the Yamanote line) is also the jumping-off point for several good daily **cruises** around Tokyo Bay, and for ferries to various points around the island of Odaiba, or across to Kasai Rinkai-kōen on the east side of the bay. In bad weather ferries and cruises are best avoided, especially if you're prone to seasickness.

Japanese addresses

Japanese addresses are described by a hierarchy of areas, rather than numbers running consecutively along named roads. A typical address starts with the largest administrative district – in Tokyo's case it's Tokyo-*to* (metropolis), but elsewhere most commonly it's the *ken* (prefecture) accompanied by a seven-digit postcode – for example, Saitama-ken 850-0072. Next comes the *ku* (ward; for example Shinjuku-ku), followed by the *chō* (district), then the *chōme* (local neighbourhood), the block and the individual building. Finally might come the building name and the floor on which the business or person is located.

Japanese addresses are therefore written in reverse order from the Western system. However, when written in English, they usually follow the Western order; this is the system we adopt in the guide. For example, the address 2-12-7 Roppongi, Minato-ku identifies building number 7, somewhere on block 12 of number 2 *chōme* in Roppongi district, in the Minato ward of Tokyo. Note that this address can also be written 12-7 Roppongi, 2-chōme, Minato-ku. Where the block is entirely taken up by one building, the address will have only two numbers, while a few addresses might contain four numbers, the first one being for a separate business within a certain part of the block.

Many buildings bear a small metal tag with their number (eg 2-12-7, or just 12-7), while lampposts often have a bigger plaque with the district name in *kanji* and the block reference (eg 2-12). The Japanese number **floors** using the American system, hence 1F is the ground floor, 2F the first floor above ground, B1F the first floor below ground.

Though the system's not too difficult in theory, actually **locating an address** on the ground can be frustrating. The consolation is that even Japanese people find it tough. The best strategy is to have the address written down, preferably in Japanese, and then get to the nearest train or bus station. Once in the neighbourhood, start asking; local police boxes (*kōban*) are a good bet and have detailed maps of their own areas. If all else fails, don't be afraid to phone – often someone will come to meet you. In addition, technology is coming to the rescue: Japan's latest generation of mobile phones use a combination of GPS, the Internet and QR bar codes to help with navigation (see box, p.46).

By taxi

For short hops around the centre of Tokyo, **taxis** are often the best option. The basic rate is ¥660 for the first 2km, after which the meter racks up ¥80 every 274m, plus a time charge when the taxi is moving at less than 10km per hour. Between 11pm and 5am, rates are about twenty percent higher.

Most taxis have a limit of four passengers. There's never any need to open or close the passenger doors since they are operated by the taxi driver. It's a good idea to have the name and address of your destination clearly written on a piece of paper to hand to the driver, but don't expect him to know where he's going; a stop at a local police box may be necessary to locate the exact address.

Taxis can be flagged down on most roads. A red light next to the driver means the cab is free; green means it's occupied. There are designated stands in the busiest parts of town, but after the trains stop at night, be prepared for long queues, especially in areas such as Roppongi and Shinjuku. The major taxi firms are Daiwa (☏03/3503-8421); Hinomaru Limousine (☏03/3212-0505, ⑩www.hinomaru.co.jp); Kokusai (☏03/3452-5931) and Nippon Kōtsū (☏03/3799-9220 24hr English answering service).

Sightseeing tours

For a quick overview of Tokyo there are several **bus tours**, ranging from half-day jaunts around the central sights to visits out to Kamakura, Nikkō and Hakone. The tours are a hassle-free way of covering a lot of ground with English-speaking guides, though all the places they visit are easy enough to get to independently. If bus tours are not your cup of tea, but you still fancy having a guide on hand, there are also various **walking** or **cycling** tours, while a few companies now offer upscale customized tours. See also p.178 for details of culinary tours and activities, and opposite for sightseeing ferries.

Asahi Helicopter ☏03/5569-7372, ⑩www .asahi-heli.co.jp. If the sky's no limit, treat yourself to a helicopter ride over the city, soaring over Ginza, Shinjuku and Asakusa. Prices start at ¥7500 per person for a day-time flight and ¥8000 at night, or you can charter a romantic moonlight flight from ¥29,000 for two.

Bespoke Tokyo ☏03/3462-2663, ⑩www .bespoketokyo.jp. Upmarket customized tours, aimed at business visitors and anyone who has a specific interest in Tokyo, are offered by two journalists, both long-time expat residents with an intimate knowledge of the city.

Experience Tokyo ☏03/5328-4030, ⑩www .j-experience.com. Try your hand at calligraphy, *taiko* drumming or wielding a samurai sword, all part of the range of cultural experiences offered by local tour company HIS. Small-group and customized options available.

Japan Gray Line ☏03/3595-5939, ⑩www .jgl.co.jp/inbound/traveler/traveler.htm. Offers full-day and half-day city tours with English-speaking guides. The full-day tour (¥9600 including lunch) takes you to Tokyo Tower, Meiji-jingū, by ferry up the Sumida-gawa to Asakusa and back via Ueno and Akihabara. The company also runs a one-day Fuji–Hakone excursion (from ¥10,000).

Odakyū Q-Tours ☏03/5321-7887, ⑩www .odakyu.jp/english. Located in Tokyo's Shinjuku Station, Odakyū offers unaccompanied one- or two-day excursions (¥9000 and ¥18,500 respectively) to Hakone, including the rail fare, meals and overnight accommodation as relevant, and an English-language guidebook.

Sky Bus ☏03/3215-0008, ⑩www.skybus.jp. Mini-tours (daily 10am-6pm; 1hr; ¥1200) in an open-top double-decker bus around the outside of the Imperial Palace grounds and through Ginza. Buses depart on the hour from outside the ticket office, in the Mitsubishi Building opposite Tokyo Central Post Office (see map on p.60). English audio-phone available. Note that services do not run in wet weather.

Sunrise Tours ☏03/5796-5454, ⑩www.jtbgmt .com/sunrisetour. Run by leading local travel agent JTB (Japan Travel Bureau), and offering a broad range of options, all with English-speaking guides. Most popular is the half-day Cityrama Tokyo Morning tour (¥4000), covering Meiji-jingū, the Imperial Palace East Garden and Asakusa, while the full-day Dynamic Tokyo tour (¥12,000 including lunch) takes in Tokyo Tower, Asakusa, a tea ceremony, a river cruise and a drive through Ginza. One- and two-day excursions start at ¥9,900 for a day in Kamakura, ¥10,000 by bus round Fuji and Hakone, and ¥10,000 for a trip to Nikkō.

Superfuture ⑩www.superfuture.com. Their concierge service offers high-end tailored tours aimed at people with an interest in art and design, fashion and the latest shopping trends.

Tokyo Great Cycling Tour ☏03/4590-2995, ⑩www.tokyocycling.jp. Sign up for a spin round Nihombashi, Tsukiji, Odaiba and Tokyo Tower. Tours for

up to ten people depart every Saturday from outside the *Marunouchi Hotel* (see map, p.60) and cost ¥10,000 including bike rental, helmet, inusrance, guide and lunch. Reservations required.
Tokyo Tour Guide Services ☎03/5321-3077, ⓦwww.tourism.metro.tokyo.jp/english/ guideservice/. Ten walking tours accompanied by volunteer guides under the auspices of Tokyo

Metropolitan Government. Tours last about three hours, departing Monday to Friday at 1pm from the tourist information centre in the Metropolitan Government Building in Shinjuku (see p.105). Itineraries range from Harajuku and Meiji-jingū (around ¥650) to Hama Rikyū Teien and Odaiba (around ¥3500).

The media

Tokyo is nirvana for media junkies, especially if they can understand and read Japanese. There are scores of daily newspapers and hundreds of magazines covering practically every topic under the rising sun. English newspapers and magazines are readily available, while on TV and radio there are some programmes presented in English or with an alternative English soundtrack, such as the main news bulletins on NHK.

Throughout this guide we list **websites** wherever useful, though note that some will be in Japanese only. If you have a yen to explore further, we can give no greater recommendation than going straight to *Japanzine*'s excellent annual rundown of the best websites (ⓦwww.seekjapan.jp/article-1/866/Japan +on+the+Web).

Newspapers and magazines

The English-language daily **newspaper** you'll most commonly find at Tokyo's newsstands is *The Japan Times* (¥160; ⓦwww .japantimes.co.jp). It has comprehensive coverage of national and international news, a major situations vacant section every Monday, as well as occasionally interesting features, some culled from the world's media. A far better read and almost as widely available is *The International Herald Tribune* (¥150; ⓦwww.asahi.com/english/ index.html), published in conjunction with the English-language version of the major Japanese newspaper *Asahi Shimbun*.

Doing a reasonable job on the features front is the *Daily Yomiuri* (¥120; ⓦwww .yomiuri.co.jp/dy), with a decent arts and

entertainment supplement on Thursdays. Also worth a look is the Japan edition of the *Financial Times* and the online-only *Mainchi Daily News* (ⓦmdn.mainichi-msn.co.jp), which includes the fun Wai-Wai section covering all the latest gossip.

The best English-language **listings magazine** is the free weekly *Metropolis* (ⓦwww.metropolis.co.jp), which is packed with reviews and listings of film and music events. An excellent quarterly publication is *KIE* (Kateigaho International Edition; ¥1260; ⓦint.kateigaho.com) a gorgeous glossy magazine which covers cultural matters, with many travel features and in-depth profiles of areas of Tokyo and other parts of Japan.

Also worth a look are a few more freesheets: the irreverent national monthly magazine *Japanzine* (ⓦwww.seekjapan.jp /japanzine.php), which has a Tokyo listings and review section; *Weekender* (ⓦwww .weekenderjapan.com), which caters to expat readers; and *Tokyo Notice Board* (ⓦwww.tokyonoticeboard.co.jp) is another free weekly devoted almost entirely to classifieds. You might also find the quarterly *Tokyo Journal* (¥600; ⓦwww.tokyo.to) of interest for its features on the city. You'll find all these at the tourist information centres, larger hotels, foreign-language bookstores and bars or restaurants frequented by *gaijin*. Bookstores such as Kinokuniya and Maruzen stock extensive ranges of imported and local magazines; Tower Records is the cheapest place to buy magazines.

Radio

You can listen to FM **radio** in Tokyo the regular way (though you'll need a radio built for the local market, as the 76–90 MHz FM spectrum here is unique to Japan) or via the Internet, where you're likely to hear more interesting music on stations such as **Samurai FM** (Ⓦ www.samurai.fm), which links up DJs in London and Tokyo. There's also **Radio Japan** Online (Ⓦ www.nhk.or.jp /rj/index_e.html), which streams programmes in 22 different languages from Japan's national broadcaster.

The pop and rock station **Inter FM** (76.1MHz; Ⓦ www.interfm.co.jp) is the main source of English-language news on the radio; listen to its "Good Morning Garage" show (Mon–Fri 7–9am). Other major stations with some English programming include

J-WAVE (81.3MHz; Ⓦ www.j-wavemusic. com); **FM Yokohama** (84.1MHz); **Tokyo FM** (80.0MHz); and **Bay FM** (78.0MHz).

Television

Japanese **television**'s notorious reputation for silly game shows and *samurai* dramas is well earned. If you don't speak Japanese, you're likely to find many TV shows totally baffling – and only a little less so once you have picked up the lingo. **NHK**, the state broadcaster, has two channels (in Tokyo, NHK on channel 1 and NHK Educational on channel 3). Many TV sets can access a bilingual soundtrack, and thus it's possible to tune into English-language commentary for NHK's nightly 7pm news; films and imported TV shows on both NHK and the commercial channels are also sometimes broadcast with an alternative English soundtrack. In Tokyo, the other main channels are Nihon TV (channel 4), TBS (6), Fuji TV (8), TV Asahi (10) and TV Tokyo (12), all flagship channels of the nationwide networks, with little to choose between them. **Satellite** and **cable** channels available in all top-end hotels include BBC World, CNN and MTV.

Festivals

No matter when you visit Tokyo, chances are there'll be a religious festival (matsuri) taking place somewhere; the TIC (see p.47) publishes a monthly round-up of festivals in and around the city. You'll also find details of upcoming events on Ⓦ www.tourism.metro.tokyo.jp/english/event and Ⓦ www.tcvb.or.jp. The dates given in the listing of festivals below can vary, so check ahead if you wish to attend a particular event.

Of the major events listed, by far the most important is **New Year**, when most of the city closes down for a week (roughly Dec 28–Jan 3). Tokyo also hosts three grand **sumo tournaments** each year (see p.216), as well as film, theatre and music festivals. Several non-Japanese festivals which have also caught on include **Valentine's Day**

(February 14), when women give men gifts of chocolate; on **White Day** (March 14) men get their turn with chocolates (white, of course), perfume or racy underwear. **Christmas** is celebrated in Japan as an almost totally commercial event, with plastic holly and tinsel in profusion; Christmas Eve, in particular, is one of the most popular date nights of the year, when all the most expensive and trendiest restaurants are booked solid. By contrast, **New Year's Eve** is a fairly subdued, family-oriented event.

January

Ganjitsu (or Gantan) January 1. The *hatsu-mōde* – the first shrine visit of the year – draws the crowds to Meiji-jingū, Hie-jinja, Kanda Myōjin and other city shrines to pray for good fortune. Performances of traditional dance and music take place at Yasukuni-jinja. National holiday.

Kōkyo Ippan Sanga January 2. Thousands of loyal Japanese – and a few curious foreigners – troop into the Imperial Palace grounds to greet the emperor. The royal family appear on the balcony several times from 9.30am to 3pm.

Dezomeshiki January 6. At Tokyo Big Sight in Odaiba, firemen in Edo-period costume pull off dazzling stunts atop long bamboo ladders.

Seijin-no-hi (Adults' Day) Second Monday in January. A colourful pageant of 20-year-old women, and a few men, in traditional dress, visiting city shrines to celebrate their entry into adulthood. At Meiji-jingū various ancient rituals are observed, including a ceremonial archery contest. National holiday.

February

Tokyo International Arts Festival February and March ⓦwww.tif.anj.or.jp. Major festival of performing arts, at various venues.

Hanami parties

With the arrival of spring in late March or early April, a pink tide of **cherry blossom** washes north over Tokyo, lasting little more than a week. The finest displays are along the moat around the Imperial Palace (particularly the section close by Yasukuni-jinja), in Ueno-kōen, Aoyama Cemetery, the riverside Sumida-kōen and on the banks of the Meguro-gawa west of Meguro Station, where every tree shelters a blossom-viewing (*hanami*) party. The blossom is best seen at night, under the light of hanging paper lanterns, though this is also the rowdiest time as revellers, lubricated with sake, croon to the backing of competing karaoke machines.

Setsubun February 3 or 4. On the last day of winter by the lunar calendar, people scatter lucky beans around their homes and at shrines or temples, to drive out evil and welcome in the year's good luck. The liveliest festivities take place at Sensō-ji, Kanda Myōjin, Zōjō-ji and Hie-jinja.

March

Hina Matsuri (Doll Festival) March 3. Families with young girls display beautiful dolls of the emperor, empress and their courtiers dressed in ancient costume. Department stores, hotels and museums often put on special displays at this time.

Hi Watari Second Sunday in March. A spectacular fire-walking ceremony held at the foot of Mount Takao.

April

Hana Matsuri April 8. The Buddha's birthday is celebrated in all Tokyo's temples with either parades or quieter celebrations, during which a small statue of Buddha is sprinkled with sweet tea.

Jibeta Matsuri Mid-April. In this celebration of fertility, an iron phallus is forged and giant wooden phalluses are paraded around Kanayama-jinja, in the southern Tokyo suburb of Kawasaki, amid dancing crowds, including a group of demure transvestites.

Kamakura Matsuri Mid-April. Kamakura's week-long festival includes traditional dances, costume parades and horseback archery.

May

Design Festa May and November or December ⓦwww.designfesta.com. Hundreds of young and aspiring artists converge on Tokyo Big Sight in Odaiba for this twice-yearly weekend celebration of design.

Kodomo-no-hi (Children's Day) May 5. Families fly carp banners, symbolizing strength, outside their homes. National holiday.

Kanda Matsuri Mid-May. One of the city's top three festivals, taking place in odd-numbered years at Kanda Myōjin, during which people in Heian-period costume escort eighty gilded *mikoshi* (portable shrines) through the streets.

Tōshō-gū Haru Matsuri May 17–18. Huge procession of one thousand armour-clad warriors and three *mikoshi*, commemorating the burial of Shogun Tokugawa Ieyasu in Nikkō in 1617.

Sanja Matsuri Third weekend in May. Tokyo's most boisterous festival, when over one hundred *mikoshi* are jostled through the streets of Asakusa, accompanied by lion dancers, geisha and musicians.

June

Sannō Matsuri Mid-June. In even-numbered years the last of the big three *matsuri* (after Kanda and Sanja) takes place, focusing on colourful processions of *mikoshi* through Akasaka.

July

International Lesbian and Gay Video and Film Festival Mid-July (dates can vary) Ⓦ www .tokyo-lgff.org. One of the best Tokyo film festivals, dedicated to queer film and roundly supported by the international community. Films are screened at the Spiral Hall in Aoyama.

Hanabi Taikai Late July and early August. The summer skies explode with thousands of fireworks, harking back to traditional "river-opening" ceremonies to mark the start of the summer boating season. The Sumida-gawa display is the most spectacular (view it from river boats or Asakusa's Sumida-kōen on the last Sat in July), but those in Edogawa, Tamagawa, Arakawa and Harumi come close. Kamakura has its *hanabi taikai* on August 10.

August

Fukagawa Matsuri Mid-August. Every three years Tomioka Hachiman-gū, a shrine in Fukagawa (east across the Sumida River from central Tokyo), hosts the city's wettest festival, when spectators throw buckets of water over a hundred *mikoshi* being shouldered through the streets. There's one scheduled for 2008.

Obon Mid-August. Families gather around their ancestral graves and much of Tokyo closes down, while many neighbourhoods stage dances in honour of the deceased.

Summer Sonic Mid-August Ⓦ www.summersonic .com. Two-day rock festival; see p.200.

Asakusa Samba Carnival Last Saturday in August Ⓦ asakusa-samba.jp. Rio comes to the streets of Asakusa with this spectacular parade of sequinned and feathered dancers. Teams compete and the crowds come out in force to support them.

September

Tsurugaoka Hachiman-gū Matsuri September 14–16. Annual shrine festival of Tsurugaoka Hachiman-gū in Kamakura. The highlight is a demonstration of horseback archery on the final day.

Ningyō Kuyō September 25. A funeral service for unwanted dolls is held at Kiyomizu Kannon-dō in Ueno-kōen, after which they are cremated.

October

Kawagoe Grand Matsuri October 14–15. One of the liveliest festivals in the Tokyo area, involving some 25 ornate floats and hundreds of costumed revellers.

Tōshō-gū Aki Matsuri October 17. Repeat of Nikkō's fabulous procession held for the spring festival, minus the horseback archery displays.

Tokyo Designer's Week Late October and early November Ⓦ www.c-channel.co.jp/en/exhibition. Catch the best of contemporary Japanese design at this event, held at a variety of venues, generally around Aoyama.

November

Daimyō Gyōretsu November 3. Re-enactment of a feudal lord's procession along the Tōkaidō (the great road linking Tokyo and Kyoto), accompanied by his doctor, accountant, tea master and road sweepers. At Sōun-ji, near Hakone-Yumoto.

Tokyo International Film Festival Early November Ⓦ www.tiff-jp.net. Japan's largest film festival, held mainly in Shibuya; see p.209.

Tori-no-ichi Mid-November. Fairs selling *kumade*, bamboo rakes decorated with lucky charms, are held at shrines on "rooster days" in the zodiacal calendar. The main fair is at Ōtori-jinja (Iriya Station).

Shichi-go-san-no-hi November 15. Children aged 7, 5 and 3 don traditional garb to visit the shrines, particularly Meiji-jingū, Hie-jinja and Yasukuni-jinja.

December

Gishi-sai December 14. Costume parade in Nihombashi re-enacting the famous vendetta of the 47 *rōnin* (see p.131), followed by a memorial service for them at Sengaku-ji.

Hagoita-ichi December 17–19. The build-up to New Year begins with a battledore fair outside Asakusa's Sensō-ji.

Ōmisoka December 31. Leading up to midnight, temple bells ring out 108 times (the number of human frailties according to Buddhist thinking), while thousands gather at Meiji-jingū, Hie-jinja and other major shrines to honour the gods with the first visit of the New Year. If you don't like crowds, head for a small local shrine.

Culture and etiquette

Japan is famous for its complex web of social conventions and rules of behaviour, which only someone who has grown up in the society could hope to master. Fortunately, allowances are made for befuddled foreigners, but it will be greatly appreciated – and even draw gasps of astonishment – if you show a grasp of the basic principles. The two main danger areas are to do with footwear and bathing (for more on the latter, see p.238), which, if you get them wrong, can cause great offence. For tips on eating and drinking etiquette, see p.164 and p.188.

The Japanese treat most foreigners with incredible, even embarrassing, kindness. There are endless stories of people going out of their way to help, or paying for drinks or even meals after the briefest of encounters. That said, foreigners will always remain **gaijin** (outsiders) no matter how long they've lived in Japan or how proficient they are in the language and social niceties. On the positive side, this can be wonderfully liberating: you're expected to make mistakes, so don't get too hung up about it. The important thing is to be seen to be trying. As a general rule, when in doubt simply follow what everyone else is doing. Conversely, it should also be said that racial discrimination can be a problem, especially for non-whites, though it is mainly directed at immigrant workers rather than tourists.

Some general pointers

In this very male, strictly hierarchical society, men always take precedence over women, so ladies shouldn't expect doors to be held open or seats vacated. **Sexual discrimination** is widespread, and foreign women working in Japan can find the predominantly male business culture hard going.

Although meticulously polite within their own social group, the Japanese relish pushing and shoving on trains or buses. Never respond by getting angry or showing **aggression**, as this is considered a complete loss of face. By the same token, don't make your **opinions** too forcefully or contradict people outright; it's more polite to say "maybe" than a direct "no".

The meaning of "yes" and "no" can in themselves be a problem, particularly when asking questions. For example, if you say "Don't you like it?", a positive answer means "Yes, I agree with you, I don't like it", and "No" means "No, I don't agree with you, I *do* like it". To avoid confusion, try not to ask negative questions – stick to "Do you like it?" And if someone seems to be giving vague answers, don't push too hard unless it's important. There's a good chance they don't want to offend you by disagreeing or revealing a problem.

It's quite normal to see men urinating in the streets in Japan, but **blowing your nose** in public is considered extremely rude – just keep sniffing until you find somewhere private. Finally, you'll be excused for not **sitting** on your knees, Japan-style, on tatami mats. It's agony for people who aren't used to it, and many young Japanese now find it uncomfortable. If you're wearing trousers, sitting cross-legged is fine; otherwise, tuck your legs to one side.

Meetings and greetings

Some visitors to Japan complain that it's difficult to meet local people, and it's certainly true that many Japanese are shy of foreigners, mainly through a fear of being unable to communicate. A few words of Japanese will help enormously, and there are various opportunities for fairly formal contact, such as through the Goodwill Guides (see p.47). Otherwise, try popping into a local bar, a *yakitori* joint or suchlike; the chances are someone emboldened by alcohol will strike up a conversation.

Whenever Japanese meet, express thanks or say goodbye, there's a flurry of **bowing**.

The precise depth of the bow and the length of time it's held for depend on the relative status of the two individuals – receptionists are sent on courses to learn the precise angles required. Foreigners aren't expected to bow, but it's terribly infectious and you'll soon find yourself bobbing with the best of them. The usual compromise is a slight nod or a quick half-bow. Japanese more familiar with Western customs might offer you a hand to shake, in which case treat it gently – they won't be expecting a firm grip.

Japanese **names** are traditionally written with the family name first, followed by a given name, which is the practice used throughout this book (except where the Western version has become famous, such as Issey Miyake). When dealing with foreigners, however, they may well write their name the other way round. Check if you're not sure because, when **addressing people**, it's normal to use the family name plus -san; for example, Suzuki-san. San is an honorific term applied to others, so you do not use it when introducing yourself or your family. As a foreigner, you can choose whichever of your names you feel comfortable with; inevitably they'll tack a -san on the end. You'll also often hear -chan or -kun as a form of address; these are diminutives reserved for very good friends, young children and pets. The suffix -sama is the most polite form of address.

Japanese people tend to **dress** smartly, especially in Tokyo. Tourists don't have to go overboard, but will be better received if they look neat and tidy, while for anyone hoping to do business, a snappy suit is de rigueur. It's also important to be **punctual** for social and business appointments.

Business meetings invariably go on much longer than you'd expect, and rarely result in decisions. They are partly for building up the all-important feeling of trust between the two parties (as is the after-hours entertainment in a restaurant or karaoke bar). An essential part of any business meeting is the swapping of meishi, **name cards**. Always carry a copious supply, since you'll be expected to exchange a card with everyone present. It's useful to have them printed in Japanese as well as English; if necessary, you can get this done at major hotels. Meishi are offered with both hands, held so that the recipient can

read the writing. It's polite to read the card and then place it on the table beside you, face up. Never write on a meishi, at least not in the owner's presence, and never shove it in a pocket – put it in your wallet or somewhere suitably respectful.

Hospitality, gifts and tips

Entertaining, whether it's business or purely social, usually takes place in bars and restaurants. The host generally orders and, if it's a Japanese-style meal, will keep passing you different things to try. You'll also find your glass continually topped up. It's polite to return the gesture but if you don't drink, or don't want any more, leave it full.

It's a rare honour to be invited to someone's home in Japan, and if this happens you should always take a small **gift**. Fruit, flowers, chocolates or alcohol (wine, whisky or brandy) are safe bets, as is anything from your home country, especially if it's a famous brand-name. The gift should always be wrapped, using plenty of fancy paper and ribbon if possible. Most shops gift-wrap purchases automatically and anything swathed in paper from a big department store has extra cachet.

Japanese people love giving gifts, and you should never refuse one if offered, though it's good manners to protest at their generosity first. Again it's polite to give and receive with both hands, and to belittle your humble donation while giving profuse thanks for the gift you receive. However, it's not the custom to open gifts in front of the donor, thus avoiding potential embarrassment.

If you're fortunate enough to be invited to a **wedding**, it's normal to give money to the happy couple. This helps defray the costs, including, somewhat bizarrely, that of the present you'll receive at the end of the meal. How much you give depends on your relationship with the couple, so ask a mutual friend what would be appropriate. Make sure to get crisp new notes and put them in a special red envelope available at stationers. Write your name clearly on the front and hand it over as you enter the reception.

Tipping is not expected in Japan, and if you press money on a taxi driver, porter or bellboy it can cause offence. If someone's been particularly helpful, the best approach is to give a small present, or offer some money discreetly in an envelope.

Shoes and slippers

It's customary to change into **slippers** when entering a Japanese home or a ryokan, and not uncommon in traditional restaurants, temples and, occasionally, in museums and art galleries. In general, if you come across a slightly raised floor and a row of slippers, then use them; leave your shoes either on the lower floor (the *genkan*) or on the shelves (sometimes lockers) provided. Slip-on shoes are easier for such manoeuvres than lace-ups and, tricky though it can be because of the often narrow space, try not to step on the *genkan* with bare or stockinged feet.

Once inside, remove your slippers before stepping onto tatami, the rice-straw flooring, and remember to change into the special **toilet slippers** lurking inside the bathroom door when you go to the toilet.

Toilets

Traditional Japanese **toilets** (*toire* or *otearai*; トイレ／お手洗い) are of the Asian squat variety. Though these are still quite common in homes, old-style restaurants and many public buildings, Western toilets are gradually becoming the norm. Look out for nifty enhancements such as a heated seat – glorious in winter – and those that flush automatically as you walk away. Another handy device plays the sound of flushing water to cover embarrassing noises. These are either automatic or are activated with a button, and were invented because so much water was wasted by constant flushing.

Increasingly, you'll be confronted by a hi-tech Western toilet known as a **Washlet**, with a control panel to one side. It's usually impossible to find the flush button, and instead you'll hit the temperature control, hot-air dryer or, worst of all, the bidet nozzle, resulting in a long metal arm extending out of the toilet bowl and spraying you with warm water.

In some places toilets are still communal, so don't be alarmed to see a urinal in what you thought was the women's room, and note that some public toilets rarely provide paper. There are lots of public lavatories on the street, but if you can't find one, then dive into the nearest department store or big shop, all of which have bathroom facilities for general use.

Travelling with children

Tokyo has no shortage of places to take the kids, rain or shine, and with standards of health, hygiene and safety so high, it's is a great place to travel with your kids. At museums and other sights, school-age children usually get reduced rates, which may be up to half the adult price. Children under 6 ride free on trains, subways and buses, while those aged 6–11 pay half fare.

If you have young children in tow, it's recommended to bring a lightweight, easily collapsible **stroller**. You'll find yourself walking long distances and, while many subway and train stations now have elevators, there are still plenty of stairs. It goes without saying that travelling with a stroller or young children at rush hour is to be avoided.

It's hard to find **hotels** offering family rooms taking more than three, though the international chain hotels may have one or two larger rooms. Otherwise, your best bet is a Japanese-style ryokan or *minshuku* where you can share a big tatami room. In either case, you'll need to book well ahead. However, only at the more upmarket Western-style hotels will you be able to arrange **babysitting**.

Tokyo for kids

The Japanese capital has a whole swath of educational **museums**, the best ones being Ueno's National Science Museum (see p.94) and Odaiba's MeSci (see p.140), plus Edo-Tokyo Museum in Ryōgoku (see p.73). Midway between a theme-park and a life-class, KidZania creates a parallel world run by kids (see p.138). For animal lovers, there's the fabulous aquarium at Kasai Rinkai-kōen (see p.141) and Ueno **zoo** might also be of interest (see p.92).

The city also boasts Tokyo Disneyland, of course (see p.142), and the thrill of the rides at Tokyo Dome City (see p.69) as well as the wonderful Ghibli Museum, Mitaka (see p.112), a short train ride from Shinjuku. If your children are 6 or under, the National Children's Castle (see p.120) and the Tokyo Metropolitan Children's Hall (see p.124) will keep them occupied for many an hour.

See p.233 for a list of **shops** featuring the latest hit toys and Japanese crazes. For older, tech-savvy kids, the electronic emporia of Akihabara will be a must (see p.68).

All the products you need – such as **nappies** and **baby food** – are easily available at shops and department stores, though not necessarily imported varieties. If you need a particular brand of something, it would be wise to bring it with you. While **breastfeeding** in public is generally accepted, it's best to be as discreet as possible. Most Japanese women who breastfeed use the private rooms provided in department stores and public buildings and in many shops, or find a quiet corner.

Although it's rather dated now, Kodansha's *Japan for Kids* (see "Books", p.310) still contains a lot of useful general information.

Travel essentials

Costs

Despite its reputation as an outrageously expensive city, prices in Tokyo have dropped or at least stabilized in recent years, and with a little planning it is a manageable destination even for those on a fairly modest budget. The key is to do what the majority of Japanese do: eat in local restaurants, avoid the ritzier bars and take advantage of any available discounts.

By staying in hostels and eating in the cheapest local restaurants, the absolute minimum **daily budget** for food and accommodation is ¥8000–¥10,000. By the time you've added in some transport costs, a few entry tickets, meals in classier restaurants and one or two nights in a ryokan or business hotel, you'll be reaching an expenditure of at least ¥15,000 per day.

Before leaving home, it's worth checking JNTO's website ⓦ www.jnto.go.jp for tips on how to save money. One recommendation is to buy the **GRUTT Pass**, a ¥2000 ticket which affords entry to 49 public, national and private institutions, including all Tokyo's major museums, and also gives discounts on special exhibitions at the museums. Valid for two months after first being used, the ticket can be bought at participating venues and the Tokyo Metropolitan Government tourist information centre in Shinjuku (see p.47), among other outlets; more details of the

A **consumption tax** (*shōhizei*) of five percent is levied on virtually all goods and services in Japan, including restaurant meals and accommodation. The law now requires that this tax is included in the advertised price, though you'll occasionally come across hotels which haven't quite got round to it yet; double-check to be on the safe side.

pass appear on the Japanese-only website Ⓦ www.rekibun.or.jp/grutto.

Holders of the **International Student Identity Card** (ISIC; Ⓦ www.isiccard.com) are eligible for discounts on some transport and admission fees, as are children. If you're planning to stay in one of the establishments run by Japan Youth Hostels (Ⓦ www.jyh .or.jp), it's worth buying a **Hostelling International card** (Ⓦ www.iyhf.org) in your home country, which gives you a ¥600 reduction on rates.

Crime and personal safety

Tokyo boasts one of the lowest crime rates in the world. On the whole, the Japanese are honest and law-abiding, there's little theft, and drug-related crimes are relatively rare. Nonetheless, it always pays to be careful in crowds and to keep money and important documents stowed in an inside pocket or money belt, or in your hotel safe.

The presence of **police boxes** (*kōban*) in every neighbourhood helps discourage petty crime, and the local police seem to spend the majority of their time dealing with stolen bikes (bicycle theft is rife) and helping bemused visitors – Japanese and foreigners – find addresses. This benevolent image is misleading, however, as the Japanese police are notorious for forcing confessions and holding suspects for weeks without access to a lawyer. Amnesty International have consistently criticized Japan for its treatment of illegal immigrants and other foreigners held in jail.

In theory, you should carry your **passport** or ID at all times; the police have the right to arrest anyone who fails to do so. In practice, however, they rarely stop foreigners. If you're found without your ID, the usual procedure

is to escort you back to your hotel or apartment to collect it. Anyone found **taking drugs** will be treated less leniently; if you're lucky, you'll simply be fined and deported, rather than sent to prison.

The generally low status of women in Japan is reflected in the amount of **groping** that goes on in crowded commuter trains – there are even pornographic films and comics aimed at gropers. If you do have the misfortune to be groped, the best solution is to grab the offending hand, yank it high in the air and embarrass the guy as much as possible. Fortunately, more violent **sexual abuse** is rare, though harassment, stalking and rape are seriously under-reported; rape may be up to ten times more common than the current statistics suggest (under 2500 cases per year). Women should exercise the same caution about being alone with a man as they would anywhere. Violent crimes against women do occur, as the murder in Tokyo of hostess-club workers Carita Ridgway in 1992 and Lucie Blackman in 2000, and that in 2007 of English-language teacher Lindsay Ann Hawker sadly prove.

In **emergencies**, phone ☏ 110 for the police or ☏ 119 for an ambulance or fire engine. You can call these numbers free from any public phone by pressing the red button before dialling. Better still, ask someone to call for you, since few police speak English, though Tokyo Metropolitan Police do run an English-language hotline on ☏ 03/3501-0110 (Mon–Fri 8.30am–5.15pm). Two other useful options are Tokyo English Language Lifeline (TELL; ☏ 03/5774-0992, Ⓦ www.telljp.com; daily 9am–11pm) and Japan Helpline (☏ 0570/000-911, Ⓦ www.jhelp.com; 24hr).

Earthquakes

Earthquakes are a part of life in Japan. The country is home to one-tenth of the world's active volcanoes and the site of one-tenth of its major earthquakes (over magnitude 7 on the Richter scale). At least one quake is recorded every day somewhere in the country, though fortunately the vast majority consist of minor tremors which you probably won't even notice.

There's a sequence of major quakes in Tokyo every seventy-odd years. The last really big quake to hit Tokyo was in 1923, when the **Great Kantō Earthquake** devastated the city, killing an estimated 140,000 people. While everyone's been talking about the next "Big One" for at least a decade, Tokyo is already equipped with some of the world's most sophisticated earthquake sensors, and architects employ mind-boggling techniques to try to ensure the city's new high-rises remain upright.

If you do have the misfortune to experience more than a minor rumble, follow the safety procedures listed below:

• Extinguish any fires and turn off electrical appliances.

• Open any doors leading out of the room, as they often get jammed shut, blocking your exit later.

• Stay away from windows because of splintering glass. If you have time, draw the curtains to contain the glass.

• Don't rush outside (many people are injured by falling masonry), but get under something solid, such as a ground-floor doorway, or a desk.

• If you are outside when the quake hits, beware of falling objects and head for the nearest park or other open space.

• If the earthquake occurs at night, make sure you've got a torch (all hotels and ryokan provide flashlights in the rooms).

• When the tremors have died down, go to the nearest park, playing field or open space, taking your documents and other valuables with you. It's also a good idea to take a cushion or pillow to protect your head against falling glass.

• Eventually, make your way to the designated neighbourhood emergency centre for information, food and shelter.

• Ultimately, get in touch with your embassy.

Beware of aftershocks, which may go on for a long time and can topple structures that are already weakened, and note that most casualties are caused by fire and traffic accidents, rather than collapsing buildings. In the aftermath of a major earthquake, it may be impossible to contact friends and relatives for a while, since the phone lines are likely to be down or reserved for emergency services, while Internet servers may be hit by power cuts.

Electricity

The mains **electricity** in the part of Japan covered by this guide is 100V, 50Hz AC. Japanese plugs have two flat pins or, less commonly, three pins (two flat and one rounded, earth pin). If you are arriving from North America or Canada, the voltage difference should cause no problems with computers, digital cameras, cell phones and the like. Appliances such as hair dryers, curling irons and travel kettles should also work, but not quite as efficiently, in which case you may need a converter. And, while Japanese plugs look identical to North American plugs, there are subtle differences, so you may also need an adaptor. Large hotels can often provide voltage converters and adaptors.

Entry requirements

All visitors to Japan must have a passport valid for the duration of their stay. Citizens of Ireland, the UK and certain other European countries can stay in Japan for up to ninety days without a visa provided they are visiting for tourism or business purposes. This stay can be extended for another three months (see below). Citizens of Australia, Canada, New Zealand, and the US can also stay for up to ninety days without a visa, though this is not extendable and you are required to be in possession of a return air ticket. Anyone from these countries wishing to stay longer will have to leave Japan and then re-enter.

Citizens of certain other countries must apply for a **visa** in advance in their own country. Visas are usually free, though in certain circumstances you may be charged a fee of around ¥3000 for a single-entry visa. The rules on visas do change from time to time, so check first with the nearest Japanese embassy or consulate, or on the Japanese Ministry of Foreign Affairs website ⓦwww.mofa.go.jp.

To get a **visa extension** you'll need to fill in two copies of an "Application for Extension of Stay", available from the Tokyo immigration bureau (see p.241). These must be returned along with passport photos, a letter explaining your reasons for wanting to extend your stay, and a fee of ¥4000. In addition, you may be asked to show proof of sufficient funds to support your stay, and a valid onward ticket out of the country. If you're not a national of one of the few countries with six-month reciprocal visa exemptions (these include Ireland and the UK), expect a thorough grilling from the immigration officials. An easier option – and the only alternative available to nationals of those countries who are not eligible for an extension – may be a short trip out of the country, say to South Korea or Hong Kong, though you'll still have to run the gauntlet of immigration officials on your return.

Citizens of the UK, Ireland, Canada, Australia, New Zealand, South Korea, France and Germany aged between 18 and 30 can apply for a **working holiday visa**, which grants a stay of up to one year and entitles the holder to take paid employment as long as your stay is "primarily deemed to be a holiday"; working in clubs and bars, for example, is prohibited. Since the number of visas issued each financial year (beginning in April) is limited, you need to apply early, and at least three weeks before departure. And you must be able to show evidence of sufficient funds, which effectively means a return ticket (or money to buy one) plus around US$2000 or the equivalent to live on while you look for work. Contact your local Japanese embassy or consulate to check the current details of the scheme.

British nationals are also eligible for the **volunteer visa scheme**, which allows holders to undertake voluntary work for charitable organizations in Japan for up to one year. Your application must include a letter from the host organization confirming details of the voluntary work to be undertaken and the treatment the volunteer will receive (pocket money and board and lodging are allowed, but formal remuneration is not). You must also be able to show evidence of sufficient funds for your stay in Japan. Contact your local embassy or consulate to check the current details of the scheme.

Foreigners staying in Japan for more than ninety days must obtain **alien registration status** before the ninety days is up; apply at the local government office for the area where you are staying. The alien registration card (often referred to as a *gaijin* card) includes your photograph and must be

carried at all times. In addition, if you're on any sort of working visa and you leave Japan temporarily, you must get a **re-entry visa** before you leave if you wish to continue working on your return. Re-entry visas are available from local immigration bureaus.

Japanese embassies and consulates

You'll find a full list of embassies and consulates on ⓦwww.mofa.go.jp/about.

Australia 112 Empire Circuit, Yarralumla, Canberra ⓣ02/6273 3244, ⓦwww.au.emb-japan.go.jp; 17th Floor, Comalco Place, 12 Creek St, Brisbane ⓣ07/3221 5188, ⓦwww.brisbane.au.emb-japan .go.jp; 45F Melbourne Central Tower, 360 Elizabeth St, Melbourne ⓣ03/9639 3244; 21F The Forrest Centre, 221 St George's Terrace, Perth ⓣ08/9480 1800; Level 34, Colonial Centre, 52 Martin Place, Sydney ⓣ02/9231 3455.

Canada 255 Sussex Drive, Ottawa ⓣ613/241-8541, ⓦwww.ca.emb-japan.go.jp; 2300 Trans Canada Tower, 450-1st Street SW, Calgary ⓣ403/294-0782; 600 Rue de la Gauchetière West, Suite 2120, Montreal ⓣ514/866-3429; Suite 3300, Royal Trust Tower, 77 King St West, Toronto ⓣ416/363-7038; 800-1177 West Hastings St, Vancouver ⓣ604/684-5868.

China 7 Ri Tan Rd, Jian Guo Men Wai, Beijing ⓣ010/6532-2361, ⓦwww.cn.emb-japan.go.jp; 37F Metropolitan Tower, 68 Zourong Rd, Central District, Chongqing ⓣ023/6373-3585; Garden Tower, 368 Huanshi Dong Lu, Guangzhou ⓣ020/8334-3009; 46–47F One Exchange Square, 8 Connaught Place, Central, Hong Kong ⓣ2522-1184, ⓦwww.hk.emb-japan.go.jp; 8 Wan Shan Rd, Shanghai ⓣ021/5257-4766.

Ireland Nutley Building, Merrion Centre, Nutley Lane, Dublin ⓣ01/202 8300, ⓦwww.ie .emb-japan.go.jp.

New Zealand Level 18, Majestic Centre, 100 Willis St, Wellington ⓣ04/473 1540, ⓦwww.nz .emb-japan.go.jp; Level 12, ASB Bank Centre, 135 Albert St, Auckland ⓣ09/303 4106; Level 5, Forsyth Barr House, 764 Colombo St, Christchurch ⓣ03/366 5680.

Singapore 16 Nassim Rd ⓣ6235-8855, ⓦwww.sg.emb-japan.go.jp.

South Africa 259 Baines St, Groenkloof, Pretoria ⓣ012/452 1500, ⓦwww.japan.org.za; 2100 Main Tower, Standard Bank Center, Heerengracht, Cape Town ⓣ021/425 1695.

South Korea 18-11 Junghak-dong, Jongno-gu, Seoul ⓣ02/2170-5200, ⓦwww.kr.emb-japan .go.jp; 1147-11, Choryang-dong, Dong-ku, Busan ⓣ051/465-5101.

Thailand 177 Witthayu Road, Lumphini, Pathum Wan, Bangkok ☎02/207-8500, ⓦwww.th-emb -japan.go.jp.
UK 101–104 Piccadilly, London ☎020/7465 6500, ⓦwww.uk.emb-japan.go.jp; 2 Melville Crescent, Edinburgh ☎0131/225 4777, ⓦwww.edinburgh .uk.emb-japan.go.jp.
US 2520 Massachusetts Ave NW, Washington DC ☎202/238-6700, ⓦwww.us.emb-japan.go.jp; One Alliance Center, Suite 1600, 3500 Lenox Rd, Atlanta ☎404/240-4300; Federal Reserve Plaza, 14th Floor, 600 Atlantic Ave, Boston ☎617/973-9774; Olympia Centre, Suite 1100, 737 North Michigan Ave, Chicago ☎312/280-0400; 1225 17th Street, Suite 3000, Denver ☎303/534-1151; 1742 Nuuanu Ave, Honolulu 96817-3201 ☎808/543-3111; 2 Houston Center Building, 909 Fannin St, Suite 3000, Houston ☎713/652-2977; 350 South Grand Ave, Suite 1700, Los Angeles ☎213/617-6700; Brickell Bay View Centre, Suite 3200, 80 SW 8th St, Miami ☎305/530-9090; 639 Loyola Ave, Suite 2050, New Orleans, LA 70113 ☎504/529-2101; 299 Park Ave, New York ☎212/371-8222; 50 Fremont St, Suite 2300, San Francisco ☎415/777-3533; 601 Union St, Suite 500, Seattle ☎206/682-9107.

Insurance

It's essential to take out a good **travel insurance** policy, particularly one with comprehensive medical coverage, due to the high cost of hospital treatment in Japan (for a list of Tokyo hospitals and clinics, see p.240). Rough Guides has teamed up with Columbus Direct to offer you travel insurance that can be tailored to suit your needs. Products include a low-cost **backpacker** option for long stays; a **short break** option for city getaways; a typical **holiday package** option; and others. There are also annual **multi-trip** policies for those who travel regularly. Different sports and activities can be usually be covered if required.

See ⓦwww.roughguidesinsurance.com for eligibility and purchasing options. Alternatively, UK residents should call ☎0870/033 9988; Australians should call ☎1300/669 999 and New Zealanders should call ☎0800/55 9911. All other nationalities should call ☎+44 870/890 2843.

Internet access

Cybercafés can be found across Tokyo – often as part of a 24-hour computer-game and *manga* centre – and increasingly there's

wireless access (free at many metro stations, for example). Connection charges, if you have to pay, are around ¥200–400 per hour. Cybercafés come and go fairly swiftly, although the copyshop Kinko's is pretty reliable, and has branches (some 24hr) throughout Tokyo; call their toll-free number ☎0120-001966 or check ⓦwww.kinkos .co.jp to find the one nearest you. Many **hotels** offer broadband access in every room, often for free or for a small daily fee (typically ¥1000). Others may provide at least one terminal for guests travelling without their own computer, generally for free, though a nominal rate may apply at budget hotels and hostels.

At the time of writing the following places were offering free or cheap (for the cost of a cup of coffee) Internet connections: Marunouchi Café (Mon–Fri 8am–9pm, Sat & Sun 11am–8pm), 1F, Shin Tokyo Building, 3-3-1 Marunouchi, Chiyoda-ku; Apple Ginza Store, 3-5-12 Ginza, Chūō-ku (daily 10am– 9pm); Café Add+Ress, 6F Parco, 1-28-2 Minami-Ikebukuro, Toshima-ku (daily 10am– 9pm); and Wired Cafes (ⓦwww.cafecompany .co.jp/ourcafe/wiredcafe.html) with branches in Aoyama Itchōme, Harajuku, Nihombashi, Shibuya, Shinjuku among other places. Marunouchi Café allows you to plug in your own computer if you have one. Note that you will need your passport or other ID to use the computers at some of these establishments.

Manga-café crash pads

In all the main areas of the city there are also 24-hour manga and computer-games parlours where you can get online. The fees can be quite steep during the day, but these places come into their own in the wee small hours when they function as unofficial crash pads for anyone waiting for the first train home in the morning after they've been partying.

There are a couple of chains to look out for. One of the best is **Gera Gera** (ⓦwww .geragera.co.jp), where you can surf the Web, play video games, watch DVDs and leaf through over fifty thousand comics, as well as consume all the soft drinks you want for an extra ¥180. From Monday to Thursday their charges start at ¥280 for half an hour (then ¥80 for every extra 10min); there are also package rates of three hours in the day or five hours at night for ¥1080. From Friday to Sunday all rates are slightly higher. You'll find them at B1 Remina Bldg, 3-17-4 Shinjuku, Shinjuku-ku; and at many other locations, listed on their website.

Bagus (ⓦ www.bagus-comic.com) is another major chain, which also has English-language DVDs. A couple of their most convenient branches are in Shibuya (28-6 Udagawa-chō, Shibuya-ku), on the sixth floor of the same building as HMV Records, and on the twelfth floor of the Roi Building in Roppongi (5-5-1 Roppongi). Their rates start at ¥420 for the first hour and then ¥100 for every extra 15 minutes. From 11pm to 8am you can park yourself here for six hours for ¥1260, drinks included.

Laundry

All hotels provide either a laundry service or, at the lower end, coin-operated machines. These typically cost cost ¥100 for a wash (powder ¥30–50) and ¥100 for ten minutes in the drier.

Living in Tokyo

Employment opportunities for foreigners have shrunk since the Japanese economy took a nosedive, though finding employment is far from impossible, especially if you have the right qualifications (a degree is essential) and appropriate visa. In fact the number of well-qualified, Japanese-speaking *gaijin* in the country employed in specialist jobs has increased.

Citizens of the UK, Ireland, Canada, Australia, New Zealand, South Korean France and Germany aged between 18 and 30 can apply for a **working holiday visa** (see p.40). All other foreigners working in Japan must apply for a **work visa** *outside* the country, for which the proper sponsorship papers from your prospective employer will be necessary. Work visas do not need to be obtained in your home country, so if you get offered a job, it's possible to sort out the paperwork in South Korea, for example. A few employers may be willing to hire you before the proper papers are sorted, but you shouldn't rely on this, and if you arrive without a job make sure you have plenty of

funds to live on until you find one. Anyone staying in Japan more than ninety days must also apply for alien registration status (see p.40). For some tips on finding long-term **accommodation** in the capital, see p.157.

The most common job available to foreigners is **teaching English**. The big employers are the national school chains, such as NOVA (ⓦ www.teachinjapan.com), ECC (ⓦ www.japanbound.com), GEOS (ⓦ www.geoscareer.com) and AEON (ⓦ www.aeonet.com); some of these organize recruiting drives abroad. However, some of the smaller schools are far from professional operations (and even the biggies get lots of complaints), so before signing any contract it's a good idea to talk to other teachers and, if possible, attend a class and find out what will be expected of you. If you have a professional teaching qualification, plus experience, or if you also speak another language such as French or Italian, your chances of getting one of the better jobs will be higher.

Another option is to get a place on the government-run **Japan Exchange and Teaching Programme** (JET; ⓦ www .jetprogramme.org), aimed at improving foreign-language teaching in schools and promoting international understanding. The scheme is open to graduates aged under 40, preferably holding some sort of language-teaching qualification. Benefits include a generous salary, help with accommodation, return air travel to Japan and paid holidays. Applying for the JET programme is a lengthy process for which you need to be well prepared. Application forms for the following year's quota are available from late September, the deadline for submission being early December. Interviews are held in January and February, with decisions made in March. After health checks and orientation meetings, JETs head off to their posts in late July on year-long contracts, which can be renewed for up to two more years by mutual consent.

A much more limited job option for *gaijin* is rewriting or editing English **translations** of Japanese text for technical documents, manuals, magazines and so on. For such jobs, it's a great help if you have at least a little Japanese. Other options include **modelling**, for which it will be an asset to have a professional portfolio of photographs, and **bar work and hostessing** – though the usual caveats about the dangers inherent in this kind of work apply. Whatever work you're looking for – or if you're doing any sort of business in Japan – a smart set of clothes will give you an advantage, as will following other general rules of social etiquette (see p.34).

Employment resources

Apart from the websites (listed below) the main places to look for job adverts are Monday's edition of *The Japan Times* and the free weekly magazines *Metropolis* (Ⓦmetropolis.japantoday.com; jobs listings posted on Fridays) and *Tokyo Notice Board*.
GaijinPot Ⓦwww.gaijinpot.com Classifieds focused on English-language teaching.
Japan Association for Working Holiday Makers Ⓦwww.jawhm.or.jp Job referrals for people on working holiday visas.
Jobs in Japan Ⓦwww.jobsinjapan.com Broad range of classified ads.
Work in Japan Ⓦwww.daijob.com/wij Japan's largest bilingual jobs website.

Studying Japanese language and culture

Tokyo offers all sorts of opportunities to study Japanese language and culture, from pottery to playing the *shakuhachi* (a traditional flute). In order to get a student or **cultural visa**, you'll need various documents from the institution where you plan to study and proof that you have sufficient funds to support yourself, among other things. Full-time courses are expensive, but once you have your visa you may be allowed to undertake a minimal amount of paid work.

Japan's Ministry of Education, Culture, Sports, Science and Technology (MEXT; Ⓦwww.mext.go.jp) offers various **scholarships** to foreign students wishing to further their knowledge of Japanese or Japanese studies, or to enrol at a Japanese university. You'll find further information on the informative Study in Japan website (Ⓦwww.studyjapan.go.jp), run by the Ministry of Foreign Affairs, or by contacting your nearest Japanese embassy or consulate.

Tokyo has numerous **Japanese language schools** offering intensive and part-time courses. Among the most established are Berlitz (Ⓦwww.berlitz.co.jp), with over thirty schools in central Tokyo, and Tokyo Kogakuin Japanese Language School (5-30-16 Sendagaya, Shibuya-ku; ☏03/3352-3851, Ⓦwww.technos-jpschool.ac.jp). The monthly bilingual magazine *Hiragana Times* (Ⓦwww.hiraganatimes.com) and the listings magazines *Metropolis* and *Tokyo Journal* also carry adverts for schools, or check out the Association for the Promotion of Japanese Language Education (2F Ishiyama Bldg, 1-58-1 Yoyogi, Shinjuku-ku; ☏03/4304-7815, Ⓦwww.nisshinkyo.org), whose website lists accredited institutions.

Mail

Japan's **mail** service is highly efficient and fast, with post offices easily identified by their red-and-white signs showing a T with a parallel bar across the top, the same symbol that you'll find on the red letterboxes. All post can be addressed in Western script (*rōmaji*) provided it's clearly printed.

The Tokyo **Central Post Office** is on the west side of Tokyo Station (Mon–Fri 9am–7pm, Sat 9am–5pm, Sun 9am–12.30pm; 24hr service for stamps and parcels). The **International Post Office**, 2-3-3 Ōtemachi (same hours) is a bit less convenient, but usually quieter. Other post offices tend to work 9am to 5pm on weekdays, closing at weekends and also on national holidays, though a few open on Saturdays from 9am to 3pm, sometimes longer; larger offices may also open on Sundays.

If you need to send bulkier items or **parcels** back home, all post offices sell reasonably priced special envelopes and boxes for packaging. The maximum weight for an overseas parcel is 30kg (less for some destinations). A good compromise between expensive air mail and slow sea mail is Surface Air Lifted (SAL) mail, which takes around three weeks to reach most destinations, and costs somewhere between the two. For English-language information about postal services, including postal fees, see the Post Office website Ⓦwww.post.japanpost.jp.

Poste restante (*tomeoki* or *kyoku dome yūbin*; 留置郵便/局留郵便) is available only at the Tokyo Central Post Office, whose postal address is 2-7-2 Marunouchi, Chiyoda-ku, Tokyo 100. To pick up post, go to the basement counter (Mon–Fri 8am–8pm, Sat 8am–5pm, Sun 9am–12.30pm) and take your passport. Mail is held for thirty days before being returned.

Maps

Decent free **maps** of the city are available from any of the tourist information centres (see p.47). If you're going to be in Tokyo for more than just a few days or want to wander off the beaten track, it's well worth investing in Kodansha's bilingual *Tokyo City Atlas* (¥2100), which gives more detail and, importantly, includes *chōme* and block numbers to help pin down addresses (see box, p.28). Bilingual maps on public notice boards outside the main exits to most subway and train stations are handy for getting your immediate bearings.

Money

The **Japanese currency** is the **yen** (*en* in Japanese). Notes are available in denominations of ¥1000, ¥2000, ¥5000 and ¥10,000, while coins come in values of ¥1, ¥5, ¥10, ¥50, ¥100 and ¥500. Apart from the ¥5 piece, a copper-coloured coin with a hole in the centre, all other notes and coins indicate their value in Western numerals. At the time of writing the **exchange rate** was approximately ¥120 to US$1, ¥240 to £1 and ¥160 to €1.

Though **credit and debit cards** are far more widely accepted than they were a few years ago, Japan is still very much a cash society. The most useful cards to carry are Visa and American Express, followed closely by MasterCard, then Diners Club; you should be able to use these in hotels, restaurants, shops and travel agencies accustomed to serving foreigners. However, many retailers only accept locally issued cards.

ATMs

The simplest way of obtaining cash in Japan is by making an **ATM** withdrawal on a credit or debit card. Both the post office and Seven Bank operate ATMs which accept foreign-issued cards, including Visa, PLUS, Master-Card, Maestro, Cirrus and American Express, with instructions provided in English. You'll need your PIN to make a withdrawal, which can be anywhere between ¥1000 and ¥1,000,000, depending on the issuer and your credit limit. If the machine doesn't allow you to withdraw money in the first instance, try again with a smaller amount.

Seven Bank machines are located in 7-Eleven stores near major hotels and in the main tourist areas, and are often accessible 24 hours. You'll find post office ATMs not only in post offices, but also in stations, department stores and the like throughout the city – they're identified with a sticker saying "International ATM Service". Their ATMs have more restricted hours than the Seven Bank machines, but the ones in major post offices can be accessed at weekends and after the counters have closed, though none is open round the clock. If you need money out of hours, you can also try Citibank (Ⓦwww.citibank.co.jp), which operates a number of ATM corners in Tokyo. Most are accessible outside normal banking hours, and some are open 24 hours. If you're having problems, pick up the phone beside the ATM and ask to speak to someone in English.

Changing money

You can change cash and traveller's cheques at the exchange counters (*ryōgae-jo*; 両替所) of main post offices and certain banks – the bigger branches of Tokyo-Mitsubishi UFJ and SMBC (Sumitomo Mitsubishi Banking Corporation) are your best bet. The post office handles cash and traveller's cheques in six major currencies, including American, Canadian and Australian dollars, sterling and euros; the most widely accepted brands of cheque are American Express, Visa, Thomas Cook and MasterCard. There's little variation in rates between banks and the post office and there are no commission fees, though post office exchange counters have slightly longer opening hours (generally Mon–Fri 9am–4pm); banks open Monday to Friday from 9am to 3pm, but some don't open their exchange desks until 10.30 or 11am. Big **department stores** often have an exchange desk, which can be useful at other times, though most only handle dollars or a limited range of currencies and might charge a small fee. **Hotels** are only supposed to change money for guests, but some might be persuaded to help in an emergency. Remember to take your passport along in case it's needed, and allow plenty of time, since even a simple transaction can take twenty minutes or more. Finally, when changing money, ask for a few ¥10,000 notes to be broken into lower denominations; these come in handy for ticket machines and small purchases.

Opening hours and public holidays

Business hours are generally Monday to Friday 9am to 5pm, though private companies often close much later in the evening and may also open on Saturday mornings. Department stores and bigger **shops** tend to open around 10am and shut at 7 or 8pm. Local shops, however, will generally stay open later, while many convenience stores stay open 24 hours. Most shops take one day off a week, not necessarily on a Sunday.

The majority of **museums** close on a Monday, but stay open on Sundays and national holidays; last entry is normally thirty minutes before closing. Most museums and department stores stay open on **national holidays** and take the following day off instead. However, during the New Year festival (January 1–3), Golden Week (April 29–May 5) and Obon (the week around August 15), almost everything shuts down. Around these periods all transport and accommodation is booked out weeks in advance, and all major tourist spots get overrun.

Public holidays

If one of the holidays listed below falls on a Sunday, then the Monday is also a holiday.
New Year's Day Jan 1
Coming of Age Day Second Mon in Jan
National Foundation Day Feb 11
Spring Equinox March 20/21
Showa Day April 29
Constitution Memorial Day May 3
Greenery Day May 4
Children's Day May 5
Marine Day Third Mon in July
Respect the Aged Day Third Mon in Sept
Autumn Equinox Sept 23/24
Health and Sports Day Second Mon in Oct
Culture Day Nov 3
Labour Thanksgiving Day Nov 23
Emperor's Birthday Dec 23

Phones

You're rarely far from a payphone in Tokyo, but only at certain ones – usually grey or metallic silver and bronze colour, with a sign in English – can you make **international calls**. These phones can be difficult to find; try a major hotel or international centre.

The vast majority of payphones take both coins (¥10 and ¥100) and **phonecards** (*terefon kādo;* テレフォンカード). The latter come in ¥500 (50-unit) and ¥1000 (105-unit) versions and can be bought in department and convenience stores and at station kiosks. Virtually every tourist attraction sells specially decorated phonecards, which come in a vast range of designs, though you'll pay a premium for these, with a ¥1000 card only giving ¥500 worth of calls.

Payphones don't give change, but do return unused coins, so for local calls use ¥10 rather than ¥100 coins. For international calls, it's best to use a phonecard and to call between 7pm and 8am Monday to Friday, or at any time at weekends or holidays, when rates are cheaper. Alternatively, use a prepaid calling card, such as KDDI's Super World card (@www.kddi.com/english /telephone/card/), Primus (@www.primustel .co.jp), or Brastel (@www.brastel.com); all are available at convenience stores such as Lawson, Mini Stop and Family Mart.

Everywhere in Japan has an **area code**, which can be omitted if the call is a local one. Tokyo's area code is ☎03. All toll-free numbers begin with either ☎0120 or 0088. In a few cases you may come across codes such as ☎0570, which are not region-specific and thus should always be dialled wherever in Japan you're calling from. Numbers starting with ☎080 or ☎090 belong to mobiles.

Mobile phones

Practically everyone in Tokyo seems to have a **mobile phone** (*keitai-denwa*, sometimes shortened to *keitai*; 携帯電話). Text messaging is phenomenally popular in Japan, not only because sending a text is cheap, but also because messages can be jazzed up with special symbols, emoticons, even animation. Furthermore, the humble mobile phone is being turned into a pocket dynamo by a host of new technologies, including GPS navigation and the ability to use the phone as a stored-value Suica or PASMO ticket on Tokyo's subway and trains. The latest trend is for mobile phones to be able to read QR barcodes, which feature a square black-and-white pattern rather than a series of lines. QR codes, increasingly seen on advertisements and in shops, usually have links to a website or email address that the phone can access, or might contain an address, telephone numbers and map of a particular place. Meanwhile, Sony and NTT DoCoMo have been working together on the FeliCa, which allows users to charge up their phone account with credit, then use the phone like a debit or credit card when making payments in convenience stores or at the more advanced vending machines.

All this advanced technology also means that in general you cannot bring your mobile phone to Japan and expect it to work. The solution is to **rent** a Japan-compatible mobile phone (buying a prepaid one once generally requires you to show proof of local residency). Phones can be rented at the airport, in Tokyo or online. One recommended option is **GoMobile** (⊛www.gomobile.co.jp), who will deliver your phone to a nominated address in Japan such as your hotel. Their tariff packages include a certain number of local calls, after which you pay a reasonable ¥85 per minute for local calls, and generally ¥100 per minute for international calls. Other mobile phone operators include industry-biggie **DoCoMo** (⊛www.nttdocomo.com) and **Softbank** (⊛www.softbank-rental.jp), both of which have rental booths at Narita Airport (if you have a 3G handset from abroad, it should work with either of these networks), and travel company **HIS** (see ⊛j-kaleidoscope.com for more details).

Phoning abroad from Japan

The main companies in Japan offering **international phone calls** are KDDI (☎001), Japan Telecom (☎0041), Cable & Wireless IDC (☎0061) and NTT (☎0033). If you want to call abroad from Japan from any type of phone, choose a company (there's little difference between them all as far as rates are concerned) and dial the relevant access code, then the country code (UK ☎44; Ireland ☎353; US and Canada ☎01; Australia ☎61; New Zealand ☎64; South Africa ☎27), then the area code minus the initial zero, then the number. For operator assistance for overseas calls, dial ☎0051. You can make international operator-assisted calls by calling ☎0051 via KDDI.

Phoning Japan from abroad

To **call Japan** from abroad, dial your international access code (UK and Ireland ☎00; US ☎011; Canada ☎011; Australia ☎0011; New Zealand ☎00; South Africa ☎09), plus the country code 81, then the area code minus the initial zero, then the number.

Smoking

Smoking is banned on all public transport and in most public buildings, shops, offices, restaurants, bars, cafés, cinemas and the like, though in some cases smoking is allowed in designated areas. Smoking in the street is also being clamped down on, including large areas of Chūō-ku (especially around Tokyo Station), Chiyoda-ku and Shinjuku-ku, with the possibility of other wards following suit. Again, you can light up in designated areas – look for the smoke-swathed huddle around the pavement ashtrays. Fines for smoking where it's prohibited start at ¥2000, though at the moment you are more likely to get away with a warning.

Time

Tokyo is nine hours ahead of Greenwich Mean Time, fourteen hours ahead of New York, seventeen hours ahead of Los Angeles and two hours behind Sydney. There is no daylight-saving, so during British Summer Time, for example, the difference drops to eight hours.

Tourist information

The **Japan National Tourist Organization** (**JNTO**; @www.jnto.go.jp) maintains a number of overseas offices stocked with a wealth of free maps and leaflets, covering everything from Japanese culture to detailed area guides, accommodation lists and practical information about local transport. You'll find a selection of the same material on their website. The official sources for Tokyo information are the excellent websites of the Tokyo Convention and Visitors Bureau (@www.tcvb.or.jp) and the Tokyo Metropolitan Government (@www.tourism.metro.tokyo.jp).

In Tokyo itself, there are several tourist information centres (TICs), the best being the **Tokyo Tourist Information Centre**, 1F Tokyo Metropolitan Government No. 1 Building, 2-8-1 Nishi-Shinjuku (daily 9.30am–6.30pm; ☎03/5321-3077; Tochō-mae Station). It has small branches at Haneda Airport (daily 9am–10pm; ☎03/5757-9345) and in the Kesei line station at Ueno (daily 9.30am–6.30pm; ☎03/3836-3471).

JNTO's main Tokyo office (Mon–Fri 9am–5pm, Sat 9am–noon; ☎03/3201-3331) is on the tenth floor of Tokyo Kotsu Kaikan, immediately east of Yūrakuchō Station in the heart of the city. There are multilingual staff here, a **Welcome Inn** desk (@www.itcj.jp) for booking accommodation across Japan and a notice board with some information on upcoming events. A more comprehensive monthly list of festivals is available on request. There are tourist information kiosks in the arrivals halls of both terminals at Narita Airport.

A couple more information sources are the **Asakusa Culture and Sightseeing Centre** (☎03/3842-5566; daily 9.30am–8pm), near Asakusa Station and across from Kaminari-mon; and the **Odakyū Sightseeing Service Center** (daily 8am–6pm; ☎03/5321-7887, @www.odakyu.jp/english), at ground level on the west side of Shinjuku Station.

Another useful source of English-language information are the **Goodwill Guides**, groups of volunteer guides who offer their services free – although you're expected to pay for their transport, entry tickets and any meals you have together. Their language abilities vary, but they do provide a great opportunity to learn more about Japanese culture and to visit local restaurants, shops and so forth with a Japanese-speaker. You can contact members of the Tokyo Metropolitan Goodwill Guides (@www2.ocn.ne.jp/~sgg) through the JNTO and Asakusa information offices; try and give at least two days' notice.

JNTO offices abroad

Apart from the following, there are also JNTO offices in France, Germany, Singapore, South Korea and Thailand; see the JNTO website for details.

Australia Level 18, Australia Square Tower, 264 George St, Sydney ☎02/9251 3024, @www.jnto.go.jp/syd/.

Canada 481 University Ave, Toronto ☎416/366-7140, @www.jnto.go.jp/canada.

China 6F, Chang Fu Gong Office Building, 26 Jianguomenwai Dajie, Chaoyang-qu, Beijing ☎010/6513-9023, @www.jnto.go.jp/chs; Suite 3704-05, 37F, Dorset House, Taikoo Place, Quarry Bay, Hong Kong ☎2968-5688; Room 1412, Ruijing Building, M205 Maoming South Road, Shanghai ☎021/5466-2808.

UK Heathcoat House, 20 Savile Row, London ☎020/7734 9638, @www.seejapan.co.uk.

US One Rockefeller Plaza, Suite 1250, New York ☎212/757-5640, @www.japantravelinfo.com; 515 Figueroa St, Suite 1470, Los Angeles ☎213/623-1952.

Travellers with disabilities

Disability has always been something of an uncomfortable topic in Japan, with disabled people generally hidden from public view. In recent years, however, there has been a certain shift in public opinion, particularly following the publication in 1998 of Ototake

Hirotada's *No One's Perfect* (Kodansha International), the upbeat, forthright autobiography of a 23-year-old student born without arms or legs, which became an instant bestseller.

The government is spearheading a drive to provide more accessible hotels and other facilities (referred to as "barrier-free" in Japan). All train and subway **stations** now have an extra-wide manned ticket gate and an increasing number have escalators or lifts. Some **trains**, such as the Narita Express from Narita International Airport into Tokyo, have spaces for wheelchair users, but you should reserve well in advance. For travelling short distances, regular **taxis** are an obvious solution, though they are not adapted to take wheelchairs, and few drivers will offer help getting in or out of the car.

Hotels are now required to provide accessible facilities. Your best bet is one of the international chains or modern Western-style business hotels, which are most likely to provide fully adapted rooms, ramps and lifts; check ahead to ensure the facilities meet your requirements. Similarly, most modern shopping complexes, museums and other public buildings are equipped with ramps, wide doors and accessible toilets.

But while things are improving, Tokyo is not an easy place to get around for anyone using a wheelchair, or for those who find it difficult to negotiate stairs or walk long distances. The sheer crush of people can also be a problem at times. Although it's usually possible to organize assistance at stations, you'll need a Japanese-speaker to phone ahead and make the arrangements. For further information and help, contact the Japanese Red Cross Language Service Volunteers (c/o Volunteers Division, Japanese Red Cross Society, 1-1-3 Shiba Daimon, Minato-ku, Tokyo 105-8521). You'll find useful, if slightly outdated, information on their website Ⓦaccessible.jp.org.

The City

The City

The Imperial Palace and around

n a green swath of central Tokyo, wrapped round with moats and broad avenues, the enigmatic **Imperial Palace** (*kōkyo*; 皇居) lies at the city's geographical and spiritual heart. The site of the palace is as old as Tokyo. In 1457 Ōta Dōkan (see p.303) built a fortress here overlooking Tokyo Bay, which in those times lapped up to where the district of Hibiya is today. After Ōta's assassination in 1486 the castle was left to fall into ruin, and it wasn't until the 1590s that its fortunes were revived under the patronage of Tokugawa Ieyasu, the warlord whose family was destined to rule Japan for close on three hundred years. Little remains of the original Edo Castle save for three fortified towers and some massive stone walls within the palace's 284-acre grounds. When the Tokugawa shogunate collapsed in 1868, the Meiji emperor moved his court here from Kyoto and Edo became Tokyo.

Home to the emperor and his family, the palace hides behind a wall of trees and is closed to the public, but the nearby parks are a natural place to start any exploration of Tokyo. The most attractive is **Higashi Gyoen**, the East Garden, where remnants of the old Edo Castle still stand amid formal gardens, while to its north **Kitanomaru-kōen** is a more natural park containing a motley collection of museums, the best of which is the **National Museum of Modern Art**.

Just outside the park's northern perimeter, the nation's war dead are remembered at the controversial shrine of **Yasukuni-jinja**, while life in Japan during World War II is portrayed at the nearby **Shōwa-kan**. Southwest of the palace is the **National Diet Building**, Japan's seat of government.

The Imperial Palace

Huge and windswept, the **Imperial Plaza** forms a protective island in front of the modern royal palace. In earlier times the shogunate's most trusted followers were allowed to build their mansions here, but after 1899 these were razed to make way for today's austere expanse of spruce lawns and manicured pine trees. The primary reason to follow the groups of local tourists straggling across the broad avenues is to view one of the palace's most photogenic corners, **Nijūbashi**, where two bridges span the moat and a jaunty little watchtower perches on its grey stone

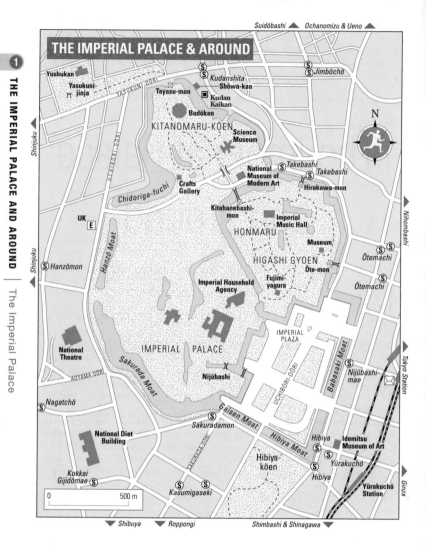

THE IMPERIAL PALACE & AROUND

Map labels:

Suidōbashi ▲   Ochanomizu & Ueno ▲

Yushukan
Yasukuni-jinja
YASUKUNI-DŌRI
Tayasu-mon
Kudanshita
Shōwa-kan
Jimbōchō
Kudan Kaikan
Budōkan
KITANOMARU-KŌEN
Science Museum
Shinjuku
Chidoriga-fuchi
Crafts Gallery
National Museum of Modern Art
Takebashi
Takebashi
Hirakawa-mon
Kitahanebashi-mon
Imperial Music Hall
UK
Nihombashi
HONMARU
Museum
HIGASHI GYOEN
Ōtemachi
Hanzōmon
Hanzō Moat
Ōte-mon
Ōtemachi
Fujimi-yagura
Imperial Household Agency
IMPERIAL PALACE
IMPERIAL PLAZA
Babasaki Moat
National Theatre
Sakurada Moat
UCHIBORI-DŌRI
Nijūbashi-mae
Tokyo Station
AOYAMA-DŌRI
Nijūbashi
Gaisen Moat
Nagatchō
Sākuradamon
Hibiya Moat
Hibiya
Idemitsu Museum of Art
National Diet Building
SAKURADA-DŌRI
Hibiya-kōen
Yūrakuchō
Ginza
Kokkai Gijidōmae
Kasumigaseki
Hibiya
Yūrakuchō Station

0   500 m

▼ Shibuya   ▼ Roppongi   Shimbashi & Shinagawa ▼

pedestal beyond. Though this double bridge is a late nineteenth-century embellishment, the tower dates back to the seventeenth century and is one of the castle's few original structures. The present palace is a long, sleek, 1960s structure, built to replace the Meiji palace burnt down in the 1945 bombing raids. The imperial **residences** themselves, built in the early 1990s, are tucked away out of sight in the thickly wooded western section of the grounds.

Twice a year (on December 23, the emperor's official birthday, and on January 2) thousands of well-wishers file across Nijūbashi to greet the royal family, lined up behind bullet-proof glass, with a rousing cheer of "Banzai" ("May you live 10,000 years"). Outside these two days, the general public is only admitted to the palace grounds on pre-arranged **official tours**, conducted in Japanese but with English-language brochures and audio-guides available. The tours are a bit of a hassle to

Descendants of the Sun Goddess

Japan's **imperial family** is the world's longest-reigning dynasty – at least according to die-hard traditionalists, who believe Emperor Akihito, the 125th incumbent of the Chrysanthemum Throne, traces his ancestry back to 660 BC and Emperor Jimmu, great-great-grandson of the Sun Goddess Amaterasu, a key mythological figure. Most scholars, however, now acknowledge that the first emperor for whom there is any historical evidence is the fifth-century Emperor Ojin.

Until the twentieth century, emperors were regarded as living deities whom ordinary folk were forbidden to set eyes on, or even hear. But on August 15, 1945, a stunned nation listened to the radio as Emperor Hirohito's quavering voice announced Japan's surrender to the Allies, and a few months later he declared that emperors no longer held divine status.

Today the emperor is a symbolic figure, a head of state with no governmental power, and the family is gradually abandoning its cloistered existence. **Emperor Akihito** was the first to benefit: as crown prince, he had an American tutor and studied at Tokyo's elite Gakushūin University, followed by a stint at Oxford University. In 1959 he broke further with tradition by marrying a commoner, **Empress Michiko**, whom he supposedly met on a tennis court.

His children have continued the modernizing trend without denting the public's deep respect for the imperial family, though the more radical papers are becoming bolder in their criticism. Akihito's daughter-in-law, **Crown Princess Masako** (before her marriage a high-flying Harvard-educated diplomat) has been the subject of an unusual amount of press interest over the fact that she and her husband **Crown Prince Naruhito** had failed to produce a male heir. Following a miscarriage, in 2001 she eventually gave birth to a baby girl, **Aiko**, but rejoicing turned to sadness as the crown princess has barely been seen in public since, suffering from a variety of stress-related illnesses, officially termed an "adjustment disorder". Crown Prince Naruhito has gone so far as to suggest that his wife was made ill by efforts to crush her personality – not just by the media but also by the powerful Imperial Household Agency, the government body that effectively runs the imperial institution.

Adding grist to the mill, in 2007 an unauthorized biography by Australian journalist Ben Hills, entitled *Princess Masako: Prisoner of the Chrysanthemum Throne*, alleged that the princess "has been persecuted by the Imperial Household bureaucrats, and driven into a deep state of depression". Not surprisingly, the Imperial Household Agency denounced the book and a Japanese edition was pulled at the last minute. Meanwhile, Empress Michiko is also said to be suffering from recurring health problems related to stress.

Matters have not been helped by an impending "crisis" over succession to the throne. While Japan has been ruled by empresses in the past, a law introduced in the Meiji era prohibits female succession. Since no males have been born in the imperial family for 41 years, however, the male line was about to die out. The situation was so serious that in 2006 the then prime minister Junichiro Koizumi was preparing a bill to alter the law in favour of female succession. The crisis was averted – or at least postponed – when **Princess Kiko**, wife of Naruhito's younger brother, gave birth to **Prince Hisahito** in September 2006; he becomes third in line to the throne.

get on, but there is a certain fascination in taking a peek inside this secret world, and the pre-tour video shows tantalizing glimpses of vast function rooms and esoteric court rituals. You can apply online up to two months in advance via the Imperial Household Agency website (Ⓦ www.kunaicho.go.jp/e17/ed17 -03.html) or by calling ☎03/3213-1111 ext 3485 (Mon–Fri 8.45am–noon & 1–5pm). In the latter case, you need to go to their office inside the palace grounds at least one day before the appointed date to collect a permit, taking along your

△ A watchtower guards Nijūbashi bridge, one of the entrances to the Imperial Palace

passport. Tours are free, last eighty minutes and take place on weekdays at 10am & 1.30pm; there are no tours from December 28 to January 4 and from July 21 to August 31.

Higashi Gyoen

The finest of Edo Castle's remaining watchtowers, three-tiered **Fujimi-yagura**, stands clear above the trees to the north of the Imperial Plaza. Built in 1659 to protect the main citadel's southern flank, these days it ornaments what is known as **Higashi Gyoen** or East Garden (東御苑; Tues–Thurs, Sat & Sun 9am–4pm; closed occasionally for court functions; free). Hemmed round with moats, the garden was opened to the public in 1968 to commemorate the completion of the new Imperial Palace. It's a good place for a stroll, though there's little to evoke the former glory of the shogunate's castle, beyond several formidable gates and the towering granite walls.

The main gate to the garden – and formerly to Edo Castle itself – is **Ōte-mon**. On entry you'll be given a numbered token to hand in again as you leave. The first building ahead on the right is a small **museum** (free), exhibiting a tiny fraction of the eight thousand artworks in the imperial collection, and worth a quick look.

From here a path winds gently up, beneath the walls of the main citadel, and then climbs more steeply towards **Shiomizaka**, the Tide-Viewing Slope, from where it was once possible to gaze out over Edo Bay rather than the concrete blocks of Ōtemachi. You emerge on a flat grassy area, empty apart from the stone foundations of **Honmaru** (the "inner citadel"), with fine views from the top, and a scattering of modern edifices, among them the bizarre, mosaic-clad **Imperial**

Music Hall. Designed by Imai Kenji, the hall commemorates the sixtieth birthday of the (then) empress in 1963 and is used for occasional performances of court music.

Kitanomaru-kōen

The northern citadel of Edo Castle is now occupied by the park of **Kitanomaru-kōen** (北の丸公園), home to a couple of interesting museums. The main one to head for, immediately to the right as you emerge from the Higashi Gyoen through the Kitahanebashi-mon gate, is the **National Museum of Modern Art** (Kokuritsu Kindai Bijutsukan; 国立近代美術館; Tues–Sun 10am–5pm, Fri until 8pm; ¥420, or ¥800 including the Crafts Gallery; ☎03/5777-8600, ⓦwww .momat.go.jp). Its excellent collection showcases Japanese art since 1900, including Gyokudo Kawa's magnificent screen painting *Parting Spring* and works by Kishida Ryusei, Fujita Tsuguharu and postwar artists such as Yoshihara Jiro.

A short walk away on the west side of Kitanomaru-kōen, the **Crafts Gallery** (Kōgeikan; 工芸館; Tues–Sun 10am–5pm, Fri until 8pm; ¥420; ☎03/5777-8600, ⓦwww.momat.go.jp) exhibits a selection of top-quality traditional Japanese craft works, many by modern masters. Erected in 1910 as the headquarters of the Imperial Guards, this neo-Gothic red-brick pile is one of very few Tokyo buildings dating from before the Great Earthquake of 1923.

To the west of the gallery, **Chidoriga-fuchi** marks where an ancient pond was incorporated into Edo Castle's moat. Rowing boats can be rented here and, with its ninety-odd cherry trees, it's a popular viewing spot come *hanami* time.

The park's last major building is the **Budōkan** hall, built in 1964 to host Olympic judo events. The design, with its graceful, curving roof and gold topknot, pays homage to a famous octagonal hall at Hōryū-ji temple in Nara, near Kyoto, though the shape is also supposedly inspired by that of Mount Fuji. Today the huge arena is used for sports meetings, graduation ceremonies and, most famously, big-name rock concerts.

Yasukuni-jinja and Shōwa-kan

Across the road from Kitanomaru-kōen, a monumental red steel *torii*, claimed to be Japan's tallest, marks the entrance to **Yasukuni-jinja** (靖国神社; ⓦwww .yasukuni.or.jp). This shrine, whose name means "for the repose of the country", was founded in 1869 to worship supporters of the emperor killed in the run-up to the Meiji Restoration. Since then it has expanded to include the legions sacrificed in subsequent wars, in total nearly 2.5 million souls, of whom some two million died in the Pacific War alone; the parting words of kamikaze pilots were said to be "see you at Yasukuni".

Despite its highly controversial nature (see box, p.56), every year some eight million Japanese visit Yasukuni to remember family and friends who died in the last, troubled century. Its surprisingly unassuming Inner Shrine stands at the end of a long avenue lined with cherry and ginkgo trees, and through a simple wooden gate. The architecture is classic Shinto styling, solid and unadorned except for two gold imperial chrysanthemums embossed on the main doors.

The problem with Yasukuni

Ever since its foundation as part of a Shinto revival promoting the new emperor, Yasukuni-jinja has been a place of high controversy. In its early years the shrine became a natural focus for the increasingly aggressive nationalism that ultimately took Japan to war in 1941. Then, in 1978, General Tōjō, prime minister during World War II, and thirteen other "Class A" war criminals were enshrined here, to be honoured along with all the other military dead. Japan's neighbours, still smarting from their treatment by the Japanese during the war, were outraged.

This has not stopped top politicians from visiting Yasukuni on the anniversary of Japan's defeat in World War II (August 15). Because Japan's postwar constitution requires the separation of state and religion, ministers have usually maintained that they attend as private individuals, but in 1985 Nakasone, in typically uncompromising mood, caused an uproar when he signed the visitors' book as "Prime Minister". Recent PMs have continued to visit Yasukuni – always in an "unofficial" capacity – despite continued protests both at home and abroad. But there's a hint of change in the air as the need to improve relations with an increasingly powerful China forces Japan's leaders to adopt a more conciliatory stance.

To the right of the Inner Shrine you'll find the **Yūshūkan** (daily 9am–5pm; ¥800; ☎03/3261-8326), a military museum established in 1882. The displays are well presented, with plentiful information in English, but the problem is as much what is left out as what is included. Events such as the Nanking Massacre ("Incident" in Japanese) and other atrocities by Japanese troops are glossed over, while the Pacific War is presented as a war of liberation, freeing the peoples of Southeast Asia from Western colonialism. The most moving displays are the ranks of faded photographs and the "bride dolls" donated by the families of young soldiers who died before they were married. You exit through a hall full of military hardware, including a replica of the gliders used by kamikaze pilots on their suicide missions, its nose elongated to carry a 1200-kilo bomb, while a spine-chilling, black *kaiten* (manned torpedo) lours to one side.

As an antidote, take a walk through the little Japanese **garden** lying behind the shrine buildings. The sunken enclosure next door is the venue for a sumo tournament during the shrine's spring festival, when top wrestlers perform under trees laden with cherry blossom. It's also well worth visiting in early July during the shrine's lively summer *matsuri*, when the precincts are illuminated by thousands of paper lanterns and there's dancing, parades and music nightly.

Shōwa-kan

There's scarcely a mention of bombs or destruction at the **Shōwa-kan** (昭和館; Tues–Sun 10am–5.30pm; ¥300; ☎03/3222-2577, ⓦwww.showakan.go.jp), a corrugated, windowless building east along Yasukuni-dōri from Yasukuni-jinja – which is odd, since this museum is devoted to life in Japan during and after World War II. To be fair, the government originally wanted the museum to document the war's origins but ran into bitter opposition from pacifists, insistent on tackling the hot-potato issue of responsibility, and a right-wing lobby opposed to any hint that Japan was an aggressor during the conflict. After twenty years of argument, they eventually decided on a compromise that pleases almost no one by sticking to a sanitized portrayal of the hardships suffered by wives and children left behind. Nevertheless, there's some interesting material, most notably that concerning life during the occupation. For Japanese-speakers, they have also amassed a vast archive of war-related documents.

The National Diet Building

The main point of interest over on the south side of the Imperial Palace grounds is the squat, three-storey **National Diet Building** (Kokkai Gijidō; 国会議事堂; Ⓦwww.sangiin.go.jp), dominated by a central tower block decorated with pillars and a pyramid-shaped roof. The Diet is supposedly based on the Senate Building in Washington DC, though Japan's style of government has more in common with the British parliamentary system. On the left stands the House of Representatives, the main body of government, while on the right, the House of Councillors, which is similar to Britain's House of Lords, is open for forty-minute **tours** (Mon–Fri 9am–4pm unless the House of Councillors is in session – call Ⓣ03/3581-3100 to check; free).

There's an Edwardian-style grandeur to the Diet's interior, especially in the carved-wood debating chamber and the central reception hall, decorated with paintings reflecting the seasons and bronze statues of significant statesmen. The room the emperor uses when he visits the Diet is predictably ornate, with detailing picked out in real gold. The tour finishes at the Diet's front garden, planted with native trees and plants from all of Japan's 47 prefectures.

Ginza and around

Walk east from the Imperial Palace, across Babasaki Moat, and you're plunged straight into the hurly-burly of downtown Tokyo, among grey-faced office blocks, swanky department stores and streets full of rush-hour crowds which are transformed at dusk into neon-lit canyons. The heart of the area is **Ginza**, Tokyo's most exclusive shopping and dining district. There are no must-see sights here, but it's a compact area where you can happily spend an hour exploring a single high-rise stacked with boutiques and cafés, or rummaging in the backstreets. Even the most anonymous building can yield a specialty store or avant-garde gallery, while some wonderfully atmospheric eating and drinking places lurk under the train tracks that split the district from north to south.

West of the tracks, **Yūrakuchō, Marunouchi** and **Hibiya** are theatre- and business-land, and also home to airline offices, banks and corporate headquarters, as well as the dramatic modern architecture of the **Tokyo International Forum**. Marunouchi is enjoying a stylish reinvention with the opening of several new shopping and restaurant complexes and the long-term redevelopment of Tokyo Station. Hibiya's highlight is its Western-style **park**, a refreshing oasis of greenery.

On Ginza's southern flank is the new suburb of **Shiodome**, where a brace of sparkling skyscrapers harbour hotels, restaurants and a few bona fide tourist sights, the best of which is **ADMT**, a museum dedicated to advertising. Head northwards from Ginza along Chūō-dōri, and you'll hit the high-finance district of **Nihombashi**, once the heart of boisterous, low-town Edo but now the preserve of blue-suited bankers. Here you'll find the original **Mitsukoshi** department store and a couple of fine-art museums: the new **Mitsui Memorial Museum** and the **Bridgestone Museum of Art**.

A **free bus** service (daily 10am–8pm; every 15min) runs in a loop from Hibiya to Tokyo Station and up to Ōtemachi, across to the *Palace Hotel* and then back south along the Imperial Palace moat to Hibiya.

Ginza

Ginza (銀座), the "place where silver is minted", took its name after Shogun Tokugawa Ieyasu started making coins here in the early 1600s. It was a happy association – Ginza's Chūō-dōri grew to become Tokyo's most stylish shopping street. The unusually regular pattern of streets here is due to British architect Thomas Waters, who was given the task of creating a less combustible city after a fire in 1872 destroyed virtually all of old, wooden Ginza. His "Bricktown", as it soon became known, proved an instant local tourist attraction, with its rows of two-storey brick houses, tree-lined avenues, gaslights and brick pavements. But since the airless buildings were totally unsuited to Tokyo's hot, humid climate, people were reluctant to settle until the government offered pepper-corn rents.

Most of the first businesses here dealt in foreign wares, and in no time Ginza had become the centre of all that was modern, Western and therefore fashionable – Western dress and hairstyles, watches, cafés and beer halls. Bricktown itself didn't survive the Great Earthquake of 1923, but by then Ginza's status was well established. In the 1930s the height of sophistication was simply to stroll around Ginza, and the practice still continues, particularly on Sunday afternoons, when Chūō-dōri is closed to traffic and everyone turns out for a spot of window-shopping. Though some of its shine has faded and cutting-edge fashion has moved elsewhere, Ginza retains much of its elegance and its undoubted snob appeal. Here you'll find the greatest concentration of exclusive shops, and restaurants in the city, the most theatres and cinemas, branches of most major department stores, and a fair number of art galleries.

The area is packed into a compact rectangular grid of streets completely enclosed by the Shuto Expressway. Three broad avenues run from north to south, **Chūō-dōri** being the main shopping street, while **Harumi-dōri** cuts across the centre from the east. In the west, Ginza proper begins at the Sukiyabashi crossing, where Sotobori-dōri and Harumi-dōri intersect. The **Sony Building** (daily 11am–7pm; free; ℡03/3573-2371, ⓦwww.sonybuilding.jp), occupying the crossing's southeast corner, is primarily of interest for techno-freaks, with four of its eleven storeys showcasing the latest Sony gadgets. Continuing east along Harumi-dōri, you'll reach the intersection with Chūō-dōri known as **Ginza Yon-chōme crossing**, which marks the heart of Ginza. Awesome at rush hour, this spot often features in films and documentaries as the epitome of this overcrowded yet totally efficient city. A number of venerable emporia cluster round the junction. **Wakō**, now an exclusive department store, started life over a century ago as the stall of a young, enterprising watchmaker who developed a line called Seikō (meaning "precision"); its clock tower, built in 1894, is one of Ginza's most enduring landmarks.

Immediately north of Wakō on Chūō-dōri, **Kimuraya bakery** was founded in 1874, while **Mikimoto Pearl** opened next door a couple of decades later. South of the crossing, just beyond the cylindrical, glass San'ai Building, **Kyūkyodō** has been selling traditional paper, calligraphy brushes and inkstones since 1800, and is filled with the dusty smell of *sumi-e* ink.

Further east down Harumi-dōri, **Kabuki-za** (歌舞伎座) has been the city's principal Kabuki theatre since its inauguration in 1889. Up until then Kabuki had belonged firmly to the lowbrow world of Edo's Shitamachi, but under the Meiji it was cleaned up and relocated to this more respectable district. The original, European-style Kabuki-za made way in 1925 for a Japanese design, of which the present building is a 1950s replica. See p.206 for details of performances.

Yūrakuchō and Marunouchi

Immediately west of Ginza and east of the Imperial Palace is **Yūrakuchō** (有楽町), home to the main JNTO tourist office (see p.47) and the **Tokyo**

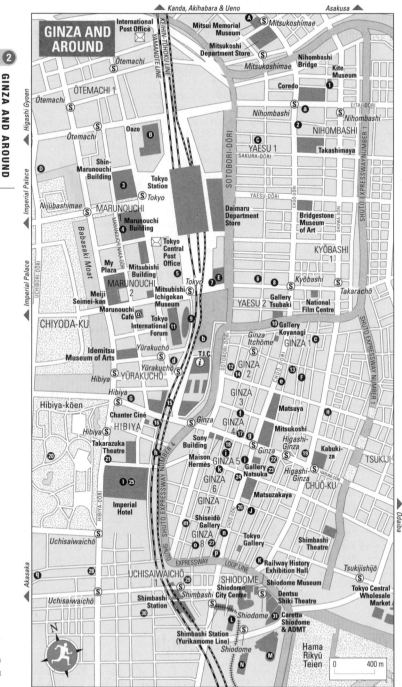

GINZA AND AROUND

Kanda, Akihabara & Ueno ▲   *Asakusa* ▲

GINZA AND AROUND

International Post Office

Ōtemachi

ŌTEMACHI 1

Higashi Gyoen ◀

Ōtemachi

Ōtemachi

Oazo **B**

Shin-Marunouchi Building **3**

Nijūbashimae

MARUNOUCHI

Imperial Palace ◀

Marunouchi Building **4**

My Plaza
Mitsubishi Building
Meiji Seimei-kan

Imperial Palace ◀

MARUNOUCHI 2

Marunouchi Café

Tokyo Central Post Office **5**

Mitsubishi Ichigokan Museum

CHIYODA-KU

Uchibori-dōri ◀
Imperial Palace ◀

Idemitsu Museum of Arts

Tokyo International Forum **11**

Yūrakuchō

Yūrakuchō

YŪRAKUCHŌ

T.I.C.

Hibiya

Hibiya-kōen

Hibiya

Chanter Ciné

Hibiya
Akasaka ◀

HIBIYA

Takarazuka Theatre **21**

20

1 25

Imperial Hotel

Uchisaiwaichō

Uchisaiwaichō

UCHISAIWAICHŌ 1

28

29

Shimbashi Station
30

Shimbashi Station (Yurikamome Line)

N

Mitsui Memorial Museum
Mitsukoshimae **A** Mitsukoshimae

Mitsukoshi Department Store

Mitsukoshimae

SOTOBORI-DŌRI

Nihombashi Bridge
Kite Museum
Coredo **1**

Nihombashi **a** Nihombashi

EITAI-DŌRI

YAESU 1
SAKURA-DŌRI **C**

NIHOMBASHI

Takashimaya

2

CHUŌ-DŌRI

SHOWA-DŌRI

SHUTO EXPRESSWAY NUMBER 1

YAESU-DŌRI

Tokyo Station

Tokyo

Daimaru Department Store

Bridgestone Museum of Art

KYŌBASHI 1

Tokyo

E **7**

6 **8** Kyōbashi

YAESU 2

Gallery Tsubaki
National Film Centre

Takarachō

9

10 Gallery Koyanagi

Ginza Itchōme

GINZA 1 **c**

b

12 GINZA 2 **e**
14

13 **F**

GINZA 3

f

Matsuya

H

GINZA 4

16 **17** **g**

Mitsukoshi

Sony Building

Ginza

Higashi-Ginza

Kabuki-za

Maison Hermès

GINZA 5 **18** **j**

22 Ginza

Gallery Natsuka **k**

23 Higashi-Ginza

TSUKIJI

19

CHUŌ-KU

GINZA 6 **24**

Matsuzakaya

Odaiba ▶

GINZA 7 **26** **J**

Shiseidō Gallery

m

GINZA 8 **o** **27** **n**

Tokyo Gallery

p

Railway History Exhibition Hall **K**

Shimbashi Theatre

SHUTO EXPRESSWAY NUMBER 4

SHUTO EXPRESSWAY

LOOP LINE

SHIODOME

Shiodome Museum

Dentsu Shiki Theatre

Shimbashi City Centre

Shimbashi

Shiodome

Caretta Shiodome & ADMT **31**

Tsukijishijō

Tokyo Central Wholesale Market

L

Shiodome

M

Hama Rikyū Teien

N

0   400 m

60

Shinagawa ▼   ▼ *Odaiba*

International Forum (東京国際フォーラム; www.t-i-forum.co.jp), a stunning creation by American architect Rafael Viñoly, which hosts concerts and conventions, plus the Ōedo Antique Market (see p.220). The boat-shaped main hall consists of a sixty-metre-high atrium sheathed in 2600 sheets of earthquake-resistant glass, with a ceiling ribbed like a ship's hull – it looks magical at night.

Immediately north and west of the International Forum, the business-focused **Marunouchi** (丸の内) district has been broadening its appeal with a raft of sleek, new multistorey developments combining offices, hotels, shopping plazas and all manner of restaurants and cafés. The 36-storey **Marunouchi Building** (www.marubiru.jp), affectionately known as Maru Biru, was first off the blocks, followed by the **Oazo** complex (www.oazo.jp), home to Maruzen's new flagship bookstore among other things. Next in line will be the Mitsubishi Ichigokan Museum, focusing on nineteenth-century European art. Due to open early 2010, it will be housed in a reconstruction of British architect Josiah Conder's (see box, p.68) original red-brick office block, erected on the same site in 1894, only to be demolished in 1968.

Tokyo Station (東京駅) is also undergoing major redevelopment, scheduled for completion by 2011, though the original, red-brick station can still be seen amid the towering office blocks. Over on the west side of Marunouchi, another building from the first half of the twentieth century has been incorporated into the My Plaza building. Completed in 1934, the **Meiji Seimei-kan** (明治生命館; Sat & Sun 11am–5pm; free; ☏03/3283-9252) is now home to the Meiji Yasuda life insurance company, but on weekends you're allowed in to admire the highly polished marble floors and plaster detailing. Upstairs is a parquet-floored and -panelled conference room, where the Allied Council of Japan met in the aftermath of World War II, and a dining room complete with dumbwaiters.

Two blocks south of here, the **Imperial Theatre** hosts big-budget Western musicals. Above it, on the ninth floor, the **Idemitsu Museum of Arts** (出光美術館; Tues–Thurs, Sat & Sun 10am–5pm, Fri 10am–7pm; ¥1000; ☏03/5777-8600, www.idemitsu.co.jp/museum) houses a magnificent collection of mostly Japanese art, though only a tiny proportion is on show at any one time. The collection includes many historically important pieces, ranging from fine examples of early Jōmon (10,000 BC–300 BC) pottery to Zen Buddhist calligraphy, hand-painted scrolls, richly gilded folding screens and elegant, late seventeenth-century *ukiyo-e* paintings. The museum also owns valuable collections of Chinese and Korean ceramics, as well as slightly incongruous works by French painter Georges Rouault and American artist Sam Francis.

Hibiya

The area south of where Edo Castle once stood was occupied by the Tokugawa shogunate's less favoured *daimyō*. The land was cleared after 1868, but was too waterlogged to support modern buildings, so in 1903 **Hibiya-kōen** (日比谷公園), Tokyo's first European-style park, came into being. These days the tree-filled park is a popular lunchtime spot for office workers and courting couples, and makes a very pleasant escape from the bustle of nearby Ginza and Shimbashi.

Across the road is the celebrated **Imperial Hotel**, first opened in 1890, when it was Tokyo's first Western-style hotel. The original building was subsequently replaced by an Art Deco, Aztec-palace creation by American architect Frank Lloyd Wright, a stunning building which famously withstood both the Great Kantō Earthquake (which struck the city on September 1, 1923, the day after the hotel's formal opening) and World War II. After all this, Wright's building finally fell victim to the 1960s property development boom, when it was replaced by the current looming tower. Today, just a hint of Wright's style exists in the *Old Imperial Bar* (see p.191), incorporating some of the original brickwork.

Tokyo's top parks and gardens

Look at any map of central Tokyo and you'll quickly realize that there isn't much in the way of parkland: just 5.3 square metres of park per resident compared to 29 square metres in New York and 26 square metres in Paris – and two of the biggest central patches of greenery (those immediately around the Imperial Palace and the Akasaka Detached Palace) are largely off-limits to the general public. What's left is often covered by cemeteries, as in Aoyama and Yanaka, or public buildings, as in Ueno. If you need a quick escape from the concrete and neon, here are our top ten picks; see ⓦ www.tokyo-park.or.jp for further suggestions.

Hama Rikyū Teien (p.136) Once the duck-hunting grounds of the shogun, now a beautiful bayside retreat.

Happōen (p.130) Harbours a gracious Japanese villa, bonsai trees and a teahouse by a pretty pond.

Hibiya-kōen (above) Relatively spacious Western-style park with fountain and bandstand.

Higashi Gyoen (p.54) The tranquil east garden of the Imperial Palace.

Kyū Furukawa Gardens (p.102) An Italianate terrace with rose beds tumbles down to a traditional Japanese-style garden laid out around an ornamental pond.

Meiji-jingū Inner Garden (p.115) Peaceful grounds surrounding Tokyo's most important Shinto shrine.

National Park for Nature Study (p.130) Limited daily admissions help preserve this park's natural serenity; a haven for solitude seekers.

Rikugi-en (p.102) Tokyo's best example of an Edo-period stroll-garden.

Shinjuku Gyoen (p.111) English, French and Japanese garden styles combine harmoniously at this spacious park.

Yoyogi-kōen (p.116) A modern park, next to Meiji-jingū shrine, and popular with families and couples.

Shiodome

Follow the railway tracks south from Ginza to reach **Shiodome** (汐留), where a clutch of ultra-modern skyscrapers now occupy the site of Japan Railways' old freight terminal. Known collectively as **Shiodome Sio-Site** (汐留シオサイト), the towers are home to some of Japan's top companies, including Nippon TV and Kyodo News.

While the overall design of Shiodome may not be as successful as its rival mega-development of Roppongi Hills (see p.81), with little to soften the alienating concrete environment, there are a few attractions worth checking out, as well as numerous restaurants and four major hotels. The most interesting sight is the hi-tech Advertising Museum Tokyo, or **ADMT** (Tues–Fri 11am–6.30pm, Sat 11am–4.30pm; free; ℡03/6218-2500, ⓦwww.admt.jp), on the B1 floor of the **Caretta Shiodome** skyscraper, the sleek headquarters of the Dentsu ad agency. In the small permanent exhibition a montage of ads provides a fascinating flick through some of the twentieth century's most arresting commercial images. It's fun to watch videos of past award-winning TV commercials and see what's happening in the online ad world. Afterwards, zip up to the top of the Caretta Shiodome building in the glass-fronted lifts to the restaurants on the 46th and 47th floors for a free panoramic view across Tokyo Bay and the Hama Rikyū Teien traditional garden.

Immediately west of Caretta Shiodome is Shiodome's second major tower complex, **Shiodome City Centre**. Back in 1872, this was the site of the original Shimbashi Station, the terminus of Japan's first railway line. A faithful reproduction of the station building, designed by American architect R. P. Bridgens, now rests incongruously at the foot of the tower and contains the **Railway History Exhibition Hall** (Tues–Sun 11am–6pm; free; ℡03/3572-1872). Part of the foundations of the original building, uncovered during excavations on the site, have been preserved, and you can also see some engaging videos (in English) about Japan's early railways, as well as woodblock prints and old photos of how the area once looked.

△ The Yurikamome monorail glides beneath Shiodome's skyscrapers

Of more minor interest is the **Shiodome Museum** (Tues–Sun 10am–6pm; ¥500; ℡03/6218-0078, ⓦwww.mew.co.jp/corp/museum), a small gallery with changing exhibitions focusing primarily on interior design, alongside a few works by the French religious artist Georges Rouault. It's in the headquarters of **Matsushita Electric Works**, where you might have more fun admiring the latest in kitchen and bathroom technology, including the newest electronically controlled toilets.

From Shiodome, you can easily continue on to the Tsukiji fish market (see p.134), or pick up the Yurikamome monorail to Odaiba (see p.138).

Nihombashi

North of Ginza, **Nihombashi** (日本橋) was once the heart of Edo's teeming Shitamachi (see p.303), growing from a cluster of riverside markets in the early seventeenth century to become the city's chief financial district. The early warehouses and moneylenders subsequently evolved into the banks, brokers and trading companies that line the streets today.

Since 1603, the centre of Nihombashi, and effectively of all Japan, was an arched red-lacquer-coated **bridge** – a favourite of *ukiyo-e* artists – which marked the start of the Tōkaidō, the great road running between Edo and Kyoto. The original wooden structure has long gone, but distances from Tokyo are still measured from a bronze marker at the halfway point of the present stone bridge, erected in 1911. Although it's now smothered by the Shuto Expressway, it's still worth swinging by here to see the bronze dragons and wrought-iron lamps that decorate the bridge.

A little further north on Chūō-dōri is the most traditional of Japan's department stores, **Mitsukoshi** (三越). The shop traces its ancestry back to a dry-goods store opened in 1673 by Mitsui Takatoshi, who revolutionized retailing in Edo and went on to found the Mitsui business empire. This was the first store in Japan to offer a delivery service, the first to sell imported goods, and the first with an escalator, though until 1923 customers were still required to take off their shoes and don Mitsukoshi slippers. The most interesting part of today's store is the north building, which dates from 1914 and whose main atrium is dominated by a weird and wonderful statue, carved from 500-year-old Japanese cypress, of Magokoro, the Goddess of Sincerity.

The block north of Mitsukoshi is home to Mitsui's headquarters and the **Mitsui Memorial Museum** (三井記念美術館; Tues–Sun 10am–5pm; ¥800; ℡03/5777-8600, ⓦwww.mitsui-museum.jp), where just some of the company's superb collection spanning three hundred years of Japanese and Asian art is on display; you'll find the entrance in the new Nihonbashi Mitsui Tower next door. Changing exhibitions follow a seasonal theme, but there's always a section devoted to tea-ceremony utensils, centred on a replica of the Jo'an teahouse, held to be one of the finest examples of teahouse architecture. The museum closes between exhibitions, so phone ahead to check.

Heading south along Chūō-dōri from the bridge, turn left immediately before the Coredo tower block – another new shopping, dining and office complex – to locate the cluttered little **Kite Museum** (凧の博物館; Mon–Sat 11am–5pm; ¥200; ℡03/3275-2704, ⓦwww.tako.gr.jp); there's no English sign, but it's on the fifth floor above *Taimeiken* restaurant. Since 1977 the restaurant's former owner has amassed over three hundred kites of every conceivable shape and size, from one no bigger than a postage stamp to a monster 18m square. If you have kids in tow, they can try making their own out of bamboo and *washi* paper.

As you return to Chūō-dōri, a row of cheerful red awnings on the left-hand side announces another of Tokyo's grand old stores, **Takashimaya** (高島屋), which started off as a kimono shop in the seventeenth century and is worth popping into for its lovely old-fashioned lifts. Further south, at the junction of Chūō-dōri and Yaesu-dōri, is the **Bridgestone Museum of Art** (ブリヂストン美術館; Tues–Sat 10am–8pm, Sun 10am–6pm; ¥800; ☎03/3563-0241, Ⓦ www.bridgestone -museum.gr.jp). This superb collection focuses on the Impressionists and continues through all the great names of early twentieth-century European art, plus a highly rated sampler of Meiji-era Japanese paintings in Western style. It's not an extensive display, but offers a rare opportunity to enjoy works by artists such as Renoir, Picasso and Van Gogh in what is often an almost deserted gallery.

From here Yaesu-dōri heads west towards the east entrance to Tokyo Station, known as the Yaesu entrance. Here you'll find the main entrance to the Shinkansen platforms, while limousine buses for Narita and Haneda airports stop across the road, on the east side of Sotobori-dōri.

Kanda, Akihabara and around

Kanda (神田), the region immediately north and west of Nihombashi, straddles Tokyo's crowded eastern lowlands – the former Shitamachi (see p.303) and the more expansive western hills. The area's scattered sights reflect these contrasting styles, kicking off at **Ochanomizu** with the lively Shinto shrine of Kanda Myōjin, and an austere monument to Confucius at Yushima Seidō. Below them lie the buzzing, neon-lit streets of **Akihabara**, Tokyo's "Electric City", dedicated to technological wizardry and anime.

West on the JR Sōbu line, Suidōbashi has a couple of minor attractions in the form of Tokyo's foremost baseball stadium, an upmarket spa complex and funfair, and a classic seventeenth-century garden, while a studious hush prevails among the secondhand bookshops of Jimbōchō, to the south.

Kanda

Kanda's two great shrines lie on the north bank of the Kanda-gawa river and are within easy reach of both **Ochanomizu's** (御茶の水) JR and Marunouchi subway line stations. Some woods hide the distinctive shrine of **Yushima Seidō** (湯島聖堂; daily: May–Oct 9.30am–5pm, Nov–April 9.30am–4pm; free), dedicated to the Chinese sage Confucius. The Seidō (Sacred Hall) was founded in 1632 as an academy for the study of the ancient classics at a time when the Tokugawa were promoting Confucianism as the state's ethical foundation. In 1691 the hall was moved to its present location, where it became an elite school for the sons of samurai and high-ranking officials, though most of these buildings were lost in the fires of 1923. Today, the quiet compound contains an eighteenth-century wooden gate and, at the top of broad steps, the Taisen-den, or "Hall of Accomplishments", where the shrine to Confucius is located. This imposing, black-lacquered building was rebuilt in 1935 to the original design; look up to see panther-like guardians poised on the roof tiles.

Follow the road round to the north of Yushima Seidō to find a large, copper *torii* and a traditional wooden shop, Amanoya (daily 9am–5.30pm), selling sweet, ginger-laced sake (*amazake*). Beyond, a vermilion gate marks the entrance to **Kanda Myōjin** (神田明神; 9am–4.30pm; free; ☎03/3254-0753,

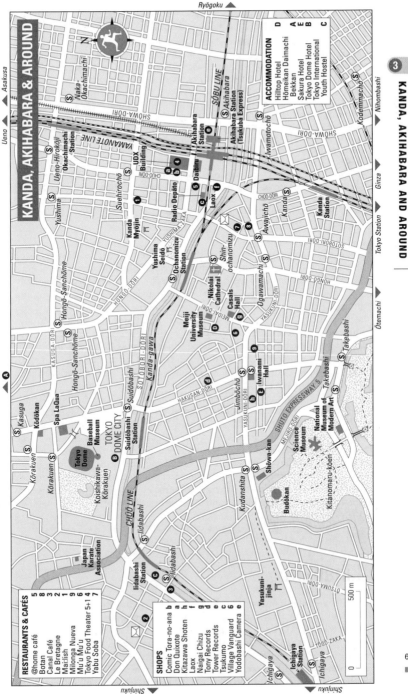

KANDA, AKIHABARA & AROUND

ACCOMMODATION

Hilltop Hotel	D
Hōmeikan Daimachi	A
Bekkan	E
Sakura Hotel	B
Tokyo Dome Hotel	B
Tokyo International	C
Youth Hostel	

RESTAURANTS & CAFÉS

@home café	5
Botan	8
Canal Café	3
Le Bretagne	2
Mai'ish	1
Milonga Nueva	9
Mu'u Mu'u	6
Tokyo Food Theater 5+1	4
Yabu Soba	7

SHOPS

Comic Tora-no-ana	b
Don Quixote	a
Kitazawa Shoten	f
Laox	g
Naigai Chizu	d
Tony Records	c
Tower Records	e
Tsukumo	c
Village Vanguard	6
Yodobashi Camera	e

Josiah Conder

Of the many Western architects invited by the Meiji government to Japan to help it modernize, Josiah Conder is considered to have had the greatest impact. When he arrived in 1877, a freshly graduated 25-year-old, his position was to teach architecture at what would become the Faculty of Engineering at Tokyo University. By the time he died in Tokyo in 1920 he had designed over fifty major buildings including the original Imperial Museum at Ueno, and the Nikolai Cathedral in Ochanomizu. His crowning glory is generally considered to be the Rokumeikan reception hall in Hibiya, a synthesis of Japanese and Western architectural styles. This was torn down in 1940, but a model of it can be seen in the Edo–Tokyo Museum (see p.73). His students Tatsuno Kingo and Katayama Tōkuma went on to design Tokyo Station and the Akasaka Detached Palace respectively.

In the West, Conder is perhaps best known for his study of Japanese gardens and his book *Landscape Gardens in Japan*, published in 1893. Kyū Iwasaki-tei in Ueno (see p.95) and Kyū Furukawa near Komagome (see p.102) are two houses he designed with gardens which are open to the public.

Ⓦ www.kandamyoujin.or.jp), one of the city's oldest shrines and host to one of its top three festivals, the **Kanda Matsuri** (see p.32), which takes place in mid-May every odd-numbered year. Founded in 730 AD, the shrine originally stood in front of Edo Castle, where it was dedicated to the gods of farming and fishing (Daikoku and Ebisu). Later, the tenth-century rebel Taira no Masakado – who was beheaded after declaring himself emperor – was also enshrined here; according to legend, his head "flew" to Edo, where he was honoured as something of a local hero. When Shogun Tokugawa Ieyasu was strengthening the castle's fortifications in 1616, he took the opportunity to move the shrine, but mollified Masakado's supporters by declaring him a guardian deity of the city.

If you're in the area in the afternoon, take a quick detour south along Hongō-dōri to visit the Russian Orthodox **Nikolai Cathedral** (ニコライ堂; Tues–Sun: April–Sept 1–4pm; Oct–March 1–3.30pm; ¥300; Ⓣ 03/3295-6879). Founded by Archbishop Nikolai Kasatkin, who came to Japan in 1861 as chaplain to the Russian consulate in Hokkaidō, the cathedral took seven years to complete (1884–91); the plans were sent from Russia but the British architect Josiah Conder (see box above) supervised the project and gets most of the credit. It's not a large building but its Byzantine flourishes stand out well against the characterless surrounding blocks, and the refurbished altarpiece positively glows in the soft light.

Akihabara

Some 500m southeast of Kanda Myōjin, following Yushima-zaka as it drops steeply downhill, a blaze of adverts and a cacophony of competing audio systems announce **Akihabara** (秋葉原). Akiba, as it's popularly known, is Tokyo's foremost discount shopping area for electrical and electronic goods of all kinds, from computers and plasma-screen TVs to digital cameras and "washlets" – electronically controlled toilet-cum-bidets with an optional medical analysis function. In recent years Akiba has also become a mecca for fans of anime and manga (see box, p.6), a showcase for all the weird and wonderful fashions on the cutting edge of Japanese cool, and the spawning ground for the decidedly surreal "maid cafés" (see box, p.181). On Sundays the main road is closed to traffic and wannabe pop artists strut their stuff with varying degrees of skill and conviction.

In fact Akiba is undergoing a bit of a facelift all round. Yodobashi Camera's vast store and the terminus of the Tsukuba Express railway line have brought new life to the east side of Akihabara JR station. Over on the west side, the **Akihabara Crossfield** complex (Ⓦwww.akiba-cross.jp) bills itself as a "dynamic crossroads of ideas and action". The southerly Daibiru ("Big Building") hosts a branch of **Digital Hollywood**, a university specializing in digital content, while some of the latest anime releases are on show at the ultra-hi-tech **Akiba 3D Theater** (generally Sat & Sun, times vary; ¥1000) on the fourth floor of the neighbouring UDX Building. The theatre is part of the **Tokyo Anime Center** (daily 11am–7pm; free; Ⓣ03/5298-1188, Ⓦwww.animecenter.jp), little more than a glorified shop selling anime novelties, plus a multi-screen monitor screening recent anime films.

The rest of Akiba is devoted to shopping. Today's electronic stores are direct descendants of a postwar black market in radios and radio parts that took place beneath the train tracks around Akihabara Station. You can recapture some of the atmosphere in the narrow passages under the tracks just west of the station, or among the tiny stalls of **Tōkyō Radio Depāto** (東京ラジオデパート) – four floors stuffed with plugs, wires, boards and tools for making or repairing radios; walk west along the north side of the Sōbu line tracks from Akihabara Station to find the store just off Chūō-dōri.

Suidōbashi and Jimbōchō

Two stops west of Akihabara, the Sōbu line rumbles into **Suidōbashi** (水道橋), where the stadium and thrill rides of **Tokyo Dome City** (Ⓦwww.tokyo-dome .co.jp) punctuate the skyline. The centrepiece is the plump, white-roofed **Tokyo Dome** (東京ドーム), popularly known as the "Big Egg", Tokyo's major baseball venue and home ground of the Yomiuri Giants. The Dome's **Baseball Hall of Fame and Museum** (Tues–Sun: March–Sept 10am–6pm, Oct–Feb 10am–5pm; ¥500; Ⓣ03/3811-3600, Ⓦwww.baseball-museum.or.jp) is for die-hard fans only, who'll appreciate the footage of early games and all sorts of baseball memorabilia, including one of Babe Ruth's jackets; you'll find the entrance by gate 21 of the stadium.

On the west side of the site is the **Tokyo Dome City Attractions** (daily 10am–10pm; Ⓦwww.laqua.jp), a complex of three amusement parks rolled into one. Best of the 17 rides are those in the most northerly **LaQua** section, where the highlight is Thunder Dolphin (¥1000), a high-speed roller coaster guaranteed to get you screaming. If you haven't got the stomach for that, the Big O, the world's first hubless and spokeless ferris wheel (it's spun by the two supports below), provides a gentler ride (¥800) and plenty of time to take a photo of the passing view. Also here is the hokey 13 Doors (¥800), a Japanese house of horrors. A one-day pass (¥4000; or ¥2800 after 5pm) gets you access to all the park's rides. Alternatively, skip the rides and soak away your stress at the excellent **Spa LaQua** (see p.239).

Immediately to the west of Tokyo Dome is **Koishikawa-Kōrakuen** (小石川後楽園; daily 9am–5pm; ¥300; Ⓣ03/3811-3015), a fine example of an early seventeenth-century stroll-garden. Winding paths take you past waterfalls, ponds and stone lanterns, down to the shores of a small lake draped with gnarled pines and over daintily humped bridges, where each view replicates a famous beauty spot. Zhu Shun Shui, a refugee scholar from Ming China, advised on the design, so Chinese as well as Japanese landscapes feature, the most obvious being the Full Moon Bridge, echoing the ancient stone bridges of Western China, and Seiko Lake, modelled on Hangzhou's West Lake. The garden attracts few visitors, though intrusive announcements from Tokyo Dome, looming over the trees, mean it's not always totally peaceful. The main entrance gate lies in the garden's southwest corner, midway between Suidōbashi and Iidabashi stations.

Jimbōchō

A lively student centre, **Jimbōchō** (神保町) is also home to dozens of secondhand **bookshops** around the intersection of Yasukuni-dōri and Hakusan-dōri. From Suidōbashi, it's a one-stop ride on the Toei Mita subway, or a one-kilometre walk south down Hakusan-dōri; you could also cover it as a side trip from Kitanomaru-kōen (see p.55). The best bookstops are along the south side of Yasukuni-dōri in the blocks either side of Jimbōchō subway station, where racks of dog-eared novels and textbooks sit outside shops stacked high with dusty tomes. Most are in Japanese, but some dealers specialize in English-language books – both new and old – while a bit of rooting around might turn up a volume of old photographs or cartoons in one of the more upmarket antiquarian dealers.

Last stop in the area is the **Meiji University Museum** (明治大学博物館; daily 10am–4.30pm; closed Aug 10–16 & Dec 26–Jan 7; free; ☎03/3296-4448, Ⓦwww.meiji.ac.jp/museum), in the basement of the university's Academy Common Building, about five minutes' walk northeast of Jimbōchō Station up Meidai-dōri. Meiji University started life in 1881 as a law school, and the most interesting – and spine-chilling – exhibits belong in the "criminal zone". After breaking you in gently with examples of Edo-era laws and edicts, the displays move on to tools used by the police to arrest miscreants: goads, the U-shaped "military fork" and the delightfully named "sleave entangler". Then it's a rapid descent into prints showing instruments of torture and methods of punishment, including some truly gruesome ways of carrying out the death penalty. There's also a guillotine and the Iron Maiden of Nuremberg, a body-shaped iron case fitted with vicious inward pointing spikes. The other two zones cover archeology and traditional crafts; all zones are well laid out and there's a fair amount of information in English.

If you carry on up Meidai-dōri from here, you can wander past shops specializing in guitars and other musical instruments, eventually arriving at Ochanomizu Station.

4

Ryōgoku and around

Across the Sumida-gawa, **Ryōgoku** is a sort of sumo town; here shops sell outsize clothes and restaurants serve flavourful tureens of *chanko-nabe*, the wrestlers' traditional body-building hotpot, packed with meat, seafood, tofu and vegetables. The area is also home to the absorbing, ultra-modern **Edo–Tokyo Museum**, where you could easily spend half a day. A short train ride to the south south, and all within walking distance of each other, are **Kiyosumi Teien**, a pleasant Meiji-era garden; the delightful **Fukagawa Edo Museum**, an atmospheric re-creation of a mid-nineteenth-century Shitamachi neighbourhood; and the **Museum of Contemporary Art**, gathering together the best of post-1945 Japanese art in one spacious, top-class venue.

Ryōgoku

Ryōgoku (両国), two stops from Akihabara on the Sōbu rail line, is the heartland of sumo, and three times a year major sumo tournaments fill the **National Sumo**

△ Sumo wrestlers strut their stuff at the start of a national sumo tournament

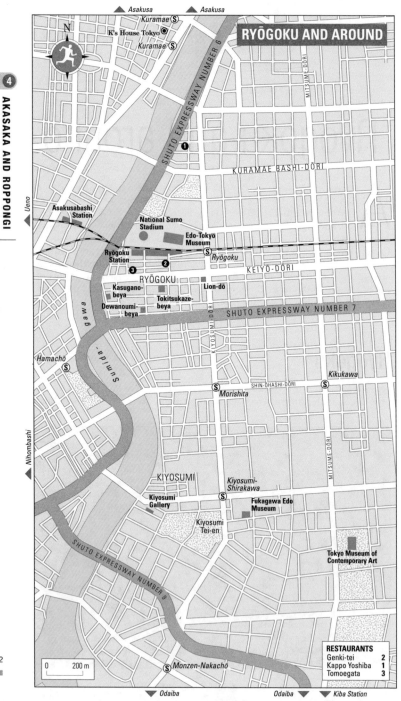

Asakusa   Asakusa

Kuramae Ⓢ

K's House Tokyo ◉

Kuramae Ⓢ

RYŌGOKU AND AROUND

N

SHUTO EXPRESSWAY NUMBER 6

❶

KURAMAE BASHI-DŌRI

MITSUME-DŌRI

Ueno

Asakusabashi
Station

National Sumo
Stadium

Edo-Tokyo
Museum

Ⓢ Ryōgoku

Ryōgoku
Station

KEIYŌ-DŌRI

❸

❷

RYŌGOKU

Kasugano-
beya

Lion-dō

Dewanoumi-
beya

Tokitsukaze-
beya

KIYOSUMI-DŌRI

SHUTO EXPRESSWAY NUMBER 7

Sumida-gawa

Hamachō
Ⓢ

Kikukawa

Ⓢ

SHIN-ŌHASHI-DŌRI

Ⓢ

Nihombashi

Ⓢ Morishita

MITSUME-DŌRI

KIYOSUMI

Kiyosumi-
Shirakawa

Ⓢ

Kiyosumi
Gallery

Fukagawa Edo
Museum

Kiyosumi
Tei-en

Tokyo Museum of
Contemporary Art

SHUTO EXPRESSWAY NUMBER 9

0   200 m

Ⓢ Monzen-Nakachō

RESTAURANTS	
Genki-tei	2
Kappo Yoshiba	1
Tomoegata	3

Odaiba   Odaiba   Kiba Station

Stadium (Kokugikan; 国技館), outside Ryōgoku Station's west exit, with a two-week pageant of thigh-slapping, foot-stamping and arcane ritual (see p.215 for more on sumo and buying tickets). The one-room historical **museum** (Mon–Fri 10am–4.30pm; closed during tournaments; free) beside the stadium is for die-hard fans only; better to simply wander the streets immediately south of the train tracks, which until recently housed many of the major "stables" where wrestlers lived and trained. Though rising land prices have forced most of them out, there's still a good chance of bumping into some junior wrestlers, with slicked-back hair and wearing their *yukata* and wooden *geta*, popping out to a store – such as sumo-size clothing specialist **Lion-dō** (ライオン堂; Mon–Sat 9.30am–6.30pm; ☎03/3631-0650, ⓦwww.liondo.co.jp), southeast of Ryōgokū Station – or for a quick snack of *chanko-nabe*. If you're feeling peckish yourself, the *Kappo Yoshiba* and *Tomoegata* restaurants (see p.174 & p.175) are two of the best places to sample the stew.

Edo-Tokyo Museum

You'll need plenty of stamina for the **Edo–Tokyo Museum** (江戸東京博物館; Tues–Fri & Sun 9.30am–5.30pm, Sat 9.30am–7.30pm; ¥600; ☎03/3626-9974, ⓦwww.edo-tokyo-museum.or.jp), housed in a colossal building – supposedly modelled on a *geta* – behind the Sumo Stadium; the ticket lasts a whole day, so you can come and go. With plenty of information in English, including a free audio-guide, the museum tells the history of Tokyo from the days of the Tokugawa shogunate to postwar reconstruction, using life-size replicas, models and holograms, as well as more conventional screen paintings, ancient maps and documents.

The museum starts on the sixth floor, where a bridge (a replica of the original Nihombashi; see p.64) takes you over the roofs of famous Edo landmarks – a Kabuki theatre, *daimyō* residence and Western-style office – on the main exhibition floor below. The displays then run roughly chronologically; they're particularly strong on life in Edo's Shitamachi, with its pleasure quarters, festivals and vibrant popular culture, and on the giddy days after 1868, when Japan opened up to the outside world.

Fukagawa Edo Museum and around

Two stops south of Ryōgoku on the Ōedo line is Kiyosumi-Shirakawa Station, where exit A3 emerges in front of the beautifully landscaped Edo-era garden, **Kiyosumi Teien** (清澄庭園; daily 9am–5pm; ¥150; ☎03/3641-5892). Surrounding a large pond and studded with artfully placed rocks from all over Japan, the gardens are particularly worth visiting in spring for their cherry blossom and azaleas.

From the gardens head east along a neighbourhood shopping street, past shops and a spruce public toilet (it's been voted one of the ten best in Japan), to the captivating **Fukagawa Edo Museum** (深川江戸資料館; daily 9.30am–5pm, closed second and fourth Mon of the month; ¥300; ☎03/3630-8625), which re-creates a Shitamachi neighbourhood. The museum's one-room exhibition hall could be a film set for nineteenth-century Edo and contains seven complete buildings: the homes of various artisans and labourers, a watchtower and storehouses. As you walk through the rooms furnished with the clutter of daily life, you're accompanied by the cries of street vendors and birdsong, while the lighting shifts from dawn through to a soft dusk. It's worth investing in the English-language guidebook (¥500) before going in.

Museum of Contemporary Art

Continue east from the Fukagawa Edo Museum until you reach the major road Mitsuni-dōri. A block south of here a severe glass-and-grey-steel building houses Tokyo's premier modern art venue, the **Tokyo Museum of Contemporary Art** (東京都現代美術館; Tues–Sun 10am–6pm; ¥500; ℡03/5245-4111, ⓦwww .mot-art-museum.jp). The museum can also be reached from Kiba Station on the Tozai line, from where it's a fifteen-minute walk north.

The vast white spaces inside provide the perfect setting for a fine collection of works by Japanese and Western artists (notably Roy Lichtenstein) from the post-1945 avant-garde through the 1950s abstract revolution to pop art, minimalism and beyond. Only 150 pieces are displayed at a time but you can see the rest of the collection (some 3800 items) in the audiovisual library. Other facilities include a museum shop, cafés and a well-stocked art library. Note that the museum closes twice a year for two weeks while the permanent exhibits are changed, so it's a good idea to check before setting off.

Akasaka and Roppongi

t used to be that Akasaka and Roppongi, both southwest of the Imperial Palace, were pretty much all about nightlife, nocturnal playgrounds for bureaucrats and politicians in the former, and younger Japanese and *gaijin* in the latter. They still are, but with the opening of the ambitious Tokyo Midtown complex in the midst of both areas, and further commercial developments on the way, all that is changing. Roppongi, in particular, is one area of Tokyo you really shouldn't miss. Styling itself as Tokyo's new arts hub, it's home to several major new art galleries, including the National Art Center, the Suntory Museum of Art, and the Mori Art Museum, the last of which sits atop the area's other mega-development, Roppongi Hills.

Both districts have longer established attractions, too. Akasaka's premier shrine, **Hie-jinja**, with its attractive avenue of red *torii*, is a distinct link to the past, as is **Zōjō-ji,** near Roppongi, once the temple of the Tokugawa clan. There are pretty **Japanese gardens** at Akasaka's *New Otani Hotel* and both the Tokyo Midtown and Roppongi Hills sites. And while the **Tokyo Tower** is no longer the most elevated viewing spot in the city, it is arguably the city's most iconic structure, a visual beauty that, like fine wine, grows more interesting with age.

Akasaka

Southwest of the Imperial Palace, beside the government areas of Kasumigaseki and Nagatachō, is **Akasaka** (赤坂). This was once an agricultural area where plants that produce a red dye were farmed – hence the locality's name, which means "red slope". Akasaka developed as an entertainment district in the late nineteenth century, when *ryōtei* restaurants, complete with performing geisha, started opening to cater for the modern breed of politicians and bureaucrats. The area still has its fair share of exclusive establishments, shielded from the hoi polloi by high walls and even higher prices. Their presence, along with the TBS Broadcasting Centre and some of Tokyo's top hotels, lends Akasaka a certain cachet, though prices at many restaurants and bars are no worse than elsewhere in Tokyo. The TBS compound has recently undergone a major redevelopment to incorporate the new 180-metre-tall **Akasaka Biz Tower** (Ⓦ www.akasakabiztower.com) and

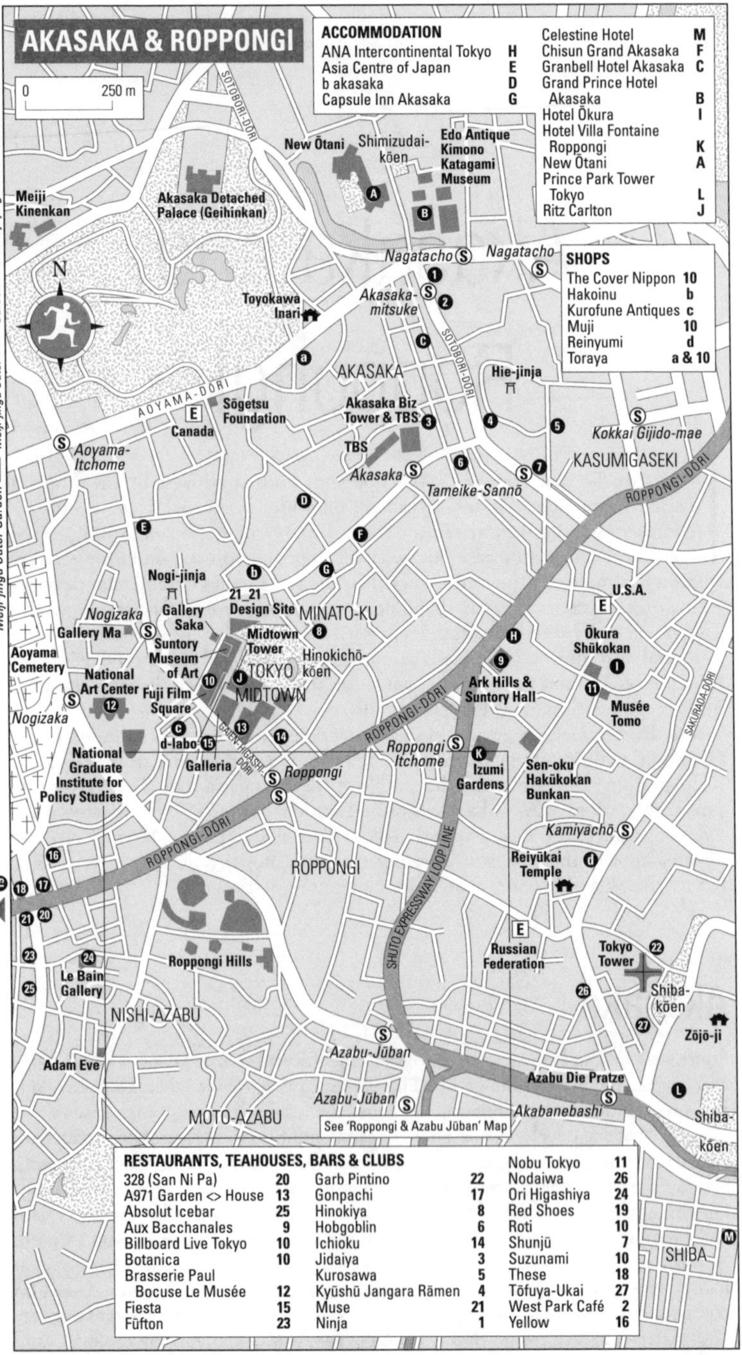
AKASAKA & ROPPONGI
0 250 m
ACCOMMODATION
ANA Intercontinental Tokyo H
Asia Centre of Japan E
b akasaka D
Capsule Inn Akasaka G
Celestine Hotel M
Chisun Grand Akasaka F
Granbell Hotel Akasaka C
Grand Prince Hotel Akasaka B
Hotel Ōkura I
Hotel Villa Fontaine Roppongi K
New Ōtani A
Prince Park Tower Tokyo L
Ritz Carlton J
SHOPS
The Cover Nippon 10
Hakoinu b
Kurofune Antiques c
Muji 10
Reinyumi d
Toraya a & 10
RESTAURANTS, TEAHOUSES, BARS & CLUBS
328 (San Ni Pa) 20
A971 Garden <> House 13
Absolut Icebar 25
Aux Bacchanales 9
Billboard Live Tokyo 10
Botanica 10
Brasserie Paul Bocuse Le Musée 12
Fiesta 15
Fūfton 23
Garb Pintino 22
Gonpachi 17
Hinokiya 8
Hobgoblin 6
Ichioku 14
Jidaiya 3
Kurosawa 5
Kyūshū Jangara Rāmen 4
Muse 21
Ninja 1
Nobu Tokyo 11
Nodaiwa 26
Ori Higashiya 24
Red Shoes 19
Roti 10
Shunjū 7
Suzunami 10
These 18
Tōfuya-Ukai 27
West Park Café 2
Yellow 16
N
Meiji-jingū Outer Garden
Meiji Kinenkan
Akasaka Detached Palace (Geihinkan)
Sotobori-dōri
New Ōtani
Shimizudai-kōen
Edo Antique Kimono Katagami Museum
Nagatacho
Akasaka-mitsuke
Toyokawa Inari
Aoyama-dōri
AKASAKA
Hie-jinja
Sōgetsu Foundation
Canada
Akasaka Biz Tower & TBS
TBS
Akasaka
Tameike-Sannō
Kokkai Gijido-mae
KASUMIGASEKI
Aoyama-Itchome
Roppongi-dōri
Nogi-jinja
21_21 Design Site
MINATO-KU
Nogizaka
Gallery Saka
Gallery Ma
Suntory Museum of Art
Midtown Tower
Hinokichō-kōen
TOKYO MIDTOWN
Aoyama Cemetery
National Art Center
Fuji Film Square
d-labo
Galleria
Gaien-Higashi-dōri
U.S.A.
Ōkura Shūkokan
Musée Tomo
Ark Hills & Suntory Hall
Sakurada-dōri
National Graduate Institute for Policy Studies
Roppongi
Roppongi Itchome
Izumi Gardens
Sen-oku Hakūkokan Bunkan
Kamiyachō
Reiyūkai Temple
ROPPONGI
Shuto Expressway Loop Line
Roppongi Hills
Russian Federation
Tokyo Tower
Shiba-kōen
Zōjō-ji
Le Bain Gallery
NISHI-AZABU
Adam Eve
Azabu-Jūban
Azabu Die Pratze
Akabanebashi
MOTO-AZABU
See 'Roppongi & Azabu Jūban' Map
SHIBA

associated complex, which promises to inject new life into the area in the same way Roppongi Hills and Tokyo Midtown have done up the road.

Hie-jinja

At the southern end of Akasaka's main thoroughfare, Sotobori-dōri, stands a huge stone *torii* gate, beyond which is a picturesque avenue of red *torii* leading up the hill to the **Hie-jinja** (日枝神社; ⓦ www.hiejinja.net), a Shinto shrine dedicated to the god Ōyamakui-no-kami, who is believed to protect against evil. Although the ferro-concrete buildings date from 1967, Hie-jinja's history stretches back to 830 AD, when it was first established on the outskirts of what would become Edo. The shrine's location shifted a couple more times before Shogun Tokugawa Ietsuna placed it here in the seventeenth century as a source of protection for his castle (now the site of the Imperial Palace). In February 1936, the Hie-jinja became the command centre for an attempted coup by a renegade group of 1400 soldiers, intent on restoring power to the emperor, who was being increasingly marginalized by the military-controlled government. Government buildings were seized and two former premiers and the inspector general of military training were killed, before the insurrection crumbled after just four days. The soldiers surrendered and nineteen of their leaders were executed.

The main entrance to the shrine is through the large stone *torii* on the east side of the hill. Fifty-one steps lead up to a spacious enclosed courtyard, in which roosters roam freely. To the left of the main shrine, look for the carving of a female monkey cradling its baby, a symbol that has come to signify protection for pregnant women.

Hie-jinja hosts one of Tokyo's most important festivals, the **Sannō Matsuri** (June 10–16). The highlight is a parade on June 15, involving four hundred participants dressed in Heian-period costume and, in even-numbered years, carrying fifty sacred *mikoshi* (portable shrines).

The New Ōtani Hotel and Edo Katagami Museum

Heading north from the shrine along Sotobori-dōri and across Benkei-bashi, the bridge that spans what was once the outer moat of the shogun's castle, you'll soon reach the **New Ōtani** hotel. Within its grounds is a beautiful traditional Japanese **garden**, originally designed for the *daimyō* Kato Kiyomasa, lord of Kumamoto in Kyūshū over four hundred years ago. You can stroll freely through the garden or admire it while sipping tea in the *New Ōtani*'s lounge. The hotel also has its own small **art gallery** (Tues–Sun 10am–6pm; ¥500, free to guests), with works by Japanese and European artists, including Chagall and Modigliani, and a tea-ceremony room, where tea is served in the traditional way (Thurs–Sat 11am–4pm; ¥1050).

A traditional tea room is also part of the delightful **Edo Katagami Museum** (江戸型紙ミュージアム; Tues, Thurs–Sun 11am–7pm; ¥700; 3-32 Kioichō, Chiyoda-ku; ⓣ 03/3265-4001, ⓦ www.kioi.jp), tucked away in an apartment building behind the *Akasaka Prince Hotel*. Well worth seeking out, the light-flooded museum and gallery display a dazzling collection of intricately carved stencils used for making patterns on kimono. Some of the stencils are used for original gifts in the museum shop, and the curator, who speaks good English, is happy to explain the collection. It's best to call ahead – especially if you want to book a tea ceremony (¥1000) – as the gallery does keep erratic hours.

Toyokawa Inari and around

Walking southwest from Benkei-bashi along Aoyama-dōri, you'll soon encounter the colourful **Toyokawa Inari** (or Myōgon-ji; 豊川稲荷神社), an example of a combined temple and shrine which was much more common across Japan before the Meiji government forcibly separated Shinto and Buddhist places of worship. The temple's compact precincts are decked with red lanterns and banners, while the main hall is guarded by statues of pointy-eared foxes wearing red bibs – the messengers of the Shinto god Inari, found at all Inari shrines.

Toyokawa Inari borders the extensive grounds of the grand, European-style **Akasaka Detached Palace** (Geihinkan; 迎賓館), which serves as the official State Guest House. When it was completed in 1909, this vast building, modelled on Buckingham Palace on the outside and Versailles on the inside, had only one bathroom in the basement, and the empress's apartments were in a separate wing from her husband's; this was fine by the emperor since he was in the habit of taking his nightly pick from the ladies-in-waiting. Some members of the imperial family, including the crown prince, still live within the palace grounds, which puts it firmly off-limits to visitors.

If you follow Aoyama-dōri west from Toyokawa Inari, with the detached palace on your right, you'll soon come to the **Sōgetsu Foundation** (草月会館; 7-2-21 Akasaka, Minato-ku; ⊤03/3408-1209, ⓦwww.sogetsu.or.jp), in a glass-fronted building designed by Tange Kenzō. This famous school of *ikebana*, traditional Japanese flower-arranging, was founded by Sofu Teshigahara in 1927 and holds classes in English (every Monday at 10am except during August; 2hr; book by emailing ⓔkyoshitsu@sogetsu.or.jp); the fee is ¥3800 including materials. Besides strikingly contemporary *ikebana* displays, the lobby also features sculptures by the renowned American-Japanese artist Isamu Noguchi.

Musée Tomo and around

Returning to Sotobori-dōri and heading southeast past Hie-jinja brings you to Roppongi-dōri. Turn south along this road to reach the **Ark Hills** (アークヒルズ) complex, a precursor of the Mori Corporation's Roppongi Hills, housing the *ANA InterContinental Hotel* and the classical-music venue Suntory Hall (see p.201). Up the hill behind here is the *Hotel Ōkura*, next to which is the **Ōkura Shūkokan** (大倉集古館; Tues–Sun 10am–4.30pm; ¥500, free to hotel guests), an art museum housing an intriguing display of Oriental ceramics, paintings, prints and sculptures, from a collection of over 1700 traditional works of art amassed by the self-styled Baron Ōkura Tsuruhiko.

Turn onto the Edomi-zaka slope running between the *Hotel Ōkura* and its annexe, and you'll soon hit the classy **Musée Tomo** (Tomo Bijutsukan; 智美術館; Tues–Sun 11am–6pm; ¥1300; ⊤03/5733-5131, ⓦwww.musee-tomo.or.jp). Home to the outstanding contemporary Japanese ceramics collection of Tomo Kikuchi, this new gallery – featuring a stunning stairwell with a barley-sugar-like banister and slivers of *washi* paper decorating the walls – is as elegant as many of the fifty-odd pieces carefully spotlit as *objets d'art*. Out front is the old Kikuchi family home, an incongruous Taisho-era villa overshadowed by the new Toranomon Tower complex. The museum's fancy French café and restaurant *Voie Lactée* provides a lovely view on to the old home's tranquil garden.

To return to Roppongi you can make a short cut through the Izumi Garden Tower complex, beside which is yet another gallery, the **Sen-oku Hakukokan Bunkan** (泉屋博古館分館; Tues–Sun 10am–4.30pm; ¥520, more for special exhibitions; 1-5-1 Roppongi, ⊤03/5777-8600, ⓦwww.sen-oku.or.jp). It displays part of the collection of the Kyoto-based museum of the same name, the core of which are antique items of Chinese bronzeware, as well as Japanese paintings, ceramics and calligraphy. There are only two rooms and exhibitions often change, so check if what's on is of interest before making a special trip.

Roppongi

Roppongi (六本木), its name meaning "six trees", was once reputed to be home to six *daimyō*, all of whom coincidentally had the Chinese character for "tree" in their names. From the Meiji era onwards, Roppongi was a military stamping ground,

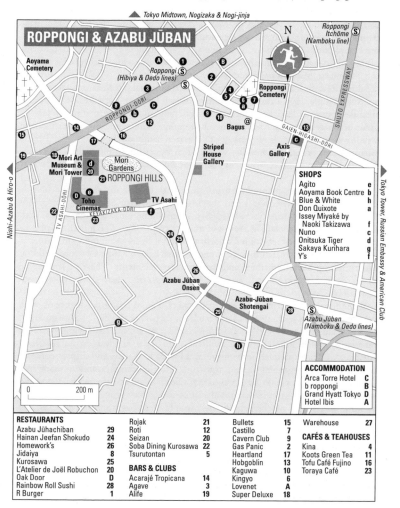

▲ *Tokyo Midtown, Nogizaka & Nogi-jinja*

SHOPS

Agito	e
Aoyama Book Centre	b
Blue & White	h
Don Quixote	a
Issey Miyaké by Naoki Takizawa	f
Nuno	c
Onitsuka Tiger	d
Sakaya Kurihara	g
Y's	f

ACCOMMODATION

Arca Torre Hotel	C
b roppongi	B
Grand Hyatt Tokyo	D
Hotel Ibis	A

RESTAURANTS					
Azabu Jūhachiban	29	Rojak	21	Bullets	15
Hainan Jeefan Shokudo	24	Roti	12	Castillo	7
Homework's	26	Seizan	20	Cavern Club	9
Jidaiya	8	Soba Dining Kurosawa	22	Gas Panic	2
Kurosawa	25	Tsurutontan	5	Heartland	17
L'Atelier de Joël Robuchon	20			Hobgoblin	13
Oak Door	D	**BARS & CLUBS**		Kaguwa	10
Rainbow Roll Sushi	28	Acarajé Tropicana	14	Kingyo	6
R Burger	1	Agave	3	Lovenet	A
		Alife	19	Super Deluxe	18

Warehouse	27		
CAFÉS & TEAHOUSES			
Kina	4		
Koots Green Tea	11		
Tofu Café Fujino	16		
Toraya Café	23		

first for the imperial troops and then, during the American Occupation, for US forces. Thus the *gaijin* community started hanging out here, and today's entertainment district was born.

Roppongi is still principally a nightlife district, but three recent major developments – Roppongi Hills in 2003 and the National Art Centre and Tokyo Midtown in 2007 – are recasting the area in a far more refined light. What follows are Roppongi's highlights; some of the smaller galleries are covered on pp.236–237. Roppongi Station is the principal access point for the area, although you can also use Nogizaka for the National Art Center and Kamiyachō for Tokyo Tower.

Tokyo Midtown

In a textbook example of Japanese efficiency, the consortium that developed the mammoth **Tokyo Midtown** (Ⓦ www.tokyo-midtown.com), covering the former Defence Agency site of nearly 70,000 square metres, opened its doors to the public bang on schedule at the end of March 2007. A block northwest of the main Roppongi crossing along Gaien-Higashi-dōri, Midtown is an enormous mixed-use complex of offices, shops, apartments, a convention centre, two museums and other public facilities, plus the small park Hinokichō-koen, all revolving around the 248-metre **Midtown Tower**, Tokyo's tallest building.

Taking its design and visual influences from traditional Japanese architecture and art, the complex has a more streamlined overall look, subtle and less confusing than Roppongi Hills. The influence of a *torii* gate can be discerned in the rectangular archway entrance to the Galleria shopping mall, while the pattern of the windows on the tower is reminiscent of a woven bamboo fence. Midtown Tower, with its slightly bulbous middle, was inspired by an Isamu Noguchi sculpture – head to the top of Mori Tower or the *ANA InterContinenal Hotel* to get the best bird's-eye view of it all.

Landscaped gardens planted with 140 trees nestle behind and along the west side of the complex, where you'll find the **Suntory Museum of Art** (サントリー美術館; Mon & Sun 10am–6pm; Wed–Sat 10am–8pm; entrance fee varies with exhibition; Ⓣ 03/3470-1073, Ⓦ www.suntory.co.jp/sma). The museum's philosophy is to highlight "art in life", and to this end it hosts changing exhibitions of ceramics, lacquerware, paintings and textiles, in a Kengo Kuma-designed building incorporating both traditional and contemporary elements. There's a traditional tea-ceremony room, as well as a café serving special wheat-gluten cakes from Kanazawa.

At the northwest corner of the garden, the two giant triangular planes of steel, concrete and glass peaking out of a green lawn are part of the **21_21 Design Sight** (daily 11am–8.30pm; ¥1000; Ⓣ 03/3475-2121, Ⓦ www.2121designsight.jp), a fascinating collaboration between architect Andō Tadao and fashion designer Issey Miyake, which is intended to be more of a forum to discuss and display contemporary design in general than a museum. The building's seamless shape was inspired by Miyake's A-POC ("A Piece Of Cloth") line, and the main gallery digs one floor into the ground to provide an elevated, airy space in which to view exhibitions on a single theme. The first couple of shows were on chocolate and water, with designers from all walks of life tackling the subject in their own literal or abstract way.

There are also a couple of smaller exhibition halls to check out. Tucked away on the seventh floor of Midtown Tower is **d-labo** (Mon–Fri 11am–7pm, Sat & Sun 10am–6pm; free; Ⓣ 03/5411-2363, Ⓦ www.d-labo-midtown.com), a quirky combination of gallery, hi-tech library and modern technology centre, attached to the offices of the Suruga bank. The gallery, housed in a wall of safe-deposit-style

Shrines and temples

While few Japanese consider themselves particularly religious, most take part in some form of ritual observance over the course of a year. Japan's main religions are the indigenous Shinto, combining ancient animism with ancestor-worship, and Buddhism. The two coexist happily, fulfilling distinct roles in society: people visit a Shinto shrine to pray for academic success or to get married, for example, whereas funerals are almost always held at a Buddhist temple. Every neighbourhood has at least one of each.

Shinto shrines

Although Shinto's myriad gods (*kami*) are believed to be present in all natural things, the focus of worship is the **shrine** (*-jinja*, *-jingū* or *-gū*). It stands in an area of sacred ground entered via one or more *torii* (literally "bird perch"), gates comprising two gently inclined uprights, topped with one or two crosspieces and symbolizing the passage from the profane to the sacred. In Tokyo, both Meiji-jingū and Yasukuni-jinja boast particularly impressive *torii*. Though *torii* are traditionally made of wood, nowadays you'll also find examples of stone, metal and concrete. Most are left unpainted, but look out for the bright red *torii* which indicate a shrine dedicated to Inari, the god of harvests.

Inside the compound, you often find pairs of human or animal **statues**. At Inari shrines, these are of pointy-eared foxes wearing red bibs, depicting his messenger. In other cases they represent austere dignitaries in ancient costumes, lion-dogs (*koma-inu*) or ferocious guardian gods borrowed from Buddhist temples. Another common feature is a **sacred tree**, marked by the twisted straw rope, *shimenawa*, tied round it and sporting zigzags of white paper. In larger shrines there are shops selling **amulets** and **fortune papers**

▲ Portable shrine

Shrine festivals

Worth seeking out are the colourful festivals which take place at every shrine at least once a year. Typically, these involve the *kami* being carried at breakneck speed around the area in a portable shrine (*mikoshi*), dispensing blessings. The bearers jostle the *mikoshi* this way and that, shouting "*wasshoi, wasshoi*" with great gusto – fuelled by copious amounts of alcohol; apparently, the *kami* enjoy all the frantic noise and activity.

(*omikuji*), which you twist round tree branches to make the predictions come true, and wooden **votive tablets** (*ema*) – write your request on the tablet and tie it up alongside the others.

Traditionally, the main **sanctuary** is a rather austere building of unpainted cypress wood, though some are much more elaborate, with perhaps red paintwork and ornate carvings, showing Chinese and Korean influences. Before approaching, worshippers purify themselves by rinsing their hands and mouth at the large **water basin** nearby. Then, standing in front of the sanctuary, they throw some coins into the wooden box (¥5 coins are considered luckiest), shake the bell-rope to attract the *kami*'s attention, and pray: the standard practice is to bow deeply twice, clap twice, pray with eyes closed and finish with another low bow.

Although it's not normally possible to enter the sanctuary, from the doorway you'll see an **offering table**, on which rests a stick with more white-paper zigzags attached, and a purification wand made of either a sprig of the sacred *sakaki* tree or of thin

◄ Fortune papers tied to wires

paper strips and flax. Hanging behind the table sometimes is a **mirror**, symbolizing not only the stainless mind of the *kami* but also the faithfulness of the worshipper, since it reflects everything truthfully. Also behind, the **inner chamber** conceals a sacred object such as a sword or another mirror, symbolizing the presence of the *kami*. Since the object loses its religious power if anyone sets eyes on it, it's kept firmly under lock and key.

Buddhist temples

Compared to shrines, **Buddhist temples** (*-tera*, *-dera*, *-ji* or *-in*) are usually much grander affairs, of which the outstanding example is Asakusa's Sensō-ji. The most distinctive

► Praying at the incense bowl in front of Sensō-ji

feature is the entry **gate**, which in some cases is as imposing as the temple itself. It typically consists of a two-storey wooden structure flanked by a pair of brightly coloured, fearsome **Niō**, or guardian gods. Despite their appearances, Niō are actually quite good-natured – except to evil spirits.

As with Shinto sanctuaries, the **main hall** (*kon-dō* or *hon-dō*) at the centre of the compound is traditionally built of unadorned wood. This is where you'll find the principal image of the Buddha (which may be hidden from public view) and a table for offerings. Again, people often purify themselves with water before approaching the Buddha, and will toss coins in the wooden coffer, but in the case of temples it's usually possible to enter the prayer hall.

Some temples, such as Sensō-ji and Kamakura's Ryūkō-ji, have a **pagoda**, usually three or five storeys high, with a roof dividing each storey and a metal spire on top. Depending on the temple's size, you might also find an ancient iron **bell** and other buildings such as a study hall, treasure houses, living quarters and a shop.

Many temples also boast beautiful **gardens**. Those belonging to the **Zen** sect are particularly famous for their stunning rock and landscape gardens designed to aid meditation. Kenjō-ji in Kamakura, where Zen Buddhism flourished during the thirteenth century, is home to Japan's oldest-surviving Zen garden.

Buddhism has no festivals or rites to match Shinto, focusing instead on simple prayer and chants wreathed in the heady perfume of smouldering incense. Nevertheless, Buddhism does mark certain annual events, the most important of which is **Obon** (late July to mid-August), when ancestral spirits return to earth and families traditionally gather to welcome them home. But probably the biggest celebration is **Shōgatsu** (January 1), as much a Shinto event as a Buddhist one. The long public holiday allows plenty of time for sake drinking and general merriment, though many people also make sure to visit the local temple or shrine to pray for good fortune in the coming year.

Lesser-known shrines and temples

In addition to the major religious edifices mentioned here, you'll stumble across any number of minor shrines and temples as you wander the streets of Tokyo or Kamakura. It's often worth taking a peek inside – some of them are real gems. Below we list a few of our favourites off the beaten track:

■ **Toyokawa Inari** (p.78) Dozens of fox statues wearing jaunty red bibs guard this colourful shrine-cum-temple.

■ **Tokudai-ji** (p.95) A haven of peace in the midst of raucous Ameyoko-chō market.

■ **Kōgan-ji** (p.102) The "thorn-removing" Kannon statue attracts a constant queue of petitioners.

■ **Baiso-in** (see map p.118) Designed by Kuma Kengo in 2003 and as sleek as the designer boutiques along nearby Omotesandō.

■ **Zeniarai Benten** (p.279) An atmospheric cave-shrine in the hills above Kamakura.

▼ A worshipper at Zeniarai Benten washing money (tradition says this ensures it will double)

cabinets, is the most innovative part of the enterprise; artists get to display their pieces in each cabinet, an electronic number display at the front showing how often it has been opened. At the front of the Midtown complex, facing Gaien-Higashi-dōri, is **Fujifilm Square** (daily 11am–8pm; free; Ⓦfujifilmsquare.jp), with photography exhibitions which change on a monthly basis; there's also a shop selling fine photographic prints and a small museum of cameras and photographic equipment.

National Art Center

A couple of minutes' walk southwest of Tokyo Midtown, just off Gaien-Higashi-dōri, is the stunning new **National Art Center Tokyo** (国立新美術館; daily except Tues 10am–6pm; entrance fee varies with exhibition; ☎03/6812-9900, Ⓦwww.nact.jp), one of the three principal points on the **Roppongi Art Triangle** formed with the Suntory Museum of Art and Mori Art Museum. A billowing wave of pale green glass ripples across the facade of the Kurokawa Kisha-designed building which, at 48,000 square metres, is Japan's largest such museum, the huge halls allowing for some very ambitious works to be displayed. Of the twelve exhibition rooms, two are devoted to curated shows (the centre has no collection of its own), the rest to ones organized by various art associations from across Japan – which can make for a very eclectic mix. While you're here, it's worth lingering in the main atrium to admire the conical pods that soar up three storeys, and exploring the excellent museum shop.

Nogi-jinja

A five-minute walk north of Tokyo Midtown and next to Nogizaka subway station is **Nogi-jinja** (乃木神社), a small shrine and terraced garden honouring the Meiji-era **General Nogi Maresuke**, a hero in both the Sino-Japanese and Russo-Japanese wars. When the Emperor Meiji died, Nogi and his wife followed the samurai tradition and committed suicide in his house within the shrine grounds. The house is still here and is open just two days a year (Sept 12 & 13 9.30am–4.30pm; free); on other days you'll have to squint through the windows to catch sight of the general's blood-soaked shirt. On the second Sunday of every month, there's a good antique flea market in the shrine grounds.

Gallery Ma

Opposite General Nogi's house, there's often an interesting exhibition on at **Gallery Ma** (Tues–Thurs & Sat 11am–6pm, Fri 11am–7pm; free; ☎03/3402-1010, Ⓦwww.toto.co.jp/gallerma), on the third floor of the TOTO Nogizaka building, belonging to Japan's largest manufacturer of toilets. The gallery specializes in interior design and architecture both from Japan and overseas, and has an excellent bookstore carrying TOTO-published titles on art, design and architecture.

Roppongi Hills

It took seventeen years for property magnate Mori Minoru to realize his dream of an "Urban New Deal" for Tokyo, in the form of **Roppongi Hills** (Ⓦwww.roppongihills.com). The overhead utility cables that plague the rest of Tokyo have been banished here, and there's a good dose of open space and greenery, so unusual in this land-starved city. A Japanese garden and pond, a liberal sprinkling of funky street sculptures, an open-air arena for free performances, several roof gardens and even a rice paddy on the roof above the state-of-the-art multiplex cinema are all part of the mix. Louise Bourgeois' **Maman**, an iconic giant bronze, stainless steel and marble spider, squats at the base of the 54-storey, Kohn Pedersen Fox-designed **Mori Tower**. If you approach Roppongi Hills through the main Metro Hat entrance from Roppongi Station, you'll see the spider at the top of the escalators.

Directly ahead of the spider is the "Museum Cone", a glass structure enclosing a swirling staircase which forms the entrance to Roppongi Hills' highlight, the **Mori Art Museum** (MAM; Mon, Wed, Thurs & Sun, 10am–10pm, Tues 10am–5pm, Fri & Sat 10am–midnight; ¥1500; ⓣ03/6406-6100, ⓦwww.mori.art.museum). It occupies the prime top floors of the Mori Tower, in line with Mori's philosophy of combining culture with commercialism in what he fancifully calls an "artelligent city". MAM puts on exhibitions of works gathered from around Japan and abroad, with a particular focus on the best contemporary art and design, and on Asian artists. The museum also includes the **Tokyo City View** observation deck, Tokyo's highest viewpoint (daily 9am–1am, last entry midnight; ¥1500; ⓦwww.tokyocityview.com); on some evenings the café here morphs into the sophisticated **Mado Lounge** (ⓦwww.ma-do.jp), hosting DJ events, launch parties and the like.

Tokyo Tower

Heading back to Roppongi crossing and continuing east along Gaien-Higashi-dōri for around 1km will eventually bring you to **Tokyo Tower** (東京タワー; daily 9am–10pm; main observatory ¥820, top observatory ¥1420; ⓣ03/3433-5111, ⓦwww.tokyotower.co.jp), something of a retro icon for the city. Built during an era when Japan was becoming famous for producing cheap copies of foreign goods, this 333-metre red-and-white copy of the Eiffel Tower, opened in 1958, manages to top its Parisian role model by several metres. The uppermost observation deck, at 250m, has been supplanted as the highest viewpoint in Tokyo by the roof deck of Roppongi Hills' Mori Tower (which, incidentally, provides the best view of the Tokyo Tower, especially when illuminated at night). More attractions, most incurring additional fees and none really worth seeing in their own right,

△ Zōjō-ji with the Tokyo Tower in the background

have been added over the years, including a plethora of the usual souvenir shops – to the point where the place feels like an amusement arcade. There are good views of Tokyo Bay from here, but the wise save their cash for a drink at the rooftop bar of the nearby *Prince Park Tower Tokyo* hotel (see p.150).

Zōjō-ji

Tokyo Tower stands on the western flank of **Shiba-kōen** (芝公園), a park whose main point of interest is **Zōjō-ji** (増上寺), the family temple of the Tokugawa clan. Dating from 1393, Zōjō-ji was moved to this site in 1598 by Tokugawa Ieyasu (the first Tokugawa shogun) in order to protect southeast Edo spiritually and provide a waystation for pilgrims approaching the capital from the Tōkaidō road. This was once the city's largest holy site, with 48 sub-temples and over a hundred other buildings. Since the fall of the Tokugawa, however, Zōjō-ji has been razed to the ground by fire three times, and virtually all the current buildings date from the mid-1970s.

The main remnant of the past is the imposing **San-gadatsu-mon**, a 21-metre-high gateway dating from 1612 and the oldest wooden structure in Tokyo. The name translates as "Three Deliverances Gate" (Buddhism is supposed to save believers from the evils of anger, greed and stupidity) and the gate is one of Japan's Important Cultural Properties. As you pass through, keep an eye out for the tower with a large bell, said to have been made from melted metal hairpins donated by the ladies of the shogun's court. Look out too for the pair of Himalayan cedar trees, one planted by US President General Grant when he visited the temple in 1879 and the other by the then Vice-President George Bush in 1982. Ahead lies the **Taiden** (Great Main Hall), while to the right are ranks of *jizō* statues, capped with red bonnets and decorated with plastic flowers and colourful windmills that twirl in the breeze. Amid this army of mini-guardians lie the remains of six shogun, behind a wrought-iron gate decorated with dragons.

Asakusa

Asakusa (浅草) is best known as the site of Tokyo's most venerable Buddhist temple, **Sensō-ji**, whose towering worship hall is filled with a continual throng of petitioners and tourists. Stalls before the temple cater to the crowds, peddling trinkets and keepsakes as they have done for centuries; old-fashioned craft shops display exquisite hair combs, paper fans and calligraphy brushes; and all around is the inevitable array of restaurants, drinking places and fast-food stands. It's the infectious, carnival atmosphere that makes Asakusa so appealing: this is the area of Tokyo where you'll find the most vivid reminders of Edo's Shitamachi and the popular culture it spawned – one which seems to be constantly in the throes of some celebration or other. The biggest bash is the Sanja Matsuri in May, but there are numerous smaller festivals; ask at the **information centre** (daily 9.30am–8pm; English-language assistance daily 10am–5pm; ☏03/3842-5566) in front of Sensō-ji's main gate if there's anything in the offing. Staff here also organize Sunday walking tours of the area with English-speaking guides (11am & 2pm; free).

Though you can easily get to Asakusa by subway (it's on the Ginza and Asakusa lines), one of the best ways of getting here – or away – is by **ferry** on the Sumida-gawa (see p.28). On the downriver leg from Asakusa you can take advantage of the stop at the gardens of Hama Rikyū Teien (see p.136), and then walk into nearby Ginza should you wish.

Sensō-ji

Walking west from the river or the Ginza line subway station, you can't miss the solid red-lacquer Kaminari-mon gate, with its monstrous paper lantern, that marks the southern entrance to **Sensō-ji** (浅草寺). This magnificent temple, also known as Asakusa Kannon, was founded in the mid-seventh century to enshrine a tiny golden image of Kannon, the goddess of mercy, which had turned up in the nets of two local fishermen. Though most of the present buildings are postwar concrete reconstructions, there's a great sense of atmosphere as you draw near the main hall with its sweeping, tiled roofs.

The main approach starts under **Kaminari-mon**, or "Thunder Gate", which shelters statues of the guardian gods of Thunder and Wind (named Raijin and Fūjin), and proceeds along Nakamise-dōri, a colourful parade of small shops packed with gaudy souvenirs, tiny traditional dolls, kimono accessories and sweet-scented piles of *sembei* rice crackers. A double-storeyed treasure gate, Hōzō-mon, stands astride the entrance to the main temple complex; the treasures,

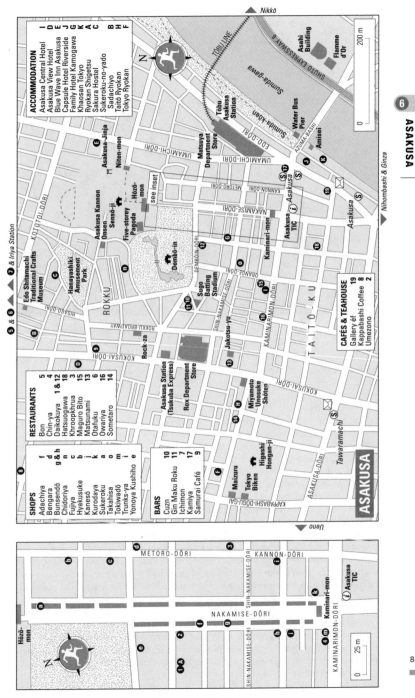

ASAKUSA

ASAKUSA

▲ *Nikkō*

Sumida-gawa

TOBU LINE

TŌBU
Asakusa
Station

Matsuya
Department
Store

Asahi
Building

Flamme
d'Or

SHUTO EXPRESSWAY 6

Sumida-gawa

Water Bus
Pier

AZUMA-BASHI

Amisei

EDO-DŌRI

UMAMICHI-DŌRI

UMAMICHI-DŌRI

Asakusa-Jinja

Niten-mon

Asakusa Kannon
Onsen

Senso-ji

Five-storey
Pagoda

Hōzō-
mon

See inset

Dembō-in

Edo Shitamachi
Traditional Crafts
Museum

Hanayashiki
Amusement
Park

ROKKU

Rock-za

METORO-DŌRI

KANNON-DŌRI

NAKAMISE-DŌRI

Asakusa
TIC

Kaminari-mon

Asakusa

Asakusa

DEMBŌIN-DŌRI

ORANGE-DŌRI

KAMINARIMON-DŌRI

Sugo
Batting
Stadium

SHIN-NAKAMISE-DŌRI

Jakotsu-yu

Asakusa Station
(Tsukuba Express)

Rox Department
Store

Miyamoto
Unosuke
Shōten

Higashi
Hongan-ji

Maizuru

Tokyo
Biken

KAPPABASHI-DŌGU-GAI

ASAKUSA-DŌRI

KOKUSAI-DŌRI

KOKUSAI-DŌRI

HISAGO-DŌRI

KOTOTOI-DŌRI

Tawaramachi

TAITŌ-KU

▼ Nihombashi & Ginza

▼ Ueno

⑤ & ⑥ ▲ ▲ ▲ ⑦ & Iriya Station

ACCOMMODATION
Asakusa Central Hotel	I
Asakusa View Hotel	D
Blue Wave Inn Asakusa	E
Capsule Hotel Riverside	J
Family Hotel Kamogawa	G
Khaosan Tokyo	K
Ryokan Shigetsu	A
Sakura Hostel	C
Sukeroku-no-yado	B
Sadachiyo	H
Taitō Ryokan	F
Tokyo Ryokan	

SHOPS
Adachiya	f
Bengara	d
Bunsendō	g & h
Chidoriya	n
Fujiya	c
Hyakusuke	b
Kanesō	j
Kurodaya	k
Sukeroku	a
Takahisa	o
Tokiwadō	m
Trunks-ya	i
Yonoya Kushiho	e

RESTAURANTS
Bon	5
Chin-ya	4
Daikokuya	1 & 12
Hatsuogawa	18
Khroopkhrua	3
Maguro Bito	15
Matsunami	13
Otafuku	6
Owariya	16
Sometaro	14

BARS
Cuzn	10
Gin Maku Roku	11
Ichimon	7
Kamiya	17
Samurai Café	9

CAFÉS & TEAHOUSE
Gallery éf	19
Kappabashi Coffee	8
Umezono	2

0 ___ 200 m

Inset map

Hōzō-
mon

METORO-DŌRI

KANNON-DŌRI

NAKAMISE-DŌRI

SHIN-NAKAMISE-DŌRI

KAMINARIMON-DŌRI

Kaminari-mon

Asakusa TIC

0 ___ 25 m

△ Pilgrims and sightseers make their way along Nakamise-dōri to Sensō-ji

fourteenth-century Chinese sutras, are locked away on the upper floor. Its two protective gods – Niō, the traditional guardians of Buddhist temples – are even more imposing than those at Kaminari-mon; look out for their enormous rice-straw sandals slung on the gate's rear wall.

Beyond, there's a constant crowd clustered around a large, bronze incense bowl where people waft the pungent smoke – considered the breath of the gods – over themselves for its supposed curative powers. There's nothing much to see inside the temple itself, since the little Kannon – said to be just 7.5cm tall – is a *hibutsu* or hidden image, considered too holy to be put on view. The hall, however, is full of life, with the rattle of coins being tossed into a huge wooden coffer, the swirling plumes of incense smoke and the constant bustle of people coming to pray, buy charms and fortune papers or to attend a service. Three times a day (6.30am, 10am & 2pm) drums echo through the hall into the courtyard as priests chant sutras beneath the altar's gilded canopy.

Like many Buddhist temples, Sensō-ji accommodates Shinto shrines in its grounds, the most important being **Asakusa-jinja** (浅草神社), dedicated to the two fishermen brothers who netted the Kannon image, and their overlord. The shrine was founded in the mid-seventeenth century by Tokugawa Iemitsu and the original building still survives, though it's hard to tell under all the restored paintwork. More popularly known as Sanja-sama, "Shrine of the Three Guardians", this is the focus of the tumultuous **Sanja Matsuri**, Tokyo's biggest festival, which takes place every year on the third weekend in May. The climax comes on the second day, when over one hundred *mikoshi* (portable shrines) are manhandled through the streets of Asakusa by a seething crowd, among them the three *mikoshi* of Asakusa-jinja, each weighing around 1000kg and carried by at least seventy men.

Sensō-ji's eastern entrance is guarded by the attractively aged Niten-mon. Originally built in 1618, this gate is all that remains of a shrine honouring Tokugawa Ieyasu, which was relocated to Ueno in 1651 after a series of fires. Niten-mon has since been rededicated and now houses two seventeenth-century Buddhist guardians of the south and east. The road heading east leads to a narrow strip of

Asakusa's traditional craft shops

Wander the arcades and backstreets of Asakusa and you'll come across all sorts of traditional **craft shops** which haven't changed much over the last hundred years. The following are just a selection of what's on offer.

Adachiya 安立屋 Nakamise-dōri, Taitō-ku ☎03/3844-1643. This shop sells clothes and other accessories for dogs – not exactly traditional, but in tune with the commercial (and sometimes kitsch) spirit of Asakusa. Daily 9am–6pm.

Bengara べんがら 1-35-6 Asakusa, Taitō-ku ☎03/3841-6613, ⓦwww.bengara.com. The best place to look for *noren*, the split curtain which can be seen hanging outside every traditional shop or restaurant. Daily 10am–6pm; closed third Sun of month.

Bunsendō 文扇堂 Nakamise-dōri, Taitō-ku ☎03/3844-9711. A specialist in high-quality paper fans. Daily 10.30am–6pm, closed one Mon each month.

Fujiya ふじ屋 2-2-15 Asakusa, Taitō-ku ☎03/3841-2283. Hand-printed cotton towels (*tenugui*) designed by octogenarian Kawakami Keiji and his son. Some Fujiya towels are collectors' items. Daily except Wed 10am–6pm.

Hyakusuke 百助 2-2-14 Asakusa, Taitō-ku ☎03/3841-7058. Geisha and Kabuki actors have been coming here for over a century to buy cosmetics, which include a skin cleanser made from powdered nightingale droppings. Daily except Tues 11am–5pm.

Kanesō かね惣 1-18-12 Asakusa, Taitō-ku ☎03/3844-1379. A mind-boggling array of knives, scissors, shears and files, crafted by the Hirano family over five generations. Daily 10.30am–7pm.

Kurodaya 黒田屋 1-2-5 Asakusa, Taitō-ku ☎03/3844-7511. Kurodaya has been selling woodblock prints and items made of traditional washi paper since 1856. Tues–Sun 11am–7pm.

Sukeroku 助六 Nakamise-dōri, Taitō-ku ☎03/3844-0577. Pint-sized shop famous for its miniature, handmade plaster dolls in Edo-period costume, joined nowadays by models of TV stars and other *aidoru* (idols). Daily 10am–6pm.

Takahisa 高久 Shin-Nakamise-dōri, 1-21-7 Asakusa, Taitō-ku ☎03/3844-1257. Rows of richly decorated battledores (*hagoita*), traditionally used by young girls playing shuttlecock at New Year. Daily 9am–8pm.

Tokiwadō 常盤堂 1-3-2 Asakusa, Taitō-ku ☎03/3841-5656, ⓦwww.tokiwado.com. Various types of *kaminari okoshi* ("thunder crackers") – just rice crackers, disappointingly enough, but tasty nonetheless. Daily 9am–9pm.

Trunks-ya とらんくすや 2F, 1-19-10 Asakusa, Taitō-ku ☎03/5806-3255, ⓦwww.trunks-ya.com. Not so traditional, but very Asakusa are this outlet's designer boxer shorts variously covered with writhing dragons, the gods of wind and thunder, Hokusai's 36 *Views of Mount Fuji*, and other fun motifs. Daily 10am–8pm.

Umezono 梅園 1-31-12 Asakusa, Taitō-ku ☎03/3841-7580. Umezono has been tempting shoppers with its mouthwatering array of traditional sweets since 1854. There's also a teahouse attached (see p.185). Daily 10am–7.30pm.

Yonoya Kushiho よのや櫛舗 1-37-10 Asakusa, Taitō-ku ☎03/3844-1755. Tokyo's finest hand-crafted boxwood combs and hair decorations. Daily except Wed 10.30am–6pm.

park, Sumida-kōen (隅田公園); the river here provides the stage for one of the city's great summer firework displays (*hanabi taikai*), held on the last Saturday in July.

West of Sensō-ji

When Kabuki and *bunraku* were banished from central Edo in the 1840s, they settled in the area known as **Rokku** ("Block 6"), between Sensō-ji and today's Kokusai-dōri. Over the next century almost every fad and fashion in popular entertainment started life here, from cinema to cabaret and striptease. Today a handful of the old venues survive, most famously **Rock-za**, with its daily strip show, and there are loads of cinemas, pachinko parlours, gambling halls and drinking dives. It's not all lowbrow, though: several small theatres in the area, such as Asakusa Engei Hall, still stage *rakugo*, a centuries-old form of comic monologue in which familiar jokes and stories are mixed with modern satire.

One block east of the Rox department store, above a covered games pitch, listen for the crack of wood on leather. In a nation besotted with baseball but short on space, the answer is indoor batting cages, such as the ones here at **Sugo Batting Stadium** (daily 10am–1am; from ¥300 for sixteen balls; ☎03/3845-5515). The idea is to try and hit balls hurtling towards you at up to 130km per hour. It's tremendous fun, especially on weekdays when it's quieter, and a great way to work up a thirst.

Behind Rox, the rather grandly named Rokku Broadway leads past betting shops and strip joints north into **Hisago-dōri**, a covered shopping street with a few interesting traditional stores. At the top end is **Edo Shitamachi Traditional Crafts Museum** (Edo Shitamachi Dentō-kōgei-kan; 江戸下町伝統工芸館; daily 10am–8pm; free; ☎03/3842-1990), where at weekends different artisans can be seen at work, while on weekdays there are video presentations about crafts production. There's also a selection of crafts on sale.

Drum Museum

The wide avenue of Kokusai-dōri forms the western boundary of Rokku. Near its southerly junction with Kaminarimon-dōri, just south from the Rox department store, **Miyamoto Unosuke Shōten** (宮本卯之助商店; daily except Tues 9am–6pm; ☎03/3874-4131, ⓦwww.miyamoto-unosuke.co.jp) is easily identifiable from the elaborate *mikoshi* in the window. The shop is an Aladdin's cave of traditional Japanese percussion instruments and festival paraphernalia: masks, shortened kimono-style *happi* coats, flutes, cymbals and, of course, all kinds of *mikoshi*, the largest with a price tag over ¥3 million. Since 1861, however, the family passion has been drums, resulting in an impressive collection from around the world which now fills the fourth-floor **Drum Museum** (Wed–Sun 10am–5pm; ¥300; ☎03/3842-5622). There's every type of percussion material and, best of all, you're allowed to have a go on some. A red dot on the name card indicates those not to be touched; blue dots mean you can tap lightly, just with your hands; and the rest have the appropriate drumsticks ready and waiting.

Kappabashi

Continuing westwards from the Drum Museum brings you after a few blocks to another main road, Kappabashi-dōgu-gai. Locally known as **Kappabashi** (かっぱ橋),

or "Kitchenware Town", this is the best-known of several wholesale markets in northeast Tokyo where you can kit out a whole restaurant. You don't have to be a bulk-buyer, however, and this is a great place to pick up unusual souvenirs, such as the plastic food displayed outside restaurants to tempt the customer. This practice, originally using wax, dates from the nineteenth century but came into its own about thirty years ago when foreign foods were being introduced to a puzzled Japanese market. The best examples, not cheap, are absolutely realistic; try Maizuru (まいづる; daily 9am–6pm; ⓣ03/3843-1686, ⓦwww.maiduru.co.jp) or Tokyo Biken (東京美研; Mon–Sat 9am–5.30pm, Sun 11am–5pm; ⓣ03/3842-5551, ⓦwww.sample-koikoi.com) if you're looking for an unusual souvenir. Note that many shops along here close on Sunday.

Ueno and around

Most people visit **Ueno** (上野) for its **park**, one of Tokyo's largest open spaces and home to a host of good museums, as well as a few relics from a vast temple complex that once occupied this hilltop. After a stroll through the park, your first stop should be the prestigious **Tokyo National Museum**, which alone could easily fill a day, though there's also the entertaining **Science Museum** and the **Museum of Western Art**. Save time, too, for the endearing **Shitamachi Museum**, which harks back to Ueno's proletarian past.

Much of downtown Ueno has a rough-and-ready feel, especially round the station and the bustling **Ameyokochō market**, which extends south under the train tracks. Further west, there's a more sedate atmosphere in the **Kyū Iwasaki-tei Gardens**, set around one of Tokyo's few remaining Meiji-era mansions, and among the worshippers at Yushima Tenjin and the students at **Tokyo University**'s ivory towers.

North of the university campus are **Nezu** and **Yanaka**, two of Tokyo's most charmingly old-fashioned areas and a world away from the usual hustle and bustle of the city. A highlight is the historic and tranquil shrine of **Nezu-jinja**, but the whole area is strewn with small temples, craft shops and other attractions, such as the picturesque and historic **Yanaka Cemetery**, the beautiful **Asakura Sculpture Museum** and the old-style shopping street of **Yanaka Ginza**. There are also a couple of good traditional Japanese-style hotels around here (see pp.154–155) for those who really want to soak up the Shitamachi atmosphere.

Some history

In 1624 the second shogun, Tokugawa Hidetada, chose Ueno hill for a magnificent temple to protect his castle's northeast quarter (northeast traditionally being the direction from which evil forces come). **Kan'ei-ji** became the city's prime Buddhist centre, with 36 sub-temples extending over a square kilometre. The complex incorporated the Tokugawas' mortuary temple and a major shrine dedicated to Ieyasu, first of the line, as well as the tombs of six subsequent shogun. When the shogunate collapsed early in 1868, this was the natural place for Tokugawa loyalists to make their last stand, in what became the Battle of Ueno. Though the shogun had already resigned and the castle surrendered peacefully, roughly two thousand rebel samurai occupied Kan'ei-ji until the emperor's army finally attacked. Nearly all the temple buildings were destroyed by fires caused by the shelling or deliberate arson on either side, although ironically Ieyasu's shrine was spared. In 1873 the new Meiji government designated the now desolate hilltop one of Tokyo's first five **public parks**. Ten years later, a station was built nearby and for many years Ueno served as the terminus for trains from the poor, northern provinces, bringing in migrants in search of jobs.

From 1869 to 1888, **Nezu** earned a certain notoriety for its licensed "pleasure quarters", though these were closed down soon after the Imperial University

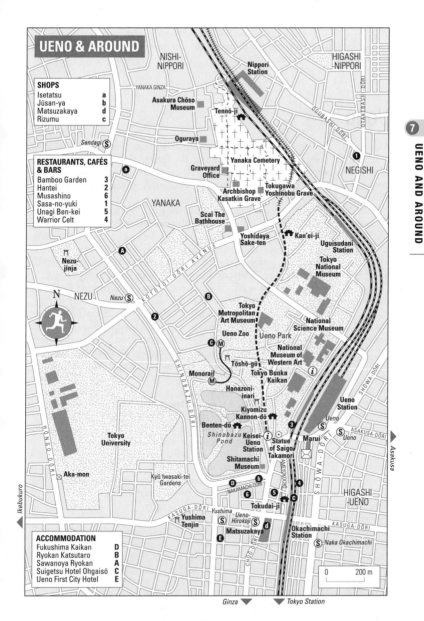

UENO & AROUND

SHOPS	
Isetatsu	**a**
Jūsan-ya	**b**
Matsuzakaya	**d**
Rizumu	**c**

RESTAURANTS, CAFÉS & BARS	
Bamboo Garden	**3**
Hantei	**2**
Musashino	**6**
Sasa-no-yuki	**1**
Unagi Ben-kei	**5**
Warrior Celt	**4**

ACCOMMODATION	
Fukushima Kaikan	**D**
Ryokan Katsutaro	**B**
Sawanoya Ryokan	**A**
Suigetsu Hotel Ohgaisō	**C**
Ueno First City Hotel	**E**

NISHI-NIPPORI

HIGASHI-NIPPORI

Nippori Station

YANAKA GINZA

Asakura Chōso Museum

Tennō-ji

Oguraya

Sendagi Ⓢ

Yanaka Cemetery

Graveyard Office

NEGISHI

Archbishop Kasatkin Grave

Tokugawa Yoshinobu Grave

YANAKA

Scai The Bathhouse

Yoshidaya Sake-ten

Kan'ei-ji

Uguisudani Station

Nezu-jinja

Tokyo National Museum

NEZU

Nezu Ⓢ

KOTOTOI-DŌRI AVENUE

Tokyo Metropolitan Art Museum

Ueno Zoo

National Science Museum

Ueno Park

National Museum of Western Art

SHINOBAZU-DŌRI

Tōshō-gū

Monorail

Tokyo Bunka Kaikan

Hanazono-inari

Kiyomizu Kannon-dō

Ueno Station

Benten-dō

Shinobazu Pond

Keisei-Ueno Station

Tokyo University

Shitamachi Museum

Statue of Saigo Takamori

Marui

HONGŌ-DŌRI

Ueno

Ueno

ASAKUSA-DŌRI

Aka-mon

Kyū Iwasaki-tei Gardens

NAKAMACHI-DŌRI

SHŌWA-DŌRI

HIGASHI-UENO

Ikebukuro

KASUGA-DŌRI

Yushima

Ueno-Hirokoji Ⓢ

Tokudai-ji

Yushima Tenjin

Matsuzakaya

CHUŌ-DŌRI

Okachimachi Station

KASUGA-DŌRI

Naka Okachimachi Ⓢ

Asakusa

0   200 m

Ginza ▼   ▼ Tokyo Station

moved into the neighbourhood in the 1880s, as it was felt the students were being distracted from their studies.

Ueno was flooded with the destitute in 1945, when firebombs destroyed huge swaths of the city and thousands lived in the underground passages beneath the station or made makeshift homes in the park. For several years a **black market** flourished under the railway arches, reaching its peak as the economy boomed in the early 1950s. Though the market has largely been cleaned up and the *yakuza* are less obvious these days, this is still one of the cheapest places to shop in the city, and a world away from genteel Ginza.

Ueno

Although it's far from being the city's most attractive park, **Ueno Park** (上野公園) is where all Tokyo seems to flock during the spring cherry-blossom season. Outside this brief period, however, the park only gets busy at weekends, and during the week it can be a pleasant place for a stroll, particularly around the Shinobazu Pond.

From Ueno Station there are two routes into the park: "Park Exit" takes you to the main, east gate where you'll also find an **information desk** (daily 9am–5pm); while the "Shinobazu Exit" brings you out closer to the southern entrance, above Keisei-Ueno Station, where trains depart for Narita Airport. If you take the southerly option, at the top of the steps leading up to the park from the street you'll find a bronze statue of **Saigo Takamori** (see box opposite) out walking his dog.

As you follow the main path northwards, the red-lacquered **Kiyomizu Kannon-dō** comes into view on the left. Built out over the hillside, this temple is a smaller, less impressive version of Kyoto's famous Kiyomizu-dera temple, but has the rare distinction of being one of Kan'ei-ji's few existing remains, dating from 1631. The temple is dedicated to **Senju Kannon** (the thousand-armed Kannon), whose image is displayed only in February, although the second-rank **Kosodate Kannon** receives more visitors as the Bodhisattva in charge of conception. Hopeful women leave dolls at the altar during the year, following which the dolls are all burnt at a rather sad memorial service on September 25.

The temple faces westwards over a broad avenue lined with ancient cherry trees towards **Shinobazu Pond**. Once an inlet of Tokyo Bay, the pond is now a wildlife protection area and, unlikely as it may seem in the midst of a city, hosts a permanent colony of wild black cormorants as well as temporary populations of migrating waterfowl. A causeway leads out across its reeds and lotus beds to a small, leafy island occupied by an octagonal-roofed temple, **Benten-dō**, dedicated to the goddess of good fortune, water and music (among other things). Inside the dimly lit worship hall you can just make out Benten's eight arms, each clutching a holy weapon, while the ceiling sports a snarling dragon.

From here, you can head back into the park on the tree-lined avenue which marks the approach to Tokugawa Ieyasu's shrine, **Tōshō-gū** (東照宮). Ieyasu died in 1616 and is buried in Nikkō, but this was his main shrine in Tokyo, founded in 1627 and rebuilt on a grander scale in 1651. For once it's possible to penetrate beyond the screened entrance and enclosing walls to take a closer look inside (daily 9am–sunset; ¥200). A path leads from the ticket gate clockwise round the polychrome halls and into the worship hall, whose faded decorative work contrasts sharply with the burnished black and gold of Ieyasu's shrine room behind. Before leaving, take a look at the ornate, Chinese-style front gate, where two golden dragons carved in 1651 by Hidari Jingorō – he of Nikkō's sleeping cat (see p.250) – attract much attention; so realistic is the carving that, according to local tradition, the pair sneak off at midnight to drink in Shinobazu Pond.

The seventeenth-century, five-storey pagoda rising above the trees to the north of Tōshō-gū is actually marooned inside **Ueno Zoo** (上野動物園; Tues–Sun 9.30am–5pm; ¥600; ☎03/3828-5171, ⓦwww.tokyo-zoo.net). Considering this

The last samurai

Saigo Takamori's life story was the inspiration for the Tom Cruise movie *The Last Samurai*. Born in 1827, the "Great Saigo", as he later became known, was leader of the Restoration army, which helped bring Emperor Meiji to power. Later, though, he grew increasingly alarmed at the loss of traditional values and eventually left the government to set up a military academy in his home town of Kagoshima in the southern island of Kyūshū. In January 1877 he led an army of forty thousand against the government in what came to be known as the Satsuma Rebellion. The imperial forces prevailed and on September 24, with the enemy closing in, a severely wounded Saigo asked one of his comrades to kill him. General Saigo's popularity was such, however, that he was rehabilitated in 1891 and his statue in Ueno Park was unveiled a few years later. A military uniform, however, was deemed inappropriate – hence the *yukata* and dog.

△ General Saigō Takamori strikes a relaxed pose in Ueno Park

zoo is over a century old and in the middle of a crowded city, it's less depressing than might be feared. In recent years the pens have been upgraded – though they're still small and predominantly concrete – and there's plenty of vegetation around, including some magnificent, corkscrewing lianas. The main attractions are the reptile house and the Giant Pandas, who snooze away on their concrete platform, blithely unaware they're supposed to be performing for the hordes of excited school children. Try to avoid visiting at weekends, when you'll hardly be able to see the animals for the crowds.

Tokyo National Museum

Dominating the northern reaches of Ueno Park is the **Tokyo National Museum** (Tokyo Kokuritsu Hakubutsukan; 東京国立博物館; April–Sept Tues–Fri 9.30am–5pm, Sat & Sun 9.30am–6pm; Oct–March Tues–Sun 9.30am–5pm; ¥420; ⊤03/3822-1111, ⓦwww.tnm.go.jp), containing the world's largest collection of Japanese art, plus an extensive collection of Oriental antiquities. Though the new galleries are a great improvement, backed up by an unusual amount of information in English, the museum style tends to old-fashioned reverential dryness. Nevertheless, among such a vast collection there's something to excite everyone's imagination. Displays are rotated every few months from a collection of 110,000 pieces, and the special exhibitions are usually worth seeing if you can stand the crowds.

It's best to start with the **Hon-kan**, the central building, where you'll find an English-language floor guide at the lobby information desk and a good museum shop in the basement. The Hon-kan presents the sweep of Japanese art, from Jōmon-period pottery (pre-fourth century BC) to early twentieth-century painting, via theatrical costume for Kabuki, Nō and *bunraku*; colourful Buddhist mandalas; *ukiyo-e* prints; samurai swords; exquisite lacquerware and even seventeenth-century Christian art from southern Japan.

In the building's northwest corner look out for a passage leading to the **Heisei-kan**, where you'll find the splendid Japanese Archeology Gallery containing important recent finds. Though some of the ground it covers is the same as at the Hon-kan, modern presentation really brings the objects to life – the best are refreshingly simple and burst with energy. Highlights are the chunky, flame-shaped Jōmon pots and a collection of super-heated Sue stoneware, made using a technique introduced from Korea in the fifth century. Look out, too, for the bug-eyed, curvaceous clay figures (*dogū*) of the Jōmon period and the funerary *haniwa* from the fourth to sixth centuries AD – these terracotta representations of houses, animals, musicians and stocky little warriors were placed on burial mounds to protect the deceased lord in the afterlife.

In the southwest corner of the compound, behind the copper-domed Hyōkei-kan of 1908 (used for talks and exhibitions), lurks the **Hōryū-ji Hōmotsu-kan**. This sleek new gallery contains a selection of priceless treasures donated over the centuries to the Hōryū-ji temple in Nara. The most eye-catching display comprises 48 gilt-bronze Buddhist statues in various poses, each an island of light in the inky darkness, while there's also an eighth-century Chinese zither, inkstand, water container and spoons said to have been used by Prince Shōtoku when annotating the lotus sutra.

The museum's final gallery is the **Tōyō-kan**, on the opposite side of the compound, housing a delightful hotchpotch of Asian antiquities, with Javanese textiles and nineteenth-century Indian prints rubbing shoulders with Egyptian mummies and a wonderful collection of Southeast Asian bronze Buddhas. The Chinese and, particularly, the Korean collections are also interesting for their obvious parallels with Japanese art.

National Science Museum and National Museum of Western Art

A minute's walk from the National Museum, the **National Science Museum** (国立科学博物館; Tues–Thurs, Sat & Sun 9am–5pm, Fri 9am–8pm; ¥600; ⓣ03/3822-0111, ⓦwww.kahaku.go.jp) is easily identified by a life-size statue of a romping blue whale outside. The museum offers lots of videos and interactive displays, though sadly nothing's labelled in English – make sure you pick up an audio-guide by the ticket desk (¥300). To get you in the mood, take a whirl in a space/time capsule back to the age of the dinosaurs in the 3D theatre, then head for the basement of the new building at the back of the museum to marvel at their extraordinary skeletons. Displays here, over six floors, cover natural history as well as science and technology. In the "exploration space" on the second floor pendulums, magnets, mirrors and hand-powered generators provide entertainment for the mainly school-age audience.

South of here is the **National Museum of Western Art** (国立西洋美術館; Tues–Sun 9.30am–5pm, Fri to 8pm; ¥420; ⓣ03/3828-5131, ⓦwww.nmwa .go.jp), instantly recognizable from the Rodin statues populating the forecourt of the gallery designed by Le Corbusier and erected in 1959 to house the mostly French Impressionist paintings left to the nation by Kawasaki shipping magnate Matsukata Kōjirō. Since then, works by Rubens, Tintoretto, Max Ernst and Jackson Pollock have broadened the scope of this impressive collection.

Tokyo Metropolitan Art Museum and Shitamachi Museum

A short stroll west across the park towards the zoo is the **Tokyo Metropolitan Art Museum** (東京メトロポリタン美術館; daily 9am–5pm, closed third Mon of the month; admission price varies; ℡03/3823-6921, ⓦwww.tobikan.jp), which hosts various temporary exhibitions. At the southern end of the park, the **Shitamachi Museum** (下町風俗資料館; Tues–Sun 9.30am–4.30pm; ¥300; ℡03/3823-7451, ⓦwww.taitocity.net/taito/shitamachi) is set in a distinctive, partly traditional-style building beside Shinobazu Pond. The museum opened in 1980 to preserve something of the Shitamachi while it was still within living memory. A reconstructed merchant's shop-house and a 1920s tenement row, complete with sweet shop and coppersmith's workroom, fill the ground floor. The upper floor is devoted to rotating exhibitions focusing on articles of daily life – old photos, toys, advertisements and artisans' tools, with plenty of information in English. All the museum's exhibits have been donated by local residents; take your shoes off to explore the shop interiors and it's possible to handle most items.

Ameyokochō

Ueno town centre lies to the south of the park, a lively mix of discount outlets, street markets, drinking clubs, a sprinkling of upmarket stores and craft shops, "soaplands" (a euphemism for brothels), love hotels and restaurants. While it's not strong on sophistication or culture, there's a greater sense of raw vitality here than elsewhere in Tokyo.

The biggest draw for both bargain-hunters and sightseers is the bustling **market** area south of Ueno Station, **Ameyokochō** (アメ横丁), which extends nearly half a kilometre along the west side of the elevated JR train lines down to Okachimachi Station, spilling down side alleys and under the tracks. The name is an abbreviation of "Ameya Yokochō", or "Candy Sellers' Alley", dating from the immediate postwar days when sweets were a luxury and hundreds of stalls here peddled mostly sweet potatoes coated in sugar syrup. Since rationing was in force, black-marketeers joined the candy sellers, dealing in rice and other foodstuffs, household goods, personal possessions – whatever was available. Later, American imports also found their way from army stores onto the streets here, especially during the early 1950s Korean War. By then the market had been legalized, and over the years the worst crime has been cleaned up, but Ameyokochō still retains a flavour of those early days: gruff men with sandpaper voices shout out their wares; stalls selling bulk tea and coffee, Korean foods, cheap shoes, ready-peeled fruit, jewellery and fish are all jumbled up, cheek by jowl; and under the arches a clutch of *yakitori* bars still tempt the market crowds. In the thick of all this it's not surprising to stumble across a temple, **Tokudai-ji** (徳大寺), dedicated to a goddess offering prosperity and abundant harvests. Look out for the temple's fluttering banners, up on the second floor two blocks before the southern limit of Ameyokochō.

Kyū Iwasaki-tei Gardens

The west side of central Ueno is dominated by seedy love hotels and dubious bars. A short walk past Yushima Station, however, you'll discover a remnant of a much more genteel past. The **Kyū Iwasaki-tei Gardens** (旧岩崎邸庭園; daily 9am–5pm; ¥400; ℡03/3823-8340, ⓦwww.tokyo-park.or.jp) date from 1896 and surround an elegant **house**, designed by British architect Josiah Conder (see box, p.68), which combines a *café au lait*-painted, Western-style two-storey mansion with a traditional single-storey Japanese residence. The wooden Jacobean and Moorish-style arabesque interiors of the Western-style mansion are in fantastic condition – in stark contrast to the severely faded screen paintings of the Japanese section. The lack of furniture in both houses makes them a little lifeless, but it's nonetheless an impressive artefact in a city where such buildings are increasingly rare. You can take tea in the Japanese section (¥500) or sit outside and admire the gardens, which also combine Eastern and Western influences.

Yushima Tenjin and Tokyo University

From the gardens it's a short walk west along the main road to **Yushima Tenjin** (湯島天神; also known as Yushima Tenmangū), a shrine dedicated to Tenjin, the god of scholarship. The best time to visit is in late February when the plum trees are in blossom and candidates for university entrance exams leave mountains of *ema* (wooden votive tablets) inscribed with their requirements.

The shrine stands a few minutes' walk south of the nation's top-ranking **Tokyo University** (東京大学), whose graduates fill the corridors of power. Founded in 1869, Tōdai – as it's commonly known – occupies the former estate of the wealthy Maeda lords, though there's little sign of their mansion beyond a scummy pond and the one-storey, red-lacquer gate, **Aka-mon**, which forms the front (west) entrance into the university's sleepy and decidedly unkempt campus.

Nezu

The old Tokyo district of **Nezu** (根津), meaning "Water's Edge", is a short walk north of Tōdai. Its main sight, the venerable, cedar-shaded shrine **Nezu-jinja** (根津神社), lies tucked off Shinobazu-dōri, five minutes' walk north of Nezu Station on the Chiyoda subway line. Nezu-jinja dates from the early eighteenth century when it was built in honour of the sixth Tokugawa shogun, Ienobu. The ornate and colourfully decorated shrine is notable for its corridor of vermilion *torii* and a hillside bedecked with some three thousand azalea bushes which bloom in a profusion of pinks and reds during late April and early May, attracting throngs of camera-toting visitors. At other times the shrine is serene and peaceful. While you're in the neighbourhood you may also want to visit the traditional *kushiage* restaurant *Hantei* (see p.178).

Five minutes northeast of Nezu Station along the major road Kototoi-dōri is **Yoshidaya Sake-ten** (吉田屋酒店; Tues–Sun 9.30am–4.30pm; free), an early twentieth-century sake store which was moved here in 1987 and is now an annexe of the Shitamachi Museum (see p.95). After a glimpse inside at the giant glass bottles, china barrels and other accoutrements of the trade, you can take the small road heading north, looking out at the next corner on the left for a bizarre little contemporary art gallery called **SCAI The Bathhouse**, which occupies a 200-year-old public bath (see p.237). Immediately uphill from here is the southern edge of Yanaka Cemetery.

Yanaka

After the Long Sleeves Fire of 1657, many temples relocated to the higher ground of **Yanaka** (谷中), where they remain today, alongside old wooden buildings that seem to have miraculously escaped the ensuing centuries' various calamities. It's a charming area to explore on foot, and you could spend many hours rambling through its narrow, quiet streets, discovering small temples, shrines and traditional craft shops. Sunrise Tours (see p.29) offer guided **walking tours** of Yanaka (Tues, Thurs & Sat at 1.40pm; 3hr 30min; ¥3500) from Ueno Park via Yanaka Cemetery, ending at the Isetatsu paper shop (see p.221).

The area is dominated by **Yanaka Cemetery** (谷中霊園), one of Tokyo's oldest and largest graveyards. If you're not walking here from Nezu, the cemetery is most easily reached from the west side of Nippori Station on the Yamanote line. A couple of minutes' walk south of the Nippori entrance to the cemetery, you'll find one the area's most attractive temples, **Tennō-ji** (天王寺), beside which stands a large copper Buddha dating from 1690. Head southwest down the cemetery's main avenue from here to reach the **graveyard offices** (daily 8.30am–5pm), opposite the public toilet, where you can pick up a Japanese map locating various notables, including the last Tokugawa shogun, Yoshinobu, in a large plot on the southern edge of the cemetery, while Archbishop Nikolai Kasatkin, founder of the Russian Orthodox Nikolai Cathedral (see p.68), lies immediately to the west.

Return to the Nippori entrance to the cemetery, turn west and walk a few hundred metres uphill to reach another of Yanaka's many gems, the **Asakura Chōso Museum** (朝倉彫塑館; Tues–Thurs, Sat & Sun 9.30am–4.30pm; ¥400; ☎03/3821-4549), the well-preserved home and studio of sculptor **Asakura Fumio** (1883–1964), often referred to as the Rodin of Japan. Completed in 1935, the house successfully combines a modernist concrete building, used by the artist as his studio, with a wood-and-bamboo Japanese-style home. A lovely Japanese garden occupies the centre, while on the roof of the studio is an equally delightful Western-style garden with great views across the rooftops. Many of Asakura's works are on display, including some incredibly lifelike sculptures of his beloved cats.

On leaving the museum, turn left and continue along an attractive residential street to reach **Oguraya** (小倉屋; Wed–Sun 10am–8pm, free; ☎03/3828-0562, Ⓦwww.oguraya.gr.jp), a pawnbroker's shop dating from 1847, now a gallery-cum-shop. Of more interest, however, is the architecture, particularly the three-storey wooden *dozō* (storehouse). It's worth popping inside just to see this lovingly preserved and increasingly rare type of architecture.

Retrace your steps towards Nippori, but when you hit the "main road" at the top of the hill, instead of turning right for the station, head left and then down some stone steps to find the pedestrianized shopping street known as **Yanaka Ginza**. The antithesis of trendy Tokyo malls, this appealing shopping promenade is worth exploring to find small family businesses selling *sembei* (rice crackers), tofu and other food specialities. Sendagi Station on the Chiyoda subway line is close by.

Ikebukuro and northern Tokyo

Marsh and farmland until a hundred years ago, **Ikebukuro** (池袋) is a product of the train age. Its first station was completed in 1903, and six lines now connect the area with central Tokyo and the low-cost dormitory suburbs to the north and east. Cheap accommodation and good transport have attracted an increasing number of expatriates, typically Chinese and Taiwanese, but also including a broad sweep of other nationalities, which lends Ikebukuro a faintly cosmopolitan air. It's by no means as trendy or hip as Shinjuku or Shibuya, and for the short-term visitor there are no compelling reasons to visit. However, to some this very lack of star status and cool pretension is Ikebukuro's appeal.

The two largest department stores in Japan – Tōbu and Seibu – square off against each other from opposite sides of Ikebukuro's confusing station. The area west of the train tracks, **Nishi-Ikebukuro** (西池袋), is the more interesting to explore, particularly the wedge of streets spreading out towards the attractive **Rikkyō University** campus, if only for its plethora of bars and restaurants. Across the tracks, **Higashi-Ikebukuro** (東池袋) is the main shopping centre and has good discount stores, with cameras and electronic goods at prices rivalling Akihabara. Apart from a fairly low-brow entertainment district, Higashi-Ikebukuro's only other draw is the **Sunshine City** complex, home to the monstrous, sixty-storey Sunshine 60 building and the Ancient Orient Museum.

Two stops east on the Yamanote line is **Sugamo**, a popular gathering spot for Tokyo's old folk, who flock to visit the local temple, **Kōgan-ji**, where they seek relief from the gods for their physical ailments. One stop east of Sugamo is **Komagome**, where you can visit **Rikugi-en**, one of the city's most attractive Edo-period gardens, and the equally lovely **Kyū Furukawa Gardens**, combining Western and Japanese styles of horticulture.

West Ikebukuro

Ikebukuro Station handles around one million passengers per day – second only to Shinjuku – and its warren of connecting passages, shopping arcades and countless exits is notoriously difficult to negotiate. It's even worse on the west side, when the helpfully colour-coded signs mutate to blue, indicating you are now in **Tōbu**

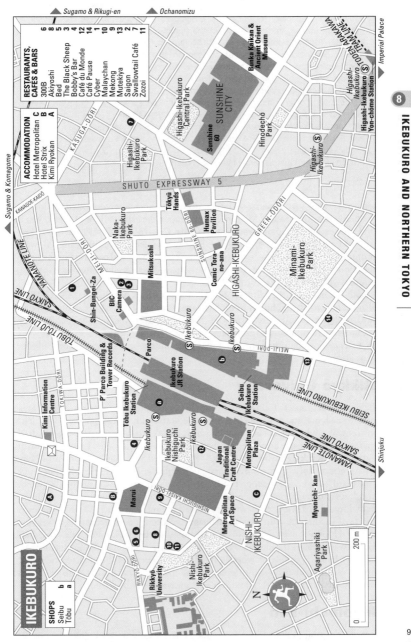

IKEBUKURO

SHOPS
- b Seibu
- a Tōbu

ACCOMMODATION
- C Hotel Metropolitan
- B Hotel Strix
- A Kimi Ryokan

RESTAURANTS, CAFÉS & BARS
300B	6
Akiyoshi	8
Bed	5
The Black Sheep	3
Bobby's Bar	4
Café du Monde	12
Café Pause	14
Cyber	1
Malaychan	10
Mekong	9
Mutekiya	13
Saigon	2
Swallowtail Café	7
Zozoi	11

▲ Sugamo & Rikugi-en   ▲ Ochanomizu

◀ Sugamo & Komagome

Imperial Palace ▶

SHUTO EXPRESSWAY 5

Bunka Kaikan & Ancient Orient Museum

Higashi-Ikebukuro Central Park

SUNSHINE CITY

Sunshine 60

Hinodechō Park

Higashi-Ikebukuro

Higashi-Ikebukuro Station

Higashi-Ikebukuro Yon-chōme Station

TŌDEN ARAKAWA TRAMLINE

Higashi-Ikebukuro Park

KASUGA-DŌRI

MEIJI-DŌRI

SUNSHINE 60-DŌRI

GREEN-ŌDŌRI

Minami-Ikebukuro Park

Tōkyū Hands

Naka-Ikebukuro Park

Mitsukoshi

Humax Pavilion

HIGASHI-IKEBUKURO

Comic Tora-no-ana

Shin-Bungei-Za

BIC Camera

KAWAGOE-KAIDŌ

YAMANOTE LINE

SAIKYO LINE

TŌBU TŌJŌ LINE

TOKIWA-DŌRI

Kimi Information Centre

P' Parco Building & Tower Records

Parco

Tōbu Ikebukuro Station

Ikebukuro JR Station

Ikebukuro

Ikebukuro

Ikebukuro Nishiguchi Park

Japan Traditional Craft Centre

Metropolitan Plaza

Seibu Ikebukuro Station

MEIJI-DŌRI

SEIBU IKEBUKURO LINE

Shinjuku ▶

Metropolitan Art Space

Marui

NISHIGUCHI KAISEI-DŌRI

RIKKYO-DŌRI

NISHI-IKEBUKURO

Myonichi-kan

Rikkyō University

Nishi-Ikebukuro Park

Agariyashiki Park

YAMANOTE LINE

SAIKYO LINE

N

0   200 m

8   IKEBUKURO AND NORTHERN TOKYO

Tokyo's last tramline

Early twentieth-century Tokyo boasted a number of tramlines, or *chin chin densha* ("ding ding trains", from the sound of the trams' bells), of which only the twelve-kilometre **Toden-Arakawa Line** (都電荒川線) remains, running north from Waseda to Minowa-bashi. The most interesting section lies along a short stretch from **Kōshinzuka Station**, a fifteen-minute walk northwest of Sugamo Station, from where the line heads southwest towards Higashi-Ikebukuro, rocking and rolling along narrow streets and through Tokyo backyards.

Most of the original tramlines were private enterprises and have gradually been replaced with subways. The Arakawa Line, built purely to take people to the spring blossoms in Asukayama Park, will probably survive for its nostalgia value if nothing else. PASMO, Suica and SF Metro cards can be used on the system, as can Toei day tickets. Ordinary tickets cost ¥160, however far you travel; you pay as you enter. Station signs and announcements are in English.

territory. This vast department store occupies three interconnected buildings, including the glass-fronted Metropolitan Plaza, on the ground floor of which you'll find the excellent **Japan Traditional Craft Centre** (全国伝統的工芸品センター; daily 11am–7pm; free; T03/5954-6066, Wwww.kougei.or.jp). Charged with promoting "authentic" crafts, the centre showcases a large and continually changing selection of hand-made items from all over Japan. Though all the items are for sale, you are welcome just to come and look.

Both the nearby *Hotel Metropolitan* and **Metropolitan Art Space** (東京芸術劇場) also belong to the Tōbu empire. The latter, facing Tōbu store across an open square, hosts regular concerts and theatre performances, plus occasionally rewarding exhibitions. Its main claim to fame, though, is its long **escalator**, best experienced on the way down for a dizzying, ninety-second descent beneath the glass atrium.

Rikkyō University

Behind the Art Space, follow any of the small roads heading west through an area of lanes rich in restaurants and bars until you hit tree-lined Rikkyō-dōri. Turn left, in front of a white clapboard wedding hall, and continue for just over a hundred metres until you see a square, red-brick gateway on the left. This is the main entrance to **Rikkyō University** (立教大学), founded as St Paul's School in 1874 by an American Episcopalian missionary. Through the gateway, the old university courtyard has an incongruous Ivy League touch in its vine-covered halls, white windows and grassy quadrangle, making it a favourite venue for film crews. Originally located in Tsukiji, the university moved to Ikebukuro in 1918 and weathered the 1923 earthquake with minimal damage except for one toppled gate tower; the lopsided look was left, so it's said, as a memorial to those who died, but a deciding factor was perhaps the sheer lack of bricks. Other original buildings include All Saint's Chapel, a couple of wooden missionary houses and the congregation hall, now a nicotine-stained canteen opposite the main gate with a quote from Cicero over the door: "Reason should direct and appetite obey".

Myonichi-kan

Fans of the American architect Frank Lloyd Wright should track down one of his lesser-known but still very distinctive buildings, the **Myonichi-kan**, or "House of

Tomorrow" (明日館; Tues–Sun 10am–4.30pm, closed occasionally during functions; ¥400, or ¥600 including Japanese tea and sweets; ☏03/3971-7535, ⓦwww.jiyu .jp). While working on the *Imperial Hotel* (see p.62), Wright and his assistant Endo Arata also designed this complex to house the Jiyū Gakuen school. The geometric windows and low-slung roofs are trademark Wright features, but the buildings are best appreciated from inside, where you get the full effect of the clean, bold lines, echoed in the hexagonal chairs, light fittings and other original furnishings. The easiest way to find the school is to start at the Metropolitan Art Space, then walk south for about five minutes, looking out for the signs as you go.

East Ikebukuro

Over on the east side of Ikebukuro Station, **Seibu** rules. This is the company's flagship store, claiming to be the largest in Japan, though there's only a matter of inches in it. While the group has been retrenching in recent years, Seibu has a history of innovation and spotting new trends. Apart from the main store, there are also branches of Parco, Loft and Wave, Seibu offshoots specializing in fashion, household goods and music respectively.

Heading east from Ikebukuro Station, you can't miss the monstrous sixty storeys of **Sunshine 60**, which at 240m was Japan's tallest building until it was pipped by Yokohama's Landmark Tower. An underground passage leads from the basement here into the Sunshine 60 tower, just one of four buildings comprising the **Sunshine City** complex of shops, offices, exhibition space, a hotel and various cultural centres – though compared to the city's newer developments, it all looks rather dowdy. The tower's sixtieth-floor **observatory** (10am–9.30pm; ¥620) may be a shade higher than its Shinjuku rivals, but you have to pay, and unless it's a really clear day there's not a lot to see anyway.

Sunshine City's most easterly building, Bunka Kaikan, houses the **Ancient Orient Museum** (daily 10am–5pm; ¥500; ☏03/3989-3491) on its seventh floor, displaying archeological finds from the Middle East (Syria in particular) and elsewhere. While there are the inevitable bits of old pot, the collection focuses on more accessible items such as statues, jewellery, icons and other works of art, including some superb Gandhara Buddhist art from Pakistan and a smiling, wide-eyed goddess made in Syria around 2000 BC.

A short walk south of Sunshine City is Higashi-Ikebukuro Yon-chōme Station, where you can hop on Tokyo's last tramway, the Toden-Arakawa Line (see box opposite). From here you can head southwest to Waseda or east to Kōshinzuka, to come into Sugamo from the north.

Sugamo and Komagome

Two stops east of Ikebukuro on the Yamanote line is **Sugamo** (巣鴨). On the north side of the JR station a shopping street, **Jizō-dōri**, branches left off the main road, marked by an arch with orange characters. The street is nicknamed *obāchan no Harajuku* or "old ladies' Harajuku", an ironic reference to Tokyo's epicentre of young fashion. Jizō-dōri is, of course, anything but fashionable; shops here sell floral aprons, sensible shoes, long johns and shopping trolleys, interspersed with speciality food, household products and traditional and Western medicines.

This all arose because of a temple, **Kōgan-ji** (高岩寺), 100m up on the right, dedicated to "thorn-removing" Togenuki Jizō, who provides relief from both physical pain and the metaphorical suffering of the soul. In case a prayer doesn't work, people also queue up in front of a small Kannon statue, known as the Migawari Kannon, tucked into a corner of the temple forecourt. Each person in turn pours water over the statue and wipes whatever part of its anatomy corresponds to their own ailment, thus transferring it to the Kannon. Until recently people used brushes but now it's hand towels only, as the poor goddess was being scrubbed away. Despite the sad undertones, there's a good atmosphere, enlivened by a number of quack doctors who set up stalls outside.

Jizō-dōri continues north as far as Kōshinzuka Station (庚申塚駅), less than ten minutes' walk from the temple, where you can pick up a **tram** (streetcar) on the **Toden Arakawa Line** (see box, p.100).

Rikugi-en

One stop east along the Yamanote line from Sugamo is **Komagome** (駒込). This is where you'll find **Rikugi-en** (六義園; daily 9am–5pm; ¥300), Tokyo's best surviving example of a classical Edo-period stroll-garden. In 1695 the fifth shogun granted one of his high-ranking feudal lords, Yanagisawa Yoshiyasu, a tract of farmland to the north of Edo. Yanagisawa was both a perfectionist and a literary scholar: he took seven years to design his celebrated garden – with its 88 allusions to famous scenes, real or imaginary, from ancient Japanese poetry – and then named it Rikugi-en, "garden of the six principles of poetry", in reference to the rules for composing *waka* (poems of 31 syllables). After Yanagisawa's death, Rikugi-en fell into disrepair until Iwasaki Yatarō, founder of Mitsubishi, bought the land in 1877 and restored it as part of his luxury villa. The family donated the garden to the Tokyo city authorities in 1938, since when it has been a public park.

Not surprisingly, few of the 88 landscapes have survived – the guide map issued at the entrance identifies a mere eighteen. Nevertheless, Rikugi-en still retains its rhythm and beauty, and is large enough to be relatively undisturbed by surrounding buildings and traffic noise. The entrance lies five minutes' walk south of the station on Hongō-dōri (take a right turn one block before the next major junction). The park kicks off with an ancient, spreading cherry tree, then slowly unfolds along paths that meander past secluded arbours and around the indented shoreline of an islet-speckled lake. In contrast, there are also areas of more natural woodland and a hillock from which to admire the whole scene.

Kyū Furukawa Gardens

While you're in the Komagome area, it would be a great shame to miss out on another beautifully maintained garden. Designed by Ogawa Jihei, a famed gardener from Kyoto, the **Kyū Furukawa Gardens** (旧古河庭園; daily 9am–5pm; ¥150) combine delightful Japanese-style grounds with an Italian-style terrace of rose beds and artfully shaped azalea bushes. The gardens cascade down the hill from the mansion designed in 1914 by British architect Josiah Conder (see box, p.68), who was also responsible for the similar Kyū Iwasaki-tei house and gardens in Ueno (see p.95). It's possible to take tea and cake in the mansion and to go on a tour of the empty (and frankly boring) rooms, but it's much more enjoyable to sample *matcha* and traditional Japanese sweets (¥500) in the teahouse in the Japanese part of the garden. The best times to visit are in late April, when the azaleas bloom,

△ The Kyū Furukawa Gardens combine Western and Japanese elements

and in mid-May, when the roses are out in full force. To reach the entrance to the gardens, walk back from Rikugi-en to Komagome Station and keep following Hongō-dōri uphill for about five minutes.

Shinjuku and western Tokyo

Some 4km due west of the Imperial Palace, **Shinjuku** (新宿) has a long and illustrious history of pandering to the more basic of human desires. A day and an evening spent in the area will show you Tokyo from high to low: the love hotels and hostess bars of **Kabukichō**, the no-frills bars of **Shomben Yokochō**, the shop-till-you-drop department stores and dazzlingly designed skyscrapers – it's all here in Shinjuku.

Shinjuku is split in two by a thick band of train tracks. The western half, **Nishi-Shinjuku**, with its soaring towers, including the monumental **Tokyo Metropolitan Government Building**, is a showcase for contemporary architecture; the raunchier eastern side, **Higashi-Shinjuku**, is a nonstop red-light and shopping district – though it's also home to one of Tokyo's most attractive parks, **Shinjuku Gyoen**.

Heading west from the station, the JR Chūō line will transport you to two must-see sights for anime fans: the **Suginami Animation Museum** and the **Ghibli Museum** at Mitaka.

Some history

The district takes its name from the "new lodgings" (*shin juku*) which were set up west of the city centre in the seventeenth century for travellers en route to Edo. These were shut down in 1718 after a fracas in a brothel involving an influential samurai and it took sixty years for Shinjuku to recover, by which time it had become one of Edo's six **licensed quarters**, catering mainly to the lower classes. By the late nineteenth century, the area had been nicknamed "Tokyo's anus", due to the transportation of human waste through its streets to the countryside – and had the most prostitutes of any area in the city.

Making sense of Shinjuku Station

Shinjuku Station, the busiest in the world, is a messy combination of three terminals (the main **JR station**, plus the **Keiō** and **Odakyū** stations beside their respective department stores on the west side) and three connecting subway lines. There's also the separate **Seibu Shinjuku Station**, northeast of the JR station. At least two million commuters are fed into these stations every day and spun out of sixty exits, and the rivers of people constantly flowing along the station's many underground passages only add to the confusion. It's easy to get hopelessly lost; if this happens, head immediately for street level and get your bearings from the skyscrapers to the west.

A turning point came in 1885 when the opening of the railway encouraged people to move out of the city into the increasingly fashionable western suburbs – and the hordes of commuters passing through also made Shinjuku the ideal location for the department stores which sprang up here during the early twentieth century. The earthquake of 1923 left the area relatively unscathed, but most of Shinjuku had to be rebuilt after the air raids of 1945 and there were plans to relocate Tokyo's Kabuki theatre to the east side of the station. Such relatively sophisticated entertainment was not really Shinjuku's style, however, so although the area adopted the name **Kabukichō**, the black market stayed put, the red-light trade resumed and the Kabuki theatre was rebuilt in Ginza.

In the immediate postwar decades Shinjuku's seediness attracted a bohemian population of writers, students and radical intellectuals, who hung out in its jazz bars and coffee shops. In October 1968 passions bubbled over into riots and paving stones were ripped up and hurled at the police in an anti-Vietnam demo. Meanwhile, on the western side of the station another type of revolution was under way. The area's first **skyscraper**, the 47-storey *Keiō Plaza Hotel*, opened in 1971 and was swiftly followed by several more earthquake-defying towers, while Tange Kenzō's Tokyo Metropolitan Government Building set the modernist seal on the area two decades later. It has since been joined by his Shinjuku Park Tower on the south side of Shinjuku Chūō-kōen and, further west, the arty performance halls of Tokyo Opera City and the New National Theatre, the latest attempt to bring respectability to the area.

Nishi-Shinjuku

West of the station, **Nishi-Shinjuku** is dominated by towers of glass, concrete and steel, including the vast Tokyo Metropolitan Government Building complex, from which the Tokyo prefecture is administered. Few are worth spending much time exploring, though most have free observation rooms on their upper floors, along with a wide selection of restaurants and bars with good views. Collectively, however, their impact is striking, mainly because their scale, coupled with the spaciousness of the surroundings, is so unusual for Tokyo – despite the recent boom of high-rise buildings, this remains predominantly a low-rise city. To reach Nishi-Shinjuku, either head for the west exit at Shinjuku Station, or hop out of the subway at Tochōmae Station, on the Ōedo line.

Tokyo Metropolitan Government Building

On the left-hand side of Chūō-dōri as you emerge at the end of the tunnel is the monumental **Tokyo Metropolitan Government Building** (TMGB; 東京都庁), a 400,000-square-metre complex designed by Tange Kenzō. Thirteen thousand city bureaucrats go to work each day at the TMGB, and the entire complex – which includes twin 48-storey towers, an adjacent tower block, the Metropolitan Assembly Hall (where the city's councillors meet) and a sweeping, statue-lined and colonnaded plaza – feels like Gotham City. Tange was actually aiming to evoke Paris's Notre Dame, and there's certainly something of that cathedral's design in the shape of the twin towers. But the building's real triumph is that it is unmistakably Japanese; the dense crisscross pattern of its glass and granite facade is reminiscent of both traditional architecture and the circuitry of an enormous computer chip.

On the ground floor of the No. 1 Tower you'll find the excellent Tokyo Tourist Information Centre (see p.47); free **tours** (Mon–Fri 10am–3pm) of the complex depart from here. Both the towers have **observation rooms** on their forty-fifth

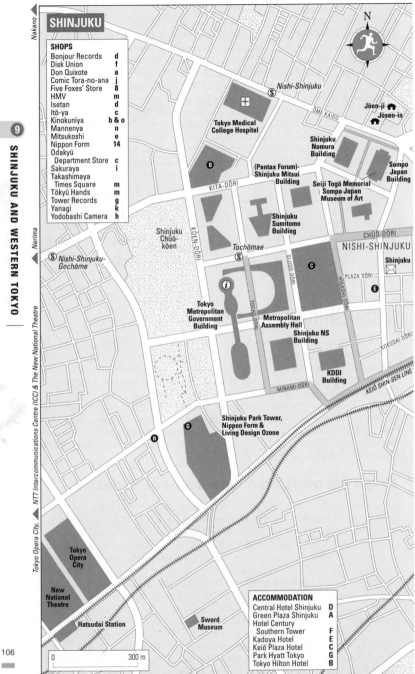

SHINJUKU

SHOPS
Bonjour Records	d
Disk Union	f
Don Quixote	a
Comic Tora-no-ana	j
Five Foxes' Store	8
HMV	m
Isetan	d
Itō-ya	c
Kinokuniya	b & o
Mannenya	n
Mitsukoshi	e
Nippon Form	14
Odakyū Department Store	c
Sakuraya	i
Takashimaya Times Square	m
Tōkyū Hands	m
Tower Records	g
Yanagi	k
Yodobashi Camera	h

Nakano

Nerima

Nishi-Shinjuku

ŌME KAIDŌ

Jōen-ji
Jōsen-in

Tokyo Medical
College Hospital

Shinjuku
Nomura
Building

Sompo
Japan
Building

B

(Pentax Forum)-
Shinjuku Mitsui
Building

Seiji Tōgō Memorial
Sompo Japan
Museum of Art

KITA-DŌRI

Shinjuku
Sumitomo
Building

CHŪŌ-DŌRI

NISHI-SHINJUKU

Shinjuku
Chūō-
kōen

Nishi-Shinjuku-
Gochōme

Tochōmae

C

Shinjuku

PLAZA DŌRI

E

i

Tokyo
Metropolitan
Government
Building

Metropolitan
Assembly Hall

Shinjuku NS
Building

KOKUSAI-DŌRI

KDDI
Building

KEIŌ SHIN-SEN LINE

MINAMI-DŌRI

Shinjuku Park Tower,
Nippon Form &
Living Design Ozone

G

D

Tokyo
Opera
City

New
National
Theatre

Hatsudai Station

Sword
Museum

ACCOMMODATION
Central Hotel Shinjuku	D
Green Plaza Shinjuku	A
Hotel Century Southern Tower	F
Kadoya Hotel	E
Keiō Plaza Hotel	C
Park Hyatt Tokyo	G
Tokyo Hilton Hotel	B

Tokyo Opera City, ◀ NTT Intercommunications Centre (ICC) & The New National Theatre

0   300 m

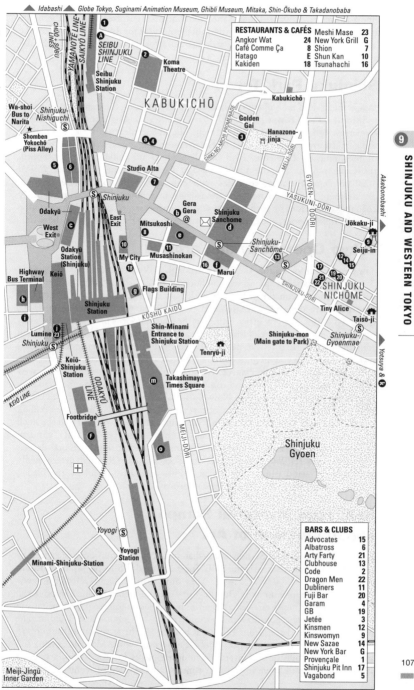

RESTAURANTS & CAFÉS

Angkor Wat	24	Meshi Mase	23
Café Comme Ça	8	New York Grill	G
Hatago	E	Shion	7
Kakiden	18	Shun Kan	10
		Tsunahachi	16

9

SHINJUKU AND WESTERN TOKYO

KABUKICHŌ

SHINJUKU NICHŌME

BARS & CLUBS

Advocates	15
Albatross	6
Arty Farty	21
Clubhouse	13
Code	2
Dragon Men	22
Dubliners	11
Fuji Bar	20
Garam	4
GB	19
Jetée	3
Kinsmen	12
Kinswomyn	9
New Sazae	14
New York Bar	G
Provençale	1
Shinjuku Pit Inn	17
Vagabond	5

floors (Mon–Fri 9.30am–10pm, Sat & Sun 9.30am–7pm; free); the southern one is preferable as it has a café. It's worth timing your visit for dusk, so you can see the multicoloured lights of Shinjuku spark into action as the setting sun turns the sky a deep photochemical orange.

Shinjuku Park Tower

Beside the TMGB is Shinjuku Chūō-kōen, a dusty park, on the south side of which is **Shinjuku Park Tower** (新宿パークタワー), another building across which Tange's modernist signature is confidently written. The style credentials of this complex of three linked towers, all topped with glass pyramids, are vouched for by the presence of the luxurious *Park Hyatt Hotel* (which occupies the building's loftiest floors), the Conran Shop and the **Living Design Centre Ozone** (daily except Wed 10.30am–7pm; entrance fee varies with exhibition; ☎03/5322-6500, ⓦwww .ozone.co.jp), a spacious museum specializing in interior design, with regularly changing exhibitions by both Japanese and Western designers. A regular free shuttle bus runs from opposite the Odakyū department store to the south side of the tower.

Tokyo Opera City and around

The best reason for visiting the 234-metre-high **Tokyo Opera City** (東京オペラシティ; ⓦwww.operacity.jp/en), with 54 floors of offices, shops and restaurants, plus a state-of-the-art concert hall (see p.201), is to see what's showing at the **NTT Intercommunication Centre** (ICC; Tues–Sun 10am–6pm, Fri until 9pm; ¥800; ☎0120-144199, ⓦwww.ntticc.or.jp), on the fourth floor. This is one of the most innovative interactive exhibition space in Tokyo, and there's almost always something interesting to see: past displays of hi-tech art have included a sound-proof room where you listen to your own heartbeat, and light-sensitive robots you can control with your brain waves. Tokyo Opera City is a ten-minute walk west of the Shinjuku Park Tower, and connected to Hatsudai Station on the Keiō line. Directly behind the tower is the **New National Theatre** (Shin-kokuritsu Gekijō; 新国立劇場), an ambitious complex of three performing arts auditoria (see p.208).

From Hatsudai Station, you can duck south into the backstreets to find the small but intriguing **Sword Museum** (Tōken Hakubutsukan; 刀剣博物館; Tues–Sun 10am–4.30pm; ¥525; ☎03/3379-1386). Fans of swashbuckling samurai dramas and Tarantino's *Kill Bill* films will love this place, and even if you're determinedly anti-violence you'll still admire the incredible decorative detail on the blades, handles and sheaths of the lethal weapons displayed.

Seiji Togō Memorial Sompo Japan Museum of Art

Back towards Shinjuku Station, immediately north of Chūō-dōri and close by Odakyū department store, is the **Seiji Togō Memorial Sompo Japan Museum of Art** (損保ジャパン東郷青児美術館; Tues–Sun 10am–5.30pm; ¥1000; ⓦwww .sompo-japan.co.jp/museum). On the forty-second floor of the Sompo Japan Building, it's the home of one in the series of *Sunflowers* paintings by Vincent van Gogh as well as other top-draw impressionist pieces by Cézanne and Gauguin. The *Sunflowers* canvas, dating from 1888, was bought for the astronomical sum of ¥5 billion during the height of Japan's "bubble economy" years. More interesting and unusual is the collection of over two hundred pieces by Togō Seiji, a popular Japanese artist best known for his soft, contoured depictions of women.

Shomben Yokochō

Still on the west side of Shinjuku Station, squashed up against the train tracks running north from the Odakyū department store, are the narrow, *akachochin* (red lantern)-lit alleyways of the **Shomben Yokochō** (しょんべん横丁), also known as Omoide Yokocho. Shomben Yokochō translates as "Piss Alley", but don't be put off visiting this atmospheric four-block neighbourhood of tiny bars and cramped *yakitori* and noodle joints – this is a cheap place to eat, and you're less likely to be ripped off for a drink here than in the similar Golden Gai district of nearby Kabukichō. Enjoy it while you can, as there's talk of redeveloping the area. A pedestrian tunnel at the southern end of the alleys, just to the right of the cheap clothes outlets, provides a short cut to the east side of Shinjuku Station and Studio Alta.

Higashi-Shinjuku

Some days it seems as if all of Tokyo is waiting at Shinjuku's favourite meeting spot, beneath the huge TV screen on the **Studio Alta** building on the east side of the JR station. If you arrange to meet anyone there, it's worth bearing in mind that the plaza opposite Studio Alta is generally less crowded, from where you can soak up the supercharged atmosphere, especially at night, when the district is ablaze with neon. To the southeast of here is **Shinjuku-dōri**, along which you'll find some of the classier department stores and shops, such as Mitsukoshi and Isetan (see p.225), which has excellent food halls in its basement, a good range of restaurants on its top floor and an art gallery that frequently holds notable exhibitions (check local English-language newspapers and magazines for details). In addition, beneath the pounding feet of pedestrians on Yasukuni-dōri lies an extensive subterranean shopping complex, **Shinjuku Subnade**, while a tunnel with exits to all the major shops runs the length of Shinjuku-dōri from the main JR station to the Shinjuku-Sanchōme subway station.

Pachinko

Could one in four Japanese be wrong? Throughout the country a staggering ¥30 trillion is spent each year on **pachinko**, a pinball game that is one of Japan's top pastimes – and also one of its major industries. Tokyo has thousands of pachinko parlours, and you'll find plenty in Shinjuku. They're easy to spot since they look like mini Las Vegas casinos on steroids, all flashing lights and big neon signs. Inside, the atmosphere is no less in-your-face. The noise of thousands of steel balls clattering through the upright electronic bagatelles is deafening, yet rows of players sit mesmerized as they control the speed with which balls fall through the machine – though the game requires a fair amount of luck and only limited skill.

The aim is to make the balls drop into the right holes so that more balls can be won. These are traded in for prizes such as cigarette lighters and calculators, and although it's illegal for the parlours to pay out cash, there's always a cubby-hole close by where prizes can be exchanged for money, a charade that the authorities have long turned a blind eye to. The initial cost of indulging in this mechanized mayhem can be as little as ¥100 for 25 ball bearings; just remember to take your earplugs too.

Kabukichō

Directly to the north of Studio Alta, across the wide boulevard of Yasukuni-dōri, lies the red-light district **Kabukichō** (歌舞伎町), at the heart of which is the Koma Theatre, where modern musicals and samurai dramas are performed. The tatty

△ The Studio Alta building

plaza in front of the theatre is lined with cinemas, many showing the latest Hollywood blockbusters.

The streets radiating around the theatre contain a wide range of bars and restaurants, but stray a block or so further north and you're deep in the raunchier side of Kabukichō, with soaplands, hostess bars and girly shows lining the narrow lanes. Though you stand a good chance of spotting members of the *yakuza* crime syndicates at work (the tight-perm hairdos and garish 1970s-style fashions are giveaway signs) around here, the overall atmosphere is not unlike London's Soho, where the porn industry and illicit goings-on nestle unthreateningly beside less salacious entertainment.

Local shopkeepers come to pray for business success at Kabukichō's attractive **Hanazono-jinja** (花園神社). This shrine predates the founding of Edo by the Tokugawa, but the current granite and vermilion buildings are modern recreations. It's worth paying a visit at night, when spotlights give the shrine a special ambience. From here, you're well poised to take a stroll through the **Golden Gai** (ゴールデン街), the low-rent drinking quarter where intellectuals and artists have rubbed shoulders with Kabukichō's demimonde since the war. In this compact grid of streets there are around two hundred bars, no larger than broom cupboards and presided over by no-nonsense *mama-sans* and *masters*. You probably won't want to stop for a drink here unless you speak good Japanese: most bars welcome regulars only, while the others will fleece you rotten. There are, however, a couple of exceptions, listed on p.195. The cinderblock buildings are constantly under threat from both property developers and from their own shoddy construction.

Shinjuku Gyoen and around

The largest, and arguably the most beautiful, garden in Tokyo is **Shinjuku Gyoen** (新宿御苑; Tues–Sun 9am–4.30pm, last entry 4pm; ¥200; @ www.shinjukugyoen .go.jp), its main entrance close by the Shinjuku-gyoenmae subway station. There's an alternative entry point through the western gate, a five-minute walk under and alongside the train tracks from Sendagaya Station.

The grounds, which once held the mansion of Lord Naitō, the *daimyō* of Tsuruga on the coast of the Sea of Japan, became the property of the Imperial Household in 1868, and the park was opened to the public after World War II. Apart from spaciousness, the gardens' most notable feature is the variety of design. The southern half is traditionally Japanese, with winding paths, stone lanterns, artificial hills and islands in ponds linked by zigzag bridges, and is home to *Rakuutei*, a pleasant **teahouse** (10am–4pm; ¥700). At the northern end of the park are formal, French-style gardens, with neat rows of tall birch trees and hedge-lined flowerbeds. Clipped, broad lawns dominate the middle of the park, modelled on English landscape design. On the eastern flank next to the large greenhouse (11am–3.30pm), packed with subtropical vegetation and particularly cosy on a chilly winter's day, an imperial wooden **villa** from 1869 has been reconstructed (open second and fourth Sat of the month 10am–3pm). In spring, the whole park bursts with pink and white cherry blossoms, while in early November kaleidoscopic chrysanthemum displays and golden autumn leaves are the main attractions. There are several **cafés** within the gardens where you can grab a reasonable lunch for around ¥900, but it's much nicer to bring a picnic and relax in the tranquil surroundings.

Walking back towards Shinjuku Station will take you past the gay and lesbian district of **Shinjuku Nichōme** (新宿二丁目). During the day the area is inconspicuous, but come nightfall a multitude of bars (see pp.203–204) spring into action, catering to every imaginable sexual orientation. Close by is **Taisō-ji** (太宗寺), a temple founded in 1668, which has the city's largest wooden statue of Yama, the

King of Hell. The statue is kept company by a large copper Buddha dressed in a red bib and cap. You have to press a button to illuminate the 5.5-metre Yama, whose fearsome expression is difficult to take seriously once you've spotted the offerings at his feet – a couple of tins of fruit are the norm.

West of Shinjuku: animation museums

Returning to Shinjuku Station, take the JR Chūō line six stops west to Ogikubo (荻窪), the closest station to **Suginami**, an area long associated with the animation industry, with several production houses and many key artists resident. It's also home to the **Suginami Animation Museum** (杉並アニメーションミュージアム; Tues–Sun 10am–5.30pm; free; Ⓦwww.sam.or.jp), which can be reached by a five-minute bus journey from either platform 0 or 1 outside Ogikubo Station. Astroboy, Gundam and many other anime characters are all present and correct at this well-organized museum atop a retro-looking function hall, with colourful displays tracing the development of animation in Japan, from the simple black-and-white 1917 feature *Genkanban-no-maki* (The Gatekeepers) to recent digital escapades such as *Blood: The Last Vampire*. Videos with English subtitles explain how anime are made, while interactive computer games allow you to create your own animations. You can watch anime screenings in the small theatre, and there's also a library packed with manga and DVDs (some with English subtitles).

The Ghibli Museum

Three stops further west along the Chūō line is **Mitaka** (三鷹), near where you'll find the charmingly inventive **Ghibli Museum, Mitaka** (ジブリミュージアム三鷹; daily except Tues 10am–6pm; ¥1000, reductions for children; ☎0570-055-777, Ⓦwww.ghibli-museum.jp), located at the southwest corner of leafy Inokashira Park. The museum celebrates the work of the Ghibli animation studio, responsible for some of Japan's biggest-ever movies, including *My Neighbour Totoro*, *Princess Mononoke* and the Oscar-winning *Spirited Away*. Beautifully designed throughout, the museum gives visitors an insight not only into Ghibli's films but also the anima-tor's art in general. There's also a small movie theatre where original short animated features, exclusive to the museum, are screened. Kids will love it, and it's a guaran-teed fun day out that will probably have you scurrying to the video shop later.

In order to keep the museum free of crowds, only 2400 **tickets** are available daily; all must be purchased in advance and are for a specified time. The museum's website lists details in English of how to apply for tickets overseas. This is much easier than applying for tickets in Japan itself, where you'll have first to make a reservation by phone (☎0570-084-633), then go to one of the country's 7600 Lawson convenience stores within three days to pick up your ticket; you'll need to specify the date and time (10am, noon, 2pm or 4pm) you would like to visit. Given the massive popularity of Ghibli's movies the museum can be booked out for weeks at a time, particularly during school holidays and over weekends.

The museum is a short walk or bus ride from the south exit of Mitaka Station. Follow the canal for about fifteen minutes towards **Inokashira Park** (井の頭公園), looking out for signs for the museum, or take the regular bus (¥200). It's a good idea to combine a visit here with a stroll around the park, which has a pleasant carp-filled lake, tree-shaded walks and a small zoo. Long a favourite haunt of courting couples, the park is mobbed by everyone during *hanami* season, when the numerous cherry trees produce a profusion of pink blossoms.

Tokyo architecture

Following mass destruction at the end of World War II, Tokyo has been reborn as the ultimate concrete, glass, steel and neon-illuminated metropolis. There's seldom been much of a grand plan to its built environment, resulting in the city's cluttered, ad hoc look. However, the capital's great wealth and relative lack of planning restrictions have given architects almost unparalleled freedom to realize their wildest dreams. The results have often been, quite simply, out of this world, and to date have helped three Japanese architects win the **Pritzker Prize**, the architecture world's equivalent of a Nobel Prize.

Postwar rebuilding

In the late 1940s and early 1950s, as Tokyo set about reconstruction, the priority was not aesthetic appeal but developing a functioning infrastructure. This led to the creation of one of Tokyo's most defining visual elements, the sinuous concrete ribbons of the Shuto Expressway, built across and over many of the rivers and canals that run through the capital.

The city was also gearing up for the 1964 Olympic Games, giving the late **Tange Kenzō** the chance to start making his mark on Tokyo with the iconic Olympic Stadium in Yoyogi, whose profile suggests a twentieth-century version of Noah's Ark.

▼ Fuji TV's headquarters

Awarded the Pritzker Prize in 1987, Tange has been strongly influenced by architects such as Le Corbusier and Walter Gropius; his work has modern structural and technological references, but is also firmly rooted in traditional Japanese design. His monumental Tokyo Metropolitan Government Building in Shinjuku – resembling a cross between an enormous computer chip and Notre Dame – has been described as the last great edifice of postmodernism, though some would argue that he went one step further with the otherworldly Fuji TV building in Odaiba, which looks like something out of a sci-fi anime.

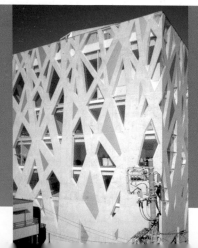

Natural inspiration

The Japanese love of nature is reflected in modern Tokyo architecture. The roof of Tokyo Budōkan, the martial-arts mecca designed by **Rokkaku Kijō**, evokes traditional paintings of overlapping mountains fading into the mists. The striking buildings of **Toyo Ito** – such as Tod's Omotesandō, with a concrete and glass facade that mimics the pattern of the avenue's zelkova trees, and the pink Mikimoto Ginza 2 building, with its windows that look like leopard spots – also have natural references.

◀ Tod's Omotesandō, built for the Italian shoe and leather goods company

Respecting tradition

Tange's synthesis of old and new design elements has been taken up by several other key Japanese architects of the postwar period, among them **Maki Fumihiko**, a former student of his. The recipient of the 1993 Pritzker Prize, Maki has a preference for glass and steel in his designs. His masterwork is Hillside Terrace, a complex of homes, offices and shops, its courtyards and vistas paying homage to ancient Japanese and Buddhist concepts of space. Developed over a 23-year period in ritzy Daikan'yama, it's considered a model of sympathetic small-scale urban development. For a contrast, search out his Spiral Hall in Aoyama, with its fragmented facade and an interior dominated by a seemingly freestanding spiral walkway.

▲ The Omotesandō Hills complex incorporates homes and upmarket shops

The art of Andō

Self-trained **Andō Tadao** has a particular way with concrete, which he frequently uses both rough and polished, so it becomes like the rarest of stone. The winner of the 1995 Pritzker Prize, Andō hails from Ōsaka, but it's his Tokyo edifices that have recently been attracting attention. His designs play with space in masterful ways – witness the atrium, with its off-kilter walkway, of the commercial and residential development Omotesandō Hills; the intriguing subterranean galleries of the 21_21 Design Sight at Tokyo Midtown, and the interior design shop Hhstyle.com/casa, the walls and ceilings folding in on themselves like a giant piece of origami.

▲ 21_21 Design Sight

Foreign flair

Tokyo's taste for daring (and sometimes daft) architecture reached its zenith in the boom years of the 1980s, when money was no object. Tempting financial offers attracted star overseas architects and designers to the city, including **Philippe Starck**, who created the Super Dry Hall in Asakusa, with its giant rooftop sculpture, officially called Flamme d'Or (but often referred to as the "golden turd"). Infinitely more elegant is the light-flooded glass hall of **Rafael Viñoly's** Tokyo International Forum in Yūrakuchō. **Sir Norman Foster's** Century Tower near Ochanomizu incorporates the vernacular design of the *torii* (shrine gate), ten of which appear to be piled on top of each other on the building's facade. Poke around Shinjuku and you'll be surprised by **Sir Richard Rogers'** Kabukichō Building, hidden on a side street and swathed in a framework of stainless-steel rods.

Among the outstanding designs of the new millennium is **Jacques Herzog** and **Pierre de Meuron's** Prada building on Omotesandō, a jewel-like edifice of rhomboid crystals, cuddled on one side by a velvety, moss-covered wall. Also doing amazing things with glass is Tokyo-based British architect **Benjamin Warner**, whose Audi Forum looks like a giant iceberg adrift on Meiji-dōri in Harajuku.

Towering ambitions

One of the most densely packed cities on earth, until recently Tokyo has also been predominantly low rise, partly due to the fear of earthquakes. Engineering advances, plus a re-energized economy, mean that skyscrapers are now sprouting across the city like giant sunflowers. Among the most striking is the Kohn Pedersen Fox-designed Mori Tower, the high point of Roppongi Hills; admire it from afar and you'll notice how the building partly resembles an enormous samurai helmet. Also noteworthy is the Skidmore Owings & Merrill-designed Midtown Tower, the apex of Tokyo Midtown, and inspired by a sculpture by the Japanese-American artist Isamu Noguchi. This is currently the city's tallest building, at 248m, but it will be eclipsed in 2011 by Andō Tadao and Sukmikawa Kiichi's New Tokyo Tower, in Sumida-ku. Like its predecessor, this will primarily be a communications tower and, at 610m, it will be the world's tallest man-made structure.

Further exploration

The quirky ⓦaruki-tect.moo.jp website celebrates the full range of modern Tokyo architecture. It has downloadable maps, some in English, pointing out key buildings; the people behind the site also arrange occasional guided tours. Also useful is *The Architectural Map of Tokyo*, published by TOTO and available at the bookshop at Gallery Ma (see p.81), with details of 534 notable buildings constructed since 1980, though note that it's in Japanese, apart from the addresses. It comes in a handy pocket size, as does Tajima Noriyuki's *Tokyo: A Guide to Recent Architecture*, which remains one of the best architecture guides around, despite missing out on some of the past decade's additions to the city's skyline.

10

Harajuku and Aoyama

The super-chic shopping and entertainment districts of **Harajuku** (原宿) and **Aoyama** (青山) are a collective showcase for contemporary Tokyo fashion and style. Consumer culture reigns supreme in these streets, packed with smart cafés, designer boutiques and hip young spenders in search of the latest fashions and the most desirable labels. Youthful and creative, Harajuku caters to the funky, adventurous fashionista, while those with gilt-edged credit cards will feel more at home among the established fashion houses and antique shops of Aoyama – although in recent years the two worlds have been blurring, as witnessed by the sprouting of big brand boutiques along **Omotesandō**, the area's key tree-lined boulevard, often referred to as Tokyo's Champs Elysées.

Even if shopping's not your bag, there are other good reasons for coming here, the best being the verdant grounds of the city's most venerable shrine, **Meiji-jingū**. Neighbouring **Yoyogi-kōen** was the focus of the 1964 Olympics, and several of the stadia surrounding it are a legacy of that event. Just off Omotesandō are a clutch of interesting **galleries**, including the **Ōta Memorial Museum of Art**, dedicated to *ukiyo-e* prints, and the anarchic **Design Festa Gallery**. Finally, the peaceful grounds of **Aoyama Cemetery**, containing the graves of many Tokyo notables, are particularly worth strolling through during the cherry-blossom season, but are worth a visit at any time of year.

Meiji-jingū

Covering parts of both Aoyama and Harajuku is **Meiji-jingū** (明治神宮; Ⓦ www .meijijingu.or.jp), Tokyo's premier Shinto shrine, a memorial to Emperor Meiji, who died in 1912, and his empress Shōken, who died in 1914. Together with the neighbouring shrines to General Nogi and Admiral Tōgō (see p.117), Meiji-jingū was created as a symbol of imperial power and Japanese racial superiority. Rebuilt in 1958 after being destroyed during World War II, the shrine remains the focus of several annual **festivals** (see box, p.115). Apart from the festivals, Meiji-jingū is best visited midweek, when its calm serenity can be appreciated without the crowds.

The shrine is split into two sections about a kilometre apart. The **Outer Garden**, between and south of Sendagaya and Shinanomachi stations, contains the Meiji Memorial Picture Gallery and several sporting arenas, including the National Stadium and Jingū Baseball Stadium, while the more important **Inner Garden**, beside Harajuku Station, includes the emperor's shrine, the empress's iris gardens, the imperial couple's Treasure House and extensive wooded grounds.

114

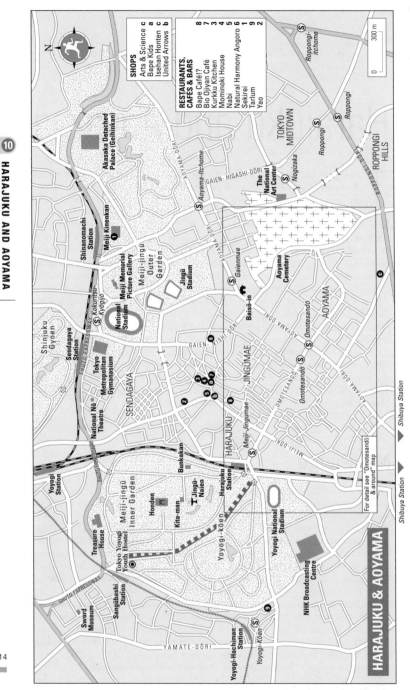

HARAJUKU & AOYAMA

SHOPS

Arts & Science	c
Bape Kids	a
Isehan Honten	c
United Arrows	b

RESTAURANTS, CAFES & BARS

Bape Café!?	8
Bio Ojiyan Café	7
Kurkku Kitchen	3
Mominoki House	4
Nabi	5
Natural Harmony Angoro	6
Sekirei	1
Tarlum	9
Yao	2

0   300 m

N

Sword Museum

Yoyogi-Hachiman Station

Yoyogi-Kōen

YAMATE-DŌRI

Sangūbashi Station

SHUTO EXPRESSWAY

Treasure House

Yoyogi Station

Meiji-jingū Inner Garden

Honden

Kita-mon

Jingū-Naien

Tokyo Yoyogi Youth Hostel

Yoyogi-Kōen

NHK Broadcasting Centre

Yoyogi National Stadium

Bunkakan

Harajuku Station

Meiji-jingū-mae

HARAJUKU

Meiji-Jingūmae

MEIJI-DŌRI

For detail see "Omotesandō & around" map

Shinjuku Gyoen

Sendagaya Station

National Nō Theatre

Tokyo Metropolitan Gymnasium

SENDAGAYA

Kokuritsu-Kyōgijō

National Stadium

SHUTO EXPRESSWAY

Shinanomachi Station

Meiji Kinenkan

Meiji Memorial Picture Gallery

Meiji-jingū Outer Garden

Jingū Stadium

GAIEN-NISHI-DŌRI

JINGŪMAE

Aoyama-Itchome

AOYAMA-DŌRI

GAIEN-HIGASHI-DŌRI

Akasaka Detached Palace (Geihinkan)

Baisō-in

Gaienmae

OMOTESANDŌ

Omotesandō

Omotesandō

AOYAMA-DŌRI

Aoyama Cemetery

AOYAMA

AOYAMA-DŌRI

The National Art Center

Nogizaka

Roppongi

Roppongi

TOKYO MIDTOWN

ROPPONGI HILLS

Roppongi

Roppongi-itchome

Festivals at Meiji-jingū

Meiji-Jingū is the focus of several important festivals during the year, the most popular of which is **Hatsu-mōde** (literally, "first shrine visit of the year"), held on January 1 and attracting three million visitors – traffic lights are set up within the shrine grounds to control the crowds on the day.

More entertaining is **Seijin-no-hi** (Adults' Day), on the second Monday in January. On this day, 20-year-olds attend the shrine to celebrate their coming of age and to seek blessings from the gods; the women often dress in elaborate long-sleeved kimono, with fur stoles wrapped around their necks, while Meiji-jingū's gravel approach is lined with ice sculptures and there's a colourful display of traditional *momoteshiki* archery by costumed archers.

From April 29 to May 3 and November 1 to 3, *bugaku* (court music and dances) are performed on a stage erected in the shrine's main courtyard, while **Shichi-go-san-no-hi** (Seven-Five-Three Day), on November 15, provides an opportunity to see children of these ages dressed in delightful mini-kimono.

The Outer Garden and around

Although Meiji-jingū's Outer Garden can be accessed from Shinanomachi JR station or Kokuritsu-kyōgijō on the subway, the main entrance is from the south, via the long ginkgo-tree-lined approach road close to Aoyama-itchōme subway station. To the left are rugby and baseball stadiums, to the right the wedding hall and restaurant complex **Meiji Kinenkan** (home to the delightful summer beer garden *Sekirei*; see p.192). At the head of the avenue is the **Meiji Memorial Picture Gallery** (Meiji Kaigakan; 明治絵画館; daily 9am–5pm; ¥500; ☎03/3401-5179) built in a similar Western style to the National Diet Building, with a marble-clad entrance hall which soars up to a central dome. On either side are halls containing forty paintings which tell the life story of Emperor Meiji, though they're of interest more for their depiction of Japan emerging from its feudal past than for their artistic merits.

Next to the gallery looms the 75,000-seater **National Stadium**, Japan's largest sporting arena, built for the 1964 Olympics. On the western side of the stadium – and best viewed from outside Sendagaya Station – is the Outer Garden's most striking feature: the **Tokyo Metropolitan Gymnasium**, designed by Maki Fumihiko. At first glance the building looks like a giant alien spacecraft, though on closer examination it becomes obvious that the inspiration is a traditional samurai helmet. The corrugated stainless-steel-roofed building houses the main arena, while in the block to the right, crowned with a glass pyramid roof, are public swimming pools and a subterranean gym (entry ¥450).

Following the railway line and road west leads you to a sign pointing to the **National Nō Theatre** (Kokuritsu Nōgakudō; 国立能劇場), set back from the street in a walled compound. Built in 1983, the theatre incorporates traditional Japanese architectural motifs, particularly in the design of its slightly sloping roofs. This is one of the best places in which to see a production of Nō, Japan's oldest and most stylized form of theatre – and something of an acquired taste. Return to the main road and follow the raised expressway as it crosses over the railway lines, then veer off left up the hill to Meiji-jingū's Inner Garden northeastern entrance.

The Inner Garden

The most impressive way to approach the **Inner Garden** is through the southern gate next to Jingū-bashi, the bridge across from Harajuku's station, a toy-town-like building complete with mock-Tudor clock tower. From the gateway a wide gravel path runs through densely forested grounds to the twelve-metre-high **Ō-torii**, the largest Myōjin-style gate in Japan, made from 1500-year-old cypress pine trees from Taiwan. Just before the gate, on the right, is the **Bunkakan**, a modern complex housing a restaurant, café, gift shop and the generally uninteresting annexe of the **Treasure House** (daily: Jan–March & Dec 9.30am–3.30pm; April–Nov 8.30am–4pm; ¥500 entry for both buildings); this is where you'll alight from your bus if you visit on an organized tour. To the left of the Ō-torii is the entrance to the **Jingū Naien** (神宮内苑; daily 8.30am–5pm; ¥500), a traditional garden – said to have been designed by the Emperor Meiji for his wife – which is at its most beautiful (and most crowded) in June, when over one hundred varieties of **irises**, the empress's favourite flowers, pepper the lush greenery with their purple and white blooms.

From the garden's main entrance, the gravel path turns right and passes through a second wooden *torii*, **Kita-mon** (north gate), leading to the impressive **honden** (central hall). With their Japanese cypress wood and green copper roofs, the buildings are a fine example of how Shinto architecture can blend seamlessly with nature. There are exits from the courtyard on its eastern and western flanks; follow either of the paths northwards through the woods to arrive at the pleasant grassy slopes and pond before the main **Treasure House** (same hours as annexe). Don't bother going in, though – the contents of the museum are no more thrilling than the lumpen grey concrete building that houses them.

Yoyogi-kōen

Apart from the wooded grounds of Meiji-jingū, Harajuku is also blessed with Tokyo's largest park, **Yoyogi-kōen** (代々木公園), a favourite spot for joggers and bonneted groups of kindergarten kids with their minders. Once an imperial army training ground, the park was dubbed "Washington Heights" after World War II, when it was used to house US military personnel. In 1964 the land was used for the Olympic athletes' village, after which it became Yoyogi-kōen. Two of the stadia, built for the Olympics, remain the area's most famous architectural features. The main building of Tange Kenzō's **Yoyogi National Stadium** (Ⓦ www.naash .go.jp/yoyogi) is a dead ringer for Noah's ark, and its steel suspension roof was a structural engineering marvel at the time. The smaller stadium, used for basketball, is like the sharp end of a giant swirling seashell.

Omotesandō and around

Harajuku's most elegant boulevard, **Omotesandō** (表参道), leads from the main entrance to Meiji-jingū to the cluster of contemporary designer boutiques on the other side of Aoyama-dōri. On either side are dense networks of streets, packed with funky little shops, restaurants and bars. One of the most famous roads is **Takeshita-dōri** (竹下通り), whose hungry mouth gobbles up teenage fashion victims as they swarm out of the north exit of Harajuku Station and spits them out the other end on Meiji-dōri, minus their cash. Selling every kind of tat imaginable, the shops here are hugely enjoyable to root around in and provide an intriguing window on Japanese teen fashion. On Sundays the crush of bodies on the street is akin to that on the Yamanote line at rush hour.

Serious bargain-hunters never miss out on the outdoor antiques market held on the first and fourth Sundays of each month in the precincts of **Tōgō-jinja** (東郷神社),

△ The entrance to the Inner-garden, near Harajuku station

just off Takeshita-dōri. The market sells everything from fine *tansu* (traditional Japanese chests) to old kimono and crockery. You'll need to know what you're looking for to avoid being ripped off, but it's also possible to snag bargains if you come at the end of the day when the stalls are packing up and the sellers are prepared to haggle. The **shrine** itself, with a pretty pond and garden fronting onto Meiji-dōri, is dedicated to Admiral Tōgō Heihachirō, who led the victorious Japanese fleet against the Russians in the Russo–Japanese War of 1904–1905.

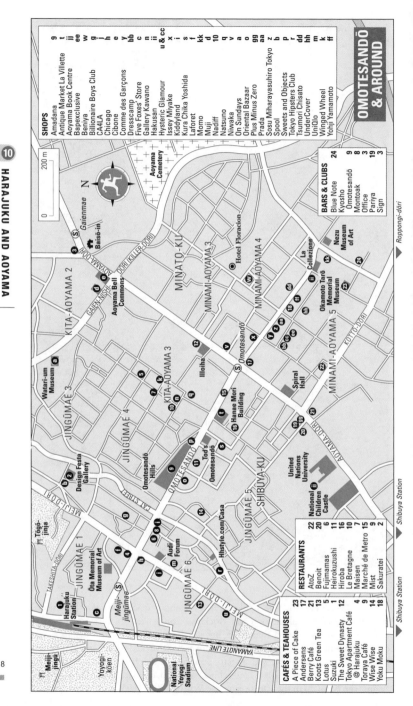

OMOTESANDŌ & AROUND

SHOPS

Amadana	g
Antique Market La Villette	t
Aoyama Book Centre	jj
Bapexclusive	ee
Beniya	w
Billionaire Boys Club	g
CA4LA	j
Chicago	h
Cibone	e
Comme des Garçons	y
Dresscamp	bb
Five Foxes' Store	c
Gallery Kawano	n
Hakusan	ii
Hysteric Glamour	u & cc
Issey Miyake	x
Kiddyland	i
Kura Chika Yoshida	s
Laforet	f
Momo	kk
Muji	d
Nadiff	10
Natsuno	q
Niwaka	v
On Sundays	a
Oriental Bazaar	o
Plus Minus Zero	gg
Prada	aa
Sosu Miharayasuhiro Tokyo	z
Spool	b
Sweets and Objects	p
Tokyo Hipsters Club	r
Tsumori Chisato	dd
UnderCover	hh
UniQlo	m
Winged Wheel	k
Yohji Yamamoto	ff

BARS & CLUBS

Blue Note	24
Kyosho Omotesandō	9
Montoak	8
Office	3
Pariya	19
Sign	3

RESTAURANTS

AtoZ	22
Benoit	20
Fujimamas	6
Heirokuzushi	11
Hiroba	16
Le Bretagne	10
Maisen	7
Marché de Metro	15
Mist	9
Sakuratei	2

CAFÉS & TEAHOUSES

A Piece of Cake	23
Andersens	17
Berry Café	21
Koots Green Tea	13
Lotus	5
Suzuki	1
The Sweet Dynasty	12
Tokyo Apartment Café @ Harajuku	4
Toraya Café	9
Wise Wise	14
Yoku Moku	18

Back towards the crossing with Omotesandō, look out for Laforet, a trendy boutique complex, behind which is the excellent **Ōta Memorial Museum of Art** (Ōta Kinen Bijutsukan; 太田記念美術館; Tues–Sun 10.30am–5pm; fee varies with exhibition; ☎03/3403-0880, Ⓦwww.ukiyoe-ota-muse.jp). You'll have to leave your shoes in the lockers and put on slippers to wander the small galleries on two levels, featuring *ukiyo-e* paintings and prints from the private collection of the late Ōta Seizō, an insurance tycoon. The art displayed comes from a collection of twelve thousand pieces, including masterpieces by Utamaro, Hokusai and Hiroshige.

In complete contrast to all this is the **Design Festa Gallery** (デザイン・フェスタ・ギャラリー; daily 11am–8pm; free; ☎03/3479-1442, Ⓦwww.designfesta.com), an anything-goes art space sprouting out of the funky backstreets of Harajuku like some bargain-basement Pompidou Centre. The gallery is an offshoot of Design Festa, Japan's biggest art and design event, held twice a year at Tokyo Big Sight (see p.139). It's hard to believe that beneath the day-glo paintings, graffiti, mad scaffolding and traffic cones, swarming over the building's front like some alien metal creeper, lies a block of ordinary apartments. Inside the art is no less eclectic, ranging from sculpture to video installations – even the toilet is plastered from floor to ceiling with artworks. Behind it is a good *okonomiyaki* café and bar. To find the gallery, take the street directly opposite the eastern Meiji-dōri end of Takeshita-dōri, then turn north at the second junction on your left.

Omotesandō Hills

Sheltering behind the zelkova trees on the northern flank of Omotesandō is the Andō Tadao-designed **Omotesandō Hills** (Ⓦwww.omotesandohills.com), a glitzy complex of upmarket designer shops, restaurants and residences that's part of the Mori Corporation's family of new Tokyo developments. At the southeastern corner Andō has recreated part of the Dojunkai Aoyama Apartments, as a homage to the much-loved housing block that once stood on the site. In their later years, the original crumbling apartments were occupied by all manner of artists and small boutiques, and many felt that something of the district's bohemian spirit had been lost when they were destroyed to make way for Omotesandō Hills.

While Omotesandō Hills' atrium, with open walkways winding down several levels, is impressive, a more dazzling Andō creation lies close by, along sinewy Cat Street heading towards Shibuya. Here you'll find his **Hhstyle.com/Casa** building (6-14-5 Jingūmae, Shibuya-ku), an angular concrete and black-corrugated-iron construction that's as startling as some of the area's high-fashion apparel.

Aoyama

Harajuku's chaotic creativity finally gives way to Aoyama's sleek sophistication, as Omotesandō crosses Aoyama-dōri and narrows to a two-lane street lined with the boutiques of many of Japan's top designers. The most striking building of all, though, is the glass bubble designed by Jacques Herzog and Pierre de Meuron for **Prada** – a tourist attraction in its own right.

At the far eastern end of Omotesandō, the road to the left leads round into Tokyo's most important graveyard, officially entitled Aoyama Reien (青山霊園), but generally known as **Aoyama Bochi**. Everyone who was anyone, including Hachikō the faithful dog (see p.121), is buried here, and the graves, many decorated with elaborate calligraphy, are interesting in their own right. Look out for the section where foreigners are buried: their tombstones provide a history of early *gaijin* involvement in Japan. Despite this being a cemetery, many locals enjoy partying here during the *hanami* season under the candyfloss bunches of pink cherry blossoms.

Turning right (south) at the end of Omotesandō brings you first to the entrance to the **Nezu Institute of Fine Arts** (Nezu Bijutsukan; 根津美術館; ☏03/3400-2536, Ⓦwww.nezu-muse.or.jp). Founded by Nezu Kaichiro of Tobū railways and department store fame, it houses a classy collection of Oriental arts, but is closed for renovations until the autumn of 2009. When it's open, the museum's nicest feature is its garden, which slopes gently away around an ornamental pond and features several traditional teahouses.

Continue for one long block and turn right again to reach the quirky **Okamoto Tarō Memorial Museum** (Okamoto Tarō Kinenkan; 岡本太郎記念館; daily except Tues 10am–5.30pm; ¥600; Ⓦtaro-okamoto.or.jp), once the studio of the avant-garde artist (1911–96) whose most famous creation is the *Tower of the Sun* sculpture, the symbol of Ōsaka's Expo in 1970. The museum houses examples of his intriguing, often whimsical work as well as a pleasant café (see p.183), while another of his bizarre, cartoon-like sculptures can be seen outside the nearby National Children's Castle (see below). There's another, larger, museum devoted to him at Kawasaki (Ⓦwww.taromuseum.jp), between Tokyo and Yokohama.

Taking the first left after leaving the museum will quickly bring you to **Kottō-dōri** (骨董道り), "antique street"; you'll find several shops selling old (and generally overpriced) wares along here, as well as more designer boutiques. At its southern end Kottō-dōri merges with Roppongi-dōri, while at its northern end it joins back with Aoyama-dōri. Immediately the right of the latter junction is the **Spiral Hall**, a striking piece of architecture which includes a gallery, a couple of restaurants and a trendy card shop. The interior, with its sweeping, seemingly free-standing ramp walkway, is worth a look.

Heading left (southwest) from Kottō-dōri along Aoyama-dōri will take you towards Shibuya, passing the Tange Kenzō-designed **United Nations University**, a research arm of the UN, and the very uncastle-like **National Children's Castle** (こどもの城; Tues–Fri 12.30–5.30pm, Sat & Sun 10am–5pm; ¥500; ☏03/3797-5666, Ⓦwww.kodomono-shiro.or.jp), housing a large kids' playground and featuring a hotel (see p.151) and swimming pool (¥300 extra).

⑪

Shibuya

As a mind-blowing introduction to contemporary Tokyo, it's hard to beat **Shibuya** (渋谷), birthplace of a million-and-one consumer crazes. Here teens and 20-somethings throng Centre Gai, the shopping precinct that splits the district's rival department-store groups: **Tōkyū** (who own the prime station site, the Mark City complex and the Bunkamura arts hall) and **Seibu** (whose outlets include the fashionable, youth-oriented Loft and Parco stores). Although there are a few interesting museums in the area – most particularly the **Japan Folk Crafts Museum** – Shibuya is primarily an after-dark destination, when the neon signs of scores of restaurants, bars and cinemas battle it out with five-storey-tall TV screens for the attention of passers-by.

The plaza on the west side of Shibuya Station was the famous waiting spot of the ever-faithful mutt **Hachikō** (see box below) and is the best place from which to take in the area's evening buzz. Head to the upper floors of the adjacent **Shibuya Mark City**, a restaurant and hotel complex, for a bird's-eye view of the area. Opposite, to the west, the **109 Building** stands at the apex of Bunkamura-dōri and Dōgenzaka, the latter leading up to **Dōgenzaka** (道玄坂), one of Tokyo's most famous love-hotel districts. This area is named after Owada Dōgen, a thirteenth-century highwayman who robbed travellers on their way through the then isolated valley. Running parallel to the north of Bunkamura-dōri is the pedestrianized **Centre Gai** (センター街), always packed with trend-obsessed Tokyoites gathering to create or spot the latest look.

Hachikō: a dog's life

The story of **Hachikō** the dog proves that fame in Japan comes to those who wait. Every morning, the Akita pup faithfully accompanied his master Ueda Eisaburō, a professor in the Department of Agriculture at the Imperial University, to Shibuya Station, and returned to the station in the evening to greet him. In May 1925, Professor Ueda died while at work, but Hachikō continued to turn up every day at the station. By 1934, Hachikō had waited patiently for nine years, and locals were so touched by the dog's devotion that a bronze statue was cast of him.

In 1935, Hachikō was finally united in death with his master and was buried with Ueda in Aoyama cemetery. The stuffed skin of a second dog was used to create a doppelgänger Hachikō, which can be seen at the National Science Museum. During World War II, the original Hachikō statue was melted down for weapons, but a replacement was reinstated beside the station in 1948. Today, this is the most famous rendezvous in all Tokyo, though the throngs of people around the small statue and the rats that rummage through the rubbish in the surrounding bushes mean that it's not a particularly convivial place to hang out.

SHIBUYA

▲ NHK Studio Park   ▲ Omotesandō

▼ Japan Folk Crafts Museum, Shimo-Kitazawa ⓟ   ▼ Tōguri Museum of Art

ACCOMMODATION

Arimax Hotel	A
Capsule Land Shibuya	E
Cerulean Tower Tōkyū Hotel	F
Granbell Hotel	G
National Children's Castle Hotel	C
Shibuya Creston Hotel	B
Shibuya Excel Hotel Tōkyū	D

RESTAURANTS & CAFÉS

Beacon	4
Christon Café	19
Gaya	17
Gonpachi	25
Kaikaya	28
Kurage	2
Lion	23
Moph	5
Respekt	8
Sonoma	16
Underground	7
Mr Zoogunzoo	15
Wired Café	

BARS & CLUBS

Belgo	27
Chestnut and Squirrel	24
Club Asia	18
Club Quattro	9
Coins Bar	3
Crocodile	1
Cozmos Café & Bar	12
Harlem	22
Fujiya Honten	26
JZ Brat	F
Karaoke-kan	10
La Fabrique	11
Legato	25
Pink Cow	6
Red Bar	13
The Ruby Room	16
Shibuya O-East	20
Womb	21
Xanadu	14

SHOPS

HMV	g
Itō-ya	k
Loft	j
Mandarake	h
Nihon Mingeikan	p
Parco	e & f
Pink Dragon	d
Recofan	n
Seibu	i
Three Minute	b
Happiness	m & o
Tōkyū	c
Tōkyū Hands	l
Tower Books	d
Tower Records	a

Aoyama Hospital

National Children's Castle

Tokyo Metropolitan Children's Hall

Mitake-kōen

Miyashita-kōen

Shibuya Post Office

Shibuya Station

Bus Terminal

Hachiko the Dog Statue

Bus Terminal

TEPCO Electric Energy Museum

Tobacco and Salt Museum

Cinema Rise

Bagus

O-Front Building

109 Building

The Prime

Uplink

Bunkamura

Tōkyū

Shiespa (closed)

JINGŪMAE

SHIBUYA-KU

JINNAN 1

SHIBUYA 1

KŌEN-DŌRI

MEIJI-DŌRI

INOKASHIRA-DŌRI

AOYAMA-DŌRI

SHIBUYA 3

MEIJI-DŌRI

TAMAGAWA SHUTO EXPRESSWAY NUMBER 3

TAMAGAWA-DŌRI

DŌGEN-ZAKA

DŌGENZAKA

DŌGENZAKA 2

BUNKAMURA-DŌRI

SPAIN-ZAKA

UDAGAWACHO

NONBEI YOKOCHO

YAMANOTE LINE

TŌYOKO LINE

INOKASHIRA LINE

0   200 m

N

△ The Hachikō statue

Bunkamura and around

At the western end of Bunkamura-dōri is the main entrance to the **Bunkamura** (Ⓦwww.bunkamura.co.jp), an arts complex with an excellent gallery, showing temporary exhibitions of mainly Western art; a couple of cinemas, the 2000-seater Orchard Hall, home of the Tokyo Philharmonic Orchestra; and the Theatre Cocoon, which hosts some of the city's more avant-garde productions. The ticket counter is on the first floor (daily 10am–7.30pm; Ⓣ03/3477-3244 for programme information).

Walk a few minutes uphill behind the Bunkamura to reach the **Toguri Museum of Art** (Toguri Bijutsukan; 戸栗美術館; Tues–Sun 9.30am–5.30pm; ¥1000; Ⓣ03/3465-0070, Ⓦwww.toguri-museum.or.jp), which displays Edo-era and Chinese Ming-dynasty (1368–1644) ceramics. This small but exquisitely displayed exhibition, comprising selections from a collection of some six thousand pieces, is a must for those interested in pottery. Carefully positioned mirrors enable you to inspect the fine detail of work on the underside of displayed plates and bowls, and there's a pretty garden beside the lobby which you can gaze out on while sipping tea or coffee. Check the website for discount admission coupons.

North to NHK Studio Park

Heading directly north from the station past Seibu department store, veer left up Kōen-dōri to find the quirky **Tobacco and Salt Museum** (Tabako-to-Shio Hakubutsukan; たばこと塩の博物館; Tues–Sun 10am–5.30pm; ¥100; Ⓣ03/3476-2041, Ⓦwww.jti.co.jp/Culture/museum). Take the lift to the fourth floor, which has temporary exhibitions, and work your way down past displays on the third, which focus on the harvesting of salt from the sea and other sources of sodium. The second floor has the tobacco exhibits, including two thousand packets from around the world, and dioramas showing how the leaves were prepared for smoking in the past. It's all in Japanese, and only on the ground floor are you actually allowed to light up a fag.

At the top of Kōen-dōri, 200m north of the Tobacco and Salt Museum and opposite the Shibuya Ward Office and Public Hall, is the NHK Broadcasting Centre, housing Japan's equivalent of the BBC. You can take an entertaining tour around part of the complex by visiting the **NHK Studio Park** (NHKスタジオパーク; daily 10am–6pm, closed third Mon of the month; ¥200; ℡03/3485-8034, ⓦwww.nhk .or.jp/studiopark). Although it's all in Japanese, much of the exhibition is interactive: you get to try your hand as a newsreader and weather presenter and mess around on multimedia gadgets.

The Electric Energy Museum and the Metropolitan Children's Hall

If you've got kids in tow, there are a couple of places worth searching out close to Shibuya Station. On Fire Street, the **TEPCO Electric Energy Museum** (TEPCO Denryokukan; TEPCO電力館; daily except Wed 10am–6pm; free; ℡03/3477-1191, ⓦwww.denryokukan.com) has seven floors of exhibits relating to electricity. The English brochure says "Let's make friends with electricity" and TEPCO, Tokyo's power company, goes out of its way to convince you that this is possible, from hosting free movie screenings to cookery events. Magical Square on the fifth floor and the Energy World displays on the sixth will provide maximum distraction for inquisitive children.

Nip under the train tracks and across Meiji-dōri to reach **Tokyo Metropolitan Children's Hall** (Tōkyō-to Jidō Kaikan; 東京都児童会館; daily 9am–5pm; free; ℡03/3409-6361, ⓦwww.fukushihoken.metro.tokyo.jp/jidou), an excellent government-sponsored facility for kids, including a rooftop playground (Sat, Sun & holidays 10am–4pm), library, music room and craft-making activities.

Japan Folk Crafts Museum

Just two stops from Shibuya on the Keiō Inokashira line to Komaba-Tōdaimae Station, or a twenty-minute walk west of Dōgenzaka to Komaba-kōen, lies the

---

Shimokitazawa

The countercultural stronghold of **Shimokitazawa** (下北沢) is an interesting diversion, four stops west of Shibuya on the Keiō Inokashira line, and can also be reached from Shinjuku on the Odakyū line. Like Ueno, following World War II, Shimo (as it's affectionately called) became a black market centre. Its unruly bohemian atmosphere and bazaar-like structure, a warren of tangled streets packed with all manner of funky no-brand shops, cafés, bars and performance spaces, has remained, making it the antithesis of areas such as Ginza and Aoyama. Come here to browse for vintage clothes, furniture, old LPs and books.

Locals fear, however, that Shimo's distinctive atmosphere will be irreparably damaged following the planned construction of Route 54 through its midst. This longstanding local-authority objective has been made possible by a project (already under way) to run the currently overground Odakyū rail line underground. The plans for the new road will lay waste to many of the narrow streets clustered around the station and inevitably bring a level of gentrification so far scorned by Shimo. To battle the changes a pressure group, **Save The Shimokitazawa**, has been formed; their website ⓦwww.stsk.net has details in English of what is planned. For more information in Japanese on the area see ⓦwww.shimokitazawa.org, the website of Setagaya-ku, the local ward.

outstanding **Japan Folk Crafts Museum** (Mingeikan; 民芸館; Tues–Sun 10am–5pm; ¥1000; ☎03/3467-4527, ⓦwww.mingeikan.or.jp). Set in a handsome stone-and-stucco building, it's the best museum in the Shibuya area and a must-see for Japanese-craft fans, with an excellent collection of pottery, textiles and lacquerware. The gift shop is a fine source of souvenirs, and an annual competition and sale of new craft works is held between November 23 and December 3.

Opposite the museum stands a nineteenth-century **nagayamon** (long gate house), brought here from Tochigi-ken prefecture in northern Honshū by the museum's founder, Yanagi Soetsu, father of the famous designer Yanagi Sori.

⑫

Ebisu to Shinagawa

E bisu, like Shibuya just to the north, is best visited at night, when its many bars and restaurants are at their liveliest. The area is the home of the old Yebisu brewery, now developed into **Ebisu Garden Place**, a forerunner of Roppongi Hills and Shiodome as an integrated living, working, shopping and entertainment area; here you'll find the excellent **Tokyo Metropolitan Photography Museum**. Stroll uphill to the west of Ebisu and you'll hit **Daikan'yama**, one of Tokyo's classiest districts and a great place to chill out at a pavement café or do a spot of window-shopping. From here, you can dip downhill again to explore the edgy creative hot spot of **Naka-Meguro**.

South along the Meguro River from here is **Meguro**, home to a couple of offbeat museums and the splendid wedding hall of **Meguro Gajoen**, as well as the tranquil **National Park for Nature Study** and the serene gardens of **Happōen**. Equally restrained and peaceful is the **Hatakeyama Collection** of tea-ceremony implements, overlooking an attractive traditional garden.

The booming transport and hotel hub of **Shinagawa**, east of Meguro, is the location of one of the original checkpoints on the Tōkaidō, the major highway into Edo during the reign of the shoguns. Nearby are the historic temple **Sengaku-ji**, a key location in Tokyo's bloodiest true-life samurai saga, and the **Hara Museum of Contemporary Art**, housing an interesting collection of modern art and a lovely café.

Ebisu

Named after the Shinto god of good fortune, **Ebisu** (恵比寿) is easily accessed either on the overground Yamanote line or the underground Hibiya line. The main focus of the area is **Yebisu Garden Place** (恵比寿ガーデンプレイス; Ⓦ www .gardenplace.jp), a huge shopping, office and entertainment complex, connected to the station by a long moving walkway. The complex is built on the site of the nineteenth-century Sapporo brewery that was once the source of the area's fortunes, and includes the glitzy *Westin Hotel*, a 39-storey tower, a cinema, a performance hall and a mock French chateau housing a Joël Robuchon restaurant.

Slated by professionals as an architectural cock-up, Yebisu Garden Place is nevertheless worth visiting for a couple of interesting museums. The best of these is the **Tokyo Metropolitan Museum of Photography** (Tōkyō-to Shashin Bijutsukan;

東京都写真美術館; Tues–Sun 10am–6pm, Thurs & Fri until 8pm; admission charges vary; ☎03/3280-0031, ⓦwww.syabi.com), on the west side of the complex. This has excellent changing exhibitions of shots by major Japanese and Western photographers, along with study rooms and an experimental photography and imaging room. The museum's policy of concentrating on one photographer at a time in its exhibitions allows you to see the artist's work develop and gain an understanding of the motivations behind it.

On the western side of the complex, behind the Mitsukoshi department store, the history of beer in Japan – and of the brewery that used to be here – is detailed at the lively **Yebisu Beer Museum** (Tues–Sun 10am–6pm; free; ☎03/5423-7255, ⓦwww.sapporobeer.jp/brewery/ebisu). Look out for the touchscreen video displays and a computer simulation, where one of the people taking part in the tour is chosen to be the leader of a virtual-reality tour around different aspects of the brewing process. There's also an opportunity to sample some of Sapporo's beers, at ¥200 for a small glass.

If you have time, head for the restaurants on the thirty-eighth and thirty-ninth floors of the **Yebisu Tower**, next to the photography museum; you don't need to eat or drink here to enjoy the spectacular free views of the city.

Daikan'yama and Naka-Meguro

Daikan'yama (代官山) is home to some of the city's classiest homes, shops and watering holes, and the village-like area's laid-back atmosphere is a refreshing break from the frenzy of nearby Shibuya, to which it's linked by the Tōkyū Tōyoko line. It's also possible to get here by taking a ten-minute stroll uphill from Ebisu Station, heading west along Komazawa-dōri.

Daikan'yama's contemporary style has been defined by the smart **Hillside Terrace** complex, designed by Maki Fumihiko (see *Tokyo architecture* colour section). Strung along leafy Kyū-yamate-dōri, the various stages of Hillside Terrace were developed over nearly a quarter-century; the **Hillside Gallery** here (Tues–Sun 10am–5pm; free), opposite the Danish Embassy, has interesting modern art exhibitions. Closer to the station are the smart **Daikan'yama Address** and **La Fuente** complexes, where you'll find more groovy boutiques and ritzy restaurants and cafés.

Immediately to the southwest (if you're walking along Komazawa-dōri, continue downhill from Daikan'yama, following the Hibiya line train tracks as they emerge above ground) is **Naka-Meguro** (中目黒), currently one of Tokyo's trendiest areas, with a laid-back, boho feel. Liberally sprinkled with eclectic boutiques and small cafés and bars, the district hugs the banks of the Meguro-gawa, a particularly lovely spot to head during cherry-blossom season and in the height of summer, when the waterway provides some natural air-conditioning. Just wandering along the river bank is a pleasure, but if you need an aim for your perambulations, you could cross to the southern bank and work your way uphill through the warren of streets to the low-key **Museum of Contemporary Sculpture** (Gendai Chōkoku Bijutsukan; 現代彫刻美術館; Tues–Sun 10am–5pm, closed mid-Dec to mid-Jan; free; 4-12-18 Naka-Meguro, Meguro-ku; ☎03/3792-5858, ⓦwww.museum-of-sculpture.org). This small and somewhat dowdy facility, surrounded by an outdoor sculpture garden on several levels, focuses on Japanese sculptors from the latter half of the last century.

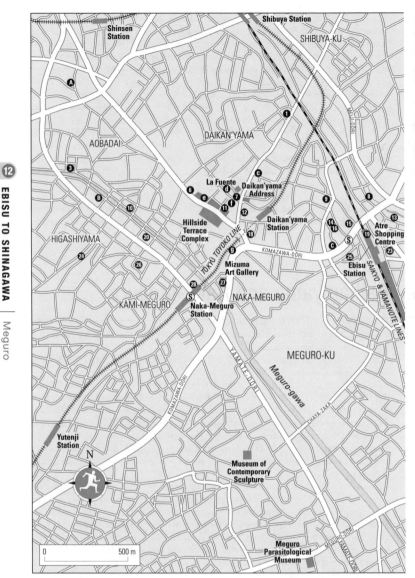

Meguro

The next station along the Yamanote line from Ebisu is **Meguro** (目黒); if you're at Yebisu Garden Place you only have another 500m to walk to reach here, passing a curious building with a giant red ball on its roof (it's a driving school).

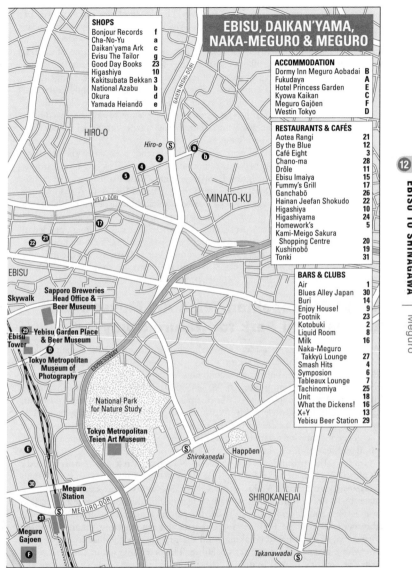

SHOPS

Bonjour Records	f
Cha-No-Yu	a
Daikan'yama Ark	c
Evisu The Tailor	g
Good Day Books	23
Higashiya	10
Kakitsubata Bekkan	3
National Azabu	b
Okura	d
Yamada Heiandō	e

EBISU, DAIKAN'YAMA, NAKA-MEGURO & MEGURO

ACCOMMODATION

Dormy Inn Meguro Aobadai	B
Fukudaya	A
Hotel Princess Garden	E
Kyowa Kaikan	C
Meguro Gajōen	F
Westin Tokyo	D

RESTAURANTS & CAFÉS

Aotea Rangi	21
By the Blue	12
Café Eight	3
Chano-ma	28
Drôle	11
Ebisu Imaiya	15
Fummy's Grill	17
Ganchabō	26
Hainan Jeefan Shokudo	22
Higashiya	10
Higashiyama	24
Homework's	5
Kami-Meigo Sakura Shopping Centre	20
Kushinobō	19
Tonki	31

BARS & CLUBS

Air	1
Blues Alley Japan	30
Buri	14
Enjoy House!	9
Footnik	23
Kotobuki	2
Liquid Room	8
Milk	16
Naka-Meguro Takkyū Lounge	27
Smash Hits	4
Symposion	6
Tableaux Lounge	7
Tachinomiya	25
Unit	18
What the Dickens!	13
X+Y	13
Yebisu Beer Station	29

HIRO-O

Hiro-o Ⓢ

MINATO-KU

EBISU

Sapporo Breweries Head Office & Beer Museum

Skywalk

Yebisu Garden Place & Beer Museum

Ebisu Tower

Tokyo Metropolitan Museum of Photography

EXPRESSWAY

National Park for Nature Study

Tokyo Metropolitan Teien Art Museum

Shirokanedai Ⓢ   Happōen

SHIROKANEDAI

Meguro Station Ⓢ

MEGURO-DORI

Meguro Gajoen

Takanawadai Ⓢ

From Meguro Station, follow the road southwest downhill, towards the towering wedding hall complex of **Meguro Gajōen** (目黒雅叙園; ☎03/5434-3920, ⓦwww.megurogajoen.co.jp). The current building replaced the original wedding hall, built in the very early twentieth century and known as Ryūgū-jō (Fairytale Dragon Palace). All that remains of that is the *hyakudan kaidan* which, despite its name ("one-hundred-step stairway") has 99 steps, leading to a series of spectacular rooms decorated in ornate style. Much of the year the *hyakudan kaidan* is off-limits to visitors, but occasionally the wedding hall runs special tours, including a slap-up lunch (courses starting at around ¥6300) at one of several restaurants here. You can still get a taste of the old wedding hall's fantastic nature in the rest of the complex, where many restored painted wooden carvings (huge *ukiyo-e*-style panoramas of kimonoed ladies and samurai warriors) and lacquer and mother-of-pearl inlaid scenes of flowers and birds, culled from the old building, decorate the enormous interior – big enough to host some twenty-odd weddings simultaneously. Visit at the weekend and the place buzzes with bridal parties. The complex also has a good hotel (see p.147).

Return to Meguro-dōri and walk a few blocks further west across the Meguro-gawa and up the hill just beyond Yamate-dōri to reach Tokyo's most curious "date" destination – the **Meguro Parasitological Museum** (Meguro Kiseichū-kan; 目黒寄生虫館; Tues–Sun 10am–5pm; free; ☎03/3716-1264). Any ideas you had of Japan being a healthy place to live will quickly be dispelled by these two floors of exhibits, which emphasize the dangers of creepy-crawlies in uncooked food. Specimens include record-breaking tapeworms (one is 8.8m long), pickled in jars, along with some gruesome photographs of past victims, including one poor fellow whose swollen testicles scrape the ground. For a bizarre reason the museum has developed a reputation as place to visit for courting couples, so don't be surprised if you feel a little like a gooseberry if you wander around alone.

Tokyo Metropolitan Teien Art Museum and the National Park for Nature Study

Approachable from either Meguro or Shirokanedai stations, the elegant **Tokyo Metropolitan Teien Art Museum** (Tōkyō-to Teien Bijutsukan; 東京都庭園美術館; daily 10am–6pm, but closed second and fourth Wed of the month; entrance fee depends on the exhibition; ☎03/3443-0201, ⓦwww.teien-art-museum.ne .jp). This Art Deco building is the former home of Prince Asaka Yasuhiko, Emperor Hirohito's uncle, who lived in Paris for three years during the 1920s, where he developed a taste for the European style. It's worth popping in to admire the gorgeous interior decoration and landscaped grounds, with Japanese gardens, pond and tea-ceremony house (entry to gardens only is ¥200).

Next to the grounds is the spacious **National Park for Nature Study** (Kokuritsu Shizen Kyōikuen; 国立自然教育園; Tues–Sun 9am–4.30pm, May–Aug until 5pm; ¥300; ☎03/3441-7176, ⓦwww.ins.kahaku.go.jp), an attempt to preserve the original natural features of the countryside before Edo was settled and developed into Tokyo. It partially succeeds – among the eight thousand trees in the park are some that have been growing for five hundred years; frogs can be heard croaking amid the grass beside the marshy ponds; and the whole place is a bird-spotter's paradise. The best thing about the park is that entry at any one time is limited to three hundred people, making it one of the few public areas in Tokyo where you can really escape the crowds. The closest subway station to the park is Shirokanedai.

Happōen and the Hatakeyama Collection

Shirokanedai Station is also the handiest jumping-off point for the lovely **Happōen** (八芳園; daily 10am–5pm; free). The garden's name means "beautiful from any angle" and, despite the addition of a modern wedding hall on one side, this is still true. A renowned adviser to the shogunate, Hikozaemon Okubo, lived here during the early seventeenth century, but most of the garden's design dates from the early twentieth century, when a business tycoon bought up the land, built a classical Japanese villa (still standing by the garden's entrance) and gave the garden its present name. Take a turn through its twisting pathways and you'll pass two 100-year-old bonsai trees, a stone lantern said to have been carved eight hundred years ago by the Heike warrior Taira-no Munekiyo, and a central pond. Nestling amid the trees is the delightful **teahouse** (daily 11am–5pm; ¥800), where ladies in kimonos will serve you *matcha* and *okashi*. At weekends the whole scene is enlivened by many smartly dressed wedding parties, lining up for group photos against the verdant backdrop.

Around 600m south of Happōen, in the midst of a quiet residential area, is another pretty Japanese garden overlooked by the formal restaurant *Hannya-en*, specializing in *kaiseki-ryōri* cuisine (see p.162), and the **Hatakeyama Collection** (畠山記念館; Tues–Sun: April–Sept 10am–5pm; Oct–March 10am–4.30pm; ¥500; ℡03/3447-5787, ⓦ www.ebara.co.jp/socialactivity/hatakeyama). Devoted to the art of the tea ceremony, this compact but appealing museum houses the collection of business magnate Hatakeyama Issei, who made his fortune manufacturing waste incinerators and pumps. Hatakeyama had exquisite taste and his collection contains many lovely pieces, including implements used in the tea ceremony and works of art; he also designed the building, which reflects the structure of a traditional teahouse, albeit on a much larger scale. Tea (¥400) is served in the exhibition hall until thirty minutes before closing. The closest subway station is Takanawadai, a couple of minutes' walk southeast of the museum.

Shinagawa

East of Meguro is the transport and hotel hub of **Shinagawa** (品川), the location of one of the original checkpoints on the Tōkaidō, the major highway into Edo during the reign of the shoguns. The opening in 2003 of a new Shinkansen station

The 47 rōnin

Celebrated in Kabuki and *bunraku* plays, as well as on film, *Chūshingura* is a true story of honour, revenge and loyalty. In 1701, a young *daimyō*, Asano Takumi, became embroiled in a fatal argument in the shogun's court with his teacher and fellow lord Kira Yoshinaka. Asano had lost face in his performance of court rituals and, blaming his mentor for his lax tuition, drew his sword within the castle walls and attacked Kira. Although Kira survived, the shogun, on hearing of this breach of etiquette, ordered Asano to commit *seppuku*, the traditional form of suicide, which he did.

Their lord having been disgraced, Asano's loyal retainers, the **rōnin** – or masterless samurai – vowed revenge. On December 14, 1702, the 47 *rōnin*, lead by **Oishi Kuranosuke**, stormed Kira's villa (the remains of which are in Ryōgoku), cut off his head and paraded it through Edo in triumph before placing it on Asano's grave in Sengaku-ji. Although their actions were in line with the samurai creed, the shogun had no option but to order the *rōnin*'s deaths. All 47 committed *seppuku* on February 14, 1703, including Oishi's 15-year-old son. They were buried with Asano in Sengaku-ji, and today their graves are still wreathed in the smoke from the bundles of incense placed by their gravestones.

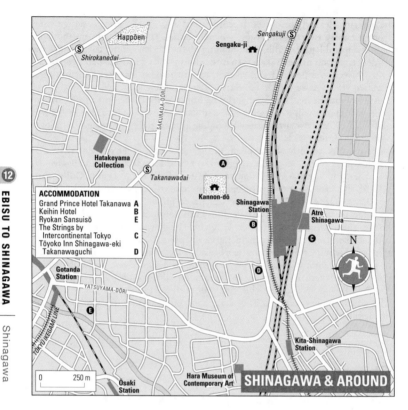

ACCOMMODATION
Grand Prince Hotel Takanawa   A
Keihin Hotel   B
Ryokan Sansuisō   E
The Strings by
  Intercontinental Tokyo   C
Tōyoko Inn Shinagawa-eki
  Takanawaguchi   D

SHINAGAWA & AROUND

here is revitalizing the area, mainly east of the tracks, where a clutch of modern towers reach for the sky, though none is particularly interesting to visit.

The best reason to head here is to visit the eclectic **Hara Museum of Contemporary Art** (Hara Bijutsukan; 原美術館; Tues–Sun 11am–5pm, Wed until 8pm; ¥1000; ☎03/3445-0651, ⓦwww.haramuseum.or.jp). Based in a 1938 Bauhaus-style house in a quiet residential area around 800m south of the station, the museum has a small permanent collection including quirky installations, such as *Rondo*, by Morimura Yasumasa, whose self-portrait occupies the downstairs toilet. The building itself, designed by Watanabe Jin, the architect responsible for Ueno's Tokyo National Museum and the Wakō department store in Ginza, is worth a look, as are the tranquil sculpture gardens overlooked by the museum's pleasant café.

Immediately west of Shinagawa Station is a compound containing three *Prince* hotels, built on the combined grounds of three imperial palaces, sold off after World War II. It's a pleasant diversion to duck into the Grand *Prince Hotel* Takanawa and walk through the gardens, parts of which are unchanged since they were the property of the emperor's family. Here you can see the **Kannon-dō**, a Kamakura-period temple rebuilt here in the 1954, and the neighbouring **Ean Tea House**, sadly not open to public viewing unless you can afford to rent it out for a meal or tea ceremony.

Sengaku-ji

Around a kilometre north of Shinagawa is the famous temple of **Sengaku-ji** (泉岳寺), home to the graves of **Asano Takumi** and his **47 rōnin** (see box, p.131); the closest station is Sengaku-ji on the Toei Asakusa line. Most of the temple was destroyed during the war and has since been rebuilt, but a striking gate dating from 1836 and decorated with a metalwork dragon remains. The statue and grave of **Oishi Kuranosuke**, the avenging leader of the 47 *rōnin*, are in the temple grounds. A **museum** (daily 9am–4pm; ¥200; ℡03/3441-5560, Ⓦwww.sengakuji.or.jp) to the left of the main building contains the personal belongings of the *rōnin* and their master Asano, as well as a receipt for the severed head of Kira.

Bayside Tokyo

S
o thoroughly urban is Tokyo that it can come as something of a surprise to many visitors (and some residents) that the city is actually beside the sea. Yet many of the *ukiyo-e* masterpieces of Hokusai and Hiroshige depict waterside scenes around **Tokyo Bay**, and several of the city's prime attractions are to be found here. An early-morning tour of the vast **Tsukiji** fish market can be followed with a visit to the serene traditional gardens **Hama Rikyū Teien**, or to **Tsukudashima**, a pocket of traditional wooden homes and shops dating from the Edo period. Across the bay to the south lies **Odaiba**, a residential community built on vast islands of reclaimed land, its principal sights being a couple of excellent museums and a raucous onsen complex, as well as some of Tokyo's most futuristic architecture.

Around 9km east from Tsukiji across Tokyo Bay, some of the city's older recreational facilities still pull in the crowds. The open spaces of **Kasai Rinkai-kōen** are a good place to catch the sea breeze, but the park's greatest attraction is its aquarium. From the park, the Cinderella spires of **Tokyo Disney Resort** are clearly visible to the west. Though not everyone's cup of tea, this little bit of America can make a hugely entertaining day out, even if you're not travelling with kids.

Tsukiji and around

A dawn visit to the vast **Tokyo Metropolitan Central Wholesale Market** (東京都中央卸売市場; Mon–Sat 4am–noon but check the website for occasional holidays; ⓦ www.tsukiji-market.or.jp/tukiji_e.htm), on the edge of Tokyo Bay, is one of the highlights of any trip to Tokyo and a must for raw-fish fans, who can breakfast here on the freshest sashimi and sushi. The closest subway station to the market is Tsukiji-Shijō (築地市場) on the Ōedo line, although Tsukiji on the Hibiya line is also convenient. If you want to witness the frantic auctions that start at 5am you'll have to catch a taxi or walk here.

Covering a quarter of a square kilometre of south of Ginza, and some 2km southeast of the Imperial Palace, the market is popularly known as **Tsukiji** ("reclaimed land"). The area the market stands on was cleared in the wake of the disastrous Furisode (Long Sleeves) Fire of 1657, after which Tokugawa Ieyasu had the debris shovelled into the marshes at the edge of Ginza, thus providing his lords with space for their mansions and gardens. In the early years of the Meiji era, after the *daimyō* had been kicked out of Tokyo, the city authorities built a special residential area for Western expats here. The market relocated to this area in from Nihombashi following the 1923 earthquake, the current complex starting

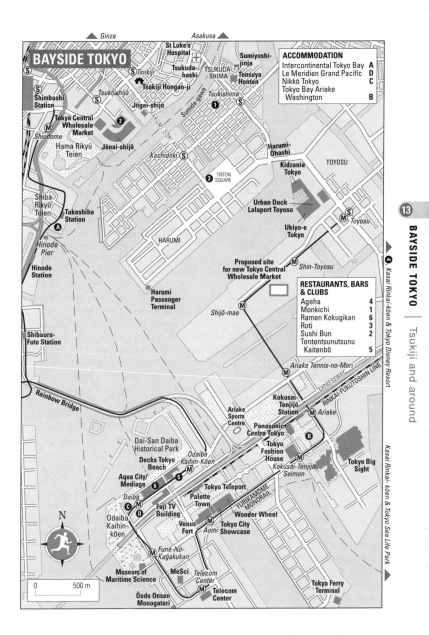

ACCOMMODATION

Intercontinental Tokyo Bay	A
Le Meridien Grand Pacific	D
Nikkō Tokyo	C
Tokyo Bay Ariake	
Washington	B

RESTAURANTS, BARS & CLUBS

Ageha	4
Monkichi	1
Ramen Kokugikan	6
Roti	3
Sushi Bun	2
Tententsunutsunu Kaitenbō	5

operations in 1935. It's looking increasingly likely that the market will move again, probably around 2012 (see box, p.136).

Tsukiji's **jōnai-shijō** (main market) lies closest to the water in the crescent-shaped hangar. Sloshing through the water-cleansed pathways, dodging the mini-forklift trucks that shift the produce around, and being surrounded by piled crates of seafood (some of it still alive) is what a visit to Tsukiji is all

Tsukiji's controversial relocation

Generating ¥1.7 billion in sales daily, Tsukiji is undoubtedly big business, but during the recession of recent years the volume of trade has been dropping, along with the number of wholesalers and middlemen who work at the market. Uppermost on merchants' minds, though, is the Tokyo Metropolitan Government's plan to shift the market to reclaimed land in Toyosu, 2km across the bay. Apart from issues involving the safety of the site (it was previously used by Tokyo Gas, and the highly toxic ground must be thoroughly cleaned up before any construction starts), there's also a worry that the new market's scale, at almost twice the size of the current site, will undermine Tsukiji's chaotic charm. Furthermore, the new site will keep tourists at arm's length from the action, restricting them to walkways overlooking the wholesale fish section.

The merchants, particularly the five hundred or so in the outer market area whose living largely depends on the continued presence of the fish market, are supported by the local ward, who are also nervous about the loss of income the market's relocation will entail. However, the city government, eyeing the Tsukiji's current site as the likely location for a media centre for its 2016 Olympic bid, appears determined to shift the market out of the city centre.

about. Eels from Taiwan, salmon from Santiago and tuna from Tasmania are among the 480 different types of seafood – 2000 tonnes of it – that come under the hammer here daily. The auctions, held at the back of the market, aren't officially open to the public, but no one will stop you slipping in quietly to watch the buyers and sellers gesticulating wildly over polystyrene crates of squid, sea urchins, crab and the like. The highlight is the sale of rock-solid frozen tuna, looking like steel torpedoes, all labelled with yellow stickers indicating their weight and country of origin. Depending on the quality, each tuna sells for between ¥600,000 and ¥1 million.

From around 7am, Tokyo's restaurateurs and food retailers pick their way through the day's catch, which is put on sale at 1600 different wholesalers' stalls. As the market's official title indicates, fish is not the only item on sale at Tsukiji, which also deals in meat, fruit and vegetables. If you get peckish, head for one of the area's plentiful sushi stalls and noodle bars servicing the sixty thousand people who pass through here each day. One good choice, in one of the rows of sushi stalls directly opposite the market's fish section, is *Sushi-Bun* (see p.177).

Before leaving, weave your way through the **jōgai-shijō** (outer market), a dense grid of streets immediately to the northeast. It's heaving with fishmongers, grocers, pottery merchants and kitchenware sellers – there's activity here later into the day when the main market is winding down.

Close to Tsukiji subway station is **Tsukiji Hongan-ji** (築地本願寺; Ⓦwww.tsukijihongwanji.jp), one of the largest and most Indian-looking of Tokyo's Buddhist temples. Pop inside to see the intricately carved golden altar and cavernous interior, with room for a thousand worshippers.

Hama Rikyū Teien

The contrast between bustling Tsukiji and the traditional garden of **Hama Rikyū Teien** (浜離宮庭園; Tues–Sun 9am–4.30pm; ¥300), less than a ten-minute walk east, couldn't be more acute. This beautifully designed park once belonged to the shogunate, who hunted ducks here. These days the ducks, protected inside the garden's nature reserve, are no longer used for target practice and only have to watch out for the large number of cats that wander the idly twisting pathways.

There are three ponds, the largest spanned by a trellis-covered bridge that leads to a floating teahouse, *Nakajima-no-Chaya* (¥500 for tea). Next to the entrance is a sprawling, 300-year-old pine tree and a manicured lawn dotted with sculpted, stunted trees. One of the best times of year to come here is in early spring, when lilac wisteria hangs in fluffy bunches from trellises around the central pond. From the Tokyo Bay side of the garden, you'll get a view across to the Rainbow Bridge, and can see the floodgate which regulates how much sea water flows in and out of this pond with the tides.

By far the nicest way of approaching the gardens is to take a ferry from Asakusa, down the Sumida-gawa (see p.28 for details).

Tsukudashima

Another rewarding diversion from Tsukiji, across the Sumida-gawa, is **Tsukudashima** (佃島; meaning "island of rice fields"), a tiny enclave of Edo-period houses and shops clustered around a backwater spanned by a dinky red bridge. Sheltering in the shadow of the modern River City 21 residential tower blocks, the area has a history stretching back to 1613, when a group of Ōsaka fishermen were settled on the island by the shogun. In addition to providing food for the castle, the fishermen were expected to report on any suspicious comings and goings in the bay. For their spiritual protection, they built themselves the delightful **Sumiyoshi-jinja** (住吉神社), dedicated to the god of the sea. The roof of the well beside the shrine's *torii* has eaves decorated with exquisite carvings of scenes from the fishermen's lives.

Every three years, on the first weekend in August, the shrine hosts the Sumiyoshi Matsuri **festival**, during which a special *mikoshi* (portable shrine) is dowsed in water as it is paraded through the streets; this is symbolic of the real dunking it would once have had in the river.

The closest **subway station** is Tsukishima (月島), on the Yūrakuchō and Ōedo lines. To reach Tsukudashima on foot from Tsukiji, head for the Tsukuda-Ōhashi bridge a ten-minute walk from Tsukiji subway station, past St Luke's Hospital. The area is easily spotted on the left side of the island as you leave the bridge, and shouldn't take more than thirty minutes to explore.

Tsukudashima cuisine

Tsukudashima is famous for a couple of types of food. **Tsukudani** are delicious morsels of seaweed and fish preserved in a mixture of soy sauce, salt or sugar – eighteen different types of this speciality are served up at *Tensuya Honten* (see p.231). Heading southwest from Tsukishima Station, you'll also find Monjadōri, a colourful shopping street packed with **okonomiyaki** and **monja** restaurants. *Okonomiyaki*, a thick savoury pancake (see p.162), is common across Japan, but *monja*, with a looser consistency not dissimilar to scrambled egg, is a Tokyo speciality dating back to the early Meiji era. The current basic *monja* recipe dates from after World War II, when cooks began flavouring the batter with Worcestershire sauce and adding vegetables, squid and a range of fried ingredients to the mix. Some of the sixty-odd restaurants in this area offer more adventurous versions with curry, pizza and *kimuchi* (Korean fermented cabbage) flavourings. A good place to sample the dish is *Monkichi* (see p.177).

Harumi and Toyosu

While you're out this way, you might like to take a swing through another of Tokyo's new mini-city developments, **Triton Square** at **Harumi** (晴海), which boasts a pleasant riverside location and some relaxing places to sit outside and enjoy food or drink (including a branch of the popular Western-style restaurant *Roti*; see p.174). The closest subway station is Kachidoki, one stop south of Tsukishima on the Ōedo line.

Walking eastwards from Triton Square across the Harumi Ōhashi, you'll soon reach **Toyosu** (豊洲), the intended location for the new Tokyo Metropolitan Central Wholesale Market. One reason for visiting this neighbourhood now is to indulge in some mall shopping at the slick **Urban Dock LaLaport Toyosu** (Ⓦtoyosu.lalaport.jp). Within this bayside complex you'll find not only 190 shops and restaurants, but also a multiplex cinema and a modest attempt at high culture in the **Ukiyo-e Tokyo** (Tues–Fri noon–7pm, Sat & Sun 11am–7pm; ¥500), a permanent exhibition of classic woodblock prints. The mall also includes **KidZania Tokyo** (daily 10am–3pm & 4–10pm; Mon–Fri ¥1200, Sat & Sun ¥1500; Ⓦwww.kidzania.jp), an imaginative mini-theme park where kids run all the various shops and services (although everything is in Japanese). Toyosu is on the Yūrakuchō subway line and is also the terminus for the Yurikamome monorail through Odaiba.

Odaiba

Odaiba (お台場) is an island of reclaimed land in Tokyo Bay. The name means "cannon emplacements", referring to the defences set up in the bay by the shogun in 1853 to protect the city from Commodore Perry's threatening Black Ships (see p.304). The remains of the two cannon emplacements are now dwarfed by the huge landfill site – Rinkai Fukutoshin, of which Odaiba is a part – on which the Metropolitan Government set about constructing a twenty-first-century city in 1988. The subsequent economic slump and spiralling development costs slowed the project down and, when the **Rainbow Bridge** linking Odaiba to the city opened in 1993, the area was still a series of empty lots.

More than a decade on, Odaiba has blossomed into one of the most popular spots in the city for locals, who love its seaside location and sense of space – so rare in Tokyo. At night, the illuminated Rainbow Bridge, giant technicolour ferris wheel and twinkling towers of the Tokyo skyline make Odaiba a romantic spot – you'll see plenty of canoodling couples staring wistfully at the glittering panorama. The success of Odaiba is spurring construction of more waterside mansions, particularly in the Shinagawa area (see p.131).

There's a whole range of ways of reaching Odaiba. The simplest is to hop on the **Yurikamome monorail** (Ⓦwww.yurikamome.co.jp), which starts at Shimbashi Station and arcs up to the Rainbow Bridge on a splendid circular line, stopping at all the area's major sites before terminating at Toyosu (see above). A one-day ticket for the monorail (¥800) is a good idea if you intend to see all the island – walking across Odaiba can be a long slog. In addition, **trains** on the Rinkai line, linked with the JR Saikyō line and the Yūrakuchō subway line, run to the central Tokyo-Teleport Station on Odaiba. **Buses** from Shinagawa Station, southwest of the bay, cross the Rainbow Bridge and run as far as the Maritime Museum, stopping at Odaiba Kaihinkōen on the way. There's also a variety of bus services (some free) to the Ōedo Onsen

Monogatari. Finally, **ferries** shuttle from the pier at Hinode (日の出) to either Ariake pier on Odaiba or the Maritime Museum via Harumi and Odaiba Kaihin-kōen; the journey costs just ¥520 and doubles as a Tokyo Bay cruise.

The following description of sights starts with the east side of Odaiba and ends with a walk back across the Rainbow Bridge – easily the highlight of any trip out to this ultra-modern area.

Panasonic Center Tokyo

Less than a minute's walk from Ariake monorail station is **Panasonic Center Tokyo** (Tues–Sun 10am–6pm; free; ⊤03/3599-2600, ⓦpanasonic.net/panasonic -center/tokyo), a showroom for the electronics group Matsushita. There's an area where you can try out the latest Nintendo games on a large-screen plasma display or high-resolution projector, as well as check out the company's technologies of tomorrow. The centre includes the fun "digital network museum" **Risupia** (¥500), at which you're issued with an electronic tag upon entering the hi-tech display hall; as you learn about science and mathematics from the computer games and simulations within, the tag keeps track of how well you're doing.

Tokyo Big Sight

Outside the Kokusai Tenjijō Seimon Station, you won't fail to see the Tokyo International Exhibition Centre, better known as the **Tokyo Big Sight** (東京ビッグサイト; ⊤03/5530-1111, ⓦwww.bigsight.jp). With an entrance composed of four huge inverted pyramids, this is one of Japan's largest venues for business fairs and exhibitions; in front stands a 15.5-metre sculpture of a saw, sticking out of the ground as if left behind by some absent-minded giant. Check their website for details of events, which include huge antique fairs, the twice-yearly Design Festa (see p.119) and the annual Tokyo Anime Fair in March.

Palette Town

Aomi Station is the stop for the vast **Palette Town** shopping and entertainment complex (パレットタウン; ⓦwww.palette-town.com), which offers something for almost everyone. On the east side, car enthusiasts will approve of the **Toyota City Showcase** (daily 11am–9pm; free; ⊤03/3599-0808, ⓦwww.megaweb.gr.jp), displaying the automobile maker's current range. Give them a call to sign up for various activities, such as designing your own car using CAD technology, taking a virtual-reality drive (¥500) or a spin in an electric vehicle (¥200), or even selecting a Toyota model and taking it for a test drive (¥300). Just behind the showroom are some more hi-tech diversions, the best of which is the **Wonder Wheel** (daily 10am–10pm; ¥900), a candy-coloured ferris wheel, 115m in diameter, which takes sixteen minutes to make a full circuit.

The upper floor on the west side of Palette Town is dominated by **Venus Fort** (ⓦwww.venusfort.co.jp), described as a "theme park for ladies" but basically a shopping mall designed as a mock Italian city, complete with piazza, fountains and Roman-style statues – even the ceiling is painted and lit to resemble a perfect Mediterranean sky from dawn to dusk. Most of the theme-style restaurants and shops here are totally bland, but the complex is worth swinging through if only to gawk at the sheer lunacy of it all. Downstairs is Sun Walk, a more restrained shopping mall, at the back of which you'll find the **History Garage** (daily 11am–9pm; free), displaying a good range of classic cars and including a gallery with around three thousand miniature cars and an extensive range of car-related books.

MeSci

West of Palette Town is a fat finger of reclaimed land partly covered by Tokyo's container port and overlooked by the **Telecom Centre**, a wannabe clone of Paris's Grande Arche at La Défense. Nearby is Tokyo's best science museum, the **National Museum of Emerging Science and Innovation**, or **MeSci** (Nihon Kagaku Miraikan; 日本科学未来館; daily except Tues 10am–5pm; ¥500; ☎03/3570-9151, ⓦwww.miraikan.jst.go.jp). Here you can learn about the latest in robot technology, superconductivity (including maglev trains), space exploration and much more, as well as check out the weather around the world by looking up at a giant sphere covered with one million light-emitting diodes and showing the globe as it appears from space that day. All displays have English explanations and there are also plenty of English-speaking volunteer guides on hand. Directly south of MeSci is the new spa complex, **Ōedo Onsen Monogatari** (see p.239).

The Museum of Maritime Science

From MeSci it's a short walk to the excellent **Museum of Maritime Science** (船の科学館; Mon–Fri 10am–5pm, Sat & Sun 10am–6pm; ☎03/5550-1111, ⓦwww.funenokagakukan.or.jp), housed in a concrete reproduction of a sixty-thousand-tonne cruise ship. The exhibits include many detailed model boats and the engines of a giant ship. Docked outside are a couple of real boats: the *Sōya*, which undertook scientific missions to the South Pole, and the *Yōtei Marine*, a ferry refitted as an exhibition space. Admission is ¥600 for the two ships only, ¥700 for the museum and the *Yōtei Marine*, or ¥1000 for everything. Within the museum grounds you'll also find a couple of lighthouses, submarines, a flying boat and two open-air swimming pools (mid-July to end Aug; ¥2800 including admission to the museum).

Head around the waterfront from the museum, past the curiously shaped triangular tower (an air vent for the road tunnel that goes under Tokyo Bay) to reach a park, **Odaiba Kaihin-kōen**. Across the bay, the lines of red cranes at the container port look like giraffes at feeding time.

Odaiba beach

Odaiba's man-made **beach** begins as you turn the corner of the island and the Rainbow Bridge comes into view. As Japanese beaches go, it's not bad, but it's best avoided on sunny weekends, when you'll see more raw flesh than sand. Lending the beach a slightly hallucinatory feel is a scale copy of the Statue of Liberty.

Fronting the beach are a couple of linked shopping malls, **Aqua City** (ⓦwww.aquacity.co.jp) and **Decks Tokyo Beach** (ⓦwww.odaiba-decks.com). Apart from trendy shops and restaurants, the former includes the Mediage multiplex cinema, while the latter has **Joypolis** (daily 10am–11.30pm; ¥500 admission only), a multistorey arcade filled with Sega's interactive entertainment technology.

Next to the mall, a surreal, sci-fi aura hangs over Tange Kenzō's **Fuji TV Building**, a futuristic block with a huge metal sphere suspended in its middle – it looks like it's been made from a giant Meccano set. You can pay to head up to the twenty-fifth-floor **viewing platform** (Tues–Sun 10am–8pm; ¥500) or do the sensible thing and put the cash towards a cocktail in the *Sky Lounge* at the top of the neighbouring *Meridien Grand Pacific Hotel*, where the view is thrown in for free.

Rainbow Bridge

From the Sunset Beach row of restaurants beside the Decks Mall, you can stroll across onto one of the shogun's gun emplacement islands, now a public park, or

△ Tokyo Bay viewed from Odaiba

continue for an exhilarating walk along the **Rainbow Bridge**. This 918-metre-long, single-span suspension bridge has two levels, the lower for the waterfront road and the monorail, and the upper for the Metropolitan Expressway. On both sides is a pedestrian promenade linking the **observation rooms** (daily: Jan–March, Nov & Dec 10am–6pm; April–Oct 10am–9pm; ¥300) in the anchorages at either end of the bridge. The walk along the bridge takes about forty minutes and provides magnificent views across the bay, even as far as Mount Fuji if the sky is clear. One minute's walk from the exit from the shoreside observation room is **Shibaura Futō** (芝浦ふ頭) Station, where you can board the monorail.

East across Tokyo Bay

East of Odaiba, older blocks of reclaimed land sporting dormitory towns, golf links and other recreational facilities jut out into Tokyo Bay. The prime attractions are **Kasai Rinkai-kōen**, a seaside park boasting one of Tokyo's biggest aquariums and a birdwatching centre, and the enormously popular **Tokyo Disneyland**. These two sights are at adjacent stops on the JR Keiyō line from Tokyo Station, though you probably won't have time to visit both in one day. Coming from Odaiba, take the Rinkai line to Shin-Kiba Station where you change to the Keiyō line.

Kasai Rinkai-kōen

Lying between its JR station and the sea, the flat expanse of **Kasai Rinkai-kōen** (葛西臨海公園; open 24hr; free) isn't the most attractive of landscapes, but there's more to it than first appears. For many Tokyo families this is a favourite weekend spot – for picnicking, cycling or summer swimming from its small, crescent-shaped beach – while bird enthusiasts ogle waterbirds and waders in the well-designed bird sanctuary.

The park's biggest draw is its large aquarium, the **Tokyo Sea Life Park** (Tues–Sun 9.30am–5pm, last entry 4pm; ¥700; Ⓦ www.tokyo-zoo.net), set under a glass-and-steel dome overlooking the sea. Escalators take you down to two vast tanks of tuna and sharks, the aquarium's highlight, where silver shoals race round you at dizzying speeds. Smaller tanks elsewhere showcase sea life from around the world, from flashy tropical butterfly fish and paper-thin seahorses to the lumpy mudskippers of Tokyo Bay. Not everyone is here to admire the beauty of the fish – as you walk round, listen out for murmurs of *oishii* (the Japanese equivalent of "delicious!").

If you're heading back into central Tokyo from here, one of the nicest ways is to hop on a **ferry** for the 55-minute ride (¥800) via Ariake to Hinode Pier near Hamamatsuchō. Boats leave hourly from the park's western pier, with the last departure at 5pm; see p.28 for further details.

Tokyo Disney Resort

The big daddy of Tokyo's theme parks, **Tokyo Disney Resort** (東京ディズニーリゾート; Ⓣ 0570-008-632, Ⓦ www.tokyodisneyresort.co.jp) comprises two separate but adjacent attractions: **Tokyo Disneyland**, a close copy of the Californian original, and **DisneySea Park**, a water- and world-travel-themed area. This unashamed slice of Americana, plonked in commuterland east of the city centre, may not be what you came to Japan for, but it's pretty hard not to have a good time overall.

You'll probably want to devote a whole day to each park to get your money's worth. A one-day "**passport**" for either costs ¥5500, a two-day passport to both parks is ¥9800, and there are also a couple of discount passports available for Disneyland only if you enter later in the day. The resort is generally open from 8 or 9am to 10pm, but hours may vary and the park is occasionally closed for special events, so it's best to call to check times beforehand. Expect long queues: Disneyland attracts over thirty thousand visitors per day on average, many more over weekends and holidays.

The gates to Disneyland sit right in front of Maihama Station (on the JR Keiyō line, 15min from Tokyo Station), and is served by direct buses from Shinjuku and Yokohama, as well as Narita and Haneda airports. Inside, you'll find World Bazaar, with its shops and general services (pushchair rentals, bank, lockers and information), followed by the central plaza in front of Cinderella's castle, from where the six theme lands radiate; Tomorrowland's Star Tours and Space Mountain offer the most heart-stopping rides. Next door, DisneySea Park offers an additional 23 water-based attractions spread across seven zones and a grand European-style *Hotel MiraCosta*. A **monorail** encircles the two sites, stopping near Maihama Station at a shopping complex which is also home to the Art Deco *Disney Ambassador Hotel*, where die-hard fans can collect complimentary Mickey toiletries before breakfasting with the mouse himself.

Listings

Listings

Accommodation

The quality and choice of accommodation in Tokyo has improved markedly in recent years and at all levels, from luxury hotels to budget dorm bunks. Security and cleanliness are generally top-notch, and you'll nearly always find someone who speaks at least a smattering of English.

In terms of design, the majority of rooms in **hotels** are pretty characterless, and don't expect much space either; thanks to the city's notoriously high real-estate prices, everything is packed in with the greatest efficiency. A handful of new design-conscious hotels aside, you'll often find better value and far more atmosphere at a traditional, family-run **ryokan** or a **minshuku**, the Japanese equivalent of a B&B. The cheapest beds in Tokyo are to be found among the rash of new, privately run **hostels** opening up, mainly in the northern districts, and in the **capsule hotels** – worth trying once if only for the experience (see p.156). For tips on finding **long-term accommodation**, see p.157.

When choosing which **area** to stay in, bear in mind that central Tokyo (comprising Ginza, Nihombashi, Hibiya, Akasaka and Roppongi) is largely the domain of expensive, world-class establishments and upmarket business hotels. For cheaper rooms, there's a greater choice in Shinagawa, Shibuya and Shinjuku to the south and east, and especially in Asakusa, Ueno and Ikebukuro in the north. In the last few years, several top-class establishments have sprung up in Tokyo's new suburban satellites, notably the Odaiba development in Tokyo Bay.

Accommodation prices and taxes

The cheapest accommodation in Tokyo will cost you at least ¥2000 for a dorm bed in a hostel or ¥6000 for a twin or double room in a hostel or a minshuku. You'll be looking at upwards of ¥10,000 for a more comfortable en-suite double in a lower-end hotel. Mid-range rooms start in the region of ¥15,000, while top-end hotels charge at least twice that. Note that rates may increase during peak holiday periods, in particular around Christmas and New Year, the Golden Week (April 29–May 5) and Obon (the week around August 15).

Unless otherwise stated, the rates given in the accommodation reviews in this book represent prices for **double or twin rooms**. Most hotels also have single rates (in fact some business hotels mainly offer single rooms), typically a third less than for doubles. For hostels providing **dormitory** accommodation, we've given the price per person.

While all hotel rates must include five percent consumption tax, there are a couple of other **taxes** to look out for. Most top-end hotels levy a service charge of ten to fifteen percent. In addition, if your room costs over ¥10,000 per person per night, there's a Tokyo Metropolitan Government tax of ¥100 per person per night (¥200 if the room costs over ¥15,000).

Whatever your budget, it's wise to **reserve** your first few nights' accommodation before arrival. This is especially true of the cheaper places, which tend to fill up quickly, particularly over national holidays and in late February, when thousands of students head to Tokyo for the university entrance exams. Rooms are also in short supply during the cherry-blossom season in late March and early April. Rates are often slightly lower online, and it's always worth asking if there are any promotions on offer, especially among the rapidly expanding ranks of top-end hotels now competing for your custom.

If you do arrive without a room reservation, head for the Welcome Inn Reservation Centre desks (Ⓦwww.itcj.jp). which can be found in both of Narita Airport's terminals (daily 8am–8pm), and in the main Tourist Information Centre in Yūrakuchō (daily 9am–noon & 1–5pm; Ⓣ03/3286-6611, Ⓦwww.itcj .or.jp; see p.47). Note that you'll need your passport and credit card details to make a reservation through them, and that Welcome Inn accepts bookings online but not over the phone.

While most places listed below are within easy access of either a **subway** or **train station**, remember that trains stop running around midnight. If you're a night owl, aim to stay near one of the entertainment districts to avoid taxi fares. Our listings give the nearest stations for each place reviewed.

Hotels

Whether in the deluxe or business categories, hotels generally provide Western-style rooms with en-suite bathrooms, TV, phone and air conditioning. Nowadays many also offer high-speed wired Internet access, often at no charge.

Akasaka and around

The places reviewed here are shown on the map on p.76.

ANA InterContinental Tokyo
1-12-33 Akasaka, Minato-ku Ⓣ03/3505-1111, Ⓦwww.anahoteltokyo.jp. Located midway between Akasaka and Roppongi, and with great views across to the new Tokyo Midtown and the Diet Building, this very stylish and professionally run hotel has attentive staff, a swimming pool, scores of restaurants and attractive public areas. Their contemporary executive-floor rooms have the edge over the rather dated-looking suites. Tameiki-Sannō Station. From ¥36,750.

Asia Center of Japan
ホテルアジア会館
8-10-32 Akasaka, Minato-ku Ⓣ03/3402-6111, Ⓦwww.asiacenter.or.jp. The small, neat rooms are Western-style, and cheaper if you forego en-suite bathrooms. Also has an inexpensive café and broadband Internet access in rooms for an extra ¥1000. A bargain for the area, so it fills up quickly – book online for discounts. Aoyama-itchōme or Nogizaka stations. From ¥11,200.

the b akasaka
7-6-13 Akasaka, Minato-ku Ⓣ03/3586-0811, Ⓦwww.ishinhotels.com. This new boutique business hotel is a chic, good-value addition to the area. Rates include breakfast and there's a mini-day spa for additional pampering. Akasaka Station. From ¥20,000.

Chisun Grand Akasaka
6-3-17 Akasaka, Minato-ku Ⓣ03/5572-7788, Ⓦwww.solarehotels.com. The flagship of the great-value Chisun chain of business hotels is a real step up in quality. The rooms, split over two wings and decorated in warm browns and reds, are lovely, and include extra spacious bathrooms. Breakfast is served in the attached *Organic House Deli & Café*. Akasaka Station. From ¥15,000.

Granbell Hotel Akasaka
3-10-9 Akasaka, Minato-ku Ⓣ03/5575-7130, Ⓦwww.granbellhotel.jp/akasaka. Of Akasaka's recent crop of smaller business/boutique-style hotels, this is the trendiest, offering very sleek, contemporary rooms. Attached downstairs, rather incongruously, is the wood-panelled British-style *Mermaid Pub*. Akasaka-Mitsuke Station. From ¥20,000.

Grand Prince Hotel Akasaka

1-2 Kiochō, Chiyoda-ku ☎ **03/3234-1111,** ⓦ **www.princehotels.co.jp.** There's a caught in an Austin Powers-time-loop feel to this Tange Kenzō-designed tower with stunning views. Some will find the cool grey and white interior a bit chilly; others will thrill to the rooms, with their retro 1970s decoration. Akasaka-Mitsuke Station. From ¥34,000.

Hotel Ōkura

2-10-4 Toranomon, Minato-ku ☎ **03/3582-0111,** ⓦ **www.okura.com/tokyo.** Many visitors to Tokyo swear by this classic hotel, located opposite the US embassy and with a 1950s-period lobby with low chairs and a garden view. Their Grand Comfort rooms and spa are the latest addition (and a very pleasant one, too) but decor in many of the other rooms lags behind Tokyo's top design-conscious hotels. Kamiyachō Station. From ¥42,000.

New Ōtani

4-1 Kiochō, Chiyoda-ku ☎ **03/3265-1111** ⓦ **www.newotani.co.jp.** Mammoth hotel which is a tourist attraction in its own right for its traditional gardens. It also sports over thirty restaurants, cafés and bars, a tea-ceremony room, art gallery, swimming pools, tennis courts and much more. Rooms are comfortable, and most have great views. Akasaka-Mitsuke Station. From ¥33,000.

Aoyama

Hotel Floracion

4-17-58 Minami-Aoyama, Minato-ku ☎ **03/3403-1541,** ⓦ **www.floracion-aoyama.com; see map, p.118.** In a quiet residential area, with Western-style rooms of a high standard and a convenient location, handy for the designer end of Omotesandō. Omotesandō Station. From ¥20,000.

Asakusa and around

The places reviewed here are shown on the map on p.85.

Asakusa Central Hotel

1-5-3 Asakusa, Taitō-ku ☎ **03/3847-2222,** ⓦ **www.pelican.co.jp.** Modest business hotel which rises above the competition thanks to its convenient location on Asakusa's main street, its English-speaking staff and its small but well-appointed rooms, all with TV, telephone and Internet access. Asakusa Station. From ¥12,000.

Asakusa View Hotel

3-17-1 Nishi-Asakusa, Taitō-ku ☎ **03/3847-1111,** ⓦ **www.viewhotels.co.jp/asakusa.** Asakusa's grandest hotel is all sparkling marble and chandeliers. The rooms are less memorable than the public areas, but are reasonably spacious and boast great views from the higher floors. There are a couple of restaurants and a pricey swimming pool (¥3500). Asakusa (Tsukuba Express rail) or Tawara-machi stations. From ¥32,500.

Blue Wave Inn Asakusa

2-33-7 Asakusa, Taitō-ku ☎ **03/5828-4321,** ⓦ **www.bluewaveinn.jp/asakusa.** Stylish new business hotel on the east side of Sensō-ji, with views of the temple from some rooms. Single rooms (from ¥11,000) are on the small side, but the twins offer better value. Triple and family rooms are also available. Asakusa Station. From ¥18,000.

Ebisu and Meguro

The places reviewed here are shown on the map on pp.128–129.

Dormy Inn Meguro Aobadai

ドーミーイン目黒青葉台

3-21-8 Aobadai, Meguro-ku ☎ **03/3760-2211,** ⓦ **www.hotespa.net//hotels/meguro.** If you want to be within walking distance of all the trendy spots in Naka-Meguro, this functional business hotel is a good deal. Each of the rooms have a hotplate and small fridge, so it's feasible to self-cater. There's also a large communal bath and sauna on the premises. Naka-Meguro Station. From ¥9,800.

Kyowa Kaikan

協和会館

1-10-5 Ebisu-Nishi, Shibuya-ku ☎ **03/3464-2262.** This cosy and well-located place calls itself a business hotel, though the rooms are very much at the budget end of the scale. Some very pleasant, good-value tatami rooms also available. No meals. Ebisu Station. From ¥8500.

Meguro Gajoen

目黒雅叙園

1-8-1 Meguro, Meguro-ku ☎ **03/5434-3837,** ⓦ **www.megurogajoen.co.jp.** Little expense is spared in the rooms (all suites) at this luxurious hotel, attached to the amazing wedding hall of the same name (see p.129). There's a choice of Western or Japanese rooms – the latter are preferable, with their own sauna, *hinoki* wood baths and compact gravel gardens outside the windows. Meguro Station. From ¥42,000.

Hotel Princess Garden

2-23 Kami-Osaki, Shinagawa-ku ☎03/3779-1010, ℻3779-4070. The quietly elegant lobby, looking out onto a pretty garden and pond, sets the romantic tone at this mid-range hotel, well placed between Meguro and Ebisu. If you're into chintzy flower prints, go for one of their luxury rooms (from ¥23,100). Meguro Station. From ¥18,000.

Westin Tokyo

1-1-4 Mita, Meguro-ku ☎03/5423-7000, ⓦwww.westin-tokyo.co.jp. In the Yebisu Garden Place development, this opulent hotel is decorated in Art Nouveau style; the spacious rooms have high ceilings and plush furnishings. Guests have access to the Yebisu Gardens gym and pool for a fee. Ebisu Station. From ¥41,000.

Ginza and around

The places reviewed here are shown on the map on p.60.

Four Seasons Hotel Tokyo at Marunouchi

Pacific Century Place Marunouchi, 1-11-1 Marunouchi, Chiyoda-ku ☎03/5222-7222, ⓦwww.fourseasons.com. Chic interior design and superb service are two pluses for this luxury hotel in a very handy location beside Tokyo Station. And with only 57 rooms, there's a personal touch which keeps this hotel a top choice. Facilities include a spa, fitness centre and French restaurant. Tokyo Station. From ¥70,000.

Ginza Washington

7-10-1 Ginza, Chūō-ku ☎03/6686-1000, ⓦwww.ginza-wh.com. This new business hotel is one of the cheaper options in Ginza. Rooms aren't huge but they're stylish and well equipped, with Internet access. Ginza Station. From ¥21,200.

Imperial Hotel

1-1-1 Uchisaiwai-chō, Chiyoda-ku ☎03/3504-1111, ⓦwww.imperialhotel.co.jp. Facing the Imperial Palace, this is still one of Tokyo's most prestigious addresses, despite increasingly stiff competition. A refit (due to finish in early 2009) has seen the addition of the exclusive Imperial floors, with butler service and the latest technological wizardry. No fewer than thirteen top-class restaurants, three bars, a tea-ceremony room (¥1500), swimming pool (¥1050) and

fitness centre (¥1050) round out the picture. Hibiya Station. From ¥40,000.

Mandarin Oriental Tokyo

2-1-1 Nihombashi-Muromachi, Chūō-ku ☎03/3270-8950, ⓦwww.mandarinoriental.com/tokyo. No expense has been spared in this new addition to the Mandarin Oriental group, from the dramatic 37th-floor lobby to some of the biggest standard-size rooms in Tokyo, where picture windows make the most of the stunning cityscapes. There's no pool, but guests can take advantage of a fabulous (and very pricey) spa, a fitness centre and seven restaurants. Mitsukoshi-mae Station. From ¥75,000.

Marunouchi Hotel

1-6-3 Marunouchi, Chiyoda-ku ☎03/3217-1111, ⓦwww.marunouchi-hotel.co.jp. Located in the new Oazo building right outside Tokyo Station, this moderately priced hotel packs a surprisingly classy punch, with its atrium lobby, choice of restaurants and cheerful, well-furbished rooms. Tokyo or Ōtemachi stations. From ¥31,500.

Mercure Hotel Ginza

2-9-4 Ginza, Chūō-ku ☎03/4335-1111, ⓦwww.mercure.com. French flair lends a feminine appeal to this mid-range hotel, on a quiet backstreet in the heart of Ginza. Rooms are reasonably spacious and the bathrooms a cut above the average for this price range. Their *L'Echanson* bistro serves very tasty French-style food. Ginza-itchōme Station. From ¥32,500.

Mitsui Garden Hotel

8-13-1 Ginza, Chūō-ku ☎03/3543-1131, ⓦwww.gardenhotels.co.jp. Italian designer Piero Rissoni's chic boutique look for Mitsui's flagship hotel helps it stand out from the crowd. Nicely detailed rooms are decorated in earthy tones, but it's the bird's-eye views of the city and bay that grab the attention. Watch out for the ¥2000 cover charge in the bar at night, though. Shinbashi Station. From ¥25,200.

Palace Hotel

1-1-1 Marunouchi, Chiyoda-ku ☎03/3211-5211, ⓦwww.palacehotel.co.jp. Smaller and a touch less pricey than its rival, the *Imperial*, this top-end hotel overlooking the palace gardens is another Tokyo institution. The chandeliers and gleaming marble give it a retro feel, while the rooms are reasonably sized and comfortably furnished, with Internet access, satellite TV and all the standard amenities. There are seven restaurants and three bars, plus a shopping arcade, business centre and well-stocked bookshop. Ōtemachi Station. From ¥38,000.

The Peninsula Tokyo
1-8-1 Yūrakuchō, Chiyoda-ku ☎03/6270-2288, ⓦwww.peninsula.com/tokyo.html. This very swanky new addition to Tokyo's increasingly crowded luxury hotel scene offers an unbeatable location, with views right across to the emperor's pad, plus some of the city's most spacious rooms, an opulent spa and rooftop restaurant and bar, among other facilities. Hibiya or Yurakuchō stations. From ¥70,000.

Yaesu Terminal Hotel
1-5-14 Yaesu, Chūō-ku ☎03/3281-3771, ⓦwww .yth.jp. Spick-and-span little business hotel offering good rates for such a central location, though the cheaper rooms are cramped. It's in an appealing area, tucked among the backstreets just northeast of Tokyo Station. Tokyo or Nihombashi stations. From ¥17,000.

Ikebukuro

The hotels reviewed here are shown on the map on p.99.

Hotel Metropolitan
1-6-1 Nishi-Ikebukuro, Toshima-ku ☎03/3980-1111, ⓦwww.metropolitan.jp. Belonging to the Crowne Plaza group, Ikebukuro's plushest hotel offers all the facilities you'd expect, including several restaurants, an outdoor pool (mid-June to early Sept; ¥1000) and limousine bus connections to Narita Airport. The rooms are comfortable and well priced, and the hotel is located on the more interesting west side of Ikebukuro. Ikebukuro Station. From ¥27,800.

Hotel Strix
2-3-1 Ikebukuro, Toshima-ku ☎03/5396-0111, ⓦwww.strix.jp. Reasonably priced hotel in a good location on the west side of Ikebukuro Station, which packs more character than its local rivals. Rates include breakfast. Ikebukuro Station. From ¥20,000.

Kanda, Akihabara and around

The hotels reviewed here are shown on the map on p.67.

Hilltop Hotel
1-1 Kanda-Surugadai, Chiyoda-ku ☎03/3293-2311, ⓦwww.yamanoue-hotel.co.jp. Perched on a small rise above Meiji University, this small 1930s hotel was formerly the commissioned officers' quarters during the Occupation, and then became the haunt of famous writers, notably Mishima. Its rooms are far from Tokyo's grandest, but there are Art Deco touches and a friendly welcome – and oxygen and supposedly refreshing negative ions are pumped around the premises. Ochanomizu Station. From ¥25,500.

Tokyo Dome Hotel
1-3-61 Koraku, Bunkyō-ku ☎03/5805-2111, ⓦwww.tokyodome-hotels.co.jp. Good value, both for its central location and high-quality, larger-than-average rooms – hence it's often full, particularly if there's a big game or event on at the neighbouring stadium. There's an outdoor pool (mid-July to end Aug; ¥1050), seven restaurants and a clutch of bars and cafés, including one on the top (43rd) floor. Suidōbashi Station. From ¥28,000.

Odaiba and Tokyo Bay

The hotels reviewed here appear on the map on p.135.

Hotel InterContinental Tokyo Bay
1-16-2 Kaigan, Minato-ku ☎03/5404-2222, ⓦwww.ichotelsgroup.com. Luxury hotel with views across the bay to the Rainbow Bridge and inland to Tokyo Tower, and rooms decorated in earthy tones. Hinode Station (Yurikamome monorail) or Hamamatsuchō Station. From ¥28,000.

Le Meridien Grand Pacific
2-6-1 Daiba, Minato-ku ☎03/5500-6711, ⓦwww.starwoodhotels.com/lemeridien. The traditional European style of this luxury hotel's interior jars uncomfortably with the futuristic architecture of Odaiba, but the rooms are reasonable value and there are lots of facilities, including a gallery with changing exhibitions. Daiba Station (Yurikamome monorail). From ¥30,000.

Hotel Nikkō Tokyo
1-9-1 Daiba, Minato-ku ☎03/5500-5500, ⓦwww.hnt.co.jp. The most pleasant of Odaiba's hotels has a light-filled lobby, walls peppered with contemporary art and great views of the Rainbow Bridge and the city across Tokyo Bay. Rooms are spacious and have small balconies. Daiba Station (Yurikamome monorail). From ¥38,200.

Tokyo Bay Ariake Washington Hotel
3-1-28 Ariake, Minato-ku ☎03/5564-0111, ⓦwww.ariake-wh.com. Best value for the Odaiba area, this upmarket chain hotel has

decent-sized rooms and is well located for events at Tokyo Big Sight. Kokusai-tenjijō Seimon Station (Yurikamome monorail). From ¥14,000.

Roppongi and around

The places reviewed here appear on the maps on p.76 or on p.79.

Arca Torre Hotel
6-1-23 Roppongi ℡03/3404-5111, ⓦwww .arktower.co.jp. There are plenty of decent single rooms at this modern business hotel directly above the subway station. The more expensive rooms face out onto Roppongi-dōri (which is odd, since this is the noisy side of the hotel). Standard double rooms are small. Roppongi Station. From ¥14,000.

the b roppongi
3-9-8 Roppongi, Minato-ku ℡03/5412-0451, ⓦwww.ishinhotels.com. This boutique-style hotel that won't break the bank or offend the eyes (although the uninspiring plastic-unit bathrooms are present throughout). A light breakfast is included in the rate, and if you like their cool background music you can purchase the house CD. Roppongi Station. From ¥13,500.

Celestine Hotel
3-23-1 Shiba, Minato-ku ℡03/5441-4111, ⓦwww.celestinehotel.com. In a business area south of Shiba-kōen, this classy hotel has a pleasant lounge and secluded Moorish-style garden. The rooms are a good size and nicely decorated. Shiba-kōen Station. From ¥30,000.

Grand Hyatt Tokyo
6-10-3 Roppongi, Minato-ku ℡03/4333-1234, ⓦwww.grandhyatttokyo.com. Glamour is the order of the day at the Grand Hyatt. The rooms' appealing design uses wood and earthy-toned fabrics. Restaurants and bars are all very chic, particularly The Oak Door (see p.173) and the slick sushi bar Roku Roku. The Beckhams have stayed here – the modern equivalent of an imperial endorsement. Roppongi Station. From ¥49,500.

Hotel Ibis
7-14-4 Roppongi, Minato-ku ℡03/3403-4411, ⓦwww.ibis-hotel.com. A stone's throw from Roppongi crossing; the lobby is on the fifth floor, where there's also Internet access. The cheapest doubles are small but bright and have TV and fridge. There are friendly English-speaking staff, too. Roppongi Station. From ¥16,300.

The Prince Park Tower Tokyo
4-8-1 Shibakōen, Minato-ku ℡03/5400-1110, ⓦwww.prince.hotels.co.jp. This 33-floor tower offers great views of neighbouring Tokyo tower. Rooms are pleasant (and come with a choice of pillows) and the facilities – including a pool and bowling alley – are impressive. Shiba-kōen Station. From ¥25,000.

The Ritz Carlton
Tokyo Midtown, 9-7-1 Akasaka, Minato-ku ℡03/6434-8100, ⓦwww.ritzcarlton.com. The Ritz Carlton has bagged the top nine floors of the 53-floor Midtown Tower, Tokyo's tallest building, for its new ultra-luxury venture, which has a more contemporary look than most of the chain's hotels. There's a choice between deluxe rooms and even larger suites. Roppongi Station. From ¥65,000.

Hotel Villa Fontaine Roppongi
1-6-2 Roppongi, Minato-ku ℡03/3560-1110, ⓦwww.villa-fontaine.co.jp. A stylish business hotel tucked into a corner of the Izumi Garden development directly above the subway station. Rooms are larger than average, pleasantly decorated and have free Internet connections. Rates, which include a buffet breakfast, are discounted online, especially at weekends. Roppongi-itchōme Station. From ¥14,500.

Shibuya

The places reviewed here appear on the map on p.122.

Arimax Hotel
11-15 Kamiyama-chō, Shibuya-ku ℡03/5454-1122, ⓦwww.arimaxhotelshibuya.co.jp. There's an elegant European feel to this boutique hotel, a short walk from the action in Shibuya. English is spoken and it's all very professional. The suites come with their own cosy sauna. Shibuya Station. From ¥27,900.

Cerulean Tower Tōkyū Hotel
26-1 Sakuragaoka-chō, Shibuya-ku ℡03/3476-3000, ⓦwww.ceruleantower-hotel.com. The Tōkyu chain's flagship hotel is a ritzy affair. Some rooms have bathrooms with a glittering view of the city, and there's a pool and gym (free to guests on the executive floor, otherwise ¥2000), several restaurants, a jazz club and even a Nō theatre in the basement. Shibuya Station. From ¥41,600.

Granbell Hotel, Shibuya
15-17 Sakuragaoka-cho, Shibuya-ku ℡03/5457-2681, ⓦwww.granbellhotel.jp. Curtains with Ray Lichtenstein-style prints,

kettles and TVs from the trendy Plus Minus Zero range, and a cool palette of greys and crisp whites give this new boutique hotel a hip atmosphere. It's not built to last – the suites are already looking worn – but is certainly fun for now. From 2 to 6pm rooms can be rented for half the daily rate. Shibuya Station. From ¥26,000.

National Children's Castle Hotel
5-53-1 Jingūmae, Shibuya-ku ☎03/3797-5677 ⓦwww.kodomono-shiro.or.jp. On the sixth and seventh floors of a complex devoted to kids' entertainment – but you don't have to have children to stay here. The hotel offers large, comfy rooms and inexpensive singles (though without windows). They also have a couple of tatami rooms from ¥21,500. A great deal, given the fab location; the only downside is the 11pm curfew. Shibuya Station. From ¥11,400.

Shibuya Creston Hotel
10-8 Kamiyamachō, Shibuya-ku ☎03/3481-5800, ⓦwww.crestonhotel.co.jp. This business hotel is bit classier than most, with larger-than-normal rooms, a discreet atmosphere and two Japanese restaurants. Near NHK at the quiet end of Shibuya. Shibuya Station. From ¥22,200.

Shibuya Excel Hotel Tōkyū
1-12-2 Dōgenzaka, Shibuya-ku ☎03/5457-0109, ⓦwww.tokyuhotels.co.jp. Hi-tech fixtures and contemporary furnishings characterize this new skyscraper hotel atop the Shibuya Mark City complex. Women get two floors to themselves, where rooms have extra amenities such as various face creams and feather bedding. Shibuya Station. From ¥23,000.

Shinagawa and around

The places reviewed here are on the map on p.132.

Grand Prince Hotel Takanawa
3-13-1 Takanawa, Minato-ku ☎03/3447-1111, ⓦwww.princehotels.co.jp. The most appealing of the three Prince hotels in Shinagawa is the original one. The recently renovated lobby overlooks the elegant gardens created for Prince Takeda, and there's a swimming pool open from July through early September. Shinagawa Station. From ¥25,500.

Keihin Hotel
京品ホテル
4-10-20 Takanawa, Minato-ku ☎03/3449-5711,

ⓦwww.keihin-hotel.co.jp. Small, old-fashioned hotel directly opposite the station, with some Japanese-style rooms as well as standard Western ones. Shinagawa Station. From ¥13,900.

The Strings by InterContinental Tokyo
Shinagawa East One Tower, 2-16-1 Konan, Minato-ku ☎03/4562-1111, ⓦwww .stringshotel.com. Watch the Shinkansen come and go from this chic eyrie, located from 26 floors up in one of the new brace of towers next to the station. The airy atrium lobby, with its water, wood and stone combination, evokes Japan, but in a thoroughly modern way. A nice touch are the teddy bears in the club and deluxe rooms, some of which have mini-plane-tarium machines. Shinagawa Station. From ¥48,000.

Tōyoko Inn Shinagawa-eki Takanawaguchi
4-23-2 Takanawa ☎03/3280-1045, ⓦwww .toyoko-inn.co.jp. Handy branch of this bargain business hotel chain that doesn't stint on room features (including trouser press and Internet access). Rates include a continental breakfast and there are free Internet terminals in the lobby. Shinagawa Station. From ¥8800.

Shinjuku

The places reviewed here appear on the map on pp.106–107.

Central Hotel Shinjuku
3-34-7 Shinjuku, Shinjuku-ku ☎03/3354-6611, ⓕ3355-4245. Classier-than-average business hotel in an ultra-convenient location near the station, with non-smoking rooms and a café. Shinjuku Station. Doubles from ¥17,850.

Hotel Century Southern Tower
2-2-1 Yoyogi, Shinjuku-ku ☎03/5354-0111, ⓦwww.southerntower.co.jp. Part of the Odakyū Southern Tower complex, this smart, stylish hotel is better value than many of its older rivals in Nishi-Shinjuku. The views overlooking the station lend the place a *Blade Runner*-ish feel. Shinjuku Station. Doubles from ¥27,700.

Kadoya Hotel
1-23-1 Nishi-Shinjuku, Shinjuku-ku ☎03/3342-1077, ⓦwww.kadoya-hotel.co.jp. In the shadow of the Keiō Plaza, this efficient business hotel is a little charmer. Single rooms are a bargain for such a handy location, especially as rates include

breakfast and Internet access. A major plus is the lively *izekaya Hatago* (see p.176) in the basement. Shinjuku Station. Singles around ¥7600, doubles from ¥13,650.

Keiō Plaza Hotel

2-2-1 Nishi-Shinjuku, Shinjuku-ku ☎ **03/3344-0111,** Ⓦ **www.keioplaza.co.jp.** Though it's long since been knocked off its perch as the tallest, most glamorous hotel in Shinjuku, the enormous *Keiō* nevertheless retains some of its original cachet and the renovated premier rooms, in grey and brown tones, are very stylish. Ask for a room on the west side – they have the best views across to the Tokyo Metropolitan Government Building. There's also an outdoor pool in summer. Shinjuku Station. Doubles from ¥21,500.

Park Hyatt Tokyo

3-7-1-2 Nishi-Shinjuku, Shinjuku-ku ☎ **03/5322-1234,** Ⓦ **www.parkhyatttokyo.com.** Famous for its key role in the recent hit movie *Lost In Translation*, the *Park Hyatt* remains the pick of Nishi-Shinjuku's luxury hotels. The huge rooms and decor – the epitome of sophistication – hold up very well to newer rivals. All rooms, plus the restaurants and spa, pool and fitness centre, occupying the pinnacles of Tange Kenzō's tower, have breathtaking views. Tochōmae Station. Doubles from ¥56,700.

Tokyo Hilton Hotel

6-6-2 Nishi-Shinjuku, Shinjuku-ku ☎ **03/3344-5111,** Ⓦ **www.hilton.com.** In the slinky, wave-like building behind the more traditional skyscrapers of Nishi-Shinjuku. Rooms have nice Japanese design touches, such as *shōji* (paper screens) on the windows. The buffet breakfast and lunch and afternoon-tea spreads are renowned. Tochōmae Station. Doubles from ¥29,000.

Shiodome

The hotels reviewed here appear on the map on p.60.

Conrad Tokyo

1-9-1 Higashi-Shinbashi, Minato-ku ☎ **03/6388-8000,** Ⓦ **www.conradtokyo.co.jp.** This top-rank hotel easily holds its own when it comes to cutting-edge contemporary design and five-star facilities – including executive floors, a 25m indoor pool (¥2500), a spacious spa and fitness centre and four restaurants, two of them under celebrity chef Gordon Ramsay. But it's the views that really steal the show. From the lobby and

bayside rooms, feast your eyes on what are arguably the best vistas in Tokyo, taking in Hama Rikyū Gardens, Odaiba and the Rainbow Bridge. It's absolutely magical at night. Shiodome Station. From ¥65,000.

Royal Park Shiodome Tower

1-6-3 Higashi-Shinbashi, Minato-ku ☎ **03/6253-1111,** Ⓦ **www.rps-tower.co.jp.** Swish business hotel at the heart of the Shiodome complex, with some nice contemporary touches and in-room Internet access. They also run the Mandara Spa, offering a range of spa treatments – one way to soothe away the stresses of Tokyo. Shiodome Station. From ¥26,000.

Villa Fontaine Shiodome

1-9-2 Higashi-Shinbashi, Minato-ku ☎ **03/3569-2220,** Ⓦ **www.villa-fontaine.co.jp.** Despite the very upscale lobby with its soaring atrium and modern artwork, this business hotel is surprisingly affordable. There's a wide choice of rooms, including "healing rooms" equipped with foot massagers, negative-ion humidifiers and contour pillows, but make sure you ask for one looking outwards – the bay-view rooms are best and come at a fraction of the price asked by other hotels in the area. All rooms are non-smoking. Shiodome Station. From ¥14,000.

Ueno

The hotels reviewed here appear on the map on p.91.

Fukushima Kaikan

ふくしま会館

2-12-14 Ueno, Taitō-ku ☎ **03/3834-6221,** Ⓕ **3834-6216.** Friendly, functional hotel with a choice of Western- or Japanese-style accommodation, the latter quite spacious. Many rooms have great views across Shinobazu pond. Yushima Station. From ¥12,700.

Suigetsu Hotel Ohgaisō

水月ホテル鴎外荘

3-3-21 Ikenohata, Taitō-ku ☎ **03/3822-4611,** Ⓦ **www.ohgai.co.jp.** One of very few mid-range hotels with a Japanese flavour, this is built around the Meiji-period house and traditional garden of novelist Mori Ōgai. The three wings contain a mix of Western and tatami rooms (the latter offer more atmosphere). Rates with or without meals available. Nezu Station. Western rooms from ¥13,500; tatami rooms from ¥25,000.

Ueno First City Hotel

1-14-8 Ueno, Taitō-ku ☎03/3831-8215, ⓦwww
.uenocity-hotel.com. Rather faded but reasonably priced and friendly little business hotel
on the western edge of Ueno, offering a
choice of Japanese- and Western-style
rooms, all en suite. Take exit 6 from
Yushima Station, turn right and right again
at the traffic lights. Yushima Station. From
¥13,700.

Ryokan and minshuku

One of the highlights of a visit to Tokyo is staying in a **ryokan**, a family-run inn
where you'll be expected to follow local custom from the moment you arrive.
Minshuku, the Japanese equivalent of a bed-and-breakfast place, are generally
more informal, but the same basic rules apply. Just inside the front door there's
usually a row of **slippers** ready for you to change into. The bedrooms have rice-
straw matting (tatami) on the floor and little else beyond a low table and dresser,
plus a few cushions. The **bedding** is stored behind sliding doors during the day
and laid out in the evening. In top-class establishments this is done for you, but
elsewhere be prepared to tackle the task yourself. There'll be a mattress (which
goes straight on the tatami) with a sheet, a soft quilt to sleep under and a pillow
stuffed with rice husks.

All ryokan provide a *yukata*, a loose cotton robe tied with a belt, and a short
jacket in cold weather. The *yukata* can be worn in bed, when going to the bathroom
and for wandering about the ryokan – many Japanese take an outdoor evening
stroll in their *yukata* and wooden shoes (*geta*), kept in the entrance hall. It's
important always to wrap the left side of the *yukata* over the right; the opposite is
used to dress bodies for a funeral.

The traditional **Japanese bath** (*furo*), which you'll find in all ryokan and most
minshuku, is a luxurious experience with its own set of rules, for more on which see
p.238. In addition to the general points made there, note that ryokan usually have
separate bathrooms for men and women, while minshuku may only have one
bathroom, in which case there'll either be designated times for males and females, or
guests take it in turn. It's perfectly acceptable for couples and families to bathe
together, though there's not usually a lot of space. Evenings are the customary time
to bathe, but note that the bath is only filled once a day, so never pull the plug out.

Evening **meals** tend to be early, at 6 or 7pm. Smarter ryokan generally serve
meals in your room, while communal dining is the norm in cheaper places. At
night, some ryokan lock their doors pretty early, so check before going out – they
may let you have a key.

Asakusa and around

The places reviewed here appear on the
map on p.85, except where noted.

Andon Ryokan
2-34-10 Nihonzutsumi, Taitō-ku
☎03/3873-8611, ⓦwww.andon.co.jp; see
Greater Tokyo map at back of book. Creative
types and clued-up travellers all gather at
the *Andon*, a traditional-style ryokan
decorated with the owner's antique collection and housed in an ultra-modern
building, which glows invitingly like a lantern
at night. The tatami rooms share bathrooms
and are small, but come equipped with
DVD players and very comfortable futon.
There's also a Jacuzzi spa you can book for
private dips, free Internet access and
super-friendly and helpful English-speaking
staff. A tea ceremony is offered to guests
(¥500) on the first, third and fourth
Thursdays of the month. Minowa Station.
Doubles ¥8200.

Family Hotel Kamogawa
1-30-10 Asakusa, Taitō-ku ☎03/3843-2681,
ⓦwww.f-kamogawa.jp. Simple but well-
maintained tatami rooms, with or without
bath, in this welcoming minshuku one block
west of Nakamise-dōri. Asakusa Station.
From ¥11,600.

Ryokan Shigetsu
旅館指月

1-31-11 Asakusa, Taitō-ku ☎03/3843-2345, ⓦ www.shigetsu.com. Just off bustling Nakamise-dōri, this smart little ryokan is a haven of kimono-clad receptionists and tinkling *shamisen* (Japanese lute) music. It's surprisingly affordable, with a choice of small Western- or Japanese-style rooms, all en suite. There's a Japanese bath on the top floor, with views over temple roofs. Asakusa Station. Western rooms ¥14,700; Japanese rooms from ¥16,800.

🏃 Sukeroku-no-yado Sadachiyo
助六の宿 貞千代

2-20-1 Asakusa, Taitō-ku ☎03/3842-6431, ⓦ www.sadachiyo.co.jp. Step back into Edo-era Asakusa in this delightful old inn marked by a willow tree and stone lanterns and northwest of Sensō-ji temple. The elegant tatami rooms are all en suite, though you can also use the traditional Japanese-style baths. Meals available. Asakusa (Tsukuba Express railway) or Tawaramachi stations. From ¥19,000.

Taitō Ryokan

2-1-4 Nishi-Asakusa, Taitō-ku ☎03/3843-2822, ⓦ www.libertyhouse.gr.jp. Somewhere between a minshuku, a hostel and student digs, *Taitō Ryokan* offers no-frills tatami rooms (none en suite and all non-smoking) in an atmospheric, if somewhat dilapidated, wooden building. Thanks to the central location, low rates and the engaging and enthusiastic English-speaking owner, who is a fount of local knowledge, you'll need to book ahead to stay in high season. Tawara-machi Station. ¥3000 per person.

🏃 Tokyo Ryokan

2-4-8 Nishi-Asakusa, Taitō-ku ☎090/8879-3599, ⓦ www.tokyoryokan.com. Beautifully rendered traditional design elements and attention to detail make this modern, Japanese-style establishment stand out from the crowd. With just three tatami rooms above a communal lounge area and a shared bathroom, it feels like you're staying in someone's home. All this, plus exceptionally reasonable rates, means you need to book well in advance. Tawaramachi Station. ¥6000.

Ginza

🏃 Ginza Yoshimizu

3-11-3 Ginza, Chūō-ku ☎03/3248-4432, ⓦ www.yoshimizu.com. See map, p.60. Look for the bamboo sprouting in front of this discreet and very appealing inn, handily located a block from the Kabuki-za. Inside, modern and traditional Japanese style blend seamlessly to create an attractive and soothing retreat. Only natural products are used in the tatami rooms, some of which are en suite, while the meals are all organic. Rates include breakfast; dinner available on request. Higashi-Ginza Station. From ¥21,200.

Gotanda and around

In the southern part of Tokyo, Gotanda is a relatively convenient place to stay thanks to its location on the Yamanote line. The places reviewed here appear on the Greater Tokyo map at the back of the book.

Ryokan Kangetsu
旅館観月

1-2-20 Chidori Ota-ku ☎03/3751-0007, ⓦ www .kangetsu.com. The main drawback of this place is its remote location, a good 20min from Gotanda via the Tōkyū Ikegami line. This said, it's a rather pleasant place, combining a new building with an older ryokan around a terraced traditional garden with a water wheel. The atmosphere is very peaceful and there's a lovely rooftop rotemburo, too. Chidorichō Station. From ¥9000.

Ryokan Sansuisō
旅館山水荘

2-9-5 Higashi-Gotanda, Shinagawa-ku ☎03/3441-7475, ⓕ 3449-1944. This modest ryokan is beautifully maintained and run by friendly people. Only a few of the simple tatami rooms have en-suite bath, and no meals are available. It's a five-minute walk from the station, near the Meguro-gawa. Gotanda Station. Singles from ¥4900; doubles from ¥8600.

Ikebukuro, Hongō and Ueno

🏃 Hōmeikan Daimachi Bekkan
鳳明館台町別館

5-12-9 Hongō, Bunkyō-ku ☎03/3811-1187, ⓦ www.homeikan.com; see Greater Tokyo map at the back of book. Of the three ryokan under the *Hōmeikan* name, it's the *Daimachi Bekkan* that's the real looker, with its ancient carpentry and traditional design. There are no en-suite bathrooms, but all rooms have tatami mats and look out on an exquisite little Japanese garden. Service is impeccable, too. The sister establishment across the road, the Meiji-era *Honkan*, is the only inn in the city that's a listed cultural property. Hongō San-chōme or Kasuga stations. From ¥11,600.

Kimi Ryokan
2-36-8 Ikebukuro, Toshima-ku ☏03/3971-3766, Ⓦwww.kimi-ryokan.jp; see map, p.99. A great-value institution on Tokyo's budget scene and a good place to meet fellow travellers – make sure you book well ahead. There's a 1am curfew. The place is a bit tricky to find, in the backstreets of west Ikebukuro. Ikebukuro Station. From ¥6500.

Ryokan Katsutaro
旅館勝太郎
4-16-8 Ikenohata, Taitō-ku ☏03/3821-9808, Ⓦwww.katsutaro.com; see map, p.91. Handily located within walking distance of Ueno Park, this homely place has just seven slightly faded tatami rooms, some with recently revamped bathrooms, plus coin laundry and Internet access. They also run a newer annexe up the road. A good alternative if *Sawanoya* (see below) is full. Nezu Station. From ¥8400.

🏃 **Sawanoya Ryokan**
2-3-11 Yanaka, Taitō-ku ☏03/3822-2251, Ⓦwww.sawanoya.com; see map, p.91. This welcoming family-run inn is a real home-from-home in a very convivial neighbourhood within walking distance of Ueno Park. Though nothing fancy, it offers good-value tatami rooms, all with washbasin, TV, telephone and air conditioning. Only two are en suite, but the two lovely new Japanese-style baths more than compensate. The owner, Sawa-san, is something of a local character, and his son performs lion dances for guests. Free Internet access, bike hire (¥200 per day), coin laundry and complimentary tea and coffee round out the picture. Nezu Station. From ¥9500.

Meguro

Fukudaya
福田屋
4-5-9 Aobadai, Meguro-ku ☏03/3467-5833, Ⓦwww.fukudaya.com; see map, pp.128–129. Ageing-with-grace ryokan that's handy for trendy Aobadai and Naka-Meguro. Western-style rooms are available too, all with attached toilet inside but the baths are shared. The manager is friendly and speaks English. Shinsen Station, or take the bus in the direction of Ikejiri Ōhashi from Shibuya Station. Single with shared bath/own bath ¥5800/7000; doubles from ¥10,000.

Hostels

Until fairly recently, hostelling in Tokyo meant staying in one of the two municipal-run youth hostels, both efficient and with excellent facilities, though the downsides are an evening curfew and, usually, a maximum stay of three nights. Now, however, several privately run hostels have come on the scene, driving prices down and standards up. All the places listed below offer Internet access, either free or for a nominal charge, and coin-operated laundries. Wherever you opt to stay, it's best to reserve well in advance.

Khaosan Tokyo
2-1-5 Kaminarimon, Taitō-ku ☏03/3842-8286, Ⓦwww.khaosan-tokyo.com; see map, p.85. The cheapest place to bed down in central Tokyo, this popular hostel has a great position overlooking the Sumida-gawa, and has recently opened two annexes and a bar across the river. Facilities include a very cramped lounge and kitchen area, and a roof terrace. Asakusa Station. Dorms – stuffed with bunk beds – cost ¥2200 per person, and there are tiny private single rooms for ¥3700 and twins for ¥5000.

K's House Tokyo
3-20-10 Kuramae, Taitō-ku ☏03/5833-0555, Ⓦwww.kshouse.jp; see map, p.72. With a canary yellow exterior, this spick-and-span new hostel just south of Asakusa gets lots of accolades. Private rooms have TV and LAN access. There's no shortage of showers and toilets, plus an attractive lounge area with a well-equipped kitchen and a roof terrace. Kuramae Station. Bunk-bed dorms from ¥2800, singles ¥3900, doubles from ¥6800, and there's an en-suite family room from ¥9800.

🏃 **Sakura Hostel**
2-24-2 Asakusa, Taitō-ku ☏03/3847-8111, Ⓦwww.sakura-hostel.co.jp; see map, p.85. This friendly, well-run hostel occupies a

cherry-pink building a couple of minutes' walk northwest of Sensō-ji. Each floor has its own shower and toilet area and, again, there's a good kitchen and TV lounge. Asakusa (Tsukuba Express railway) or Asakusa subway stations. Bunk-bed dorms ¥2940, and there are private rooms for two (¥8300) or four people (¥11800).

Sakura Hotel
2-21-4 Kanda-Jimbōchō, Chiyoda-ku
Ⓣ**03/3261-3939,** Ⓦ**www.sakura-hotel.co.jp; see map, p.67.** With both dorm bunks and private rooms, this member of the Sakura group falls somewhere between a cheap hotel and a hostel. Also in the trademark cherry-pink, it's located a couple of blocks south of Yasukuni-dōri. Rooms are boxy and share common bathrooms, but they're spotless and good value for such a central location. All come with TV, phone, Internet access and a/c. On the ground floor is a cheap café open round the clock. Jimbōchō Station. Bunk-bed dormitories ¥3780 per person, singles around ¥7000, doubles ¥8200, bunk-bed twins ¥8400.

Tokyo International Youth Hostel
18F Central Plaza, 1-1 Kaguragashi, Shinjuku-ku
Ⓣ**03/3235-1107,** Ⓦ**www.tokyo-ih.jp; see map, p.67.** On a clear winter's day you can see Mount Fuji from this smart hostel above Iidabashi Station. Exit B2b from the subway brings you straight up into the lift lobby; alternatively, from the JR station's west exit, turn right into the Ramla Centre and keep straight ahead to find the lift. Each bunk has its own curtains and locker and there are big, Japanese-style communal bathrooms. Reception is open 3–10pm; 11pm curfew. Iidabashi Station. Dorm beds ¥3900 per night.

Tokyo Yoyogi Youth Hostel
東京代々木ユースホステル
3-1 Kamizonochō, Shibuya-ku Ⓣ**03/3467-9163,** Ⓦ**www.jyh.or.jp/english/kanto/yoyogi/index .html; see map, p.114.** Small but comfortable single rooms only, with shared bathrooms, at this modern hostel, part of the Olympic Youth Centre. The hostel is on the ground floor of the curved building at the top of the hill and towards the rear of the complex. Guests must be out between 9am and 4pm, and there's a vague 10pm curfew. Sangūbashi Station. Rooms ¥3000 (¥3600 for non-JYH members).

Capsule hotels

Another option at the bottom of the price scale, at least for the odd night, are Tokyo's **capsule hotels**, rows of coffin-like tubes with just enough room to sit up, containing a thin mattress, with a TV and radio built into the plastic surrounds. The "door" consists of a plastic curtain – which won't keep out the loudest snores – and you're completely sealed away from the outside world and daylight, making alarm clocks a necessity for waking up early. Capsule hotels are generally clustered around major train stations and cater mainly to salarymen – often in various states of inebriation – who've missed the last train. While staying in a capsule provides a quintessentially Japanese experience, they won't suit everyone – claustrophobics and anyone over two metres tall should give them a miss – and note also that the majority are for men only. Rates generally include a *yukata*, towel and toothbrush set.

Capsule Inn Akasaka
かぷせるイン赤坂
6-14-1 Akasaka, Minato-ku Ⓣ**03/3588-1811; see map, p.76.** Men-only capsule hotel with a large lounge and communal bathrooms and sauna. There are 280 capsules, so you shouldn't have a problem if you turn up late at night without a booking. Check in from 5pm; check out by 10am. Akasaka Station. ¥3500 per person.

Capsule Hotel Riverside
カプセルホテルリバーサイド
2-20-4 Kaminarimon Ⓣ**03/3844-1155,**

△ A capsule hotel

Love hotels

Love hotels – where you can rent rooms by the hour – can be a source of cheap accommodation for the adventurous. Generally located in entertainment districts, such as Shibuya, Shinjuku, Ueno and Ikebukuro, they are immediately recognizable from their ornate exteriors, incorporating cupids, crenellations or, most incongruously, the Statue of Liberty, and a sign quoting prices for "rest" or "stay". They're not as sleazy as they might sound, and the main market is young people or married couples taking a break from crowded apartments. All kinds of tastes can be indulged at love hotels, with rotating beds in mirror-lined rooms being almost passé in comparison to some of the fantasy creations on offer. The best contain moving beds, lurid murals and even swimming pools; some rooms even come equipped with video cameras so you can take home a souvenir DVD of your stay.

You usually choose your room from a back-lit display indicating those available, and then negotiate with a cashier lurking behind a tiny window (eye-to-eye contact is avoided to preserve privacy). Though daytime rates are high (from about ¥3000 for 2hr), the price of an overnight stay can cost the same as a basic business hotel (roughly ¥6000–8000), though you generally can't check in until around 10pm.

If you fancy giving it a try, you'll find dozens of love hotels listed on Ⓦwww.lovehomap.com. Though in Japanese, the website is easy to navigate, with hotels divided by area, and keyed on seven maps, giving contact details, prices and an exterior shot.

Ⓦ www.asakusa-capsule.jp; see map, p.85. One of the cheapest capsule deals in Tokyo, which gets extra points for having English-speaking staff and an instruction leaflet in English. It's mainly for men (there are just 21 capsules for women on a separate floor). Asakusa Station. ¥3000 per person.

Capsule Land Shibuya
カプセルランド渋谷
1-19-14 Dōgenzaka, Shibuya-ku Ⓣ03/3464-1777, Ⓦwww.ps-w.com/landconcept; see map, p.122. Easy to find, near crest of Dōgenzaka

– which is the main thing it has going for it. Shibuya Station. ¥3700 per person.

Green Plaza Shinjuku
グリーンプラザ新宿
1-29-2 Kabukichō, Shinjuku-ku Ⓣ03/3207-4923; see map, pp.106–107. The lobby of this large men-only capsule hotel, with room for 660 guests, is on the fourth floor, with friendly staff and a good fitness and sauna area. The rooftop spa baths cost extra. Shinjuku Station. ¥4300 per person.

Long-term accommodation

The 1990s recession took the edge off Tokyo's astronomical real-estate prices, and nowadays there is a lot more accommodation available to rent, at more affordable prices. Most newcomers start off in what's known as a **gaijin house** – a privately owned house or apartment consisting of shared or private rooms with communal kitchen and bathroom. They're usually rented by the month, though if there's space, weekly or even nightly rates may be available. Tokyo has a wide range of such places, from total fleapits to the almost luxurious, though the best places are nearly always full. One of the biggest and best known agencies for *gaijin* houses is Sakura House (9F K-1 Building, 7-2-6 Nishi-Shinjuku, Shinjuku-ku; Ⓣ03/5330-5250, Ⓦwww.sakura-house.com. For other options scan the English-language press, particularly *Metropolis*, or contact the Kimi Information Centre (8F Oscar Building, 2-42-3 Ikebukuro; Ⓣ03/3986-1604, Ⓦwww.kimiwillbe.com; see map, p.99), which runs a useful letting agency. Monthly rates start from ¥30,000–40,000 per person for a shared room and ¥50,000–60,000 for a single. A deposit may also be required.

The alternative is a private **apartment**. These are usually rented out by real-estate companies, although both Sakura House and Kimi have apartments on their books and you'll find places advertised in the media. Unfortunately, there is still some endemic prejudice among landlords towards renting to non-Japanese. Some rental agencies – such as Sakura House and Kimi – specialize in dealing with foreigners, or you could ask a Japanese friend or colleague to act as an intermediary.

When you've found a place, apart from the first month's rent you should be prepared to pay a deposit of one to two months' rent in addition to key money (usually one or two months' non-refundable rent when you move in) and a month's rent in commission to the agent. You may also be asked to provide information about your financial situation and find someone – generally a Japanese national – to act as a guarantor. Rentals in Tokyo start at ¥50,000–60,000 per month for a one-room box, or ¥100,000 for somewhere with a separate kitchen and bathroom.

For more upmarket **serviced apartments**, try Tōkyū Stay (Ⓦwww.tokyustay .co.jp), Oakwood (Ⓦwww.oakwood.com/serviced-apartments/international /JP/212/Tokyo.html), Mori Living (Ⓦwww.moriliving.com) and the very affordable apartments of Ichii Corp (Ⓦwww.japt.co.jp).

Restaurants

G et ready for the gastronomic experience of a lifetime: when it comes to eating and drinking, few places in the world can compare to Tokyo. Choose any country, from Belarus to Vietnam, and you're likely to find their cuisine somewhere in the city. And, of course, there are endless renditions and permutations of Japanese favourites such as sushi, ramen, tempura and *yakitori*.

There's no need to panic about **prices**. Even celebrity-chef-fronted restaurants offer good-value set-meal specials (particularly for lunch), and there's a plethora of fast-food options, including stand-up noodle bars and conveyor-belt sushi restaurants, many clustered around and inside train stations. There's also an enormous variety of cafés and chain restaurants offering light meals.

Japanese cuisine

To assist with **ordering**, the overview of Japanese food here is complemented by a rundown of alcoholic drinks in the "Bars" chapter, and by a culinary glossary in the Language section (see pp.313–329). These days more places are providing menus translated into English, and it's always worth asking for one (*Eigo no menu arimasuka?*) if it's not automatically presented.

Noodles

The three main types of noodle are soba, udon and ramen. **Soba** are thin brown noodles made of buckwheat flour (if the noodles are green, they've been flavoured with green tea powder). *Kake-soba* is served in a clear hot broth, often with added ingredients such as tofu, vegetables and chicken; cold soba piled on a bamboo mat, with a cold sauce for dipping (which can be flavoured with chopped spring onion, seaweed flakes and *wasabi* – grated green horseradish paste), is called *zaru-soba* or *mori-soba*. In more traditional restaurants you'll also be served a flask of the hot water (*soba-yu*) used to cook the noodles, which is added to the dipping

sauce to make a soup once you've finished the soba.

Udon are thicker noodles made with plain wheat flour, and are served in the same hot or cold styles as soba. In *yakisoba* and *yakiudon* the noodles are fried, often in a thick soy sauce, along with meat, seaweed flakes and other vegetables.

Ramen are yellow, wheat-flour noodles usually served in a steaming oily soup, which typically comes in three varieties: miso (flavoured with fermented bean paste); *shio* (salt); or *shōyu* (soy sauce). A range of garnishes, including seaweed, bamboo shoots, pork slices and swirls of fish paste, often finishes off the dish. Wherever you eat ramen, you can usually accompany them with **gyōza**, fried half-moon-shaped dumplings filled with pork or seafood.

Rice dishes

A traditional meal isn't considered finished until a bowl of rice has been eaten, and the grain is an integral part of several snack-type dishes. **Onigiri** are palm-sized triangles of rice with a filling such as tuna, salmon roe or sour *umeboshi* (pickled plum), all wrapped up in a sheet of crisp *nori* (seaweed). They can be bought at convenience stores for around ¥150 each. **Donburi** is a bowl of rice topped with a *tonkatsu* pork cutlet.

Curry rice (*karē raisu*) definitely qualifies as a top Japanese comfort food and cheap snack, though what goes into the sludgy brown curry is a mystery, and you'll often search in vain for evidence of any beef or chicken in the so-called *biifu karē* and *chikin karē*.

Fish and seafood

Fish and seafood are essential and traditional elements of Japanese cuisine, and range from slices of tuna, salmon and squid laid across slabs of sushi rice to the seaweed used in miso soup.

Restaurants specializing in **kani** (crab) or the infamous **fugu** (blowfish) are easily identified by the picture or model of a crab or balloon-like fish outside. *Fugu*'s reputation derives from its poisonous nature rather than its bland, rubbery taste. The poison is concentrated in the liver and other innards which professional chefs are trained to remove, so the risk of dropping dead at the counter is virtually nil; you're more likely to keel over at the bill, which (cheaper cultivated *fugu* apart) will be in the ¥10,000-per-person bracket. A much tastier seafood speciality is **unagi** (eel), typically basted with a thick sweet sauce of soy and sake, sizzled over charcoal and served on a bed of rice.

Meat dishes

The more expensive steak restaurants serve up the likes of **sukiyaki** (thin beef slices cooked in a soy, sugar and sake broth) and **shabu-shabu** (beef and vegetable slices cooked at the table in a light broth). **Nabe** stews (the term *nabe* refers to the cooking pot) are, like the

The Big Sushi

Culinary legend has it that **sushi** was invented in Tokyo in the early nineteenth century, and not for nothing is the city nicknamed the "Big Sushi". Varieties of sushi include *chirashi-zushi*, a layer of rice topped with fish, vegetables and cooked egg, and *maki-zushi*, which is rice, raw seafood and/or vegetables rolled in a sheet of crisp seaweed. It's a common mistake of *gaijin* to assume all sushi is fish, but the term actually refers to the way the sushi rice is prepared with vinegar (slices of raw fish and seafood on their own are known as **sashimi**).

Kaiten-zushi shops, where you choose whatever sushi you want from the conveyor belt, are a cheap, convenient way of sampling this cuisine. If you can't see what you want, you can ask the chefs to make it for you. Plates are colour-coded according to how much each one costs, and the total is totted up at the end; the bill will rarely stretch beyond ¥2000 per person. Green tea is generally free, and you can usually order beer or sake.

In a traditional sushi restaurant (**sushi-ya**), each plate is freshly made by a team of chefs working in full view of the customers. If you're not sure of the different types, order by pointing at one of the trays on show in the glass chiller at the counter, or go for the *nigiri-zushi mori-awase*, six or seven different types of fish and seafood on fingers of sushi rice. A meal at a *sushi-ya* averages ¥5000 per person.

For some of the best quality sushi and sashimi, head to the stalls within the mammoth **Tsukiji** fish market (see p.134).

Vegetarianism isn't a widely practised or fully understood concept in Japan, despite the country being the home of macrobiotic cooking. You might ask for a vegetarian (*saishoku*) dish in a restaurant and still be served something with meat or fish in it. For example, you might think the most popular tofu dish in restaurants – *hiya yakko*, a small slab of chilled tofu topped with grated ginger, spring onions and soy sauce – would be suitable, but it's usually sprinkled with flakes of *bonito* (dried tuna). If you're a committed vegetarian, things to watch out for include *dashi* stock, which contains *bonito*; breads and cakes, as these can contain lard; and omelettes, which often contain chicken stock. To get a truly vegetarian meal you will have to be prepared to spell out exactly what you do and do not eat when you order.

The **Tokyo Vegetarian Guide** (Ⓦwww.vegietokyo.com) is a great website in English, with restaurant recommendations and other information to help guide you to places that fit your dietary needs. In this chapter, check out the reviews for *Bon* (p.165), *Café Eight* (p.167), *Gaya* (p.175), *Hiroba* (p.170), *Mominoki House* (p.170), *Natural Harmony Angoro* (p.170) and *Shunjū* (p.164).

⑮

RESTAURANTS | Japanese cuisine

aforementioned dishes, prepared at the table over a gas or charcoal burner; diners throw raw meat or fish, along with vegetables, into the pot to cook. As things cook, they're fished out and eaten; the last thing to be immersed is usually some type of noodle. *Chanko-nabe* is the famous chuck-it-all-in stew used to beef up sumo wrestlers.

Yakitori are delicious skewers of grilled chicken (and sometimes other meats, offal and vegetables). At the cheapest *yakitori-ya*, you pay for each skewer individually. Not dissimilar are

kushiage, skewers of meat, seafood and vegetables, coated in breadcrumbs and deep-fried. Another popular meat dish is **tonkatsu**, fried, breadcrumbed slabs of pork, usually served on shredded cabbage with a brown, semi-sweet sauce.

Other dishes

Best eaten piping hot from the fryer, **tempura** are lightly battered pieces of seafood and vegetables, dipped in a bowl of light sauce (*ten-tsuyu*) mixed with grated *daikon* (mooli radish) and sometimes ginger. Specialist restaurants

Japan's gift to the vegetarian world is **tofu** – cakes of soya-bean curd. It comes in two main varieties, *momen-dōfu* (cotton tofu, so-called because of its fluffy texture) and the smoother, more fragile *kinugoshi-dōfu* (silk tofu). At a few specialist restaurants you can experience Buddhist cuisine (*shōjin-ryōri*), which concocts whole menus around different tofu dishes.

Miso (fermented bean paste) is another crucial ingredient of Japanese cooking, used in virtually every meal, if only in the soup *miso-shiru*. It often serves as a flavouring in vegetable dishes and comes in two main varieties, the light *shiro-miso* and the darker, stronger-tasting *aka-miso*. One of the most delicious ways of eating the gooey paste is *hōba miso*, where the miso is mixed with vegetables, roasted over a charcoal brazier, and served on a large magnolia leaf.

One question all foreigners in Japan are asked is "Can you eat **nattō**?". This sticky, stringy, fermented bean paste has a strong taste and unfamiliar texture, which can be off-putting. It's worth trying at least once, though, and is often served in little tubs as part of a traditional Japanese breakfast, to be mixed with mustard and soy sauce and eaten with rice.

have set meals which typically include whole prawns, squid, aubergines, mushrooms and the aromatic herb *shiso*, all prepared tempura-style.

Oden, a great winter dish (but available year found), tastes much more delicious than it looks. Large chunks of food, usually on skewers, are simmered in a thin broth, and often served from portable carts (*yatai*) on street corners or in convenience stores from beside the till. The main ingredients are blocks of tofu, *daikon*, *konnyaku* jelly (made from a root vegetable), *konbu* (seaweed), hard-boiled eggs and fish cakes. All are best eaten with a smear of fiery English-style mustard.

Like a cross between pizza and an omelette, **okonomiyaki** is a fun, cheap meal, comprising a pancake batter that binds shredded cabbage and other vegetables with either seafood or meat. Very similar is *monjayaki*, a savoury pancake unique to Tokyo (see p.137). DIY restaurants give you the chance to mix the ingredients and cook them on a griddle in the middle of the table. Once cooked, *okonomiyaki* is coated in a sweet brown sauce and/or mayonnaise and dusted off with dried seaweed and *bonito* flakes.

A hybrid style of cooking known as **yōshoku** ("Western food") developed as Western influences permeated Japan at the end of the nineteenth century. Examples of *yōshoku* dishes include omelettes with a filling of rice (*omuraisu*), deep-fried potato croquettes (*korokke*) and hamburger steaks in a thick sauce (*hanbāgu*). Similar in spirit is **mukokuseki** or "no-nationality" cuisine, a mishmash of world cooking styles usually found in Japanese-style pubs.

Meals

The traditional Japanese **breakfast** features miso soup, fish, pickles and rice, though many Japanese now prefer a quick *kōhii* and *tōsuto* (coffee and toast), served at most cafés on the "morning service" menu. Many ryokan and top hotels offer a choice between a Western- or Japanese-style breakfast.

Hardly any locals linger over **lunch**, usually taken around noon – but that's no reason why you should follow suit. You could grab a sandwich, *onigiri* or a **bentō** (a boxed meal, served particularly at lunchtime), but it's better to go for a hearty restaurant meal. All restaurants offer **set menus** (*teishoku*), usually at around ¥1000 for a couple of courses plus a drink, and only rarely topping ¥3000 per person. This makes lunch ideal for sampling the food at top restaurants. **Dinner**, the main meal of the day, can be eaten as early as 6pm (with many places taking last orders around 9pm), although Tokyo is not short of options for late-night dining. At both lunch and dinner you may also come across what is described as a "course menu", which is in fact a set menu of several courses and more expensive than the *teishoku*.

Kaiseki-ryōri: Japanese haute cuisine

Japan's finest style of cooking, **kaiseki-ryōri**, comprises a series of small, carefully balanced and expertly presented dishes; it's a unique dining experience which shouldn't be missed while in Tokyo.

Kaiseki-ryōri began as an accompaniment to the tea ceremony and still retains the meticulous design of that elegant ritual. At the best *kaiseki-ryōri* restaurants the ambience of the room is just as important as the food; you'll sit on tatami, a scroll decorated with calligraphy will hang in the *tokonoma* (alcove) and a waitress in kimono will serve each course on beautiful china and lacquerware.

For such a sublime experience you should expect to pay ¥10,000 or more for dinner, although a *kaiseki* bentō is a more affordable option. Good *kaiseki-ryōri* restaurants to try include *Kakiden* (see p.176), *Tōfuya-Ukai* (see p.174) and the *Park Hyatt's Kazue* (see p.176).

With traditional Japanese cuisine you'll usually get all your courses at the same time, but at more formal places rice and soup are always served at the end of the meal.

Restaurants

Tokyo has over 300,000 places to eat, from simple street food vendors to high temples of gastronomy where the eye-popping beauty of the food on the plate is paired with an equally creative approach to interior design. If style matters are of little concern, there are several unpretentious restaurant **chains** worth checking out, including good-value "family" establishments such as *Denny's*, *Royal Host* and *Jonathan's*, serving both Western and Japanese dishes and with easy-to-choose-from picture menus; most are open 24 hours, too.

The restaurant floors of **department stores**, such as Lumine and My City in Shinjuku (see p.104), or **shopping malls**, including Roppongi Hills (see p.81) and the new Galleria at Tokyo Midtown (see p.80), are also worth a look. They harbour a wide choice of cuisines under one roof, often with plastic food displays in the windows and lots of daily specials.

Japanese rarely go out just to drink, and **izakaya** (traditional bars) also serve great food; a few with especially good food are reviewed here, others in the Bars chapter.

For the most up-to-date information on Tokyo's restaurants, check out the free weekly magazine *Metropolis* or the excellent website Tokyo Food Page (Ⓦ www .bento.com); the author of this site, Robb Satterwhite, also writes *Not Just a Good Food Guide Tokyo*, a handy pocket guidebook to Tokyo's dining scene. Also useful is the Gourmet Navigator website Ⓦ www.gnavi.co.jp/en.

The restaurants reviewed in this book have been graded as **inexpensive** (under ¥1000 for a meal without alcohol); **moderate** (¥1000–4000); **expensive** (¥4000–6000) and **very expensive** (over ¥6000). **Consumption tax** (five percent) can push up the total cost if not included in the prices. Some restaurants and bars serving food, especially those in hotels, add on a **service charge** (typically ten percent). Make sure you have cash to hand; payment by **credit card** is becoming more common, but is generally restricted to upmarket restaurants and hotels. **Reservations** are advisable for many places, especially on Friday, Saturday and Sunday nights.

Akasaka

The places reviewed below appear on the map on p.76.

Aux Bacchanales
2F Ark Mori Building, 1-12-32 Akasaka, Minato-ku Ⓣ 03/3582-2225. Tucked away in the Ark Hills complex, opposite Suntory Hall, this is

Tokyo and the celebrity chef

Japan's love of international brand names has lured many internationally famous chefs and restaurateurs to set up shop in Tokyo, including Alain Ducasse, Gordon Ramsay and Sir Terence Conran. But celebrity chefs are just not that important to many Tokyo gourmands, who might well name as their favourite chef someone who grills succulent *yakitori* at their neighbourhood eatery. Top homegrown chefs who've made a splash internationally include **Nobu Matsuhisa**, who, after conquering LA, London and New York, has returned to his roots with *Nobu* (see p.173); and **Imai Koji**, who had a humble start at *Ebisu Imaiya* (see p.167), but now runs multiple operations including *Megu*, the Japanese restaurant that's the toast of Manhattan.

one of Tokyo's most authentic Parisian-style brasseries – their *steak frite* is the real thing – and it's a pleasant spot to hang out sipping coffee or red wine. Moderate. Roppongi-itchōme Station. Daily 10am–midnight.

Jidaiya
時代屋

3-14-3 Akasaka, Minato-ku ☎03/3588-0489. Charming farmhouse-style place in the heart of Akasaka, all dark wood, tatami and traditional ornaments. There's an English menu to help you select between the wide range of dishes, including a wild boar stew for ¥4000 and a *kaiseki*-style course for ¥8000. Lunch is a great deal at under ¥1000. There's also a branch in Roppongi (B1F Uni Roppongi Building, 7-15-17 Roppongi, Minato-ku; ☎03/3403-3563). Expensive. Akasaka Station. Mon–Fri 11.30am–2.30pm & 5pm–4am, Sat & Sun 5–11pm.

 Kurosawa
黒澤

2-7-9 Nagatachō, Chiyoda-ku ☎03/3580-9638. Politicos and bureaucrats are likely to spotted here dining on the quality soba and pork dishes that are the speciality of this atmospheric restaurant, whose design was inspired by the sets from Akira Kurosawa's movies *Yojimbo* and *Red Beard*. They also have a couple of other cute restaurants, one specializing in udon (6-11-16 Roppongi, Minato-ku ☎03/3403-9638) and *Soba Dining Kurosawa* (蕎麦ダイニングくろさわ; 3-2-15 Nishi-Azabu, Minato-ku ☎03/5775-9638) both near Roppongi Hills. Moderate. Tameike-sannō Station. Mon–Fri 11.30am–3pm, 5–10pm, Sat noon–9pm.

Kyūshū Jangara Rāmen
九州じゃんがらラーメン

2-12-8 Nagatachō, Chiyoda-ku ☎03/3595-2130, ⓦwww.kyusyujangara.co.jp. On Sotobori-dōri, near the entrance to the Hie-jinja, this funky noodle bar serves up large bowls of Kyūshū-style ramen in three types of soup: fish, mild and light, and greasy garlic. Branches in Akihabara (3-11-6 Soto-Kanda, Chiyoda-ku; ☎03/3512-4059), Ginza (7-11-10 Ginza, Chūō-ku; ☎03/3289-2307) and on Omotesandō near Harajuku Station (1-13-21 Jingūmae, Shibuya-ku; ☎03/3404-5572). Inexpensive. Tameike-sannō Station. Mon–Fri 11am–3pm & 5pm–12.30am.

Ninja
忍者

1F Akasaka Tōkyū Building, 2-14-31 Nagatachō, Chiyoda-ku ☎03/5157-3936. Dark, twisting corridors, waiters who jump out of secret doorways, a magician who does amazing tricks at your table – all this and more make up the fun dining experience at this upmarket *ninja*-themed *izakaya*. The modern Japanese cuisine comes in small but tasty portions. Moderate to expensive. Akasaka-Mitsuke Station. Daily 5.30pm–4am.

 Shunjū
春秋

27F San'nō Park Tower, 2-11-1 Nagatachō, Chiyoda-ku ☎03/3592-5288, ⓦwww.shunju .com/ja. The modern Japanese dining experience *par excellence*, matching stylish interior design with food made from the freshest seasonal ingredients. Lunch deals are good (although the place gets busy with office workers) while in the evening set menus kick off at ¥6000 (plus twenty percent in service and taxes). Branches around town include the more casual *Kitchen Shunjū* (☎03/5369-0377; see map pp.106–107) in Shinjuku's My City department store and *Shunjū Tsugihagi* (☎03/3595-0511; see map, p.60) opposite the *Imperial Hotel*. Expensive to very expensive. Tameike-sannō Station. Mon–Sat 11.30am–2.30pm & 5–11pm.

West Park Café
2F Akasaka Tōkyū Plaza, 2-14-3 Nagatachō, Chiyoda-ku ☎03/3580-9090. Relaxed American-style deli-café, with an outdoor terrace and an airy interior. Good for light meals and weekend brunches. There are other branches a 5min walk west of Yoyogi-kōen at 23-11 Moto-Yoyogichō, and on the fifth floor of the Maru Building, Marunouchi (see map, p.60). Moderate. Akasaka-mitsuke Station. Mon–Fri 11.30am–11pm, Sat & Sun 11.30am–3pm.

Asakusa and around

The places reviewed here appear on the map on p.85, except for a few restaurants, noted in the text, which appear on the Greater Tokyo map at the back of the book.

Bon
梵
1-2-11 Ryusen, Taitō-ku ☎03/3872-0375, ⓦwww.fuchabon.co.jp; see Greater Tokyo map. A rare chance to sample *fucha shojin-ryōri*, a distinctive style of Zen Buddhist cuisine in which each dish is traditionally served from one large bowl, and the meal begins and

ends with tea. The setting, a charming old Japanese house, and the calm service, make it an experience not to be missed. Reservations essential. Expensive to very expensive. Iriya Station. Daily except Wed noon–3pm & 5.30–7pm.

Chin-ya
ちんや
1-3-4 Asakusa, Taitō-ku ☎03/3841-0010, ⓦwww.chinya.co.jp. Founded in 1880, this famous, traditional *shabu-shabu* and *sukiyaki* restaurant offers basic menus from ¥3200. The place occupies seven floors, with cheaper, more casual dining in the basement (from ¥2600). Moderate to expensive. Asakusa Station. Daily except Tues noon–9pm.

Daikokuya
大黒家
1-38-10 Asakusa, Taitō-ku ☎03/3844-1111, ⓦwww.tempura.co.jp; branch at 1-31-10 Asakusa ☎03/3844-2222. There's always a lunchtime queue at this Meiji-era tempura restaurant, set in an attractive old building opposite Dembō-in garden. The speciality is *tendon*, a satisfying bowl of shrimp, fish and prawn fritters on a bed of rice (from ¥1470). If the main branch is too busy or closed, head for the annexe around the corner, next to *Ryokan Shigetsu*. Moderate. Asakusa Station. Open 11.30am–8.30pm; closing days vary.

Hatsuogawa
初小川
2-8-4 Kaminarimon, Taitō-ku ☎03/3844-2723. Look for the profusion of potted plants outside this tiny, rustic eel restaurant. It's

Fast-food city

When it comes to **fast food**, there's no shortage of places, from the usual Western suspects to local chains such as *Yoshinoya*, which serves reasonably tasty *gyūdon* (stewed strips of beef on rice); and *Tenya*, for tempura and rice dishes. The ubiquitous *Mos Burger* does an interesting line of burgers sandwiched by patties of rice, while newcomer *R Burger* (ⓦwww.r-burger.co.jp), which has a branch near Roppongi Crossing, serves healthy burgers made from lean pork or chicken, in between soft Chinese-style buns.

A huge hit of recent years has been *Soup Stock Tokyo* (ⓦwww.soup-stock-tokyo .com), serving a great selection of hearty broths. In a similar vein, the latest fast-food craze is for **soup curry**, a not-too-spicy concoction that hails originally from Hokkaidō; *Soup Curry Cocoro* (ⓦwww.cocoro-soupcurry.com) is one of the chains to look out for.

Convenience stores such as 7-Eleven, AM/PM and Lawson sell snacks and meals round the clock, which can be heated up in the shop's microwave. For more upmarket goodies, make your way to the basement food halls of the major department stores.

very foreigner-friendly and a lovely place to experience this most luscious of Japanese dishes. Moderate. Asakusa Station. Mon–Sat noon–2pm & 5–8pm, Sun 5–8pm.

Khroopkhrua

1-33-4 Asakusa, Taitō-ku ☏ 03/3847-3461, ⓦ www.khroopkhrua.com. Thai/Vietnamese restaurant offering fresh spring rolls, flavourful Vietnamese *pho* soup and even a Thai take on *sukiyaki*, among other delights. It's all pretty authentic and you can wash it down with a bottle of Singha, 333 Beer and other imported brews. Inexpensive to moderate. Asakusa Station. Mon–Sat 11.30am–3pm & 6–11pm, Sun noon–9pm.

Maguro Bito

まぐろ人

1-5-9 Asakusa, Taitō-ku ☏ 03/3844-8736. Fuji TV viewers voted this the top *kaiten-zushi* shop in Japan, and it's easy to see why: the quality of fish and other ingredients is excellent, the turnover fast and the decor on the ritzy side. Expect a queue (but it moves fast). Electronically price-coded plates range from ¥130 to ¥400. Inexpensive to moderate. Asakusa Station. Daily 11am–10pm

Matsunami

1-11-6 Asakusa, Taitō-ku ☏ 03/3844-3737, ⓦ www.matsunami.net. If you want to try some of Japan's melt-in-the-mouth beef, lunch at this traditional steakhouse, where the chef cooks the meat in front of you, won't break the bank; prices start at ¥1575. Moderate to expensive. Asakusa (Tsukuba Express railway) or Tawaramachi stations. Daily 11.30am–2pm & 5pm–1am, Sun until 10pm.

Nakae

中江

1-9-2 Nihonzutsumi, Taitō-ku ☏ 03/3872-5398; see Greater Tokyo map. This venerable restaurant specializes in dishes made with horse meat, including *sukiyaki* – an unusual delight, although it won't be to everyone's taste. The interior, decorated with beautiful ink paintings of horses, looks pretty much like it did a century ago when the whole area was a thriving red-light district. Next door is *Dote-no-Iseya* (土手の伊勢屋; daily except Wed 11.30am–2pm & 5–8pm) an equally atmospheric joint specializing in *tendon*. Moderate. Minowa Station. Tues–Sun 11.30am–2pm & 5–10pm.

Otafuku

大多福

1-6-2 Senzoku, Taitō-ku ☏ 03/3871-2521; see Greater Tokyo map. Customers have been coming to this charming restaurant for over eighty years to sample its delicious selection of *oden*. Wash it all down with a glass of pine-scented *tarozake* (sake). Some knowledge of Japanese would help here, but staff are very friendly and you can sit at the counter and point at what you want in the bubbling brass vats. Moderate to expensive. Iriya Station. Tues–Sun 5–11pm.

Owariya

尾張屋

1-7-1 Asakusa, Taitō-ku ☏ 03/3845-4500. This unpretentious restaurant has been dishing up delicious soba in all its variations for over a century. Nowadays it also serves tempura and rice dishes. Inexpensive to moderate. Tawaramachi Station. Daily except Fri 11.30am–8.30pm.

Sometaro

染太郎

2-2-2 Nishi-Asakusa, Taitō-ku ☏ 03/3844-9502. Homely restaurant specializing in *okonomiyaki*. One good-sized bowl costs from ¥400, depending on the ingredients, or you can opt for an "introductory set" of three varieties for ¥1575 (enough to feed two). Alternatively, try your hand at *yakisoba* (from ¥610). There's a book of English instructions and plenty of

△ Preparing *okonomiyaki*

people to offer advice. To find the place, look for a bamboo-fenced garden and lantern halfway up the street. Inexpensive. Tawaramachi Station. Tues–Sun noon–10pm.

Ebisu, Hiro-o, Meguro & Naka-Meguro

The places reviewed below appear on the map on pp.128–129.

Café Eight
T+ Bldg, 3-17-7 Aobadai, Meguro-ku ⓣ03/5458-5262, ⓦwww.cafe8.jp.
Charming café-bar with unimpeachable vegan credentials, serving a menu of salads, sandwiches and other dishes prepared mainly with organic ingredients. Even the champagne is organic. They also host interesting art exhibits. Inexpensive. Naka-Meguro Station. Tues–Sun 11am–9.30pm.

Chano-ma
6F Nakameguro Kangyō Building, 1-22-4 Kami-Meguro, Meguro-ku ⓣ03/3792-9898.
Slip off your shoes and relax on the huge padded bed-like platform, overlooking the river and train tracks, at this super-casual operation. They serve some very tasty rustic-style Japanese dishes, as well as a great selection of teas and flavoured lattes. Moderate. Naka-Meguro Station. Mon–Thurs & Sun noon–2am, Fri & Sat noon–4am.

Ebisu Imaiya
えびす今井屋
1-7-11 Ebisu-Nishi, Shibuya-ku ⓣ03/5456-0255, ⓦwww.imaiya.co.jp. The man behind New York's *Megu* started his restaurant empire at this backstreet joint serving the "ultimate chicken" – the *hinai-jidori* broiler from Akita-ken in northern Japan – as well as a choice selection of sake. Downstairs it's casual and lively; for more privacy and service from kimonoed waitresses, book a private room upstairs. Moderate to expensive. Ebisu Station; take the road opposite with Mizuho bank on the corner, and you'll find the restaurant on the right-hand side. Mon–Thurs & Sun 5pm–1am, Fri & Sat 5pm–3am.

Fummy's Grill
2-1-5 Ebisu, Shibuya-ku ⓣ03/3473-9629.
California-style cuisine with good renditions of dishes such as Caesar salad, served in a casual setting with a small open terrace overlooking a quiet street. They also offer a weekend brunch. Moderate. Ebisu Station. Daily 11am–4pm & 5.30pm–2am.

Higashiyama
東山
1-21-25 Higashiyama, Meguro-ku ⓣ03/5720-1300, ⓦwww.simplicity.co.jp. It's well worth making the hike from Naka-Meguro station to this elegant hillside restaurant and bar that's the epitome of Tokyo cool. The multi-level space has an open kitchen that allows you watch the delicious range of dishes being prepared. The course menu is a deal at ¥6000 and they have a fine selection of sake and *shōchū* to match. The same company is behind the equally stylish and appealing *Higashiya* teahouse (see p.186). Expensive to very expensive. Naka-Meguro Station. Mon–Sat 6pm–midnight.

Homework's
5-1-20 Hiro-o, Shibuya-ku ⓣ03/3440-4560.
This popular pit stop at the end of Hiro-o's main shopping street does good, chunky, home-made burgers – and the French fries are well up to scratch, too. There's also a branch near Roppongi Hills (1-5-8 Azabu-Jūban, Minato-ku; ⓣ03/3405-9884; see map, p.79). Moderate. Hiro-o Station. Mon–Sat 11am–9pm, Sun 11am–6pm.

Tonki
とんき
1-1-2 Shimo-Meguro, Meguro-ku ⓣ03/3491-9928. Tokyo's most famous *tonkatsu* restaurant, where a seemingly telepathic team make order of chaos. You'll need to queue up outside the main branch, west of the station, which is only open from 4pm; for lunch, go to *Tonki Annex* on the east side of the station, across the plaza on the second floor of the corner building. Moderate. Meguro Station. Daily except Tues 4–10.45pm.

Ginza and around

There are plenty of restaurants to choose from in the new Oazo, Marunouchi and Coredo buildings, and the Caretta Shiodome complex. The more adventurous will want to muck in with the locals at the numerous *yakitori* bars nestling under the railway tracks between Yūrakuchō and Shimbashi stations. The places reviewed below are shown on the map on p.60.

Aroyna Tabeta
あろいなたべた
3-7-11 Marunouchi, Chiyoda-ku ⓣ03/5219-6099, ⓦtabeta.com/yurakucho. Note the big

⑮

RESTAURANTS | Restaurants

¥630 sign – that's the price you'll pay for all food, including set meals, at this basic Thai place under the tracks. The cooking is heavy on the chilli (a surprise in Tokyo) but tasty, and great value. Inexpensive. Yūrakuchō Station. Open virtually 24hr daily (closed 10.30–11.20am).

Ichi-ni-san (One-Two-Three)

B2F Caretta Shiodome Building, 1-8-2 Higashi-Shinbashi, Minato-ku ☎03/5537-2123. Among a host of casual restaurants in the basement floors of the Caretta building, try this restaurant serving local "black pork" meat with *ponzu*, a sesame-laced dipping sauce, and other delicacies from Kagoshima in Kyushu. Lunch sets start at around ¥1000. Moderate. Shiodome Station. Mon–Sat 11am–9.45pm, Sun 11am–8.45pm.

Dhaba India

2-7-9 Yaesu, Chūō-ku ☎03/3272-7160. Give your taste buds a workout at this bustling South Indian restaurant, popular among the local Indian community. Specialities include a potent chicken and black pepper curry and a sweet-and-sour fish curry, and you can choose from the wide selection of set meals. They also do a mean dhosa. Moderate. Kyōbashi Station. Mon–Fri 11.15am–3pm & 5–11pm, Sat & Sun noon–3pm & 5–10pm.

G-Zone Ginza

1-2-3 Ginza, Chūō-ku. The Global Dining group has gathered together several of its concept restaurants at this complex beneath the Shuto Expressway – from the ye olde Japanese-style *Gonpachi* (☎03/5524-3641) at one end to the faux-European *La Bohème* (☎03/5524-3616) at the other, with the Mexican *Zest Cantina* (☎03/5524-3621) and Southeast Asian *Monsoon Café* (☎03/5524-3631) in the middle; all are pretty dependable. Moderate to expensive. Ginza-itchōme Station. Daily 11.30am–3.30am.

Hibiki

46F Caretta Shiodome Building, 1-8-2 Higashi-Shinbashi, Minato-ku ☎0120-55-8874. Take the ear-popping lift to the 46th floor of the Caretta building and admire the breathtaking views from the windows of this modern *izakaya*, which serves contemporary Japanese cuisine in sleek surroundings. The lunch sets (from ¥1200) are particularly good value; count on around ¥6000 a head in the evening. Moderate to expensive. Shiodome Station. Mon–Fri 11am–3pm &

5–11.30pm, Sat & Sun 11am–4pm & 5–11pm.

Little Okinawa

8-7-10 Ginza, Chūō-ku ☎03/3572-2930. The welcome at this cosy Okinawan restaurant is as warm as it would be in the southern islands. Try Ryūkyū dishes such as *champuru* (noodles with stir-fried veg) and the strong rice liquor *awamori*. There's an English menu, but the Japanese one has photos. Bookings recommended. Moderate. Shimbashi Station. Mon–Fri 5pm–3am, Sat & Sun 4pm–midnight.

Mango Tree Tokyo

35F Marunouchi Building, 2-4-1 Marunouchi, Chiyoda-ku ☎03/5224-5489. Stylish Thai restaurant with branches in Shinjuku's Lumine department store (☎03/6389-2535) as well as in Bangkok and London. The tasty lunchtime buffet (¥2625) is one of the best ways to enjoy the view from the top of the Marunouchi Building. Moderate. Tokyo Station. Daily 11am–4pm & 5–11pm.

Matsumotorō

1-2 Hibiya-kōen, Chiyoda-ku ☎03/3503-1451. On a sunny day it's a pleasure to sit on the terrace of this venerable restaurant, as old as Tokyo's first Western-style park, in which it's located. The food is pretty standard, along the lines of *omu-raisu* (rice-filled omelette), hamburgers, *croques* (French-style toasted sandwiches) and other Western "favourites". Moderate. Hibiya Station. Daily 10am–9pm.

Nair's

4-10-7 Ginza, Chūō-ku ☎03/3541-8246. This Tokyo institution has been going since 1949, and although it's perhaps not the best Indian place around, the Kerala home cooking is tasty and reasonably cheap for Ginza, even if the decor is on the tacky, Bollywood side. Moderate. Higashi-Ginza Station. Daily except Tues 11.30am–9.30pm, Sun until 8.30pm.

No-no-Budō
野の葡萄

3F Tokia Building, 2-7-3 Marunouchi, Chiyoda-ku ☎03/3215-7320. Avoid the peak lunchtime rush (11.30am–1pm) if you don't want to queue at this café-style "natural foods buffet", where you can fill up on a good spread of salads and Japanese dishes, including some organic foods. Lunch costs ¥1600, including soft drinks, while dinner is a pretty reasonable ¥2600. Moderate. Tokyo Station. Daily 11am–4pm & 5.30–11pm.

Robata Honten
爐端本店

1-3-8 Yūrakuchō, Chiyoda-ku ☎03/3591-1905. The delicious food at this rustic *izakaya* (look for the basket of veggies outside) is laid out in big plates for you to see – order what you fancy and the kimono-clad staff will whisk it off to be prepared. Moderate. Hibiya Station. Daily 5–11pm.

Taimeiken

1-12-10 Nihombashi, Chūō-ku ☎03/3271-2464. Tokyoites swoon at the nostalgia of one of Tokyo's original Western-style restaurants, whose *omu-raisu* featured in the movie *Tampopo* (see p.211). Waiting staff bustle about the cheap and cheerful cafeteria downstairs serving large portions of curry rice, *tonkatsu* and noodles. Upstairs is a more formal restaurant serving the same menu at higher prices. Inexpensive to moderate. Nihombashi Station. Mon–Sat 11am–9pm.

Takara
宝

B1 Tokyo International Forum, 3-5-1 Marunouchi, Chiyoda-ku ☎03/5223-9888. A striking red communal table defines this modern *izakaya*, specializing in sake and serving excellent modern Japanese cuisine – try their substantial lunch sets. John Gautner, Tokyo's *gaijin* sake guru, holds monthly seminars here. Moderate. Yūrakuchō Station. Mon–Fri 11.30am–2.30pm & 5–11pm, Sat & Sun 11.30am–3.30pm.

Tenmaru
天○

6-9-2 Ginza, Chūō-ku ☎03/3289-1010. Consistently good tempura restaurant in a basement just off Chūō-dōri. Expect to spend at least ¥2000 per head. Limited English menu available. Moderate. Ginza Station. Mon–Fri 11.30am–3pm & 5–9.20pm, Sat & Sun 11.30am–9.30pm.

Torigin Honten
鳥ぎん本店

B1F 5-5-7 Ginza, Chūō-ku ☎03/3571-3333, ⓦwww.torigin-ginza.co.jp. Bright, popular restaurant serving *yakitori* and *kamameshi* (kettle-cooked rice with a choice of toppings), tucked down an alley two blocks east of Ginza's Sony Building. Good for a snack or a full meal, particularly if you opt for *kamameshi* or a weekday lunch set, both from around ¥800. English menu available. Inexpensive. Ginza Station. Daily 11.30am–10pm.

Tsukiji Sushi Sen
築地すし鮮

5-9-1 Ginza, Chūō-ku ☎03/5337-2878. This outpost of the well-known *Tsukiji sushi* restaurant provides a useful pit stop any time of day or night. It's a bright and breezy place, serving up a good choice of well-priced sushi and sashimi sets, as well as à la carte food from a picture menu, with some English explanations. There's a branch on Asakusa's Kaminarimon-dōri, east of the tourist office (☎03/5830-1020). Inexpensive to moderate. Higashi-Ginza Station. Daily 24hr.

Ume-no-hana
梅の花

5F 2-3-6 Ginza, Chūō-ku ☎03/3538-2226, ⓦwww.umenohana.co.jp. Trickling streams and bamboo screens set the mood in this elegant restaurant far from the madding crowds of Ginza, below. It specializes in melt-in-the-mouth tofu creations – the tofu comes natural, deep fried, boiled, grilled or sweetened for dessert. If you can't decide, try the *yudōfu* set (¥1600), where you boil the tofu at the table, then eat it with grated ginger and a sprinkling of ground sesame, accompanied by all sorts of other delicacies. Dinner sets start from ¥4500. Moderate to expensive. Ginza-itchōme Station. Daily 11am–4pm & 5–10pm.

Harajuku and Aoyama

The places reviewed below appear on the map on p.118, except for *Kurkku Kitchen, Mominoki House, Nabi, Natural Harmony Angoro* and *Tarlum*, which appear on the map on p.114.

AtoZ

Minami Aoyama 5-8-3 ☎03/5464 0281, ⓦa-to-z.heteml.jp. Enter the offbeat world of artist Yoshitomo Nara, who has helped create this impressive café – part art installation, part kindergarten for the art-school set. The food includes tasty salads, noodle and rice dishes – all the kind of things a Japanese mum might cook up. Moderate. Omotesandō Station. Daily 11.30am–11.30pm.

Benoit

10F La Porte Aoyama, 5-51-8 Jingūmae, Shibuya-ku ☎03/5468-0883, ⓦwww.benoit -tokyo.com. The best value at this Alain Ducasse venture is the Parisian-style café, which has great views to boot, back across Aoyama towards Yoyogi-kōen. The main dining hall is above, with set menus starting at ¥4500 for lunch, ¥8000 for dinner. Expensive. Omotesandō Station. Daily 11.30am–10pm.

Fujimamas

6-3-2 Jingūmae, Shibuya-ku ☎ 03/5485-2262. There's a bit more style than substance to the East–West fusion food at this popular place, but it's generally good value and the menu is a hoot (desserts are headed "Oh, I just couldn't … but I will!"). Moderate. Meiji-jingūmae Station. Mon–Fri noon–3pm & 6–11pm, Sat & Sun noon–4pm & 6–11pm.

Heirokuzushi

平禄寿司

5-8-5 Jingūmae, Shibuya-ku ☎ 03/3498-3968. Perennially popular *kaiten-zushi* restaurant in a prime position on Omotesandō. Plates range from ¥120 to ¥240. Inexpensive. Meiji-jingūmae Station. Daily 11am–9pm.

Hiroba

広場

3-8-15 Kita-Aoyama, Minato-ku ☎ 03/3406-6409. Hearty lunch buffets with plenty of veggie options for ¥1200. It's at the Crayon House natural food shop, just off Omotesandō and around the corner from the Hanae Mori Building. Moderate. Omotesandō Station. Daily 11am–10pm.

🏃 Kurkku Kitchen

2-18-21 Jingūmae, Shibuya-ku ☎ 03/5414-0944, ⓦ www.kurkku.jp. The Kurkku (Finnish for "cucumber") complex is an ecologically sound operation comprising a café, shop, library and charming roof garden, as well as this restaurant – which makes delicious use of organic ingredients in a very stylish natural wood environment. Moderate to expensive. Meiji-jingūmae Station. Tues–Sun 11.30am–2pm & 6–10pm.

Maisen

マイ泉

4-8-5 Jingūmae, Shibuya-ku ☎ 03/3470-0071. Famous for being set in an old bathhouse, this long-running *tonkatsu* restaurant serves up great-value set meals. The actual bathhouse bit is the smoking section of the restaurant. Moderate. Omotesandō Station. Daily 11am–10pm.

Marché de Metro

Omotesandō Station. In the warren of underground tunnels that thread their way beneath Omotesandō to the metro lines is this stylish French-style food court. It's a serve-yourself affair, with stalls offering all

manner of tasty options, from crepes to freshly baked croissants or a nice glass of red. Inexpensive. Omotesandō Station. Daily 7.30am–11pm.

Mist

3F Omotesandō Hills, 4-12-10 Meiji-Jingūmae, Shibuya-ku ☎ 03/5410-1368, ⓦ www.chabuya .com. You may well wonder how good a bowl of ramen could be to justify a price tag close to ¥2000 per person, once all the extras are added on. However, this plush restaurant/bar, specializing in the humble noodle, does generally make a delicious product, though the eccentric ramen sushi doesn't really work. Moderate. Omotesandō Station. Daily 11am–11pm.

Mominoki House

モミノキハウス

2-18-5 Jingūmae, Shibuya-ku ☎ 03/3405-9144. Lots of natural ingredients are used at this macrobiotic restaurant, and in business since 1976. Plants, paintings and jazz add to the atmosphere, and a good lunch can be had for ¥1050. Dinner courses start at ¥2800. Moderate. Meiji-jingūmae Station. Mon–Sat 11am–11pm.

Nabi

B1F Accorder Jingūmae, 2-31-20 Jingūmae, Shibuya-ku, ☎ 03/5771-0071, ⓦ www.nabi -tokyo.com. Stylish Korean restaurant using mainly organic ingredients for dishes such as *do pulgogi* (smoked beef salad). Moderate. Meiji-jingūmae Station. Mon–Fri 11.30am–1am, Sat 6pm–1am, Sun 6pm–midnight.

🏃 Natural Harmony Angoro

ナチュラルハーモニーレストランアンゴロ

3-38-12 Jingūmae, Shibuya-ku ☎ 03/3405-8393. Rustically stylish, *Natural Harmony Angoro* is one of the best of Tokyo's vegetarian picks (although note that some of their dishes do include fish). Set lunches will fill you up nicely and in the evening you can wash your meal down with organic wine or beer. Moderate. Gaienmae Station. Tues–Sun 11.30am–2.30pm & 6–8.50pm.

△ Food at Natural Harmony Angoro

Sakuratei

さくら亭

3-20-1 Jingūmae, Shibuya-ku ☎03/3479-0039.
Funky cook-your-own *okonomiyaki* and
yakisoba joint behind the weird and
wonderful Design Festa gallery (see p.119).
From 11.30am to 3pm you can eat as much
as you like within 90min for ¥980, and it's
just as good value at night. Inexpensive.
Meiji-jingūmae Station. Daily
11.30am–11pm.

Tarlum

1-10-2 Tomigaya, Shibuya-ku ☎03/3466-1105,
Ⓦ **www.tarlum.com.** This appealing, modish
place calls itself an "aqua brasserie" – which
means that fish and seafood are their
mainstays. It's also open for breakfast and
has a bar area for late-night drinks. A
brunch menu is available from 11.30am to
5pm each weekend and there's a prix-fixe
dinner after 6pm. Moderate. Yoyogi-kōen
Station. Daily 8am–4am.

Ikebukuro

The places reviewed below appear on
the map on p.99.

Akiyoshi

秋吉

**3-30-4 Nishi-Ikebukuro, Toshima-ku ☎03/3982-
0601.** Unusually large *yakitori* bar with a
good atmosphere and a helpful picture
menu. You might have to queue at peak
times for the tables, but there's generally
space at the counter. Inexpensive.
Ikebukuro Station. Daily 5pm–midnight.

Malaychan

**3-22-6 Nishi-Ikebukuro, Toshima-ku ☎03/5391-
7638,** Ⓦ **www.malaychan.jp.** Unpretentious
Malay restaurant dishing up decent food,
from grilled fish on banana leaf and *mee
goreng* (fried noodles) to winter steamboats
(the Malay equivalent of *sukiyaki*). Weekday
lunch menus start at ¥840, and in general
you'll eat well for around ¥2000. The beer
pitchers are good value. Inexpensive to
moderate. Ikebukuro Station. Mon 5–11pm,
Tues–Sat 11am–2.30pm & 5–11pm, Sun
11am–11pm.

Mekong

**B1, 3-26-5 Nishi-Ikebukuro, Toshima-ku
☎03/3988-5688.** The decor may not be
much to rave about, but the tastes and
aromas will take you straight to Thailand.
The lunchtime buffet is a steal at ¥1000; at
other times you can eat well for around

¥2000 per head from their picture menu.
Moderate. Ikebukuro Station. Daily except
Tues lunchtime 11.30am–2.30pm &
5–11pm.

Mutekiya

無敵家

**1-7-1 Minami-Ikebukuro, Toshima-ku
☎03/3982-7565.** Fans of the Chinese-style
soupy noodle dish should head straight to
this ramen joint on the main road south of
the Seibu department store. The queue
(nearly always there) moves fairly quickly,
and while you wait you can decide on the
size of your helping, its flavour and whether
you want extra toppings and so forth. The
English menu is somewhat cryptic, but it's
all delicious. Inexpensive. Ikebukuro Station.
Daily 10.30am–4am.

Saigon

**3F 1-7-10 Higashi-Ikebukuro, Toshima-ku
☎03/3989-0255.** Friendly, unpretentious
place serving authentic Vietnamese food,
down to the 333 beer. *Banh xeo* (sizzling
pancake with a spicy sauce) or *bunh bo*
(beef noodle soup) are recommended, with
a side dish of *nem* (spring rolls) if you're
really hungry. Weekday lunchtime sets are
excellent value at ¥780. Inexpensive to
moderate. Ikebukuro Station. Mon–Fri
11.30am–2.30pm & 5–10.30pm, Sat & Sun
11.30am–10.30pm.

Kanda, Akihabara and around

The places reviewed below appear on
the map on p.67.

Botan

ぼたん

**1-15 Kanda-Sudachō, Chiyoda-ku ☎03/3251-
0577.** Chicken *sukiyaki* is the order of the
day at this atmospheric old restaurant,
tucked into the backstreets of Kanda. It's
not cheap at just over ¥6000 a head, but
this is the genuine article, where the
chicken, vegetables and tofu simmer gently
over individual braziers in small rooms. Very
expensive. Awajichō Station. Mon–Sat
11.30am–9pm.

Canal Café

1-9 Kagurazaka, Shinjuku-ku ☎03/3260-8068,
Ⓦ **www.canalcafe.jp.** Below the southwest
end of Iidabashi Station, this is a surprisingly
tranquil and appealing waterside spot to
enjoy a meal or alfresco drink. The scene is
particularly romantic at night, when the old
clapperboard boathouses sparkle with fairy

lights. The menu is Italian, a little pricey in the evening but of decent quality; pizzas come in at ¥1800 to ¥2600, while lunch menus start at ¥1000. Moderate. Iidabashi Station. Tues–Sat 11.30am–11pm, Sun 11.30am–9.30pm.

Le Bretagne

4-2 Kagurazaka, Shinjuku-ku ☎03/3235-3001, ⓦ**www.le-bretagne.com.** Attractive French-run restaurant, down a little dead-end street with tables outside, offering authentic crepes and buckwheat *galettes*. Also serves salads, lunchtime sets (from around ¥1500) and daily specials. There's a branch just off Omotesandō (4-9-8 Jingūmae, Shibuya-ku ☎03/3478-7855; see map, p.118). Moderate. Iidabashi Station. Tues–Sat 11.30am–10.30pm, Sun 11.30am–9pm.

Tokyo Food Theater 5+1

4F UDX Building, 4-14-1 Soto-Kanda, Chiyoda-ku; ☎03/5297-8441, ⓦ**www.foodtheater.jp.** Worried about your calorie intake or showing your age? If so, hurry along to this Akihabara concept restaurant which serves "doctors' menus" concocted to keep you young and beautiful. There's a low-calorie menu (set lunch ¥3500) and an "anti-ageing" menu (¥3000) which professes to keep the wrinkles at bay. If this all sounds too whacky, you can opt for the regular Japanese, Oriental, French and Italian menus. Moderate. Akihabara Station. Daily 11am–2.30pm & 5–10pm.

Yabu Soba

やぶそば

2-10 Kanda-Awajichō, Chiyoda-ku ☎03/3251-0287. Since 1880 soba connoisseurs have been coming here to slurp their noodles and to listen to the cheerful waiting staff's distinctive singsong cries. You might have to wait at busy times, but it doesn't take long, and there's an attractive garden to admire. Prices start at around ¥630. Inexpensive to moderate. Awajichō Station. Daily 11.30am–8pm.

Roppongi, Nishi-Azabu and Azabu-Jūban

The places reviewed here appear on the maps on p.76 or p.79. Both Tokyo Midtown and Roppongi Hills offer up scores more options; at the former the super-stylish food court and bar *Okiwari.jp* (B1F Midtown Plaza; daily 7am–11pm) is an obvious choice.

Azabu Jūhachiban

麻布十八番

Ibuse Azuba-jūban Bldg, 2-7-5 Azabu-Jūban, Minato-ku ☎03/5443-5757. Old Hollywood movies, projected on a big screen, form a moving-picture backdrop to this stylish restaurant, which follows a strict organic creed to provide supposedly "anti-ageing" cuisine. Whatever the efficacy of the fare in this regard, the tastiness of items such as tomato sherbet, organic vegetable salad, the luscious roast chicken and the home-made ice creams and sorbets is not in doubt. Moderate to expensive. Azabu-Jūban Station. Mon–Sat noon–2pm & 6–10.30pm.

Botanica

4F Garden Terrace, Tokyo Midtown, 9-7-4 Akasaka, Minato-ku ☎03/5413-3282, ⓦwww .conran-restaurants.jp. Sir Terence Conran Tokyo restaurant debut doesn't overdo the British angle, despite the presence of roast beef on the menu and afternoon tea (Mon–Fri 2.30–4.30pm, Sat & Sun 3–4.30pm; ¥3800) with assorted sandwiches, petits fours and scones. Book well in advance for the weekend and holiday brunch (¥3800), or be prepared to line up early for one of the tables scattered around the lovely terrace garden, which only become available on the day depending on the weather. Expensive to very expensive. Roppongi Station. Mon–Fri 11am–10.30pm, Sat & Sun 11am–9pm.

Brasserie Paul Bocuse Le Musée

National Arts Centre, 7-22-2, Roppongi, Minato-ku ☎03/5770-8161, ⓦwww.hiramatsu.co.jp. Admire the space-age architecture of the National Arts Centre by lunching at this classy French operation, atop one of the massive inverted cones that rises three storeys from the lobby. They don't take bookings for lunch so come early or late to avoid a long wait. Moderate to expensive. Roppongi Station. Daily except Tues 11am–9pm.

Fūton

4-1-8 Nishi-Azabu, Minato-ku ☎03/5467-2213, ⓦwww.take-5.co.jp. Cute, relaxed Korean barbecue place with an English menu. Cook salt beef short ribs above a charcoal brazier for ¥1050 or try the traditional *chijime* seafood pancake ¥840. Moderate. Roppongi Station. Mon–Sat 6pm–5am, Sun 5pm–midnight.

Garb Pintino

3-5-4 Shiba-kōen, Minato-ku ☎03/5472-1057.

There's a casual stylishness to this Italian place opposite Tokyo Tower, with a menu of pasta, salads, pizza and so on – no surprises, but nonetheless appealing. Moderate. Kamiyachō Station. Mon–Fri 11.30am–2.30pm & 6–11pm, Sat & Sun 11.30am–11pm.

Gonpachi
権八

1-13-11 Nishi-Azabu, Minato-ku ☎03/5771-0170. A faux-Edo-period storehouse is the home to this atmospheric Japanese restaurant. Take your pick between soba and grilled items on the ground and second floors, while on the third it's sushi. There's a wonderful samurai drama atmosphere, and its easy to see how the place inspired part of Quentin Tarantino's *Kill Bill Part 1*. There are also branches in *G-Zone* in Ginza (see p.168) and on the fourteenth floor of E Space Tower, 3-6 Maruyama-chō, Shibuya-ku (☎03/5784-2011; see map, p.122). Moderate. Roppongi Station. Daily 11.30am–5pm.

Hainan Jeefan Shokudo
海南鶏飯食堂

6-11-16 Roppongi, Minato-ku ☎03/5474 3200, ⓦ**www.route9g.com.** The menu at this friendly place, at the quiet end of Roppongi Hills, is made up of Singaporean street-food favourites. The portions aren't huge but it's all tasty and nicely presented. There's an equally good branch at 1-21-14 Ebisu, Shibuya-ku ☎03/3447-3615 (see map, pp.128–129). Moderate. Roppongi Station. Mon–Fri 11.30am–2pm & 6pm–midnight, Sat & Sun 11.30am–3pm & 6–11pm; closed 3rd Mon of month.

Hinokiya
檜屋

6-19-45 Akasaka Minato-ku, ☎03/6808-6815, ⓦ**www.pjgroup.jp/hinokiya.** A charming house and garden is the delightful setting for this *robatayaki* – a restaurant specializing in charcoal-grilled foods – tucked away in a quiet street to the rear of Tokyo Midtown. Expensive. Roppongi Station. Daily 6pm–midnight.

Ichioku
一億

4-4-5 Roppongi, Minato-ku ☎03/3405-9891. Look for the green-painted front of this funkily decorated *mukokuseki izakaya* close by Tokyo Midtown. Many swear by the unusual cheese *gyōza* and tofu "steaks", but there's plenty more to choose from on the picture menu. Dishes are generally made from organically grown vegetables. Moderate. Roppongi Station. Daily 11.30am–2pm & 5pm–3am.

L'Atelier de Joël Robuchon
2F Roppongi Hills Hillside, 6-10-1 Roppongi, Minato-ku ☎03/5772-7500. Of all the many restaurants in Roppongi Hills, this is the one that has created the biggest buzz. There's a no-bookings policy, so you may have to wait to get a seat at the long counter, facing the open kitchen where black-garbed chefs create culinary mini-masterpieces before your very eyes. The six-course menu is ¥6000, but it's possible to treat yourself to a couple of the *dégustation*-size dishes for less. There's also a tearoom under the same moniker in the Takashimaya department store (see p.225). Expensive to very expensive. Roppongi Station. Daily 11.30am–2.30pm & 6–10pm.

Nobu Tokyo
Toranomon Towers Office, 4-1-28 Toranomon, Minato-ku ☎03/5733-0070, ⓦwww.nobutokyo .com. A new location and dramatic Japanese-style design for Nobu Matsuhisa's latest Tokyo operation. The famous black-cod dinner (Robert de Niro's favourite) is a bargain ¥3500. For something a bit different, try *tiradito*, Nobu's South American twist on sashimi. Courses start at ¥12,000 plus ten percent service. Moderate to expensive. Kamiyachō Station. Mon–Fri 11.30am–2pm & 6–10.30pm, Sat & Sun 6–10.30pm.

Nodaiwa
野田岩

1-5-4 Higashi-Azabu, Minato-ku ☎03/3583-785. Matronly women in elegant black kimono shuffle around this 160-year-old *kura* (store-house), converted into one of Tokyo's best eel restaurants. It gets busy, but the private rooms upstairs can only be booked by parties of four or more. They may guide you to the annexe (*bekkan*) around the corner which has almost an identical interior. Moderate to expensive. Kamiyachō Station. Mon–Sat 11am–1.30pm & 5–8pm.

The Oak Door
Grand Hyatt Tokyo, 6-10-3 Roppongi, Minato-ku ☎03/4333-8888. The *Grand Hyatt* has an excellent range of restaurants, of which this is the most popular – justifiably so for its great steak dishes, New World wines and fruit tarts, temptingly displayed on the counter of the open kitchen. The clubby bar

has been taken over by the suit-and-braces expat brigade. Expensive. Roppongi Station. Daily 11.30am–11pm.

Rainbow Roll Sushi

2F Monteplaza, 1-10-3 Azabu-Jūban ☎03/5572-7689. Sushi gets a contemporary makeover at this sleekly designed restaurant, where fish is often the last thing you'll find in your California-style roll. They do great cocktails too. Moderate. Azabu-Jūban Station. Daily 11.30am–2pm & 6–11pm.

Rojak

B2F Hillside Roppongi Hills, 6-10-1 Roppongi, Minato-ku ☎03/5770-5831. There's a lovely view of the Mori Garden from this stylish, casual restaurant specializing in southeast Asian dishes. On warm days you can sit outside. Moderate to expensive. Roppongi Station. Daily noon–4pm, 6pm–midnight.

Roti

1F Piramide Building, 6-6-9 Roppongi, Minato-ku ☎03/5785-3671, ⓦwww.rotico.jp. You'd better be hungry before dining at this modern American brasserie, as portions are huge. Their speciality – rotisserie chicken – or any of their other grilled meat dishes could easily feed two. Microbrew beers and a tempting range of desserts are also available. There's a branch at the Harumi Triton complex (1-8-16 Harumi, Chūō-ku; ☎03/5144-8275; see map, p.135) and in the Garden Terrace section of Tokyo Midtown (☎03/5413-3655). Moderate. Roppongi Station. Mon–Fri 11.30am–3pm & 6–11pm, Sat noon–5pm & 6–11pm, Sun 10am–3pm & 6–10pm.

Seizan
清山

Roppongi Hills West Walk 5F, 6-10-1 Roppongi, Minato-ku ☎03/5772-2077. Part of the venerable Sushisei chain, this is the best sushi place in Roppongi Hills, with a great lunch set for ¥1300 as well as dinner sets from ¥1800. Ask to sit at the counter if you want to order directly from the chefs. Moderate. Roppongi Station. Daily 11am–11pm.

Suzunami
鈴波

B1F Galleria, Tokyo Midtown, 9-7-4 Akasaka, Minato-ku ☎03/5413-0335, ⓦwww.suzunami .co.jp. This restaurant specializing in silver cod marinated in sake is good choice among the many in Midtown. Their filling set meals are rounded off with a glass of plum wine and great value, starting off at around

¥1000. Moderate. Roppongi Station. Daily 11am–10pm.

🏃 **Tōfuya-Ukai**
とふ屋うかい

4-4-13 Shiba-kōen, Minato-ku ☎03/3436-1028, ⓦwww.ukai.co.jp. At the foot of Tokyo Tower, this stunning recreation of Edo-era mansion (incorporating huge beams from an old sake brewery) serves unforgettable tofu-based *kaiseki*-style cuisine. It's incredibly popular so book well ahead, especially for dinner (at least a month in advance). Set meals only, with lunch from ¥5500 and dinner from ¥8400. Very expensive. Akabanebashi Station. Daily 11am–8pm.

Tsurutontan
つるとんたん

3-14-12 Roppongi, Minato-ku ☎03/5786-2626, ⓦwww.tsurutontan.co.jp. Giant bowls of udon are the signature dish of this great-value chain restaurant, which also offers rice bowls, *nabe* and *shabu-shabu* in similarly epic portions. The atmosphere is slick, and there's a good selection of *shōchū*, sake and *umeshu* (plum wine) to wash it all down. Moderate. Roppongi Station. Daily 11am–8pm.

Ryōgoku

Genki-tei
元氣亭

3-24-10 Ryōgoku, Sumida-ku ☎03/3632-3933. If you're in Ryōgoku and can't face a sumo-sized stew, try this bright and breezy "ecological" restaurant above a health-food store. It serves mostly vegetarian fare; the seasonal set lunches (from ¥950) are good value and include a wholesome helping of brown rice, soup and pickles. You can spoil the effect by tucking into their home-made chocolate cake for dessert. Inexpensive to moderate. Ryōgoku Station. Mon–Sat 11.30am–8pm.

Kappo Yoshiba
割烹吉葉

2-14-5 Yokoami, Sumida-ku ☎03/3623-4480. Set in an old sumo *dōjō* (practice hall; book ahead for the prime tables around the ring), this is an atmospheric place to come for *chanko-nabe*, the wrestlers' protein-packed meat, seafood and vegetable stew, including seventeen different ingredients (from ¥2100; minimum two persons). There are also set menus at ¥6300 and ¥8500 per person. On Monday, Wednesday and Friday

RESTAURANTS | Restaurants

there's live singing of traditional songs.
Moderate to expensive. Ryōgoku Station.
Mon–Sat 11.30am–2pm & 5–10pm.

Tomoegata

巴潟

2-17-6 Ryōgoku, Sumida-ku ☎03/3632-5600, ⓦ**www.tomoegata.com.** In the heart of sumo
territory, this is a good place to sample
chanko-nabe. For around ¥3000 you can
have the full-blown meal cooked at your
table, though most people will find the
smaller, ready-made version (¥840; lunch
only) more than enough. It's two blocks
south of the station, and easy to spot from
its parade of colourful flags; when it's full
you'll be directed to the annexe on the north
side of the street. Inexpensive to moderate.
Ryōgoku Station. Daily 11.30am–2pm
& 5–11pm.

Shibuya

The places reviewed here are shown on
the map on p.122.

Beacon

1-2-5 Shibuya, Shibuya-ku ☎03/6418-0077, ⓦ**www.tyharborbrewing.co.jp/restaurants/
beacon.html.** This self-styled "urban chop
house", specializing in choice cuts of meat,
impresses with its slick contemporary look
and reassuringly expensive prices. Fortunately, the food is worth it. Expensive to
very expensive. Shibuya Station. Mon–Fri
11.30am–3pm & 6–10pm, Sat & Sun
11.30am–10pm; bar daily 6–11pm.

Christon Café

**B1F, 2-10-7 Dogenzaka, Shibuya-ku ☎03/5728-
2225.** Descend into this basement operation
to discover what could be the set for a
Hammer horror movie shot in a Gothic
cathedral. The Asian fusion food isn't so
scary and is nicely presented. Moderate.
Shibuya Station. Mon 5–11pm, Tues–Sun
5pm–5am.

Gaya

我や

2-2-5 Shibuya, Shibuya-ku ☎03/3498-8810, ⓦ**www.gaya.co.jp.** Macrobiotic food and
stylish decor rarely go hand in hand, but this
place manages the trick nicely, offering
plenty of vegetarian and vegan dishes
alongside those with meat and fish. It also
keeps late hours. Moderate. Shibuya
Station. Mon–Fri 11.30am–3pm & 5.30pm–
midnight, Sat & Sun 5.30pm–midnight.

Kaikaya

開花屋

**23-7 Maruyama-chō, Shibuya-ku ☎03/3770-
0878,** ⓦ**www.kaikaya.com.** Many *gaijin* swear
by this convivial, smoky *izakaya*, plastered
with snaps of carousing customers and
specializing in fish. There's an English menu
and the friendly staff are happy to advise on
what to order. Moderate. Shinsen Station.
Daily 11.30am–2pm & 6–11.30pm.

Kurage

1-19-8 Jin'nan, Shibuya-ku ☎03/3463-3323, ⓦ**www.jellyfish.bz/shop/tokyo/kurage/kurage.
html.** Artists and art lovers hang out at this
trendy café after taking in exhibitions at the
adjoining gallery of Tokyo Wonder Site. Their
deli lunch is excellent value at ¥840 for rice,
soup and a choice of three tasty Japanese
dishes. The photo menu helps with
ordering. Inexpensive. Shibuya Station. Daily
10am–11.30pm.

Respekt

1-11-1 Shibuya, Shibuya-ku ☎03/6418-8144, ⓦ**www.cafecompany.co.jp.** Apart from offering
filling, attractive café-style dishes, this trend-
setting place has tons of English style,
fashion mags to browse and free Internet
access. Moderate. Shibuya Station.
Mon–Thurs 11.30am–2am, Fri & Sat
11.30am–5am, Sun 11.30am–midnight.

Sonoma

**2-25-17 Dōgenzaka, Shibuya-ku ☎03/3462-
7766.** A *gaijin* hangout but none the worse for
that, with decent, good-value fusion food. It's
a little hidden away: look for the first alley off
to the right of Dōgenzaka as you walk up the
hill from the station. Eat here and you can get
into the tiny upstairs cocktail bar/club *Ruby
Room* (see p.198) for free. Moderate.
Shibuya Station. Mon–Thurs & Sun
11.30am–midnight, Fri & Sat 11.30am–4am.

Underground Mr Zoogunzoo

**B1 Aoyama City Building, 2-9-11 Shibuya,
Shibuya-ku ☎03/3400-1496,** ⓦ**www.unitedf
.com/zoogunzoo.** The earthy tones and baked
mud walls of this narrow basement space
conjure up the Australian outback, while the
menu also reflects the tastes of down under,
with Pacific-rim fusion cuisine and an
extensive selection of Antipodean wines.
They've recently launched a sister operation,
Aotea Rangi (1-21-18 Ebisu, Shibuya-ku;
☎03-3447-1496; see map, pp.128–129),
specializing in mussels and other seafood.
Expensive. Omotesandō Station.
Tues–Sun 6–11pm.

The places reviewed here are mostly shown on the map on pp.106–107.

Angkor Wat
アンコールワット

1-38-13 Yoyogi, Shibuya-ku ☏03/3370-3019. In business since 1982, this remains Tokyo's best Cambodian restaurant. There are set meals, but you can also tell the waiters your budget and let them bring you a suitable selection of dishes (allow ¥2000 per head). The sweetly spicy salads, soups and vegetable rolls are all excellent. It's a 5min walk west of Yoyogi Station; look for the pottery elephant outside the entrance on a side street. Moderate. Yoyogi Station. Mon–Fri 11am–2pm & 5–11pm, Sat & Sun 5–11pm.

Hatago
はたご

1-23-1 Nishi-Shinjuku, Shinjuku-ku ☏03/3344-3144, ⓦwww.kadoya-hotel.co.jp. Beneath the *Kadoya Hotel* is this country-style *izakaya* with a very jovial feel. Beer, sake and *sochu* are available as well as some delicious traditional food, from sashimi to meaty titbits you grill at the table on charcoal braziers. There's an English menu. Moderate. Shinjuku Station. Mon–Fri 5–11.30pm, Sat 4–11.30pm, Sun 4–10pm.

Kakiden
柿でん

8F Yasuyo Building, 3-37-11 Shinjuku, Shinjuku-ku ☏03/3352-5121. One of the best places in Tokyo to sample *kaiseki-ryōri* (see box, p.162). There's a lunch for ¥4000, but you won't regret investing in the eighteen-course dinner for ¥8000. Live performances on the thirteen-stringed *koto* take place from 6 to 8pm. Very expensive. Shinjuku Station. Daily 11am–9pm.

Meshi Mase
めしませ

6F & 7F Lumine 1, Nishi-Shinjuku 1-1-5, Shinjuku-ku. Not to be outdone by My City on the other side of the station, Lumine has brought together a collection of distinctive operations on its restaurant floor, including the *Mango Tree Café* (☏03/6380-2535) for Thai food and *Vietnam Alice* (☏03/5339-2033) for Vietnamese. Best are the contemporary Japanese-themed *Yusōshi* (☏03/5321-7233) and *Roisu* (☏03/5909-3855). Moderate. Shinjuku Station. Daily 11am–11pm.

New York Grill

Park Hyatt Tower, 3-7-1-2 Nishi-Shinjuku ☏03/5323-3458. Sitting pretty on the 52nd floor is the hotel's premier restaurant where the great views, Stateside-sized portions of American food and bustling atmosphere make for a memorable eating experience. After the ¥5000 buffet lunch you won't need to eat much else all day. Bookings essential. The hotel's *kaiseki-ryōri* restaurant *Kazue* (☏03/5323-3460), on the fortieth floor, is also a delight. Expensive to very expensive. Tochōmae Station. Daily 11.30am–2.30pm & 5.30–10.30pm.

Puan Tei
プアンテイ

2-32-3 Ōkubo, Shinjuku-ku ☏03/5272-5137; **see Greater Tokyo map at back of book.** Expat Thais and others in the know head to this tiny place for an authentic, spicy Thai food fix. There's room for just eight people at the counter bar, over which the super-friendly Thai owners keep Singha beers coming. Moderate. Shin-Ōkubo Station. Tues–Sun 5pm–2am.

Shion
しおん

1-25 Kabukichō, Shinjuku-ku. Round the corner from *Kirin City* on the west side of Shinjuku, this is one of the area's cheapest conveyor-belt sushi operations. There's often a queue, but it moves quickly. Plates cost ¥100 or ¥200 each, and you can order beer and sake. Inexpensive. Shinjuku Station. Daily 11.30am–11pm.

Shun Kan
しゅんかん

7F & 8F My City, 3-38-1 Shinjuku, Shinjuku-ku. Shun Kan is the name given to the two restaurant floors of the snazzy My City department store. The more populist seventh floor has walls decorated with an ingenious range of items – from old video recorders to flattened cardboard boxes; the eighth floor is all Zen coolness. Among the wide range of restaurants, it's worth checking out *Kowloon Ten Shin* (☏03/5360-8191), for an all-you-can-eat Chinese and dim sum buffet; *Nabbie & Kamado* (☏03/5379-1070) for Okinawan fare; and *Kitchen Shunju* (see p.164). Moderate. Shinjuku Station. Daily 11.30am–10pm.

Tsunahachi
つな八

3-31-8 Shinjuku, Shinjuku-ku ☏03/3352-1012. The main branch of the famous tempura restaurant almost always has a queue outside, though you're likely to get seated quickly if you settle for the upstairs rooms away from the frying action. Everything is freshly made, and even the ¥1300 set (including soup, rice and pickles) will fill you up. Moderate. Shinjuku Station. Daily 11.15am–10pm.

Tsukiji and Odaiba

The places reviewed here appear on the map on p.135.

Monkichi
もんきち

3-8-10 Tsukushima ☎03/3531-2380. As patronized by no less a luminary than Brad Pitt (whose photo is on the wall), this friendly place is a classic *monjayaki* restaurant on an alley just off Monja-dōri. Tsukishima Station. Daily 11am–10.30pm.

Ramen Kokugikan
5F Aqua City, 1-7-1 Daiba, Minato-ku. Six top ramen noodle chefs from around Japan square off against each other in this section of Aqua City's restaurant floor. Each provides mini portions of their product so you can take the taste test and decide the winner. Inexpensive. Odaiba Kaihin-kōen monorail station. Daily 11am–11pm.

Sushi Bun
鮨文

5 Tsukiji, Chūō-ku ☎03/3541-3860. One of the most *gaijin*-friendly options among the rows of sushi stalls within Tsukiji fish market (and there's less likely to a long line as there always as outside media favourites such as *Sushi Dai*). They have an English menu with sets starting at ¥2100. It's well worth spending ¥3675 for their top-quality ten-piece selection including creamy *uni* (sea urchin) and *shirako* (cod sperm)-topped sushi. The website ⓦwww .tsukijigourmet.or.jp gives full details of other sushi stalls in the market. Moderate. Tsukijishijō Station. Mon–Sat 6am–2.30pm, but closed during occasional market holidays.

Tententsunetsune Kaitenbō
天天常常回転坊

Decks Tokyo Beach Mall, 1-6-1 Daiba, Minato-ku; ☎03/3599-6705, ⓦwww.kaitenyamucha .com. It was only a matter of time before some bright spark saw the potential of the *kaiten* (revolving conveyor belt) for food other than sushi. Here the colour-coded plates carry dim sum, pretty tasty and keenly priced. There's a separate menu from which you can order à la carte. The place is part of a collection of Chinese restaurants

Dining on the water

Lunch and dinner cruises on **yakatabune**, low-slung traditional boats lit up with paper lanterns, are a charming Tokyo eating institution, dating back to the Edo period. Operated by several companies, the boats accommodate anything from sixteen to a hundred people on trips along the Sumida-gawa and out on Tokyo Bay.

Boats run by **Amisei** (☎03/3844-1869) set off from the southwest side of Azuma-bashi bridge, Asakusa. Their ninety-minute lunch cruises cost ¥6300, while a two-hour evening cruise costs ¥8000 (including all the tempura you can eat). More lavish menus can be ordered and, naturally, charges skyrocket for cruises on the night when Asakusa holds its annual fireworks extravaganza in July. **Funasei Yakatabune** cruises (☎03/5479-2731, ⓦwww.funasei.com) run out of Kita-Shinagawa and offer a choice of Japanese- and Western-style menus for around ¥10,000 per person. There's also the Harumi-based **Yakatabune Harumiya** (☎03/3644-1344, ⓦwww .harumiya.co.jp) which can arrange an English-speaking host if you have a group of twenty or more, and the **Tsukishima** cruises (☎03/3533-6699), where the meal features the local pancake speciality, *monjayaki*; their cruises kick off at around ¥5000 per person, including all you can eat and drink.

An affordable alternative to *yakatabune* is **Jicoo**, the night-time persona of the futuristic ferry *Himiko* (see p.28; ☎0120-049-490, ⓦwww.jicoofloatingbar.com). From Thursday to Saturday between 8 and 11pm the ferry shuttles from Hinode under the Rainbow Bridge to Odaiba and back. A night ticket (¥2500) covers entertainment, which includes a belly dancer who shimmies across the underlit floor panels; drinks (from ¥700) and snacks are served.

on the sixth and seventh floors of the mall, and has a branch in Ueno Station. Moderate. Odaiba Kaihin-kōen monorail station. Daily 11am–10.15pm.

Ueno, Nezu and around

The places reviewed here appear on the map on p.91, except *Goemon*, which is on the Greater Tokyo map at the back of the book.

Bamboo Garden
1-52 Ueno-Kōen, Taitō-ku. This new complex immediately west of Ueno Station, beside the steps up to the park, is home to three stylish contemporary restaurants. Perhaps the nicest is *Ito Ito* (☎03/5807-2244; Mon–Sat 11am–11.30pm, Sun 11am–11pm), on the middle floor, serving a broad range of Japanese favourites, from soba and *donburi* to sashimi platters (set meals ¥1300–1900). It's sandwiched between the *Korean Tokori* (☎03/5807-2255; daily 11am–midnight), on the bottom floor, and *Kamonka* (☎03/5807-2288; daily 11am–11.30pm), serving Chinese cuisine, above. Moderate. Ueno Station.

Goemon
五右衛門
1-1-26 Hon-Komagome, Bunkyō-ku ☎03/3811-2015. Cooking with tofu is raised to a fine art here in a delightful setting straight out of a woodblock print. Dine in one of the wooden pavilions fronting the rock garden and gurgling fountain, if possible. The set menu for lunch starts at ¥2700, while dinner costs from ¥5500. Expensive to very expensive. Hon-Komagome Station. Mon–Fri noon–2pm & 5–9pm, Sat noon–8pm.

Hantei
はん亭
2-12-15 Nezu, Bunkyō-ku ☎03/3828-1440. Stylish dining in a beautiful, three-storey wooden house. There's only one dish, *kushiage*, served in combination plates, six at a time: ¥2900 for the first plate (plus two appetizers); ¥1400 thereafter, until you say stop. Moderate to expensive. Nezu Station. Tues–Sat noon–2.30pm & 5–10pm, Sun noon–2.30pm & 4–9.30pm.

Musashino
武蔵野
2-8-1 Ueno, Taitō-ku ☎03/3831-1672. One of Ueno's few remaining old-style restaurants serving *tonkatsu*, for which the area was once famed. They come in big, thick, melt-in-the-mouth slabs. Choose between standard *rōsu* (fatty belly meat) and the leaner *hire* (loin fillet), both at under ¥1500 including soup, rice and pickles. Moderate. Ueno-Hirokōji Station. Daily noon–9.30pm.

Sasa-no-yuki
笹乃雪
2-15-10 Negishi, Taitō-ku ☎03/3873-1145. Three centuries ago, the chef here was said to make tofu like "snow lying on bamboo leaves", and both the name and the quality have survived, though the old wooden house is now marooned among flyovers. The interior is nowhere nearly as fancy as that at *Goemon* (see above), but calm prevails over the tatami mats as you feast on delicately flavoured silk-strained tofu. Lunch menus start at ¥1900 on weekdays (prices are higher at weekends) and dinner menus at ¥4500, with the emphasis on flavour rather than quantity. Moderate to

Learning more about Japanese cuisine

Tokyo has a good selection of English-language courses to help expand your knowledge of Japanese food and drink. **Experience Tokyo** (⊛j-experience.com) offers hands-on half-day courses on how to make sushi or soba (¥17,000) as well as a cooking class at a typical Japanese home (¥14,500) or with a master Japanese chef at his restaurant (¥30,000). **Konishi Japanese Cooking** Class (1405 Nissei Meguro-Mansion, 3-1-7 Meguro, Meguro-ku; ☎03/3714-8859, ⊛www.seiko-osp.com /private/sekigu/kjcc/index.htm) offers culinary courses (Tues–Thurs; ¥4500 per lesson or ¥38,000 for ten lessons). Food writer **Elizabeth Andoh** (☎03/5716-5751, ⊛www.tasteofculture.com) runs cooking workshops and leads highly popular trips around Japanese markets, helping you to identify all those weird and wonderful Japanese products. You'll need to book well in advance for both.

Sake courses and talks are regularly run by sake expert **John Gautner** (⊛www.sake -world.com) at *Takara* (see p.169; ¥7000 including dinner and a tasting of six sakes).

expensive. Uguisudani Station. Tues–Sun
11.30am–9pm.

Unagi Ben-kei
鰻弁慶

4-5-10 Ueno, Taitō-ku ☎03/3831-2283. Eel is
the order of the day at this informal traditional
restaurant on three floors. Try their *unagi*
donburi lunchtime set for a taster (¥1400;
Mon–Fri). They also do well-priced *sukiyaki*
meals (¥1700 for lunch), as well as tempura,
shabu-shabu, sashimi and so forth. English
menu is available. Moderate. Okachimachi
Station. Daily 11.30am–9.50pm, closed third
Mon of month.

15

RESTAURANTS | Restaurants

Cafés and teahouses

Y ou can hardly walk a block of central Tokyo these days without passing a chain **café** – as often as not a *Starbucks*, although local operations such as *Doutor*, *Mister Donuts* and *Tully's* are also pretty common. Despite all the convenience of these operations, don't miss sampling at least one of the many other individual cafés, sometimes called **kissaten**, where the emphasis is on service and creating an interesting, relaxing space, using quirky decor and unusual music, for example. Apart from drinks, many cafés serve a fine selection of food and are good places for snacks, Western-style pastries and cakes, and light meals.

If you want to experience the trendiest of Tokyo's cafés, head to fashionable areas such as Harajuku, Aoyama and Daikan'yama. Ginza is also starting a small trend in chic cafés inside boutiques.

Teahouses are thinner on the ground than cafés, but are becoming more popular as the health benefits of tea are promoted. They're a good place to sample traditional Japanese sweets, known as **wagashi** and usually made from compounded sugar or pounded rice cake (*mochi*) and red bean paste, the sweetness of which balances the bitterness of the tea. It's worth noting that while cafés often keep late hours, teahouses are generally a daytime affair.

Cafés

Harajuku, Aoyama and Daikan'yama are the centres of Tokyo's trendiest café societies. Apart from drinks, many of the cafés listed below also serve a fine selection of food and are good places for snacks and light meals.

Asakusa and around

The places reviewed here appear on the map on p.85.

Gallery éf
2-19-18 Kaminarimon, Taitō-ku
☎03/3841-0442, ⓦwww.gallery-ef.com. This café-bar is one of Asakusa's trendiest hangouts, with decent lunch sets for around ¥900. It's worth popping in, if only to see the *kura* (traditional storehouse) at the back, which has miraculously survived and now provides an intimate venue for an eclectic mix of exhibitions, concerts and performance art. Asakusa Station. Daily except Tues: café and gallery 11am–7pm, bar 6pm–midnight.

Kappabashi Coffee
3-25-11 Nishi-Asakusa, Taitō-ku ☎03/3843-9555. Chunky wooden furniture offset against white walls lend an unexpectedly sophisticated air to this café at the north end of Kappabashi-dōgu-gai, serving a big choice of coffees, teas, infusions and juices, as well as cakes and light meals. Upstairs, the interior design gallery/shop Soi is worth a quick look. Iriya or Tawaramachi stations. Daily 10am–7pm.

Ebisu, Hiro-o, Meguro & Naka-Meguro

See map on pp.128–129.
By the Blue
La Place de Daikan'yama, 20-23 Daikan'yama-cho,

Maid cafés

They go by cute nicknames such as Chocolate and Pom-Pom. They wear long black skirts covered by frilly white aprons topped off with bows, brooches, and lacy hair bands and caps. They greet you using elaborately formal language and a girly voice, addressing you as their "master" or "mistress". And when they bring your coffee or tea they kneel by your side to serve it, gently enquiring how much milk or sugar sir or madam would desire. These are the twenty-first-century maids of Tokyo, and you'll find them at the city's latest phenomenon – the **maid café**.

Also known as *maid kissa*, maid cafés debuted in Akihabara (Akiba for short) in 2001. They were inspired by a video game in which the main characters are maids at a restaurant, and the concept tapped into the popular *cosuplay* scene, in which participants dress up as their favourite Japanese pop-culture idols. To outside eyes the role-playing and costumes may seem a little kinky, but sex really has very little to do with it. In many ways the maids are like modern-day geisha, there to entertain their guests in a playful, non-sexual manner; more often than not their costumes are evocative of prim Victorian lasses.

A visit to one of the earliest examples, the friendly *Mai:lish* (2F FH Kowa Square, 3-6-2 Soto-Kanda, Chiyoda-ku; Suehirochō Station; see map, p.67; daily 11am–10pm; ☎03/5289-7310, ⓦwww.mailish.jp), will give you a good insight into what maid cafés are all about. Over at *@home café* (Mitsuwa Bldg, 1-11-4 Soto-Kanda, Chiyoda-ku; Akihabara Station; see map, p.67; daily 11.30am–10pm, closed third Tues of the month; ☎03/5294-7707, ⓦwww.cafe-athome.com) you can end up having to wait well over an hour for a seat. This place includes a wacky *sabo* (traditional teahouse) where the maids accessorize their kimono with fluffy rabbit ears and other contemporary accoutrement. Apart from ordering the standard comfort foods – milky drinks, curry rice, creamy cakes – you can also pay to play kids' toy games with the maids or have your photo taken with them (note that taking your own photos in maid cafés is forbidden).

Originally it was mainly nerdy males (*otaku*) of Akiba that frequented maid cafés, but now men and women, young and old come to relax in them. Women specifically are being courted with **butler cafés**, the first of which was *Swallowtail Café* (3-12-12 Higashi-Ikebukuro, Toshima-ku; Ikebukuro Station; see map, p.99; daily 10am–8pm; ⓦbutlers-cafe.jp), where young guys dressed like Jeeves are the solicitous waiters in a room hung with chandeliers and antique-style furniture; it's so popular that booking online is essential. As other butler cafés are set to open in Akiba, maid cafés are now popping up in South Korea and Taiwan – like many a bright Japanese idea, the concept is going global.

Shibuya-ku ☎03/5784-2903, ⓦwww .by-the-blue.com. Although it calls itself "the closet café", this relaxed affair, decked out in blue and white and with a courtyard area, is more St Tropez than gay. Crepes are the mainstay. Daikan'yama Station. Daily 11.30am–9.30pm.

Drôle
Second floor, 38-3 Sarugaku-chō, Shibuya-ku ☎03/3462-6263. A designery café in the midst of Daikan'yama's boutiques, *Drôle* is good for a quick pick-me-up while shopping or a decent lunch. Their chicken curry impresses by actually having some large pieces of chicken in it. Daikan'yama Station.

Mon–Fri 9.30am–8pm, Sat & Sun 11am–8pm.

🏃 **Kami-Meigo Sakura Shopping Centre**
1-25-5 Aobadai, Meguro-ku ⓦwww .mfs11.com. Beside the Meguro-gawa, this appealingly ramshackle complex is practically ground central for the trendsters of Naka-Meguro. Inside you'll find *Opatoca*, a good bakery and café, *Onamori*, a bistro-style café and *Continental Overseas*, a boutique and café-bar. Next door in a small van is the cute *Expresso Bar Madeleine*. Naka-Meguro Station. Mon–Thurs 11.30am–midnight, Fri & Sat 11.30am–2am.

△ Café society, Tokyo style

Ginza and around

The places reviewed here appear on the map on p.60.

100% Chocolate Café

2-4-16 Kyōbashi, Chūō-ku ☎03/3237-3184, ⓦwww.choco-cafe.jp. Indulgence is taken to new heights at this trendy Meiji-run café, where Tokyo's chocoholics are queueing out the door. A mug of their hot chocolate should satisfy the most hardcore addict, or try the chocolate fondue (served with pretzels and café au lait). Other options include waffles, tarts and cornets with a choice of chocolate fillings. The decor – by Masamichi Katayama, one of Tokyo's hottest designers – takes up the theme, from the "chocolate library" lining one wall to the chocolate-bar ceiling. To stave off withdrawal symptoms, grab a few boxes of the stuff before you go – there are 56 varieties to choose from. Kyōbashi Station. Mon–Fri 8am–8pm, Sat & Sun 11am–7pm.

Gucci Café

4-4-10 Ginza, Chūō-ku ☎03/3562-8112. Hidden away on the fourth floor of the boutique is this hyper-chic café with low table and chairs, Gucci-logo-embossed leather placemats and "light meals" for the stick-figure fashionistas. Ginza Station. Daily 11am–8pm.

Henri Charpentier

2-8-20 Ginza, Chūō-ku ☎03/3562-2721. This deep-pink Ginza boutique offers the ultimate in Tokyo patisseries on the ground floor and a *salon de thé* below. Here you can enjoy crêpe suzette flambéed at your table, as well as a range of gold-flecked chocolate morsels and seasonal specialities, to go with a choice of coffees, teas and infusions. Don't leave before checking out the toilets – if you can find them. In case you were thinking *Charpentier* is a French creation, the company actually began life in Kansai in 1969. Ginza-itchōme Station; see map, p.60/Ginza. Daily 11am–9pm.

Mikimoto Lounge

3F Mikimoto Boutique, 2-4-12 Ginza, Chūō-ku ☎03/3562-3134. The Toyo Ito-designed boutique for the pearl jewellery company has a café with drinks and very appealing Western-style desserts and cakes on the menu. Ginza Station. Mon–Sat 11am– 7.30pm, Sun 11am–7pm.

Paul

1-11 Marunouchi, Chiyoda-ku ☎03/5208-8418. The main branch of the respected French bakery, on the ground floor of Pacific Century Place, to the southeast of Tokyo Station. The baguettes, croissants, quiches and the like are *très authentique*. Tokyo Station. Daily 10am–10pm.

Wired Café News

2F Mitsui Tower, 2-2-1 Nihombashi-Muromachi, Chūō-ku ☎03/3231-5766, ⓦ www.wiredcafe.jp. Parquet floors and 1970-style leather sofas contrast with super-fast WiFi in this plush combination of café, bar, restaurant and Internet café. There's a bank of spanking new computers to use and, best of all, ordering one drink or food item buys you an hour online. Branches in Harajuku, Aoyama-Itchōme and Shibuya, among other places. Mitsukoshimae Station. Mon–Fri 7.30am–11pm, Sat 11am–8pm.

Harajuku and Aoyama

The places reviewed here appear on the map on p.118, except for *Bape Café!?*, *Bio Ojiyan Café* and *Yao*, which are on the map on p.114.

A Piece of Cake

6-1-19 Minami-Aoyama, Minato-ku ☎03/5466-0686. Looking out onto the small, funky sculpture garden in front of the Okanoto Tarō Memorial Museum (see p.120), this very laid-back place has some interesting choices, including traditional Indian *chai* and mulled wine. Omotesandō Station. Daily except Tues 11am–7pm.

Andersens

5-1-26 Aoyama, Minato-ku ☎03/3407-3333. This Tokyo outpost of Hiroshima's famed Swedish-style bakery has an excellent range of pastries and sandwiches and a reason-ably priced sit-down café – a good option for breakfast and lunch. Omotesandō Station. Daily 7am–10pm.

Bape Café!?

3-27-22 Jingūmae, Shibuya-ku ☎03/5770-6560. You bought the T-shirt or hoodie, now relax over a drink or snack at this fun café, part of the A Bathing Ape empire of trendy streetwear designer Nigo (see p.227). Meiji-jingūmae Station. Daily 11am–8pm.

Berry Café

5-10-19 Minami Aoyama, Minato-ku ☎03/5774-7130. The cakes and tarts on display at this café are guaranteed to stop you in your tracks – they look so luscious and perfect it's difficult to believe they're real until you tuck in. Omotesandō Station. Mon–Sat 11am–9pm, Sun 11am–8pm.

Bio Ojiyan Café

3-29-3 Jingumae, Shibuya-ku ☎03/3746 5990, ⓦ www.mfs11.com. Hairdressers upstairs, laid-back café-bar downstairs. The

speciality is scrambled eggs on rice with a variety of toppings. Meiji-jingūmae Station. Daily 11.45am–10pm.

Lotus

ロータス

4-6-8 Jingūmae, Shibuya-ku ☎03/5772-6077. Long opening hours, an appealing light-meal menu and a quietly trendy vibe make *Lotus* a prime choice for the style mavens of Harajuku. Omotesandō Station. Daily 10am–4am.

Tokyo Apartment Café @ Harajuku

1F Green Fantasia, 1-11-11 Jingūmae, Shibuya-ku ☎03/3401-4101. Coming here is like going to a party at a retro pad, and you can drink a coffee or cocktail in the closet, kitchen, study or dining room. Also does a good range of food, with nothing above ¥1000. Meiji-jingūmae Station. Daily 11am–4am.

Yao

Villa Blanca, 2-33-12 Jingūmae, Shibuya-ku ☎03/3475-0860, ⓦ www.cporganizing.com. This super-cool café-bar is a short walk beyond the hordes of Harajuku. Set lunches start at around ¥1200 and fruity cocktails are served in the evening. Meiji-jingūmae Station. Mon–Wed noon–1am, Thurs–Sat noon–3am, Sun noon–11pm.

Yoku Moku

ヨクモク

5-3-3 Minami-Aoyama, Minato-ku ☎03/5485-3330. Hushed café with courtyard tables, in tune with the elegant sensibilities of these designer boutiques of Omotesandō. There's also a shop selling nicely packaged cakes, chocolates and confectionery, including its famous Cigar wafer-thin rolled biscuits. Omotesandō Station. Daily 10am–7pm.

Ikebukuro

The places reviewed here appear on the map on p.99.

Café du Monde

Spice 2 Building, 1-10-10 Nishi-Ikebukuro, Toshima-ku. Bright, modern New Orleans-style coffee shop specializing in authentic chicory coffee and *beignets* (doughnuts fried in cotton-seed oil) with various dipping sauces. Ikebukuro Station. Mon–Fri 8.30am–10.30pm, Sat 9am–10.30pm, Sun 9am–10pm.

Café Pause

2-14-12 Minami-Ikebukuro, Toshima-ku ☎03/5950-6117, ⓦ www.geocities.jp/cafe_pause_ikebukuro. It's something of a surprise to find this hip gallery café in the backstreets of Ikebukuro. Besides hosting regular exhibitions, parties and events, including monthly get-togethers for local designers and artists, it's also a relaxed place for a quiet coffee. Ikebukuro Station. Mon–Sat noon–11pm, Sun noon–10pm.

Zozoi

3-22-6 Nishi-Ikebukuro, Toshima-ku T 03/5396-6676. Sheepskin-covered stools and a statue of a Beefeater are part of the eclectic decor at this amiable café offering home-made cakes and biscuits, and a pleasant view onto the park. Ikebukuro Station. Mon–Sat noon–10pm, Sun noon–9.30pm.

Kanda, Akihabara and around

The places reviewed here appear on the map on p.67.

Milonga Nueva

1-3 Kanda-Jimbōchō, Chiyoda-ku T 03/3295-1716. A rustic café tucked away on the alley running parallel to Yasukuni-dōri, and serving up tango music along with its *café au lait*. Jimbōchō Station. Mon–Fri 10.30am–10.30pm, Sat & Sun 11.30am–7pm.

Mu'u Mu'u

3-14-3 Kanda-Ogawamachi, Chiyoda-ku T 03/3518-6787. Swap the dusty books of Jimbōchō for a sunny Hawaiian vibe at this café-restaurant, decked out with surfboards and hibiscus garlands. Besides Hawaiian Kona coffee, it also serves Kona beer as well as meals. Jimbōchō Station. Daily 11am–11pm.

Roppongi, Nishi-Azabu and Azabu-Jūban

See map on p.79.

Kina
貴奈

3-13-12 Roppongi, Minato-ku T 03/3478-1678 W www.kina-roppongi.com. One of the great survivors of the Roppongi scene is this spectacular *kissaten*, dating from the early 1970s. The retro decor with its fabulously colourful lamps and comfy sofas has to be seen to be believed, and the old waiters wear bow ties and burgundy blazers with gilt buttons. Apart from coffee, they do a great tea and traditional Japanese sweet set for ¥800. Roppongi Station. Mon–Fri noon–11pm, Sat noon–9pm.

Tofu Café Fujino

1F Hollywood Beauty Plaza, 6-4-1 Roppongi, Minato-ku T 03/5771-0102. Cute bunnies are the mascot at this fun modern café. Soy milk is used in all drinks (such as the black sesame soy milk smoothie at ¥600) and there's a variety of other tofu-based desserts. Their ¥900 lunch box is good value. Roppongi Station. Daily 8am–11pm.

Shibuya

The places reviewed here appear on the map on p.122.

Lion
ライオン

2-19-13 Dōgenzaka, Shibuya-ku T 03/3461-6858. Not the place for animated conversations, this *Addams Family*-style institution amid the love hotels of Dōgenzaka is where salarymen and pensioners come to appreciate classical music with their coffee – which is hardly strong, since many of the clients seem to be asleep. Seats are arranged to face a pair of enormous speakers. Shibuya Station. Daily 11am–10.30pm.

Moph

1F Sibuya Parco Part-1, 15-1 Udagawa-chō, Shibuya-ku T 03/5456-8244, W www.moph.jp. Trendy self-service café on the ground floor of the Parco fashion store. Here you can get three kinds of tasty tapas-like nibbles plus a drink for ¥680. Shibuya Station. Daily 11am–midnight.

Shinjuku

Café Comme Ça

3-26-6 Shinjuku, Shinjuku-ku T 03/5367-5551; see map pp.106–107. Serving delicious cakes, this place has stark concrete surfaces enlivened by paintings of Buddhist deities and piles of coloured powder as bright as the clothes downstairs in the trendy Five Foxes store. Shinjuku Station. Daily noon–8pm.

Takadanobaba

Ben's Café
1-29-21 Takadanobaba, Shinjuku-ku T 03/3202-2445, W www.benscafé.com; see Greater Tokyo map. Any time is a good time to visit this laid-back New York-style café. There's a fine range of coffees, drinks and snacks, and the website has details of art events, comedy and poetry reading nights. Takadanobaba Station. Daily 11.30am–midnight.

Teahouses

Besides the venues reviewed below, there are teahouses with pretty settings in Hama Rikyū Teien (p.136), Shinjuku Gyoen (p.111), Happōen (p.130), Kyū Iwasaki-tei Gardens (p.95) and Kyū Furukawa Gardens (p.102).

Asakusa

Umezono
梅園
1-31-12 Asakusa, Taitō-ku ☎03/3841-7580; see map, p.85. This traditional teashop in the heart of Asakusa is famous for its *awa-zenzai*, millet-flour cakes wrapped in sweet adzuki-bean paste, served with seeds of Japanese basil for contrast. Alternatively, choose a bowl of *anmitsu* from the window display; it's a colourful concoction of agar jelly, adzuki beans and sticky rice topped with a variety of fruits (and, if you're really hungry, whipped cream or ice cream). Asakusa Station. Daily 10am–8pm.

Ginza and around

The places reviewed here appear on the map on p.60.
Cha Ginza
5-5-6 Ginza, Chiyoda-ku ☎03/3571-1211. This teahouse offers a pleasing new take on the business of sipping *sencha*; ¥500 gets you two cups of the refreshing green stuff, plus traditional sweets and a taste of sake or wine first to allow you to savour the contrast. Iron walls add a contemporary touch, and the rooftop area, where they serve *matcha* in fine weather, is the place to hang out with those Tokyo ladies who make shopping a career. Ginza Station. Tues–Sun 10am–6pm; closed Aug.

Yamamotoyama
山本山
2-5-2 Nihombashi, Chūō-ku ☎03/3281-0010, ⓦwww.yamamotoyama.co.jp. You can sip all grades of green tea, served with either a sweet rice cake (from ¥600) or rice cracker (from ¥400), at the back of this venerable and very traditional tea merchant's shop. Nihombashi Station. Daily 9.30am–7pm, Fri until 8pm.

The way of tea

Tea was introduced to Japan from China in the ninth century and was popularized by Zen Buddhist monks, who appreciated its caffeine kick during their long meditation sessions. Gradually, tea-drinking developed into a formal ritual known as *cha-no-yu*, the **tea ceremony**, whose purpose is to heighten the senses within a contemplative atmosphere. In its simplest form the ceremony takes place in a tatami room, undecorated save for a hanging scroll or display of *ikebana* (traditional flower arrangement). Using beautifully crafted utensils of bamboo, iron and rustic pottery, your host will whisk **matcha** – the strong powdered form of green tea – into a thick, frothy brew and present it to each guest in turn. Take the bowl in both hands, turn it clockwise a couple of inches and drink it down in three slow sips. It's then customary to admire the bowl while nibbling on a dainty sweetmeat (*wagashi*).

To attend a tea ceremony, book with the *Imperial* (see p.148), *New Ōtani* (see p.147) or *Ōkura* hotels (see p.147), all of which have traditional rooms in which such ceremonies are regularly held; the cost will be around ¥1000. A good alternative is booking a tea ceremony at the Edo Antique Kimono Katagami Museum near Akasaka (see p.77).

Japan's tea culture embraces many types of tea other than *matcha*. Whenever you sit down in a restaurant, or visit a Japanese home, you'll be offered a small cup of slightly bitter green *ocha* (honourable tea), which is always drunk plain. *Bancha*, the cheapest grade, is for everyday drinking and, in its roasted form, is used to make the smoky *hōji-cha*, or mixed with popped brown rice for the nutty *genmaicha*. Medium-grade *sencha* is served in upmarket restaurants or to favoured guests, while top-ranking, slightly sweet *gyokuro* (dewdrop) is reserved for special occasions.

Harajuku and Aoyama

The places reviewed here appear on the map on p.118.

 Suzuki
寿々木

1-15-4 Jingūmae, Shibuya-ku ☎03/3404-8007. Tucked behind teeming Takeshita-dōri, but a million miles away in atmosphere, this shop specializes in *wagashi*, and has tatami rooms, screens and manicured gardens. A frothy *matcha* and one pick from the selection of sweets costs ¥900. Harajuku Station. Mon–Sat 10.30am–8pm, Sun 10.30am–7pm.

The Sweet Dynasty

3-5-14 Kita-Aoyama, Minato-ku ☎03/5786-1555. This classy branch of a top Hong Kong café has been a huge hit with its Chinese teas and sweets, including a luscious mango pudding. They do dim sum, too. Omotesandō Station. Daily 11am–10pm.

Wise Wise

5-12-7 Jingūmae, Shibuya-ku ☎03/5467-7003. Tucked away at the rear of the Wise Wise designer interior store, this refined but unstuffy café specializes in different green teas from across Japan, each served with a small plate of rice-cracker snacks. Omotesandō Station. Tues–Sun 11am–8pm.

Naka-Meguro

The places reviewed here appear on the map on pp.128–129.

Ganchabō
岩茶房

3-15-5 Kami-Meguro, Meguro-ku ☎03/3714-7425, ⓦwww.gancha-bou.co.jp. Well off the beaten track in the backstreets off Yamate-dōri is this teashop in a lovely residential-style building, specializing in Chinese teas. They also have an interesting food menu. Naka-Meguro Station. Tues–Sun 11am–7pm.

Higashiya

1-13-12 Aobadai, Meguro-ku ☎03/5428-0240, ⓦwww.higashiya.com. Upstairs from the traditional Japanese sweet shop (see p.230) is this wonderfully rustic lounge. An iron kettle in the middle of a huge shared table provides the hot water for the range of teas on offer, each of which can be sampled with the shop's delicious sweets. There's an excellent set lunch and, as day turns into night, the space morphs into a classy bar offering a range of sake. Their *Ori Higashiya* branch is near Roppongi Hills (Le Bain, 3-16-28 Nishi-Azabu, Minato-ku; see map, p.76). Naka-Meguro Station. Daily except Tues 11am–10pm.

Roppongi

The places reviewed here appear on the map on p.79.

Koots Green Tea

6-2 Roppongi, Minato-ku ⓦwww.kootsgreentea.com. Next to the Roppongi Hills North Tower is a branch of this popular and stylish chain café, where the focus is on drinks made with green tea and traditional Japanese snacks such as *onigiri* (rice balls). They also offer various regional sakes, making it a good alternative to Roppongi's raucous bars. Branches in the Galleria at Tokyo Midtown as well as in Harajuku (6-27-4 Jingūmae, Shibuya-ku) and elsewhere. They've recently taken on *Starbucks* on their home turf, opening two Seattle outlets. Roppongi Station. Daily 7am–11pm.

Toraya Café

Keyakizaka-dōri, 6-12-2 Roppongi, Minato-ku ☎03/5789-9811. Amid the sleek designer shops of Roppongi Hills' Keyakizaka-dōri, this stylish café specializes in Japanese teas and sweets made from adzuki beans. It's usually busy with ladies lunching or sipping tea between boutique visits. There's a branch in Omotesandō Hills. Roppongi Station. Daily 10am–10pm.

Bars

Tokyo's drinking establishments run the gamut, from shoebox-sized bars for regular patrons only to sophisticated cocktail lounges at top hotels. The typical Tokyo bar – smoky, cramped, exclusively male – is the **nomiya**, often containing nothing more than a short counter and a few chairs. *Nomiya*, generally run by a genial woman called a *mama-san* (a male owner is called a master), act more like mini-private clubs rather than regular bars, and strangers are not always warmly welcomed. Furthermore, drinks prices are rarely fixed, and if you're not careful you can find yourself faced with hefty bills at the end of the night. However, if you speak Japanese or have Japanese friends who can negotiate the way, having a few drinks at a *nomiya* is recommended. Many *nomiyas* can be found under the tracks at Yūrakuchō, along Shinjuku's Shomben Yokochō and Golden Gai, and on Nonbei Yokochō, the alley running alongside the train tracks just north of Shibuya Station; *gaijin*-friendly ones are listed below. For details of gay and lesbian friendly bars, see pp.203–204.

The buzz on the Tokyo bar scene of late has been about **tachinomiya**, or standing bars – which is odd as such places have been around as long as salarymen and -women have fancied a drink after work. However, these days even Shibuya hipsters are crashing in on the *tachinomiya* scene, and venues serving not just beer and nibbles but also specialist sake, *shōchū* (a popular vodka-like spirit) and wines are opening up.

The major breweries have their own reliable chains of **izakaya** – Japanese-style pubs – which are generally quite large, serve a good range of drinks and bar snacks and often have a lively atmosphere. Ones to look out for include *Kirin City*, in Ginza, Harajuku and Shinjuku; the *Hub* in Ueno, Ikebukuro, Shibuya and Shinjuku; Sapporo's *Lions Beer Hall* in Ebisu, Ginza, Ikebukuro and Shinjuku; the identikit Irish bar *The Dubliners* in Akasaka, Ikebukuro and Shinjuku; and the faux-Victorian British pub the *Rose & Crown* in Yūrakuchō, Shinbashi and Shinjuku.

A Tokyo summer is invariably a hot and sticky experience, but there is compensation in the form of the **outdoor beer gardens** which sprout around the city from June through to the end of August. You can spot them by looking out for red lanterns and fairy lights on the roofs of buildings or in street-level gardens and plazas.

Opening hours are generally daily from 5pm to around midnight Mon to Thursday as well as Sunday, extended until 4 or 5am on Friday and Saturday; our reviews give specific hours where they depart from the norm. *Nomiya* stay open as long as there are customers.

Some bars have a cover charge of anything from ¥300 to ¥1000 (*izakaya* almost always do), added onto the bill at the end, but there's plenty of choice among those that don't, so always check the deal before buying your drink. The small snack or a plate of nuts you may be served with your first drink are often cited as the reason for the charge (though some places levy one without providing anything extra), and if there's live music you'll often pay for it through a cover charge or higher drink prices.

In many bars, in particular the small *nomiya*, you'll notice that regular customers have a bottle of their favourite tipple kept behind the counter with their name on it; this is known as the bottle-keep system.

If you're out drinking with Japanese, remember to pour your companions' drinks, but never your own; they'll take care of that. In fact, you'll usually find your glass being topped up after every couple of sips, making it difficult to judge how much you've imbibed. You can make a **toast** by lifting your glass and saying "kampai".

Asakusa and Ueno

The places listed here appear on the map on p.85, except for the *Warrior Celt*, which is on the map on p.91.

Cuzn
1-41-8 Asakusa, Taitō-ku ☎03/3842-3223. Tucked away on a quiet Asakusa street behind the Rox department store, this friendly, rustic bar has a comfy sofa area, free Internet access and sometimes shows soccer games on its big screen. The food's not bad, either. It's a bit hard to spot – look for the English signboard on the pavement. Asakusa Station.

Gin Maku Roku
銀幕ロック
2F 1-41-5 Asakusa ☎03/5828-6969. The Asakusa spirit is alive and kicking in this intimate, backstreet bar full of colourful characters and festooned with homely bric-a-brac. Somehow they even manage to squeeze in a stage for the occasional concert (around ¥1000), which could feature anything from owner Hoshyou, who plays

double bass in a rockabilly band, to Balkan gypsy music. Asakusa (Tsukuba Express railway) or Tawaramachi stations.

Ichimon
一文
3-12-6 Asakusa, Taitō-ku ☎03/3875-6800.
Traditional *izakaya* with a cosy atmosphere, specializing in various types of sake and dishes made with a range of unusual meats – including ostrich, turtle, crocodile and whale. Payment is by wooden tokens which you purchase on entering. It's round the back of the block on the northeast corner of the junction of Kokusai-dōri and Kototoi-dōri. Tawaramachi Station.

Kamiya
1-1-1 Asakusa, Taitō-ku ☎03/3841-5400.
A feature of Asakusa since 1880, this was Tokyo's first Western-style bar. It's also known for its Denkibran ("electric brandy"), first brewed in 1883 when electricity was all the rage, which is made up of a small shot of gin, wine, Curaçao and brandy – it's a potent tipple, though they also make a

"weaker" version, only 30 percent proof. The ground floor is the liveliest and most informal; pay for your round of food and drinks at the cash desk as you enter. Asakusa Station. Closed Tues.

Samurai Café
2-12-6 Asakusa, Taitō-ku ☎03/3847-0161. A friendly little bar that's popular among *gaijin* staying at Asakusa's hostels, who appreciate the English-speaking staff, happy-hour deals (5–7pm) and cheap bar snacks. The sofas upstairs make a nice place to chill out. Asakusa Station.

The Warrior Celt
3F Ito Building, 6-9-22 Ueno ☎03/3836-8588.
Things can get pretty raucous at this good-time bar in the thick of Ueno. Prime ingredients are a fine range of beers, a nightly happy hour (5–7pm), live bands (Tues, Fri & Sat from 8.30pm) and, last but not least, Ladies Night on Thursdays (when all cocktails are ¥500). Add fish 'n' chips – or a mean "raj chicken" curry – and you're away. Ueno Station.

Daikan'yama, Ebisu, Hiro-o and Meguro

The places listed here appear on the map on pp.128–129.

Buri
1-14-1 Ebisu-nishi, Shibuya-ku ☎03/3496-7744. One of the new breed of venues that kick-started Ebisu's *tachi-nomiya* boom. The parent company To-Vi has made its name by creating casual standing bars where the food is worth dropping by for just as much as the drink. The speciality here is sake; other branches (with different names; see ⓦ www.to-vi.jp for details) can be found in Shibuya and Naka-Meguro. Ebisu Station.

Enjoy House!
2F Daikan'yama Techno Building, 2-9-9 Ebisu-Nishi, Shibuya-ku ☎03/5489-1591. The unique look here is zebra prints, low velour sofas, red lace curtains and tons of shiny disco balls. The master wears shorts and Jackie Onassis-style sunglasses. It gets busy at weekends, with a suitably young and attitude-free crowd. Ebisu Station.

Footnik
1F Asahi Building, 1-11-2 Ebisu, Shibuya-ku ☎03/5795-0144, ⓦ www.footnik.net. Tokyo's only bar devoted to soccer has a game or two on the big screen every night, and

reasonable food. For popular matches you'll have to pay an entry charge. Ebisu Station.

Kotobuki
ことぶき
5-3 Hiro-o, Shibuya-ku ☎03/3473-5463. Lively, modern *izakaya* on two floors, with a ground-floor bar open to the street in the summer. It's popular with expats, and there's an English menu stretching from Mexican-style taco rice to crab pasta. Hiro-o Station.

Naka-Meguro Takkyū Lounge
中目卓球ラウンジ
1-3 Kami-Meguro, Meguro-ku ⓦ www.mfs11 .com. *Takkyū* is Japanese for ping-pong, and sure enough there's a table-tennis table in the centre of this unsigned lounge bar, on the first floor of an anonymous apartment block. In-the-know hipsters love it for its unstudied coolness, in a city packed with slickly packaged watering holes. To find it, head directly across the river from Naka-Meguro Station, take the first right at the convenience store and walk to the shop Jumpin Jack Flash; it's above here. Naka-Meguro Station.

Smash Hits

B1F M2 Hiro-o Building, 5-2-26 Hiro-o, Shibuya-ku ☎03/3444-0432, ⓦwww .smashhits.jp. This basement bar, designed as a mini-amphitheatre, is the place for karaoke exhibitionists keen to perform in front of a crowd – and with twelve thousand English songs to choose from, plus many in other languages, you'll never be stuck for a tune. Entrance costs ¥3000, including two drinks and unlimited karaoke. Hiro-o Station. Mon–Sat 7pm–3am.

Symposion

17-16 Sarugaku-chō, Shibuya-ku ☎03/5458-6324. Pure *belle époque* restaurant and bar with French-influenced food and classy wines – you almost expect Toulouse-Lautrec and a troupe of girls to come high-kicking through the Art Nouveau doors. Daikan'yama Station.

Tableaux Lounge

Sunroser Daikan'yama B1, 11-6 Sarugaku-chō, Shibuya-ku ☎03/5489-2202. Ritzy lounge bar with padded leather chairs and lots of chandeliers. Daikan'yama Station.

Tachinomiya

立呑屋

1-1-6 Ebisu, Shibuya-ku ☎03/3491-4194, ⓦwww.tachinomi-ya.com. A short hop from the station is this convivial, traditional standing bar, serving a good range of drinks and *yakitori* snacks. Ebisu Station.

What the Dickens!

4F Roob 6 Building, 1-13-3 Ebisu-Nishi, Shibuya-ku ☎03/3780-2099. There's live music nightly at this olde English pub complete with beams and candle-lit nooks, with draught Guinness and Bass pale ale. The food – a range of hearty pies served with potatoes, veggies and bread – promises to warm the cockles of a homesick heart. Ebisu Station.

🏃 X+Y

4F Yoshikawa Bldg, 1-4-11 Ebisu-nishi, Shibuya-ku ☎03/5489-0095. Designed by cult photographer Tsuzuki Kyoichi, this retro-styled place – with its gilt-framed paintings of voluptuous nudes, flock-patterned uphol-stered sofas and glitter ball, looks like a misplaced slice of the Playboy Mansion. Go with the retro theme and don dark glasses, velvet jacket and flares to feel fully at home. Ebisu Station.

Yebisu Beer Station

Yebisu Garden Place, Ebisu, Shibuya-ku. Sapporo's office and shopping development hosts several bars and *izakaya*, plus a beer garden in summer. Ebisu Station.

Ginza and around

The places reviewed here are shown on the maps on p.60.

300 Bar

B1F Fazenda Building, 5-9-11 Ginza, Chūō-ku ☎03/3572-6300, ⓦwww.300bar.com. The bargain-basement face of Ginza is this standing-only bar, where all food and drinks are ¥300. Well, it's actually ¥315 now, and you have to buy two food/drink tickets to enter, but that's still cheap by Tokyo standards. Ginza Station.

Karaoke bars

The Japanese were partial to a good singsong long before **karaoke**, literally "empty orchestra", was invented, possibly by an Ōsaka record store manager in the early 1970s. It caught on like wildfire, and was boosted further in the mid-1980s by the debut of the **karaoke box**, a booth kitted out with a karaoke system and rented out by groups or individuals wanting to brush up on their singing technique. These boxes have proved particularly popular with youngsters, women and families who shied away from the small smoky bars frequented by salarymen that were the original preserve of karaoke. Today the karaoke industry earns a staggering ¥1 trillion a year.

Amazingly, research has shown that the introduction of karaoke has coincided with a significant drop in the number of drunks taken into protective custody by the police, as salarymen drink less while relaxing over a rousing rendition of "My Way". If you fancy joining in the sing-a-thon there's no shortage of options, including *Fiesta* (see p.193), *Karaoke-kan* (see p.194), *Lovenet* (see p.194) and *Smash Hits* (see above).

Kagaya

B1F Hanasada Building, 2-15-12 Shinbashi, Minato-ku ⓣ03/3591-2347, ⓦwww1.ocn.ne.jp/~kagayayy. English-speaking Mark runs this simple basement bar as if he's hosting an 8-year-old's birthday party with alcohol. Around ¥3000 will get you plenty of drink, food and side-splittingly silly games. Phone ahead to check he's open; reservations recommended. Shinbashi Station. Closed Sun.

Kudan Kaikan

九段会館

1-6-5 Kudan-minami, Chiyoda-ku ⓣ03/3261-5521. A good rooftop beer garden. Wednesday is usually ladies' night, when women can drink as much as they like for ¥1000. Kudanshita Station. Mid-May to end Aug Mon–Fri 5–10pm, Sat & Sun 5–9pm.

Lion

7-9-20 Ginza, Chūō-ku ⓣ03/3571-2590. Opened in 1934, this beer hall, flagship of the Sapporo chain, is a rather baronial place with its dark tiles and mock wood-panelling. There are sausages, sauerkraut and other German snacks on offer alongside international pub fare, and a restaurant upstairs. You'll find other branches scattered around Tokyo. Ginza Station.

Marunouchi House

7F Shin-Marunouchi Bldg, 1-5-1 Maranouchi, Chiyoda-ku ⓦwww.marunouchi-house.com. The best thing about the funky open-plan space here, with seven different restaurants and bars, is that you can take your drinks out on to the broad, wrap-around terrace for ace views of Tokyo Station and towards the Imperial Palace. Tokyo Station. It keeps late hours, too, until 4am (11am on Sun & holidays).

Old Imperial Bar

Imperial Hotel, 1-1-1 Uchisaiwaichō, Chiyoda-ku ⓣ03/3504-1111. This recreated bar is all that remains in Tokyo of Frank Lloyd Wright's Art Deco *Imperial Hotel* from the 1920s (you can find the front and lobby in the Meiji Mura park near Nagoya, in central Honshū). To get in the spirit of the place, you might like to try a Mount Fuji cocktail – a wickedly sweet blend of gin, cream, egg white and sugar syrup with a cherry on top, which was invented here in 1924. And while you sup it, ask to see the photo albums of how the hotel once looked. Hibiya Station.

🏃 Shin Hi No Moto
新日の基

1-chōme Yūrakuchō, Chiyoda-ku ⓣ03/3214-8021. A lively English-owned *izakaya* under the tracks just south of Yūrakuchō Station. It's one of the few places to try the excellent Sapporo Red Star beer, or cheap, strong *shōchū*. The seafood and vegetables come fresh from Tsukiji. Reservations are recommended, especially at weeekends. Yūrakuchō or Hibiya stations.

Town Cryer

B1F Hibiya Central Building, 1-2-9 Nishi-Shinbashi, Minato-ku ⓣ03/3519-6690. Billed as a "Genuine British pub" (well, it's got beams and hop garlands) and run by the team behind Ebisu's *What the Dickens!*, which means the meals can be relied on to be filling. Ōtemachi Station. Closed Sat & Sun.

Harajuku and Aoyama

The places reviewed here are shown on the maps on p.114 or p.118.

Kyosho Omotesandō

B3F Omotesandō Hills, 4-12-10 Meiji-Jingūmae, Shibuya-ku ⓣ03/5785-0280. In the basement of Omotesandō Hills, this shop selling model cars has a track at the back where you can race radio-controlled cars while sipping a beer or other drink. Opposite, in the wine-shop and brasserie *Bisty's*, it's possible to sample some of the bottles at a stand-up bar before buying. Omotesandō Station. Daily 11am–9pm.

Montoak

6-1-9 Jingūmae, Shibuya-ku ⓣ03/5468-5928. Snooty but stylish café-bar, with a glass facade facing onto Harajuku's famous shopping street. DJs create a suitable loungey vibe, and there's live music sometimes at weekends. Meiji-jingūmae Station. Daily 10am–11pm.

Office

5F 2-7-18 Kita-Aoyama, Minato-ku ⓣ03/5788-1052. This trendy bar is for those who don't really want to leave the office; here you can huddle round the photocopier, squat at childishly low tables and knock back the booze without the boss raising an eye. At ground level in the same building is its sister café-bar *Sign*, where a DJ keeps punters grooving along nicely. Gaienmae Station. Closed Sun.

Pariya
3-12-14 Kita Aoyama, Minato-ku ☎03/3486-1316. Dark and with some interesting artwork and nooks and crannies, this sophisticated café-bar serves decent food, but really excels as a bolthole for a discreet assignation. Omotesandō Station. Daily 11.30am–2.30pm & 6–11pm.

Sekirei
明治記念館
Meiji Kinenkan, 2-2-23 Moto-Akasaka, Minato-ku ☎03/3746-7723, ⓦwww.meijikinenkan.gr.jp. One of the nicest beer gardens in Tokyo, sited in a real garden attached to the Meiji Kinenkan wedding hall. A bonus is the chance to watch classical Japanese dance (Nihon Buyō) nightly at around 8pm. Mon–Sat 4.30–10.30pm, Sun 5.30–10.30pm.

Ikebukuro

The places reviewed here are shown on the map on p.99.

300B
2F 3-29-4 Nishi-Ikebukuro ☎03/3986-3005. Big, bubbling *izakaya*, popular with a young crowd for its cheap prices and good food. A reliable standby. Ikebukuro Station.

The Black Sheep
B1F 1-7-12 Higashi-Ikebukuro, Toshima-ku ☎03/3987-2289. Tiny, lively, friendly bar behind BIC Camera, with a choice of seven beers on tap and great fish and chips. On Wednesday there's a special deal on

draught pale ale and weekends feature live music. Ikebukuro Station.

Bobby's Bar
3F Milano Building, 1-18-10 Nishi-Ikebukuro, Toshima-ku ☎03/3980-8875. There's a warm welcome at this *gaijin*-friendly bar run by the eponymous Bobby, who shakes a mean cocktail – try his Hellsgate and Heavensgate concoctions, or invent your own from the vast array of alcohol in stock. Bobby's home-made spicy nachos also get the thumbs-up. Ikebukuro Station.

Sake

Legend has it that Japan's ancient deities brewed **sake** from the first rice of the new year. Although sake, also known as *nihonshu*, has now been overtaken by beer as the nation's most popular tipple, over ten thousand different brands of the clean-tasting rice wine are still produced throughout the country by some two thousand breweries.

Sake primarily comes either in sweet (*amakuchi*) and dry (*karakuchi*) varieties. Some types are cloudier and less refined than others, while a few are aged. If you're after the best quality, take a look at bottles labelled *ginjō-zukuri* (or *ginjō-zō*), the most expensive and rare of the *junmai-shu* pure rice sake.

In restaurants and *izakaya* you'll be given the choice of drinking your sake warm (*atsukan*) or cold (*reishu*). *Reishu* is usually the preferred way to enable you to properly taste the wine's complex flavours; you should never drink premium sake warm. Sake is often served in a small flask (*tokkuri*), but cold sake is sometimes drunk out of a small wooden box (*masu*), with a smidgen of salt on the rim to counter the slightly sweet taste. Glasses are traditionally filled right to the brim and are sometimes placed on a saucer to catch any overflow; they're generally small because, with an alcohol content of fifteen percent or more, sake is a strong drink – and it goes to your head even more quickly if drunk warm.

For more on sake, check out the books and informative website (ⓦwww.sake -world.com) of long-time resident expert John Gautner, who often holds seminars on sake at *Takara* in Yūrakuchō (see p.169).

Roppongi and around

Roppongi easily has Tokyo's greatest concentration of foreigner-friendly bars, though many are closed on Sunday. Unless mentioned otherwise, the places reviewed here appear on the map on p.79.

A971 Garden < > House
Tokyo Midtown, 9-7-3 Akasaka, Minato-ku ☎03/5413-7340; see map, p.76. The "garden" part of this relaxed café-bar is on the ground floor at the front of the Midtown complex, while the "house" is the restaurant upstairs. With mid-twentieth-century modernist furnishings, it's quickly proved itself a popular hangout, and does a good selection of reasonably priced drinks and food. Free Internet terminals, too. Roppongi Station.

Absolut Icebar Tokyo
The Wall, 4-2-4 Nishi-Azabu, Minato-ku ☎03/5464-2160, ⓦwww.icebartokyo.com; see map, p.76. Many big cities seem to have a bar made of ice these days, and Tokyo is no different. It's all probably a passing phase, but on a scorching summer night this place could seem like a blessing. There's a hefty cover charge, for which you receive all the clothing you need to withstand the freezing temperatures. Roppongi Station.

Acarajé Tropicana
B2F Edge Building, 1-1-1 Nishi-Azabu, Minato-ku ☎03/3479-4690. Join the all-night Brazilian line-dancing sessions at this popular Latin American-style basement bar-restaurant, just off Roppongi-dōri. On Thursdays women pay ¥500 for all drinks, all night. Roppongi Station. Closed Mon.

Agave
B1F Clover Building, 7-15-10 Roppongi, Minato-ku ☎03/3497-0229. One for tequila- and cigar-lovers, this atmospheric basement bar has an authentic Latin American tang, with four hundred varieties of the Mexican tipple on the shelves and a humidor bulging with stogies. Roppongi Station. Closed Sun.

Castillo
3F Win Roppongi Bldg, 3-15-24 Roppongi, Minato-ku ☎03/3475-1629 ⓦwww.castillo -tokyo.com. Rock, disco and new wave sounds of the 1970s and 1980s at this long-running *gaijin* bar. Browse their collection of over thirty thousand discs on Tuesdays when the place doubles as a record shop. Roppongi Station. Closed Sun.

Fiesta
3F Crest Roppongi Building, 7-9-3 Roppongi, Minato-ku ☎03/5410-3008, ⓦwww.fiesta -roppongi.com; see map, p.76. *Gaijin*-friendly karaoke bar with ten thousand songs in languages other than Japanese. There's no excuse for not being able to read the lyrics when they're displayed on fifty-inch plasma screens. The ¥3150 cover charge includes three drinks. Roppongi Station.

Gas Panic
50 Togensha Building, 3-15-24 Roppongi, Minato-ku ☎03/3405-0633, ⓦwww.gaspanic .co.jp. This grungy bar and club just keeps going and going. Although it's just about the last word in sleaze (think drunken *gaijin* males groping scantily clad Japanese girls), most Tokyo residents and not a few visitors pass through here at least once. There are two branches in Shibuya, one at the station end of Centre Gai, and the other on Dōgenzaka (see map, p.122). Roppongi Station.

Heartland
1F Roppongi Hills West Walk, 6-10-1 Roppongi, Minato-ku ☎03/5772-7600, ⓦwww.heartland .jp. It's usually standing room only at this über-trendy but friendly bar in the northwest corner of Roppongi Hills. Sink one of their trademark green bottled beers and watch arty videos on the panoramic plasma screen behind the bar. Roppongi Station. Also opens for lunch.

Hobgoblin
Aoba Roppongi Building, 3-16-33 Roppongi, Minato-ku ☎03/3568-1280, ⓦwww.hobgoblin.jp. British microbrewery Wychwood serves up its fine ales at this spacious bar that's a Roppongi classic – which means you'll be part of a very boozy, noisy crowd of *gaijin* at weekends and on nights when there are major sports matches on the big-screen TVs. Its real strength is the very comforting English pub-style food, including pies and fish and chips. They also run *Legend Sports Bar* in the same building, a casual American-style bar festooned with photos of sporting heroes. There's a smaller *Hobgoblin* in Akasaka (B1F Tamondo Building, 2-13-19 Akasaka, Minato-ku; see map, p.76). Roppongi Station.

Lovenet
3F Hotel Ibis, 7-14-4 Roppongi, Minato-ku ☎03/5771-5511. Luxury karaoke-box complex with 34 different themed rooms, even including some with Jacuzzis. Food is on offer from restaurants in the complex, including *Hann*, a classy Korean place. Reckon on at least ¥4000 per head. Roppongi Station. Daily 6pm–5am.

These
2-13-19 Nishi-Azabu, Minato-ku ☎03/5466-7331, ⓦwww.these-jp.com; see map, p.76. On the second floor, this lounge bar-cum-library, pronounced "Tay-Zay", is a cool hangout for a quiet drink or a late-night bite to eat. Break the ice by asking them to show you their "secret room". Roppongi Station; Closed Sun.

Shibuya

The places listed here appear on the map on p.122.

Belgo
B1F Ichigokan Building, 3-18-7 Shibuya, Shibuya-ku ☎03/3409-4442. This bar specializes in European beers, particularly from Belgium. The dark, slimline, multi-level basement space feels a bit like a medieval dungeon. Shibuya Station. Closed third Sun of the month.

Coins Bar
300 B1F Noa Shibuya Building, 36-2 Udagawa-chō, Shibuya-ku ☎03/3463-3039. The choice at this friendly basement bar is simple: ¥300 for any drink or plate of food, or ¥2500 for as much as you like of either over a 2hr 30min period. Given how cheap it is, it's surprisingly stylish, making it a top choice if you're on a budget. Shibuya Station.

Cozmos Café & Bar
1-6-3 Shibuya, Shibuya-ku ☎03/3407-5166, ⓦwww.cozmoscafe.com. US expat Ronna Wagenheim is the dynamic creator of this popular café-bar hosting an interesting series of events, detailed on their website. Shibuya Station. Closed Sun.

Fujiya Honten
2-3 Sakuragaoka-chō, Shibuya-ku ☎03/ 3461-2128. No-frills, good-value standing bar with some fifty different wines on offer at from as little as ¥1600 a bottle, and a dozen by the glass at ¥400.

Karaoke-kan
カラオケ館
6–8F K&F Building, 30-8 Udagawachō, Shibuya-ku ☎03/3462-0785. Just off Centre Gai, this typical karaoke-box complex is the very one in which Bill Murray serenaded Scarlett Johansson in *Lost in Translation*; rooms 601 and 602 were used in the movie. An hour of karaoke costs ¥1000 Mon–Thurs, ¥1200

Fri–Sun; drinks and snacks are extra. Shibuya Station.

🏃 **Legato**
15F E-Space Tower, 3-6 Maruyama-cho, Shibuya-ku ☎03/5784-2121. A fancy Italian restaurant with a bar offering a jaw-dropping floor-to-ceiling view over Shibuya from fifteen floors up. Shibuya Station. Mon–Fri 11.30am–2pm, daily 5.30pm–4am.

Pink Cow
Villa Moderna, 1-3-18 Shibuya, Shibuya-ku ☎03/3406-5597, ⓦwww.thepinkcow.com. There's always something interesting going on – from book readings to comedy improv nights – at this funky haven for local artists and writers, run by the convivial Tracey. It stocks a good range of imported wines and, on Fri & Sat night, it serves a home-cooked buffet for ¥2500. Shibuya Station.

Red Bar
1-12-22 Shibuya, Shibuya-ku. Tucked around the corner from Shibuya's main post office is this super-compact Ali-Baba's cave, decked out with chandeliers and lamps. As with other Tokyo bars of this size it can be cliquey, but at 3am, when it hits its stride, that hardly seems to matter. Shibuya Station.

Xanadu
B1F Hontis Building, 2-23-12 Dōgenzaka, Shibuya-ku ☎03/5489-3750. Kublai Khan's pleasure dome it certainly ain't, but this hardly matters to most of the up-for-it *gaijin* and young Japanese crowd. The place keeps going all night long at weekends, when the cover charge is at least ¥1000 (including a drink). Shibuya Station.

Shinjuku and around

The places listed here appear on the map on pp.106–107.

Albatross
アルバトロス
1-2-11 Nishi-Shinjuku, Shinjuku-ku ☎03/3342-
5758. Groovy little bar (with a tiny art gallery
upstairs) set amid the pint-sized bars and
yakitori joints of the Shomben Yokochō
alley, immediately north of the station.
They're welcoming of foreigners and, with
a cover charge of ¥300 and drinks at
¥500, you're not going to get stung.
Shinjuku Station.

Clubhouse
**3F Marunaka Building, 3-7-3 Shinjuku,
Shinjuku-ku** ☎03/3359-7785. This spacious
sports bar has a jolly atmosphere and a
policy of being cheaper than the Roppongi
competition. On the menu are fish and
chips, Aussie meat pies and a good
selection of vegetarian dishes. Shinjuku-
sanchōme Station.

The Dubliners
**2F Shinjuku Lion Hall, 3-28-9 Shinjuku,
Shinjuku-ku** ☎03/3352-6606. Popular
branch of the Irish bar chain, with
Guinness and Kilkenny bitter on tap and
Irish stew on the menu. Good for a quiet
lunch or coffee as well as a rowdy night's
drinking. Shinjuku Station.

Jetée
ジュテ
2F 1-1-8, Kabukichō, Shinjuku-ku ☎03/3208-
9645. Kawai-san, the venue's *mama-san* is a
Francophile whose passion for films and
jazz are combined in this tiny, quintessential
Golden Gai bar – but don't bother turning
up during May, when she decamps to the
Cannes Film Festival. Cover charge ¥1000.
Shinjuku-sanchōme Station. Closed Sun
and in May.

New York Bar
**Park Hyatt Hotel, 3-7-1-2 Nishi-Shinjuku,
Shinjuku-ku** ☎03/5323-3458. Top-class live
jazz plus the glittering nighttime view of
Shinjuku are the attractions of this sophisti-
cated bar, attached to the *New York Grill*.
Lost in Translation buffs can relive scenes
from the movie here. Tochōmae Station.

Vagabond
1-4-20 Nishi-Shinjuku, Shinjuku-ku ☎03/3348-
9109. A Shinjuku institution, where
Matsuoka-san plays the genial host, greeting
guests and sometimes playing along with
the jazz pianists who tinkle the ivories every
night. There's a ¥500 cover charge, but the
drinks are good value and the atmosphere is
priceless. Also has a downstairs bar, without
live music. Shinjuku Station.

Bayside Tokyo

T.Y. Harbor Brewery
**Bond St, 2-1-3 Higashi-Shinagawa, Shinagawa-
ku** ☎03/5479-4555, ⓦ www.tyharborbrewing
.co.jp; see Greater Tokyo map at back of book.
Take the monorail from Hamamatsuchō to
reach this microbrewery, in a converted

Bayside warehouse, which also has an
outdoor deck and a so-so Californian-
cuisine restaurant. The main draw is the
Tennoz brand beer – varieties of which
include amber ale, porter, wheat beer and
California pale ale. Tennōzu Isle Station.

Clubs and live music

Tokyo is as important a venue on the international **clubbing** scene as London and New York, and you'll find all the latest sounds covered, from hip-hop and acid jazz to techno, trance and drum 'n' bass, with overseas DJs regularly jetting in to play gigs at the top clubs. If you prefer dancing, or just listening, to **live music**, then Tokyo is also well stocked with options – the city has an incredibly varied appetite for music from all corners of the globe, as a trip to any of the city's major CD emporiums will prove. It's not surprising, therefore, that major artists and orchestras are keen to include the capital on their schedules, and on many nights of the week you can take your pick of anything from Beethoven to Beatles tribute bands or traditional Japanese ballads to contemporary jazz.

Clubs

The chameleon-like nature of the city's nightlife, fuelled by an insatiable appetite for new trends, means that Tokyo is one of the most exciting, but also most unpredictable, places in the world to party, and while some clubs weather the vagaries of fashion, it pays to consult the media before heading out. Check the local listings, magazines and websites (see p.30) and look for the free monthly booklet of DJ schedules and discount coupons put out by the CIA (Club Information Agency; Ⓦ www.ciajapan.com), which is available at clubs and shops such as Tower Records. Most major clubs also have their schedule on their website.

All clubs levy a **cover charge**, typically ¥2500–3000, which usually includes a ticket for at least your first drink. You can often save a small amount if you pick up a flyer for the club from one of the record shops or boutiques around town, or look for the discount coupons in the CIA booklet.

The clubs listed below are open daily unless stated otherwise in the reviews. Most clubs don't really get going until after 11pm, especially at weekends, and most stay open until around 4am. The main clubbing regions are Roppongi and Shibuya. Top local DJs to look out for are **Ken Ishii**, well known for his techno sets, the hard-house-loving **Ko Kimura**, expat Brit **Mike McKenna**, an award-winner who spins house and breakbeats, and the hip-hop maestro **Krash**.

Ebisu and Daikan'yama

The places below appear on the map on pp.128–129.

Air
B1 Hikawa Building, 2-11 Sarugaku-chō, Shibuya-ku ☎ 03/5784-3386, Ⓦ www.air-tokyo .com. South of Shibuya Station on the way to Ebisu, this eclectic club has a great sound system, but is only open for special events; look out for flyers. Shibuya Station.

Milk
みるく
B1 Roob 6 Building, 1-13-3 Ebisu-Nishi, Shibuya-ku ☎ 03/5458-2826, Ⓦ www.milk -tokyo.com. *Milk* usually packs in a lively

crowd who come mainly for techno and trance nights, although they do have the occasional live band. If you get bored with the music, check out the sex toys in the chill-out room's kitchen cabinet. Ebisu Station.

Unit
Za-House Bldg, 1-34-17 Ebisu-Nishi, Shibuya-ku ☏03/5459-8630, ⓦwww .unit-tokyo.com. DJ events are mixed up with concerts by an interesting selection of artists and bands at this cool three-floor club, café and lounge bar. Ebisu or Daikan'yama stations.

Ikebukuro

Bed
B1F Fukuri Building, 3-29-9 Nishi-Ikebukuro ☏03/3981-5300, ⓦwww.ikebukurobed.com; see map, p.99. About as hip as nightlife gets in Ikebukuro. The mix of hip-hop, reggae, jungle, R&B and occasional drum 'n' bass keeps things jumping until 5am. Also stages live shows. Ikebukuro Station.

Roppongi and around

The places below appear on the map on p.76 or p.79.

328 (San Ni Pa)
3-24-20 Nishi-Azabu, Minato-ku ☏03/3401-4968, ⓦwww.3-2-8.jp. One of the eternal fixtures of the Tokyo club scene is this basement DJ bar; the entrance is next to the police box at Nishi-Azabu crossing. Generally more laid-back than many other late-night Roppongi options, but can still get packed out at weekends. Roppongi Station.

Alife
1-7-2 Nishi-Azabu, Minato-ku ☏03/5785-2531, ⓦwww.e-alife.net. Continues to be a stylish presence on the club scene. The

ground-floor café-bar is a good place to chill out after you've worked up a sweat on the large dance floor below. Roppongi Station. Thurs–Sat only.

Bullets
B1F Kasumi Bldg,1-7-11 Nishi-Azabu, Minato-ku ☏03/3401-4844, ⓦbul-lets.com. Nestling behind *Alife*, this small, cosy club hosts DJs who veer towards breakbeats. The venue has its own compilation CD, featuring various electronica, ambient and abstract tracks. Roppongi Station. Fri & Sat 10pm–5am.

Muse
1-13-3 Nishi-Azabu, Minato-ku ☏03/5467-1188, ⓦwww.muse-web.com. A pick-up joint, but an imaginatively designed one, spread across three floors, with lots of interesting little rooms to explore or canoodle in. There's also a groovy dance area at the back, which gets packed at weekends. Roppongi Station.

Super Deluxe
B1F 3-1-25 Nishi-Azabu, Minato-ku ☏03/5412-0515, ⓦwww.super-deluxe.com. Billing itself as a place for "thinking, drinking people" *Super Deluxe* is alternative-clubland central for Tokyo, hosting a wide variety of arty events. The toilets– an art project in themselves – are something to behold. Roppongi Station. Closed Sun.

Warehouse
B1F Fukuo Bldg, 1-4-5 Azabu-Jūban, Minato-ku ☏03/6230-0343, ⓦwww.a-warehouse.net. *Warehouse* is the latest incarnation for this spacious basement space. Gay-friendly events are held here as well as a range of other club nights. Azabu-Jūban Station.

Yellow
1-10-11 Nishi-Azabu, Minato-ku ☏03/3479-0690, ⓦwww.club-yellow.com. Look for the blank yellow neon sign and descend into the basement to discover one of Tokyo's

CLUBS AND LIVE MUSIC | Clubs

A creative dialogue

In 2003, Tokyo-based architects Astrid Klein and Mark Dytham started **Pecha Kucha** (ⓦwww.pecha-kucha.org), a monthly gathering of creative people both Japanese and *gaijin*, to network and publicly show their work at the club and events space *Super Deluxe*. The format allows each presenter just twenty images, each shown for no more than twenty seconds so no one can get boring or longwinded. A great success, Pecha Kucha (the name means chit-chat) has since gone global, with events happening in many other cities. Similar cross-cultural design forums are a feature of both *Café Pause* (see p.183) and the *Pink Cow* (see p.194).

most enduring clubs (it opened in 1991), offering a range of music on different nights, with weekends mainly featuring techno and house. Also known as *Space Lab Yellow*. Roppongi Station.

Shibuya

The places below appear on the map on p.122.

Club Asia

1-8 Maruyamachō, Shibuya-ku ☎03/5458-2551, ⓦwww.clubasia.co.jp. Another mainstay of the clubbing scene with the emphasis on techno and trance nights. It's in the heart of the Dōgenzaka love-hotel district and is a popular place for one-off events such as gigs by visiting DJs. Shibuya Station.

Harlem

Dr Jeekan's Building, 2-4 Maruyama-chō, Shibuya-ku ☎03/3461-8806, ⓦwww.harlem .co.jp. Spacious two-floor club specializing in hip-hop, rap and R&B, and a good spot to check out the latest in street fashion. Shibuya Station.

La Fabrique

B1F Zero Gate, 16-9 Udagawa-chō, Shibuya-ku ☎03/5428-5100, ⓦwww.lafabrique.jp. Smart, a bit snooty and oh so Parisian. Although you can come here for lunch or dinner (their speciality is *flammekueche*, wafer-thin pizza from Alsace), it's the French house that is the main selling point (Fri & Sat 11pm–5am; entrance ¥3000). Shibuya Station.

The Ruby Room

2-25-17 Dōgenzaka, Shibuya-ku ☎03/3780-3022, ⓦwww.rubyroomtokyo.com. Cosy, groovy cocktail bar/club upstairs from the casual California diner *Sonoma* (see p.175), eating at which exempts you from the club's cover charge. Shibuya Station.

Womb

2-16 Maruyama-chō, Shibuya-ku ☎03/5459-0039, ⓦwww.womb.co.jp. One of Tokyo's mega-clubs, with a spacious dance floor, enormous glitterball and a pleasant chill-out space. Top DJs work the decks, but be warned that at big events it can get dangerously crowded. Shibuya Station.

Shinjuku

See map on pp.106–107.

Code

4F Shinjuku Toho Kaikan, 1-19-9 Kabukichō, Shinjuku-ku ☎03/3209-0702, ⓦwww .clubcomplexcode.com. On the fourth floor of a Kabukichō building is one of Japan's biggest clubs, with room for two thousand people and three dance floors, including an enormous main dance area surrounded by giant video screens. Shinjuku Station.

Garam

Eighth floor, Dai-Roku Polestar Bldg, 1-16-6 Kabukichō, Shinjuku-ku ☎03/3205-8668. *Garam* is tiny, but also friendly, and a good place to head if you're into reggae. Shinjuku Station.

Bayside Tokyo

Ageha

Studio Coast, 2-2-10 Shin-kiba, Kōtō-ku ☎03/5534-2525, ⓦwww.ageha.com; see map, p.135. This giant warehouse space has been transformed into an ultra-cool mega-club with several dance areas, an outdoor pool, a body-shaking sound and a roster of high-profile events. The location is way across Tokyo Bay, but there's a free shuttle bus here from the east side of Shibuya Station – check the website for details and make sure you turn up at least half an hour before you want to depart to get a ticket to board the bus. Shin-Kiba Station.

Live music

Pop and rock acts usually play in "live houses", many of which are little more than a pub with a small stage (*What the Dickens!*, p.190, falls into this category), although some clubs such as *Super Deluxe* and *Unit* also have live music events. There are also several larger venues where top local and international acts do their thing, most notably the cavernous Tokyo Dome in Suidōbashi, affectionately known as the "Big Egg", and the Nippon Budōkan, where the Beatles played. Tickets for concerts can be bought through ticket agencies – see p.241.

Jazz and blues are incredibly popular in Tokyo, with scores of clubs across the city. The city is equally well served with **Western classical music** venues and there are usually one or two concerts of every week, either by one of

Tokyo's several resident symphony orchestras or by a visiting group, as well as occasional performances of **opera**. Tickets are available from the relevant box office or a ticket agency (see p.241), though they are often scooped up as soon as they go on sale. However, a limited number of cheap seats (sometimes half-price) often go on sale on the day of the performance – be prepared to queue if you want these.

Concerts of **traditional Japanese music**, played on instruments such as the *shakuhachi* (flute), the *shamisen* (a kind of lute that is laid on the ground), and the *taiko* (drum), are much rarer. Top groups to watch out for include Kodō, the theatrical drumming ensemble who occasionally play Tokyo venues such as the Bunkamura in Shibuya.

Rock and pop

Billboard Live Tokyo
4F Tokyo Midtown 9-7-4 Akasaka, Minato-ku ☎03/3405-1133, ⓦwww.billboard-live.com; see map, p.76. Recently launched, this is a relatively intimate space at which everyone on the three levels gets a great view of the stage. Steely Dan were the opening act, so don't expect anything too cutting edge. Roppongi Station.

Cavern Club
5-3-2 Roppongi, Minato-ku ☎03/3405-5207; see map, p.79. A meticulous re-creation of the Beatles' Liverpool venue, with pretty decent Beatles cover bands providing the entertainment. Entrance ¥1500. Roppongi Station.

Club Citta
4-1-26 Ogawachō, Kawasaki ☎044/246-8888, ⓦwww.clubcitta.co.jp. One of Tokyo's major live-music venues, in the suburb-city of Kawasaki, hosting a variety of local and international rock bands. It was given a total makeover in 2003 and is now part of a new entertainment and shopping complex called La Cittadella. It's a 5min walk south of the station, which is around 20min from central Tokyo. Kawasaki Station.

Club Quattro
5F Quattro Building, 32-13 Udagawa-chō, Shibuya-ku ☎03/3477-8750, ⓦwww.club -quattro.com; see map, p.122. Intimate rock-music venue which tends to showcase up-and-coming bands and artists, though it also plays host to well-known local and international acts. Shibuya Station.

Crocodile
6-18-8 Jingūmae, Shibuya-ku ☎03/3499-5205, ⓦwww.music.co.jp/~croco; see map, p.122/Shibuya. You'll find everything from samba to blues and reggae at this long-running basement space on Meiji-dōri, between

Harajuku and Shibuya. Cover charge ¥2000–3000. Meiji-jingūmae or Shibuya stations.

Cyber
B1, 1-43-14 Higashi-Ikebukuro ☎03/3985-5844, ⓦwww.explosionworks.net/cyber; see map, p.99. Dark, throbbing rock dive among the soaplands and love hotels north of Ikebukuro Station. The bands are variable, though you might strike lucky. Concerts start as early as 4.30pm. Entry ¥2000 and up. Ikebukuro Station.

Liquid Room
3-16-6 Higashi, Shibuya-ku ☎03/5464-0800, ⓦwww.liquidroom.net; see map, pp.128–129. A live music venue with some DJ events, usually held in their *Liquid Loft* space. Also on the premises are the groovy *Tower Café* and shop. Ebisu Station.

Red Shoes
B1F Chigau Aoyama Bldg, 6-7-14 Minami-Aoyama, Minato-ku ☎03/3486-1169, ⓦwww .redshoes.jp; see map, p.76. A little uphill from the Nishi-Azabu crossing towards Shibuya, this is a venue where fledgling bands try out their stuff. Worth a look-in. Roppongi Station.

Shibuya O-East
2-14-8 Dōgenzaka, Shibuya-ku ☎03/5458-4681, ⓦwww.shibuya-o.com; see map, p.122/Shibuya. This complex has several venues, all hosting live music events, ranging from J-pop to hard rock. International bands also play here. Shibuya Station.

Jazz and blues

Blue Note
6-3-16 Minami-Aoyama, Minato-ku ☎03/5485-0088, ⓦwww.bluenote.co.jp; see map, p.118. Tokyo's premier jazz venue, part of the international chain, attracts world-class performers (at steep ticket prices). Entry for shows at 7 and 9pm is from ¥6000

(including one drink), depending on the acts. Omotesandō Station. Closed Sun.

Blues Alley Japan

B1F Hotel Wing International Meguro, 1-3-14 Meguro, Meguro-ku ☎03/5496-4381, ⓦwww .bluesalley.co.jp; see map, pp.128–129. This offshoot of the Washington DC blues and jazz club occupies a small basement space near the station. Meguro Station.

Cotton Club

2F Tokia Building, 2-7-3 Marunouchi ☎03/3215-1555, ⓦwww.cottonclubjapan.co.jp; see map, p.60. From the same stable as the *Blue Note* is this ritzy jazz club, which has already made a name for itself showcasing the likes of Cab Calloway, Monty Alexander and The Drifters. It's run as a supper club with two shows a night (Mon–Sat 7pm & 9.30pm, Sun 5pm & 8pm) and ticket prices (¥5000–12,000) varying depending on where you sit and who's on. Tokyo Station.

JZ Brat

2F Cerulean Tower Tōkyū Hotel, 26-1 Sakuragaoka-ch, Shibuya-ku ☎03/5728-0168, ⓦwww.jzbrat.com; see map, p.122. Swanky jazz club and restaurant in Shibuya's top hotel, with a spacious contemporary design and a respectable line-up of artists. Cover charge from ¥3000. Shibuya Station.

New York Bar

Park Hyatt Hotel, 3-7-1-2 Nishi-Shinjuku, Shinjuku-ku ☎03/5322-1234; see map, pp.106–107. Top-class live jazz plus a glittering night view of Shinjuku are the attractions of this sophisticated bar attached to the *Park Hyatt's New York Grill*. There's a ¥2000 cover charge (waived if you eat at the *New York Grill*). Tochōmae Station.

Shinjuku Pit Inn

B1F Accord Shinjuku Building, 2-12-4 Shinjuku, Shinjuku-ku ☎03/3354-2024, ⓦwww.pit-inn .com; see map, pp.106–107. Serious, longstanding jazz club which has been the launch platform for many top Japanese performers and which also attracts overseas acts. Daytime shows 2–5pm (¥1300); evening sessions kick off at 8pm (¥3000 including one drink). Shinjuku Station.

Classical music and opera

Casals Hall

1-6 Kanda-Surugadai, Chiyoda-ku ☎03/3294-1229; see map, p.67. Set inside the Ochanomizu Square Building, designed by top architect Arata Isozaki, this is a major venue for piano recitals, chamber music and small ensembles. Ochanomizu Station.

NHK Hall

2-2-1 Jinnan, Shibuya-ku ☎03/3465-1751; see map, p.114. One of Tokyo's older auditoria for classical concerts, but still well thought of and home to the highly rated NHK Symphony Orchestra. It's next to the NHK Broadcasting Centre, south of Yoyogi-kōen. Harajuku or Shibuya stations.

Music festivals

July and August are the months for **rock and popular music festivals**. The most established event as far as foreign bands is concerned is **Fuji Rock** (ⓦwww.fujirockfestival .com). Going since 1997, this huge three-day event hosts a wide range of top-name acts covering musical genres from dance and electronica to jazz and blues on multiple stages. It takes place in the mountains of Niigata Prefecture at Naeba Ski Resort, easily accessible from Tokyo via Shinkansen. Tickets cost around ¥16,800 for one day or ¥39,800 for three days; it's possible to camp here or stay in the hotels that cater to the ski crowd in winter.

Even bigger in terms of crowds (it attracts an audience of well over 100,000) and simpler to get to is **Summer Sonic** (ⓦwww.summersonic.com), a two-day event held in Chiba, just across the Edo-gawa river from Tokyo. This festival showcases a good mix of both local and overseas bands and has both indoor and outdoor performances. One-day tickets cost ¥15,000, two-day tickets ¥27,500.

Rock in Japan (ⓦwww.rijfes.co.jp), focusing on domestic bands, is usually held in August at Hitachi Seaside Park, north of Tokyo in Ibaraki-ken (accessible from Ueno Station). More general in its scope is the **Tokyo Summer Music Festival** (ⓦwww .arion-edo.org/tsf), held throughout July around the city, which encompasses classical and world-music performances.

Orchard Hall

2-24-1 Dōgenzaka, Shibuya-ku ☎03/3477-9111, ⓦwww.bunkamura.co.jp; see map, p.122. In the Bunkamura Centre, up the slope from central Shibuya, this large concert hall hosts a wide range of classical music performances throughout the year and has good acoustics. Shibuya Station.

Suntory Hall

Ark Hills, 1-13-1 Akasaka, Minato-ku ☎03/3505-1001, ⓦwww.suntory.co.jp /suntoryhall; see map, p.76. Reputed to have the best acoustics in the city, this elegant concert hall has one of the world's largest pipe organs, sometimes used for free lunchtime recitals; check the website for details of this and other events. Roppongi-itchōme Station.

Tokyo Bunka Kaikan

5-45 Ueno, Taitō-ku ☎03/3828-2111, ⓦwww .t-bunka.jp; see map, p.90. The largest classical music hall in the city has a busy and varied schedule of performances.

Classical music buffs should enquire about joining their music library, which holds over 100,000 recordings, books and scores. Ueno Station.

Tokyo International Forum

3-5-1 Marunouchi, Chiyoda-ku ☎03/5221-9000, ⓦwww.t-i-forum.or.jp; see map, p.60. The Forum's four multi-purpose halls (including one of the world's largest auditoria, with over five thousand seats) host an eclectic mix of performing arts, from opera to Kabuki. Yūrakuchō Station.

Tokyo Opera City
東京オペラシティ

3-20-2 Nishi-Shinjuku, Shinjuku-ku ☎03/5353-9999, ⓦwww.operacity.jp; see map, pp.106–107. This stunningly designed concert hall, with a giant pipe organ, seats over 1600 and has excellent acoustics – though despite its name it hosts only music concerts, not full-blown opera. There's a more intimate recital hall too. Hatsudai Station.

Gay and lesbian Tokyo

ompared to other big Japanese cities such as Ōsaka, Tokyo's gay and lesbian scene is relatively open and friendly. Even so, don't expect anywhere near the same level of openness as in London, San Francisco or Sydney; gay life in Tokyo is a low-key affair and it's very rare to find same-sex couples parading their love on the streets. Shinjuku Nichōme may be one of the most densely packed areas of gay and lesbian venues in Japan (it's reckoned that there are at least two hundred bars alone here), but during the day you'd hardly know there was anything transgressive about it all.

Dates for your diary include the Tokyo Gay and Lesbian Parade (Ⓦparade.tokyo-pride.org/6th), which has been known to attract three thousand marchers and many more spectators, but has yet to establish itself as an annual event (in 2003 and 2004 there was no parade; when it does take place it's usually held in August); and the hugely popular Nichōme Matsuri (penultimate weekend in August), with drag shows and dancing in the street. The annual Tokyo International Lesbian and Gay Video and Film Festival (Ⓦwww.tokyo-lgff.org), based in Aoyama's Spiral Hall and usually held in late July, is also a permanent fixture of Tokyo's gay calendar, showing films from around the world with English subtitles.

Homosexuality in Japan

Before the Meiji Restoration and the associated influx of Western ideas and morality, there was an honourable tradition of male homosexuality in Japan. Some ancient Buddhist sects believed that love among men was preferable to love between the sexes and many an emperor, not to mention countless samurai, took male lovers.

While Japan today has no laws against homosexual activity, marriage is an almost essential step on the career ladder at many corporations, and such expectations keep many Japanese gays in the closet, often leading double lives. This said, in recent times homosexuality has come to be seen as more acceptable. In Ōsaka, assembly-woman Otsuji Kanako came out as a lesbian in 2005, while two years earlier the Kamikawa Aya was the first transsexual candidate to openly run for public office.

Among young working women, whose tastes drive a million marketing campaigns, comic books and movies with homosexual characters have been a huge success. There are gay and transvestite TV celebrities, and even bars in Tokyo staffed by butch women dressed up as men, who fawn over their female customers the way bona fide hostesses do over salarymen – only in a more macho fashion.

The quarterly magazine *Tokyo Journal* has some details of gay venues in its Cityscope listings. If you can read Japanese, search out the *Otoko Machi Map*, an annual guide to gay bars and venues, available from the bookshops in Nichōme. Other good online sources of information in English include Fridae (Ⓦwww.fridae .com); GayNet Japan (Ⓦwww.gnj.or.jp); Utopia (Ⓦwww.utopia-asia.com/tipsjapn .htm); and Out Japan (Ⓦwww.outjapan.com), a great resource for lesbians, with details of the dyke retreat weekend trips out of Tokyo. OCCUR (Japan Association for the Lesbian and Gay Movement; ☎03/3383-5556, Ⓦwww.occur.or.jp) is a grassroots gay activist organization that you might also want to touch base with.

Bars and clubs

The vast majority of gay and lesbian bars and clubs are located in Shinjuku Nichōme (see map pp.106–107 for locations, unless otherwise stated in the reviews), and are generally open daily from the late afternoon to the early hours of the morning. We've noted in the reviews where a venue is exclusively gay or lesbian; otherwise, the following bars and clubs accept all-comers.

Other clubs around the city, including *Ageha* and *Warehouse* (see the "Clubs" chapter for details), host monthly gay and lesbian dance events; ones to watch out for include gay hard-house night Red (Ⓦwww.joinac.com/red) and The Ring (both typically held at *Warehouse*), and the women-only club nights Goldfinger (Ⓦwww .goldfingerparty.com), Diamond Cutter (Ⓦdiamondcutter.jp) and Agitation+G (Ⓦwww.ag-party.com). *Metropolis* magazine (see p.30) and CIA Japan (Ⓦwww .ciajapan.com) are both good sources of information about specific dance events.

Advocates
アドボカト

7th Tenka Building, 2-18-1 Shinjuku, Shinjuku-ku ☎03/3358-3988. The place to see and be seen around Nichōme, with the area's most casual vibe – although the bar itself is barely big enough for ten people, which is why scores of patrons hang out on the street corner outside. Not to be confused with *Advocates Bar*, in a basement around the corner, where there's often a hefty cover charge for the drag show, and where they sometimes hold women-only nights. Shinjuku-sanchōme Station.

Arty Farty
アーティファーティ

2F Dai 33 Kyutei Building, 2-11-7 Shinjuku, Shinjuku-ku ☎03/5362-9720, Ⓦwww.arty-farty .net. As the night draws on, this artfully designed bar with a small dance floor becomes packed with an up-for-fun crowd. The music is generally handbag house and disco. They also have a newer annexe around the corner at 2-14-11 Shinjuku. Shinjuku-sanchōme Station.

Chestnut & Squirrel
3F Dai-ishi Bldg, 3-7-5 Shibuya, Shibuya-ku ☎090/9834-4842, Ⓦ2d-k.oops.jp/cs/cs.html; **see map, p.122.** Friendly, reasonably

spacious and a really good occasion to catch up with what's going on in the lesbian scene, with a mixed crowd of Japanese and *gaijin*. Cunningly, the name translates into Japanese as *kuri-to-risu* (clitoris, geddit?). Note that the bar's sign says *Minx* (which is the Thursday night event); there's also the lesbian bar *Liam* here Tues, Fri & Sun, when there's a ¥1000 cover charge including one drink. Shibuya Station. Wed 7pm–midnight.

Dragon Men
ドラゴン

2-11-4 Shinjuku, Shinjuku-ku ☎03/3341-0606. A long-running dance bar where patrons whoop it up to dance anthems played through a dodgy PA. Admission ¥1000 men, ¥2000 women, including one drink. Shinjuku-sanchōme Station.

Fuji Bar
富士バー

2-12-16 Shinjuku, Shinjuku-ku ☎03/3354-2707. This cosy karaoke bar (¥100 per song) in the basement of a building around the corner from *GB* has a wide selection of English songs, and attracts a mixed crowd. Shinjuku-sanchōme Station.

GB
B1F Business Hotel T Building, 2-12-3 Shinjuku, Shinjuku-ku ☎03/3352-8972. Only for the

boys, this smoky basement bar is a long-standing pick-up joint for Japanese and foreigners. The initials stand for *Ginger Bar*, after Hollywood icon Ginger Rogers. Women are only allowed in at Halloween. Shinjuku-sanchōme Station.

Kinsmen
キンズメン

2F 2-18-5 Shinjuku, Shinjuku-ku ☎03/3354-4949. Long-running and unpretentious bar – you're as likely to be carousing with a mixed group of office workers here as with a drag queen. Check out their famous *ikebana* flower displays. Shinjuku-sanchōme Station.

Kinswomyn
キンズウイメン

3F Dai-ichi Tenka Building, 2-15-10 Shinjuku, Shinjku-ku ☎03/3354-8720. Tokyo's top women-only bar, which has a more relaxed ambience (and lower prices) than many of Nichōme's other lesbian haunts. Drinks are ¥700 and there's no cover charge. Shinjuku-sanchōme Station.

New Sazae
ニューさざえ

2F Ishikawa Building, 2-18-5 Shinjuku, Shinjuku-ku ☎03/3354-1745. The antithesis of cool, this grungy, graffitied bar is nonetheless welcoming to everyone, from bright-eyed *gaijin* to hard-bitten Japanese drag queens. Shinjuku-sanchōme Station.

🏃 Townhouse Tokyo
タウンハウス東京

6F Koruteire Ginza Bldg, 1-11-5 Shimbashi, Minato-ku ☎03/3289-8558, ⓦwww13.ocn.ne.jp/~t_h_tky; see map, p.60. Spacious men-only gay bar, welcoming to *gaijin*, that's a breath of fresh air compared to many of the dingy dives of Nichōme. Saturday nights are only for the bold: that's when they have one-piece-of-clothing-only parties. On other nights be prepared for a spot of karaoke, the sweetener being that all drinks are ¥500. Shimbashi Station. Mon–Fri 6pm–2pm, Sat 4pm–midnight.

Theatre and cinema

hough language can be a problem when it comes to exploring Tokyo's **theatre**, colourful extravaganzas like **Takarazuka** or the more traditional **Kabuki** are captivating, and even the notoriously difficult **Nō** and **Butō** are worth trying once. Tokyo can also be a surprisingly good place for **English-language drama** – major international theatre groups often pass through on foreign tours, although tickets tend to be expensive and hard to come by. **Information** about current and upcoming performances is available in the English-language press and from the Tokyo TIC (see p.47). Look out, too, for the handy *Tokyo Theatre Guide*, a free monthly brochure covering the main venues, with detailed maps. As for film, there are plenty of multi-screen **cinemas** showing the latest Hollywood blockbusters – usually with Japanese subtitles – while a decent number of smaller cinemas show independent and art-house releases. See p.241 for details of **ticket agencies**.

Traditional theatre

Kabuki is by far the most accessible of Japan's traditional performing arts, and its dramatic plots, full of larger-than-life heroes, are easy to follow even without understanding a word of the dialogue. Performances last three or four hours, but single-act tickets are available at the Kabuki-za (see below).

Puppet theatre, **bunraku**, predates Kabuki but shares many of the same story-lines. Don't expect the same lightning drama as in Kabuki – the puppets need three people to manipulate them – but the artistry of the puppeteers is astounding.

Even most Japanese find **Nō**, the country's oldest form of theatre, unfathomable. Its highly stylized, painfully slow movements and archaic language don't make for a rip-roaring theatrical experience, though some find the rarefied style incredibly powerful. **Kyōgen**, short satirical plays with an earthy humour and simple plots, liven up the intervals. If you want to try Nō or Kyōgen, it's worth asking at the TIC about free performances by amateur groups.

At establishments such as the Kabuki-za and the National Theatre, it's long been possible to listen to recorded commentaries in English to gain a better understanding of what's happening on stage. Subtitles displayed on a screen beside the performers are also sometimes used. Since November 2006, the National Nō Theatre has gone one step further by installing LCD displays in the back of each seat to display subtitles in both English and Japanese (many locals, particularly the younger generation, cannot understand the archaic language of a Nō play). Apart from the lines being spoken, information on the background of the story and the characters is also provided.

△ A performance at the Kabuki-za

⑳

THEATRE AND CINEMA | Traditional theatre

Cerulean Tower Nō Theatre
セルリアンタワー能楽堂
26-1 Sakuragaoka-chō, Shibuya-ku ☎ **03/3477-6412,** ⓦ **www.ceruleantower.com; see map, p.122.** Tokyo's newest Nō theatre, in the basement of this luxury hotel, provides the elegant setting for both professional and amateur Nō and *kyōgen* performances. Shibuya Station.

Kabuki-za
4-12-15 Ginza, Chūō-ku ☎ **03/5565-6000,** ⓦ **www.shochiku.co.jp/play/kabukiza/theater; see map, p.60.** Tokyo's main Kabuki theatre stages two programmes a day on 25 days each month (usually the first three weeks), generally at 11am and 4.30pm. Prices start at around ¥2500 for the full programme, or you can buy one-act tickets (usually under

¥2000) on the day, from a separate box office to the left of the main entrance. Details, including a brief English synopsis, are available at the theatre, but it's worth investing in the excellent English-language programme (¥500). You can also rent an audio-guide (¥650 for the full programme or ¥400 for one act, plus ¥1000 deposit), but then you miss all the sound effects. A pair of binoculars is also useful if you're in the cheapest seats, which are way up at the back. Higashi-Ginza Station.

Kanze Nō-gakudō
観世能楽堂

1-16-4 Shōtō, Shibuya-ku ☎ **03/3469-5241.** The home theatre of Kanze, the best-known of Tokyo's several Nō troupes, and one of the city's most traditional Nō theatres. Shibuya Station.

National Nō Theatre
国立能楽堂

4-18-1 Sendagaya, Shibuya-ku ☎ **03/3230-3000,** ⓦ**www.ntj.jac.go.jp; see map, p.114.** The National Nō Theatre hosts performances several times a month, with tickets starting at around ¥2500. Printed English explanations

of the plot will help you make some sense of what's going on. Sendagaya Station; the theatre is a 5min walk southwest.

National Theatre
国立劇場

4-1 Hayabusachō, Chiyoda-ku ☎ **03/3230-3000,** ⓦ**www.ntj.jac.go.jp; see map, p.52.** In its two auditoria, Tokyo's National Theatre puts on a varied programme of traditional theatre and music, including Kabuki, *bunraku*, court music and dance. English-language earphones (¥650, plus ¥1000 deposit) and programmes are available. Tickets start at around ¥1500 for Kabuki and ¥4500 for *bunraku*. Hanzōmon Station.

Shimbashi Theatre
新橋演舞場

6-18-2 Ginza, Chūō-ku ☎ **03/3541-2600,** ⓦ **www.shochiku.co.jp/play/enbujyo; see map, p.60.** This large theatre on the eastern edge of Ginza stages a range of traditional dance, music and theatre, including the "Super-Kabuki" (Kabuki with all the bells and whistles of modern musical theatre) extravaganzas of veteran impressario Ichikawa Ennosuke. Higashi-Ginza Station.

Contemporary and international theatre, dance and comedy

Apart from Japanese transfers of hit Broadway shows by the likes of Andrew Lloyd Webber, the most entertaining popular theatrical experience you can have in Tokyo is **Takarazuka** (see box, p.208), the all-singing, all-dancing, all-female revue which appears occasionally at the Takarazuka Theatre. On a far more serious level, keep an eye out for performances of **Butō** (or Butoh). This highly expressive dance form, inspired by visiting American performers in the early 1950s, is minimalist, introspective, and often violent or sexually explicit. It's not to everyone's taste, but shouldn't be missed if you're interested in modern performance art.

Both Takarazuka and Butō have entered the mainstream, but there's plenty happening on the fringes. Tiny Alice and Theatre Cocoon are prime places to catch Japanese-language **avant-garde theatre**, while in February and March the **Tokyo International Festival of Performing Arts** (ⓦ www.tif.anj.or.jp) showcases the best on the current scene. In addition to the places listed below, *Super Deluxe* in Nishi-Azabu (see p.197) is an important venue for innovative performance art, while Yokohama's Akarenga Theatre puts on an interesting programme of theatre and dance (see p.296).

Tokyo is also on the tour circuit of many **international theatre companies**, who often appear at the Tokyo Globe or Shinjuku's New National Theatre, though seats sell out months in advance for the bigger names. Easier to come by are tickets for the amateur dramatic group **Tokyo International Players** (ⓦ www .tokyoplayers.org), which has been going for over a century, feeding off the ever-changing cast of foreign acting talent that passes through the city. Their website lists their productions, mounted four or five times a year, which are usually staged

Takarazuka

There's a long tradition of men performing female roles in Japanese theatre, acting out a male fantasy of how women are supposed to behave. It's not so strange, then, that actresses playing idealized men have struck such a chord with contemporary female audiences. Along with the glitter, this has been the successful formula of the 500-strong all-female **Takarazuka Review Company**, founded in 1914 in the town of the same name, 20km northwest of Ōsaka.

The company's founder, Kobayashi Ichizō, was mightily impressed by performances of Western operas he'd seen in Tokyo. He sensed that Japanese audiences were ripe for lively Western musical dramas, but he wanted to preserve something of Japan's traditional theatre, too. So, as well as performing dance reviews and musicals, Takarazuka act out classical Japanese plays and have developed shows from Western novels, including *Gone with the Wind* and *War and Peace*.

Thousands of young girls apply annually to join the troupe at the age of 16, and devote themselves to a punishing routine of classes that will enable them to embody the "modesty, fairness and grace" (the company's motto) expected of a Takarazuka member. They must also forsake boyfriends, but in return are guaranteed the slavish adoration of an almost exclusively female audience, who go particularly crazy for the male impersonators or *otoko-yaku*.

at the American Club in Kamiyachō (☎03/3224-3670); details can also be found in the English-language press.

For **comedy** in English, the **Tokyo Comedy Store** (⊛www.tokyocomedy.com) hosts shows at *Crocodile live house* (B1F Sekiguchi Building, 6-18-8 Meiji-Jingūmae, Shibuya-ku; ☎03-3499-5205) once a month, while the **Punchline Comedy Club** (⊛www.punchlinecomedy.com) occasionally brings top foreign talent to *Pizza Express* (3F, 4-30-3 Jingūmae, Shibuya-ku; ☎03/5775-3894). Finally, the **Tokyo Cynics** offer pud-style, hit-and-miss stand-ups at various bars around Tokyo – check the Tokyo Comedy Store site and English-language press for details.

Azabu Die Pratze
麻布ディープラッツ
2F 1-26-6 Higashi-Azabu, Minato-ku ☎03/5545-1385, ⊛www.geocities.jp/kagurara2000; see map, p.76. Important venue for experimental theatre in an office block near Tokyo Tower. Akabanebashi Station.

Dentsu Shiki Theatre SEA (Umi)
電通四季劇場 [海]
1F Caretta Building, 1-8-2 Higashi-Shimbashi, Minato-ku ☎0120-489444, ⊛www.shiki.gr.jp; see map, p.60. Part of the Shiodome Sio-Site development, this state-of-the-art theatre hosts long runs of blockbuster Western musicals along the lines of *Mamma Mia!* and *Phantom of the Opera*, all in Japanese. Shiodome Station.

The Globe Tokyo
東京グローブ
3-1-2 Hyakunin-chō, Shinjuku-ku ☎03/3366-4020, ⊛www.tglobe.net; see map, pp.106–107. A variety of works, including Shakespearean plays and Western-style operas, are performed in this modern-day replica of the famous Elizabethan stage in London. Follow the tracks north from the station to find it. Shin-Ōkubo Station.

New National Theatre
新国立劇場
1-20 Honmachi, Shinjuku-ku ☎03/5352-9999, ⊛www.nntt.jac.go.jp; see map, pp.106–107. Just behind Tokyo Opera City, the New National Theatre comprises three stages specially designed for Western performing arts, including opera, ballet, dance and drama. Hatsudai Station.

Plan B
B1F Monark Nakano Building, 4-26-20 Yayoi-chō, Nakano-ku ☎03/3384-2051, ⊛www.i10x .com/planb. Underground space putting on a programme of alternative music, dance, Butō and the like. Nakano-Fujimichō Station.

Setagaya Public Theatre
世田谷パブリックシアター
4-1-1 Tasihido, Setagaya-ku ☎03/5432-1526,

@www.setagaya-pt.jp. One of Tokyo's most watchable contemporary theatre companies, whose productions have includee an adaptation of Haruki Murakami's book, *The Elephant Vanishes* (a co-production with Theatre de Complicité), which has toured internationally to much acclaim. Just west of Shibuya on the Tōkyū Den'en Toshi line; Sangenjaya Station.

Shiki Theatre
四季劇場
1-10-48 Kaigan, Minato-ku ☎0120-489444, @www.shiki.gr.jp. There are three modern theatres here – named Haru (Spring), Aki (Autumn) and Jiyū (Freedom) – hosting big Western musicals and home-grown musicals and plays. Hamamatsuchō or Takeshiba stations.

Takarazuka Theatre
宝塚劇場
1-1-3 Yūrakuchō, Chūō-ku ☎03/5251-2001, @kageki.hankyu.co.jp; see map, p.60. Mostly stages Hollywood musicals, punched out by a huge cast in fabulous costumes to an audience of middle-aged housewives and star-struck teenage girls. The theatre, immediately north of the *Imperial Hotel*, also stages regular Takarazuka performances. Hibiya Station.

Theatre Cocoon
シアターコクーン
2-24-1 Dōgenzaka, Shibuya-ku ☎03/3477-9999, @www.bunkamura.co.jp; see map, p.122. Part of Shibuya's Bunkamura arts centre, this modern theatre hosts some of Tokyo's more accessible fringe productions. Shibuya Station.

Tiny Alice
タイニイアリス
2-13-6 Shinjuku-ku ☎03/3354-7307, @www .tinyalice.net; see map, pp.106–107. Well known for its cutting-edge Japanese and Asian performance art, and for its summer theatre festival. Shinjuku-Sanchōme Station.

Cabaret bars

The two cabaret bars below, both in Roppongi (see map, p.79), host shows with transvestite and drag queen performers, and make for a highly theatrical night out.

Kaguwa
香和
5-4-2 Roppongi, Minato-ku ☎03/5414-8818, @www.kaguwa.com. Big-production cabaret show with a Meiji-era theme. The show alone is at ¥3500, but it's probably better to opt for all-you-can-eat-and-drink deals from ¥6500. Roppongi Station. Tues–Sun 7.30pm & 10pm, plus Fri & Sat at 1.30am.

Kingyo
金魚
3-14-17 Roppongi, Minato-ku ☎03/3478-3000, @www.kingyo.co.jp. This is the original trans-sexual and drag show club, and its logo – a goldfish kissing a penis – gives you a clue as to the kind of surreal night you'll have inside. Expect fabulous costumes, split-level stages and plenty of glitz. Entry including food and drink is ¥6500, but check their website for occasional discount deals. Roppongi Station. Tues–Thurs 6pm– midnight, Fri & Sat 6pm–3am; shows (50min) at 7.30pm & 10pm, plus Fri & Sat 1.30am.

Cinema

Tokyoites are avid movie-goers, lapping up the latest Hollywood blockbusters at the city's ever-growing ranks of multiplexes. They're also devotees of fringe cinema; indeed, there's been something of a revival of independent art house cinemas in recent years.

The biggest of the city's several **film festivals** is the **Tokyo International Film Festival** (@www.tiff-jp.net), held each autumn at Bunkamura (see p.123), Roppongi Hills (see below) and other venues around Tokyo. It's one of the few opportunities to catch Japanese and world cinema with English subtitles, not to mention seeing some films that would never get a general release, although it's increasingly becoming a vehicle for promoting major releases from the US. Also worth catching is the annual **Tokyo Lesbian and Gay Video and Film Festival** (see "Gay and lesbian Tokyo", p.202).

Listings are published on Friday in *The Japan Times* and *Metropolis*, which also has reviews as well as maps locating all the major cinemas. Apart from those listed here, which tend to specialize in independent movies, there are many more cinemas in Ginza, Ikebukuro, Shibuya and Shinjuku, mostly showing the latest Hollywood releases. And don't forget the big-screen experiences at Tokyo's two IMAX theatres, in Shinjuku and Ikebukuro.

The best time to catch a movie is on Cinema Day, generally the first day of the month, when all **tickets** cost ¥1000, as opposed to the regular price of around ¥1800, or ¥2500 for a reserved seat (*shitei-seki*). Women can also get discounted tickets (¥1000) on Ladies Day, usually Wednesday. Otherwise, you can buy slightly reduced tickets in advance from a ticket agency such as CN Playguide and Ticket Pia (see p.241). Note that the last screening of the day is generally around 7 or 8pm, and that if it's a popular new release you'll need to be at the cinema well before the start to get a decent seat, or sometimes any seat at all.

Cinema Qualité
シネマクアリテ
Musashinokan Building, 3-27 Shinjuku, Shinjuku-ku ☎03/3354-5670; **see map, pp.106–107.** Three screens at this complex on the east side of Shinjuku Station, behind the Mitsukoshi department store. Often screens classic revivals as well as independent European hits. Shinjuku Station.

Cinema Rise
シネマライズ
13-17 Udagawa-chō, Shibuya ☎03/3464-0052, ⓦwww.cinemarise.com; **see map, p.122.** Avant-garde cinema with three screens, including Rise X, which specializes in digital film-making. A good place to catch independent movies from Japan and around the world. Shibuya Station.

Ciné Saison Shibuya
シネセゾン渋谷
6F The Prime Building, 2-29-5 Dōgenzaka, Shibuya-ku ☎03/3770-1721; **see map, p.122.** Comfy cinema which showcases a wide range of films, including classic revivals from the 1960s and 1970s. Shibuya Station.

Hibiya Chanter
シャンテ シネ
Hibiya Chanter Building, 1-2-2 Yūrakuchō, Chiyoda-ku ☎03/3591-1511, ⓦwww.chantercine .com; **see map, p.60.** The three large cinemas at this complex screen many of the higher-profile, mainstream American and British releases. Hibiya and Yūrakuchō stations.

Iwanami Hall
岩波ホール
10F, 2-1 Kanda-Jimbōchō, Chiyoda-ku ☎03/3262-5252, ⓦwww.iwanami-hall.com; **see map, p.67.** Long-established venue

showing non-commercial European films from places as diverse as Greece and Poland, as well as quirky Japanese movies. Jimbōchō Station.

Le Cinéma
ル・シネマ
Tōkyū Bunkamura, 2-24-1 Dōgenzaka, Shibuya-ku ☎03/3477-9264, ⓦwww.bunkamura.co.jp; **see map, p.122.** This classy two-screen cinema within the Bunkamura arts complex is the main venue for the Tokyo International Film Festival. Shibuya Station.

National Film Centre
東京国立近代美術館フィルムセンター
3-7-6 Kyōbashi, Chūō-ku ☎03/3272-8600, ⓦwww.momat.go.jp; **see map, p.60.** A treasure trove for film-lovers, with a small gallery on the seventh floor for film-related exhibitions and two small cinemas screening retrospectives from their vast movie archive. Most are Japanese classics, though they occasionally dust off their collection of foreign movies. Kyōbashi Station.

Shin-Bungei-za
新文芸坐
3F Maruhan-Ikebukuro Building, 1-43-5 Higashi-Ikebukuro, Toshima-ku ☎03/3971-9422, ⓦwww .shin-bungeiza.com; **see map, p.99.** Recently renovated repertory theatre among the soaplands and game parlours of Ikebukuro. The ¥2000 annual membership includes one ticket, a monthly newsletter and regular discounts on admission. All-night screenings on Saturdays. Ikebukuro Station.

Toho Cinemas Roppongi Hills
TOHOシネマズ六本木ヒルズ
Roppongi Hills, Roppongi, Minato-ku ☎03/5775-6090, ⓦwww.tohotheater.jp; **see**

map, p.79. Ultra-modern multiplex cinema with bookable seats (no more rushing to grab the best spot), late-night screenings and popular Japanese movies with English subtitles. Tickets (¥3000) include a drink. Roppongi Station.

Tokyo in the movies

Dazzlingly colourful and other-worldly Tokyo has proved an irresistible location for film-makers down the ages, as well as an inspiration for dystopian anime (Japanese animation movies). Here are a few cinematic offerings that together will give you an insight into different aspects of the city.

Babel (Alejandro González Iñárritu; 2006) The talented Mexican director's world-spanning vision captures the very essence of contemporary Tokyo. There's a particularly beautiful sequence filmed in Shibuya at the *Womb* club. Kikuchi Rinko as the mute Chieko and her father, played by Yakusho Kōji, are outstanding.

Godzilla, King of the Monsters (Honda Ishirō; 1954). Your everyday tale of a giant mutant lizard, born after a US hydrogen bomb test in the Bikini Atoll, who ends up running amok in Tokyo. It went on to spawn a long line of sequels (including a big-bucks Hollywood remake in 1998), the latest being *Godzilla: Final Wars* (2004).

Lost in Translation (Sofia Coppola; 2003). Few films have so accurately captured contemporary Tokyo as this stylish comedy drama, with Bill Murray and Scarlett Johansson teetering on the brink of romance in and out of Shinjuku's *Park Hyatt Hotel*.

Shall We Dance (Suo Masayuki; 1996). Yakusho Kōji, one of Japan's most popular actors, pops up again as the quietly frustrated salaryman who breaks out of the mould when he takes up ballroom dancing.

Tampopo (Itami Jūzō; 1985). Tampopo, the proprietress of a noodle bar, is taught how to prepare perfect ramen in this comedy about Japan's gourmet boom. From the old woman squishing fruit in a supermarket to the gangster and his moll passing a raw egg sexily between their mouths, this is packed with memorable scenes guaranteed to get the tummy rumbling.

Tokyo Godfathers (Kon Satoshi; 2003). Maverick auteur Kon is one of the most exciting of the current crop of anime film-makers. This loose remake of John Ford's classic western *Three Godfathers* takes a sympathetic look at the dark side of the city as it follows three homeless friends, including a transvestite, who discover and adopt an abandoned baby.

Tōkyō Monogatari (*Tokyo Story*; Ozu Yasujirō; 1954). An elderly couple travel to Tokyo from their seaside home in western Japan to visit their children and grandchildren. The only person who has any time for them is Noriko, the widow of their son Shōji, who was killed in the war. On their return, the mother falls ill and dies. That's about it for the plot, but Ozu's simple approach to the themes of loneliness and the breakdown of tradition, and the sincerity of the acting, make this a genuine classic.

Until the End of the World (Wim Wenders; 1993). Rambling Millennium angst road movie with an interesting premise, though it gets bogged down during its Australian outback section. The Japan scenes, contrasting frantic Tokyo and the soothing countryside, are among the best. Among the stars is the great Ryū Chishū, who played the father in *Tokyo Story*.

Walk Don't Run (Charles Walters; 1966) Cary Grant's sayonara to screen acting sees the dapper gent playing cupid to Samantha Egger and Jim Hutton during the Tokyo Olympics. George Takei (Mr Sulu in *Star Trek*) makes an appearance as a Tokyo policeman.

You Only Live Twice (Lewis Gilbert; 1967). Sean Connery's fifth outing as 007 has Bondo-san grappling with arch-enemy Blofeld and sundry Oriental villains in Tokyo and the Japanese countryside. Cool gadgets include a mini-helicopter in a suitcase (with rocket launchers, of course).

Uplink

アップリンク

37-18 Udagawachō, Shibuya-ku ☎03/6825-5502; ⓦ www.uplink.co.jp; see map, p.122.
World cinema is a staple at this arts centre, combining a couple of cinemas with a gallery, live music, bar and various workshops. Shibuya Station.

Waseda Shochiku

早稲田松竹

1-5-16 Takadanobaba, Shinjuku-ku ☎03/3200-8968. Popular with students from the nearby university, this cinema is cheaper (¥1300) and less fancy than others in town, but still shows a decent selection of mainstream and non-commercial releases. Takadanobaba Station.

Yebisu Garden Cinema

恵比寿ガーデンシネマ

Yebisu Garden Place, 4-20 Ebisu, Shibuya-ku ☎03/5420-6161; see map, pp.128–129. There are two screens at this modern cinema, with numbered seating, in the Yebisu brewery development, showing an interesting range of non-mainstream US and British releases. Ebisu Station.

Sports and martial arts

The Japanese take their sport very seriously, and it's not uncommon for parts of Tokyo to come to a complete standstill during crucial moments of a major **baseball** game as fans gather around television screens in homes, offices, shops, bars – even on the street. Baseball is the city's premier sporting obsession, but hot on its heels is **soccer**, boosted by Japan's co-hosting of the 2002 World Cup. The success of that huge sporting event has encouraged Tokyo to prepare for a bid for the 2016 Olympics (Ⓦ www.2016tokyo.jp).

Although its popularity – not to mention credibility – is slipping (see box, p.215), **sumo wrestling** also has a high profile, with big tournaments (*basho*) televised nationwide and wrestlers enjoying celebrity status. **Martial arts** such as aikido, judo and karate, all associated with Japan, are far less widely practised, though Tokyo, with its numerous *dōjō* (practice halls), is the best place in the country to watch or learn about these ancient fighting ways. Many *dōjō* allow visitors in to watch practice sessions.

Check the local media, such as *The Japan Times* and *Metropolis*, for details of events. For tickets, approach one of the major **ticket agencies** (see p.241). Major games and events tend to sell out fast, but you can always go directly to the venue on the day and see if you can get a ticket from the box office or a tout outside; expect to pay well over the odds if it's a key game.

Baseball

If you're in Tokyo during the baseball season (April–Oct), it's great fun to pitch up to a professional match; even if you're not a fan, the audience enthusiasm can be infectious. Tickets, available from the stadia or at advance ticket booths, start at around ¥1500 and go on sale on the Friday two weeks prior to a game.

It's rare to find anyone who doesn't support one of Tokyo's two main **baseball** (*yakyū*) teams, the Yomiuri Giants (Ⓦ www.giants.jp) and the Yakult Swallows (Ⓦ www.yakult-swallows.co.jp). Neighbouring Yokohama, for its part, has the Yokohama Baystars (Ⓦ www.baystars.co.jp). As well as the two professional leagues (Central and Pacific), there's the equally popular All-Japan High School Baseball Championship, and you might be able to catch one of the local play-offs before the main tournament held each summer in Ōsaka; check with the tourist office for details.

△ The Yakult Swallows in action at the Jingū Baseball Stadium

Jingū Baseball Stadium
神宮技場
**13 Kasumigaoka, Shinjuku-ku ☎03/3404-8999;
see map, p.114.** One of the stadia grouped in Meiji-jingū's Outer Gardens, this is home ground of the Yakult Swallows and the hosts the college baseball Tokyo Big Six league (Ⓦwww.big6.gr.jp). Gaienmae Station.

Tokyo Dome
東京ドーム
**1-3 Koraku, Bunkyō-ku ☎03/5800-9999,
Ⓦwww.tokyo-dome.co.jp/e/dome; see map,
p.67.** This huge covered arena, affectionately nicknamed the "Big Egg", is home to the Yomiuri Giants, and is a great place to take in a night game (naitā). Suidōbashi Station.

Soccer

The **J-League** (Ⓦwww.j-league.or.jp), Japan's first professional football league, was launched amid a multi-billion-yen promotional drive in 1993, and has firmly captured the public's imagination – not to mention wallet, with its glitzy range of associated merchandise. Following on from the success of the 2002 World Cup, hosted jointly by Japan and Korea, the game is now a huge crowd-puller; games are held between March and October, with a break in August.

Sixteen clubs play in the J1 league, twelve in the J2, and all participate in the JL Yamazaki Nabisco Cup. The local teams are FC Tokyo (Ⓦwww.fctokyo.co.jp), in the J1 league, and Tokyo Verdy 1969 (Ⓦwww.verdy.co.jp). Plenty also support the Urawa Reds in Saitama (Ⓦwww.urawa-reds.co.jp), Kawasaki Frontale (Ⓦwww.frontale.co.jp) as well as the two Yokohama-based teams Yokohama F Marinos (Ⓦwww.f-marinos.com) and Yokohama Ventforet (Ⓦwww.ventforet.co.jp).

At an amateur level, there's the Tokyo Metropolis League (Ⓦwww.footyjapan.com/tml) which sponsors organizes camps for kids, offers soccer-coaching instruction for adults and so forth. Check the website for games or if you're interested in taking part.

Ajinomoto Stadium
味の素スタジアム
**376-3 Nishimachi, Chōfu ☎ 0424/40-0555,
Ⓦ www.ajinomotostadium.com.** Head west on
the Keiō line to reach this stadium, home to
FC Tokyo and Tokyo Verdy. Tobitakyu
Station.

National Stadium
国立競技場
**10 Kasumigaoka-chō, Shinjuku-ku ☎ 03/3403-
1151; see map, p.114.** Big Japanese and
international games are held at this huge

oval stadium built for the 1964 Olympics
and seating 75,000 people. Tickets from
¥2000. Sendagaya Station.

Saitama Stadium
埼玉スタジアム
**2002 500 Nakanoda, Saitama ☎ 048/812-2002,
Ⓦ www.stadium2002.com.** The home of the
Urawa Reds, this is Japan's largest soccer-
only stadium, seating 64,000, and was the
venue for the 2002 World Cup semi-final.
Urawa Misono Station.

Sumo

Japan's national sport, **sumo**, developed out of the divination rites performed at
Shinto shrines, and its religious roots are still apparent in the various rituals which
form an integral part of a *basho*. A bout involves two huge wrestlers, each weighing
170 kilos on average and wearing nothing but a hefty loincloth, facing off in a small
ring of hard-packed clay. The loser is the first to step outside the rope or touch the
ground with any part of the body except the feet. The contest is often over in
seconds, but the pageantry and ritual make for a wonderfully absorbing spectacle.

Sumo players are ranked according to the number of wins they have had, the top
ranking wrestler being called the **yokozuna**. In a neat reversal of Japan's appropri-
ation of baseball and export of professional players to the US league, several of
sumo's most revered stars of recent years were born abroad, including Konishiki
(aka the "dump truck") and Akebono, who both hail from Hawaii, and Musashi-
maru from American Samoa. All three have retired, leaving the field open for a
new generation of *gaijin* fighters such the Bulgarian Kotooshu (born Kaloyan
Stafanov) and the current *yokozuna*, Mongolian-born Asashoryu (formerly
Dolgorsuren Dagvadorj).

Sumo scandals

These are turbulent times for sumo. Attendance at *basho* is down and even TV
viewing figures are dipping, as younger Japanese tune into faster-paced sports such
as soccer. Furthermore, claims of match-fixing are tainting the sport. At Tokyo's New
Year *basho* in January 2007 the *yokozuna* Asahoryu cruised to his twentieth tournament victory in a row, but a couple of months later, he was tumbling in the initial
rounds of the Ōsaka *basho*. Many suspected the *yokozuna* was suffering stress after
being accused by a tabloid sports paper of paying opponents to throw matches in
his favour. Some also feel that the scrutiny of Asahoryu has a lot to do with his being
Mongolian-born and the fact that he has shown less than full reverence for sumo's
strict code of conduct in the past.

Lower-ranked wrestlers are poorly paid, and it's not beyond belief that some would
be tempted to take money to throw a bout. And the rumours surrounding Asahoryu
were far from the first whisperings of match-fixing to reach the press, the most
notorious being in the mid-1990s, when an ex-wrestler claimed that the practice,
along with drug-taking, was rife in the sport. Shortly after the wrestler died in mysterious circumstances. Each time a potential scandal rears its head, the Japan Sumo
Association have conducted its own investigations and so far has always concluded
that the allegations are unfounded.

The **National Sumo Stadium** (Kokugikan; 国技館; 1-3-28 Yokoami, Kōtō-ku; ℡03/3622-1100) in Ryōgoku (see p.72) is the venue for Tokyo's three *basho* during the middle fortnights of January, May and September. Tickets go on sale a month before each tournament; they're available from ticket agencies (see p.241), or you can line up early – before 8am – outside the stadium box office for unreserved tickets which are sold on the day (¥2100). Note that tickets are particularly hard to come by on the first and last days. For further information, consult the Nihon Sumō Kyōkai website Ⓦ www.sumo.or.jp.

At other times it's possible to watch practice sessions (*keiko*) at the stables (*heya*) where the wrestlers live and train. These take place in the early morning (usually from 5 or 6am to 10.30am) except during and immediately after a *basho* or when the wrestlers are out of town. A few stables accept visitors without an appointment, but it's safest to double-check first with the Tokyo TIC to make sure they're actually training that day. Visitors are expected to watch in silence, and women must wear trousers. Recommended stables to try, shown on the Ryōgoku map on p.72, are: Dewanoumi-beya (出羽海部屋; 2-3-15 Ryōgoku, Sumida-ku; ℡03/3632-4920, Ⓦ www.dewanoumi.com), Kasugano-beya (春日野部屋; 1-7-11 Ryōgoku, Sumida-ku; ℡03/3631-1871) and Tokitsukaze-beya (時津風部屋; 3-15-4 Ryōgoku, Sumida-ku; ℡03/5600-2561).

Aikido

Half sport, half religion, **aikido** (which translates as "the way of harmonious spirit") blends elements of judo, karate and kendo into a form of self-defence without body contact. It's one of the newer martial arts, having only been created in Japan earlier last century and, as a rule, is performed without weapons. For a painfully enlightening and humorous take on the rigours of aikido training, read Robert Twigger's *Angry White Pyjamas* (see p.309). You can learn more about the sport by heading to the International Aikido Federation (全日本合気道連盟; 17-18 Wakamatsuchō, Shinjuku-ku; ℡03/3203-9236, Ⓦ www.aikikai.or.jp; Wakamatsu-Kawada Station).

Judo

Probably the martial art most closely associated with Japan, **judo** is a self-defence technique that developed out of the Edo-era style of fighting called *jujutsu*. Judo activities in Japan are controlled by the All-Japan Judo Federation (℡03/3818-4199, Ⓦ www.judo.or.jp).

Kōdōkan
講道館
1-16-30 Kasuga, Bunkyō-ku; ℡03/3818-4172, Ⓦ **www.kodokan.org; see map, p.67.** This *dōjō* has a spectators' gallery open to visitors free of charge, with classes held most evenings (Mon–Fri 5–8pm, Sat 5–7.30pm). There's also a hostel here where you can stay if you have an introduction from an authorized judo body or an approved

Japanese sponsor. Kasuga or Kōrakuen stations.

Nippon Budōkan
日本武道館
2-3 Kitanomaru-kōen, Chiyoda-ku ℡03/3216-5143, Ⓦ **www.nipponbudokan.or.jp; see map, p.52.** Around fifty free martial-arts exhibition matches are held at this large octagonal arena, an important centre for all martial arts, as well as judo. Kudanshita Station.

Keeping fit in Tokyo

The city offers plenty of ways to keep fit, from gyms to running clubs and yoga classes. Despite pretty dire air quality and a lack of open space, **running** as a form of exercise is popular, with many people jogging around the Imperial Palace or Yoyogi-kōen, and you can join running clubs such as Namban Rengo (Ⓦnamban.org) or the several Hash House Harrier groups (Ⓦtokyohash.org). If you want something to aim for, consider signing up for the Tokyo Marathon (Ⓦwww.tokyo42195.org), held in February and covering a course from Shinjuku to Odaiba.

Gyms are liberally sprinked around the city. The Tokyo Metropolitan Gymnasium (1-17-1 Sendagaya, Shibuya-ku; Ⓦwww.tef.or.jp/tmg) includes a 25-metre and 50-metre pool as well as a gym. Private chains include Tipness (Ⓦwww.tipness.co.jp), with branches in Shinjuku and Roppongi, among many others, and Gold's Gym (Ⓦwww.goldsgym.jp) with two branches in Harajuku; if you're a member overseas you can use their facilities here.

At some gyms you can take **yoga** classes, also available through Yogajaya in Daikan'yama (1-25-11 Ebisu-nishi, Shibuya-ku; ☏03-5784-3622, Ⓦwww.yogajaya.com). For general information on all forms of sport, check out the webzine *Fitness Japan* (Ⓦwww.fitnessjp.com).

Karate

Karate has its roots in China and was only introduced into Japan in 1922. Since then the sport has developed into many different styles, with several major governing bodies and federations based in Tokyo.

Japan Karate Association
日本空手協会
2-23-15 Koraku, Bunkyō-ku ☏**03/5800-3091,** Ⓦ**www.jka.or.jp; see map, p.67.** Home of the world's largest karate association teaching the Shokotan tradition. You can apply to train here, but it's best to call or email first. Iidabashi or Kōrakuen stations.

Japan Karatedō Federation
全日本空手道連盟
6F, 2 Nippon Zaidan Building, 1-11-2 Toranomon, Minato-ku ☏**03/3503-6640,** Ⓦ**www.karatedo.co.jp.** This umbrella organization can advise on the main styles of karate and the best places to see practice sessions or take lessons. Toranomon Station.

Kendo

Kendo ("the way of the sword") is Japanese fencing using a long bamboo weapon (the *shinai*) or the metal *katana* blade. This is the oldest fighting skill in Japan, dating from the Muromachi period (1392–1573). It was developed as a sport in the Edo period and is now watched over by the All-Japan Kendo Federation (全日本剣道連盟; ☏03/3211-5804, Ⓦwww.kendo.or.jp) at the Nippon Budōkan (see opposite). The Budōkan is also the venue for the All-Japan Championships each autumn, and the children's kendo competition in the summer.

Shopping

C ruising the boutiques and fashion malls while toting a couple of designer-label carrier bags is such a part of Tokyo life that it's hard not to get caught up in the general enthusiasm. There are shops to suit every taste and budget, from funky fashion boutiques and swanky department stores to some great crafts shops and wonderfully quirky souvenir and novelty stores. Antique and bargain hunters shouldn't miss out on a visit to one of the city's flea markets, which if nothing else can turn up some unusual curios. As the capital of world cool, the city is also a prime hunting ground for the latest electronic gadgets, as well as fashions that are so next year – if not next decade – elsewhere.

In general, store **opening hours** are from 10 or 11am to 7 or 8pm. Most shops close one day a week, not always on Sunday, and smaller places often shut on public holidays. Though it's always worth asking, few shops take **credit cards** and fewer still accept cards issued abroad, so make sure you have plenty of cash.

Where to shop

Ginza remains the preserve of the city's conservative elegance, and is still regarded as Tokyo's traditional shopping centre. **Shinjuku** has long put up a strong challenge, with an abundance of department stores and malls offering everything under one roof. Young and funky, **Shibuya** and **Harajuku** are probably the most enjoyable places to shop: even if you don't want to buy, the passing fashion parade doesn't get much better. The haute couture boutiques along **Omotesandō** and in nearby **Aoyama** provide a more rarefied shopping experience, while, of the northern districts, **Asakusa** figures highly for its plethora of small, traditional crafts shops, particularly on and around Nakamise-dōri. **Akihabara** has long been

---

Duty-free shopping

Foreign visitors can buy **duty-free** items (that is, without consumption tax), but only in certain tourist shops and the larger department stores. Perishable goods, such as food, drinks, tobacco, cosmetics and film, are exempt from the scheme, and most stores only offer duty-free if your total spend in that shop on a single day exceeds ¥10,000. The shop will either give you a duty-free price immediately or, in department stores especially, you pay the full price first and then apply for a refund at their "tax-exemption" counter. The shop will attach a copy of the customs document (*warriin*) to your passport, to be removed by customs officers when you leave Japan. Note, however, that you can often find the same goods elsewhere at a better price, including tax, so shop around first.

known as "electric town" thanks to its myriad hi-tech emporia, but is also now becoming a mecca for manga and anime. Ueno is famous for the lively **Ameyoko-chō** market, while **Ikebukuro** is home to Japan's two largest department stores and discount outlets. Also worth a look are the shopping malls out at **Odaiba**, such as Decks Tokyo Beach, with its retro 1960s-style arcade, and Venus Fort, a mall devoted to the tastes of young women, as well as the huge new mall Urban Dock LaLaport Toyosu.

Tokyo also has a number of wholesale districts that can be fun to poke around. The most famous are **Tsukiji** fish market, **Kappabashi** ("Kitchenware Town"). North of Asakusabashi Station, **Edo-dōri** and its backstreets specialize in traditional Japanese dolls, while further north along Edo-dōri, the area called **Kuramae** is "Toy Town", where shops sell fireworks, fancy goods and decorations, as well as cheap plastic toys of every description.

For a somewhat more relaxed shopping experience, head out to one of the residential neighbourhoods such as Daikan'yama, Naka-Meguro and Shimo-Kitazawa, all a short train ride from Shibuya. Chic **Daikan'yama** has an appealing village atmosphere and is a good place to check out up-and-coming Japanese designers. The next stop along the Tōkyū-Tōyoko line from Shibuya (and also on the Hibiya metro line) is **Naka-Meguro**, where a host of funky fashion shops line the streets beside the Meguro-gawa. **Shimo-Kitazawa** has a studenty, bohemian air and any number of boutiques, some selling secondhand clothes, where you can scoop big-name labels at bargain prices – and keep an eye open too for fashion and art creations by local students. To get there, take the Keiō-Inokashira line four stops from Shibuya, or the Odakyū line six stops from Shinjuku.

Antique and flea markets

There's at least one **flea market** in Tokyo every weekend, though you'll need to arrive early for any bargains; see below for a round-up of the main venues and ask at the TIC (see p.47) for the current schedule. Alternatively, head for the permanent **antique halls**, also listed below, which gather various dealers under one roof, and where you'll come across fine, hand-painted scrolls, and samurai armour or intricate *netsuke* among a good deal of tat.

For a really wide selection of antiques there are several good fairs. One of the biggest is the **Heiwajima Zenkoku Komingu Kottō Matsuri**, which takes place over three days about five times a year (usually in Feb/March, May, June, Sept and Dec) at the Ryūtsū Centre (6-1-1 Heiwajima, Ōta-ku; ☎03/3980-8228), one stop on the monorail from Hamamatsuchō to Haneda. Also recommended is the Ōedo Antique Fair (see below) and **Yokohama Kottō World** (Pacifico Yokohama, 1-1-1 Minato Mirai, Nishi-ku; ⓦhome.att.ne.jp/sigma/y-world/; entry ¥1000) held in Yokohama for three days, generally in April and November.

Antique Mall Ginza
アンティークモール銀座
1-13-1 Ginza, Chūō-ku ⓦwww.antiques-jp.com; **see map, p.60.** Upmarket collection of classy antiques spread across three floors, including a good selection of kimono though few bargains. Ginza-Itchōme Station. Daily except Wed 11am–7pm.

Antique Market La Villette
ルアンティークマーケット ラビレット
Hanae Mori Building, 3-6-1 Kita-Aoyama,

Minato-ku; see map, p.118. Permanent stalls selling an expensive assortment of Japanese and Western antiques. Each stall has its own speciality – woodblock prints, ceramics, jewellery and so on. Omotesandō Station. Daily 11am–8pm (some shops closed Thurs).

Hanazono-jinja
花園神社
5-17-3 Shinjuku, Shinjuku-ku; see map, pp.106–107. You're more likely to find junk than real

antiques at this market, but its setting in the grounds of a shrine on the east side of Shinjuku is attractive. Shinjuku-sanchōme Station. Sun dawn to dusk.

Nogi-jinja
乃木神社
8-11-27 Akasaka, Minato-ku; see map, p.114.
Around thirty vendors gather at this lively flea market offering the usual assortment of old kimono, bric-a-brac and the like. Nogizaka Station. Second Sun of each month from dawn to dusk.

Ōedo Antique Market
大江戸骨董市
Tokyo International Forum, 3-5-1 Marunouchi, Chiyoda-ku Ⓦwww.antique-market.jp; see map, p.60. One of the largest regular flea markets with some 250 vendors offering real antiques and interesting curios. Don't expect any bargains, though. Yūrakuchō Station. First and third Sunday of the month 9am–4pm, though closed if weather is poor.

Tōgō-jinja
東郷神社
1-5-3 Jingūmae, Shibuya-ku; see map, p.118.
One of Tokyo's best flea markets, with around 150 vendors and a good range of inexpensive items that make great souvenirs. Harajuku Station. First, fourth and fifth (if there is one) Sunday of the month 4am–3pm, but cancelled in wet weather.

Arts, crafts and souvenirs

While most department stores have at least a small **crafts** section, it's a lot more fun rummaging around in Tokyo's specialist shops. The largest concentration is in **Asakusa** (see box, p.87), though a few still survive in the thick of Ginza and Nihombashi.

All the following outlets are good places to hunt for **souvenirs**, from cheap and cheerful paper products, whacky novelties and toys to satin-smooth lacquerware and sumptuous wedding kimono. Keep an eye out, too, for the ubiquitous "¥100 Shops" (everything at ¥100), which can yield amazing gizmos for next to nothing.

Beniya
べにや民芸店
4-20-19 Minami-Aoyama, Minato-ku Ⓣ03/3403-8115, Ⓦbeniya.m78.com; see map, p.118.
Stocks one of Tokyo's best ranges of folk crafts (*mingei*) from around the country. They also stage craft exhibitions – check their website for details. Omotesandō Station. Daily except Thurs 10am–7pm.

Blue & White
2-9-2 Azabu-Jūban, Minato-ku Ⓣ03/3451-0537; see map, p.79. Quirky shop specializing in blue-and-white-coloured products made in Japan, including *yukata*, *furoshiki* (textile wrapping cloths), quilts, pottery and traditional decorations. Azabu-Jūban Station. Mon–Sat 10am–6pm.

Rental box shops

In a city where space comes at a premium, it can be difficult, if not impossible, for aspiring artists and designers to afford the rent to open their own shop. Ever ingenious, local entrepreneurs have come up with a solution: *hako-gashi* or rental-box shops. These gallery-like shops are divided into display cubes of around 30cm square, each with its own rental fee depending on its position, and each serving as a micro-shop for the "tenant" to display their wares – typically accessories, jewellery and artworks. The main shop sells the goods, in exchange for the rent and a commission. You'll generally find *hako-gashi* in areas such as Harajuku, Shibuya and Akihabara; a couple of possibilities to check out incude **Daikan'yama Ark** (B1F 23-6 Sarugaku-chō, Shibuya-ku; Ⓦwww.daikanyama-ark.com; see map, pp.128–129) and **Spool** (3-27-17 Jingūmae, Shibuya-ku; Ⓦwww.spool-store.com; see map, p.118).

Haibara
はいばら
2-7-6 Nihombashi, Chūō-ku ☎ 03/3272-3801,
Ⓦ www.haibara.co.jp; see map, p.60. This
lovely old shop has been selling traditional
washi paper – and everything made from it
– since 1806. Nihombashi Station. Mon–Fri
10am–6.30pm, Sat 9.30am–5pm.

Isetatsu
いせ辰
2-18-9 Yanaka, Taitō-ku ☎ 03/3823-1453; **see
map, p.91/Ueno.** One of the colourful craft
shops that make Yanaka such a delightful
part of Tokyo to explore. This one specializes in *chiyogami* – brightly coloured and
patterned paper products. Sendagi Station.
Daily 10am–6pm.

 Itō-ya
2-7-15 Ginza, Chūō-ku ☎ 03/3561-8311,
Ⓦ www.ito-ya.co.jp; see map, p.60. This
fabulous stationery store comprising 11 floors
and two annexes (Itō-ya 2 & 3), is a treasure
trove full of packable souvenirs such as traditional *washi* paper, calligraphy brushes, inks
and so on. There are also branches in
Shibuya (3F Tōkyū Department Store, 2-24-1
Shibuya, Shibuya-ku), Shinjuku (10F Odakyu
Department Store, 1-1-3 Nishi-Shinjuku,
Shinjuku-ku) and Ikebukuro (7F Tōbu Department Store, 1-1-25 Nishi-Ikebukuro,
Toshima-ku), among other locations. Ginza
Station. Mon, Tues & Sun 10.30am–7pm,
Wed–Sat 10.30am–8pm.

Japan Traditional Craft Centre
**Metropolitan Plaza Building, 1-11-1 Nishi-
Ikebukuro, Toshima-ku** ☎ 03/5954-6066,
Ⓦ www.kougei.or.jp; see map, p.99. This centre
showcases the works of craft associations
across the nation – everything from finely
crafted chopsticks to elegant lacquerware
and metalwork. Ikebukuro Station. Daily
11am–7pm.

Jūsan-ya
十三や
2-12-21 Ueno, Taitō-ku ☎ 03/3831-3238; **see
map, p.91.** Tiny shop across from Shinobazu
Pond, where a craftsman sits making
beautiful boxwood combs – just as succes-
sive generations have done since 1736.
Ueno-Hirokōji Station. Mon–Sat
10am–6.30pm.

Kakitsubata Bekkan
燕子花別館
2-16-7 Aobadai, Meguro-ku ☎ 03/3770-3401,
Ⓦ www.kakitsubataweb.com; see map,
pp.128–129. Stylish shop specializing in

tenugui cotton printed hand towels that can
also be framed and hung as prints. They
also run a small boutique showcasing hand-
picked products at 1-13-11 Aobadai. Naka-
Meguro Station. Daily except Tues
noon–7pm.

Natsuno
夏野
6-7-4 Ginza, Chūō-ku ☎ 03/3569-0952, Ⓦ www
.e-ohashi.com; see map, p.60. Stuffed to the
rafters with an incredible collection of over a
thousand types of chopstick, plus chopstick
rests and rice bowls. Prices range from
¥200 up to ¥35,000 or more for a pair
made from ivory. They have another store
just off Omotesandō (4-2-17 Jingūmae,
Shibuya-ku; ☎ 03/3403-6033; see map,
p.118). Ginza Station. Mon–Sat 10am–8pm,
Sun 10am–7pm.

Nihon Mingeikan
日本民芸館
4-3-33 Komaba, Meguro-ku ☎ 03/3467-4527;
see Greater Tokyo map at back of the book. The
gift shop of the Japan Folk Crafts Museum
is a bit out of the way, but displays have
original pottery and prints to die for, and it's
a fine source of souvenirs. If you're in town,
don't miss their annual sale of new work
(Nov 23–Dec 3). Komaba-Tōdaimae Station.
Tues–Sun 10am–5pm.

Oriental Bazaar
5-9-13 Jingūmae, Shibuya-ku ☎ 03/3400-3933;
see Greater Tokyo map at back of book. A bit of
a tourist trap, but its prime location on
Omotesandō makes this a very popular,
one-stop souvenir emporium, selling everything from secondhand kimono to origami
paper. Meiji-jingūmae Station. Daily except
Thurs 10am–7pm.

S Watanabe
渡邊木版美術画舗
8-6-19 Ginza, Chūō-ku ☎ 03/3571-4684,
Ⓦ www.hangasw.com; see map, p.60. Small
shop specializing in woodblock prints at a
range of prices and with both modern and
traditional designs, including original *ukiyo-e*
as well as reproductions of famous artists.
Shimbashi Station. Mon–Sat 9.30am–8pm.

Takumi
たくみ
8-4-2 Ginza, Chūō-ku ☎ 03/3571-2017, Ⓦ www
.ginza-takumi.co.jp; see map, p.60. Folk-craft
shop offering a small but select range of
bags, baskets, pots, toys, fabrics and other
items from around Japan. Shimbashi
Station. Mon–Sat 11am–7pm.

Winged Wheel
4-5-4 Jingūmae, Shibuya-ku ☎ 03/5785 0719, Ⓦ www.winged-wheel.co.jp; see map, p.118. In business since 1918, this stationery store has some beautiful and elegant designs, and also offers custom printing. Omotesandō Station. Daily except Tues 11am–8pm.

Yamada Heiandō
山田平安堂
2F Hillside Terrace, 18-12 Sarugaku-chō, Shibuya-ku ☎ 03/3464-5541, Ⓦ www.heiando .com; see map, pp.128–129. For lacquerware, the likes of which are found on tables no less distinguished than those of the Imperial Household and Japan's embassies. Designs are both traditional and contemporary and include several affordable pieces. Daikan'yama Station. Mon–Sat 10.30am–7pm, Sun 10.30am–6.30pm.

Books and magazines

Tokyo is the best place in Japan to buy books in English and a few other languages, but foreign-language books can be very pricey. Still, it can be enjoyable to browse the city's bookstores, and bookworms should also rummage around the secondhand book outlets of Jimbōchō, north of central Tokyo on the Hanzōmon, Mita and Shinjuku subway lines. Most big hotels have a shop stocking English-language books on Japan and a limited choice of fiction, as well as imported newspapers and magazines.

Aoyama Book Centre
Garden Floor 2BF Cosmos Aoyama, 5-53-67, Jingūmae, Shibuya-ku ☎ 03/5485-5511, Ⓦ www.aoyamabc.co.jp; see map, p.118. Innovative bookstore with a fine collection of titles related to design, architecture and photography. Also carries lots of foreign magazines. There's a popular branch in Roppongi (see map, p.79). Omotesandō Station. Daily 10am–10pm.

The Blue Parrot Bookshop
Third floor, Obayashi Bldg, 2-14-10 Takadanobaba, Shinjuku-ku ☎ 03/3202-3671, Ⓦ www.blueparrottokyo.com. A welcome

Manga

All types of cartoons, from comic strips to magazines, are known as **manga**, which has become a recognized art form the world over. Though some manga caters to less wholesome tastes, the form is targeted at a cross-section of society, and is frequently used to explain complicated current affairs topics and to teach high-school subjects.

Scholars of the genre acknowledge **Tezuka Osamu** as Japan's equivalent of Walt Disney. In the 1960s he created the iconic series *Astro Boy* and *Kimba, the White Lion* in the 1960s and went on to pen more challenging work such as the adventures of the mysterious renegade surgeon Black Jack and the epic wartime saga *Adorufu ni Tsugu* (*Tell Adolf*). Another big name is **Takahashi Rumiko**, the creator of *Ranma 1/2* and *Inuyasha*, both made into anime; she is reputed to be one of the richest women in Japan, and her work is immensely popular in the US where manga has pretty much moved into mainstream culture.

Manga are available just about everywhere in Tokyo, from train-station kiosks to bookstores. The bestselling publication is *Shūkan Shōnen Jump*, a weekly which regularly shifts over three million copies, but there are hundreds of other titles. There's also the *dōjinshi* phenomena – amateur manga produced by obsessive fans (*otaku*), whose works sometimes emulate the originals so faithfully that it's hard to tell them apart. In places such as Akihabara there are stores entirely devoted to *dōjinshi*. Serious fans might want to check out the website of leading manga publisher Kodansha (Ⓦ www.kodanclub.com). A couple of worthwhile books on the subject of manga are *Japanamerica* by Roland Kelts and *Dreamland Japan: Writings on Modern Manga* by Frederik L. Schodt.

addition to the Tokyo book scene is this store specializing in used books, magazines, DVDs and CDs. Takadanobaba Station. Daily 11am–9.30pm.

Comic Tora-no-ana

コミックとらのあな

4-3-1 Soto-Kanda, Chiyoda-ku ☎**03/3526-5330,** Ⓦ**www.toranoana.co.jp; see map, p.67.** Seven floors of manga and related products, including self-published works and second-hand comics on the top floor. There are branches in Ikebukuro (1-13-4 Higashi-Ikebukuro) and Shinjuku (6F Lumine Building, 1-18-1 Nishi-Shinjuku). Akihabara Station. Daily 10am–10pm.

Good Day Books

1-11-2 Ebisu, Shibuya-ku ☎**03/5421-0957** Ⓦ**www.gooddaybooks.com; see map, pp.128–129.** On the third floor of the same building as the bar *Footnik*, this is nirvana for homesick bookworms, with Tokyo's best selection of secondhand books. Their monthly author talks and book club are popular; see the website for details. Ebisu Station. Mon–Sat 11am–8pm, Sun 11am–6pm.

Kinokuniya

Takashimaya Times Square, Annex Building, 5-24-2 Sendagaya, Shinjuku-ku ☎**03/5361-3301; see map, pp.106–107.** The sixth floor of Kinokuniya's seven-storey outlet offers Tokyo's widest selection of foreign-language books and magazines. Its original shop on Shinjuku-dōri – whose forecourt is still a favourite meeting spot – is also worth a browse. Shinjuku Station. Daily 10am–8pm, closed one Wed each month.

Kitazawa Shoten

北沢書店

2F 2-5 Jimbōchō, Chiyoda-ku ☎**03/3263-0011,** Ⓦ**www.kitazawa.co.jp; see map, p.67.** The stately granite- and brick-fronted building houses one of the best selections of English-language titles among the dozens of secondhand stores in Jimbōchō. It's on Yasukuni-dōri, just west of the junction with Hakusan-dōri. Jimbōchō Station. Daily except Wed 11am–6.30pm.

Maruzen

Oazo Building, 1-6-4 Marunouchi, Chiyoda-ku ☎**03/5288-8881,** Ⓦ**www.maruzen.co.jp; see map, p.60.** Maruzen's huge new flagship store stocks a wide range of imported and locally published books, with a strong showing in art and design, plus magazines in a variety of languages on the fourth floor. It also sells stationery and gifts. Tokyo Station. Daily 9am–9pm.

Nadiff

4-9-8 Jingūmae, Shibuya-ku ☎**03/3403-8814; see map, p.118.** Known for its good selection of art and photography books, as well as art supplies, avant-garde and world-music CDs, gallery and chill-out café. Omotesandō Station. Daily 11am–8pm.

Naigai Chizu

内外地図

3-22 Kanda-Ogawamachi, Chiyoda-ku ☎**03/3291-0830; see map, p.67.** If you're heading into the hills, this specialist map shop carries a full range of detailed hiking maps, among others. Jimbōchō Station. Mon–Sat 8.30am–6.30pm, Sun 8.30am–5pm; closed first and third Sat of month.

On Sundays

Watari-um Museum of Contemporary Art, 3-7-6 Jingūmae, Shibuya-ku ☎**03/3470-1424; see map, p.118.** This stylish bookstore inside one of the city's more avant-garde galleries offers Tokyo's best choice of art, photo-graphy and architecture books, plus a fabulous selection of postcards. Gaienmae Station. Tues–Sun 11am–8pm.

Tower Books

7F Tower Records, 1-22-14 Jinnan, Shibuya-ku ☎**03/3496-3661,** Ⓦ**www.towerrecords.jp/store/store03.html; see map, p.122.** Reasonable prices and an excellent selection of imported books, magazines and papers, including Tokyo's best travel guidebook section. Tower Records in Shinjuku and Ikebukuro (see p.233) stocks a more limited range. Shibuya Station. Daily 10am–11pm.

Cameras, computers and electronic goods

Shinjuku is Tokyo's prime area for **cameras** and photographic equipment, though **Ikebukuro** also has a solid reputation for new and secondhand deals at reasonable prices, and **Akihabara** is catching up fast with the opening of Yodobashi Camera's mega-store. Akihabara also boasts Tokyo's biggest concentration of stores selling **electronic goods**, mostly on and around Chūō-dōri and spreading east of Akihabara Station. Anything you can plug in, log onto or interact with is available here from a bewildering array of stores split into several outlets, with multiple floors selling overlapping product ranges. There are also plenty of discount stores in **Shinjuku**, **Ikebukuro** and **Shibuya**.

Before buying electrical goods, do compare prices – many shops are open to bargaining – and make sure there's the appropriate voltage switch (the Japanese power supply is 100V). It's also important to check that whatever you buy will be compatible with equipment you have at home. For English-language instructions, after-sales service and guarantees, stick to export models, which you'll find mostly in the stores' duty-free sections, but bear in mind they may not be any cheaper than you would pay at home. Some of the larger Akihabara stores offering export models are listed below and on Ⓦ www.e-akihabara.jp.

BIC Camera

1-11-1 Yūrakuchō, Chiyoda-ku ☎ 03/5221-1111, Ⓦ www.biccamera.com; see map, p.60. The main branch of BIC offers hard-to-beat prices for cameras and audio and electronic goods – practically any gizmo you want can be found here, plus (strangely enough) discounted wine and liquor. You'll find other branches scattered around Tokyo's main shopping centres, including several in Ikebukuro, Shinjuku and Shibuya. Yūrakuchō Station. Daily 10am–10pm.

Laox

1-2-9 Soto-Kanda, Chiyoda-ku ☎ 03/3253-7111, Ⓦ www.laox.co.jp; see map, p.67. One of the most prominent names in Akiba and probably the best place to start browsing: they have a well-established duty-free section with English-speaking staff, and nine stores where you can buy everything from pocket calculators to plasma-screen TVs. Akihabara Station. Daily 10am–9pm.

Sakuraya

さくらや

1-1-1 Nishi-Shinjuku, Shinjuku-ku ☎ 03/5324-3636, Ⓦ www.sakuraya.co.jp; see map, pp.106–107. Next to the Odakyū department store is the flagship store of this camera and electronics chain, which has several branches around Shinjuku, including one across the road from main rival Yodobashi

Camera. There's a good selection of equipment and prices are keen. Shinjuku Station. Daily 10am–9.30pm.

Shimizu Camera

4-3-2 Ginza, Chūō-ku ☎ 03/3564-1008; see map, p.60. Reputable used-camera specialist in the backstreets of Ginza, two blocks west of the Apple Store. Ginza Station. Mon–Sat 10.30am–8pm, Sun 11am–7pm.

Tsukumo

1-9-7 Soto-Kanda, Chiyoda-ku ☎ 03/3253-5599; see map, p.67. Tsukumo is a general electrical store with three outlets – look for the one saying Robot. Upstairs you'll find a floor aimed at model enthusiasts building their very own androids, but there are also a few demonstration models of working robots and the videos are fun to watch, too. Akihabara Station. Mon–Sat 10.30am–8pm, Sun 11am–7.30pm.

Yodobashi Camera

1-11-1 Nishi-Shinjuku, Shinjuku-ku ☎ 03/3346-1010, Ⓦ www.yodobashi.co.jp; see map, pp.106–107. Claiming to be the world's largest camera shop, this place offers decent reductions and stocks the broadest range. There's another huge branch in Akihabara (1-1 Kanda-Hanaokachō, Chiyoda-ku), beside the Tsukubua Express station, selling everything from PCs to exercise bikes, by way of cameras. Shinjuku Station. Daily 9.30am–10pm.

Department stores

With impressive basement food halls right up through fashion, crafts and household items to the restaurant floors, Tokyo's massive **department stores** are likely to have almost anything you're looking for. They're also more likely to have English-speaking staff and a duty-free service than smaller shops, though prices tend to be slightly above average. Seasonal sales can offer great bargains, particularly kimono; look for adverts in the English-language press.

Isetan

3-14-1 Shinjuku, Shinjuku-ku ☎03/3352-1111, ⓦwww.isetan.co.jp; see map, pp.106–107. This stylish department store is one of the best in Shinjuku, with an emphasis on well-designed local goods and a reputation for promoting up-and-coming fashion designers. The newly renovated annexe housing men's clothing and accessories is particularly chic. English-speaking assistants are on hand if needed. Shinjuku Station. Daily 10am–8pm.

Matsuya

3-6-1 Ginza, Chūō-ku ☎03/3567-1211, ⓦwww.matsuya.com; see map, p.60. The most workaday of the big department stores, Matsuya only has one other branch, in Asakusa (1-4-1 Hanakawado, Taitō-ku). Ginza Station. Daily 10am–8pm.

Matsuzakaya

3-29-5 Ueno, Taitō-ku ☎03/3832-1111, ⓦwww.matsuzakaya.co.jp/ueno; see map, p.91. Three-hundred-year-old store based in Ueno, where its main outlet has benefited from a recent renovation. There's another, rather more fusty branch in Ginza (6-10-1 Ginza, Chūō-ku ☎03/3572-1111; Ginza Station; see map, p.60/Ginza). Ueno-Hirokōji Station. Daily 10am–7.30pm.

Mitsukoshi

1-4-1 Nihombashi-Muromachi, Chūō-ku ☎03/3241-3311, ⓦwww.mitsukoshi.co.jp; see map, p.60. Tokyo's most prestigious and oldest department store is elegant, spacious and renowned for its high-quality merchandise. Designer boutiques and more contemporary fashions are concentrated in the southerly *shin-kan* ("new building"). Branches at 4-6-16 Ginza, Chūō-ku (☎03/3562-1111; Ginza Station; see map, p.60), 1-5-7 Higashi-Ikebukuro, Toshima-ku (☎03/3987-1111; Ikebukuro Station; see map, p.99) and 3-29-1 Shinjuku, Shinjuku-ku (☎03/3354-1111; Shinjuku Station; see map, pp.106–107). Mitsukoshimae Station. Daily 10am–7.30pm.

Seibu

1-28-1 Minami-Ikebukuro, Toshima-ku ☎03/3981-0111, ⓦwww.seibu.co.jp; see map, p.99. Sprawling department store with a reputation for innovation, especially in its homeware store Loft and funky fashion offshoot Parco, whose racks and shelves groan with state-of-the-art ephemera. There's also a cluster of Seibu, Loft and Parco stores in Shibuya. Ikebukuro Station. Mon–Sat 10am–9pm, Sun 10am–8pm.

Takashimaya

2-4-1 Nihombashi, Chūō-ku ☎03/3211-4111, ⓦwww.takashimaya.co.jp; see map, p.60. Like Mitsukoshi, Takashimaya has a long and illustrious past, a great food hall and stocks a very broad range of goods, though it appeals to decidedly conservative tastes. There's a huge branch in Shinjuku at Takashimaya Times Square (5-24-2 Sendagaya, Shibuya-ku ☎03/5361-1111; see map, pp.106–107). Nihombashi Station. Daily 10am–7pm.

Tōbu

1-1-25 Nishi-Ikebukuro, Toshima-ku ☎03/3981-2211, ⓦwww.tobu-dept.jp; see map, p.99. One of Japan's largest department stores, Tōbu is mainly of interest for its excellent basement food halls on two levels and dozens of restaurants in its Spice section and the Spice 2 annexe. Ikebukuro Station. Daily 10am–8pm.

Tōkyū

2-24-1 Dōgenzaka, Shibuya-ku ☎03/3477-3111, ⓦwww.tokyu-dept.co.jp; see map, p.122. Top dog in the Shibuya department store stakes, with branches all over the area, particularly around the train station. This main store specializes in designer fashions and interior goods. They also run Tōkyū Hands (see p.232). Shibuya Station. Daily 11am–7pm.

Wakō

4-5-11 Ginza, Chūō-ku ☎03/3562-2111, ⓦwww.shop.wako.co.jp; see map, p.60. Ginza's most elegant department store, this century-old establishment (which started as the home of Seiko watches) might not have as wide a range of goods as its rivals, but it does have a sterling reputation for custom-making anything customers desire, including fine jewellery and watches. Ginza Station. Mon–Sat 10.30am–6pm.

Fashion, cosmetics & jewellery

The city's epicentre of chic is **Omotesandō**, the tree-lined boulevard cutting through Harajuku and Aoyama. The roll call of brands here – Gucci, Louis Vuitton, Armani, Chanel – reads like a who's who of fashion, and you'll also find top Japanese designers such as Issey Miyake and Comme des Garçons. The area's backstreets are prime hunting grounds for up-and-coming designers and streetwear labels, including Underground, Bapexclusive and Hysteric Glamour.

Daikan'yama, **Naka-Meguro** and **Shimo-Kitazawa** are also worth browsing around – the fashion shops in the last two areas are slightly cheaper and less precious. In addition, all Tokyo's big **department stores** have several floors devoted to clothes, from haute couture to more modest wear at affordable prices, albeit not always very uninspired.

Finding clothes that fit is becoming easier as young Japanese are, on average, substantially bigger than their parents, and foreign chains tend to carry larger sizes. **Shoes**, however, are more of a problem. While stores stock larger sizes nowadays, the range is still pretty limited. The ubiquitous ABC-Mart and Ginza's Washington shoe shop are usually your best bet. Good places to hunt for bargain footwear are Higashi-Shinjuku, especially around the Studio Alta fashion supermarket, and Ueno's Ameyokochō market.

If you had something more sparkly in mind, head for the exclusive **jewellery** stores of Ginza, notably Mikimoto and Wakō (see p.225), or the more affordable outlets in Omotesandō. Ginza is also home to the main store of the famous cosmetics chain Shiseido. For more traditional cosmetics, try Hyakusuke in Asakusa (see p.87) or Isehan Honten (see p.228).

The comeback of the kimono

In Japan, the kimono is still worn by both sexes for special occasions, such as weddings and festival visits to a shrine. But as the demand for high-class kimono declines – a result of the falling birth rate and Japan's ageing population – the one bright spot for the industry is the trend to adapt old kimono to new uses. Over the last few years the kimono has made something of a comeback in the fashion stakes, particularly among young women, who sometimes wear kimono like a coat over Western clothes or co-ordinate it with coloured rather than white *tabi* (traditional split-toed socks). At the same time, fashion designers are turning to kimono fabrics and styles for contemporary creations.

Few visitors to Japan fail to be impressed by the beauty and variety of kimono available, and every department store has a corner devoted to ready-made or tailored kimono. None is particularly cheap: the ready-made versions can easily cost ¥100,000, while ¥1 million for the best made-to-measure kimono is not uncommon. Much more affordable secondhand or antique kimono can be found at tourist shops, flea markets or in the kimono sales held by department stores, usually in spring and autumn. Prices can start as low as ¥1000, but you'll pay more for the sumptuous, highly decorated wedding kimono (they make striking wall hangings), as well as the most beautifully patterned **obi**, the broad, silk sash worn with a kimono. A cheaper, more practical alternative is the light cotton **yukata**, popular with both sexes as dressing gowns; you'll find them in all department stores and many speciality stores, along with *happi* coats – the loose jackets that just cover the upper body. To complete the outfit, you could pick up a pair of *zōri*, traditional straw **sandals**, or their wooden counterpart, *geta*.

If you want to try out the full kimono look, one option is to make an appointment at Katsura Photo Studio (4-28-4 Jingū-mae, Shibuya-ku; ☎03/3470-0027; daily 10am–6pm) for a geisha makeover (¥15,000 including three photos). Men can get in on the act, too, dressing up in what is called "samurai" style (¥5000). Incidentally, the male kimono is much less florid in design than the female version, and is usually in muted colours such as black, greys and browns.

△ The Gucci store on Omotesandō

If you want to see what the world will be wearing tomorrow, you could sign up for a **Tokyo Fashion Tour** (☎090/3680-0836, ⓦwww.fashioninjapan.com/tokyofashiontour.htm; from around ¥100,000 per day), a guided jaunt round the city's trendiest shopping districts and its coolest designer outlets.

Arts & Science

6-6-20 Minami-Aoyama, Minato-ku ☎03/3498-1091, ⓦwww.arts-science.com; see map, p.114. Sonya Park, the Korean-born, Hawaii-raised owner of this boutique, has a great eye for what works in fashion. Her collection includes original pieces alongside such things as sheepskin Scandinavian army coats and French perfumes. Her footwear collection of is available around the corner at Shoes & Things (103 Palace Aoyama, 6-16-6 Minami-Aoyama, Minato-ku). Omotesandō Station. Daily noon–8pm.

Bapexclusive

5-5-8 Minami-Aoyama, Minato-ku ☎03/3407-2145, ⓦwww.bape.com; see map, p.118. A Bathing Ape, the streetwear brand of designer Nigo (who took his inspiration from the *Planet of the Apes* movies), has a string of boutiques all over Aoyama and Harajuku, of which this is the main

showroom. Also check out the super-cute Bape Kids store (3-29-11 Jingūmae) with its playpool filled with multicoloured rubber bananas, and the groovy *Bape Cafe!?* (see p.183). One of their T-shirts will set you back at least ¥6000. Omotesandō Station. Daily 11am–8pm.

Billionaire Boys Club

4-28-22 Jingūmae, Shibuya-ku ☎03/5775-2633, ⓦwww.bbcicecream.com; see map, p.118. It looks more like a trendy club than a boutique, selling the hip-hop inspired clothes of Pharell Williams and the tutti-fruiti coloured sneaker line Ice Cream (his collaboration with Japanese designer Nigo of A Bathing Ape fame). Meiji-jingūmae Station. Daily 11am–7pm.

CA4LA

6-29-4 Jingūmae, Shibuya-ku ☎03/3406-8271; see map, p.118. The hat shop to the eternally trendy, with everything from

227

foppish fedoras and swoony sunhats to hip-hop beanies and designer baseball caps. The name is pronounced Ka-shi-ra, by the way. Meiji-jingūmae Station. Daily 11am–8pm.

Chicago
6-31-21 Jingumae, Shibuya-ku ⊤ 03/3409-5017; see map, p.118. There's a fine selection of kimono, *obi*, and so on at this highly popular thrift store, as well as rack upon rack of good used clothes. Meiji-jingūmae Station. Daily 11am–8pm.

Chidoriya
ちどり屋
2-3-24 Asakusa, Taitō-ku ⊤ 03/3841-1868; see map, p.85. Not the most stylish collection, but a decent range of men's kimono and *yukata* at prices that won't break the bank. Asakusa Station. Daily except Wed 10am–6.30pm.

Comme des Garçons
5-2-1 Minami-Aoyama, Minato-ku ⊤ 03/3406-3951; see map, p.118. More like an art gallery than a clothes shop, this beautiful store offers a suitable setting for high fashion for men and women by world-famous designer Rei Kawakubo. Omotesandō Station. Daily 11am–8pm.

Dresscamp
5-5-1 Minami-Aoyama, Minato-ku ⊤ 03/5778-3717, ⓦ www.dresscamp.org; see map, p.118. Indulge your inner rock goddess at this glitzy boutique with a very wacky style. Daily noon–9pm.

🏃 Evisu The Tailor
1-1-5 Kami-Meguro, Meguro-ku ⊤ 03/3710-1999; see map, pp.128–129. Main branch of the ultra-trendy Japanese jeans designer. Stock up here on shirts, T-shirts, sweat-shirts and a full range of accessories. Ebisu Station. Daily noon–8pm.

Five Foxes' Store
3-26-6 Shinjuku, Shinjuku-ku ⊤ 03/5367-5551; see map, pp.106–107. Stylish showcase for Comme ça de Mode, a bright and afford-able fashion brand. There's a branch opposite Harajuku station. Shinjuku Station. Mon–Sat 11am–11pm, Sun 11am–8pm.

Gallery Kawano
ギャラリー 川野
102 Flats-Omotesandō, 4-4-9 Jingūmae, Shibuya-ku ⊤ 03/3470-3305; see map, p.118. Excellent selection of vintage kimono, *yukata* and *obi*, with swatches of gorgeous kimono fabric available too. Omotesandō Station. Daily 11am–6pm.

Hayayashi Kimono
林きもの
International Arcade, 2-1-1 Yūrakuchō, Chiyoda-ku ⊤ 03/3501-4012; see map, p.60. English-speaking staff can help you find the right size of new, secondhand or vintage kimono, *obi*, *yukata* and shorter *happi* coats at this large kimono boutique. Yūrakuchō Station. Mon–Sat 10am–7pm, Sun 10am–6pm.

🏃 Hysteric Glamour
5-5-3 Minami-Aoyama, Minato-ku ⊤ 03/6419-3899, ⓦ www.hystericglamour.jp; see map, p.118. The premier outlet for this fun, retro-kitsch Americana label which has become Japan's leading youth brand. They also have a shop at 6-23-2 Jingūmae. Omotesandō Station. Daily 11am–8pm.

Isehan Honten
伊勢反本店
6-6-20 Minami-Aoyama, Minato-ku ⊤ 03/5467-3735 ⓦ www.isehan.co.jp; see map, p.114. Beni, a safflower-based lip colour, is a traditional Japanese cosmetic with a lustrous green glow in its concentrated form, though it paints on red; only one percent of the yellow flower's pigment is red, that's why it's expensive. The stuff is sold here in lovely china pots, and you can learn about its history in the small museum and enjoy complimentary tea and sweets coloured and flavoured with *beni*. Omotesandō Station. Tues–Sun 11am–7pm.

Issey Miyake
三宅一生
3-18-11 Minami-Aoyama, Minato-ku ⊤ 03/3423-1407, ⓦ www.isseymikaye; see map, p.118. One of the top names in world fashion, famous for his elegant, eminently wearable designs. Issey Miyake by Naoki Takizawa (6-12-4 Roppongi, Minato-ku ⊤ 03/5772-2777), in the Roppongi Hills development on Keyakizaka-dōri, showcases the designs of Miyake's protégé Takizawa (see map, p.79). Omotesandō Station. Daily 11am–8pm.

🏃 Kura Chika Yoshida
クラチカヨシダ
5-6-8 Jingūmae, Shibuya-ku ⊤ 03/5464-1766, ⓦ www.yoshidakaban.com; see map, p.118. Access the full range of bags, wallets and luggage at this shrine to the hip Japanese brand Porter. It's just off Omotesandō, behind Tokyo Union Church. Omotesandō Station. Daily except Wed noon–8pm.

Laforet
1-11-6 Jingūmae, Shibuya-ku ⊤ 03/3475-0411; see map, p.118. This pioneering

"fashion building" is packed with trendy boutiques, many catering to the fickle tastes of Harajuku's teenage shopping mavens. Wander through and catch the *Zeitgeist*. Meiji-jingūmae Station. Daily 11am–8pm.

Mannenya
万年屋

3-8-1 Nishi-Shinjuku, Shinjuku-ku ☎03/3373-1111, ⓦwww.mannen-ya.co.jp; see map, pp.106–107. If you want to achieve the baggy pants, split-toed pump look of a Japanese construction worker, this work clothes super-store is the place to head. Don't scoff – the likes of Jean-Paul Gaultier come shopping here and it's a great place to pick up all kinds of underwear and outdoor wear at a fraction of designer-label prices. Check the website for weekly specials. Tochōmae Station. Mon–Sat 7am–9pm, Sat & Sun 9am–7pm.

Mikimoto

4-5-5 Ginza, Chūō-ku ☎03/3535-4611, ⓦwww.mikimoto.com; see map, p.60. The famous purveyor of cultured pearls has branched out into diamonds and other jewellery lines, all shown off to perfection in its dramatic main store in the heart of Ginza. Round the corner, Mikimoto Ginza 2 (2-4-12 Ginza) focuses on high fashion clothes, accessories and beauty products – look for the pale, pearly pink building with holes punched in it, the work of architect Toyō Ito. Ginza Station. Daily 11am–7pm.

Momo

6-1-6-107 Minami-Aoyama, Minato-ku ☎03/3406-4738; see map, p.118. Boutique showcasing the designs of Masako Yamada, who creates lovely original clothes (including blouses and decorated jeans) and accessories using vintage kimono. Omotesandō Station. Tues–Sat noon–7pm, Sun noon–6pm.

Niwaka
にわか

313 Minami Aoyama Bldg, 3-13-18 Minami-Aoyama, Minato-ku ☎03/3796-0803, ⓦwww.niwaka.com; see map, p.118. Find rings and other items of jewellery decorated with traditional carving techniques at this elegant outpost of the Kyoto-based manufacturer. Omotesandō Station. Daily 11am–8pm.

Okura
おくら

20-11 Sarugaku-chō, Shibuya-ku ☎03/3461-8511, ⓦwww.hrm.co.jp; see map, pp.128–129. Visit this youthful boutique for indigo-dyed traditional and contemporary Japanese fashions, from jeans and T-shirts to kimono and *tabi* socks. Daikan'yama Station. Daily 11am–8pm.

Onitsuka Tiger

Westwalk 4F Roppongi Hills, 6-10-1 Roppongi, Minato-ku ☎03/5772-2660, ⓦwww.onitsukatiger.com; see map, p.79. Selling sneakers as seen on the most fashionable feet, this Japanese brand started business back in 1949. Branch also in Daikan'yama (20-7, Sarugaku-chō). Roppongi Station. Daily 11am–9pm.

Prada

5-2-6 Minami-Aoyama, Minato-ku ☎03/6418-0400; see map, p.118. Even if the fashion lines of Miuccia Prada don't appeal, you really should swing by this pure temple to high fashion to admire the incredible architecture of the Herzog/de Meuron-designed building. Omotesandō Station. Daily 11am–8pm.

Reinyumi
れいんゆみ

1-7-1 Azabudai, Minato-ku ☎03/3505-1031, ⓦweb.mac.com/reinyumi; see map, p.76. Reworked kimono, jeans decorated with Japanese embroidery and original print T-shirts make this an interesting boutique to check out. Kamiyachō Station. Daily 10.30am–8pm.

Shiseido

Tokyo Ginza Shiseido Building, 8-8-3 Ginza, Chūō-ku ☎03/3572-3913, ⓦwww.shiseido.co.jp; see map, p.60. You can't miss this distinctive red building occupied by cosmetics giant Shiseido. Ginza or Shimbashi stations. Mon–Sat 11.30am–7.30pm, Sun 11.30am–7pm.

Sosu Miharayasuhiro Tokyo

B1F Colonade Bldg, 5-2-6 Jingūmae, Shibuya-ku ☎03/5778-0678, ⓦwww.sosu.co.jp; see map, p.118. Nagasaki-born designer Sosu, whose colourful sneaker creations for Puma are sold worldwide, now has a clothing collection for men and women. See it here at his main store. Meiji-jingūmae Station. Mon–Fri noon–8pm, Sat & Sun 11am–8pm.

Tokyo Hipsters Club

6-12-23 Jingūmae, Shibuya-ku ☎03/5778-2081, ⓦwww.tokyohipstersclub.com; see map, p.118. Designed by Habitat's creative director Tom Dixon, this groovy concept store mines the 1960s and its counterculture for inspiration for its fashions and accessories. There's also a café. Meiji-jingūmae Station. Daily noon–8pm.

Tsumori Chisato

4-21-25 Minami-Aoyama, Minato-ku ⓉO3/3423-5170; see map, p.118. Girlish streetwear that captures the Harajuku look but with better tailoring, materials and attention to detail. Branch in Daikan'yama (La Fuente Daikan'yama, 7 Daikan'yama-chō). Omotesandō Station. Daily 11am–8pm.

UnderCover

5-3 Minami-Aoyama, Minato-ku ⓉO3/3407-1232; see map, p.118.Jun Takahashi's Under-Cover brand of clothing isn't so under-ground any more, but remains youthful and eclectic. Omotesandō Station. Daily 10am–8.30pm.

UniQlo

6-10-8 Jingūmae, Shibuya-ku ⓉO3/5468-7313; see map, p.118. The Japanese version of Gap has proved that inexpensive can still be cool. The clothes are simple but of good quality – mostly plain cotton fabrics – and come in a wide range of colours, though not huge sizes. There are branches in all Tokyo's main shopping centres. Meiji-jingūmae Station. Daily 11am–9pm.

United Arrows

3-28-1 Jingūmae, Shibuya-ku ⓉO3/3479-8180, Ⓦwww.united-arrows.co.jp; see map, p.114. Main store of the upmarket fashion chain, famous for their clean-cut men's shirts and suits. Head to the top floor to have your measurements taken for a custom-made kimono or cotton shirt. Meiji-jingūmae Station. Mon–Fri noon–8pm, Sat & Sun 11am–8pm.

Yohji Yamamoto

5-3-6 Minami-Aoyama, Shibuya-ku ⓉO3/3409-6006, Ⓦwww.yohjiyamamoto.co.jp; see map, p.118. Discreetly hidden behind a bronze facade, this is the flagship store of Japanese fashion icon Yamamoto, famed for his edgy, one-colour designs. For his more populist line of clothing, check out Y's on Keyaki-zaka-dōri in Roppongi Hills (6-12-14 Roppongi, Minato-ku; see map, p.79). Omotesandō Station. Daily 11am–8pm.

Food and drink

The best one-stop places to find unusual and souvenir food-and-drink items – such as beautifully boxed biscuits, cakes and traditional sweets (*wagashi*), and sake from across the country – are the department store **food halls** (see p.224). There are also some highly regarded food and drink shops in Tokyo, some of which have been around for centuries.

For a couple of places to buy premium **teas**, try Cha Ginza and Yamamotoyama (both on p.185). General foodstuffs and snacks are easily bought from **24-hour convenience stores** – Tokyo has thousands, often located near subway or train stations. Lawson, Family Mart, AM/PM and 7-Eleven have the widest geographical coverage.

Cha-no-Yu

茶の愉

5-16-6 Minami-Azabu, Minato-ku ⓉO3/5447-5535, Ⓦwww.cha-no-yu.com; see map, pp.128–129. Looking a bit like an arty laboratory, this shop sells leaves and herbal concoctions from around the world. You can sample them before you buy. Hiro-o Station. Daily 11am–7pm.

Fukumitsuya

福光屋

5-5-8 Ginza, Chūō-ku ⓉO3/3569-2291, Ⓦwww.fukumitsuya.co.jp; see map, p.60. Sake shop and bar representing the oldest brewery in Kanazawa (1625), in north central Japan. There are fifty different sakes on offer, from which you can taste a selection of three for ¥700. Otherwise, prices start at ¥300 a shot. Ginza Station. Mon–Sat 11am–9pm, Sun 11am–8pm.

Higashiya

1-13-12 Aobadai, Meguro-ku ⓉO3/5428-0240, Ⓦwww.higashiya.com; see map, pp.128–129. Here traditional Japanese sweets, made from pounded rice and beans, are beautiful wrapped and displayed like fine chocolates. They also sell some original pottery and sake implements. There's a teahouse/bar upstairs and a second branch Ori Higashiya near Roppongi Hills (see p.76). Naka-Meguro Station. Daily except Tues 11am–10pm.

National Azabu

4-5-2 Minami-Azabu, Minato-ku ⓉO3/3442-3181; see map, pp.128–129. Firmly geared towards the tastes of the expat community, with a great selection of international food goods and fresh veggies, fruits, meat and fish. Hiro-o Station. Daily 9.30am–8pm.

Sakaya Kurihara
さかや栗原

3-6-17 Moto-Azabu, Minato-ku ☎03/3408-5378, ⓦwww.sakaya-kurihara.jp; see map, p.79. This small shop stocks a fine selection of sake, including brands and types rarely found elsewhere, and they're used to dealing with *gaijin*. Hiro-o Station. Mon–Sat 10am–9pm.

Sake Plaza

1-1-21 Nishi-Shinbashi, Minato-ku ☎03/3519-2091; see map, p.60. Run by the Japan Sake Brewers Association, this shop and tasting room has an excellent range of sake from all over the country. It promotes a different region each season, and the range of sakes on offer changes each day. You can sample substantial slugs of five different varieties for ¥525. Toranomon or Uchisaiwachō stations. Mon–Fri 10am–6pm.

Sweets and Objects

Omotesandō Hills, 4-12-10 Meiji-Jingūmae, Shibuya-ku ☎03/5785-1790, ⓦwww .macmuseumshop.com; see map, p.118. Sells sweets and other goods, designed and packaged by Japanese contemporary artists such as Yayoi Kusama. It's in the part of Omotesandō Hills built to resemble the old Dojunkai apartments. Omotesandō Station. Daily 11am–9pm.

Tensuya Honten
てんすや本店

1-9 Tsukuda, Chūō-ku ☎03/3531-2351; see map, p.135. This ancient shop specializes in *tsukudani*, delicious morsels of seaweed and fish preserved in a mixture of soy sauce, salt and sugar. A wooden box set of six different types from their selection of eighteen costs ¥2000. The preserves last for three weeks. Tsukishima Station. Daily 9am–6pm.

 Toraya
とらや

4-9-22 Akasaka, Minato-ku ☎03/3408-4121; see map, p.76. Makers of *wagashi* (traditional confectionery often used in tea ceremonies) for the imperial family. It's not cheap, but everything is beautifully packaged and products vary with the season. There's a café downstairs where you can sample the products along with some green tea. Akasaka-mitsuke Station. Mon–Fri 11am–7pm, Sat & Sun 11am–5.30pm.

Homeware and interior design

Japan is justly famous for the delicate beauty and practicality of its interior design, particularly the ingenious way it makes the most of limited space, and for its *wabi-sabi* sensibility, which finds beauty in imperfection. Even everyday appliances items such as telephones and air-purifiers are getting contemporary design makeovers, as typified by the products of Amadana and Plus Minus Zero.

Agito

2F West Walk Roppongi Hills, 6-10-3 Roppongi, Minato-ku ☎03/5570-4411; see map, p.79. This design store within the Roppongi Hills complex exhibits a tasteful collection of contemporary Japanese interior products, from silky lacquerware to modern pottery designs and furniture. Roppongi Station. Daily 11am–9pm.

 Amadana

B3F Omotesandō Hills, 4-12-10 Jingūmae, Shibuya-ku ☎03/3408-2018, ⓦwww.amadana .com; see map, p.118. The name refers to the old area of Amadana, near Nihombashi, which was famous for lacquerware artisans during the Edo period. That craft's traditional respect for design and beauty is reflected in the look of Amadana's top-end DVD players and so forth, produced by big-name manufacturers to the designs of architect Tei Shuwa. Omotesandō Station. Mon–Sat 11am–9pm, Sun 11am–8pm.

Cibone

B1F Aoyama Bell Commons, 2-14-6 Kita-Aoyama, Minato-ku ☎03/3475-8017, ⓦwww .cibone.com; see map, p.118. All kinds of furniture and interior design goods can be purchased at this stylish store, with a strong representation of local designers as well as a books section. Gaienmae Station. Daily 11am–9pm.

 The Cover Nippon

3F Galleria, Tokyo Midtown, 9-7-3 Akasaka, Minato-ku ☎03/5413-0658, ⓦwww .thecovernippon.jp; see map, p.76. One of the best shops on Tokyo Midtown's interior design floor, The Cover Nippon has a fantastic selection of Japanese designer goods made by small, quality manufacturers – everything from cotton fabric and furniture to lacquerware. Roppongi Station. Daily 11am–9pm.

Hakusan

Floor G, From First Bldg, 5-3-10 Minami-Aoyama, Minato-ku ☎03/5774-8850, Ⓦwww1 .ocn.ne.jp/~hakusan; see map, p.118. Sophisticated, award-winning porcelain produced at the Kyūshū town of Hasami, near Nagasaki. Omotesandō Station. Daily 11am–8pm.

J.

3F Decks Tokyo Beach, 1-6-1 Daiba, Minato-ku ☎03/3599-2031, Ⓦwww.j-period.com. Contemporary design store offering the cream Japanese-made interior goods, from Isamu Nogochi lamps to modern takes on *urushi* (lacquerware). Odaiba Kaihin-kōen Station. Daily 11am–9pm.

 Muji

3-8-3 Marunouchi, Chiyoda-ku ☎03/5208-8241, Ⓦwww.mujiyurakucho.com; see map, p.60. The largest Tokyo branch of this internationally famous "no-brand" homeware, lifestyle and fashion chain has the full range of Muji goods, plus a decent café and even bikes for rent (see p.240). There are branches all over the city; Muji's latest addition at the time of writing is a sleek trend-setting store in Tokyo Midtown, while its outlet near Gaienmae Station (2-12-18 Kita-Aoyama, Minato-ku) is stylishly built from salvaged wood and steel. Yūrakuchō Station. Daily 10am–9pm.

Nippon Form

にっぽんフォルム

6F Living Design Centre Ozone, Shinjuku Park Tower, 3-7-1 Nishi-Shinjuku, Shinjuku-ku ☎03/5322-6620; see map, pp.106–107. One-stop shop for the best in Japanese homeware design, including products from the Yanagi range (see below) and Isamu Noguchi's paper lanterns, and classic modern furniture such as the spoke chair by Toyoguchi Katsuhei. Tochōmae Station. Daily except Wed 10.30am–7.30pm.

Nuno

ぬの

B1 Axis, 5-17-1 Roppongi ☎03/3582-7997; see map, p.79. In the basement of the Axis Building (which has several other good interior design shops), Nuno stocks its own range of exquisite original fabrics made in Japan, either sold on their own by the metre or made into clothes, cushions and other items. Roppongi Station. Mon–Sat 11am–7pm.

Plus Minus Zero

3-12-12 Kita-Aoyama, Minato-ku ☎03/5778-5380, Ⓦwww.plusminuszero.jp; see map, p.118. Designer Fukusawa Naoto's concept is to create household appliances, audiovisual equipment, interior furnishings and other miscellaneous items that are "not boring". In this he succeeds admirably, and you'll clock his products – such as a humidifier resembling a smooth bun – in the trendiest places. Omotesandō Station. Daily except Wed 11am–7pm.

Three Minute Happiness

3-5 Udagawachō, Shibuya-ku ☎03/5459-1851; see map, p.122. Part of the Comme Ça fashion chain, with colourful, inexpensive homeware and fashion – look in the window to see what the week's top-selling items are. There's another big branch at the Aqua City mall in Odaiba. Shibuya Station. Daily 11am–9pm.

Tōkyū Hands

12-10 Udagawachō, Shibuya-ku ☎03/5489-5111; see map, p.122. This offshoot of the Tōkyū department store is the place to head if you're planning home improvements or have a hobby of practically any type – they stock everything that a handy person or an outdoor type could want. It's also a great place to look for quirky souvenirs. Branches in Ikebukuro (1-28-10 Higashi-Ikebukuro, Toshima-ku; see map, p.99) and at Takashimaya Times Square in Shinjuku (see map, pp.106–107). Shibuya Station. Daily 10am–8pm, except second and third Wed of the month.

Yanagi

1F Edlehof Building, 8 Honshio-cho, Shinjuku-ku ☎03/3359 9721, Ⓦwww.japon.net/yanagi; see map pp.106–107. Little more than a tiny office in front of their stockroom, this is the HQ for the homeware of the legendary Yanagi Sori, whose Butterfly Stool – two elegant folds of wood – is exhibited in design museums as a classic. Yanagi cutlery, crockery and glassware are equally good-looking and reasonably affordable. Yotsuya Station. Wed–Fri 1–5.30pm.

Records and CDs

Tokyo's tastes in **CDs and records** are nothing if not eclectic, with a huge range of foreign imports – including world music, jazz and classical recordings – boosting an already mammoth local output of ephemeral pop and rock. Foreign outlets including HMV and Tower Records offer some of the best prices for imported CDs (typically under ¥2000), while CDs of foreign artists produced for the Japanese market, with translated lyrics and extra tracks, generally start in the region of ¥2300.

Shibuya is said to have the city's highest concentration of recorded music shops: head to the Udagawachō district near Tōkyū Hands to find scores of outlets specializing in hip-hop, house and techno. The tiny stores of Shimo-Kitazawa (see p.124) are another good place to root around.

Bonjour Records
24-1 Sarugaku-cho, Shibuya-ku
☎03/5458-6020, ⓦwww.bonjour.co.jp; see map, pp.128–129. It may not be the biggest CD store in Tokyo, but it's certainly the trendiest – they even sell their own designer T-shirts. Also in Shinjuku in the basement of Isetan. Daikan'yama Station. Daily 11am–7pm.

Disk Union
3-31-4 Shinjuku, Shinjuku-ku ☎03/3352-2691, ⓦwww.diskunion.co.jp; see map, pp.106–107. A broad selection of secondhand records and CDs. There are some twenty other branches scattered around Tokyo, some specializing in particular genres. Shinjuku Station. Mon–Sat 11am–8pm, Sun 11am–7pm.

HMV
24-1 Udagawachō, Shibuya-ku; ☎03/5458-3411, ⓦwww.hmv.co.jp; see map, p.122. The main outlet of the British music store has a good selection of discs, videos and DVDs. Branches in Laforet in Harajuku, Shinjuku's Takashimaya Times Square, and the Metropolitan Plaza in Higashi-Ikebukuro (1-11-1 Nishi-Ikebukuro, Toshima-ku; see map, p.99). Shibuya Station. Daily 10am–10pm.

Recofan
4F Shibuya BEAM, 31 Udagawachō, Shibuya-ku ☎03/3463-0090, ⓦwww.recofan.co.jp; see map, p.122. A mixed bag of new and used records and CDs, both imported and locally

produced, at bargain prices. Three branches in Shibuya and two in Shimo-Kitazawa, plus other outlets around the city. Shibuya Station. Daily 11.30am–9pm.

Rizumu
リズム
6-4-12 Ueno, Bunkyō-ku ☎03/3831-5135; see map, p.91. This ancient record shop squeezed under the railway track in Ueno's Ameyoko market is *the* place to come for *enka* – traditional Japanese "chanson". Owner Kobayashi-san will help you search for that haunting track you just can't get out your head. Okachimachi Station. Tues–Sun 11am–7pm.

Tony Records
1-52 Kanda-Jimbōchō, Chiyoda-ku ☎03/3294-3621; see map, p.67. Classic jazz, swing and pop platters – including all kinds of rarities – are the stock-in-trade of this store, which mainly specializes in secondhand vinyl, though it also stocks CDs. Jimbōchō Station. Mon–Sat 11am–8pm, Sun noon–7pm.

Tower Records
1-22-14 Jinnan, Shibuya-ku ☎03/3496-3661, ⓦwww.towerrecords.co.jp; see map, p.122. Tokyo's biggest music store, with six floors of CDs, records and related paraphernalia, including videos and games. Branches in Shinjuku, Ikebukuro and Akihabara. Shibuya Station. Daily 10am–10pm.

Toys, games and novelties

The land that gave the world Donkey Kong, Super Mario Brothers, the Tamigotchi and Hello Kitty is forever throwing up new must-have toys, games and novelties. Step into one of Tokyo's major toy stores, such as Kiddyland or Hakuhinkan, and you'll find the range quite amazing. These places are among the best places to hunt for unusual souvenirs and for the next big craze before it hits

The uncool shopping guide to Tokyo

The Japanese have an unrivalled affection for objects that are cloyingly cute, tackily kitsch, downright crass or just plain bizarre. If your tastes run in a similar vein, try the following as possible souvenirs of your visit:

- a T-shirt from the Parasite Museum in Meguro (see p.130) bearing the slogan "Wonderful World of the Worm".
- sumo-wrestler-shaped chocolates, from the National Sumo Stadium, Ryōgoku (see p.71).
- practically anything from über-novelty shop Don Quixote (see below) – such as leopard-print men's undies or breast-shaped pillows, to name but two.
- a soft toy of Gloomy Bear, the teddy with attitude (and blood dripping from his claws and fangs), created by Ōsaka illustrator Mori Chack. It's available from Kiddyland (see below) and other toy shops.
- a portable bidet (keitai washlet) from the household sections of Akiba's electronics stores (see pp.223–224). You simply never know when one might come in handy.
- a "golden poo" lucky charm. These little gilded piles were inspired by a play on the first syllable of the word unko, which can either mean "lucky" or "shit".

the world market. For more traditional toys and novelties, head for the nostalgia-filled stalls of Asakusa (see p.87).

Don Quixote
ドン・キホーテ

1-16-5 Kabuki-chō, Shinjuku-ku ☎03/5291-9211, ⓦwww.donki.com; see map, pp.106–107. A mind-boggling array of stuff is piled high and sold cheap here – everything from liquor to sex toys and gadgets galore. Worth visiting just for the gawp factor. There are branches in Roppongi (3-14-10 Roppongi, Minato-ku; see map, p.79) and Akihabara (4-3-3 Sotokanda, Chiyoda-ku; see map, p.67). Shinjuku Station. Daily 24 hr.

Hakoinu

Mori Bldg, 8-13-23 Akasaka, Minato-ku ☎03/3796-6044, ⓦwww.hakoinu.com; see map, p.76. Only the hard of heart would not be enchanted by Hakoinu (the name means "box dog"), a cute creation by illustrator Sato Emei, and the even cuter background story that goes with it. Proof that great toys don't need to be sophisticated or an X-box. Akasaka Station. Mon–Fri 11am–6.30pm.

Hakuhinkan Toy Park
博品館

8-8-11 Ginza, Chūō-ku ☎03/3571-8008, ⓦwww.hakuhinkan.co.jp; see map, p.60. This huge toy shop also houses a theatre staging Japanese-language shows which might entertain junior – or at least distract him from spending up a storm on your behalf.

And you might want to keep quiet about the 24hr vending machine outside. Shimbashi Station. Daily 11am–8pm.

Kiddyland

6-1-9 Jingūmae, Shibuya-ku ☎03/3409-3431, ⓦwww.kiddyland.co.jp; see map, p.118. Six floors of toys, stationery, sweets and other souvenirs. Meiji-jingūmae Station. Daily 10am–8pm, closed every third Tues.

Mandarake

5-52-15 Nakano, Nakano-ku ☎03/3228-0007, ⓦwww.mandarake.co.jp. If you're into character dolls and plastic figures (figua) based on anime and manga, this multiple outlet operation in the Broadway shopping centre is the place to head. They also have a wide range of secondhand manga as well posters, cards and even costumes if you fancy dressing up as your favourite manga character. There's also a branch in Shibuya (B2F Shibuya Beam Building, 31-2 Udagawa-chō; see map, p.122). Nakano Station. Daily noon–8pm.

Village Vanguard

B1F 3-14 Kanda-Ogawamachi, Chiyoda-ku ☎03/5281-5535; see map, p.67. This "exciting bookstore" stocks an amazing hotchpotch of toys and novelties, from inflatable bananas to Batman accessories – oh, yes, and a few fun books and CDs. Jimbōchō or Ogawamachi stations. Daily 10am–11pm.

Art galleries

Tokyo's **contemporary art galleries** are a bit of a lucky dip: some are formal affairs representing some of the brightest stars of Japan's vibrant art scene, though the vast majority are little more than a single room rented out to amateur groups or aspiring individuals. This chapter covers the best of the commercial galleries; major art museums such as the National Art Center and Mori Art Museum in Roppongi (see p.82), the Hara Museum of Contemporary Art (see p.132) and the Museum of Contemporary Art in Miyoshi (see p.74) are reviewed elsewhere.

The bulk of the commercial galleries can be found in Ginza and its northern neighbours Kyōbashi and Nihombashi, though the majority are pretty conservative in what they show. For more challenging work, search out the galleries in the Kiyosumi Gallery complex (see p.237) and in the Roppongi area, where the creation of the Roppongi Art Triangle (see p.81) is attracting new galleries to the area and refocusing attention on older ones.

The best place to look for listings of exhibitions is Ⓦ www.tokyoartbeat.com. *Metropolis* magazine also has selective art listings. Alternatively, try one of the galleries below, where you can pick up fliers for other venues around town. And if you happen to be in town during the annual **Art Fair Tokyo** (Ⓦ www.artfairtokyo .com; dates vary), it's well worth going along: the three-day event brings together around one hundred selected galleries with a strong focus on contemporary work.

Contemporary Japanese artists

The international success of artists such as **Nara Yoshitomo** and **Murakami Takashi** has shaped the world's perception of Japanese contemporary art during the last decade. Nara's imagery, which includes large-headed children with expressions ranging from angelic to evil, can be seen at *AtoZ* (see p.169), the café he helped create in Aoyama, while Murakami's colourful cartoon creations – such as smiling flowers and a blobby morphing character known as DOB – are plastered all over Roppongi Hills (see p.81).

The new wave of artists is led by **Matsuura Hiroyuki** and **Nishizawa Chiharu**. Matsuura, a one-time maker of models of manga characters, now produces ambiguous but dynamic canvases that have been described as "manga as fine art". Nishizawa's work uses the elevated point of view of traditional Japanese painting, but portrays the emptiness of modern life, sometimes featuring distant, uniform figures of salarymen, perhaps engaged in acts of violence or debauchery. Other artists to look out for include **Ito Zon**, known for his delicate drawings, embroideries and video works that explore nature; and **Yamaguchi Akira**, whose mystical paintings are rooted in traditional Asian aesthetics and display a masterful technique.

Ginza and around

The places listed below appear on the map on p.60.

Gallery Koyanagi

8F 1-7-5 Ginza, Chūō-ku ☎03/3561-1896, ⓦwww.gallerykoyanagi.com. Innovative gallery representing a varied group of Japanese and international artists. Exhibitions change monthly. Ginza-itchōme Station. Tues–Sat 11am–7pm.

Gallery Natsuka

8F 5-8-17 Ginza, Chūō-ku ☎03/3571-0130, ⓦwww.ginza.co.jp/natsuka. Well-respected gallery showcasing young local artists. Ginza Station. Mon–Sat 11.30am–6.30pm.

Gallery Tsubaki

3-3-10 Kyōbashi, Chūō-ku ☎03/3281-7808, ⓦwww.gallery-tsubaki.jp. Representing about forty artists, mostly Japanese, this interesting little place is tucked down a sidestreet just west of Chūō-dōri. Kyōbashi Station. Daily 11am–6.30pm.

Maison Hermès

8F 5-4-1 Ginza, Chūō-ku ☎03/3569-3611. At the top of the distinctive, Renzo Piano-designed "bubble-wrap" building, home to Hermès' Toky boutique, this gallery hosts themed shows of both Japanese and international art. Ginza Station. Daily 11am–7pm.

Shiseidō Gallery

B1F 8-8-3 Ginza, Chūō-ku ☎03/3572-3901, ⓦwww.shiseido.co.jp/gallery/html. Located in the distinctive red showroom of the Japanese cosmetics giant Shiseidō, this basement gallery hosts group and solo shows. Ginza or Shimbashi stations. Tues–Sat 11am–7pm, Sun 11am–6pm.

Tokyo Gallery
東京画廊

7F 8-10-5 Ginza, Chūō-ku ☎03/3571-1808 ⓦwww.tokyo-gallery.com. Dating back to 1950, Tokyo Gallery shows cutting-edge work from the Chinese and Korean contemporary art scenes (they have a branch in Beijing) as well as pieces by collectable Japanese artists, including Matsuura Hiroyuki and Nishizawa Chiharu. Shimbashi Station. Mon–Fri 11am–7pm, Sat 11am–5pm.

Kagurazaka

Kodama Gallery
児玉画廊

4F 3-7 Nishigoken-chō ⓦwww.kodamagallery .com. Representing the up-and-coming artist Ito Zon. Ongoing projects involve artists such as Tanaka Hidekazu and Nohara Kenji. Kagurazaka Station. Tues–Sat 11am–7pm.

Naka-Meguro

Mizuma Art Gallery
ミヅマアートギャラリー

2F Fujiya Bldg, 1-3-9 Kami-meguro, Meguro-ku ☎03/3793-7931, ⓦwww.mizuma-art.co.jp; see map pp.128–129. In business since 1994, this gallery represents up-and-coming Japanese and overseas artists. Naka-meguro Station. Tues–Sat 11am–7pm.

Roppongi

The galleries listed here are shown on the maps on p.76 and p.79. The following Roppongi galleries were relocating at the time of writing but may well remain in the area; check their websites for details: Taro Nasu (ⓦwww.taronasugallery. com); Weissfeld (ⓦroentgenwerke.com); magical Artroom (ⓦwww.magical -artroom.com); Gallery Min Min (ⓦwww.galleryminmin.com) and Ota Fine Arts (ⓦwww.otafinearts.com).

Axis Gallery

4F Axis Bldg, 5-17-1 Roppongi, Minato-ku ☎03/5575-8655, ⓦwww.axisinc.co.jp. Larger-than-average space on the top floor of a building housing several design-related businesses. Their monthly magazine, on sale in the basement bookshop, carries information in English on the artists they feature. Roppongi Station. Daily 11am–7pm.

Le Bain

3-16-28 Nishi-Azabu, Minato-ku ☎03/3479-3843 ⓦwww.le-bain.com. Attached to the showroom of bathroom fittings company Reliance, this gallery specializes in interior design and crafts. Also here are a boutique with design goods for sale and the beautiful Japanese sweet shop and tearoom *Ori Higashiya* (see p.186). Roppongi Station. Tues–Sun 11am–7pm.

Gallery Saka

9-5-12 Akasaka, Minato-ku ☎03/3401-6446. Created in 1988 by Yuri Sakakura as a memorial to her late husband Junzo, a celebrated Japanese architect who worked with Le Corbusier in Paris in the mid-1930s, this shows work by young artists and architects and has a lovely location bordering

Tokyo Midtown. Roppongi Station. Tues–Sat 11am–6pm.

Striped House Gallery

5-10-33 Roppongi, Minato-ku ☎03/3405-8108. Ⓦwww.striped-house.com. Taking its name from the striped brick building in which it's based, this gallery has an eclectic range of exhibitions, ranging from the alien-faced metal sculptures of Fujii Takehito to works from Poland and Cuba. Roppongi Station. Daily 11am–6.30pm.

Ryōgoku and around

Kiyosumi Gallery

1-3-2 Kiyosumi, Kōtō-ku; see map, p.72. Seven galleries above a warehouse, including Tomio Koyama Gallery (☎03/3642-4090, Ⓦwww.tomiokoyamagallery.com), which represents Murakami Takashi and Nara

Yoshitomo, among others. It's also worth checking out Shugo Arts (☎03/5621-6434, Ⓦwww.shugoarts.com), specializing in fine arts; Taka Ishii Gallery (☎03/5646-6050, Ⓦwww.takaishiigallery.com), for photo-graphs; and Hiromi Yoshii (☎03/5620-0555, Ⓦwww.hiromiyoshii.com), promoting young artists. Kiyosumi-Shirakawa Station. All Tues–Sat noon–7pm.

Yanaka

SCAI The Bathhouse

6-1-23 Yanaka, Taitō-ku ☎03/3821-1144, Ⓦwww.scaithebathhouse.com; see map, p.91. Occupying a 200-year-old bathhouse in northern Tokyo, SCAI hosts a range of exhibitions, lectures, performance art and so forth. Nezu or Nippori stations. Tues–Sat noon–7pm, though phone ahead to be sure.

Public baths, onsen and spas

Until just a few decades ago, when people began installing bathrooms at home, life in Tokyo's residential neighbourhoods focused round the **sentō**, the public bath. Though you no longer find them every few blocks, a surprising number of bathhouses survive, of which we've given a sampler below.

The *sentō* have been recently joined by a number of enormous **onsen** (hot spring) complexes, notably Spa LaQua in Suidōbashi and Ōedo Onsen Monogatari in Odaiba. Both are much more expensive than a traditional *sentō*, but offer extensive bathing facilities, a range of places to eat and relaxation areas with very comfortable reclining chairs. Then there are the **luxury spas**, often attached to top-end hotels and offering all sorts of treatments and therapies, but which aren't necessarily fed with hot-spring water. For a spot of real self-indulgence, treat yourself to one of the swanky spas in the *Grand Hyatt* (see p.150), *Park Hyatt* (see p.152), *Ritz Carlton* (see p.150), *Mandarin Oriental* (see p.148) or *Peninsula* (see p.148) hotels.

Taking a traditional Japanese bath, whether in an onsen, a *sentō* or a ryokan, is a ritual that's definitely worth mastering. Key points to remember are that everyone uses the same water and that the bathtub is only for soaking. It's therefore essential to wash and rinse the soap off thoroughly – showers and bowls are provided, as well as soap and shampoo in most cases – before stepping into the bath. Ryokan and the more upmarket public bathhouses provide small towels (bring your own or buy one on the door if using a cheaper *sentō*), though no one minds full nudity. Nowadays most baths are **segregated**, so memorize the *kanji* for male (男) and female (女).

Asakusa

Asakusa Kannon Onsen
浅草観音温泉
2-7-26 Asakusa, Taitō-ku ☎03/3844-4141; see map, p.85. This big, old ivy-covered bathhouse isn't the cheapest *sentō* around, but it's right next to Sensō-ji and uses real onsen water. The clientele ranges from *yakuza* to grannies – very Asakusa. Asakusa Station. Daily except Wed 6.30am–6pm; ¥700.

Jakotsu-yu
蛇骨湯
1-11-11 Asakusa, Taitō-ku ☎03/3841-8641, ⓦwww.jakotsuyu.co.jp; see map, p.85. Traditional neighbourhood bathhouse down a back alley just south of Rox department store. It's fed with what they call "black", mineral-rich hot-spring water; one bath is designed to give you a mild but stimulating electric shock. Each section also has a small open-air bath (*rotemburo*). Asakusa (Tsukuba Express

railway) or Tawaramachi stations. Daily except Tues 1pm–midnight; ¥430.

Odaiba

Ōedo Onsen Monogatari
大江戸温泉物語
2-57 Omi, Koto-ku ☎**03/5500-1126,** ⓦ**www .ooedoonsen.jp; see map, p.135**. More of a theme park than a bathhouse, this giant onsen on the southwestern edge of Odaiba goes in for nostalgic kitsch in a big way. There are free outdoor footbaths, though you'll have to pay extra for the one in which tiny fish nibble the dead skin from your feet, and for the hot-sand bath and the range of massages. In the large dining and relaxation area street performers keep the atmosphere jolly. There are free shuttle buses from Shinagawa and Tokyo stations. Admission fee includes a colourful *yukata* and towels. Telecom Centre Station (Yurikamome monorail). Daily 11am–9pm; ¥2872, or ¥1987 after 6pm.

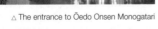

△ The entrance to Ōedo Onsen Monogatari

Roppongi and around

Adam Eve
3-5-5 Nishi-Azabu, Minato-ku ☎**03/5474-4489; see map, p.76**. Looking like a ship stranded mid-city, this long-time favourite sauna and scrub parlour is nothing fancy, but the traditional Korean-style Akasuri massage (¥4000) or bamboo salt massage (¥8000) are the real

thing. General entry is ¥3800 for the bath and sauna. Roppongi Station. Daily 24hr.

Azabu-Jūban Onsen
麻布十番温泉
1-5-22 Azabu-Jūban, Minato-ku ☎**03/3404-2610; Azabu-Jūban Station; see map, p.79**. Two options here – the no-frills ground-floor *sentō* (¥400) and the classier baths upstairs (¥1260, or ¥940 after 6pm). Either way, the brown, mineral-rich onsen water is scalding hot. Daily except Tues: *sentō* 3–11pm; upstairs baths 11am–9am.

Shu Sanctuary
2F Galleria, Tokyo Midtown 9-7-4 Akasaka, Minato-ku ☎**03/5413-7202; see map, p.76**. Make-up and beauty supremo Shu Uemura's complex of spas and cosmetic outlets occupies a pure white corridor down one side of Midtown. Here you might want to check out the first overseas branch of the men's grooming spa The Refinery London (☎03/5413-7202 ⓦwww .the-refinery.jp), whose signature face and body treatment package (¥27,000) has been a hit with Tokyo's metro-sexual males. Roppongi Station. Daily 11am–11pm.

Suidōbashi

Spa LaQua
6F 1-1-1 Kasuga, Bunkyō-ku ☎**03/5800-9999,** ⓦ**www.laqua.jp; see map, p.67**. Spread over five floors, this is by far the most sophisticated of Tokyo's bathing complexes, and uses real onsen water pumped from 1700m underground. Admission includes towels and loose pyjamas to wear around the complex. It's also a great place to pass the time if you miss the last train home. Suidōbashi Station. Daily 11am–9am; Mon–Fri ¥2565, Sat & Sun ¥2880; ¥1890 surcharge midnight–6am. Access to the Healing Baden set of special therapeutic saunas (11am–1pm) costs ¥525 extra.

Directory

Airlines Aeroflot ☎03/5532-8701; Air Canada ☎03/5404-8800; Air China ☎03/5251-0711; Air France ☎03/3570-8577; Air India ☎03/3508-0261; Air New Zealand ☎03/5521-2727; Air Pacific ☎03/5208-5171; Alitalia ☎0476/32-7811; American Airlines ☎03/4550-2111; ANA ☎0120-029709; Asiana Airlines ☎03/5812-6600; British Airways ☎03/3570-8657; Cathay Pacific ☎03/5159-1700; China Airlines ☎03/5520-0333; China Eastern Airlines ☎03/3506-1166; Continental Airlines ☎03/5464-5050; Delta Airlines ☎03/3593-6666; Dragonair ☎03/5159-1715; Garuda Indonesia ☎03/3240-6171; Ibex Airlines ☎03/6471-6688; Japan Airlines (JAL) ☎0120-255931; KLM ☎03/3570-8770; Korean Air ☎03/5443-3311; Lufthansa ☎00120-051844; Malaysian Airlines ☎03/5733-2111; Northwest Airlines ☎0476/31-8000; Philippine Airlines ☎03/5157-4362; Qantas ☎03/3593-7000; Singapore Airlines ☎03/3213-3431; Thai Airways International ☎03/3503-3311; United Airlines ☎03/3817-4411; Virgin Atlantic ☎03/3499-8811. JAL and ANA also operate domestic services, as do the following: Air Do ☎03/6741-1122; Skymark Airlines ☎03/3433-7670; Skynet Asia Airways ☎03/5757-8107; Starflyer ☎03/5641-1489.

Bike rental The cheapest place to rent bikes is in the underground Sumida Park bicycle park beside the bridge in Asakusa (daily 6am–8pm; ¥200 for 24hr, ¥500 for 7 days; ☎03/5246-1305); they only have 30 bikes, so you'll need to get there early at weekends and on public holidays. Muji in Yūrakuchō (see p.232) rents bikes for ¥525 per day (¥1050 on Saturdays, Sundays and holidays), plus a ¥3000 cash deposit. Otherwise, you'll find rental outfits listed on ⊛cycle-tokyo.cycling.co.jp, as

well as lots of useful information about cycling in Tokyo.

Embassies Australia, 2-1-14 Mita, Minato-ku ☎03/5232-4111; Canada, 7-3-38 Akasaka, Minato-ku ☎03/5412-6200; China, 3-4-33 Moto-Azabu, Minato-ku ☎03/3403-3380; Ireland, 2-10-7 Kōjimachi, Chiyoda-ku ☎03/3263-0695; New Zealand, 20-40 Kamiyamachō, Shibuya-ku ☎03/3467-2271; Russian Federation, 2-1-1 Azabudai, Minato-ku ☎03/3583-4224; South Africa, 2-7-9 Hirakawachō, Chiyoda-ku ☎03/3265-3366; South Korea 1-2-5 Minami-Azabu, Minato-ku ☎03/3452-7611; UK, 1 Ichibanchō, Chiyoda-ku ☎03/5211-1100; US, 1-10-5 Akasaka, Minato-ku ☎03/3224-5000.

Emergencies Police ☎110; fire and ambulance ☎119. The Tokyo Metropolitan Police have an English-language hotline on ☎03/3501-0110 (Mon–Fri 8.30am–5.15pm). Japan Helpline (☎0570-000-911, ⊛www .jhelp.com/en/jhlp.html) provides 24hr general advice in English. Tokyo English Life Line (TELL; ☎03/5774-0992, ⊛www.tel jp .com) provides telephone counselling (daily 9am–11pm).

Hospitals and clinics To find an English-speaking doctor and the hospital or clinic best suited to your needs, phone the Tokyo Medical Information Service (☎03/5285-8181, ⊛www.himawari.metro.tokyo.jp; Mon–Fri 9am–8pm); they can also provide emergency medical translation services over the phone. Two major hospitals with English-speaking doctors are St Luke's International Hospital, 9-1 Akashichō, Chūō-ku (☎03/3541-5151, ⊛www.luk.or .jp) and Tokyo Adventist Hospital, 3-17-3 Amanuma, Suginami-ku (☎03/3392-6151); their reception desks are open Monday to Friday 8.30 to 11am for non-emergency cases. Among several private clinics with

English-speaking staff, try Tokyo Medical and Surgical Clinic, 32 Shiba-kōen Building, 3-4-30 Shiba-kōen, Minato-ku (T03/3436-3028, Wwww.tmsc.jp; by appointment only Mon–Fri 8.30am–5.30pm, Sat 8.30am–noon), or the International Clinic, 1-5-9 Azabudai, Minato-ku (T03/3583-7831; Mon–Fri 9am–6pm).

Immigration To renew tourist or student visas, apply to the Tokyo Regional Immigration Bureau, 5-5-30 Konan, Minato-ku (T03/5796-7112, Wwww.immi-moj.go.jp; Mon–Fri 9am–noon & 1–4pm). To reach it, take the Konan exit from Shinagawa Station and then bus #99 from bus stop 8. Go early in the day since the process takes forever.

Left luggage Most hotels will keep luggage for a few days. If not, the baggage room (daily 8am–8pm) at Tokyo Station takes bags for up to fifteen days at a daily rate of ¥410 for the first five days and ¥820 per day thereafter. At the time of writing the baggage room was located at the far southeast end of the station, beyond the Highway Bus stops, but it may be moved once the redevelopment of the station is complete. Note that coin lockers (¥300–800 depending on the size) can only be used for a maximum of three days.

Lost property If you've lost something, try the local police box (kōban). Alternatively, ask your hotel to help call the following offices to reclaim lost property: taxis T03/3648-0300; JR T03/3231-1880; Tokyo Metro T03/3834-5577; Toei bus and subway T03/3812-2011. If all else fails, contact the Metropolitan Police Lost and Found Office on T03/3501-0110.

Pharmacies The American Pharmacy, Marunouchi Building, 2-4-1 Marunouchi, Chiyoda-ku (Mon–Fri 9am–9pm, Sat 10am–9pm, Sun 10am–8pm; T03/5220-7716), has English-speaking pharmacists and a good range of drugs and general medical supplies. It also has outlets in Ikebukuro (B1F Alpa, Sunshine City, 3-1 Higashi-Ikebukuro, Toshima-ku) and Ueno station (Atré Mall, 7-1-1 Ueno, Taitō-ku). Alternatively, try the National Azabu Pharmacy (T03/3442-3495), above the National Azabu supermarket (nearest subway station Hiro-o). Major hotels usually stock a limited array of common medicines.

Ticket agencies To buy tickets for theatre performances, concerts and sporting events, it's best, in the first instance, to approach one of the major advance ticket agencies. Ticket Pia (T03/5237-9999, Wt.pia.co.jp) has outlets in the main city areas, such as Ginza, Ikebukuro, Shibuya and Shinjuku, or try phoning Lawson (T0570-000-777, Wwww2.lawsonticket.com) or CN Playguide (T03/5802-9999, Wwww.cnplayguide.com). Major events sell out quickly; don't expect to be able to buy tickets at the venue door.

Travel agents For international tickets, try one of the following English-speaking agents: No. 1 Travel (7F Don Quixote Building, 1-16-5 Kabuki-chō, Shinjuku-ku T03/3200-6073, Wwww.no1-travel.com); A'cross Traveller's Bureau (2F Yamate-Shinjuku Building, 1-19-6 Nishi-Shinjuku, Shinjuku-ku T03/3340-6745, Wwww.across-travel.com); and Hit Travel (5F Okayama Building, 7-5-11 Nishi-Shinjuku, Shinjuku-ku T03/53484363, Wwww.hittravel.co.jp). The main domestic travel agents, with branches all over Tokyo, are Japan Travel Bureau (JTB; T03/5620-9500, Wwww.jtb.co.jp); Nippon Travel Agency (T03/3572-8744, Wwww.nta.co.jp); and Kinki Nippon Tourist (T03/3255-7137, Wwww.knt.co.jp).

Beyond the city

Beyond the City

26

Nikkō and around

I f you make one trip from Tokyo, it should be to the pilgrim town of
NIKKŌ (日光), 128km north of the capital, where the World Heritage-listed
Tōshō-gū shrine complex sits amid mountains crisscrossed by outstanding
hiking trails within the Nikkō National Park. Tōshō-gū attracts masses of
Japanese tourists year round, who tramp dutifully around the shrine and the
surrounding holy buildings. After you've done the same, it's worth investigating
the far less crowded **Nikkō Tōshō-gū Museum of Art**, and the **Nikkō
Tamozawa Imperial-villa Memorial Park**, then crossing the Daiya-gawa to
explore the dramatically named **Ganman-ga-fuchi abyss**, which is in fact a
tranquil riverside walk. The most beautiful parts of the national park are around
Chūzenji-ko lake, some 17km from Nikkō, and the quieter resort of **Yumoto**,
higher in the mountains.

With a very early start from Tokyo you could attempt to see both Tōshō-gū and
Chūzenji-ko in a long day-trip, though cramming both into one day during the
peak summer and autumn seasons is impossible. It's best to stay **overnight** to get
the most out of the excursion; Nikkō has plenty of accommodation, covering all
categories, and is the best base for seeing the area. If you want to be closer to
nature or are looking for a quieter environment, consider staying up at Chūzenji-
ko or Yumoto.

Access to Nikkō

The simplest way of reaching Nikkō is to take a Tōbu-Nikkō from Asakusa in
Tokyo (the station is in the basement of the Matsuya department store and
connected by tunnel to Asakusa subway station). An alternative access point for
this line is Kita-Senju Station on both the Hibiya and Chiyoda subway lines.
Kaisoku (rapid) trains make the journey in around two hours and twenty
minutes and cost ¥1320 one way. The "Spacia" *tokkyū* (limited express) takes
just under two hours, and costs ¥2740. On some trains you'll need to change
at Shimo-Imaichi. Tōbu also run one early morning direct train to Nikkō
from Shinjuku and Ikebukuro, but the Nikkō Pass (see below) isn't valid for
travel on it.

Tōbu offers various **travel passes** covering the return trip from Tokyo and
transport around the Nikkō area. These tickets, which can only be bought at Tōbu
stations, include the fare from Asakusa to Nikkō (express train surcharges for the
Spacia still apply), unlimited use of local buses, and discounts on entrance charges
at many of the area's attractions, including the cable cars and boat trips at
Chūzenji-ko. It's not worth buying the pass if you only intend to visit Tōshō-gū,
but if you're planning a trip out to Chūzenji-ko, the most useful ticket is the two-
day All Nikkō Pass (¥4400). For further details of all the passes and train times, see
Ⓦwww.tobuland.com/foreign/english/nikkopass.html.

You can also reach Nikkō on JR trains but the fares are higher, so travelling with JR only makes sense if you have a rail pass from them. The fastest route (around 2hr total) is by Shinkansen from either Tokyo or Ueno to **Utsunomiya** (宇都宮), where you change to the JR Nikkō line for a local train to the JR Nikkō terminus, a minute's walk east of the Tōbu station.

Arrival, information and accommodation

Tōbu Nikkō Station, resembling a giant Swiss chalet, and the JR Nikkō Station, a historic wooden building designed by Frank Lloyd Wright, are side by side, at the foot of the town, next to a small plaza surrounded by gift shops; the main road in the western corner runs up to Tōshō-gū. Inside both stations there are luggage lockers and, at Tōbu, an information desk (daily 8.30am–5pm; ☎0288/53-4511), where the assistant speaks some English and can provide you with maps and leaflets on the area. **Buses** up to the lake and on to Yumoto run at fairly frequent intervals from the train stations between 6am and 6pm. If you haven't bought a Tōbu pass, it's still possible to save money on transport by buying a two-day **bus pass** at either train station. For unlimited return trips to Chūzenji the cost is ¥2000, while to Yumoto it's ¥3000.

The main **tourist office** is the Nikkō Kyōdo Centre (daily 8.30am–5pm; ☎0288/54-2496, ⓦ www.nikko-jp.org), on the main road from the station to the Tōshō-gū complex; from 11am there's usually an English-speaking volunteer here. The centre has an attached gallery (daily 8.30am–5pm) showcasing local art and showing short videos – with English commentaries – on Nikkō. If you're planning on walking in the area, pick up copies of the excellent English-language *Guidebook for Walking Trails* (¥150) and the free *Tourist Guide of Nikkō*, both of which feature good maps and pictures of local flora and fauna.

Internet access (¥100 per 30min) is also available at the centre, and at the restaurants *Asian Garden* and *Hippari Dako* (see p.252). The main **post office** (Mon–Fri 8.45am–7pm, Sat & Sun 9am–5pm), on the approach road to Tōshō-gū, has an **ATM** which accepts foreign-issued cards, as do the ones in the post offices opposite Tōbu Station and up at Chūzenji; otherwise, it's near impossible to use credit cards in the town.

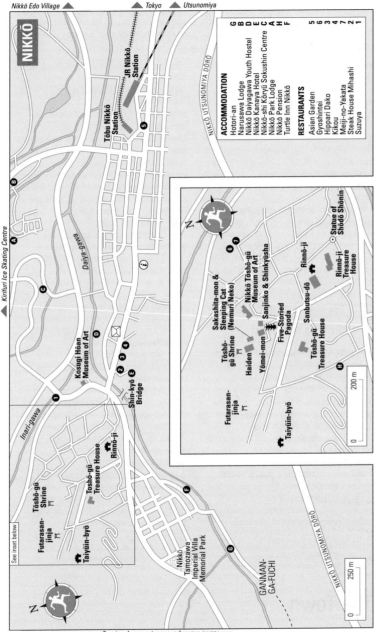

NIKKŌ

Nikkō Edo Village ▲   ▲ Tokyo   ▲ Utsunomiya

Kirifuri Ice Skating Centre ▲

Yashio Municipal Onsen, Chūzenji-ko, Kegon Falls & Yumoto ▲

ACCOMMODATION

Hotori-an	G
Narusawa Lodge	B
Nikkō Daiyagawa Youth Hostel	D
Nikkō Kanaya Hotel	E
Nikkō-shi Kōryū Sokushin Centre	C
Nikkō Park Lodge	A
Nikkō Pension	H
Turtle Inn Nikkō	F

RESTAURANTS

Asian Garden	5
Gyoshintei	6
Hippari Dako	3
Kikou	4
Meiji-no-Yakata	7
Steak House Mihashi	2
Suzuya	1

JR Nikkō Station

Tōbu Nikkō Station

NIKKŌ UTSUNOMIYA DŌRO

Daiya-gawa

Kosugi Hōan Museum of Art

Shin-kyō Bridge

Inari-gawa

Tōshō-gū Shrine

Futarasan-jinja

Tōshō-gū Treasure House

Rinnō-ji

Taiyūin-byō

See inset below

Nikkō Tamozawa Imperial Villa Memorial Park

GANMAN-GA-FUCHI

NIKKŌ UTSUNOMIYA DŌRO

0   250 m

Futarasan-jinja

Tōshō-gū Shrine

Haiden

Yōmei-mon

Sakashita-mon & Sleeping Cat (Nemuri Neko)

Nikkō Tōshō-gū Museum of Art

Sanjinko & Shinkyūsha

Five-Storied Pagoda

Tōshō-gū Treasure House

Sanbutsu-dō

Rinnō-ji

Rinnō-ji Treasure House

Statue of Shōdō Shōnin

Taiyūin-byō

0   200 m

N

Accommodation

Reservations are essential to stay in Nikkō in peak holiday seasons and autumn. Rates at virtually all places are slightly higher in August, from October to early November, and during major holidays. Note that there are also several good places to stay up at Chūzenji and Yumoto (see p.254).

Hotori-an
ほとり庵

8-28 Takumi-chō ☎ 0288/53-3663, ⓦ www .turtle-nikko.com. The modern annexe to the *Turtle Inn* (see below) is set in a tranquil location beside the path to the Ganman-ga-fuchi abyss and has good-value en-suite tatami rooms. There's a pottery shop and a bath with forest views. Dinner is served at the *Turtle Inn*. From ¥12,400.

Narusawa Lodge
鳴沢ロッジ

1 Tokorono ☎ & Ⓕ 0288/54-1630, ⓦ www .nikko-narusawa.com. A delightful minshuku, surrounded by flowers and set well away from the tourist throng. The tatami rooms are lovely, the shared bathrooms are spotless and the people who run it are very friendly and speak a little English. They'll also let you take their pet beagle for a walk. Prices drop by ¥300 per person if you stay more than one night. From ¥7500.

Nikkō Daiyagawa Youth Hostel
日光大谷川ユースホステル

1075 Naka-Hatsuishi-machi ☎ 0288/54-1974, ⓦ www.jyh.or.jp. From the main road to Tōshō-gū, you can follow English signposts pointing the way down a narrow back path to this cosy hostel, facing the river. It's run by a very hospitable family and deservedly gets rave reviews. Dinner (¥840; book ahead) is good. Dorms ¥2730 per person.

Nikkō Kanaya Hotel

1300 Kami-Hatsuishi-machi ☎ 0288/54-0001, ⓦ www.kanayahotel.co.jp. This charming heritage property, practically a museum piece, remains Nikkō's top Western-style hotel, harking back to the glamorous days of early twentieth-century travel. There are some cheaper rooms with en-suite shower or just a toilet (the hotel has a communal bath) but for the full effect, splash out on the deluxe grade. From ¥14,000.

Nikkō-shi Kōryū Sokushin Centre
日光市交流促進センター

2854 Tokorono ☎ 0288/54-1013, ⓦ www.city .nikko.tochigi.jp/nyh. On the far side of the Daiya-gawa from the town, this hostel/hotel has a secluded location behind the high school. The en-suite tatami rooms are excellent and have good views of the town, and there are also Western-style rooms, a laundry and a small kitchen for self-caterers. Curfew at 10pm. From ¥8000.

Nikkō Park Lodge

2828-5 Tokorono, ☎ 0288/53-1201, ⓦ www.nikkoparklodge.com. A great new hostel, owned by genial Ken Sakamoto (who speaks fluent English), in a lovely spot high up on the north bank of the river. Vegan dinners are ¥1500 and they offer a daily Zen yoga class at 7am (guests/non-guests ¥300/500). Dorm beds ¥2990; single rooms from ¥3990; doubles from ¥8000.

Nikkō Pension
日光ペンション

10-9 Nishi-sandō ☎ 0288/53-3636, ⓦ www .nikko-pension.jp. Eccentric decorations (including an organ, stained-glass windows and mock-Tudor facade) enliven this small Western-style hotel close by Tōshō-gū. The rooms are comfy and excellent value, and there's also French-influenced cooking and an onsen. From ¥11,600.

Turtle Inn Nikkō

2-16 Takumi-chō ☎ 0288/53-3168, ⓦ www .turtle-nikko.com. Popular pension run by an English-speaking family in a quiet location next to the Daiya-gawa. There are small, plain tatami rooms with common bathrooms, and en-suite Western-style rooms, plus a cosy lounge. Add ¥2100 for the evening meal. From ¥9000.

The Town

First impressions of Nikkō as you come out of either train station aren't great – the uphill approach to the shrine is lined with tatty shops and houses. However, the walk along the town's main street takes no more than fifteen minutes, and frequent buses head towards the main approach to Tōshō-gū.

Despite its popularity as a tourist destination today, barely a century ago, in the wake of the Meiji Restoration, Nikkō was running to seed. It was foreign diplomats and businesspeople who began to favour it as a highland retreat from the heat of summer in Tokyo; grand villas such as the Meiji-no-Yakata (see p.251) were built and the *Kanaya Inn* – now the *Nikkō Kanaya Hotel* – was founded by Zenichiro Kanaya in 1873.

Shin-kyō bridge and Rinnō-ji

At the top of the main street is one of the town's most famous landmarks, the red-lacquered **Shin-kyō bridge** (神橋; ¥300; daily 9am–4pm). Legend has it that when the Buddhist priest Shōdō Shōnin visited Nikkō in the eighth century he was helped across the Daiya-gawa at this very spot by the timely appearance of two snakes, who formed a bridge and then vanished. The original arched wooden structure first went up in 1636, but has been reconstructed many times since, most recently in 2005. Unless you must have a close-up shot of the bridge, there's little need to pay the entrance fee, as the structure is clearly visible from the road.

Take the left-hand path uphill across from the bridge and you'll emerge in front of the main compound of **Rinnō-ji** (輪王寺; April–Oct 8am–4.30pm; Nov–March 8am–3.30pm; ¥400), a Tendai Buddhist temple founded in 766 by Shōdō Shōnin; his statue stands on a rock at the entrance. The large, red-painted hall, **Sanbutsu-dō**, houses three giant gilded statues: the thousand-handed Kannon, the Amida Buddha and the fearsome horse-headed Kannon. It's worth paying to view these awe-inspiring figures from directly beneath their lotus-flower perches (entry is included in the combination ticket, which you can buy at the booth outside). Rinnō-ji's **Treasure House** (Hōmotsuden; 宝物殿; daily 8am–5pm; ¥300), opposite the Sanbutsu-dō, has some interesting items on display, but its nicest feature is the attached Shōyō-en, an elegant garden with a strolling route around a small pond.

Tōshō-gū

Although Nikkō has been a holy place in the Buddhist and Shinto religions for over a thousand years (a hermitage was built here in the eighth century), its fortunes only took off with the death of **Tokugawa Ieyasu** in 1616. In his will, the shogun requested that a shrine be built here in his honour. However the complex, completed in 1617, was deemed not nearly impressive enough by Ieyasu's grandson, **Tokugawa Iemitsu**, who ordered work to begin on the elaborate mausoleum seen today. Iemitsu's dazzling vision was driven by practical as well as aesthetic considerations: he wanted to stop rival lords amassing money of their own, so he ordered the *daimyō* to supply the materials for the shrine, and to pay the thousands of craftsmen.

You can save money if you buy the right ticket for Nikkō's main temples and shrines. If you intend to see Rinnō-ji, Tōshō-gū and Futarasan-jinja, buy the ¥1000 *nisha-ichiji* **combination ticket**, which includes entrance to the Taiyūin-byō and the roaring dragon hall (Honji-dō) in Tōshō-gū, but not the area of Tōshō-gū containing the sleeping cat carving and Ieyasu's tomb (these last two can be tacked onto the combination ticket for an additional ¥520). The combination ticket can be bought from booths beside the Sanbutsu-dō hall in Rinnō-ji and outside the Omote-mon gate to Tōshō-gū.

The mausoleum was completed in 1634, and ever since the jury has been out on its over-the-top design, the antithesis of the usually austere Shinto shrines, and often considered overbearingly gaudy. Whatever you make of it, **Tōshō-gū** (the name means "sunlight") – along with the slightly more restrained Taiyūin-byō mausoleum of Iemitsu – is entirely successful at conveying the immense power and wealth of the Tokugawa dynasty.

The shrine complex

Broad, tree-lined Omotesandō leads up to the main **entrance** to Tōshō-gū (東照宮; daily: April–Oct 8am–4.30pm; Nov–March 8am–3.30pm), just to the west of Rinnō-ji. You'll pass under a giant stone *torii* gate (one of the few remaining features of the original 1617 shrine), while on the left is an impressive red and green five-storey pagoda, an 1819 reconstruction of a 1650 original, which burned down. Ahead is the Omote-mon gate, the entrance to the main shrine precincts, where you'll need to hand over a section of your combination ticket or Tōshō-gū and sleeping cat-only ticket (¥1300), either of which can be bought from the booth in front of the gate.

Inside the precincts, turn left to reach the **Three Sacred Storehouses** (Sanjinko) on the right and the **Sacred Stables** (Shinkyūsha) on the left. There's usually a crowd of amateur photographers in front of the stables jostling to capture one of Tōshō-gū's many famous painted woodcarvings – the "hear no evil, see no evil, speak no evil" **monkeys**, which represent the three major principles of Tendai Buddhism. The route leads to the steps up to the dazzling **Yōmei-mon** (Sun Blaze Gate), with wildly ornate carvings, gilt and intricate decoration. Impressive as it is, the gate has less dramatic impact than the detailed panels on the flanking walls, which are adorned with fantastic flowers and birds. A belfry and drum tower stand alone in front of the gate. Behind the drum tower is the **Honji-dō** (¥50). This small hall is part of Rinnō-ji temple and contains a ceiling painting of a "roaring dragon"; a priest will demonstrate how to make the dragon roar by standing beneath its head and clapping to create an echo.

It's better to pay the small charge to see the roaring dragon rather than fork out ¥520 for the less impressive **sleeping cat** (*nemuri neko*) beyond the Yōmei-mon. You'd easily miss this minute carving, just above the Sakashita-mon gate to the right of the inner precinct, if it wasn't for the gawping crowd. Two hundred stone steps lead uphill from the gate to the surprisingly unostentatious **tomb of Ieyasu**, amid a glade of pines, and about the only corner of the shrine where tourists are generally absent.

Directly in front of the Yōmei-mon is the serene white and gold gate of **Kara-mon**, beyond which is the **Haiden**, or hall of worship. The side entrance to the hall is to the right of the gate; you'll need to remove your shoes and stop taking photographs. Inside, you can walk down into the Honden, the shrine's central hall, still decorated with its beautiful original paintwork.

Every year, on May 18, the **Grand Festival** re-stages the spectacular burial of Ieyasu at Tōshō-gū, with a cast of over one thousand costumed priests and warriors taking part in a colourful procession through the shrine grounds, topped off with horseback archery. It's well worth attending, as is the smaller-scale festival on October 17 – this doesn't have the archery and only lasts half a day, but does coincide with "Light Up Nikkō" (Oct 16–20), during which the major temple buildings are illuminated at night to great effect.

Nikkō Tōshō-gū Museum of Art and around

Before rushing off, check out the **Nikkō Tōshō-gū Museum of Art** (日光東照宮 美術館; daily: April–Oct 8am–5pm; Nov–March 8am–4pm; ¥800), at the back of the shrine complex, to the left as you walk out of the Omote-mon gate. This traditional, impressively simple wooden mansion dates from 1928 and is the former head office of the shrine. Inside, the sliding doors and screens were decorated by the top Japanese painters of the day and together constitute one of the most beautiful collections of this type of art that you'll see in Japan.

Not far east of here are the grounds of **Meiji-no-Yakata** (明治の館), the early twentieth-century holiday home of the American trade representative F.W. Horne. The various houses amid the trees are now fancy restaurants (see p.252), but it's worth wandering around even if you don't eat here to take in the pretty gardens and sylvan setting.

Following the road down hill from here towards the river will bring you to the modern, terracotta-coloured **Kosugi Hōan Museum of Art** (小杉放庵美術館; Tues–Sun 9.30am–4.30pm; ¥700), which displays the dreamily beautiful figurative and landscape paintings of local artist Hōan (1920–64). Concerts are occasionally held here in the evenings – ask at tourist information.

Futarasan-jinja and Taiyūin-byō

A trip around Tōshō-gū is likely to quench your appetite for sightseeing, but it's worth pressing on to some of the other temples and shrines in the surrounding woods. On leaving the main shrine, take the path next to Tōshō-gū's pagoda, and head west to the **Futarasan-jinja** (二荒山神社), whose simple red colour scheme comes as a relief to the senses. This shrine, originally established by the priest Shōdō Shōnin in 782, is the main one dedicated to the deity of Nantai-san, the volcano whose eruption created nearby Chūzenji-ko. There are some good paintings of animals and birds on votive plaques in the shrine's main hall, while the attached garden (¥200) offers a quiet retreat, with a small teahouse serving *matcha* green tea and sweets for ¥350. You can also inspect the *bakemono tōrō*, a "phantom lantern" made of bronze in 1292 and said to be possessed by demons.

Just beyond Futarasan-jinja, and bypassed by the tourist mêlée, is the charming **Taiyūin-byō** (大猷院廟; ¥550), which contains the mausoleum of the third shogun, Tokugawa Iemitsu, who died in 1651. This complex – part of Rinnō-ji and hidden away on a hillside, surrounded by lofty pines – was deliberately designed to be less ostentatious than Tōshō-gū. Look out for the green god of wind and the red god of thunder in the alcoves behind the Niten-mon gate, and the beautiful Kara-mon (Chinese-style gate) and fence surrounding the gold and black lacquer inner precincts.

Nikkō Tamozawa Imperial Villa Memorial Park and the Ganman-ga-fuchi abyss

In stark contrast to Nikkō's temples and shrines is the Zen-like simplicity of the beautifully restored **Nikkō Tamozawa Imperial Villa** (日光田母沢御用邸記念公園; daily except Tues 9am–4pm; ¥500). A ten-minute walk west of the Shin-kyō bridge along the main road, this 106-room residence, surrounded by manicured gardens (including a 400-year-old weeping cherry tree), combines buildings of widely different heritage, some parts dating back to 1632. Three emperors have lived in it, including the Emperor Akihito, who was evacuated here during the war. As you stroll the corridors, take time to appreciate the intricate details and the gorgeous screen paintings.

Another tranquil escape is close at hand. From the villa, take the road heading south down to the Daiya-gawa; five minutes' walk west along the river is the Ganman-bashi, a small bridge across from which begins the riverside pathway through the **Ganman-ga-fuchi abyss** (含満ヶ淵). Part of this restful walk, along the attractive and rocky river valley, is lined by the Narabi-jizō, some fifty decaying stone statues of Jizō, the Buddhist saint of travellers and children.

Eating

Avoid the bland tourist restaurants clustered around Nikkō's train and bus stations, and chances are you'll **eat** pretty well. The area's speciality is *yuba-ryōri* – thin, tasty strips of tofu, usually rolled into tubes and cooked in various stews; you're likely to be served this at your hotel or pension. Note that most restaurants here shut around 8pm.

Besides the establishments reviewed below, there's also the lovely second-floor dining room at the *Nikkō Kanaya Hotel* (see p.248), a meal in which will set you back at least ¥3500 for lunch and ¥6000 for dinner. The first-floor *Maple Leaf* coffee shop is cheaper, but much less glamorous. Best value is the *Yashio* Japanese restaurant, behind the coffee shop, which has set lunches for under ¥2000. The dark and cosy hotel **bar** is Nikkō's best spot for a nightcap.

Asian Garden
Opposite Tobu Nikkō Station. Indian restaurant with a good vegetarian set menu (¥950) and reasonably priced meat-based set meals from ¥1200. Inexpensive. Daily 11am–11pm.

Gyoshintei
尭心亭
☎0288/53-3751. Sample exquisitely prepared *shōjin-ryōri* vegetarian food (bentō ¥3230, course menu from ¥4050) in a traditional tatami room that's part of the Meiji-no-Yakata complex (see below). The waitresses wear kimono and you can gaze out on a lovely garden. Expensive. Daily except Thurs 11.30am–7pm.

Hippari Dako
ひっぱり凧
Classic *yakitori* and noodle café – look for the giant kite outside – popular with just about every *gaijin* who has ever set foot in Nikkō, as the written recommendations and *meishi* that plaster the walls testify. The menu has plenty of vegetarian options, plus beer and sake. Inexpensive.

Kikou
希光
Just before *Hippari Dako* if you approach from the station, this small Korean restaurant has tatami mat seating and hearty set meals under ¥1000. Inexpensive. Open till midnight.

Meiji-no-Yakata
明治の館
☎0288/53-3751. The dishes, such as curry rice, are simple, but the charming stone villa, once a Meiji-era holiday home, is a nostalgic treat. It's nice to enjoy coffee and cakes on their terrace, while behind the main house, *Yūan san Bō* serves more upmarket set courses. Moderate.

Suzuya
鈴家
Just before you cross over the bridge up the slope from the Kosugi Hōan Museum of Art. This stand-alone restaurant is a good place to sample *yuba-ryōri*; the set lunch costs ¥1400 and includes tempura, rice, noodles and rolled tofu. Moderate. Daily 11am–3pm.

Chūzenji-ko and the Kegon Falls

Some 10km west of Nikkō lie **Chūzenji-ko** (中禅寺湖) and the dramatic **Kegon Falls** (華厳の滝) that flow from it. Local buses run east along Route 120 and up the twisting, one-way road to reach **CHŪZENJI**, the lakeside resort. Both the lake and waterfalls were created thousands of years ago, when nearby **Mount Nantai** (男体山; 2486m) erupted, its lava plugging the valley. The best way of seeing the evidence of this geological event is to hop off the bus at Akechi-daira, the stop before Chūzenji, where a **cable car** (daily 9am–4pm; ¥390 one way, ¥710 return) will whisk you up to a viewing platform. From here it's a 1500-metre walk uphill and across the Chanoki-daira plateau, where there are sweeping views of Chūzenji-ko, Mount Nantai and the falls. An even better view of the falls can be had from the viewing platform at their base (daily: Jan, Feb & Dec 9am–4.30pm; March, April & Nov 8am–5pm; May–Sept 7.30am–6pm; Oct 7.30am–5pm; ¥530). The lift to this vantage point lies east across the car park behind the Chūzenji bus station; don't be put off by the queues of tour groups – a shorter line is reserved for independent travellers. The lift drops 100m through the rock to the base of the falls, where you can see over a tonne of water per second cascading from the Ojiri River, which flows from the lake.

Walking west along the shore for around 1km brings you to the second **Futarasan-jinja** (二荒山神社) of the Nikkō area. This colourful shrine, which once bore the name Chūzenji, has a pretty view of the lake, but is nothing extraordinary. There's also a third Futarasan-jinja, on the actual summit of the volcano; to reach it you'll have to pay ¥500 to climb the peak, which is owned by the shrine. The hike up takes around four hours and should only be attempted in good weather.

Head in a southerly direction around the lake, past several of the compounds still reserved for diplomatic retreats, and you come to the **Italian Embassy Villa Memorial Park** (April–June & Sept–Nov 9am–4pm, July & Aug 9am–5pm; free). The handsome lakeside villa here, designed by Anotonin Raymond and built in 1928, was used by the Italian ambassador up until 1997. Standing here, it's easy to imagine the languid atmosphere of summer house parties and yacht races.

△ Chūzenji-ko, with Mount Nantai in the background

Practicalities

Local **buses** from Nikkō (¥1100 each way) usually take less than an hour to get here, though travelling times can easily double – or even triple – during *kōyō* in mid-October, the prime time for viewing the changing autumn leaves, when traffic is bumper-to-bumper.

Overlooking the lake five minutes' walk from the bus station is the *Petit Pension Friendly* (⌾0288/55-0027, ⑤55-0549; from ¥16,000), a homely family-run **hotel** and café with both Western- and Japanese-style rooms, the cheaper ones not en suite; rates include two meals. The most luxurious place to stay on the lake is *Chūzenji Kanaya*, 2482 Chugushi (⌾0288/51-0001, ⓦwww.kanayahotel.co.jp; from ¥28,000), a couple of kilometres away from the tourist village, en route to the Ryūzu Falls, and specially designed to blend in with the woodland surroundings.

In a log house next to the *Chūzenji Kanaya Hotel* is the *Coffee House Yukon* (May–Oct daily 11am–6pm), a convivial spot for lunch or a snack. Another place where you can **eat** is *Chez Hoshino* (daily 11.30am–3pm & 6–8pm), an elegant, European-style restaurant on way to the shrine from the bus station, and facing the lake; set lunches cost from ¥1570 and the restaurant has a real log fire in winter and an English menu.

Yumoto

Many buses from Chūzenji continue northwest to terminate at the onsen village of **YUMOTO** (湯元), which nestles cosily at the base of the mountains on the northern shore of lake **Yuno-ko**. Five minutes' walk from the bus terminal at the back of the village is the **Yu-no-daira**, a field where bubbling water breaks through the ground – this is the source of the sulphur smell that hangs so pungently in the air. Nearby **Onsen-ji** (温泉寺) is a small temple notable for its onsen bath, which you can use. There's also a free footbath, great for soaking weary feet, near the *Yumoto Hillside Inn* (see below).

A lovely way to take in the scenery is to rent a rowing boat (¥1000 for 50min; May–Oct only) at the lakeside *Yumoto Rest House* (also a restaurant). Alternatively, you could walk around the lake in about an hour. If you're feeling energetic, it's worth embarking on the easy and enjoyable ten-kilometre **hike** from Yumoto across the **Senjōgahara marshland plateau** (戦場ヶ原), past two spectacular waterfalls and back to Chūzenji-ko. First, follow the west bank of Yuno-ko around to the steps down to the picturesque Yudaki Falls (湯滝), where you can stop off at the lodge serving delicious grilled fish and rice cakes (*mochi*) dipped in sweet miso paste. The trail continues along the Yu-gawa through shady woods before emerging beside the Izumiyado, a large pond and the start of a two-hour tramp across the raised walkways above the Senjōgahara marshland, which blooms with many wild flowers during the summer.

Roughly one hour further on, at the Akanuma junction, you can branch off back to the main road or continue along the riverside path for thirty minutes to the main road and bridge overlooking the spectacular **Ryūzu Falls** (竜頭の滝), with clear views of Chūzenji-ko. At the base of the falls are found several gift shops and noodle bars, one of which is superbly located, overlooking the water as it gushes into the lake. A lakeside path continues back to Chūzenji, finally emerging on the main road around 1km before Futarasan-jinja. A more relaxing way of completing

Nikkō Edo Village

There are several onsen resorts dotted along the Kinu-gawa, which flows through the mountains northeast of Nikkō. Avoid the touristy Kinugawa Onsen, where multistorey concrete hotels line the riverbank, and head instead for **Nikkō Edo Village** (日光江戸村; daily: Jan–March & Dec 9.30am–4pm; April–Nov 9am–5pm; ¥4500; ⓦwww .edomura.net), a fantasy recreation of eighteenth-century life complete with bewigged samurai guides and entertaining shows, many of which are great for kids. Half a day here will fly by, though to get the jokes in the geisha and comedy shows you'll need to know some Japanese. The live ninja aerial action display is a real hoot.

A free shuttle **bus** runs here from JR Nikkō Station. Alternatively, go one stop from Nikkō to Tōbu Shimo-Imaichi Station, and change to a train on the Tōbu Kinugawa line (¥290); get off at Shin-Takatoku Station and cross the road to catch another free bus to Nikkō Edo Village, five minutes' ride away.

---

this last section is to board a **boat** at Shobugahama, the jetty near the base of the Ryūzu Falls, and cruise for twenty minutes back to Chūzenji.

Yumoto is a very pleasant and generally quiet place to **stay**. A couple of good choices are *Yumoto Hillside Inn* (☎0288/62-2434, ⓦwww.hillsideinn.jp; from ¥23,400 including two meals), a Western-style hotel in a wooden chalet with an outdoor deck, English-speaking owners, a small heated swimming pool and indoor and outdoor onsen; and ⚜ *Yu-no-Mori* (ゆの森; ☎0288/62-2800, ⓦwww .okunikko-yunomori.com; from ¥36,000 including two meals), a stylish modern ryokan that combines Zen traditionalism with contemporary Western decor. Each of the rooms here has a bathtub made from *hinoki*, a type of pine, on its balcony.

Fuji Five Lakes

The best reason for heading 100km west from Tokyo towards the area known as **FUJI FIVE LAKES** is to climb Mount Fuji (富士山), Japan's most sacred volcano and, at 3776m, its highest mountain. Fuji-san, as it's respectfully known by the Japanese, has long been worshipped for its latent power (it last erupted in 1707) and near-perfect symmetry; it is most beautiful from October to May, when the summit is crowned with snow. The climbing season is basically July and August; even if you don't fancy the rather daunting ascent, just getting up close to Japan's most famous national symbol is a memorable experience. Apart from Fuji-san, the single most interesting sight is the wonderfully atmospheric shrine **Fuji Sengen-jinja**, in the area's transport hub of **Fuji-Yoshida**.

During the summer, the **five lakes** in the area are packed with urbanites fleeing the dust and grime of Tokyo. The best lake to head for is **Kawaguchi-ko**: as well as being a popular starting point for climbing Mount Fuji, it features a kimono museum and the easily climbable Mount Tenjō, which has outstanding views of Fuji-san and the surrounding lakes. The smallest of the other four lakes, horseshoe-shaped **Shōji-ko** (精進湖), 2km west of Kawaguchi-ko, is by far the prettiest. The largest lake, **Yamanaka-ko** (山中湖), southeast of Fuji-Yoshida, is just as developed as Kawaguchi-ko and has fewer attractions, while **Motosu-ko** (本栖湖) and **Sai-ko** (西湖) – the best for swimming and camping – are fine, but not so extraordinary that they're worth the trouble of visiting if you're on a short trip.

Fuji-Yoshida and around

FUJI-YOSHIDA (富士吉田), some 100km west of Tokyo, lies so close to Mount Fuji that when the dormant volcano eventually blows her top the local residents will be toast. For the time being, however, this small, friendly town acts as an efficient transport hub for the area, as well as the traditional departure point for journeys up the volcano, with frequent buses leaving for Fuji-san's fifth station (see box, p.258) from outside the train station.

The volcano aside, the town's main attraction is its Shinto shrine. To reach it, head southwest from the station uphill along the main street, Honchō-dōri, which will take you past several ornate **pilgrims' inns** (*oshi-no-ie*). These old lodging houses, where pilgrims used to stay before climbing Mount Fuji, are set back from the road, their entrances marked by narrow stone pillars; some still operate as minshuku today.

Where the road hits a junction, turn left and after a couple of hundred metres you'll see a giant *torii* and a broad gravel pathway lined with stone lanterns leading

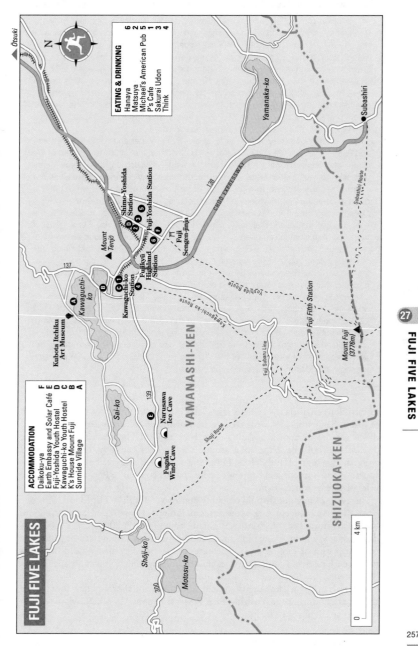

FUJI FIVE LAKES

ACCOMMODATION

Daikoku-ya	F
Earth Embassy and Solar Café	E
Fuji-Yoshida Youth Hostel	D
Kawaguchi-ko Youth Hostel	C
K's House Mount Fuji	B
Sunnide Village	A

EATING & DRINKING

Hanaya	6
Matsuya	2
Michael's American Pub	5
P's Café	1
Sakurai Udon	3
Think	4

Kubota Itchiku
Art Museum

Kawaguchi-
ko

Mount
Tenjō

Shimo-Yoshida
Station

Fuji-Yoshida Station

Fujikyu
Highland
Station

Kawaguchi-ko
Station

Fuji
Sengen-jinja

Sai-ko

Narusawa
Ice Cave

Fugaku
Wind Cave

Shoji-ko

Motosu-ko

Yamanaka-ko

CHUO EXPRESSWAY

Subashiri

Subashiri Route

Yoshida Route

Kawaguchi-ko Route

Fuji Subaru Line

Fuji Fifth Station

Mount Fuji
(3776m)

Shoji Route

YAMANASHI-KEN

SHIZUOKA-KEN

Otsuki

N

137

138

139

300

27

FUJI FIVE LAKES

0   4 km

257

"A wise man climbs Fuji once. A fool climbs it twice", says the Japanese proverb. Don't let the sight of children and grannies trudging up lull you into a false sense of security: this is a tough climb. There are several **routes** up the volcano, with the ascent divided into sections known as **stations**. Most people take a bus to the Kawaguchi-ko fifth station (*go-gōme*), about halfway up the volcano, where a Swiss-chalet-style gift shop marks the end of the road. The traditional hike, though, begins at Fuji-Yoshida; walking from here to the fifth station takes around five hours, and it's another six hours before you reach the summit. Many choose to climb at night to reach the summit by dawn; during the season, the lights of climbers' torches resemble a line of fireflies trailing up the volcanic scree.

Essential items to carry include at least one litre of water and some food, a torch and batteries, a raincoat and extra clothes; however hot it might be at the start of the climb, the closer you get to the summit the colder it becomes, with temperatures dropping to well below freezing, and sudden rain and lightning strikes are not uncommon. You can rest en route at any of seventeen **huts**, most of which provide dorm accommodation from around ¥5000 per night for just a bed (no need for a sleeping bag), and ¥7000 with dinner, though it's essential to book in advance; the huts also sell snacks and stamina-building dishes, such as curry rice. For a full list of the huts, with contact numbers, go to the Fuji-Yoshida city website (ⓦwww.city .fujiyoshida.yamanashi.jp), which also has lots of information on climbing the mountain. Once you're at the summit, it will take around an hour to make a circuit of the crater. Otherwise you can take part in the time-honoured tradition of making a phone call or mailing a letter from the post office.

Mount Fuji's official **climbing season**, when all the facilities on the mountain are open, including lodging huts and phones at the summit, runs from July 1 to August 27. For more details, pick up a free copy of the *Mount Fuji Climber's Guide Map*, which is published by the Fuji-Yoshida city hall and available at the local tourist office (see opposite) or from the website above. You can climb outside these dates, but don't expect all, or indeed any, of the facilities to be in operation, and be prepared for snow and extreme cold towards the summit.

to **Fuji Sengen-jinja** (富士浅間神社), a large, colourful shrine set in a small patch of forest. Sengen shrines, dedicated to the worship of volcanoes, encircle Fuji, and this is the most important, dating right back to 788. The beautiful main shrine (*honden*) was built in 1615. Look around the back for the jolly, brightly painted wooden carvings of the deities Ebisu the fisherman and Daikoku, the god of wealth, good humour and happiness, who appears content to let a rat nibble at the bales of rice he squats upon.

These fun-loving gods would certainly approve of **Fujikyū Highland** (富士急ハイランド; all year except Aug Mon–Fri 9am–5pm, Sat 9am–7pm, Sun 9am–6pm, but closed third Tues of month; Aug daily 8am–9pm; ¥1200 entry, ¥4800 one-day pass; ⓦwww.fujikyu.co.jp), an appealingly ramshackle amusement park. One train stop west of Fuji-Yoshida, it features the terrifying Fujiyama and Eejanaika roller coasters. Avoid coming at weekends or holidays unless you enjoy standing in long queues.

If you're in town late August, you'll find the main thoroughfare illuminated spectacularly during the **Yoshida Fire Festival** (August 26 & 27), when seventy bonfires are lit along its length.

Kawaguchi-ko

At first glance, there doesn't seem to be a whole lot to commend the shabby lakeside resort of **KAWAGUCHI-KO** (河口湖), a couple of kilometres west of Fuji-Yoshida. With its cruise boats and crass souvenir shops, this is the tourist hub of the area and is often choked with traffic during the holiday season. However, the fabulous view of Mount Fuji and lake Kawaguchi-ko from the top of **Tenjō-zan** (天上山) make a trip here worth the effort. You can either take a three-minute cable-car ride up to the lookout (daily: March–Nov 9am–5.10pm, Dec–Feb 9.30am–4.40pm; ¥700 return) or get some exercise by hiking up, which takes around 45 minutes.

Kawaguchi-ko's other highlight is the **Kubota Itchiku Art Museum** (久保田一竹美術館; Jan & Feb daily except Tues 10am–5pm; March & Dec daily 10am–5pm; April–Nov daily 9.30am–5.30pm; ¥1300; Ⓦwww.itchiku-tsujigahana.co.jp), on the northern shore of the lake. This small museum, in a Gaudí-esque-style building, houses the work of Kubota Itchiku, who has refined the traditional *tsujigahana* textile-patterning technique and applied it to kimono. Inside the pyramid-shaped building are pieces from the artist's *Symphony of Light* series, a continuous mountain landscape through the seasons, formed when the kimono are placed side by side. The museum is some 4km west of the town and can be reached by bus from both Fuji-Yoshida and Kawaguchi-ko.

Practicalities

The easiest way to reach the Fuji Five Lakes area is to take the **bus** (¥1700; 1hr 45min in good traffic) from the Shinjuku bus terminal in Tokyo, on the west side of the train station; during the climbing season there are frequent services, including at least three a day that run directly to the fifth station on Mount Fuji. The **train** journey from Shinjuku Station involves transferring from the JR Chūō line to the Fuji Kyūkō line at Ōtsuki, from where a local train chugs first to Fuji-Yoshida and then on to Kawaguchi-ko. On Sundays and public holidays, an early-morning train from Shinjuku does the trip in just over two hours (¥2390). A comprehensive system of **buses** will help you get around once you've arrived at either Fuji-Yoshida or Kawaguchi-ko.

If you're going to be touring the area, it's worth buying the **Rail and Go-ko Free Pass** (¥3800) at Shinjuku or as soon as you arrive at Ōtsuki. Valid for three days, it covers all rail travel and buses around the five lakes, plus tickets for the cable car. For just travelling around Kawaguchi-ko, the **Retrobus** two-day pass (¥1000) is a good buy. If you want to combine the Fuji Five Lakes area with a trip around Hakone, buy the **Fuji Hakone Pass** (see p.261).

Tons of **information**, in English, is available from both the Fuji-Yoshida Tourist Information Service (daily 9am–5.30pm; ℡0555/22-7000, Ⓦwww.city.fujiyoshida.yamanashi.jp), to the left as you exit Fuji-Yoshida Station; and at Kawaguchi-ko Tourist Information Centre (daily 9am–4.30pm; ℡0555/72-6700), outside Kawaguchi-ko Station.

Accommodation

Fuji-Yoshida and Kawaguchi-ko have plenty of good **places to stay**, including youth hostels and hotels. Fuji climbers could consider overnighting in one of the mountain huts (see p.258), but the claustrophobic should stick to the roomier accommodation at the base of the mountain. There are also several campsites around the lakes.

Daikoku-ya
大国屋
Honchō-dōri, Fuji-Yoshida ℡ **0555/22-3778.** This original pilgrims' inn on the main road still takes guests in its very traditional and beautifully decorated tatami rooms (though the owner prefers guests who can speak some Japanese). Rate includes two meals. Closed Oct–April. From ¥14,000 including two meals.

Earth Embassy and Solar Café
Narusawa-mura 8529-74 ℡ **0555/85-2576,** ⓦ **www.earthembassy.org.** This rustic organic café and farm is run by volunteers who give cooking and farming workshops as well as providing basic dorm accommodation and camping space. Note there's no running hot water (they take you to the local onsen for a bath) and that reservations are essential as it sometimes closes up in winter. Add ¥2000 for a vegetarian dinner and breakfast. The *Embassy* is on Route 139 towards Shoji-ko, 300m past the Koyodai-iriguchi bus stop; the last bus here from Kawaguchi-ko Station is around 5.30pm. Dorm beds ¥3000, camping ¥2000 per person, or ¥1500 with your own tent.

Fuji-Yoshida Youth Hostel
富士吉田ユースホステル
2-339 Shimo Yoshida Hon-chō, Fuji-Yoshida-shi ℡ **0555/22-0533,** ⓦ **www.jyh.or.jp.** Small, appealing hostel with tatami rooms in a family home. It's a 20min walk from Fuji-Yoshida

Station, less from Shimo-Yoshida, the preceding station. English is spoken and meals are available. Dorm beds ¥3200.

Kawaguchi-ko Youth Hostel
河口湖ユースホステル
2128 Funatsu, Kawaguchi-ko-machi ℡ **0555/72-1431,** ⓦ **www.jyh.or.jp.** Large and somewhat institutional hostel with a 5min walk southwest of Kawaguchi-ko Station, with tatami rooms and bunks, and bikes for rent (¥800 per day). Closed November–April. Dorm beds ¥3360.

K's House Mount Fuji
6713-108, Funatsu, Kawaguchi-ko-machi ℡ **0555/83-5556,** ⓦ **www.kshouse.jp/fuji-e.** The winning formula here is a choice of either bunk-bed dorms or private tatami-style rooms, some en suite. Also on offer are a well-equipped kitchen, comfy lounge, Internet access, laundry and bike rental. They'll even pick up from the station for free (8am–8pm). Dorm beds ¥2700; doubles from ¥6800.

Sunnide Village
Kawaguchi-ko ℡ **0555/76-6004,** ⓦ **www.sunnide** **.com.** This attractive complex of hotel and holiday cottages, with spectacular views across the lake towards Mount Fuji, offers a great "backpackers plan" starting at ¥4200 per person. They have lovely public baths too. It's on the north side of the lake, towards the Itchiku Kubota Art Museum. From ¥8400.

Eating

Fuji-Yoshida is renowned for its thick handmade *teuchi* udon noodles, topped with shredded cabbage and carrot. It's prepared and served in people's homes at lunchtime only; the tourist office can provide a Japanese list and map of the best places. One of the easiest to locate is the convivial *Hanaya* (花屋), towards the top of Honchō-dōri, but it's also worth searching out *Sakurai Udon* (桜井うどん; closed Sun) downhill from the train station, just off Honchō-dōri to the right when you reach the watch shop. Both serve just three types of dishes: *yumori*, noodles in a soup; *zaru*, cold noodles; and *sara*, warm noodles dipped in hot soup. Also down this way is the cute café *Matsuya* (まつや; Tues–Sun 10am–7pm), where you can access the **Internet**.

If you're staying overnight in Fuji-Yoshida, a warm welcome is guaranteed at *Michael's American Pub* (daily except Thurs 8pm–2am, lunch 11.30am–3pm; ⓦ www.mfi.or.jp/michael), while over in Kawaguchi-ko *Think* (daily 11am–midnight; ⓦ www.e-think.info) is a great café, restaurant and bar rolled into one cool whole; it's five minutes' walk from the youth hostel. There's an area where you can play with the owner's radio-controlled model cars and there's also Internet access. Finally, *P's Café* in Kawaguchi-ko Station is a pleasant Internet café (daily 8am–8pm), where the speciality of the house is udon topped with horsemeat.

Hakone

S outh of Mount Fuji and 90km west of Tokyo is the lakeland, mountain and onsen area known as **HAKONE** (箱根), always busy at weekends and holidays. Most visitors follow the well-established day-trip route, which is good fun and combines rides on several trains or buses, a funicular, a cable car and a sightseeing ship, styled as a seventeenth-century galleon, across the **lake**, Ashino-ko. However the scenery is so pretty, and there's so much else to do – such as seeing great art at the Hakone Open-Air Museum and the Pola Museum of Art, not to mention soaking in numerous onsen – that an overnight stay is encouraged. Weather permitting, you'll also get great views of nearby Mount Fuji.

The traditional day-trip itinerary, described below, runs anticlockwise from **Hakone-Yumoto**, gateway to the **Fuji-Hakone-Izu National Park**, then over **Mount Sōun**, across the length of **Ashino-ko** to **Moto-Hakone**, and back to the start. Approaching Hakone from the west, you can follow a similar route clockwise from Hakone-machi, on the southern shore of Ashino-ko, to Hakone-Yumoto.

Access to Hakone

Most people visit Hakone aboard the Odakyū-line **train** from Shinjuku, using one of the company's excellent-value travel passes (see box below). Alternatively, you can

Hakone passes and the Fuji Hakone Pass

If you plan to follow the traditional Hakone route, invest in either the three-day **Hakone Freepass** (¥5500 from Shinjuku) or the two-day **Hakone Winter Weekday Pass** (¥4700), valid December through mid-March Monday to Thursday, not including public holidays. Both cover a return journey on the Odakyū line from Shinjuku to Odawara, and unlimited use of the Hakone-Tozan line, Hakone-Tozan funicular railway, cable car, boat across the lake and most local buses. Besides saving you money on the total cost of all these trips, the passes give discounts at many of Hakone's attractions. The same passes from Odawara cost ¥4130 and ¥3410 respectively; there's also a ¥2000 one-day ticket from here that doesn't cover the cable car or the boat. For ¥870 extra one way, you can take the more comfortable "Romance Car" which goes directly from Shinjuku through to Hakone-Yumoto in ninety minutes.

If you're going directly from Hakone to the neighbouring Fuji Five Lakes area (or vice versa) then the three-day **Fuji Hakone Pass** (¥7200) is the way to go. This offers the same deal as a Hakone Freepass and covers a one-way express bus trip to or from Kawaguchi-ko, plus bus connections between the lakeland area and Hakone. For full details of all passes go to ⓦ www.odakyu.jp/English, or visit the Odakyū Sightseeing Service Centre (daily 8am–6pm) at the west exit of Shinjuku Station, where you'll find English-speaking staff and can also make reservations for tours and hotels.

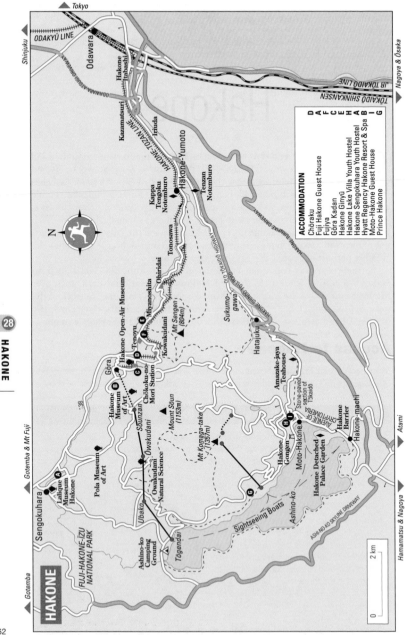

HAKONE

Tokyo

ODAKYŪ LINE

Shinjuku

Odawara

Hakone Itabashi

Kazamatsuri

Iriuda

JR TŌKAIDŌ LINE

TŌKAIDO SHINKANSEN

Nagoya & Ōsaka

HAKONE-TŌZAN LINE

ODAWARA-ATSUGI DRIVEWAY

Hakone-Yumoto

Kappa Tengoku Notemburo

Tenzan Notemburo

Tonosawa

Miyanoshita

Ōhiridai

Kowakudani

Mt Sengen (804m)

Hakone Open-Air Museum

Tenyu

Gōra

Chōkoku-no-Mori Station

OLD TŌKAIDO HIGHWAY

Sukumo-gawa

Hatajuku

HAKONE SHINDO TOLL ROAD

Amazake-jaya Teahouse

Hakone Museum of Art

Sōunzan

Pola Museum of Art

Mount Sōun (1153m)

Mt Komaga-take (1357m)

Owakudani Natural Science

Ōwakudani

Ubako

Stone-paved section of Tōkaidō

AVENUE OF CRYPTOMERIA

Hakone Gongen

Moto-Hakone

Hakone-machi

Hakone Barrier

Atami

Lalique Museum Hakone

Sengokuhara

FUJI-HAKONE-IZU NATIONAL PARK

Gotemba & Mt Fuji

Gotemba

Ashino-ko Camping Ground

Tōgendai

Ashino-ko

Sightseeing Boats

Hakone Detached Palace Garden

ASHI-NO-KO SKYLINE DRIVEWAY

Hamamatsu & Nagoya

N

HAKONE

ACCOMMODATION

Chōraku	D
Fuji Hakone Guest House	A
Fujiya	F
Gōra Kadan	C
Hakone Ginyū	E
Hakone Lake Villa Youth Hostel	H
Hakone Sengokuhara Youth Hostel	A
Hyatt Regency Hakone Resort & Spa	B
Moto-Hakone Guest House	I
Prince Hakone	G

0   2 km

take the Odakyū express **bus** (¥1950) from Shinjuku bus terminal, which will get you to Ashino-ko in a couple of hours. If you're using a JR rail pass (see p.27), the fastest route is to take a Shinkansen to **Odawara** (小田原), from where you should transfer to an Odakyū train or bus into the national park area. It's also possible to visit from the Fuji Five Lakes area, in which case you'll enter Hakone through **Sengoku-hara** to the north, passing through the major town of **Gotemba**.

You can pick up a map of the area and plenty of other **information** at the very friendly Hakone Tourist Information Office (daily: April–Nov 9.30am–6pm, Dec–March 9am–5.30pm; ☎0460/85-5700, ⓦwww.hakone.or.jp), across the street from Hakone-Yumoto Station, in the buildings at the bus terminal.

Accommodation

Excellent transportation links allow you to stay pretty much anywhere in the national park and still get around easily. There's a good range of budget options and some top-grade ryokans that are well worth saving up for, as well as the *Fujiya Hotel*, certainly one for heritage buffs.

Chōraku
長楽
Chōkoku-no-Mori ☎0460/82-2192, ℉82-4533. This appealing, modern ryokan has simple tatami rooms, onsen baths and a friendly manager who speaks a little English. From ¥15,000 with two meals.

Fuji-Hakone Guesthouse
富士箱根ゲストハウス
912 Sengokuhara ☎0460/84-6577, ⓦhakone.syuriken.jp/hakone. This convivial guesthouse, run by the friendly, English-speaking Takahashi-san and his family, has tatami rooms and onsen water piped into a communal bath; only breakfast is available. From ¥10,500.

Fujiya Hotel
富士屋ホテル
Miyanoshita ☎0460/82-2211, ⓦwww.fujiyahotel.co.jp. The first Western-style hotel in Japan, the *Fujiya* is a living monument to a more glamorous era of travel, and boasts lots of Japanese touches, including traditional gardens and decorative gables like those you find in temples. The plush 1950s-style decor is retro-chic and the rooms are good value, especially from Sunday to Friday, when foreign guests qualify for a cheaper rate. From ¥10,700.

Gōra Kadan
強羅花壇
Gōra ☎0460/82-3333, ⓦwww.gorakadan.com. One of Hakone's most exclusive ryokans is the stuff of legend, which means you might have wait an eternity to secure a reservation. Expect beautiful tatami rooms, antiques, exquisite meals and a serene

atmosphere. From ¥90,000 including two meals.

Hakone Ginyu
Miyanoshita ☎0460/82-3355, ⓦwww.hakoneginyu.co.jp. Another of Hakone's outstanding luxury ryokans where guests are spared little comfort. The views across the valley are stunning and the interiors are a tasteful blend of old and new. Huge *hinoki* wood tubs on private verandas are a plus. From ¥90,000 with two meals.

Hakone Lake Villa Youth Hostel
Motohakone ☎0460/83-1610, ⓦwww.jyh.or.jp. In a secluded spot, surrounded by woods above Ashino-ko, this pleasant hostel has tatami and Western-style dorms, a lounge with a large outdoor deck, a bath filled with onsen water, and good-value meals. Dorm beds ¥3000.

Hakone Prince Hotel
Motohakone ☎0460/83-1111, ⓦwww.princehotels.co.jp/hakone-e. With a prime location on the Komaga-take side of Ashino-ko and a multitude of facilities, this is very 1970s as with many Prince hotels – but in a good way. The nicest rooms are in the Japanese-style annexes. From ¥25,000.

Hakone Sengokuhara Youth Hostel
Sengokuhara ☎0460/84-8966, ⓦwww.jyh.or.jp. Directly behind the *Fuji-Hakone Guesthouse*, and run by the same family, this hostel offers good dorm accommodation in a lovely wooden building. Dorm beds ¥2950.

Hyatt Regency Hakone Resort & Spa
Gōra ☎0460/82-2000, ⓦwww.hakone.regency.hyatt.com. This slickly designed new hotel is a treat, offering some of the largest rooms in

Hakone and elegant facilities, including lounge, two restaurants and the Izumi onsen spa. For those who can't bear to be parted with their poodle, there are even dog-friendly stone-floored rooms. From ¥38,000.

Moto-Hakone Guesthouse
Moto-Hakone ⓣ 0460/83-7880,

ⓦ **hakone.syuriken.jp/hakone.** A short bus ride (get off at Ashinokoen-mae) or stiff 10min walk uphill from the village, the reward for the journey being spotless Japanese-style rooms. Singles ¥5000, doubles from ¥10,500; breakfast is an extra ¥800 per person.

Hakone-Yumoto to Chōkoku-no-Mori

HAKONE-YUMOTO (箱根湯元), the small town nestling in the valley at the gateway to the national park, is marred by scores of concrete-block hotels and *bessō*, vacation villas for company workers, not to mention the usual cacophony of souvenir shops. It does, however, have some good **onsen** which are ideal for unwinding after a day's sightseeing around the park.

Up the hill from the station is the **Kappa Tengoku Notemburo** (かっぱ天国野天風呂; daily 10am–10pm; ¥750), a small, traditional outdoor onsen, which can get crowded. More stylish is **Tenzan Notemburo** (天山野天風呂; daily 9am–11pm; ¥1000), a luxurious public onsen complex at Oku-Yumoto, 2km southwest of town. The main building has separate male and female outdoor baths, including waterfalls and Jacuzzi in a series of rocky pools. There's also a clay-hut sauna for men, and for ¥200 extra on weekdays (¥1000 at weekends) both men and women can use the wooden baths in the building across the car park. A free shuttle bus runs to the baths from the bridge just north of Hakone-Yumoto Station.

Hakone-Yumoto is stacked with good places to **eat**. *Yama Soba*, on the main road between the station and the tourist office, serves up soba sets from ¥1100. *Chikuzen*, across the road, is the best of the town's udon restaurants. There are also three good-value restaurants at the *Tenzan Notemburo*, serving rice, *shabu-shabu* and *yakiniku* (grilled meat) dishes.

Miyanoshita and around

Rising up into the mountains, the Hakone-Tozan switchback railway zigzags for nearly 9km alongside a ravine from Hakone-Yumoto to the village of Gōra. There are small traditional inns and temples at several of the stations along the way, but the single best place to alight is the village onsen resort of **MIYANOS-HITA** (宮ノ下). Interesting antique and craft shops are dotted along its main road, and there are several hiking routes up 804-metre **Mount Sengen** on the eastern flank of the railway – one path begins just beside the station. At the top you'll get a great view of the gorge below. Afterwards you can relax in the rotemburo at the attractive day-onsen **Tenoyu** (てのゆ; daily 10am–10pm; weekday/weekend ¥1600/¥2100), a short walk out of the village along the main road to Gōra. But Miyanoshita's real draw is its handful of splendid **hotels**, the most historic of which is the *Fujiya* (see p.263), which opened for business in 1878. It's well worth a look even if you're not staying, and its *Orchid Lounge* is great for afternoon tea, while the ornate French **restaurant** is an excellent, if pricey, choice for lunch or dinner. The *Picot Bakery* on the main road outside the *Fujiya* is a good place to pick up bread and cakes for breakfast or lunch.

Travelling two more stops on the Hakone-Tozan railway brings you to **Chōkoku-no-Mori**, where you should alight if you want to visit the nearby **Hakone Open-Air Museum** (彫刻の森美術館; daily: March–Nov 9am–5pm;

Dec–Feb 9am–4pm; ¥1600; ⓦwww.hakone.oam.or.jp). This worthwhile museum is packed with sculptures, ranging from works by Rodin and Giacometti to Michelangelo reproductions and bizarre modern formations scattered across the landscaped grounds, which have lovely views across the mountains to the sea. There's an enclave of 26 pieces by Henry Moore; a "Picasso Pavilion", which houses over three hundred paintings, lithographs, ceramics and sculptures by the Spanish artist; and four galleries featuring works by Chagall, Miró and Renoir, plus works by modern Japanese artists such as Umehara Ryuzaburo and Takeshi Hayashi. You can rest between galleries at several restaurants or cafés, and there's also a traditional Japanese teahouse here.

Heading towards Gōra along the main road from the museum, you'll soon pass the excellent *Gyōza Centre* (daily except Thurs 11.30am–2.30pm & 5–8.30pm). This two-floor **restaurant** usually has a long line of customers waiting to sample the thirteen types of delicious home-made dumplings, including ones stuffed with prawns and *nattō*. A set meal with rice and soup costs around ¥1150.

West and north from Gōra

The Hakone-Tozan railway terminates at **GŌRA** (強羅), another possible place to stay overnight or have lunch. Continuing west on the day-trip route, you'll transfer to a **funicular tram** (¥410), which takes ten minutes to cover the short but steep distance to **Sōunzan**, the start of the cable car across Mount Sōun. On the way, you might want to stop at **KŌEN-KAMI** (公園上), a couple of stops from Gōra. Here the **Hakone Museum of Art** (箱根美術館; daily except Thurs 9am–4pm; ¥900) and its collection of ancient ceramics is likely to appeal to experts only, but the delicate moss gardens and the view from the traditional teahouse across the verdant hills is captivating.

From Sōunzan, the **cable car** (¥1330 one way) floats like a balloon on its thirty-minute journey high above the mountain to the Tōgendai terminal beside Ashino-ko, stopping at a couple of points along the way. If the weather is playing ball, you should get a good glimpse of Mount Fuji in the distance as you pop over the hill at the first stop, **ŌWAKUDANI** (大湧谷). This is the site of a constantly bubbling and steaming valley formed by a volcanic eruption three thousand years ago. You can hike up the valley through the lava formations to the bubbling pools where eggs are boiled until they are black and scoffed religiously by every Japanese tourist, for no better reason than it's the done thing when visiting Ōwakudani.

Pola Museum of Art and Sengokuhara

If volcanic activity and a cable car isn't your thing, once you get to Gōra you can transfer to the bus bound for the splendid **Pola Museum of Art** (ポーラ美術館; daily 9am–5pm; ¥1800; ⓦ www.polamuseum.or.jp). This diverse and eclectic collection of Western art and glasswork (predominantly French Impressionists and Ecole de Paris artists) and Japanese works, among them paintings and ceramics, includes some outstanding pieces by the likes of Renoir, Monet, Picasso, Van Gogh, Cezanne and Gallé. They're all displayed in modern galleries in a stunning building that blends beautifully with the surrounding forest, with a café and restaurant on site too.

Continuing north on the same bus, you soon reach the pleasant village of **SENGOKUHARA** (仙石原), another possible place to stay the night. Several museums here aim to cater to the rarefied tastes of Japanese women, of which perhaps the most interesting – and certainly the most beautifully situated – is the **Lalique Museum Hakone** (箱根ラリック美術館; daily 9am–5pm; ¥1500; ⓣ 0406/84-2225, ⓦ www.lalique-museum.com), dedicated to the delicate glass pieces of the French artist René Lalique. At the entrance a parked Orient Express Pullman train carriage is kitted out with Lalique's glass panels; entry is by reservation and costs ¥2100, including drinks and dessert. Also at the museum is café-restaurant *Lys*, which boasts a wonderful setting with a view of the mountains and garden seating in summer; lunch here will run to around ¥2000.

From opposite the museum a reasonably frequent **bus** heads south towards the Tōgendai cable-car terminus.

Ashino-ko and around

From **Tōgendai** (桃原台), a shoreline trail winds along the western side of **Ashino-ko** (芦ノ湖) to the small resort of Hakone-machi some 8km south, taking around three hours to cover. The western lakeshore, forming part of the Prince empire of hotels and resorts, is not covered by the Hakone Free Pass (see p.261) and so is somewhat marginalized – and all the more peaceful for it. However, most visitors – and most likely you, too – hop straight from the cable car on to one of the colourful sightseeing ships (¥840), modelled after the seventeenth-century man-o'-war *The Sovereign of the Seas*, that regularly sail the length of the lake in around thirty minutes. Boats also run from Tōgendai to the *Prince* hotel resort at **Hakone-en**, midway down the east side of the lake, where there's a cable car up the 1357-metre **Komaga-take** (駒ヶ岳), from where there's a fabulous view.

A cluster of upmarket hotels and ryokan can be found at **Hakone-machi**, where the sightseeing boats dock. This is also the location of the **Hakone Barrier** (箱根関所; daily 9am–4.30pm; ¥300) through which all traffic on the **Tōkaidō**, the ancient

In 1618 the second shogun, Tokugawa Hidetada, put up the **Hakone Barrier** (Sekisho) – actually more of a large compound than a single gate – which stood at Hakone-machi until 1869. The shogun decreed that all his lords' wives and their families live in Edo (now Tokyo) and that the lords themselves make expensive formal visits to the capital every other year, a strategy designed to ensure no one attempted a rebellion. The Tōkaidō, on which the barrier stands, was one of the major routes in and out of the capital, and it was here that travellers were carefully checked to see how many guns they were taking into the Edo area, and that the lords' families were stopped from escaping. Any man caught trying to dodge the barrier was crucified and then beheaded, while accompanying women had their heads shaved and were, according to contemporary statute, "given to anyone who wants them".

road linking Kyoto and Edo, once had to pass (see box above). What stands here today is a reproduction, enlivened by waxwork displays which provide the historical background. There's nothing much to keep you here, though; instead, stroll north of the barrier around the wooded promontory, past the bland reconstruction of the Emperor Meiji's Hakone Detached Palace, and take in the views of the lake.

Part of the Tōkaidō, shaded by 420 lofty cryptomeria trees planted in 1618, and now designated "Natural Treasures", runs for around 1km beside the road leading from the Hakone Barrier to the lakeside **MOTO-HAKONE** (元箱根) tourist village. The prettiest spot around here is the vermilion *torii* gate, standing in the water just north of Moto-Hakone – a scene celebrated in many an *ukiyo-e* print and modern postcard. The gate belongs to the **Hakone Gongen** (箱根権現) and is the best thing about this small Shinto shrine, set back in the trees, where samurai once came to pray.

Back to Hakone-Yumoto

From either Hakone-machi or Moto-Hakone you can take a **bus** back to Hakone-Yumoto or Odawara (see p.263). Far more rewarding, however, is the eleven-kilometre **hike** along part of the Tōkaidō, which begins five minutes up the hill from the Hakone-Tozan bus station in Moto-Hakone; watch for the spot where large paving stones are laid through the shady forests. After the first couple of kilometres the route is all downhill and takes around four hours. When the path comes out of the trees and hits the main road, you'll see the **Amazake-jaya Teahouse** (甘酒茶屋; daily 7am–5.30pm) where you can rest, just as travellers did hundreds of years ago, and sip a restorative cup of the milky, sweet and alcoholic rice drink *amazake*, with some pickles, for ¥400.

From the teahouse, the path shadows the main road to the small village of **HATAJUKU** (畑宿), where since the ninth century craftsmen have perfected the art of *yosegi-zaiku*, or marquetry. The wooden boxes, toys and other objects inlaid with elaborate mosaic patterns make great souvenirs and there are workshops throughout the village, including one right where the path emerges onto the main road. Hatajuku is a good place to pick up the bus the rest of the way to Hakone-Yumoto if you don't fancy hiking any further. From here the path descends to the **Sukumo-gawa** and past several old temples, as well as the Tenzan Notemburo (see p.264), before ending up in the centre of Hakone-Yumoto.

Mount Takao and Mitake

W est from Shinjuku Station are several pleasant day-trip opportunities, the best of which is **Mount Takao**, crowned by a picturesque temple, **Yakuo-in**, which hosts a spectacular fire-walking festival annually. The rest of the year, pilgrims are joined by multitudes of hikers who meander along the many easy trails around the mountain; several more challenging paths lead further afield to Chichibu-Tama National Park to the northwest. If you're heading directly to the park, **Mitake** is a main gateway. As at Takao, the nearby **Mount Mitake** (930m) is home to an ancient, picturesque shrine.

En route you could stop off at the **Edo-Tokyo Open Air Architectural Museum**, an annexe of the Edo-Tokyo Museum, to view prime examples of vernacular architecture saved from the wrecking ball. Closer into the city you'll pass through Mitaka (not to be confused with Mitake), home to the Ghibli Museum (see p.112).

Mount Takao

Only an hour west of Shinjuku, **Mount Takao** (高尾山; 600m), also referred to as Takao-san, is a particularly pleasant place midweek for a quick escape from Tokyo, and a starting point for longer trails into the mountains, though you'd be well advised to avoid it at the weekend, when the main trails are clogged with day-trippers and picnic parties cover the slopes.

The Keiō line from Shinjuku provides the simplest and cheapest way of reaching the terminus of Takao-san-guchi (1hr; ¥370). If you take the slower and far more expensive JR Chūō line, you'll need to change to the Keiō line at Takao to go one last stop to Takao-san-guchi. It comes as something of a relief to arrive here, as the unremitting city sprawl is brought to a halt by the verdant slopes of the Takao Quasi National Park.

There are seven marked trails on the mountain of various lengths and difficulties, with the longest three starting from Takao-san-guchi; all are detailed on a map (in Japanese) provided by the Keiō train company, or in English from the tourist offices in Tokyo (see p.47) or the Takao Visitor Centre at the top of the mountain. To reach the start of these trails, turn right outside the station and follow the riverside path for 100m, past the noodle restaurants, to the **cable car** and **chairlifts** (both ¥470 one way, ¥900 return). Taking either of these will save a kilometre or so of slogging up the main no. 1 trail.

Rejoining the no. 1 trail at the top of the cable-car station, you can continue to the ranks of red-painted lanterns leading up to **Yakuo-in** (薬王院). Founded in the eighth century, the temple is notable for the ornate polychromatic carvings which decorate its main hall, very reminiscent of those in Nikkō. In front of the hall and dotted around the temple grounds are striking statues of Tengu, the winged, Pinocchio-nosed deity of the mountains. Just before climbing the stairs to the main hall, you can pause to sample the *okashi* (sweets) and nuts offered at a temple stall – good hiking snacks for later in the day. Yakuo-in also has a small temple beside the Biwataki falls on the no. 6 trail, and hosts a spectacular **fire ritual** annually on the second Sunday in March back in Takao-san-guchi, where you can watch priests and pilgrims march across hot coals – and even follow them yourself.

From the temple, it doesn't take very long to reach Takao's summit, where you'll find a cluster of soba stalls and the **visitor centre** (Tues–Sun 10am–4pm; ☎0426/64-6157), which has some nature displays, though all the information is in Japanese. On a fine day there are good views back towards the city and, in the opposite direction, if you're really lucky, of Mount Fuji. However, those hoping for a real hiking workout would be forgiven for feeling somewhat short-changed. If you want to continue, take the path down the hill behind the visitor centre and pick up the undulating trail to **Mount Kobotoke Shiroyama** (小仏城山; 670m), another 45 minutes away, where the panoramic views of Lake Sagami make up for the ugly telecommunications tower.

Of the several routes back from the visitor centre to Takao-san-guchi, no. 6 trail is particularly attractive, passing through a range of forest habitats and then hugging the side of a stream (and at one point running down its rocky centre). On the way you'll pass the **Biwataki**, a freezing waterfall under which religious ascetics take a shower. This route remains within the trees; if you want country-side views, follow the Inariyama trail. Neither route should take more than ninety minutes at a steady pace.

While there are plenty of places to **eat** along the trails and at Takao-san-guchi, with rustic cafés dishing up soba and udon noodles, there's little to choose between them. At the base of the mountain, however, it's a different story. Here in a sylvan setting you'll find the delightful ⚑ *Ukai Toriyama* (うかい鳥山; Mon–Fri 11am– 9.30pm, Sat 11am–8pm, Sun 11am–7pm; ☎042/661-0739, ⓦwww.ukai.co.jp /toriyama), a traditional restaurant specializing in charcoal-broiled chicken and Hida beef. The food is served by kimono-clad waitresses in small tatami rooms, with set menus starting at ¥4730. Also worth searching out is the new *Toumai* (657 Tatemachi, Hachioji-shi; Tues–Sun 11.30am–9pm; ☎042/667-1424, ⓦwww .toumai.jp), the relaxed café and events space of world-traveller Yuki Shirakawa; it's a ten-minute walk south of Takao Station.

Mitake

The mountains in the 1263-square-kilometre **Chichibu–Tama National Park** (秩 父多摩国立公園) provide the headwaters for several fast-flowing rivers, including the Tama-gawa. The attractively rocky gorge that this flows through as it passes **MITAKE** (御岳) is what sets this sleepy town apart from nearby Takao. Otherwise, Mitake shares many features with Takao: a cable car up a sacred mountain, an attractive temple and plenty of easy-to-follow hiking trails which get packed out on weekends and holidays.

Heading here from Shinjuku Station, you need to take the JR Chūō line, then branch off at Hajima Station onto the Ome line. This runs alongside the Tamagawa, providing fine views of the river and **gorge**; to get up close, alight at Ikusabata or Sawai station and follow the riverside walk to Mitake Station, where you'll find the **Mitake Information Centre** (Tues–Sun 8am–4pm; ☎0428/78-8836), which has maps of the area. The assistants are unlikely to speak English, but they will point out the stop across the road at which you can catch a bus (¥270) heading to the cable car up Mount Mitake. Buses are fairly frequent, but if you have time to kill it's worth crossing the bridge over to the river's south side and visiting the **Gyokudō Art Museum** (玉堂美術館; Tues–Sun 10am–5pm; ¥500; ☎0428/78-8335), home to some fine paintings by Gyokudo Kawai (1873–1957) and a serene Zen rock garden.

The **cable car** (¥570 one way) deposits you near the summit of the 929-metre sacred mountain, about twenty minutes' walk from the 1250-year-old **Mitake-jinja** (御岳神社). The statue in front of this picturesque shrine is of the Kamakura-era hero Hatakeyama Shigetada; his armour is on display in the shrine's treasure house (daily 9.30am–4.30pm; ¥300), but it's not that interesting that you'd want to pay to see it. On the way to the shrine from the cable car you'll pass another **visitor centre** (Tues–Sun 9am–4.30pm; ☎0428/78-9363). The assistants here have more maps and can help you find a good hiking route or accommodation on the mountain at one of several attractively thatched traditional houses. These include the reasonable *Mitake Youth Hostel* (御岳ユースホステル; ☎0428/78-8774; Ⓦwww.jyh.or.jp; dorm beds ¥2880), a quiet place to hang out for a day or two. If you're hungry, try a traditional dish of noodles at *Momiji-ya* (紅葉屋), a simple café by the approach to the shrine.

Edo-Tokyo Architectural Museum

A kind of retirement home for old Tokyo buildings which have proved surplus to requirements in modern times, the **Edo-Tokyo Open Air Architectural Museum** (江戸東京建物公園; Tues–Sun: April–Sept 9.30am–5.30pm; Oct–March 9.30am–4.30pm; ¥400; Ⓦwww.tatemonoen.jp) is worth swinging by on your way to or from Takao or Mitaka. The museum was the inspiration for the abandoned theme park in Studio Ghibli's Oscar-winning *Spirited Away*, and is set within the parkland of Koganei-kōen, a twenty-minute walk or five-minute bus ride (¥170) north of Musashi Koganei Station. Some 35 buildings of varying degrees of interest are gathered here, plus an exhibition hall with archeological artefacts and folk crafts. You can enter most of the buildings (taking your shoes off first), whose interiors have been faithfully preserved or recreated.

On the west side of the sprawling complex, the most engaging structure is the very grand **Mitsue residence**, an 1852 mansion moved from Kyoto and furnished with painted screens, lacquered shrines and chandeliers. There are also several thatched farmhouses. On the east side a Shitamachi (downtown Tokyo) street of houses and shops has been reconstructed, including a tailor's shop and stationers, plus kitchenware and flower stores. The highlight is a public bathhouse, a veritable palace of ablutions with magnificent Chinese-style gables and a lakeside view of Fuji painted on the tiled wall inside. Also look out for the Uemura-tei, a 1927 shophouse, its copper cladding pocked by shrapnel from World War II bombings.

30

Kawagoe and around

Sophisticated Tokyoites tend to view Saitama-ken, the prefecture immediately northeast of the capital, as an achingly dull place that's notable only for the dormitory communities of the capital's worker bees. This is a gross generalization and, if anything, heading in this direction should be high on your list of things to do because it's home to the old castle town of **KAWAGOE** (川越), an interesting and highly enjoyable day-trip, only 40km north of Tokyo. Although it doesn't look promising on arrival, Kawagoe's compact area of sights, around 1km north of the main station, is aptly described as a "Little Edo", and can easily be toured in a few hours, and once you've browsed the many traditional craft shops and paused to sample the town's culinary delights, you'll probably find the day has flown by. This would certainly be the case on the third Saturday and Sunday of October, when Kawagoe's grand *matsuri* is held, one of the most lively festivals in the Tokyo area, involving some 25 ornate floats (called *dashi*) and hundreds of costumed revellers.

Kawagoe's fortunes owe everything to its strategic position on the Shingashi River and Kawagoe-kaidō, the ancient highway to the capital. If you wanted to get goods to Tokyo, then called Edo, they more than likely had to go via Kawagoe, and the town's merchants prospered as a result, accumulating the cash to build fireproof **kurazukuri**, the black, two-storey shophouses the town is now famous for. At one time there were over two hundred of these houses, but their earthen walls didn't prove quite so effective against fire as hoped (nor were they much use in the face of Japan's headlong rush to modernization). Even so, some thirty still remain, with sixteen prime examples clustered together along Chūō-dōri, around 1km north of the JR and Tōbu stations.

Other Saitamai-ken sights worth checking out range from **Saitama** city's **John Lennon Museum**, which Yoko Ono was instrumental in helping establish, gifting it many personal items, to the new state-of-the-art **Railway Museum** in Ōmiya.

The town and around

Heading north up Chūō-dōri from Kawagoe's central train stations, you'll pass a small shrine, **Kumano–jinja** (熊野神社), around 200m before the main enclave of *kurazukuri*; beside the shrine is a tall storehouse containing a magnificent *dashi* float. At the next major crossroads, on the left-hand side, is the old Kameya *okashi* (sweet) shop, warehouse and factory. These buildings now house the **Yamazaki Museum of Art** (山崎美術館; daily except Thurs 9.30am–5pm; ¥500), dedicated to the works of Meiji-era artist Gaho Hashimoto. Some of his elegant screen paintings hang in the

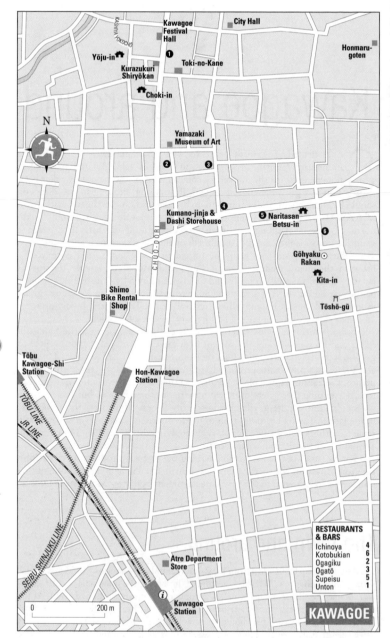

Kawagoe Festival Hall

City Hall

KASHIYA YOKOCHO

Yōju-in

Kurazukuri Shiryōkan

Choki-in

Honmaru-goten

❶ Toki-no-Kane

N

Yamazaki Museum of Art

❷ ❸

❹

Kumano-jinja & Dashi Storehouse

❺ Naritasan Betsu-in

❻

Gōhyaku Rakan

Kita-in

CHUO-DORI

Shimo Bike Rental Shop

Tōshō-gū

Tōbu Kawagoe-Shi Station

Hon-Kawagoe Station

TŌBU LINE

JR LINE

SEIBU SHINJUKU LINE

Atre Department Store

Kawagoe Station

0   200 m

RESTAURANTS & BARS

Ichinoya	4
Kotobukian	6
Ogagiku	2
Ogatō	3
Supeisu	5
Unton	1

KAWAGOE

main gallery, while there are artistic examples of the sugary confections once made here in the converted *kura* (storehouses); entry includes a cup of tea and *okashi*.

Continuing up Chūō-dōri, you'll come to several craft shops, including Machikan, which specializes in knives and swords (costing anything from ¥20,000 to ¥800,000), and Sōbiki Atelier, which sells woodwork. On the left, take a moment to duck into **Chōki-in** (長喜院), a temple with a statue of an emaciated, Gandhara-style Buddha in its grounds along with a pretty lily pond and sculpted bushes and trees.

Back on the main street, the **Kurazukuri Shiryōkan** (蔵造り資料館; Tues–Sun 9am–4.30pm; ¥100) is a museum housed inside an old tobacco wholesaler's, one of the first *kurazukuri* to be rebuilt after the great fire of 1893. In the upstairs living quarters you can squeeze around the tiny twisting staircase that leads down to ground level, and one of the *kura* contains antique firefighting uniforms and woodblock prints of the fires that ravaged the town. Just north of here on the main road is the **Kawagoe Festival Hall** (川越まつり会館; daily 9.30am–4.30pm but closed second and fourth Wed of the month; ¥500) which houses two magnificent *dashi* floats along with videos of past festivals and various displays, though there are no English descriptions.

Opposite the Kurazukuri Shiryōkan, just off Chūō-dōri, you won't miss the **Toki-no-Kane** (時の鐘), the wooden bell tower rebuilt in 1894, that was used to raise the alarm when fires broke out. An electric motor now powers the bell, which is rung four times daily. Returning to Chūō-dōri and taking the first street off to the west will bring you to **Yōju-in** (養寿院), another handsomely wrought temple with pleasant grounds. Just north of here is the **Kashiya Yokochō** (菓子屋横町), or confectioners' alley, a picturesque pedestrian street still lined with several colourful sweet and toy shops – another great place to browse for souvenirs.

It's a 500-metre hike east of the Kurazukuri Shiryōkan, along the main road, to reach the scant remains of **Kawagoe Castle** (川越城), now mainly parkland and the grounds of the senior high school, but still containing the vast **Honmaru-goten** (本丸御殿), the former residence of the *daimyō*. There's a

△ An old kurazukuri

museum inside (Tues–Sun 9am–5pm; ¥100) containing mainly archeological artefacts, but it's building itself, dating from 1848, that is the main attraction, with its Chinese-style gabled roof, spacious tatami rooms and gorgeous painted screens.

Heading south from the castle grounds, you'll soon reach **Naritasan Betsu-in** (成田山別院), an otherwise unremarkable shrine that comes to life on the twenty-eighth of each month, when it hosts a busy flea market.

Kita-in

Some 100m southeast of Naritasan Betsu-in lies **Kita-in** (喜多院), the main temple complex of the Tendai Buddhist sect and one of Kawagoe's highlights. There's been a temple on these grounds since 830, and it gained fame when the first Tōkugawa shogun, Ieyasu, declared the head priest Tenkai Sōjō a "living Buddha". Such was the reverence in which the priests here were held that, when the temple burnt down in 1638, the third shogun, Iemitsu, donated a secondary palace from Edo Castle (on the site of Tokyo's present-day Imperial Palace) as a replacement building. This was dismantled and moved here piece by piece, and is now the only remaining structure from Edo Castle which survives anywhere.

You have to pay an entry fee to view the palace part of the temple (March–Nov 8.50am–4.30pm, Dec–Feb 8.50am–4pm; ¥400), but it's well worth it. The room with a painted floral ceiling is believed to be where Iemitsu was born. Serene gardens surround the palace and a covered wooden bridge leads across into the temple's inner sanctum, decorated with a dazzling golden chandelier. The entry fee also includes access to the **Gohyaku Rakan**, a remarkable grove of stone statues. Although the name translates as "500 Rakans", there are actually 540 of these enigmatic dwarf disciples of Buddha, and no two are alike. Should you know your Chinese birth sign, it's fun to search the ranks for it, as twelve of the statues include the Chinese zodiac symbols of animals and mythical beasts. Kita-in also has its own mini **Tōshō-gū** which, like its famous cousin in Nikkō, enshrines the spirit of Tokugawa Ieyasu and is decorated with bright colours and elaborate carvings.

John Lennon Museum

Around 23km from Kawagoe lies the absorbing **John Lennon Museum** (ジョンレノンミュジアム; daily except Tues 11am–6pm; ¥1500; ☎048/601-0009, Ⓦwww.taisei.co.jp/museum). The imaginative displays makes a genuine attempt to honour one of the twentieth century's most iconic pop artists, despite the tendency to idealize Lennon and Yoko Ono's life together, and anyone with even a casual interest in pop culture will enjoy seeing Lennon's original sketches, scribbled lyrics, instruments and much more. Keep an eye too on Yoko Ono's art exhibit "Telephone Peace": if this white telephone rings when you pass it, pick it up and you'll find yourself chatting with the artist – apparently Ono calls from time to time to find out how things are going.

The closest **train station** is Saitama Shintoshin on the Keihin Tōhoku, Utsunomiya and Takasaki lines from Ueno in Tokyo (around 30min); the museum is a five-minute walk from the station. Kita-yono station, on the Saikyo line from Shinjuku and Ikebukuro, and five stops from Kawagoe, is also close by.

Railway Museum

The new **Railway Museum** (Tetsudō Hakubutsukan; 鉄道博物館; daily except Tues 10am–6pm; ¥1000; Ⓦwww.railway-museum.jp) in Ōmiya (大宮), which should be open by the time you read this, looks set to add a thrill to many a trains-potters' heart. Some 36 different pieces of rolling stock, including beautifully detailed antique carriages and late nineteenth-century steam trains, tell the story of the development of Japan's railways from 1872. Ōmiya Station is most easily accessed from Ueno in Tokyo; from here the museum can be reached by a regular rail service to Tetsudo Hakubutsukan Station.

Practicalities

Of the three **train lines** to Kawagoe, the fastest is the express on the Tōbu line from Ikebukuro (32min; ¥450); you can get off either at Kawagoe Station (which is also on the slower JR Saikyō line) or at Tōbu Kawagoe-shi, which is marginally closer to Chūō-dōri. Seibu Shinjuku-line trains run from Shinjuku to Hon-Kawagoe Station (43min; ¥480), which is the most convenient of the lot for the *kurazukuri*. The staff at the **tourist office** (daily 9am–4.30pm; ☎049/222-5556, ⓦ www.koedo.or.jp) at Kawagoe Station may speak some English and can provide you with a map of the town and an English pamphlet on the sights.

Immediately northwest of the main square, in front of the Seibu line terminus, is the Shimo bicycle store (daily except Wed 9am–7.30pm; also closed second Thurs of the month), where you can rent **bicycles** (¥700 per day) – handy if you plan to see all of Kawagoe's somewhat scattered sights. Note that there's an unrelated bicycle repair shop (which doesn't rent out bikes) confusingly close to the Shimo store.

Eating and drinking

Local gourmands flock to Kawagoe for eel, most famously sampled at the venerable *Ichinoya* (いちのや; 1-18-10 Matsue-chō), where there are two floors of tatami rooms in which to scoff set courses of broiled eel – the recommended one clocks up at ¥3150. Less pricey, but just as tasty, are the *unagi* restaurants *Ogatō* (小川藤) and *Ogagiku* (小川菊), both a short walk southeast of the *kurazukuri*. The area is also known for its *satsaimo* (sweet potato) dishes; sample some at the confectionry shop and café *Kurazukuri Honpo* (くくらづくり本舗) on Chūō-dōri.

Kotobukian (寿庵; closed Tues), beside Kita-in, is good for soba. For udon, try the popular *Unton* (うんとん), behind the soy-sauce store Kinbue on Chūō-dōri, opposite the Kawagoe Festival Hall. If you happen to still be in town in the evening, consider dropping by *Supeisu* (スペイス; daily 7pm–2am), a cool **bar** in an old wooden building fronted by a small bamboo grove, near Naritasan Betsu-in.

Kamakura and Enoshima

An hour's train ride south of Tokyo lies the small, relaxed town of **Kamakura**, trapped between the sea and a circle of wooded hills. The town is steeped in history, and many of its 65 temples and 19 shrines date back some eight centuries, when, for a brief and tumultuous period, it was Japan's political and military centre. Its most famous sight is the **Daibutsu**, a glorious bronze Buddha surrounded by trees, but the town's ancient **Zen temples** are equally compelling. Kamakura's prime sights can be covered on a day-trip from Tokyo, but the town more than justifies a two-day visit, allowing you time to explore the enchanting temples of **east Kamakura**, to follow one of the gentle "hiking courses" up into the hills, or to ride the Enoden line a few kilometres west to tiny **Enoshima** island. If at all possible, avoid weekends and national holidays and July and August, when both Kamakura and Enoshima are swamped with tourists. In summer, the coast here is a favourite spot for windsurfing.

Kamakura

If you're visiting **KAMAKURA** (鎌倉) on a day-trip, you could reasonably start with the temples of **Kita-Kamakura**, the town's northern suburb, and then walk south to the sights of **central Kamakura**, before finishing up at the Great Buddha in **Hase** on its western outskirts. Make sure you get an early start: most sights close early (generally 4 or 4.30pm in winter and only a little later in summer).

The town's biggest **festivals** take place in early April (second Sun to third or fourth Sun) and mid-September, including displays of horseback archery and costume parades, though the summer fireworks display (second Tues in Aug) over Sugami Bay is the most spectacular event. Kamakura is also well known for its spring blossoms and autumn colours, while many temple gardens are famous for a particular flower – for example, Japanese apricot at Zuisen-ji and Tōkei-ji (February) and hydrangea at Meigetsu-in (mid-June).

Some history

In 1185 the warlord **Minamoto Yoritomo** became the first permanent shogun and the effective ruler of Japan. Seven years later he established his military government – known as the Bakufu, or "tent government" – in Kamakura. Over the next century, dozens of grand monuments were built here, notably the great Zen temples founded by monks fleeing Song-dynasty China. Zen Buddhism flourished under the patronage of a warrior class who shared similar ideals of single-minded devotion to duty and rigorous self-discipline.

The Minamoto rule was brief and violent. Almost immediately, Yoritomo turned against his valiant younger brother, Yoshitsune, who had led the clan's armies, and hounded him until Yoshitsune committed ritual suicide (*seppuku*) – a favourite tale of Kabuki theatre. Both the second and third Minamoto shoguns were murdered, and in 1219 power passed to the Hōjō clan, who ruled as fairly able regents behind puppet shoguns. Their downfall followed the Mongol invasions in the late thirteenth century, and in 1333 Emperor Go-Daigo wrested power back to Kyoto; as the imperial armies approached Kamakura, the last Hōjō regent and an estimated eight hundred retainers committed *seppuku*. Kamakura remained an important military centre before fading into obscurity in the late fifteenth century. Its temples, however, continued to attract religious pilgrims until Kamakura was "rediscovered" in the last century as a tourist destination and a desirable residential area within commuting distance of Tokyo.

Kita-Kamakura

As the Tokyo train nears Kita-Kamakura Station, urban sprawl gradually gives way to gentle, forested hills which provide the backdrop for some of Kamakura's greatest Zen temples. Chief among these are **Kenchō-ji** and the wonderfully atmospheric **Engaku-ji**. It takes over an hour to cover the prime sights, walking south along the main road, the Kamakura-kaidō, to the edge of central Kamakura. With more time, follow the Daibutsu Hiking Course up into the western hills to wash your yen at an alluring temple dedicated to **Zeniarai Benten**.

Engaku-ji

The second most important but most satisfying of Kamakura's major Zen temples, **Engaku-ji** (円覚寺; daily: April–Oct 8am–5pm; Nov–March 8am–4pm; ¥300) lies buried among ancient cedars just two minutes' walk east of Kita-Kamakura Station. It was founded in 1282 to honour victims (on both sides) of the ultimately unsuccessful Mongolian invasions in 1274 and 1281. The layout follows a traditional Chinese Zen formula – a pond and bridge (now cut off by the train tracks), followed by a succession of somewhat austere buildings – but the encroaching trees and secretive gardens add a gentler touch.

The first building inside the compound, Engaku-ji's two-storeyed main gate, **San-mon**, is a magnificent structure, rebuilt in 1783, beneath which the well-worn flagstones bear witness to generations of pilgrims. Beyond, the modern **Butsu-den** (Buddha Hall) houses the temple's primary Buddha image, haloed in soft light, while behind it the charming **Shari-den** lies tucked off to the left past an oblong pond. This small reliquary, usually closed to visitors, is said to contain a tooth of the Buddha brought here from China in the early thirteenth century. It's also considered Japan's finest example of Song-dynasty Zen architecture, albeit a sixteenth-century replica. The main path continues gently uphill to another pretty thatched building, **Butsunichi-an** (¥100), where regent Hōjō Tokimune was buried in 1284; in fine weather green tea is served in its attractive garden (¥500 including entrance). Finally, tiny **Ōbai-in** enshrines a pale-yellow Kannon statue, but its best attribute is a nicely informal garden with a grove of Japanese apricot.

On the way out, follow signs up a steep flight of steps to the left of San-mon to find Kamakura's biggest bell, **Ōgane**, forged in 1301 and an impressive 2.5m tall.

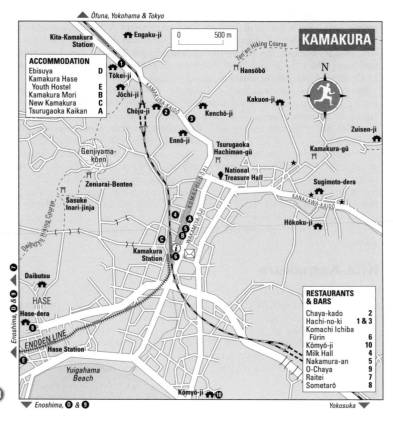

At the top of the map:

▲ Ōfuna, Yokohama & Tokyo

KAMAKURA

N

0   500 m

Kita-Kamakura Station
Engaku-ji
Ten'en Hiking Course
Hansōbō
Tōkei-ji
Jōchi-ji
Chōju-ji
Kenchō-ji
Kakuon-ji
Zuisen-ji
Ennō-ji
Genjiyama-kōen
Tsurugaoka Hachiman-gū
Kamakura-gū
National Treasure Hall
Zeniarai-Benten
Sugimoto-dera
Sasuke Inari-jinja
Daibutsu Hiking Course
KANAZAWA-KAIDŌ
Hōkoku-ji
Daibutsu
Kamakura Station
HASE
Hase-dera
ENODEN LINE
Hase Station
Yuigahama Beach
Kōmyō-ji

ACCOMMODATION

Ebisuya	D
Kamakura Hase Youth Hostel	E
Kamakura Mori	B
New Kamakura	C
Tsurugaoka Kaikan	A

RESTAURANTS & BARS

Chaya-kado	2
Hachi-no-ki	1 & 3
Komachi Ichiba Fūrin	6
Kōmyō-ji	10
Milk Hall	4
Nakamura-an	5
O-Chaya	9
Raitei	7
Sometarō	8

▼ Enoshima, **D** & **9**   Yokosuka ▼

At the adjacent teahouse you can enjoy a cup of *matcha* (¥600) while admiring the view across the valley to Tōkei-ji, the next stop.

Tōkei-ji and Jōchi-ji

One minutes' walk along the main road from Engaku-ji, **Tōkei-ji** (東慶寺; daily: March–Oct 8.30am–5pm; Nov–Feb 8.30am–4pm; ¥100) was founded as a nunnery in 1285 by the young widow of Hōjō Tokimune. It's an intimate temple, with a pleasing cluster of buildings and a profusion of flowers at almost any time of year: Japanese apricot in February, magnolia and peach in late March, followed by peonies and then irises in early June; September is the season for cascades of bush clover.

Tōkei-ji is more popularly known as the "Divorce Temple". Up until the mid-nineteenth century, when women were given the legal right to seek divorce, this was one of the few places where wives could escape domestic ill-treatment. If they reached the sanctuary, which many didn't, they automatically received a divorce after three years according to traditional temple law. Husbands could be summoned to resolve the dispute or, ultimately, sign the divorce papers. Some of these documents are preserved, along with other temple treasures, in the **Treasure House** (Mon–Fri 9.30am–3pm; ¥300), including two books detailing the women's reasons for seeking sanctuary – unfortunately, not translated. At the back of the temple, take a walk round the peaceful, mossy cemetery hidden among stately cryptomeria trees, where many famous and forgotten nuns lie buried.

Further along the main valley almost as far as the train tracks, a sign to the right indicates **Jōchi-ji** (浄智寺; daily 9am–4.30pm; ¥200), the fourth most important of Kamakura's great Zen temples. Founded by the nephew of Hōjō Tokimune in 1283, Jōchi-ji was almost completely levelled by the 1923 earthquake. Nevertheless, it's worth walking up the lane to see its beautifully proportioned Chinese-style gate which doubles as a bell tower. The small worship hall contains a trinity of Buddhas while, at the back, there's another graveyard, this time sheltered by a bamboo grove.

Zeniarai Benten and the Daibutsu Hiking Course

Follow the lane running south beside Jōchi-ji and you'll find the steps which mark the start of the **Daibutsu Hiking Course** (大仏ハイキングコース). This meandering ridge-path (2.2km) makes an enjoyable approach to Hase's Great Buddha (see p.282), but in any case it's well worth taking a diversion as far as the captivating cave-shrine dedicated to the goddess **Zeniarai Benten** (銭洗弁天), the "Money-Washing Benten", an incarnation of the goddess of good fortune, music and water. From Jōchi-ji, follow the somewhat erratic signs for Genjiyama-kōen (源氏山公園) along a trail heading southeast through the park, to a road junction where the main trail turns right. Here, you'll pick up signs pointing steeply downhill to where a *torii* and banners mark the shrine entrance. Duck under the tunnel to emerge in a natural amphitheatre filled with a forest of *torii* wreathed in incense and candle-smoke.

A constant stream of hopeful punters come here, despite its being so hidden, to test the goddess's powers. According to tradition, money washed in the spring, which gushes out of a cave on the opposite side from the entrance, is guaranteed to double at the very least, though not immediately. It's worth a shot – your notes won't dissolve – but let the money dry naturally to retain the beneficial effects.

If you're following the Daibutsu Hiking Course all the way to Hase, then rather than retracing your steps, take the path heading south under a tunnel of tightly packed *torii*, zigzagging down to the valley bottom. Turn right at a T-junction to find another avenue of vermilion *torii* leading uphill deep into the cryptomeria forest. At the end lies a simple shrine, **Sasuke Inari-jinja** (佐助稲荷神社), dating from before the twelfth century and dedicated to the god of harvests. His messenger is the fox; as you head up the steep path behind, to the left of the shrine buildings, climbing over tangled roots, you'll find fox statues of all shapes and sizes peering out of the surrounding gloom. At the top, turn right and then left at a white signboard to pick up the hiking course for the final 1500m to the Daibutsu (see p.283).

South to Kenchō-ji and Ennō-ji

Back at the main road near Jōchi-ji, walk southwest for another five minutes to find the greatest of Kamakura's Zen temples, **Kenchō-ji** (建長寺; daily 8.30am–4.30pm; ¥300), headquarters of the Rinzai sect and Japan's oldest Zen training monastery. More formal than Engaku-ji and a lot less peaceful, largely because of the neighbouring high school, Kenchō-ji contains several important buildings, most of which have been relocated here from Tokyo and Kyoto to replace those lost since the temple's foundation in 1253. Again, the design of the layout shows a strong Chinese influence; the founding abbot was another Song Chinese émigré, in this case working under the patronage of Hōjō Tokiyori, the devout fifth regent and father of Engaku-ji's Tokumine.

Zazen, or sitting meditation, is a crucial aspect of Zen Buddhist training, particularly among followers of the Rinzai sect. Several temples in Kamakura hold public *zazen* sessions at various levels, of which the most accessible are those at Engaku-ji (daily: April–Oct at 5.30am; Nov–March at 6am in the Butsu-den; second and fourth Sunday of month at 10am in the Hōjō, or abbot's hall; ℡0467/22-0478) and Kenchō-ji (Fri & Sat 5pm in the Hōjō; ℡0467/22-0981). These hour-long sessions are free and no reservations are required, though it's best to check the current schedule with the temple or Kamakura information office (see p.284) before setting out, and you should get there at least fifteen minutes early. Though non-Japanese speakers are welcome, you'll get much more out of it if you take an interpreter.

The main complex begins with the towering, copper-roofed **San-mon**, an eighteenth-century reconstruction, to the right of which hangs the original temple **bell**, cast in 1255 and considered one of Japan's most beautiful. Beyond San-mon, a grove of gnarled and twisted juniper trees hides the dainty, nicely dilapidated **Butsu-den**. The main image is, unusually, of Jizō (the guardian deity of children) seated on a lotus throne, his bright, half-closed eyes piercing the gloom. Behind is the **Hattō**, or lecture hall, one of Japan's largest wooden Buddhist buildings. The curvaceous Chinese-style gate, **Kara-mon**, and the **Hōjō** hall beyond are much more attractive structures. Walk round the latter's balcony to find a **pond-garden** generally attributed to a thirteenth-century monk, making it Japan's oldest-surviving Zen garden, though it's recently been spruced up considerably.

Behind the Hōjō, a path heads the up steep steps past **Hansōbō**, a shrine guarded by statues of long-nosed, mythical *tengu*. This is the start of the **Ten'en Hiking Course** (天園ハイキングコース). It takes roughly one and a half hours to complete the five-kilometre trail from Kenchō-ji, which loops round the town's northeast outskirts to Zuisen-ji (see p.282); for a shorter walk (2.5km), you can cut down earlier to Kamakura-gū (see opposite).

Sticking to the main road, however, from Kenchō-ji there's one last temple to visit before you hit central Kamakura. **Ennō-ji** (円応寺; daily: March–Nov 9am–4pm; Dec–Feb 9am–3pm; ¥200) looks fairly insignificant, but inside its hall reside the red-faced King of Hell, Enma, and his ten cohorts. This ferocious crew are charged with deciding the appropriate level of reincarnation in your next life and their wonderfully realistic expressions are meant to scare you into better ways. The statues are actually reproductions – the originals are in safekeeping in the National Treasure Hall (see opposite), but usually only one is displayed there, whereas here you get to see the whole gang.

From Ennō-ji it's only another five minutes through the tunnel and downhill to the side entrance of Tsurugaoka Hachiman-gū (see opposite).

Central Kamakura

Modern Kamakura revolves around its central **train station** and a couple of touristy streets leading to the town's most important shrine, Tsurugaoka Hachiman-gū. The traditional approach to this grand edifice lies along **Wakamiya-ōji**, which runs straight from the sea to the shrine entrance. Shops here peddle a motley collection of souvenirs and crafts, the most famous of which is *kamakura-bori*, an 800-year-old method of laying lacquer over carved wood. More popular, however, is *hato*, a pigeon-shaped French-style biscuit first made by Toshimaya bakers a century ago. You can buy them all over town, but walk up Wakamiya-ōji to find their main shop (daily except Wed 9am–7pm), with telltale ironwork pigeons on the outside, halfway along. Shadowing Wakamiya-ōji to the west is **Komachi-dōri**, a narrow, pedestrian-only shopping street, packed with more souvenir shops, restaurants and increasingly trendy boutiques.

Tsurugaoka Hachiman-gū

A majestic, vermilion-lacquered *torii* marks the front entrance to **Tsurugaoka Hachiman-gū** (鶴岡八幡宮), the Minamoto clan's guardian shrine since 1063. Hachiman-gū, as it's popularly known, was moved to its present site in 1191, since when it has witnessed some of the more unsavoury episodes of Kamakura history. Most of the present buildings date from the early nineteenth century, and their striking red paintwork, combined with the parade of souvenir stalls and the constant bustle of people, create a festive atmosphere in sharp contrast to that of Kamakura's more secluded Zen temples.

Three humpback bridges lead into the shrine compound between two connected ponds known as **Genpei-ike**. These were designed by Minamoto Yoritomo's wife, Hōjō Masako, and are full of heavy, complicated symbolism, anticipating the longed-for victory of her husband's clan over their bitter enemies, the Taira; strangely, the bloodthirsty Masako was of Taira stock. The **Mai-den**, an open-sided stage at the end of a broad avenue, was the scene of another unhappy event in 1186, when Yoritomo forced his brother's mistress, Shizuka, to dance for the assembled samurai. Yoritomo wanted his popular brother, Yoshitsune, killed and was holding Shizuka prisoner in the hope of discovering his whereabouts; instead, she made a defiant declaration of love and only narrowly escaped death herself, though her newborn son was murdered soon after. Her bravery is commemorated with classical dances and Nō plays during the shrine **festival** (Sept 14–16), which also features demonstrations of horseback archery on the final day.

Beyond the Mai-den, a long flight of steps leads up beside a knobbly, ancient ginkgo tree, reputedly 1000 years old and scene of the third shogun's murder by his vengeful nephew, to the **main shrine**. It's an attractive collection of buildings set among trees, though, as with all Shinto shrines, you can only peer in. Appropriately, the principal deity, Hachiman, is the God of War.

The **Hōmotsu-den** (daily 8.30am–4.30pm; ¥200), in a corridor immediately left of the shrine, contains a missable exhibition of shrine treasures. Instead, head back down the steps and turn left to find the beautifully restrained, black-lacquered **Shirahata-jinja**, dedicated to the first and third Kamakura shoguns, then take the path south to the modern **Kamakura National Treasure Hall** (鎌倉国宝館; Tues–Sun 9am–4.30pm; ¥300; English-language leaflet ¥250). This one-room museum is noted for its collection of Kamakura- and Muromachi-period art (1192–1573), mostly gathered from local Zen temples. Unfortunately, only a few of the priceless pieces are on display at any one time.

East Kamakura

The eastern side of Kamakura contains a scattering of less-visited shrines and temples, including two of the town's most enchanting corners. Though it's possible to cover the area on foot in a half-day, less if you hop on a bus for the return journey, by far the best way to explore these scattered locations is to rent a bicycle (see p.284 for information on buses and bikes).

If you're starting from Hachiman-gū, you can work your way eastwards through a quiet suburban area north of the main highway, the Kanazawa-kaidō, until you find signs indicating an optional left turn for **Kamakura-gū** (鎌倉宮). Mainly of interest for its history and torchlight Nō dramas in early October, this was founded by Emperor Meiji in 1869 to encourage support for his new imperial regime. The shrine is dedicated to Prince Morinaga, a forgotten fourteenth-century hero who helped restore his father, Emperor Go-Daigo, briefly to the throne. The prince was soon denounced, however, by power-hungry rivals and held for nine months in a Kamakura cave before being executed. The small cave and a desultory treasure house (daily: Jan–Nov 9am–4.30pm; Dec 9am–4pm; ¥300) lie to the rear of the classically styled shrine, but don't really justify the entry fee.

A road heading north from Kamakura-gū marks the beginning – or end – of the shortcut to the Ten'en Hiking Course (see p.280), though the main trail starts 900m further east, near **Zuisen-ji** (瑞泉寺; daily: April–Sept 9am–5pm; Oct–March 9am–4.30pm; ¥100). The temple's fourteenth-century Zen garden, to the rear of the main building, is rather dilapidated, but the quiet, wooded location and luxuriant gardens in front of the temple make it an attractive spot.

From here you have to drop south and join the main road for the last short stretch to Kamakura's oldest temple, **Sugimoto-dera** (杉本寺; daily 8am–4.30pm; ¥200), at the top of a steep, foot-worn staircase lined with fluttering white flags. Standing in a woodland clearing, the small, thatched temple, founded in 734, exudes a real sense of history. Inside its smoke-blackened hall, spattered with pilgrims' prayer stickers, you can slip off your shoes and take a look behind the altar at the three wooden statues of Jūichimen Kannon, the eleven-faced Goddess of Mercy. The images were carved at different times by famous monks, but all three are at least 1000 years old. According to legend, they survived a devastating fire in 1189 by taking shelter – all by themselves – behind a giant tree; since then the temple has been known as Sugimoto ("Under the Cedar").

Just a couple of minutes further east along Kanazawa-kaidō, turn right over a small bridge to reach the entrance to **Hōkoku-ji** (報国寺; daily 9am–4pm; closed Dec 29–Jan 3; ¥200), or Take-dera, the "Bamboo Temple". The well-tended gardens and simple wooden buildings are attractive in themselves, but the temple is best known for a grove of evergreen bamboo protected by the encircling cliffs. This dappled forest of thick, gently curved stems, where tinkling water spouts and the soft creaking of the wind-rocked canes muffle the outside world, would seem the perfect place for the monks' meditation. Too soon, though, the path emerges beside the manicured rear garden, which was created by the temple's founding priest in the thirteenth century.

To return to central Kamakura, you can catch a bus for the two-kilometre ride from opposite Sugimoto-dera. Alternatively, take the small lane to the left in front of Hōkoku-ji and follow it west through an attractive residential area, which cuts off at least a chunk of the highway.

Hase-dera and the Daibutsu

The west side of Kamakura, an area known as **Hase** (長谷), is home to the town's most famous sight, the Daibutsu (Great Buddha), cast in bronze nearly 750 years ago. On the way, it's worth visiting Hase-dera to see an image of Kannon, the Goddess of Mercy, which is said to be Japan's largest wooden statue. Both these sights are within walking distance of Hase Station, three stops from Kamakura Station (¥190) on the private Enoden line.

Hase–dera (長谷寺; daily: March–Sept 8am–5pm; Oct–Feb 8am–4.30pm; ¥300; ⓦ www.hasedera.jp) stands high on the hillside a few minutes' walk north of Hase Station, with good views of Kamakura and across Yuigahama beach to the Miura peninsula beyond. Though the temple's present layout dates from the mid-thirteenth century, according to legend it was founded in 736, when a

wooden eleven-faced Kannon was washed ashore nearby. The statue is supposedly one of a pair carved from a single camphor tree in 721 by a monk in the
original Hase, near Nara; he placed one Kannon in a local temple and pushed the
other out to sea.

Nowadays the **Kamakura Kannon** – just over 9m tall and gleaming with gold
leaf (a fourteenth-century embellishment) – resides in an attractive, chocolate-
brown and cream building at the top of the temple steps. This central hall is flanked
by two smaller buildings: the right hall houses a large Amidha Buddha carved in
1189 for Minamoto Yoritomo's 42nd birthday to ward off the bad luck traditionally associated with that age; while that on the left shelters an early fifteenth-
century statue of Daikoku-ten, the cheerful God of Wealth. In fact the statue here
is a copy. The real one is in the small **treasure hall** (Tues–Sun 9am–4pm) immediately behind, alongside the original temple bell, cast in 1264. The next building
along is the Sutra Repository, where a revolving drum contains a complete set of
Buddhist scriptures – one turn of the wheel is equivalent to reading the whole lot.
Ranks of Jizō statues are a common sight in Hase-dera, some clutching sweets or
"windmills" and wrapped in tiny, woollen mufflers; these sad little figures
commemorate stillborn or aborted children. Finally, a cave in the far northern
corner of the complex contains statues of the goddess Benten (also known as
Benzaiten) and her sixteen children, or disciples, though it can't compete with the
atmospheric setting of the Zeniarai Benten cave-shrine (see p.279).

The Daibutsu

From Hase-dera, turn left at the main road and follow the crowds north for a few
hundred metres to find the **Daibutsu** (大仏; daily: April–Sept 7am–6pm; Oct–
March 7am–5.30pm; ¥200), in the grounds of Kōtoku-in temple. After all the
hype, the Great Buddha can seem a little disappointing, but as you approach, and
his serene, rather aloof face comes into view, the magic begins to take hold. He sits
on a stone pedestal, a broad-shouldered figure lost in deep meditation, with his
head slightly bowed, his face and robes streaked grey-green by centuries of sun,
wind and rain. The thirteen-metre-tall image represents Amida Nyorai, the future
Buddha who receives souls into the Western Paradise, and was built under the
orders of Minamoto Yoritomo to rival the larger Nara Buddha, near Kyoto.
Completed in 1252, the statue is constructed of bronze plates bolted together
around a hollow frame – you can climb inside for ¥20 (daily 8am–4.30pm) – and
evidence suggests that, at some time, it was covered in gold leaf. Amazingly, it has
withstood fires, typhoons, tidal waves and even the Great Earthquake of 1923. Its
predecessor, however, was less successful: the wooden statue was unveiled in 1243,
only to be destroyed in a violent storm just five years later. Various attempts to
build a shelter suffered similar fates until, happily, they gave up after 1498 and left
the Daibutsu framed by trees and an expanse of sky.

Practicalities

The easiest way of **getting to Kamakura** is either the JR Yokosuka line from
Tokyo Station via Yokohama, or the JR Shōnan-Shinjuku line from Shinjuku
via Shibuya and Yokohama (1hr; ¥890); from Tokyo Station, make sure you
board a Yokosuka- or Kurihama-bound train to avoid changing at Ōfuna. Trains
stop at Kita-Kamakura before pulling into the main Kamakura Station three
minutes later. For a two-day outing it's worth considering the Kamakura-
Enoshima Free Kippu (¥1970), a discount ticket covering the return trip by JR
services from Tokyo, and unlimited travel on the Enoden line and Shōnan
monorail (see p.287).

Outside the main, eastern exit of Kamakura Station, and immediately to the right, there's a small **tourist information** window (daily 9am–5pm; ☏ 0467/22-3350, ⊛ www.kcn-net.org/kamakura) with English-speaking staff. They hand out free maps with the main sights marked in English, or you can buy a slightly more detailed colour map along with a booklet (¥200) outlining suggested itineraries and the hiking trails; though it's mostly in Japanese, basic details are provided in English.

Local **buses** depart from the main station concourse. Given the narrow roads and amount of traffic, however, it's usually quicker to use the trains as far as possible and then walk. The only time a bus might come in handy is for the more far-flung restaurants or the eastern sites; in the latter case you want stand 4 for Kamakura-gū and stand 5 for Sugimoto-dera (¥190 minimum fare). To make three or more journeys by bus, you'll save money by buying a Kamakura Free Kippu (¥550), a day-pass available from the JR ticket office. The pass also covers JR trains from Kamakura to Kita-Kamakura and Enoden line services as far as Hase.

A better, but more expensive, option is to rent a **bike** from the outfit outside the station's east exit; turn right as you emerge and it's up the slope on the south side of the square (daily 8.30am–5pm). Rates are on a sliding scale, from ¥500 for the first hour to ¥1500 for a day on weekdays and ¥550 and ¥1600 respectively on weekends and national holidays, when you should try to get there early. You'll need to show a passport and give the name of your hotel.

On the west side of Kamakura Station are ticket machines and platforms for the private **Enoden line** (⊛ www.enoden.co.jp) to Hase and Enoshima, with trains running roughly every twelve minutes from 6am to 11pm. If you plan to hop on and off the Enoden line a lot – for example, going from Kamakura to Hase to Enoshima and back, or on to Fujisawa to pick up a Tokyo-bound train – and haven't got any other form of discount ticket, it's worth investing in the "One Day Free Ticket" (¥580), which entitles you to unlimited travel on the Enoden line.

There's an international ATM (Mon–Fri 8am–9pm, Sat & Sun 8am–7pm) at the post office on Wakamiya-ōji, and you can change money at Yokohama Bank outside the station's east exit.

Accommodation

Central Kamakura offers little budget accommodation, but a fair choice of mid-range hotels. Another option is to stay on Enoshima (see p.286) and enjoy the island when the crowds have gone. Many places charge higher rates at weekends and during peak holiday periods, when it's hard to get a room in any case.

Hotel Kamakura Mori
3F, 1-5-21 Komachi ☏ 0467/22-5868, ⊛ www1.ocn.ne.jp/~hotelkm. A short walk up Wakamiya-ōji from the station, the *Mori* offers clean, decent-sized twin or triple rooms with TV and en-suite bathrooms, though rates are expensive at ¥19,000 for two and ¥14,200 for single use.

Hotel New Kamakura
13-2 Onarimachi ☏ 0467/22-2230. The nicest place to stay in Kamakura is this welcoming hotel in an early twentieth-century, Western-style building, a minute's walk north of Kamakura Station – take the west exit and follow the train tracks. Don't be put off by the car park out front: inside the rooms are light and airy, with a choice of Western or Japanese style. Prices start at a very reasonable ¥11,000 for a twin with shared bathroom, or ¥15,000 en suite.

Hotel Tsurugaoka Kaikan
2-12-27 Komachi ☏ 0467/24-1111, ⊛ www.tsurugaoka-kaikan.com. Big, old-fashioned hotel on Wakamiya-ōji, which doubles as the wedding venue "Kamakura Marriage Avenue" – hence the glitzy chandeliers and expanses of floral wallpaper. The comfortable twin rooms are more restrained, with Western beds, a tatami sitting area and small en-suite bathroom. Prices start at around ¥18,000 on a weekday with no meals, rising to ¥32,000 for two meals on a

Saturday, when it's usually booked solid with weddings. Single rooms are expensive at ¥13,500 and ¥24,000 respectively.

Kamakura Hase Youth Hostel
鎌倉長谷ユースホステル
5-11 Sakanoshita ☎0467/24-3390, ⓦwww1
.kamakuranet.ne.jp/hase_yh. Small hostel with

bunk-bed dorms, a 3min walk from Hase Station – follow the tracks heading away from Kamakura. Reception is open 3.30–8pm and they serve breakfast and dinner. HI members ¥3000 per person; non-members ¥4000.

Eating and drinking

Kamakura is famous for its beautifully presented Buddhist vegetarian cuisine, known as **shōjin ryōri**, though there's plenty more casual dining on offer at local restaurants. For a picnic, Kinokuniya has a good food hall on the west side of Kamakura Station, or try Union Store on Wakamiya-ōji. In summer, funky wooden bars line the beaches from Kamakura to Enoshima.

Chaya-kado
茶屋かど
1518 Yamanouchi. This homely soba restaurant, on the opposite side of the main road just north of the entrance to Kenchō-ji, makes a good pit stop on the temple trail. Try *chikara* udon, which comes with a couple of filling *mochi* (steamed pounded rice cakes), for ¥1100. Dishes from ¥700. Inexpensive to moderate. Daily 10am–6pm.

Hachi-no-ki Honten
鉢の木本店
7 Yamanouchi ☎0120/22-8719; **also opposite Tōkei-ji in Kita-Kamakura** ☎0120-23-3722. Reservations are recommended for this famous *shōjin ryōri* restaurant beside the entrance to Kenchō-ji, though it's easier to get a table at their newer Kita-Kamakura branch. Whichever you opt for, prices start at around ¥3000 for a course menu. Moderate to expensive. Tues–Fri 11am–2pm, Sat & Sun 11am–3pm; Kita-Kamakura branch daily except Wed 11am–7pm.

Komachi Ichiba Fūrin
こまち市場風凛
2F, 1-1-1 Komachi. This surprisingly stylish *izakaya* above JR Kamakura Station is justifiably popular for its warm welcome and extensive choice of well-priced dishes, from salads to sashimi. Inexpensive to moderate. Daily 11am–10pm.

Kōmyō-ji
光明寺
6-1-19 Zaimokuza ☎0467/22-0603. Enjoy the full *shōjin ryōri* experience in this temple set in beautiful gardens on the coast in southern Kamakura. Prices start at ¥4000 for a minimum of two people. Reservations required at least a day in advance. Expensive. Open for lunch only.

Milk Hall
ミルクホール
2-3-8 Komachi ☎0467/22-1179. Relaxed, jazz-playing coffee house-cum-antique shop buried in the backstreets west of Komachi-dōri. Best for a coffee and cake, or an evening beer, rather than as a place to eat. Occasional live music. Daily 11am–10.30pm.

Nakamura-an
なかむら庵
1-7-6 Komachi. A homely restaurant that has them queuing up outside at weekends for the handmade soba. To find it, walk up Wakamiya-ōji and take the first left after the Union Store. Dishes start at ¥700. Inexpensive to moderate. Daily except Tues 11am–4.30pm.

Raitei
櫑亭
Takasago ☎0467/32-5656, ⓦwww.raitei.com. Atmospheric restaurant in an old farmhouse set in gardens among the hills west of Kamakura, with views to Fuji if you're lucky. Basic soba set meals start at ¥700 and there's a choice of beautifully presented *bentō* from ¥2600 up; the garden entry fee (¥500) is discounted from your bill. Though a bit off the beaten track, it's worth the effort; take bus #4 or #6 from stand 6 outside Kamakura Station to the Takasago stop (2–3 hourly; 20min; ¥230). Moderate to expensive. Daily 11am–dusk.

Sometarō
染太郎
2F, 3-12-11 Hase. Traditional DIY *okonomiyaki* restaurant in front of Hase-dera. A bowl of ingredients costs around ¥900. *Teppanyaki* is also available. Inexpensive to moderate. Daily 11.30am–10pm.

Enoshima

Tied to the mainland by a 600-metre-long bridge, the tiny, sacred island of **Enoshima** (江の島) has a few sights – some shrines, a botanical garden and a couple of missable caves – but its prime attraction is as a pleasant place to walk away from motor traffic. If you're here in early August, you can also catch an excellent fireworks display on the first Tuesday of the month.

As the Enoden line train rattles into Enoshima Station from Kamakura, look out on the right for the copper-clad roofs of **Ryūkō-ji** (龍口寺). This temple was built on the spot where the monk Nichiren, founder of the eponymous Buddhist sect, was nearly beheaded in 1271 for his persistent criticisms of the government and rival sects. According to legend, as the executioner's sword was about to fall, a fortuitous bolt of lightning split the blade in two, just in time for the shogun's messenger to arrive with a reprieve. Ryūkō-ji was founded a few years later and the main hall, its Buddha image surrounded by a sea of gold, is a good example of the sect's striking decorative style. To the left of the hall there's a statue of Nichiren in the cave (more a hollow in the rock) where he was imprisoned, while steps to the right of the hall lead to where a magnificent five-storey pagoda, erected in 1910, seems part of the surrounding forest.

From Enoshima Station it's roughly fifteen minutes' walk southwest to the island, via a bridge constructed over the original sand spit. Enoshima's eastern side shelters a yacht harbour and car parks, but otherwise the knuckle of rock – less than 1km from end to end – is largely covered with woods and a network of well-marked paths. From here, walk straight ahead under the bronze *torii* and uphill past restaurants and souvenir shops to where the steps begin; though the climb's easy enough, there are three escalators tunnelled through the hillside (¥350, or pay for each separately).

Enoshima is mostly famous for a naked **statue of Benten**, sitting in an octagonal hall halfway up the hill (daily 9am–4.30pm; ¥150). Though the pale-skinned, purple-haired beauty strumming her lute is said to be 600 years old and is ranked among Japan's top three Benten images, it's a little hard to see what all the fuss is about. Continuing round the hill, you'll pass several other shrine buildings belonging to **Enoshima-jinja**, founded in the thirteenth century and dedicated to the guardian of sailors and fisherfolk, before emerging beside a nicely laid-out **botanical garden**, known as the Samuel Cocking Park (April–June, Sept & Oct Mon–Fri 9am–6pm, Sat & Sun 9am–8pm; July & Aug daily 9am–8pm; Nov–March Mon–Fri 9am–5pm, Sat & Sun 9am–8pm; ¥200) after the English merchant and horticulturalist who built Japan's first greenhouse here in 1880. If it's clear, you'll get good views south to Ōshima's smoking volcano and west to Fuji from the lighthouse (an extra ¥300) inside the garden.

The path then drops down steeply past restaurant-bars perched over the cliff – great for a sunset beer in fine weather – to the island's rocky west shore and two caves known as **Iwaya** (岩屋; daily: March–Oct 9am–5pm; Nov–Feb 9am–4pm; ¥500). Though it's an attractive walk, you might want to give these very artificial grottoes, with their piped music and roaring dragons, a miss.

Instead of retracing your steps from here, on weekends you can hop on one of the small **boats** shuttling tourists back to the mainland, weather permitting (Sat & Sun 10am–4pm; ¥300).

Practicalities

Enoshima is 25 minutes west of Kamakura Station on the Enoden line (¥250). There are three options if you're heading directly back **to central Tokyo** from

Enoshima. The most straightforward is the Odakyū-Enoshima line direct to Shinjuku, though note that weekday services are few and far between. The trains depart from Katase-Enoshima Station (片瀬江ノ島駅); from the island causeway, turn left across the river to find the station with its distinctive Chinese-style facade. A pleasant alternative is to take the Shōnan monorail to Ōfuna, on the main JR lines to central Tokyo via Yokohama; Shōnan-Enoshima Station (湘南江ノ島駅) is located just north of the Enoden line station. The last option is to hop on the Enoden line west to its terminal in Fujisawa, where you have to change stations for JR services to central Tokyo.

You can pick up an English-language map of the island at the small **tourist office** (daily 10am–5pm; ℡0466/26-9544, ⓦwww.cityfujisawa.ne.jp/kankou), on the left as you come off the bridge. It's possible to **stay** on Enoshima at the *Ebisuya* (恵比寿屋; 1-4-16 Enoshima ℡0466/22-4105, ⓦwww.ebisuyaryokan.jp; doubles from ¥30,000 including two meals), a good-value ryokan. Just under the bronze *torii* and down an alley on the left, it offers well-maintained Western and tatami rooms, plus traditional baths and excellent meals.

If you're looking for somewhere to **eat**, head left (southeast) along the seafront from the causeway to find *O-Chaya* (おちゃや; 1-6-8 Enoshima; daily 9am–9pm), a bright, modern noodle shop overlooking the yacht harbour. It's nothing fancy but serves tasty soba and udon dishes (from ¥800), with the added advantage that it's away from the main drag.

Yokohama

O n its southern borders Tokyo merges with **YOKOHAMA** (横浜), Japan's second most populous city (home to 3.6 million people) and a major international port. Yokohama feels far more spacious and airy than the capital thanks to its open harbour frontage and generally low-rise skyline, and though it can't claim any outstanding sights, the place has enough of interest to justify a day's outing from Tokyo. Locals are proud of their city's international heritage, and there's definitely a cosmopolitan flavour to the place, with its scattering of Western-style buildings, Chinese temples and world cuisines, and its sizeable foreign community. It might seem strange to come all this way to look at nineteenth-century European-style architecture, but the upmarket suburb of **Yamate** is one of the city's highlights, an area of handsome residences, church spires and bijou teashops. Yamate's "exotic" attractions still draw Japanese tourists in large numbers, as do the vibrant alleys and speciality restaurants of nearby **Chinatown**. There's a clutch of assorted **museums** along the seafront, and north to where **Kannai** boasts a few grand old Western edifices, in complete contrast to the **Minato Mirai 21** development's hi-tech skyscrapers in the distance.

Yokohama promises to be particularly lively in 2009, with all sorts of events planned to celebrate the one-hundred-and-fiftieth anniversary of the **founding of the port** on June 2.

Some history

When Commodore Perry sailed his "Black Ships" into Tokyo Bay in 1853, Yokohama was a mere fishing village of some eighty houses on the distant shore. But it was this harbour, well out of harm's way as far as the Japanese were concerned, that the shogun designated one of the five **treaty ports** open to foreign trade in 1858. At first foreign merchants were limited to a small compound in today's Kannai – allegedly for their protection from anti-foreign sentiment – but eventually they moved up onto the more favourable southern hills.

From the early 1860s until the first decades of the twentieth century, Yokohama flourished on the back of raw silk exports, a trade dominated by British merchants. During this period the city provided the main conduit for new ideas and inventions into Japan: the first bakery, photographers, ice-cream shop, brewery and – perhaps most importantly – the first railway line, which linked today's Sakuragichō with Shimbashi in central Tokyo in 1872. Yokohama was soon established as Japan's major international port and held pole position until the **Great Earthquake** levelled the city in 1923, killing more than 40,000 people. It was eventually rebuilt, only to be devastated again in air raids at the end of World War II. By this time Kōbe in western Japan was in the ascendancy and, though Yokohama still figures among the world's largest ports, it never regained its hold over Japanese trade.

Arrival, information and city transport

The best way to get to Yokohama **from central Tokyo** is on a Tōkyū-Tōyoko-line **train** from Shibuya Station (every 5min; 30min; ¥260), which calls at Yokohama Station before heading off underground to Minato Mirai and terminating at the Motomachi-Chūkagai Station. If you're coming from Tokyo Station, you can choose from the Tōkaidō or Yokosuka lines (both every 5–10min; 30min; ¥450), or the Keihin-Tōhoku line (every 5–10min; 40min; ¥450). All three are JR lines; the first two terminate at Yokohama Station, while the latter continues to Sakuragichō, Kannai and Ishikawachō. From Shinjuku, JR's Shōnan-Shinjuku line brings you into Yokohama Station (every 20–30min; 30min; ¥540).

Yokohama's plethora of tourist **information** centres, with English-speaking staff, puts Tokyo's to shame. The most useful is the one immediately outside **Sakuragichō Station**'s east entrance (daily 9am–7pm; ☎045/211-0111). Other options include the office in the harbour-front **Sanbo Centre** east of Kannai Station (Mon–Fri 9am–5pm; ☎045/641-4759) and the booth in the underground concourse of **Yokohama Station** (daily 9am–7pm; ☎045/441-7300). They all provide free **city maps** and brochures, and can help with hotel reservations. There's also no shortage of information online at ⓦwww.welcome.city .yokohama.jp/eng/tourism, run by Yokohama Convention and Visitors Bureau; ⓦwww.kanagawa-kankou.or.jp, the website of Kanagawa Prefectural Tourist Association; and the city's home page, ⓦwww.city.yokohama.jp/en.

City transport

Getting around central Yokohama is best done on either the Tōkyū-Tōyoko line or the JR Negishi line (the local name for Keihin-Tōhoku trains); trains on both lines run every five minutes, with a minimum fare of ¥180. A single **subway** line connects Kannai and stations north to Shin-Yokohama, on the Shinkansen line, but services only run every five to fifteen minutes and the minimum fare is ¥200.

Another good option is the "Akai Kutsu" **sightseeing bus**, a retro-style red bus that runs from outside Sakuragichō Station's east exit via Minato Mirai, Akarenga complex, Chinatown and Yamashita-kōen to Harbour View Park, then loops back via Ōsanbashi pier. Services run every half-hour on weekdays and every twenty minutes at weekends from 10am to 6pm (May–Oct until 7pm). Individual tickets cost ¥100, but you'll probably be better off buying a day-pass (¥300), available from tourist offices or on the bus.

But perhaps the most enjoyable way of getting about the city are the *Sea Bass* **ferries** (ⓦwww.yokohama-cruising.jp) that shuttle between Yokohama Station (from a pier in the Bay Quarter shopping complex) and southerly Yamashita-kōen, with some services stopping at Minato Mirai and Akarenga on route. There are departures every fifteen minutes (roughly 10.30am–7pm, or 8pm March–Nov), with one-way tickets costing ¥600 to Yamashita-kōen, ¥350 to Minato Mirai and ¥500 to Akarenga.

From Yamashita-kōen you can also join the *Marine Shuttle* or *Marine Rouge* for a variety of **sightseeing cruises** round the harbour (from ¥900 for 40min; ⓦwww.yokohama-cruising.jp); the *Marine Rouge* also offers lunch and dinner cruises (¥2500 plus ¥5000–10,000 for food). In addition, the bigger and more luxurious *Royal Wing* cruise ship (☎045/662-6125, ⓦwww.royalwing.co.jp) runs lunch, tea and dinner cruises from Ōsanbashi pier (¥1600–2100 plus ¥2100–6,000 for food).

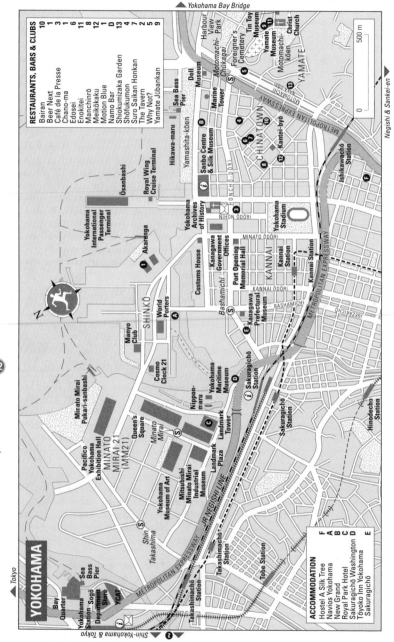

YOKOHAMA

▲ *Tokyo*

▲ *Yokohama Bay Bridge*

Bay Quarter

Sea Bass Pier

Yokohama Station Sōgō Department Store

YCAT

▲ *Shin-Yokohama & Tokyo*

Ōsanbashi

Royal Wing Cruise Terminal

Yokohama International Passenger Terminal

Akarenga

Manyo Club

Yokohama Passenger Terminal

SHINKŌ

World Porters

Customs House

Cosmo Clock 21

Nippon-maru

Yokohama Maritime Museum

Landmark Plaza

Landmark Tower

Queen's Square

MINATO MIRAI 21 (MM21)

Minato Mirai

Pacifico Yokohama Exhibition Hall

Minato Mirai Pukari-sanbashi

Yokohama Museum of Art

Mitsubishi Minato Mirai Industrial Museum

Shin Takashima

JR NEGISHI LINE

METROPOLITAN EXPRESSWAY

Takashimachō Station

Takashimachō Station

Tōbe Station

Sakuragichō Station

Sakuragichō Station

Hikawa-maru

Yamashita-kōen

Sea Bass Pier

Doll Museum

Marine Tower

Yokohama Archives of History

NIHON ŌDŌRI

Kanagawa Government Offices

Port Opening Memorial Hall

Kanagawa Prefectural Museum

Bashamichi

Bashamichi

BASHAMICHI

MINATO ŌDŌRI

KANNAI

Yokohama Stadium

Kannai Station

Kannai Station

Kannai Station

KANNAI ŌDŌRI

Sanbo Centre & Silk Museum

MOTOMACHI

CHINATOWN

Kantei-byō

Foreigner's Cemetery

Motomachi-Chūkagai

YAMATE

Harbour View Park

Tin Toy Museum

Yamate Museum

Christ Church

Motomachi-kōen

METROPOLITAN EXPRESSWAY

MOTOMACHI

METROPOLITAN EXPRESSWAY

Negishi & Sankei-en ▶

Ishikawachō Station

ISEZAKICHŌ

Hinodechō Station

0   500 m

RESTAURANTS, BARS & CLUBS

Bairan	10
Beer Next	1
Café de la Presse	3
Chano-ma	1
Edosei	6
Enokitei	11
Manchinrō	8
Meikōkaku	12
Motion Blue	1
Namo Bar	D
Shiokumizaka Garden	13
Shōfukumon	4
Suro Saikan Honkan	7
The Tavern	2
Why Not?	5
Yamate Jūbankan	9

ACCOMMODATION

Hostel A Silk Tree	F
Navios Yokohama	A
New Grand	B
Royal Park Hotel	C
Sakuragichō Washington	D
Tōyoko Inn Yokohama Sakuragichō	E

Accommodation

Yokohama's luxury **hotels**, all located in the Minato Mirai 21 district, are a tourist attraction in their own right. You'll need a reservation at the weekend (when premium rates also usually apply), though weekdays shouldn't be a problem. Lower down the scale, there are a few reasonable business hotels scattered round the city centre and some welcome new budget options.

Hostel A Silk Tree
8F 3-9-4 Matsukage-chō, Naka-ku ☎045/719-1541, ⓦ www.silktree.biz. Spotlessly clean hostel in a tenement block three minutes' walk from Ishikawachō Station. The rooms are basic, tatami-mat boxes, which will just about fit two at a squeeze, but all come with TV and a/c. Other facilities include a kitchen corner, Internet access, coin-operated showers (on the ground floor; ¥200) and laundry and bike rental (¥300 per day). Singles ¥3000, doubles ¥4500 including a small breakfast.

Hotel New Grand
10 Yamashita-chō, Naka-ku ☎045/681-1841, ⓦ www.hotel-newgrand.co.jp. Built in the late 1920s in European style, the main building retains some of its original elegance, while many rooms in the newer tower offer bay views. All come with satellite TV and en-suite bath, and there's a choice of three restaurants. Doubles from ¥38,000, or ¥43,000 with full bay views.

Navios Yokohama
Shinkō-chō, Naka-ku ☎045/633-6000, ⓦ www.navios-yokohama.com. The light, spacious rooms and reasonable rates make this one of the best-value options in Yokohama. Ask for a room facing the Landmark Tower for the best night-time views. Facilities include free Internet access, a restaurant and the *International Seamen's Club* bar. Western-style double rooms start at ¥15,000; Japanese-style ¥19,000.

Royal Park Hotel
2-2-1-3 Minato Mirai, Nishi-ku ☎045/221-1111, ⓦ www.yrph.com. The gargantuan Landmark Tower houses the *Royal Park* guest rooms on its fifty-second to sixty-seventh floors, so spectacular views are guaranteed. The rooms, which are gradually being modernized and jazzed up with wooden floors and contemporary art, are fairly spacious and come with good-sized bathrooms. As well as a fitness club and swimming pool (¥2100–5250), facilities include a tea-ceremony room (¥1000), the *Sirius Sky Lounge* bar on the seventieth floor, and French, Chinese and Japanese restaurants. Doubles from ¥45,000.

Sakuragichō Washington
1-1-67 Sakuragi-chō, Naka-ku ☎045/683-3111, ⓦ wh-rsv.com/english/yokohama_2. It's worth paying a little extra for a sea-view room at this business hotel conveniently located across the road from Sakuragichō Station, above the Cross Gate shopping mall. Rooms are relatively spacious and come with the usual amenities, including high-speed Internet access, fridge and a/c. Doubles from ¥16,000, or ¥18,000 with sea view.

Tōyoko Inn Yokohama Sakuragichō
東横イン横浜桜木町
6-55 Hon-chō, Naka-ku ☎045/671-1045, ⓦ www.toyoko-inn.co.jp. One of several Yokohama branches of this Japan-wide chain of budget business hotels, with good-value rooms, free Internet access and breakfast. Doubles from Y9300.

The City

Yokohama retains a few European-style buildings from its days as a treaty port, some of which lie scattered around **Kannai**, the traditional city centre. For a more evocative atmosphere, climb up to **Yamate** (also known as "the Bluff"), a genteel residential area of clapboard houses, tennis clubs and church spires on the southern hills. **Chinatown**, back down on the levels, makes for a lively contrast, with its hordes of colourful trinket shops and bustling restaurants. From here it's a short stroll down to the harbour-front **Marine Tower** and a couple of nearby museums, or a train ride north to where the aptly named **Landmark Tower**, Japan's tallest building, pinpoints the futuristic **Minato Mirai 21** (MM21) development. There are a couple of specific sights among its gleaming hotels, shopping malls and conference centres, notably a modern art museum and an incongruous four-masted barque, the **Nippon-maru**.

All these central sights can be covered in an easy day's outing; the account below starts with Yokohama's southern districts and heads north. With a little extra time **Sankei-en**, south of Yamate, makes a good half-day excursion. This extensive Japanese garden provides a perfect backdrop for its collection of picturesque temples and other ancient buildings.

Motomachi and Yamate

Southeast of central Yokohama, just before the land rises to Yamate hill, **Motomachi** (元町; Ⓦ www.motomachi.or.jp) is a chic shopping street from prewar days which used to serve the city's expatriate community. The narrow, semi-pedestrianized lane still exudes a faint retro flavour with its European facades, though the small boutiques and family stores are gradually giving way to the regular national and international chains. Nowadays, you'll get more of the old Motomachi feel in the two streets to either side, particularly Naka-dōri (仲通り), to the south, with its funky cafés and galleries.

At the northeast end of Motomachi, a wooded promontory marks the beginning of the Yamate (山手) district. Take any of the paths heading uphill through **Harbour View Park** to find a lookout point where the British and French barracks once stood – the panoramic view of the harbour and its graceful Bay Bridge is particularly beautiful at night. Turning inland and walking through the park will bring you to the **Foreigners' Cemetery** (Gaikokujin Bochi; 外国人墓地; late March to third week of Dec Sat & Sun noon–4pm; ¥200; Ⓦ www.yfgc-japan.com) on the western hillside. Over 4500 people from more than forty countries are buried here, the vast majority either British or American. Wandering among the crosses and sculpted angels, look out for Edward Morel, chief engineer on the Yokohama–Tokyo railway, who died of TB at the age of 30, and Charles Richardson, a British merchant whose murder in 1862 provoked a war between Britain and the Satsuma clan. You'll also find more modern tombstones – an average of twenty foreigners a year are still buried on Yamate.

If you head south along the cemetery's eastern perimeter, you'll pass a handsome row of houses, including the turreted Yamate Jūbankan – now a French restaurant (see p.298) – and, next door to it, the city's oldest wooden building. The latter, erected in 1909 for a wealthy Japanese family, now houses the **Yamate Museum** (daily 11am–4pm; ¥200), most interesting for its collection of cartoons from *Japan Punch*, a satirical magazine published in Yokohama for a while in the late nineteenth century. Just beyond, the square tower of **Christ Church**, founded in 1862 but rebuilt most recently in 1947, adds a village-green touch to the neighbourhood, which is still the most popular residential district for Yokohama's wealthy expatriates.

Just behind the church, the **Tin Toy Museum** (ブリキのおもちゃ博物館; Mon–Sat 9.30am–6pm, Sun 9.30am–7pm; ¥200) houses a wonderful collection of 13,000 tin toys from the 1890s to the 1960s. It also sells reproductions and other old-fashioned toys and, in a separate shop next door, you can buy a huge variety of Christmas decorations and stocking fillers at any time of year.

Down to the harbour

From Yamate, drop down through Motomachi-kōen and cross Motomachi shopping street to find one of the several colourful entrance gates to **Chinatown** (Chūka-gai; 中華街; ⓦ www.chinatown.or.jp). Founded in 1863, Yokohama's Chinatown is the largest in Japan: its streets contain roughly two hundred restaurants and over three hundred shops, while some eighteen million tourists pass through its narrow byways every year to browse stores peddling Chinese herbs or cooking utensils, groceries and garish souvenirs. Few leave without tasting what's on offer, from steaming savoury dumplings to a full-blown meal in one of the famous speciality restaurants (see p.297).

The fortunes of the Chinese community based here (around two thousand strong) have followed the vagaries of mainland history. During the late nineteenth and early twentieth centuries hundreds of radicals (most famously, Sun Yat-sen and Chiang Kai-shek) sought refuge here, while Communist and Nationalist factions polarized Chinatown in the 1940s and later during the Cultural Revolution. The focus of community life is **Kantei-byō** (関帝廟; daily 9am–7pm; free; ⓦ www.yokohama-kanteibyo.com), a shrine dedicated to Guan Yu, a former general and guardian deity of Chinatown. The building is a bit cramped, but impressive nonetheless, with a colourful ornamental gateway and writhing dragons wherever you look. Inside, a red-faced, long-haired Guan Yu sits on the main altar, gazing over the heads of supplicants petitioning for health and prosperity; you can pay ¥500 to enter, but you don't really see much more. The best times to visit are during the major festivities surrounding Chinese New Year (Jan or Feb), Guan Yu's birthday (the twenty-fourth day of the sixth lunar month; June or July) and Chinese National Day (Oct 1).

From the eastern edge of Chinatown it's a short hop down to the harbour – aim for the pink-grey **Marine Tower**. This 106-metre-high tower, built in 1961 to celebrate the port's centenary, is supposedly the world's tallest lighthouse. It's due to reopen after renovations in time for the city's one-hundred-and-fiftieth anniversary in 2009, though it's better to save your money for the Landmark Tower's much higher observation deck (see p.294). In front of the tower, **Yamashita-kōen** is a pleasant seafront park – more grass than trees – created as a memorial to victims of the Great Earthquake. Here you can pick up a *Sea Bass* ferry or take a harbour cruise (see p.289) from the pier beside the **Hikawa-maru**. This retired passenger liner, also known as the *Queen of the Pacific*, was built in 1930 for the NYK line Yokohama–Seattle service, though it was commandeered as a hospital ship during the war. In recent years it has served as a museum, though it is closed at the time of writing for restoration.

At the south end of Yamashita-kōen, the **Doll Museum** (Ningyō no Ie; 人形の 家; daily 10am–6.30pm, but closed third Mon of month; ¥500; ⓦ www.museum .or.jp/yokohama-doll-museum) offers a more diverting display of dolls from around the world. The vast collection ranges from American "blue-eyed friendship dolls", sent to Japan in the 1920s at a time of increasing tension between the two countries, to Japanese folk and classical dolls. Don't miss the exquisite, ceremonial *hina* dolls, traditionally displayed around the Hina Matsuri (Doll Festival) on March 3.

North to the administrative district

Yokohama's rapid growth in the late nineteenth century was underpinned by a flourishing export trade in raw silk. You can learn about the practical aspects of silk production, from the rearing of silkworms to the weaving and dyeing of gorgeously coloured kimono, at the **Silk Museum** (シルク博物館; Tues–Sun 9am–4.30pm; ¥500; ⓦ www.silkmuseum.or.jp), in the Sanbo Centre at the north end of Yamashita-kōen.

Opposite the museum, the Ōsanbashi (大さん橋) pier is where cruise ships pull up to berth at Yokohama's International Passenger Terminal. Originally dating from the late nineteenth century, the pier was rebuilt in 2002 to a beautifully fluid, low-slung design inspired by ocean waves. It's a popular spot for an evening stroll, providing fabulous views of MM21 in one direction and Yokohama Bay Bridge in the other.

Continuing north from the Silk Museum across a leafy square, you come to a modern, windowless building which houses the **Yokohama Archives of History** (横浜開港資料館; Tues–Sun 9.30am–5pm; ¥200). The museum details the opening of Yokohama (and Japan) to the outside world after 1853 through an impressive collection of photos, artefacts and documents, including contemporary newspaper reports from London, helped by an unusual amount of English translation.

You're now in the thick of Yokohama's administrative district, where several European-style facades still survive. Kanagawa government offices occupy the next block north, while the biscuit-coloured **Customs House**, opposite, is a more attractive structure, topped by a distinguished, copper-clad dome. A road north of here leads to Shinkō island (see opposite), but for now follow the road heading inland, Minato Ōdori, to find the graceful **Port Opening Memorial Hall**; erected in 1918, this red-brick neo-Renaissance building now serves as public function rooms. In front of the hall, turn north again, onto Honchō-dōri, to reach the last and most ornate of Yokohama's European-style facades, with Neoclassical flourishes. The building was completed in 1904 as the headquarters of a Yokohama bank, and then later converted into the **Kanagawa Prefectural Museum of Cultural History** (神奈川県立歴史博物館; Tues–Sun 9.30am–5pm; ¥300). Much improved after a recent refurbishment, the museum takes a broad sweep from prehistoric times to the present day. Though much of the material is devoted to Yokohama, including woodblock prints of the Black Ships and big-nosed, red-haired foreigners, exhibits also cover Kamakura's Zen temples and local folk culture. The museum is woefully short of information in English, but there are enthusiastic, English-speaking guides on hand to answer questions.

Minato Mirai 21 (MM21)

In a bid to beat Tokyo at its own game, Yokohama now boasts Japan's tallest building and is in the process of creating a mini-city of apartment blocks, offices, recreational and cultural facilities: **Minato Mirai 21** (みなとみらい21; ⓦ www.minatomirai21.com) – or **MM21** as it's better known. This development is rapidly changing the face of Yokohama, and will eventually occupy over two square kilometres of reclaimed land and disused dockyards.

MM21 can be accessed from either Minato Mirai Station on the Tōkyū-Tōyoko line or Sakuragichō train and subway station, from where a covered moving walkway whisks you towards the awesome, 296-metre-tall **Landmark Tower**. Inside, an ear-popping, forty-second ride by lift takes you up to the sixty-ninth-floor **Sky Garden observation deck** (July & Aug daily 10am–10pm; Sept–June Mon–Fri & Sun 10am–9pm, Sat 10am–10pm; ¥1000). On clear days, when Fuji is flaunting her beauty, superb views more than justify the entry fee. Alternatively, if you don't mind missing the thrill of the lift, you can enjoy a coffee for about the same price in the opulent *Sirius Sky Lounge* on the seventieth floor of the *Royal Park Hotel*, or splash out on an early evening cocktail as the city lights spread their magic; note that after 5pm there's an additional live music charge of ¥1000–¥2000.

Next door, the **Landmark Plaza** consists of a swanky shopping mall set around a five-storey atrium. Here you'll find flash boutiques, the Yurindo bookstore on the fifth floor – with an excellent foreign-language section – and plenty of restaurants, bars and coffee shops, some of which are built into the stone walls of an old dry dock. Off to the east, the stepped towers of **Queen's Square** – another vast complex of shops, offices, a concert hall and the sail-shaped *Intercontinental Hotel* – fill the skyline.

The Yokohama Maritime Museum

A water-filled dock in front of Landmark Tower is now home to the sleek **Nippon-maru** training sail ship, part of the enjoyable **Yokohama Maritime Museum** (横浜マリタイムミュージアム; Tues–Sun: March–June, Sept & Oct 10am–5pm; July & Aug 10am–6.30pm; Nov–Feb 10am–4.30pm; ¥600). The *Nippon-maru* was built in 1930 and saw service up until 1984, during which time she sailed the equivalent of 45 times round the world; when her pristine white sails are hoisted (around ten times a year), it's clear why she's more familiarly known as the *Swan of the Pacific*. You can explore the entire vessel, from the engine room to the captain's wood-panelled cabin. There's copious English labelling and alternating Japanese and English commentary over the loudspeakers.

The museum's main exhibition rooms occupy a purpose-built underground hall beside the ship. In addition to well-designed coverage of Yokohama's historical development, there's also a lot about the modern port and the technical side of sailing, though little in English. Nevertheless, you can still test your navigational skills at a mock-up bridge with a simulator, or have a bash at unloading a container vessel.

The Yokohama Museum of Art and the Industrial Museum

MM21's two major museums are to be found in the blocks immediately north of Landmark Tower. Head first for the splendid **Yokohama Museum of Art** (横浜美術館; Mon–Wed, Sat & Sun 10am–6pm, Fri 10am–8pm; ¥500; varying prices for special exhibitions; Ⓦwww.yaf.or.jp/yma), in which mostly twentieth-century Japanese and Western art is set off to fine effect by designer Tange Kenzō's cool, grey space. In fact, the architecture – particularly the magnificent central atrium – grabs your attention as much as the exhibits. The photography galleries are always worth checking out, while the Art Library contains a wealth of international art and design publications.

Kids will be in their element at the **Mitsubishi Minato Mirai Industrial Museum** (三菱みなとみらい技術館; Tues–Sun 10am–5.30pm; ¥300; Ⓦwww .mhi.co.jp/museum) in the neighbouring block. The museum's six well-laid-out zones illustrate technological developments, from today's power generators, oil platforms and deep-sea probes to the space stations of tomorrow. There are plenty of models and interactive displays, with English-speaking staff on hand if needed, but the biggest draws are the "Sky-Walk Adventure" – a helicopter simulator which takes you swooping and soaring over Yokohama – and the 3D theatre up on the second floor, on which you're immersed in an adventure set in 2050; you'll need to book times for these when you arrive.

Shinkō Island

Between MM21 and Ōsanbashi is **Shinkō** island, which was reclaimed about a hundred years ago as part of Yokohama's then state-of-the-art port facilities. The

△ The Cosmo Clock ferris wheel and the MM21 complex showcase the modern face of Yokohama

slowly revolving **Cosmo Clock 21** (generally Mon–Fri 11am–9pm; Sat & Sun 11am–10pm; occasionally closed on Thurs; ¥700) here is one of the world's largest ferris wheels, with a diameter of 112m; one circuit takes around fifteen minutes, allowing plenty of time to take in the view, which is particularly spectacular at night.

Cosmo Clock's changing colours provide a night-time spectacle in their own right, and one of the best places from which to admire them is the rooftop of the **Manyo Club** (万葉倶楽部; daily 10am–9am; ¥2620, plus ¥1680 after 3am; Ⓦ www .manyo.co.jp/mm21), a spa complex in the next block east. Spread over five floors, it offers a variety of hot-spring baths – the water is trucked in from Atami onsen down the coast – in addition to massages and treatments, restaurants and relaxation rooms; you could easily spend half a day here. Its best feature, though, is the circular rooftop footbath. Get a spot facing west for a grandstand view over MM21.

On the other side of Shinkō island, two handsome red-brick warehouses dating from 1911 now form the attractive **Akarenga** (赤レンガ) shopping, dining and entertainment complex. Live music concerts and other events often take place in summer and at weekends in the plaza, which transforms into a skating rink in winter.

Sankei-en

In the late nineteenth century a wealthy silk merchant, Hara Tomitaro, established his residence in sculptured parkland on Yokohama's southern hills and filled it with rare and beautiful buildings from Kamakura and the Kansai region. Today **Sankei-en** (三溪園; daily 9am–5pm; ¥500; Ⓦ www.sankeien.or.jp) is divided into an outer garden and a smaller inner core, where most of the famous structures are located. To reach Sankei-en, take bus #148, or the slower #8, from Yokohama or Sakuragichō stations to Honmoku Sankeien-mae, from where the garden is a three-minute walk, or hop on a JR Negishi-line train to Negishi Station (根岸駅) and then a bus as far as the Honmoku stop, 600m north of the main gate.

From the gate, follow the well-marked route to the **inner garden**, where **Rinshunkaku** – an elegant, lakeside mansion built for one of the Tokugawa lords in 1649 – is the only structure of its kind still in existence. Another Tokugawa legacy, dating from 1623, sits beside a picturesque stream a few minutes further on; named **Choshukaku**, it originally served as a tea-ceremony house in the grounds of Kyoto's Nijō Castle. **Tenju-in** may not be as famous, but it's worth walking up beside the stream to see its fine carving. This little seventeenth-century temple dedicated to Jizō, the guardian deity of children, hails from Kamakura.

In the less formal **outer garden**, thatched farm roofs blend with bamboo thickets and groves of twisted plum trees, above which rises a graceful three-tiered pagoda. The most interesting building here is **Old Yanohara House**, the former home of a wealthy farmer, where you can take a close look at the vast roof built in *gassho* style – no nails but plenty of rope. Don't bother climbing up the hill to Shofukaku: the concrete viewing platform has great views of billowing chimney stacks and industrial dockyards.

Eating, drinking and nightlife

One of Yokohama's highlights is sampling the enormous variety of restaurants and snack-food outlets cramming the streets of **Chinatown**. In Yamate and Motomachi, European cuisine predominates, while the restaurants in the new developments of MM21 cater to every taste and budget. In fine weather, the casual little eating places on the ground floor of Akarenga are a good option, if only because you can take your food to the tables outside.

Though it's generally less boisterous than Tokyo, Yokohama has no shortage of lively drinking holes. The west side of Yokohama Station comprises the main **nightlife** area, but the area around Chinatown and across to Kannai Station also has a sprinkling of bars.

Restaurants and cafés

Besides the establishments listed below, there are shopping malls such as Landmark Plaza, Queen's Square, Cross Gate and Shinkō-chō's World Porters, all of which make happy culinary hunting grounds.

Chinatown

Bairan
梅蘭
133-10 Yamashita-chō ☎ **045/651-6695,** ⓦ **www
.bairan.jp.** Small, unpretentious restaurant tucked in the backstreets and known for its Bairan *yakisoba*, stir-fried noodles served like a sort of pancake, crispy on the outside and with a juicy pork or beef stuffing (¥900 and ¥1260 respectively) – unless you're very hungry, it's plenty big enough for two. They also serve a full range of other soba and rice dishes. Inexpensive to moderate. Mon-Fri 11.30am–3pm & 5–10pm, Sat & Sun 11.30am–10pm.

Edosei
江戸清
192 Yamashita-chō ☎ **045/681-3133.** Mega-size steamed dumplings are this shop's speciality, stuffed with interesting ingredients including black bean and walnut, onion and seafood, and shrimp and chilli, as well as the usual barbecued pork. Inexpensive. Daily 9am–8pm.

Manchinrō
萬珍樓
153 Yamashita-chō ☎ **045/681-4004,** ⓦ **www
.manchinro.com.** This famous restaurant, with its wonderfully extravagant exterior, has

been serving tasty Cantonese cuisine since 1892. Though prices are a touch on the high side, the portions are generous. Noodle and fried-rice dishes start at around ¥1100, lunch sets at ¥2500 and evening course menus at ¥5000. The branch behind serves a full range of dim sum. Moderate to expensive. Daily 11am–10pm.

Ryokuen
緑苑

220 Yamashita-chō ☏ 045/651-5651. Simple, stylish Chinese teashop with some thirty types of tea on the menu, from ¥800 for a pot serving up to six small cups. Daily except Thurs noon–8pm.

Shōfukumon
招福門

81-3 Yamashita- chō ☏ 045/664-4141,
Ⓦ **www.shofukumon.com.** Multistorey restaurant offering eat-all-you-can dim sum deals for ¥2625, including 32 types of dim sum to choose from, plus fried rice and soup – worth considering if you've worked up a healthy appetite. Moderate. Mon–Fri 11.30am–10pm, Sat & Sun 11am–10pm.

Sigoroku Saikan Honkan
四五六菜館本館

190 Yamashita-chō ☏ 045/681-3456. Decorated with gorgeous mosaics, this place is popular for its reliable Shanghai cuisine. Weekday lunch sets start at under ¥700, course menus from around ¥3500, lunch or dinner. Moderate to expensive. Mon–Fri 11.30am–11.30pm, Sat & Sun 11am–11.30pm.

The rest of the city

Café de la Presse
2F Media Centre Building, 11 Nihon-dōri
☏ 045/650-8228. Pretty authentic-looking Viennese-style café in the corner of one of Yokohama's grand old buildings. The house speciality is macaroons, though they also serve cakes, sandwiches and light meals (set lunch ¥1100). There's also a smarter restaurant attached. Moderate. Tues–Sun 10am–9pm.

Chano-ma
3F Akarenga 2, 1-1-2 Shinkō, Naka-ku
☏ 045/650-8228. Sit back with a cocktail and nibble interesting modern Japanese dishes at this large, relaxed restaurant-cum-tea-room with a very contemporary vibe. Lunch sets from ¥1000. Moderate. Mon–Thurs & Sun 11am–11pm, Fri & Sat 11am–5am.

Enokitei
89-6 Yamate-chō ☏ 045/623-2288. Set in a venerable Yamate home, this cute English-style café serves dainty sandwiches and home-made cakes. You can sit in the front garden and watch the world pass by. Moderate. Tues–Fri 11am–7pm, Sat & Sun 11am–8pm.

Shiokumizaka Garden
汐汲坂ガーデン

3-145 Motomachi, Naka-ku ☏ 045/641-5310. This café-restaurant has a slightly bohemian air – very Motomachi – and serves nicely presented dishes with an Italian twist, plus a big range of scrumptious home-made cakes. Set lunches from ¥1260; in the evening count on around ¥2500. Choose between tables in the plant-filled courtyard or in the homely wooden chalet behind. Moderate. Mon 11am–6pm, Tues–Thurs & Sun 11am–11pm, Fri & Sat 11am–midnight.

Yamate Jūbankan
247 Yamate-chō ☏ 045/621-4466. Pleasant French restaurant in a pretty clapboard house opposite the Foreigners' Cemetery. There's a formal restaurant upstairs (set lunches from ¥3500) and more casual dining on the ground floor, where you can snack on a sandwich or *croque* (¥800) or a more filling lunch platter (¥2000). In July and August they run a popular beer garden. Moderate. Daily 11am–9pm.

Bars and clubs

Beer Next
3F Akarenga 2, 1-1-2 Shinkō, Naka-ku
☏ 045/226-1961. Stylish beer hall and restaurant in a warehouse conversion. Their own-brew Spring Valley beer (¥550) is refreshing,
and they also have Guinness on tap. Daily 11am–11pm.

Motion Blue
3F Akarenga 2, 1-1-2 Shinkō, Naka-ku
☏ 045/226-1919, Ⓦ www.motionblue.co.jp. In

the renovated Akarenga buildings, this cool jazz club attracts top acts – for which you'll pay top prices. There's no charge, though, to park yourself at the attached *Bar Tune*'s long counter and soak up the ambience. Also hosts several free performances each month. Mon–Sat 5–11.30pm, Sun 4–10.30pm; closing days vary.

Namo Bar

2F Cross Gate, 1-1-67 Sakuragi-chō, Naka-ku ☏045/210-9201. Sleek, modern *izakaya* offering over three hundred types of *shōchū* (distilled liquor) and around forty plum wines. The food menu features Nagoya-style cuisine. Mon–Thurs 5pm–1am, Fri & Sat 5pm–4am, Sun 5–11pm.

The Tavern

B1F 2-14 Minami Saiwai-chō ☏045/322-9727, Ⓦ**www.the-tavern.com**. This British-style pub, popular with local expats, is a good place to kick off an evening in the nightlife district west of Yokohama Station; turn left out of the station, behind Takashimaya department store, to find it opposite the Daiei store. It serves the sort of bar food that will appeal to homesick Brits, including an all-you-can-eat Sunday roast lunch (¥1500). Mon–Thurs 6pm–midnight, Fri 6pm–5am, Sat noon–5am, Sun noon–midnight.

Why Not?

B1 1-31 Motomachi, Naka-ku ☏045/663-2955, Ⓦ**www.clubwhynot.com**. Surprisingly spacious basement bar-cum-dance club with DJs on Friday and Saturday nights (entry ¥1000–2000) and occasional salsa nights. The rest of the week it's a regular bar. All-night happy hour on Tuesdays. Daily 7pm–5am.

Contexts

Contexts

A brief history of Tokyo

Although Tokyo's founding date is usually given as 1457, the year when **Ōta Dōkan**, a minor lord, built his modest castle on a bluff overlooking the river, there have been people living on the Kantō plain for well over two thousand years. Today's restless metropolis, sprawling round the western shores of Tokyo Bay, began life as a humble fishing village called **Edo**, lost among the marshes of the Sumida-gawa. The name Edo, meaning "river-gate", was granted in the twelfth century by Edo Shigenaga, a member of the Taira clan who held control of the Kantō district at the time.

The most significant date in the city's early history was 1590, when the ambitious warlord **Tokugawa Ieyasu** established his power base in this obscure castle town, far from the emperor in Kyoto. For more than a century Japan had been torn apart by political and social unrest, but in little over a decade Ieyasu succeeded in reuniting the country, taking the title of **shogun**, effectively a military dictator. Though the emperor continued to hold court in Kyoto, Japan's real centre of power would henceforth lie in Edo.

Under the Tokugawa

The **Tokugawa** dynasty set about creating a city befitting their new status, initiating massive construction projects – a trend which has continued to the present day. By 1640 Edo Castle was the most imposing in all Japan, complete with a five-storey central keep, a double moat and a complex, spiralling network of canals. Instead of perimeter walls, however, there were simple barrier gates and then a bewildering warren of narrow, tortuous lanes, sudden dead-ends and unbridged canals to snare unwelcome intruders. At the same time drainage work began on the surrounding marshes, where embankments were raised to protect the nascent city against flooding.

The shogun protected himself further by requiring his *daimyō* (feudal lords) to split the year between their provincial holdings and Edo, where their families were kept as virtual hostages. Maintaining two households with two sets of retainers, travelling long distances and observing prescribed ceremonies on the way left them neither the time nor money to raise a serious threat. But the *daimyō* also enjoyed numerous privileges: within Edo they were granted the most favourable land to the west of the castle, in the area known as **Yamanote**. Artisans, merchants and others at the bottom of the established order, meanwhile, were confined to **Shitamachi**, a low-lying, overcrowded region to the east. Though growing less distinct, this division between the "high" and "low" city is still apparent today. Mid-eighteenth-century Edo was the world's largest city, with a population well over one million, of whom roughly half were squeezed into Shitamachi at an astonishing 70,000 people per square kilometre.

During more than two hundred years of peace, the shogunate grew increasingly conservative and sterile, while life down in Shitamachi was buzzing. Peace had given rise to an increasingly wealthy merchant class and a vigorous, often bawdy subculture where the pursuit of pleasure was taken to new extremes. In Shitamachi, where rank counted for little, the arbiters of fashion were the irrepressible, devil-may-care *Edo-ko*, the "children of Edo", with their earthy humour and delight in practical jokes. Inevitably, there was also a darker side to life and the

Edo-ko knew their fair share of squalor, poverty and violence. Licensed brothels, euphemistically known as "pleasure quarters", flourished, and child prostitution was common.

Shitamachi's tightly packed streets of thatch and wood dwellings usually suffered worst in the great fires which broke out so frequently that they were dubbed *Edo no hana*, the "flowers of Edo". In January 1657, the **Fire of the Long Sleeves** – so named because it started at a temple where the long-sleeved kimono of women who had recently died were being burnt – laid waste to three-quarters of the district's buildings and killed an estimated one hundred thousand people. Subsequent precautions included earth firewalls, manned watchtowers and local firefighting teams, who were much revered for their acrobatic skills and bravery. The fires continued, however, and the life expectancy of an Edo building averaged a mere twenty years.

The Meiji Restoration and modernization

Since the early seventeenth century Japan had been a **closed country**; the shogun, distrusting the success of earlier Christian missionaries and fearful of colonization by their European backers, banned virtually all contact with the outside world. Within this vacuum, by the early nineteenth century the highly conservative shogunate had become a weak and inept regime. When it failed to deal effectively with **Commodore Perry**, the American who insolently sailed his "Black Ships" into Edo Bay in 1853 and 1854 to secure trading rights, the shoguns' days were numbered. Opposition forces gradually rallied round the emperor until, after a brief civil war, the fifteenth Tokugawa shogun surrendered in November 1867. A few months later, in what came to be called the **Meiji Restoration**, power was fully restored to the emperor, and in 1869 Emperor Meiji took up permanent residence in the city now known as **Tokyo**, Japan's "eastern capital".

The first years of **Meiji rule** saw another, very different, revolution. Determined to modernize, Japan embraced the ideas and technologies of the West with startling enthusiasm. Tokyo stood at the centre of Japanese innovation: brick buildings, electric lights, trams, trains and then cars all made their first appearance here. Within a few decades the castle lost its outer gates and most of its grounds, canals were filled in or built over and the commercial focus shifted to Ginza, while Shitamachi's wealthier merchants decamped for the more desirable residential areas of Yamanote, leaving the low city to sink into slow decline.

Beneath its modern veneer, however, Tokyo remained largely a city of wood, still regularly swept by fire and rocked by earthquakes, most disastrously by the **Great Kantō Earthquake**, which struck the city at noon on September 1, 1923. Half of Tokyo – by then a city of some two million – was destroyed, while a hundred thousand people lost their lives in the quake itself and in the blazes sparked by thousands of cooking-fires.

The war and its aftermath

The city rose from its ashes and for a while development continued apace, but nationalism was brewing and before long Tokyo, like the rest of Japan, was gearing up for war. The first bombs hit the city in April 1942, followed as the Allied forces drew closer by more frequent raids throughout 1944, reaching a crescendo in March 1945. During three days of sustained **incendiary bombing** an estimated one hundred thousand people died, most of them on the night of March 9, when great swaths of the city burnt to the ground. The physical devastation surpassed even that of the Great Earthquake: Meiji-jingū, Sensō-ji and Edo Castle were all destroyed, and Shitamachi all but obliterated; from Hibiya it was possible to see clear across the eight kilometres to Shinjuku.

From a prewar population of nearly seven million, Tokyo in 1945 was reduced to around three million residents living in a state of near-starvation. This time, however, regeneration was fuelled by an influx of American dollars and food aid under the **Allied Occupation** led by General MacArthur. A **Security Pact** was signed allowing the US to keep bases in Japan in exchange for providing military protection. Not surprisingly, the liveliest sector of the economy during this period was the black market, first in Yūrakuchō and later in Ueno and Ikebukuro.

In 1950 the **Korean War** broke out, and central Tokyo underwent extensive redevelopment on the back of a manufacturing boom partly fuelled by the war, while immigrants flooded in from the provinces to fill the factories. With economic recovery well on the way, political tensions surfaced in the late 1950s. Anti-American **demonstrations** occurred sporadically throughout the decade, but in May 1960 more serious rioting broke out over ratification of the revised Security Pact. The crisis passed, though student discontent continued to rumble on for a long time – so much so that in 1968 the authorities closed Tokyo University for a year – and heavily armed riot police became a familiar sight on the streets. But the situation was never allowed to threaten the major event of the postwar period when, on October 10, 1964, Emperor Hirohito opened the eighteenth **Olympic Games**. The first Olympics ever held in Asia, the games marked Japan's return to economic health and to international respectability. Visitors to the games were surprised by the previously war-torn country's rapid transformation, epitomized by the new Shinkansen trains zipping between Tokyo and Kyoto.

Like the rest of the industrialized world, Japan suffered during the oil crisis of the 1970s, but by the following decade her economy was the envy of the world. The late-1980s **boom** saw land prices in Tokyo reach dizzying heights, matched by excesses of every conceivable sort, from gold-wrapped sushi to mink toilet-seat covers. The heady optimism was reflected in ambitious building projects such as the Metropolitan Government offices in Shinjuku, the Odaiba reclamation and the vast development of Makuhari Messe on the east side of Tokyo Bay.

The bubble bursts

By 1992, with the stock market rapidly sinking and businesses contracting, it was clear the economic bubble had burst. The sudden sobering-up and subsequent loss of confidence was compounded by revelations of deep-seated political corruption and by the **AUM Shinrikyō** terrorist group releasing deadly sarin gas on Tokyo commuter trains in 1995 – a particularly shocking event which left twelve dead and thousands injured.

Recession was officially announced in 1998, and newspaper headlines during the late 1990s announced a seemingly endless stream of financial misdealings, resignations and suicides. By February 1998, a manual on how to commit suicide had sold an incredible 1.1 million copies, and over 30,000 people – the majority middle-aged men facing unemployment – killed themselves that year, followed by a record 33,000 in 1999. Another type of death – the murder of Lucy Blackman, a young British woman working as a hostess in Roppongi – hit the headlines in 2000, alerting the world to the fact that life in Tokyo wasn't quite as safe as had been imagined.

The new millennium brought glimmerings of **recovery** – hardly surprising after trillions of yen had been pumped into the economy through various government packages. But Tokyo would never quite be the same, and the blue-tarpaulin tent compounds of the **homeless** have become commonplace in the capital's parks.

Soccer and style

The **2002 World Cup** saw Tokyo swamped with visitors and everyone go football crazy. There was the inevitable anticlimax after the final had been played at Yokohama, but it was clear that the soccer jamboree had done the country no end of good in tackling the lingering notion that Japan is an expensive country in which to travel. Japanese exports began to pick up again in 2003 and with the economy steadily growing again, Tokyo has been a major beneficiary, renewed growth fuelling the city's taste for redevelopment, with districts from Akihabara to Roppongi getting structural makeovers.

It's not all good news – in early 2007 several gruesome murder cases laid bare the underlying stress of Tokyo society. A demographic time bomb is also ticking away in the city in the shape of a stubbornly low birth rate (under one percent per year, even less than the Japanese average of 1.24 percent) and growing numbers of elderly folk.

On a more positive note, Japan is aiming to boost overseas visitor numbers to ten million by 2010, and Tokyo is pitching in by becoming a far more foreigner-friendly place, with far more English (and other languages) being seen on city signs, maps and restaurant menus. All this is part of a strategy to help the city snag the **Olympics** for a second time in 2016.

Books

Many of the titles below are published by Kodansha and Charles E. Tuttle, both in Japan and abroad. For Japanese authors, the Japanese convention of placing the family name first is followed. Titles marked with a ⚹ are particularly recommended.

History

Pat Barr *The Coming of the Barbarians*. Entertaining and very readable tales of how Japan opened up to the West at the beginning of the Meiji Restoration.

⚹ **Ian Buruma** *The Wages of Guilt*. In which Buruma, an eloquent Dutch scholar of things Japanese, skilfully explains how and why Germany and Japan have come to terms so differently with their roles in World War II.

Ian Buruma *Inventing Japan*. An examination of the country's history between 1853 and 1964, the period which saw the country go from a feudal, isolated state to a powerhouse of the modern world economy.

John Dower *Embracing Defeat: Japan in the Aftermath of World War II*. This accessible Pulitzer Prize-winner looks at the long-lasting impact of the American occupation on Japan. First-person accounts and snappy writing bring the book alive.

Edward Seidensticker *Tokyo Central: A Memoir*. This leading translator of ancient and modern Japanese literature has had a ringside seat to the changes in the city over the last half-century, and his memoirs make for fascinating reading. His out-of-print works *Low City, High City* and *Tokyo Rising: The City Since the Great Earthquake* tackle Tokyo's history – from its humble beginnings to the Great Kantō quake of 1923 in the first book, to the capital's postwar experiences in the second.

Richard Storry *A History of Modern Japan*. Ideal primer for the basics and themes of Japanese history.

Richard Tames *A Traveller's History of Japan*. This clearly written and succinct volume romps through Japan's history and provides useful cultural descriptions and essays.

⚹ **Paul Waley** *Tokyo: City of Stories*. An intimate, anecdotal history of the capital, delving into Tokyo's neighbourhoods and uncovering some fascinating stories in the process.

Business, economics and politics

Jacob M. Schlesinger *Shadow Shoguns*. Cracking crash course in Japan's political scene, scandals and all, from *Wall Street Journal* reporter Schlesinger, who spent five years at the newspaper's Tokyo bureau.

⚹ **Karel Van Wolferen** *The Enigma of Japanese Power*. Standard text on the triad of Japan's bureaucracy, politicians and business, and how the jockeying for power among them has left the country with a power vacuum. A weighty, thought-provoking tome, worth wading through.

Arts, culture and society

Ian Buruma *A Japanese Mirror* and *The Missionary and the Libertine*. The first book is an intelligent, erudite examination of Japan's popular culture, while the latter collects a range of the author's essays, including pieces on Japan-bashing; Hiroshima; Pearl Harbor; the authors Mishima Yukio, Tanizaki Junichirō and Yoshimoto Banana; and the film director Ōshima Nagisa.

Veronica Chambers *Kickboxing Geishas*. Using interviews with a broad cross-section of women, from Hokkaidō DJs via "charismatic housewives" to top executives, journalist Veronica Chambers argues that modern Japanese women are not the submissive characters so often portrayed in the media, but in fact a strong force for change. A sympathetic and insightful book.

Liza Dalby *Geisha*. In the 1970s, anthropologist Dalby became a geisha, thus immersing herself in a fast-disappearing world. This book is the fascinating account of her experience and those of her teachers and fellow pupils. *Kimono*, her history of the most Japanese of garments, is also worth a look.

Lesley Downer *The Brothers* and *Madame Sadayakko*. The former is a gripping saga of fabulous wealth, illegitimacy and the fabled hatred between the two half-brothers, Tsutsumi Yoshiake and Tsutsumi Seiji, who inherited the Seibu business empire. In the latter Downer applies her narrative skills to the life of Sadayakko, one of Japan's most celebrated geisha at the turn of the last century, who took to the stage – the first woman in Japan to do so for 250 years – and wowed audiences around the world with her passionate performances.

Edward Fowler *San'ya Blues*. Fowler's experiences living and working among the casual labourers of Tokyo's San'ya district makes fascinating reading, revealing the dark underbelly of Japan's economic miracle and blowing apart a few myths and misconceptions on the way.

Robin Gerster *Legless in Ginza*. A funny and spot-on account of the writer's two-year residence at Japan's most prestigious university, Tokyo's Todai. Gerster writes with an Aussie verve and notices things that many other expat commentators ignore.

Gunji Masakatsu *Kabuki*. Excellent, highly readable introduction to Kabuki by one of the leading connoisseurs of Japanese drama. It's illustrated with copious annotated photos of the great actors and the most dramatic moments in Kabuki theatre.

Alex Kerr *Lost Japan*. Although it's part of the usually tedious "Japan's not what it once was" school of writing, this book won a prestigious literature prize when first published in Japanese, and the translation is just as worthy of praise. Kerr, the son of a US naval officer, first came to Japan as a child in the 1960s and has been fascinated by it ever since. This beautifully written and thoughtfully observed set of essays covers aspects of his life and passions, including Kabuki, art collecting and cities such as Kyoto and Ōsaka.

Alex Kerr *Dogs and Demons*. A scathing and thought-provoking attack on Japan's economic, environmental and social policies of the past decades.

Simon May *Atomic Sushi*. In which British Professor of Philosophy Simon May looks back over his year as a guest lecturer at the prestigious Tokyo University. The result is a highly readable book full of finely observed insights as he muses over life in Japan, from coping with the surreal bureaucracy to the intricacies of gift-giving.

Karin Muller *Japanland*. Documentary filmmaker and travel writer Muller heads to Japan in search of *wa* – the Japanese concept of harmony. The interesting cast of characters she meets in the year she spends there – part of that time spent just south of Tokyo – are what makes this book rise above similar efforts.

Donald Richie *Public People, Private People*; *A Lateral View* and *Partial Views*. These three books, all collections of essays by a man whose love affair with Japan began when he arrived with the US occupying forces in 1947, set the standard other expat commentators can only aspire to. *Public People* is a set of sketches of famous and unknown Japanese, including profiles of novelist Mishima and the actor Mifune Toshiro. In *A Lateral View* and *Partial Views*, Richie tackles Tokyo style, avant-garde theatre, pachinko, and the Japanese kiss, among many other things. For an overview of the immense Ritchie oeuvre dip into *The Donald Richie Reader: 50 Years of Writing on Japan*.

Mark Schilling *The Encyclopedia of Japanese Pop Culture*. Forget sumo, samurai and *ikebana*; Godzilla, pop idols and instant ramen are really where Japan's culture's at. Schilling's book is an indispensable, spot-on guide to late twentieth-century Japan.

Frederik L. Schodt *Dreamland Japan: Writings on Modern Manga*. A series of entertaining and informative essays on the art of Japanese comic books, profiling the top publications, artists, animated films and English-language manga.

Joan Stanley-Baker *Japanese Art*. Highly readable introduction to the broad range of Japan's artistic traditions (though excluding theatre and music), tracing their development from prehistoric to modern times.

Robert Twigger *Angry White Pyjamas*. An intense, forensic account of the daily trials, humiliations and triumphs of becoming a master of aikido. The subtitle "An Oxford poet trains with the Tokyo riot police" gives you the gist, although Twigger's writing is more prose than poetry.

Rey Ventura *Underground in Japan*. The non-Caucasian *gaijin* experience in Japan is brilliantly essayed by Ventura, who lived and worked with fellow Filipino illegal immigrants in the dockyards of Yokohama.

Robert Whiting *Tokyo Underworld*. This well-researched tale follows the ups and downs of Nick Zapapetti, a larger-than-life Italian American who arrived with the occupying forces in 1945 and stayed on to become "the king of Roppongi" and Tokyo's Mafia boss. In the process, Whiting also charts the history of the *yakuza* in postwar Japan.

Guides and reference books

John Carroll *Trails of Two Cities*. Enjoyable and informative walking guide to Yokohama and Kamakura by a long-time resident, full of fascinating historical detail and local insights.

Enbutsu Sumiko *Old Tokyo: Walks in the City of the Shogun*. Tokyo's old Shitamachi area is best explored on foot, and Enbutsu's guide, illustrated

with charcterful block prints, helps bring the city's history alive.

Thomas F. Judge and Tomita Hiroyuki *Edo Craftsmen*. Beautifully produced portraits of some of the traditional craftsmen still working in the backstreets of Tokyo. A timely insight into a disappearing world.

Caroline Pover *Being a Broad in Japan*. The subtitle, *Everything a Western woman needs to thrive and survive*, sums it up. Pover proves a sassy guide to the various perils and pitfalls of life in Japan from a female perspective, covering everything from finding day care to getting divorced.

Robb Satterwhite *What's What in Japanese Restaurants*. Handy guide to all things culinary; the menus annotated with Japanese characters are particularly useful. Satterwhite, a Tokyo-based epicure, is also the author of *Not Just a Good Food Guide Tokyo*, one of the more up-to-date English guides to the city's restaurant scene, and manages the excellent resource ⓦwww.bento.com/tokyofood.html.

Tajima Noriyuki *Tokyo: A Guide to Recent Architecture*. Although it's out of date, this compact, expertly written and nicely illustrated book remains a useful companion on any modern architectural tour of the capital.

Gary D'A. Walters *Day Walks Near Tokyo*. Slim volume of strolls and hikes, all within easy reach of the capital, to help get you off the beaten tourist path. The maps are clear, as are the practical details and directions.

Diane Wiltshire Kanagawa and **Jeanne Huey Erickson** *Japan for Kids*. Immensely practical guide covering everything from vocabulary for the labour ward to where to hire a Santa. Aimed mainly at expat parents living in Tokyo, but also full of practical tips and recommendations for visitors with kids, though some information is getting a bit dated.

Japanese fiction

Alfred Birnbaum ed. *Monkey Brain Sushi*. Eleven often quirky short stories by contemporary Japanese authors. A good introduction to modern prose writers.

Kawabata Yasunari *Snow Country*; *The Izu Dancer*; and other titles. Japan's first Nobel Prize winner for fiction writes intense tales of passion, usually about a sophisticated urban man falling for a simple country girl.

Kirino Natsuo *Out*. Four women working in a bentō factory just outside Tokyo discover that committing murder is both easier and much more complicated than they could ever have imagined, in this dark, superior thriller that mines a very dark seam of Japan's underbelly.

Mishima Yukio *After the Banquet*; *Confessions of a Mask*; *Forbidden Colours*; and *The Sea of Fertility*. Novelist Mishima sealed his notoriety by committing ritual suicide after leading a failed military coup in 1970. He left behind a highly respectable, if at times melodramatic, body of literature, including some of Japan's finest postwar novels. Themes of tradition, sexuality and militarism run through many of his works.

Miyabe Miyuki *All She Was Worth*. When a young man's fiancée goes missing, a trail of credit-card debts and worse turns up. There's more to this clever whodunnit set in contemporary Tokyo than immediately meets the eye.

Murakami Ryū *Coin Locker Babies* and *In the Miso Soup*. Murakami burst onto Japan's literary scene in the mid-1980s with *Almost Transparent Blue*, a hip tale of student life mixing reality and fantasy. *Coin Locker Babies* is his most ambitious work, spinning a revenger's tragedy about the lives of two boys dumped as babies in adjacent coin lockers, while *In the Miso Soup* is a superior thriller along the lines of *American Psycho*, set in Tokyo.

Natsume Sōseki *I am a Cat* and *Kokoro*. The three volumes of *I am a*

One of Japan's most entertaining contemporary writers, Haruki Murakami (Ⓦwww .harukimurakami.com) has been hailed as a postwar successor to the great novelists Mishima, Kawabata and Tanizaki, and talked of as a future Nobel laureate. And yet the Kyoto-born writer and marathon runner (he's run one a year for the past twenty-odd years, and is planning a book on the subject) shuns the media spotlight and is happy that few people recognize him.

Translated into some thirty languages and increasingly well known and respected overseas, Murakami lives in Tokyo, but has spent large parts of his career abroad, including five years teaching in the US. The contemporary edge to his writing, which eschews the traditional clichés of Japanese literature, has been fuelled by his work as a translator of books by John Irving, Raymond Carver, Truman Capote and Paul Theroux among others.

Many of Murakami's books are set in Tokyo, drawing on his time studying at Waseda University in the early 1970s and running a jazz bar in Kokubunji, a place that became a haunt for literary types and, no doubt, provided inspiration for his jazz-bar-running hero in the bittersweet novella *South of the Border, West of the Sun*. A good introduction to Murakami is the two-volume *Norwegian Wood*, a tender coming-of-age love story of two students, that has sold over five million copies. The truly bizarre *A Wild Sheep Chase* and its follow-up *Dance Dance Dance* are funny but disturbing modern-day fables, dressed up as detective novels. Considered among his best works are *The Wind-Up Bird Chronicle*, a hefty yet dazzling cocktail of mystery, war reportage and philosophy, and the truly bizarre *Kafka on the Shore*, a murder story in which cats talk to people and fish rain from the sky. His latest work published in English is *After Dark*, a modern-day fable set in the dead of the Tokyo night, which has the usual trademark flourishes, from quirky characters to metaphysical speculation.

Cat see one of Japan's most famous novelists (his image is on the ¥1000 note) adopting a wry feline point of view on the world. *Kokoro* – about an ageing *sensei* (master or teacher) trying to come to terms with the modern era – is considered his best book.

Ōe Kenzaburō *Nip the Buds, Shoot the Kids*; *A Personal Matter* and *A Healing Family*. Ōe won Japan's second Nobel Prize for literature in 1994. His first full-length novel was *Nip the Buds*, published in 1958, a tale of lost innocence concerning fifteen reformatory school boys evacuated in wartime to a remote mountain village; they are left to fend for themselves when a threatening plague frightens away the villagers. *A Personal Matter* sees Ōe tackling the trauma of his handicapped son Hikari's birth, while *A Healing Family* catches up with Hikari thirty years later documenting his trials and triumphs. Never an easy read, but always startlingly honest.

Tokyo in foreign fiction

Alan Brown *Audrey Hepburn's Neck*. Beneath this rib-tickling, acutely observed tale of a young guy from the sticks adrift in big-city Tokyo are several important themes, including the continuing impact of World War II and the confused relationships between the Japanese and *gaijin*.

Ian Fleming *You Only Live Twice*. Bondo-san on the trail of arch-enemy Blofeld in trendy mid-1960s Tokyo and the wilds of Kyūshū, assisted by Tiger Tanaka and Kissy Suzuki.

William Gibson *Idoru* and *Pattern Recognition*. In *Idoru*, Cyberpunk novelist Gibson's sci-fi vision of Tokyo's future – a world of non-intrusive DNA checks at airports and computerized pop icons (the *idoru* of the title) – rings disturbingly true. In his more recent *Pattern Recognition* Tokyo plays a memorable walk-on part in the heroine's search for an elusive movie-maker.

Gavin Kramer *Shopping*. British lawyer Kramer's zippy first novel is on the bleak side, but captures the turn-of-the-millennium zeitgeist of Tokyo, where schoolgirls trade sex for designer labels and *gaijin* flounder in a sea of misunderstanding.

David Mitchell *Ghostwritten* and *number9dream*. Mitchell's debut

Ghostwritten is a dazzling collection of interlocked short stories, a couple of which are set in Japan. *number9dream*, shortlisted for the Booker Prize in 2001, conjures up a postmodern Tokyo of computer hackers, video games, gangsters and violence. A demanding, dark yet compulsive read.

Peter Tasker *Silent Thunder*; *Buddha Kiss*; *Samurai Boogie* and *Dragon Dance*. This series of fun, throwaway thrillers are the work of a Tokyo-based British financial analyst. They're mainly set in Tokyo, with James Bond-like set pieces and lively Japanese characters, especially Mori, the down-at-heel gumshoe who's the central character.

Language

Language

Language

First the good news: picking up a few words of Japanese, even managing a sentence or two, is not difficult. **Pronunciation** is simple and standard and there are few exceptions to the straightforward **grammar** rules. With a couple of weeks' effort you should be able to read the words spelled out in **hiragana** and **katakana**, Japanese phonetic characters, even if you can't understand them. And any time spent learning Japanese will be amply rewarded by the thrilled response you'll elicit from the locals, who'll always politely comment on your fine linguistic ability.

The bad news is that it takes a very great effort indeed to become halfway proficient in Japanese, let alone master the language. One of the main stumbling blocks is the thousands of **kanji** characters that need to be memorized, most of which have at least two pronunciations, depending on the sentence and their combination with other characters. Another tricky area is the multiple levels of **politeness** embodied in Japanese, married with different sets of words used by men and women. Finally, there are also different **dialects** to deal with, involving whole new vocabularies.

Japanese characters

The exact origins of Japanese are a mystery, and until the sixth century it only existed in the spoken form. Once the Japanese imported Chinese characters, known as *kanji*, they began to develop their own forms of written language.

Japanese is now written in a combination of three systems. The most difficult of the three to master is **kanji** (based on Chinese ideograms), which originally developed as mini-pictures of the word they stand for. To be able to read a newspaper, you'll need to know around two thousand *kanji*, much more difficult than it sounds, since what each one means varies with its context.

The easier writing systems to pick up are the phonetic syllabaries, **hiragana** and **katakana**. Both have 46 regular characters (see box overleaf) and can be learned within a couple of weeks. *Hiragana* is used for Japanese words, while *katakana*, with the squarer characters, is used mainly for "loan words" borrowed from other languages (especially English) and technical names. Increasingly, **rōmaji** (see p.317), the roman script used to spell out Japanese words, is also used in advertisements and magazines.

The first five letters in *hiragana* and *katakana* (**a**, **i**, **u**, **e**, **o**) are the vowel sounds (see Pronunciation, p.317). The remainder are a combination of a consonant and a vowel (eg **ka**, **ki**, **ku**, **ke**, **ko**), with the exception of **n**, the only consonant that exists on its own. While *hiragana* provides an exact phonetic reading of all Japanese words, it's a mistake to think that *katakana* does the same for foreign loan words. Often words are abbreviated, hence television becomes *terebi* and sexual harassment *sekuhara*. Sometimes, they become almost unrecognizable, as with *kakuteru*, which is cocktail.

Traditionally, Japanese is written in vertical columns and read right to left. However, the Western way of writing from left to right, horizontally from top to bottom is increasingly common. In the media and on signs you'll see a mixture of the two ways of writing.

The Japanese script consists of **hiragana**, **katakana** and ideograms based on Chinese characters *(kanji)*. *Hiragana* and *katakana* are two phonetic syllabaries represented by the characters shown below. *Katakana*, the squarer characters in the table immediately below, are used for writing foreign "loan words". The rounder characters in the bottom table, *hiragana*, are used for Japanese words, in combination with, or as substitutes for, *kanji*.

Katakana

a	ア	i	イ	u	ウ	e	エ	o	オ
ka	カ	ki	キ	ku	ク	ke	ケ	ko	コ
sa	サ	shi	シ	su	ス	se	セ	so	ソ
ta	タ	chi	チ	tsu	ツ	te	テ	to	ト
na	ナ	ni	ニ	nu	ヌ	ne	ネ	no	ノ
ha	ハ	hi	ヒ	fu	フ	he	ヘ	ho	ホ
ma	マ	mi	ミ	mu	ム	me	メ	mo	モ
ya	ヤ			yu	ユ			yo	ヨ
ra	ラ	ri	リ	ru	ル	re	レ	ro	ロ
wa	ワ							wo	ヲ
n	ン								

Hiragana

a	あ	i	い	u	う	e	え	o	お
ka	か	ki	き	ku	く	ke	け	ko	こ
sa	さ	shi	し	su	す	se	せ	so	そ
ta	た	chi	ち	tsu	つ	te	て	to	と
na	な	ni	に	nu	ぬ	ne	ね	no	の
ha	は	hi	ひ	fu	ふ	he	へ	ho	ほ
ma	ま	mi	み	mu	む	me	め	mo	も
ya	や			yu	ゆ			yo	よ
ra	ら	ri	り	ru	る	re	れ	ro	ろ
wa	わ							wo	を
n	ん								

Grammar

There are several significant **grammatical** differences between Japanese and European languages. **Verbs** do not change according to the person or number, so that *ikimasu* can mean "I go", "he/she/it goes", or "we/they go". **Pronouns**, such as I and they, are usually omitted, since it's generally clear from the context who or what the speaker is referring to. There are no **definite articles**, and **nouns** stay the same whether they refer to singular or plural words.

From the point of view of English grammar, Japanese **sentences** are structured back to front. An English-speaker would say "I am going to Tokyo" which in Japanese would translate directly as "Tokyo to going". Placing the sound "*ka*" at the end of a verb indicates a **question**, hence *Tokyo e ikimasu-ka* means "Are you going to Tokyo?" There are also levels of **politeness** to contend with, which alter the way the verb is conjugated, and sometimes change the word entirely. For the most part, stick to the polite *-masu* form of verbs and you'll be fine.

If you want to learn more about the language and have a wider range of expressions and vocabulary at your command than those listed below, invest in a phrasebook or dictionary. *Japanese: A Rough Guide Phrasebook* is user-friendly and combines essential phrases and expressions with a dictionary section and menu reader. The phonetic translations in this phrasebook are rendered slightly differently from the standard way *rōmaji* is written in this book, as an aid to pronunciation. One of the best books for learning Japanese more thoroughly is *Japanese For Busy People* (Kodansha), which comes in three parts and is often used as a set text in Japanese-language classes. A worthy alternative, although more difficult to buy outside of Japan, is *Communicative Japanese for Time Pressed People* (Aratake Publishing).

Pronunciation

Throughout this book, Japanese words have been transliterated into the standard Hepburn system of romanization, called **rōmaji**. Pronunciation is as follows:

a as in rather	ai as in Thai
i as in macaroni, or ee	ei as in weight
u as in put, or oo	ie as in two separate sounds, ee-eh
e as in bed; e is always pronounced, even at the end of a word	ue as in two separate sounds, oo-eh
	g, a hard sound as in girl
o as in not	s as in mass (never z)
ae as in the two separate sounds, ah-eh	y as in yet

A bar (macron) over a vowel or "ii" means that the vowel sound is twice as long as a vowel without a bar. Only where words are well known in English, such as Tokyo, Kyoto, judo and shogun, have we not used a bar to indicate long vowel sounds. Sometimes, vowel sounds are shortened or softened; for example, the verb *desu* sounds more like *des* when pronounced, and *sukiyaki* like *skiyaki*. Apart from this, all syllables in Japanese words are evenly stressed and pronounced in full. For example, Nagano is Na-ga-no, not Na-GA-no.

Useful words and phrases

Basics

Yes	*hai*	はい
No	*iie/chigaimasu*	いいえ／違います
OK	*daijōbu/ōkē*	大丈夫／オーケー
Well . . . (as in making things less definite)	*chotto*	ちょっと
Please (offering something)	*dōzo*	どうぞ
Please (asking for something)	*onegai shimasu*	お願いします
Excuse me	*sumimasen/shitsurei shimasu*	すみません／失礼します
I'm sorry	*gomen nasai/sumimasen*	ごめんなさい／すみません
Thanks (informal)	*dōmo*	どうも
Thank you	*arigatō*	ありがとう

Thank you very much	dōmo arigatō gozaimasu	どうもありがとうございます
What?	nani?	なに
When?	itsu?	いつ
Where?	doko?	どこ
Who?	dare?	だれ
This	kore	これ
That	sore	それ
That (over there)	are	あれ
How many?	ikutsu?	いくつ
How much?	ikura?	いくら
I want (x)	Watashi wa (x) ga hoshii desu	私は(x)が欲しいです
I don't want (x)	Watashi wa (x) ga irimasen	私は(x)がいりません
Is it possible . . . ?	. . . koto ga dekimasu ka	。。。ことができますか
Is it . . . ?	. . . desu ka	。。。ですか
Can you please help me?	Tetsudatte kuremasen ka	手伝ってくれませんか
I don't speak Japanese	Nihongo wa hanashimasen	日本語は話せません
I don't read Japanese	Nihongo wa yomimasen	日本語は読めません
Can you speak English?	Eigo ga dekimasu ka	英語ができますか
Is there someone who can interpret?	Tsūyaku wa imasu ka	通訳はいますか
Could you please speak more slowly?	Motto yukkuri hanashite kuremasen ka	もっとゆっくり話してくれませんか
Please say that again	Mō ichido itte kuremasen ka	もう一度言ってくれませんか
I understand/I see	Wakarimasu/Naruhodo	わかります／なるほど
I don't understand	Wakarimasen	わかりません
What does this mean?	Kore wa dōiu imi desu ka	これはどういう意味ですか
How do you say (x) in Japanese?	Nihongo de (x) o nan-te yomimasu ka	日本語で(x)を何て言いますか
What's this called?	Kore wa nan-to iimasu ka	これは何と言いますか
How do you pronounce this character?	Kono kanji wa nan-te yomimasu ka	この漢字は何て読みますか
Please write in English/Japanese	Eigo/Nihongo de kaite kudasai	英語／日本語で書いてください
Clean/dirty	kirei/kitanai	きれい／きたない
Hot/cold	atsui/samui	あつい／さむい
Fast/slow	hayai/osoi	はやい／おそい
Pretty/ugly	kirei/minikui	きれい／醜い
Interesting/boring	omoshiroi/tsumaranai	おもしろい／つまらない

Greetings and basic courtesies

Hello/Good day	Konnichiwa	今日は
Good morning	Ohayō gozaimasu	おはようございます
Good evening	Konbanwa	今晩は
Good night (when leaving)	Osaki ni	お先に
Good night (when going to bed)	Oyasuminasai	おやすみなさい

How are you?	O-genki desu ka	お元気ですか
I'm fine (informal)	Genki desu	元気です
I'm fine, thanks	Okagesama de	おかげさまで
How do you do/Nice to meet you	Hajimemashite	はじめまして
Don't mention it /you're welcome	Dō itashimashite	どういたしまして
I'm sorry	Gomen nasai	ごめんなさい
Just a minute please	Chotto matte kudasai	ちょっと待ってください
Goodbye	Sayonara	さよなら
Goodbye (informal)	Dewa mata/Jā ne	では又／じゃあね

Chitchat

What's your name?	Shitsurei desu ga o-namae wa	失礼ですがお名前は
My name is (x)	Watashi no namae wa (x) desu	私の名前は(x)
Where are you from?	O-kuni wa doko desu ka	お国はどこですか
Britain	Eikoku/Igirisu	英国／イギリス
Ireland	Airurando	アイランド
America	Amerika	アメリカ
Australia	Ōsutoraria	オーストラリア
Canada	Kanada	カナダ
New Zealand	Nyū Jiirando	ニュージーランド
Japan	Nihon	日本
Outside Japan	Gaikoku	外国
How old are you?	O-ikutsu desu ka	おいくつですか
I am (age)	(age) sai desu	(age) 才です
Are you married?	Kekkon shite imasu ka	結婚していますか
I am married/not married	Kekkon shite imasu/imasen	結婚しています／いません
Do you like . . . ?	. . . suki desu ka	...好きですか
I do like	. . . suki desu	...好きです
I don't like	. . . suki dewa arimasen	...好きではありません
What's your job?	O-shigoto wa nan desu ka	お仕事は何ですか
I work for a company	Kaishain desu	会社員です
I'm a tourist	Kankō kyaku desu	観光客です
Really?	Hontō	本当
That's a shame	Zannen desu	残念です
It can't be helped	Shikata ga nai/shō ga nai (informal)	仕方がない／しょうがない

Numbers, time and dates

There are special ways of **counting** different things in Japanese. The safest option is to stick to the most common first translation, used when counting time and quantities and measurements, with added qualifiers such as minutes (*pun/fun*) or yen (*en*). The second translations are sometimes used for counting objects, as in *biiru futatsu, onegai shimasu* (two beers, please). From ten, there is only one set of numbers. For four, seven and nine alternatives to the first translation are used in some circumstances.

Zero	*zero*		0	
One	*ichi*	*hitotsu*	一	ひとつ
Two	*ni*	*futatsu*	二	ふたつ
Three	*san*	*mittsu*	三	みっつ
Four	*yon/shi*	*yottsu*	四	よっつ
Five	*go*	*itsutsu*	五	いつつ
Six	*roku*	*muttsu*	六	むっつ
Seven	*shichi/nana*	*nanatsu*	七	ななつ
Eight	*hachi*	*yattsu*	八	やっつ
Nine	*ku/kyū*	*kokonotsu*	九	ここのつ
Ten	*jū*	*tō*	十	とう
Eleven	*jū-ichi*		十一	
Twelve	*jū-ni*		十二	
Twenty	*ni-jū*		二十	
Twenty-one	*ni-jū-ichi*		二十一	
Thirty	*san-jū*		三十	
One hundred	*hyaku*		百	
Two hundred	*ni-hyaku*		二百	
Thousand	*sen*		千	
Ten thousand	*ichi-man*		一万	
One hundred thousand	*jū-man*		十万	
One million	*hyaku-man*		百万	
One hundred million	*ichi-oku*		一億	

Now	*ima*	今
Today	*kyō*	今日
Morning	*asa*	朝
Evening	*yūgata*	夕方
Night	*yoru*	夜
Tomorrow	*ashita*	明日
The day after tomorrow	*asatte*	あさって
Yesterday	*kinō*	昨日
Week	*shū*	週
Month	*gatsu*	月
Year	*nen/toshi*	年
Monday	*Getsuyōbi*	月曜日
Tuesday	*Kayōbi*	火曜日
Wednesday	*Suiyōbi*	水曜日
Thursday	*Mokuyōbi*	木曜日
Friday	*Kin'yōbi*	金曜日
Saturday	*Doyōbi*	土曜日
Sunday	*Nichiyōbi*	日曜日

What time is it?	*Ima nan-ji desu ka*	今何時ですか
It's 10 o'clock	*Jū-ji desu*	十時です
10.20	*Jū-ji ni-juppun*	十時二十分

10.30	*Jū-ji han*	十時半
10.50	*Jū-ichi-ji juppun mae*	十一時十分前
AM	*gozen*	午前
PM	*gogo*	午後

Getting around

Aeroplane	*hikōki*	飛行機
Airport	*kūkō*	空港
Bus	*basu*	バス
Bus stop	*basu tei*	バス停
Train	*densha*	電車
Station	*eki*	駅
Subway	*chikatetsu*	地下鉄
Ferry	*ferii*	フェリー
Left-luggage office	*ichiji azukarijo*	一時預かり所
Coin locker	*koin rokkā*	コインロッカー
Ticket office	*kippu uriba*	切符売り場
Ticket	*kippu*	切符
One-way	*kata-michi*	片道
Return	*ōfuku*	往復
Bicycle	*jitensha*	自転車
Taxi	*takushii*	タクシー

Map	*chizu*	地図
Where is (x)?	*(x) wa doko desu ka*	(x)はどこですか
Straight ahead	*massugu*	まっすぐ
In front of	*mae*	前
Right	*migi*	右
Left	*hidari*	左
North	*kita*	北
South	*minami*	南
East	*higashi*	東
West	*nishi*	西

Places

Temple	*otera/odera/-ji/-in*	お寺／-寺／-院
Shrine	*jinja/jingū/-gū/-taisha*	神社／神宮／-宮／-大社
Castle	*-jō*	城
Park	*kōen*	公園
River	*kawa/gawa*	川
Street	*tōri/dōri/michi*	通り／道
Bridge	*hashi/bashi*	橋
Museum	*hakubutsukan*	博物館
Art gallery	*bijutsukan*	美術館
Garden	*niwa/teien/-en*	庭／庭園／-園

Island	shima/-jima/-tō	島
Slope	saka/-zaka	坂
Hill	oka	丘
Mountain	yama/-san/-take	山／岳
Hot spring spa	onsen	温泉
Lake	-ko	湖
Bay	-wan	湾

Accommodation

Hotel	hoteru	ホテル
Traditional-style inn	ryokan	旅館
Guesthouse	minshuku	民宿
Youth hostel	yūsu hosuteru	ユースホステル
Single room	shinguru rūmu	シングルルーム
Double room	daburu rūmu	ダブルルーム
Twin room	tsuin rūmu	ツインルーム
Dormitory	kyōdō/ōbeya	共同／大部屋
Japanese-style room	washitsu	和室
Western-style room	yōshitsu	洋室
Western-style bed	beddo	ベッド
Bath	o-furo	お風呂

Do you have any vacancies?	Kūshitsu wa arimasu ka	空室はありますか
I'd like to make a reservation	Yoyaku o shitai no desu ga	予約をしたいのですが
I have a reservation	Yoyaku shimashita	予約しました
I don't have a reservation	Yoyaku shimasen deshita	予約しませんでした
How much is it per person?	Hitori ikura desu ka	一人いくらですか
Does that include meals?	Shokuji wa tsuite imasu ka	食事はついていますか
I would like to stay one night/two nights	Hitoban/futaban tomaritai no desu ga	一晩／二晩泊まりたいのですが
I would like to see the room	Heya o misete kudasaimasen ka	部屋を見せてくださいませんか
Key	kagi	鍵
Passport	pasupōto	パスポート

Shopping, money and banks

Shop	mise/-ten/-ya	店／屋
How much is it?	Kore wa ikura desu ka	これはいくらですか
It's too expensive	Taka-sugimasu	高すぎます
Is there anything cheaper?	Mō sukoshi yasui mono wa arimasu ka	もう少し安いものはありますか
Do you accept credit cards?	Kurejitto kādo wa tsukaemasu ka	クレジットカードは使えますか
I'm just looking	Miru dake desu	見るだけです
Yen	Yen/-en	￥／-円
UK pounds	pondo	ポンド

Dollars	*doru*	ドル
Foreign exchange	*gaikoku-kawase*	外国為替
Bank	*ginkō*	銀行
Traveller's cheque	*toraberāzu chekku*	トラベラーズチェック

Post and telephones

Post office	*yūbinkyoku*	郵便局
Letter	*tegami*	手紙
Postcard	*hagaki*	葉書
Stamp	*kitte*	切手
Airmail	*kōkūbin*	航空便
Poste restante	*tomeoki*	留置
Telephone	*denwa*	電話
International telephone call	*kokusai-denwa*	国際電話
Reverse charge/collect call	*korekuto-kōru*	コレクトコール
Telephone card	*terefon kādo*	テレフォンカード
I would like to call (place)	*(place) e denwa o kaketai no desu*	(place) へ電話をかけたいのです
I would like to send a fax to (place)	*(place) e fakkusu shitai no desu*	(place) へファックスしたいのです

Health

Hospital	*byōin*	病院
Pharmacy	*yakkyoku*	薬局
Medicine	*kusuri*	薬
Doctor	*isha*	医者
Dentist	*haisha*	歯医者
I'm ill	*byōki desu*	病気です

Food and drink

Basics

Bar	*nomiya*	飲み屋
Standing-only bar	*tachinomiya*	立ちのみ屋
Café/coffee shop	*kissaten*	喫茶店
Cafeteria	*shokudō*	食堂
Pub	*pabu*	パブ
Pub-style restaurant	*izakaya*	居酒屋
Restaurant	*resutoran*	レストラン
Restaurant specializing in charcoal-grilled foods	*robatayaki*	炉端焼
Breakfast	*asa-gohan*	朝ご飯
Lunch	*hiru-gohan*	昼ご飯
Dinner	*ban-gohan*	晩ご飯

Boxed meal	*bentō*	弁当
Set meal	*teishoku*	定食
Daily special set meal	*higawari-teishoku*	日替り定食
Menu	*menyū*	メニュー
Do you have an English menu?	*eigo no menyū arimasu ka*	英語のメニューありますか
How much is that?	*ikura desu ka*	いくらですか
I would like (a) . . .	*(a) . . . o onegai shimasu*	(a)をお願いします
May I have the bill?	*okanjō o onegai shimasu*	お勘定をお願いします

Staple foods

Bean curd tofu	*tōfu*	豆腐
Butter	*batā*	バター
Bread	*pan*	パン
Dried seaweed	*nori*	のり
Egg	*tamago*	卵
Fermented soyabean paste	*miso*	味噌
Garlic	*ninniku*	にんにく
Oil	*abura*	油
Pepper	*koshō*	こしょう
Rice	*gohan*	ご飯
Salt	*shio*	塩
Soy sauce	*shōyu*	しょうゆ
Sugar	*satō*	砂糖

Fruit, vegetables and salads

Fruit	*kudamono*	果物
Apple	*ringo*	りんご
Banana	*banana*	バナナ
Grapefruit	*gurēpufurūtsu*	グレープフルーツ
Grapes	*budō*	ぶどう
Japanese plum	*ume*	うめ
Lemon	*remon*	レモン
Melon	*meron*	メロン
Orange	*orenji*	オレンジ
Peach	*momo*	桃
Pear	*nashi*	なし
Persimmon	*kaki*	柿
Pineapple	*painappuru*	パイナップル
Strawberry	*ichigo*	いちご
Tangerine	*mikan*	みかん
Watermelon	*suika*	すいか
Vegetables	*yasai*	野菜
Salad	*sarada*	サラダ
Aubergine	*nasu*	なす

Beans	mame	豆
Beansprouts	moyashi	もやし
Carrot	ninjin	にんじん
Cauliflower	karifurawā	カリフラワー
Green pepper	piiman	ピーマン
Green horseradish	wasabi	わさび
Leek	negi	ねぎ
Mushroom	kinoko	きのこ
Onion	tamanegi	たまねぎ
Potato	poteto, jagaimo	ポテト,じゃがいも
Radish	daikon	だいこん
Sweetcorn	kōn	コーン
Tomato	tomato	トマト

Fish and seafood dishes

Fish	sakana	魚
Shellfish	kai	貝
Raw fish	sashimi	さしみ
Sushi	sushi	寿司
Sushi mixed selection	nigiri-zushi	にぎり寿司
Sushi rolled in crisp seaweed	maki-zushi	まき寿司
Sushi topped with fish, egg and vegetables	chirashi-zushi	ちらし寿司
Abalone	awabi	あわび
Blowfish	fugu	ふぐ
Cod	tara	たら
Crab	kani	かに
Eel	unagi	うなぎ
Herring	nishin	にしん
Horse mackerel	aji	あじ
Lobster	ise-ebi	伊勢海老
Octopus	tako	たこ
Oyster	kaki	かき
Prawn	ebi	えび
Sea bream	tai	たい
Sea urchin	uni	うに
Squid	ika	いか
Sweet smelt	ayu	あゆ
Tuna	maguro	まぐろ
Yellowtail	buri	ぶり

Meat and meat dishes

Meat	niku	肉
Beef	gyūniku	牛肉
Chicken	toriniku	鶏肉

Lamb	*ramu*	ラム
Pork	*butaniku*	豚肉
Breaded, deep-fried slice of pork	*tonkatsu*	とんかつ
Chicken, other meat and vegetables grilled on skewers	*yakitori*	焼き鳥
Skewers of food dipped in breadcrumbs and deep-fried	*kushiage*	串揚げ
Stew including meat (or seafood), vegetables and noodles	*nabe*	鍋
Thin beef slices cooked in broth	*shabu-shabu*	しゃぶしゃぶ
Thin beef slices braised in a sauce	*sukiyaki*	すきやき

Other dishes

Buddhist-style vegetarian cuisine	*shōjin-ryōri*	精進料理
Chinese-style noodles	*rāmen*	ラーメン
Chinese-style dumplings	*gyōza*	ぎょうざ
Fried noodles	*yakisoba/udon*	焼そば／うどん
Stewed chunks of vegetables and fish on skewers	*oden*	おでん
Thin buckwheat noodles	*soba*	そば
Soba in a hot soup	*kake-soba*	かけそば
Cold soba served with a dipping sauce	*zaru-soba/mori-soba*	ざるそば／もりそば
Thick wheat noodles	*udon*	うどん
Fried rice	*chāhan*	チャーハン
Lightly battered seafood and vegetables	*tempura*	天ぷら
Meat, vegetable and fish cooked in soy sauce and sweet sake	*teriyaki*	照り焼き
Mild curry served with rice	*karē raisu*	カレーライス
Octopus in balls of batter	*takoyaki*	たこやき
Pounded rice cakes	*mocihi*	もち
Rice topped with fish, meat or vegetable	*donburi*	どんぶり
Rice triangles wrapped in crisp seaweed	*onigiri*	おにぎり
Savoury pancakes	*okonomiyaki*	お好み焼き
Chinese food	*Chūka-/Chūgoku-ryōri*	中華／中国料理
French food	*Furansu-ryōri*	フランス料理
Italian food	*Itaria-ryōri*	イタリア料理
Japanese-style food	*washoku*	和食
Japanese haute cuisine	*kaiseki-ryōri*	懐石料理
Korean food	*Kankoku-ryōri*	韓国料理
"No-nationality" food	*mukokuseki-ryōri*	無国籍料理

| Thai food | *Tai-ryōri* | タイ料理 |
| Western-style food | *yōshoku* | 洋食 |

Drinks

Beer	*biiru*	ビール
Black tea	*kōcha*	紅茶
Coffee	*kōhii*	コーヒー
Distilled liquor	*shōchū*	焼酎
Fruit juice	*jūsu*	ジュース
Green tea	*sencha*	煎茶
Milk	*miruku*	ミルク
Oolong tea	*ūron-cha*	ウーロン茶
Powdered green tea	*matcha*	抹茶
Water	*mizu*	水
Whisky	*uisukii*	ウイスキー
Whisky and water	*mizu-wari*	水割り
Sake (rice wine)	*sake/nihon-shu*	酒／日本酒
Wine	*wain*	ワイン

Glossary

anime animated movies.

banzai Traditional Japanese cheer, meaning "10,000 years".

-bashi Bridge.

basho Sumo tournament.

bodhisattva Buddhist who has forsaken nirvana to work for the salvation of all humanity.

bunraku Puppet theatre.

-chō, or **machi** Subdivision of the city, smaller than a ku.

-chōme Area of the city consisting of a few blocks.

dai Big or great.

daimyō Feudal lords.

-dōri Main road.

Edo Pre-1868 name for Tokyo.

furo Traditional Japanese bath.

futon Bedding.

gaijin Foreigner.

-gawa River.

geisha Traditional female entertainer accomplished in the arts.

geta Wooden sandals.

hanami Cherry-blossom viewing.

Heian Period when Japan was ruled from Heian-kyō, now Kyoto (794–1185).

higashi East.

-ji Buddhist temple.

ji-biiru Beer produced in local microbreweries.

-jingū, or **-jinja** Shinto shrine.

Jizō Buddhist protector of children, travellers and the dead.

-jō Castle.

JR Japan Railways.

kabuki Traditional theatre.

kaiseki Japanese haute cuisine.

kampai "Cheers" when drinking.

kanji Japanese script derived from Chinese characters.

Kannon Buddhist Goddess of Mercy.

katakana Phonetic script used mainly for writing foreign words in Japanese.

kimono Literally "clothes" but usually referring to women's traditional dress.

kita North.

kōban Local police box.

-kōen/gyoen Public park.

-ku Principal administrative division of the city, usually translated as "ward".

manga Comics.

matsuri Festival.

Meiji Period named after the Emperor Meiji (1868–1912).

mikoshi Portable shrine used in festivals.

minami South.

minshuku Family-run lodge, similar to a bed and breakfast, cheaper than a ryokan.

mon Gate.

netsuke Small, intricately carved toggles for fastening the cords of cloth bags.

nishi West.

Nō Traditional theatre.

noren Split curtain hanging in shop and restaurant doorways.

obi Wide sash worn with kimono.

okashi Japanese sweets.

onsen Hot spring, generally developed for bathing.

pachinko Vertical pinball machines.

rōnin Masterless samurai.

rotemburo outdoor hot-spring bath.

ryokan Traditional Japanese inn.

ryōtei Restaurant serving *kaiseki*.

samurai Warrior class who were retainers of the *daimyō*.

sembei Rice crackers.

sentō Neighbourhood public bath.

shamisen Type of lute.

Shinkansen Bullet train.

Shinto Japan's indigenous religion, based on the premise that gods inhabit all natural things, both animate and inanimate.

Shitamachi Low-lying, working-class districts of east Tokyo, nowadays usually referring to Asakusa and Ueno.

shogun The military rulers of Japan before 1868.

shōji Paper-covered sliding screens used to divide rooms or cover windows.

soaplands Brothel.

sumi-e Ink paintings.

sumo Japan's national sport, a form of heavyweight wrestling which evolved from ancient Shinto divination rites.

tatami Rice-straw matting, the traditional covering for floors.

tansu Traditional chest of drawers.

-tera/-dera/-ji Buddhist temple.

torii Gate to a Shinto shrine.

ukiyo-e "Pictures of the floating world", colourful woodblock prints which became particularly popular in the late eighteenth century.

washi Japanese paper.

yakuza Professional criminal gangs.

yukata Loose cotton robe worn as a dressing gown in a ryokan.

Travel store

D: Rough Guide **DIRECTIONS** for short breaks

Available from all good bookstores

Kenya
Marrakesh **D**
Morocco
South Africa, Lesotho
& Swaziland
Syria
Tanzania
Tunisia
West Africa
Zanzibar

Travel Specials
First-Time Africa
First-Time Around
the World
First-Time Asia
First-Time Europe
First-Time Latin
America
Travel Health
Travel Online
Travel Survival
Walks in London
& SE England
Women Travel
World Party

Maps
Algarve
Amsterdam
Andalucia
& Costa del Sol
Argentina
Athens
Australia
Barcelona
Berlin
Boston & Cambridge
Brittany
Brussels
California
Chicago
Chile
Corsica
Costa Rica
& Panama
Crete
Croatia
Cuba
Cyprus
Czech Republic
Dominican Republic
Dubai & UAE
Dublin
Egypt

Florence & Siena
Florida
France
Frankfurt
Germany
Greece
Guatemala & Belize
Iceland
India
Ireland
Italy
Kenya & Northern
Tanzania
Lisbon
London
Los Angeles
Madrid
Malaysia
Mallorca
Marrakesh
Mexico
Miami & Key West
Morocco
New England
New York City
New Zealand
Northern Spain
Paris
Peru
Portugal
Prague
Pyrenees & Andorra
Rome
San Francisco
Sicily
South Africa
South India
Spain & Portugal
Sri Lanka
Tenerife
Thailand
Toronto
Trinidad & Tobago
Tunisia
Turkey
Tuscany
Venice
Vietnam, Laos
& Cambodia
Washington DC
Yucatán Peninsula

Dictionary Phrasebooks
Croatian
Czech
Dutch
Egyptian Arabic
French
German
Greek
Hindi & Urdu
Italian
Japanese
Latin American
Spanish
Mandarin Chinese
Mexican Spanish
Polish
Portuguese
Russian
Spanish
Swahili
Thai
Turkish
Vietnamese

Computers
Blogging
eBay
iPhone
iPods, iTunes
& music online
The Internet
Macs & OS X
MySpace
PCs and Windows
PlayStation Portable
Website Directory

Film & TV
American
Independent Film
British Cult Comedy
Chick Flicks
Comedy Movies
Cult Movies
Film
Film Musicals
Film Noir
Gangster Movies
Horror Movies
Kids' Movies
Sci-Fi Movies
Westerns

Lifestyle
Babies
Ethical Living
Pregnancy & Birth
Running

Music Guides
The Beatles
Blues
Bob Dylan
Book of Playlists
Classical Music
Elvis
Frank Sinatra
Heavy Metal
Hip-Hop
Jazz
Led Zeppelin
Opera
Pink Floyd
Punk
Reggae
Rock
The Rolling Stones
Soul and R&B
Velvet Underground
World Music
(2 vols)

Popular Culture
Books for Teenagers
Children's Books,
5-11
Conspiracy Theories
Crime Fiction
Cult Fiction
The Da Vinci Code
His Dark Materials
Lord of the Rings
Shakespeare
Superheroes
The Templars
Unexplained
Phenomena

Science
The Brain
Climate Change
The Earth
Genes & Cloning
The Universe
Weather

Visit us online

www.roughguides.com

Information on over 25,000 destinations around the world

- **Read** Rough Guides' trusted travel info
- **Access** exclusive articles from Rough Guides authors
- **Update** yourself on new books, maps, CDs and other products
- **Enter** our competitions and win travel prizes
- **Share** ideas, journals, photos & travel advice with other users
- **Earn** points every time you contribute to the Rough Guide
  community and get rewards

BROADEN YOUR HORIZONS

Small print and

Index

A Rough Guide to Rough Guides

Published in 1982, the first Rough Guide – to Greece – was a student scheme that became a publishing phenomenon. Mark Ellingham, a recent graduate in English from Bristol University, had been travelling in Greece the previous summer and couldn't find the right guidebook. With a small group of friends he wrote his own guide, combining a highly contemporary, journalistic style with a thoroughly practical approach to travellers' needs.

The immediate success of the book spawned a series that rapidly covered dozens of destinations. And, in addition to impecunious backpackers, Rough Guides soon acquired a much broader and older readership that relished the guides' wit and inquisitiveness as much as their enthusiastic, critical approach and value-for-money ethos.

These days, Rough Guides include recommendations from shoestring to luxury and cover more than 200 destinations around the globe, including almost every country in the Americas and Europe, more than half of Africa and most of Asia and Australasia. Our ever-growing team of authors and photographers is spread all over the world, particularly in Europe, the USA and Australia.

In the early 1990s, Rough Guides branched out of travel, with the publication of Rough Guides to World Music, Classical Music and the Internet. All three have become benchmark titles in their fields, spearheading the publication of a wide range of books under the Rough Guide name.

Including the travel series, Rough Guides now number more than 350 titles, covering: phrasebooks, waterproof maps, music guides from Opera to Heavy Metal, reference works as diverse as Conspiracy Theories and Shakespeare, and popular culture books from iPods to Poker. Rough Guides also produce a series of more than 120 World Music CDs in partnership with World Music Network.

Visit www.roughguides.com to see our latest publications.

Rough Guide travel images are available for commercial licensing at www.roughguidespictures.com

ROUGH
GUIDES

SMALL PRINT

Rough Guide credits

Text editor: Richard Lim
Layout: Umesh Aggarwal, Jessica Subramanian
Cartography: Karobi Gogoi
Picture editor: Mark Thomas
Production: Rebecca Short
Proofreader: Karen Parker and Rika Baggett
Cover design: Chloë Roberts
Photographer: Martin Richardson
Editorial: **London** Kate Berens, Claire Saunders, Ruth Blackmore, Alison Murchie, Karoline Densley, Andy Turner, Keith Drew, Edward Aves, Nikki Birrell, Alice Park, Sarah Eno, Lucy White, Jo Kirby, James Smart, Natasha Foges, Róisín Cameron, Emma Traynor, Emma Gibbs, James Rice, Joe Staines, Duncan Clark, Peter Buckley, Matthew Milton, Tracy Hopkins, Ruth Tidball; **New York** Andrew Rosenberg, Steven Horak, AnneLise Sorensen, Amy Hegarty, April Isaacs, Ella Steim, Anna Owens, Joseph Petta, Sean Mahoney; **Delhi** Madhavi Singh, Karen D'Souza
Design & Pictures: **London** Scott Stickland, Dan May, Diana Jarvis, Jj Luck, Chloë Roberts, Nicole Newman, Sarah Cummins; **Delhi** Ajay Verma, Ankur Guha, Pradeep Thapliyal, Sachin Tanwar, Anita Singh, Nikhil Agarwal

Production: Vicky Baldwin
Cartography: **London** Maxine Repath, Ed Wright, Katie Lloyd-Jones; **Delhi** Jai Prakash Mishra, Rajesh Chhibber, Ashutosh Bharti, Rajesh Mishra, Animesh Pathak, Jasbir Sandhu, Amod Singh, Alakananda Bhattacharya, Swati Handoo
Online: **New York** Jennifer Gold, Kristin Mingrone; **Delhi** Manik Chauhan, Narender Kumar, Rakesh Kumar, Amit Verma, Rahul Kumar, Ganesh Sharma, Debojit Borah
Marketing & Publicity: **London** Liz Statham, Niki Hanmer, Louise Maher, Jess Carter, Vanessa Godden, Vivienne Watton, Anna Paynton, Rachel Sprackett; **New York** Geoff Colquitt, Megan Kennedy, Katy Ball
Manager India: Punita Singh
Series Editor: Mark Ellingham
Reference Director: Andrew Lockett
Publishing Coordinator: Helen Phillips
Publishing Director: Martin Dunford
Commercial Manager: Gino Magnotta
Managing Director: John Duhigg

Publishing information

This fourth edition published February 2008 by
Rough Guides Ltd,
80 Strand, London WC2R 0RL
345 Hudson St, 4th Floor,
New York, NY 10014, USA
14 Local Shopping Centre, Panchsheel Park,
New Delhi 110017, India
Distributed by the Penguin Group
Penguin Books Ltd,
80 Strand, London WC2R 0RL
Penguin Group (USA)
375 Hudson Street, NY 10014, USA
Penguin Group (Australia)
250 Camberwell Road, Camberwell,
Victoria 3124, Australia
Penguin Books Canada Ltd,
10 Alcorn Avenue, Toronto, Ontario,
Canada M4V 1E4
Penguin Group (NZ)
67 Apollo Drive, Mairangi Bay, Auckland 1310,
New Zealand

Cover concept by Peter Dyer.

Typeset in Bembo and Helvetica to an original design by Henry Iles.

Printed and bound in China

© Jan Dodd and Simon Richmond

No part of this book may be reproduced in any form without permission from the publisher except for the quotation of brief passages in reviews.

352pp includes index

A catalogue record for this book is available from the British Library

ISBN: 978-1-84353-908-7

ROUGH GUIDES

SMALL PRINT

Help us update

We've gone to a lot of effort to ensure that the fourth edition of **The Rough Guide to Tokyo** is accurate and up to date. However, things change – places get "discovered", opening hours are notoriously fickle, restaurants and rooms raise prices or lower standards. If you feel we've got it wrong or left something out, we'd like to know, and if you can remember the address, the price, for hours, the phone number, so much the better.

Please send your comments with the subject line "**Rough Guide Tokyo Update**" to email@roughguides.com. We'll credit all contributions and send a copy of the next edition (or any other Rough Guide if you prefer) for the very best emails. Have your questions answered and tell others about your trip at **ⓦcommunity.roughguides.com**

Acknowledgements

Jan: Thanks are due to Tabata Naoka at TCVB for her endless patience and enthusiasm; Yamada Takanari of JNTO for answering yet more questions; Kylie Clark in JNTO London; Sawa-san and family for providing the usual warm welcome and a home from home; and to Kenichi, Shiila Takaoka, Elliott Samuels, Rob Henderson, Dominic al-Badri and Rob Schwartz for great tips and excellent company. Will, Shimizu-san, Michael and Mizukoshi Kaeko also gave much appreciated help along the way. As always, it's a pleasure to work with Simon. Many thanks, too, to Richard for pulling this edition into shape.
Simon: I owe a great deal of thanks to the following people: Kylie Clark and her colleagues at JNTO; the dynamic duo of Tabata Naoko and Homma Yuko at TCVB; Charlie Spreckley, Steve Trautline, Rob Swarz, Gardner Robinson and Jean Snow all for generously sharing their contacts and city knowledge; the ever-erudite Giles Murray; Rob Henderson and Koga Sayuri at ANA; Mark Holguin and Fujiyoshi Eri at Solare Hotels; Yoshiba Taiki at HIS; Ashley Rawlings and Paul Baron from Tokyo Art Beat; my friends Toshiko and Kenichi who are always ready with great advice and assistance; my co-author Jan and editor Richard. For sake, sembei and wasabi loving Tonny who was with me in spirit all the way.

Readers' letters

Thanks to all the readers who have taken the time to write in with comments and suggestions (and apologies if we've inadvertently omitted or misspelt anyone's name):

Thanks to all the readers who wrote in with comments and suggestions: Andri van den Berg, Cap'n Billy, Toby Bricheno, Alison Brown, Francia Castaneda, Rhian Chapman, James Clarke, Murray Dickson, Lorna Duke, Carla Francis, Carl Gerrard, Catherine Midori Gollery, Stuart Gordon, Mark Heaney, Stefan Heller, Jonathan Hughes, Mark Janssen, Stuart Kerr, Gerry Knoch, Amy Knopf, Brian Knox, Dan Lawes, Wei-Yun Mak, Ketki Marthak, T Mcnamara, Andy McVitty, Matt Metcalfe, Hannah Mitchell, Wendy Moor, David Murphy, Tim Neal, Matthew Paetz, Tim Passey, Dante Pinto, Sarah Riches, Ian & Freda Rickword, Jason Rix & Rebecca Amboaje, Wendy Schaffer, Sapna Shah, Taro Kumashiro, Maria Tempe, Marie Verlingo, Peter Wieringa, Daniel Witvoet, Derek Wolfson.

Photo credits

All photos © Rough Guides except the following:

Introduction
Pedestrian crossing in Shibuya © Mark Thomas
Happōen © Simon Richmond
Sushi © Mark Thomas
The Shin-kyō Bridge in the Nikkō National Park
    © Mark Thomas
Artwork in an underpass © Simon Richmond
Businessmen passing manga advertising
    © Alice/Getty Images
Women with pet dogs in prams, Ginza
    © Jon Arnold Images/Alamy

Things not to miss
01 Rikugi-en © JTB Photo Communications/
    Alamy
03 The Daibutsu, Kamakura © Mark Thomas
04 Happōen © Simon Richmond
05 Shinjuku Gyoen National Gardens
    © Mark Thomas
06 Tokyo National Art Center © Simon Richmond
07 Bathers at an onsen © Jeremy Sutton Hibbert/
    Alamy
08 Harajuku © James Leynse/Corbis
09 The Rainbow Bridge © Mitchell Coster/Axiom
10 Tsukiji Market © Mark Thomas
11 Naka-Meguro © Simon Richmond
12 Kabuki © Kankuro Nakamura/Corbis
14 The Sun Blaze Gate, Tōshō-gū Shrine, Nikkō
    © Mark Thomas
15 Hanami party © Mark Thomas
16 Meiji-jingū © Mark Thomas
17 River tour along the Sumida
    © JTB Communications/Alamy
18 Sensō-ji Temple, Asakusa © Mark Thomas
19 Fireworks over Tokyo © JTB Communications/
    Alamy
20 Studio Ghibli Museum © Tom Wagner/Corbis
22 Yanaka © Iain Masterton/Alamy

Shrines and temples colour section
The pagoda at Sensō-ji © Mark Thomas
Torii gateway © Mark Thomas
Crowd with a portable shrine © John Draks/
    Corbis
Prayer papers © Mark Thomas
Woman praying © Bob Jensen/Alamy
The Zeniarai Benten Shrine, Kamakura
    © TW photo/Corbis

Tokyo architecture colour section
Prada Building © Mark Thomas
Tokyo Metropolitan Government Building © Mark
    Thomas
Fuji TV Building © Mark Thomas
Tod's Omotesandō Building © Edmund Summer/
    View Pictures/Alamy
Omotesandō Hills © Simon Richmond
21_21 Design Sight © Simon Richmond
Tokyo International Forum © Mark Thomas

Black and whites
p.63 Monorail train passing through Shiodome
    © Mark Thomas
p.93 Statue of Saigō Takamori, Ueno Park
    © Mark Thomas
p.103 Kyū Furukawa Garden © JTB Photo
    Communications
p.110 Studio Alta building, Shinjuku © Peter M
    Wilson/Alamy
p.117 The entrance to Meiji-jingū, Harajuku
    © Mark Thomas
p.123 Crowds meeting at the Hachikō dog
    sculpture, Shibuya © Jim Holmes/Axiom
p.141 View across Tokyo Bay from Odaiba
    © Simon Richmond
p.156 Capsule hotel © Louie Psihoyas/Corbis
p.166 Okonomiyaki © Christian Kober/Alamy
p.170 Food at the Natural Harmony restaurant
    © Simon Richmond
p.182 Coffee house in Shinjuku © Jonah
    Calinawan/Alamy
p.206 Kabuki © Jim Holmes/Axiom
p.227 Gucci store, Omotesandō © Mark Thomas/
    Axiom
p.239 Entrance to Oedo Onsen Monogatari
    © Jeremy Sutton Hibbert/Alamy
p.252 Chūzenji-ko, Nikkō © Simon Richmond
p.265 The Hakone Open Air Museum © Christian
    Kober/Alamy
p.273 Old merchant's house © JTB Photo
    Communications/Alamy
p.296 Yokohama waterfront © Paul Quayle/Axiom

Index

Map entries are in colour.

INDEX

341

I

J

K

S

INDEX

INDEX

INDEX

Y

Z

Map symbols

maps are listed in the full index using coloured text

— ··	Provincial boundary	◉	Accommodation
▬	Expressway	▣	Restaurant/bar
=	Major road	@	Internet
=	Minor road	(i)	Tourist office
▬	Pedestrianized street	E	Embassy
....	Road under construction	Ⓢ	Subway station
- - - -	Path	★	Bus stop
—	River	⊠	Gate
— —	Ferry route	⊞	Hospital
●- - -●	Cable car and stations	⊠	Post office
══	JR line	✈	Airport
═══	Shinkensen line	⌣	Bridge
┉┉┉	Private rail line	⊙	Statue
....	Funicular railway	♀	Museum
—Ⓜ—	Monorail with station	⚶	Pagoda
- - - -	Tram line	卅	Shrine
)········(	Railway tunnel	♠	Buddhist temple
▬▬▬	Wall	▬	Building
▲	Peak	⊞	Church
⌂	Cave	▢	Market
𝄃	Waterfall	⬭	Stadium
♦	Place of interest	⁺⁺⁺	Cemetery
⊤	Garden	▨	Park
⚠	Campsite		

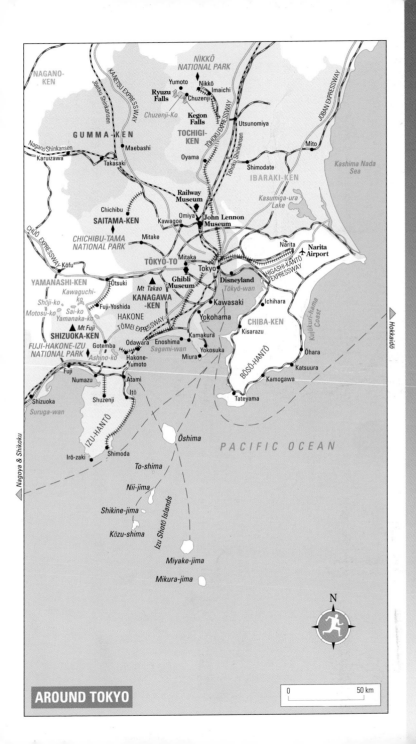

NAGANO-KEN

NIKKŌ
NATIONAL PARK

Yumoto
Nikkō
Imaichi

Ryuzu
Falls
Chuzenji

Chuzenji-Ko
Kegon
Falls

Utsunomiya

KANETSU EXPRESSWAY

Jõetsu Shinkansen

GUMMA-KEN

TOCHIGI-KEN

TŌHOKU EXPRESSWAY

Tōhoku Shinkansen

Mito

Kashima Nada
Sea

Maebashi

Nagano Shinkansen
Karuizawa

Takasaki

Oyama

Shimodate

IBARAKI-KEN

Kasumiga-ura
Lake

Chichibu

SAITAMA-KEN

Railway
Museum

CHŪO EXPRESSWAY

CHICHIBU-TAMA
NATIONAL PARK

Mitake

Omiya
Kawagoe
John Lennon
Museum

Kōfu

TŌKYŌ-TO

Ōtsuki

Mt Takao

Mitaka
Tokyo

Ghibli
Museum

Narita

Narita
Airport

YAMANASHI-KEN

Kawaguchi-
ko

Shōji-ko
Motosu-ko
Sai-ko
Yamanaka-ko

Fuji-Yoshida

KANAGAWA
-KEN

Disneyland
Tōkyō-wan

HIGASHI-KANTO
EXPRESSWAY

Ichihara

Kawasaki

HAKONE

Mt Fuji

TŌMEI EXPRESSWAY

Yokohama

Kamakura

Kisarazu

CHIBA-KEN

Kujūkuri-hama Coast

SHIZUOKA-KEN

Gotemba

FUJI-HAKONE-IZU
NATIONAL PARK

Ashino-ko

Odawara
Hakone-
Yumoto

Enoshima
Sagami-wan

Yokosuka
Miura

Ōhara

BŌSŌ-HANTŌ

Katsuura

Fuji

Numazu

Atami

Kamogawa

Shizuoka

Shuzenji

Itō

Suruga-wan

Shimoda

IZU-HANTŌ

Tateyama

Irō-zaki

Ōshima

PACIFIC OCEAN

To-shima

Nii-jima

Shikine-jima

Kōzu-shima

Izu Shotō Islands

Miyake-jima

Mikura-jima

◁ Nagoya & Shikoku

▷ Hokkaidō

N

0   50 km

AROUND TOKYO

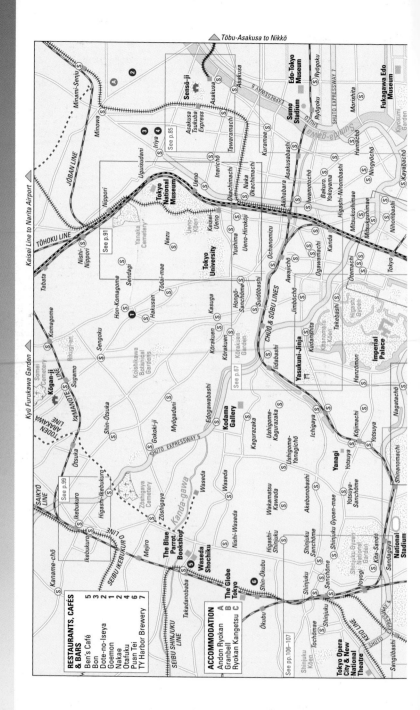

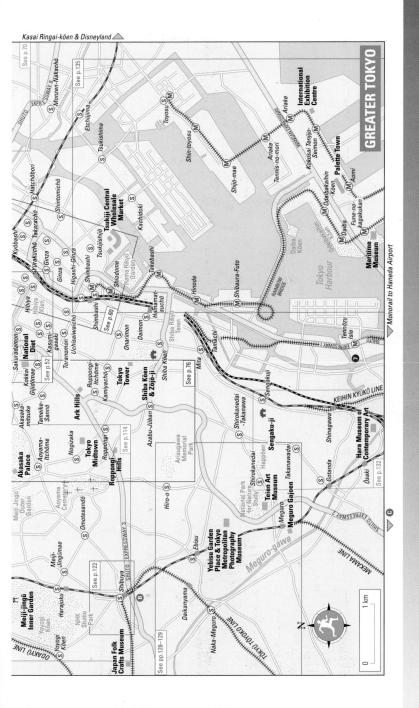

Kasai Ringai-kōen & Disneyland

GREATER TOKYO

See p.70
See p.135

SHUTO EXPRESSWAY 9

Monzen-Nakachō (S)

Etchūjima (S)

Hatchōbori (S)

Tsukishima (S)

Shintomichō (S)

Takaracho (S)

Kyōbashi (S)

Yūrakuchō (S)

Ginza (S)

Higashi-Ginza (S)

Tsukijishijō (S)

Toyosu (S) (M)

Shin-toyosu (M)

Ariake (M)

Ariake-Tennis-no-mori (M)

Kokusai Tenjijō-Seimon (M)

International Exhibition Centre

Palette Town

Aomi (M)

Fune-no-kagakukan (M)

Daiba (M)

Ōdaibakaihin (M)

Daiba Kōen

Maritime Museum

Tennōzu Isle (M)

SHUTO EXPRESSWAY 1

Tsukiji Central Wholesale Market

Kachidoki (S)

Hama Rikyū Garden

Takebashi (M)

Shiodome (M) (S)

Shimbashi (S) (M)

See p.60

Hamamatsu-chō (M) (S)

Shibaura-Futo

Daimon (S)

Onarimon (S)

Shiba Rikyū Teien

Hinode (M)

Shiba Kōen

See p.76

Mita (M) (S)

RAINBOW BRIDGE

Tokyo Harbour

Shibaura-Futo (M)

Tamachi (M) (S)

Sakuradamon (S)

National Diet

Kokkai-Gijidōmae (S)

See p.52

Kasumi-gaseki (S)

Uchisaiwaichō (S)

Toranomon (S)

Kamiyachō (S)

Tokyo Tower

Shiba Kōen & Zōjō-ji

Ark Hills

Roppongi-Itchōme (S)

Akasaka-mitsuke (S)

Tameike-Sannō (S)

Hibiya (S)

Hibiya Kōen

Shirokanedai-Takanawa (S)

Sengakuji (S)

Sengaku-ji

KEIHIN KYŪKŌ LINE

Shinagawa (S)

Akasaka Palace

Aoyama-Itchōme (S)

Nogizaka (S)

Tokyo Midtown

Roppongi Hills

Roppongi (S)

See p.114

Azabu-Jūban (S)

Arisugawa Memorial Park

Hiro-o (S)

Shirokanedai (S)

Happōen

Hara Museum of Contemporary Art

Gotanda (S)

See p.132

Ōsaki (S)

Meiji Jingū Outer Garden

Aoyama Cemetery

Omotesandō (S)

National Park for Nature Study

Teien Art Museum

Meguro (S)

Takanawadai (S)

Meguro Gajoen

SHUTO EXPRESSWAY 2

MEKAMA LINE

Meiji-jingū Inner Garden

Yoyogi Kōen

Harajuku (S)

Meiji-Jingūmae (S)

NHK Studio Park

See p.122

Shibuya (S) (B)

SHUTO EXPRESSWAY 3

Ebisu (S)

Yebisu Garden Place & Tokyo Metropolitan Photography Museum

Daikanyama (S)

Naka-Meguro (S)

TOKYŪ TŌYOKO LINE

Meguro-gawa

ODAKYŪ LINE

Yoyogi Kōen

Japan Folk Crafts Museum

See pp.128–129

N

0   1 km

Monorail to Haneda Airport

7

C

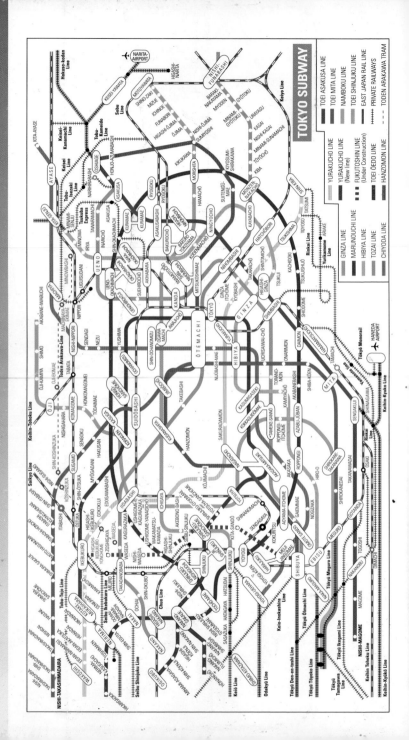